Lecture Notes in Computer Science 9189

Commenced Publication in 1973
Founding and Former Series Editors:
Gerhard Goos, Juris Hartmanis, and Jan van Leeuwen

More information about this series at http://www.springer.com/series/7409

Norbert Streitz · Panos Markopoulos (Eds.)

Distributed, Ambient, and Pervasive Interactions

Third International Conference, DAPI 2015
Held as Part of HCI International 2015
Los Angeles, CA, USA, August 2–7, 2015
Proceedings

 Springer

Editors
Norbert Streitz
Smart Future Initiative
Frankfurt
Germany

Panos Markopoulos
Eindhoven University of Technology
Eindhoven
The Netherlands

ISSN 0302-9743   ISSN 1611-3349 (electronic)
Lecture Notes in Computer Science
ISBN 978-3-319-20803-9   ISBN 978-3-319-20804-6 (eBook)
DOI 10.1007/978-3-319-20804-6

Library of Congress Control Number: 2015942808

LNCS Sublibrary: SL3 – Information Systems and Applications, incl. Internet/Web, and HCI

Springer Cham Heidelberg New York Dordrecht London

Printed on acid-free paper

Springer International Publishing AG Switzerland is part of Springer Science+Business Media
(www.springer.com)

Foreword

The 17th International Conference on Human-Computer Interaction, HCI International 2015, was held in Los Angeles, CA, USA, during 2–7 August 2015. The event incorporated the 15 conferences/thematic areas listed on the following page.

A total of 4843 individuals from academia, research institutes, industry, and governmental agencies from 73 countries submitted contributions, and 1462 papers and 246 posters have been included in the proceedings. These papers address the latest research and development efforts and highlight the human aspects of design and use of computing systems. The papers thoroughly cover the entire field of Human-Computer Interaction, addressing major advances in knowledge and effective use of computers in a variety of application areas. The volumes constituting the full 28-volume set of the conference proceedings are listed on pages VII and VIII.

I would like to thank the Program Board Chairs and the members of the Program Boards of all thematic areas and affiliated conferences for their contribution to the highest scientific quality and the overall success of the HCI International 2015 conference.

This conference could not have been possible without the continuous and unwavering support and advice of the founder, Conference General Chair Emeritus and Conference Scientific Advisor, Prof. Gavriel Salvendy. For their outstanding efforts, I would like to express my appreciation to the Communications Chair and Editor of HCI International News, Dr. Abbas Moallem, and the Student Volunteer Chair, Prof. Kim-Phuong L. Vu. Finally, for their dedicated contribution towards the smooth organization of HCI International 2015, I would like to express my gratitude to Maria Pitsoulaki and George Paparoulis, General Chair Assistants.

May 2015

Constantine Stephanidis
General Chair, HCI International 2015

HCI International 2015 Thematic Areas
and Affiliated Conferences

Thematic areas:

- Human-Computer Interaction (HCI 2015)
- Human Interface and the Management of Information (HIMI 2015)

Affiliated conferences:

- 12th International Conference on Engineering Psychology and Cognitive Ergonomics (EPCE 2015)
- 9th International Conference on Universal Access in Human-Computer Interaction (UAHCI 2015)
- 7th International Conference on Virtual, Augmented and Mixed Reality (VAMR 2015)
- 7th International Conference on Cross-Cultural Design (CCD 2015)
- 7th International Conference on Social Computing and Social Media (SCSM 2015)
- 9th International Conference on Augmented Cognition (AC 2015)
- 6th International Conference on Digital Human Modeling and Applications in Health, Safety, Ergonomics and Risk Management (DHM 2015)
- 4th International Conference on Design, User Experience and Usability (DUXU 2015)
- 3rd International Conference on Distributed, Ambient and Pervasive Interactions (DAPI 2015)
- 3rd International Conference on Human Aspects of Information Security, Privacy and Trust (HAS 2015)
- 2nd International Conference on HCI in Business (HCIB 2015)
- 2nd International Conference on Learning and Collaboration Technologies (LCT 2015)
- 1st International Conference on Human Aspects of IT for the Aged Population (ITAP 2015)

Conference Proceedings Volumes Full List

1. LNCS 9169, Human-Computer Interaction: Design and Evaluation (Part I), edited by Masaaki Kurosu
2. LNCS 9170, Human-Computer Interaction: Interaction Technologies (Part II), edited by Masaaki Kurosu
3. LNCS 9171, Human-Computer Interaction: Users and Contexts (Part III), edited by Masaaki Kurosu
4. LNCS 9172, Human Interface and the Management of Information: Information and Knowledge Design (Part I), edited by Sakae Yamamoto
5. LNCS 9173, Human Interface and the Management of Information: Information and Knowledge in Context (Part II), edited by Sakae Yamamoto
6. LNAI 9174, Engineering Psychology and Cognitive Ergonomics, edited by Don Harris
7. LNCS 9175, Universal Access in Human-Computer Interaction: Access to Today's Technologies (Part I), edited by Margherita Antona and Constantine Stephanidis
8. LNCS 9176, Universal Access in Human-Computer Interaction: Access to Interaction (Part II), edited by Margherita Antona and Constantine Stephanidis
9. LNCS 9177, Universal Access in Human-Computer Interaction: Access to Learning, Health and Well-Being (Part III), edited by Margherita Antona and Constantine Stephanidis
10. LNCS 9178, Universal Access in Human-Computer Interaction: Access to the Human Environment and Culture (Part IV), edited by Margherita Antona and Constantine Stephanidis
11. LNCS 9179, Virtual, Augmented and Mixed Reality, edited by Randall Shumaker and Stephanie Lackey
12. LNCS 9180, Cross-Cultural Design: Methods, Practice and Impact (Part I), edited by P.L. Patrick Rau
13. LNCS 9181, Cross-Cultural Design: Applications in Mobile Interaction, Education, Health, Transport and Cultural Heritage (Part II), edited by P.L. Patrick Rau
14. LNCS 9182, Social Computing and Social Media, edited by Gabriele Meiselwitz
15. LNAI 9183, Foundations of Augmented Cognition, edited by Dylan D. Schmorrow and Cali M. Fidopiastis
16. LNCS 9184, Digital Human Modeling and Applications in Health, Safety, Ergonomics and Risk Management: Human Modeling (Part I), edited by Vincent G. Duffy
17. LNCS 9185, Digital Human Modeling and Applications in Health, Safety, Ergonomics and Risk Management: Ergonomics and Health (Part II), edited by Vincent G. Duffy
18. LNCS 9186, Design, User Experience, and Usability: Design Discourse (Part I), edited by Aaron Marcus
19. LNCS 9187, Design, User Experience, and Usability: Users and Interactions (Part II), edited by Aaron Marcus
20. LNCS 9188, Design, User Experience, and Usability: Interactive Experience Design (Part III), edited by Aaron Marcus

Distributed, Ambient, and Pervasive Interactions

Program Board Chairs: Norbert Streitz, Germany and Panos Markopoulos, The Netherlands

- Michael Cohen, Japan
- Adrian David Cheok, UK
- Boris de Ruyter, The Netherlands
- Dimitris Grammenos, Greece
- Nuno Guimarães, Portugal
- Achilles Kameas, Greece
- Javed Vassilis Khan, The Netherlands
- Shin'ichi Konomi, Japan
- Irene Mavrommati, Greece
- Ingrid Mulder, The Netherlands
- Anton Nijholt, The Netherlands
- Fabio Paternó, Italy
- Carsten Röcker, Germany
- Reiner Wichert, Germany
- Woontack Woo, Korea
- Xenophon Zabulis, Greece

The full list with the Program Board Chairs and the members of the Program Boards of all thematic areas and affiliated conferences is available online at:

http://www.hci.international/2015/

HCI International 2016

The 18th International Conference on Human-Computer Interaction, HCI International 2016, will be held jointly with the affiliated conferences in Toronto, Canada, at the Westin Harbour Castle Hotel, 17–22 July 2016. It will cover a broad spectrum of themes related to Human-Computer Interaction, including theoretical issues, methods, tools, processes, and case studies in HCI design, as well as novel interaction techniques, interfaces, and applications. The proceedings will be published by Springer. More information will be available on the conference website: http://2016.hci.international/.

General Chair
Prof. Constantine Stephanidis
University of Crete and ICS-FORTH
Heraklion, Crete, Greece
Email: general_chair@hcii2016.org

http://2016.hci.international/

Contents

Natural Interaction

Design and Development of Distributed, Ambient and Pervasive Interactions

Smart Devices, Objects and Materials

Location, Motion and Activity Recognition

Smart Cities and Communities

Humor in Ambient Intelligence

Designing and Developing Intelligent Environments

Visualizing Human-Environment Interactions: Integrating Concepts and Techniques from HCI, Human Factors and Media Psychology

Bimal Balakrishnan[1(✉)], Loukas Kalisperis[2], and Danielle Oprean[2]

[1] University of Missouri, Columbia, MO, USA
balakrishnanb@missouri.edu
[2] The Pennsylvania State University, State College, PA, USA
{lnk,dxo12}@psu.edu

Abstract. As architecture becomes increasingly integrated with information technology, we need to envision new approaches for architectural visualization. In this paper, we describe an evolving approach for architectural visualization that integrates affordable virtual reality tools, motion capture technology and psychophysiological measurement tools. We start by tracing the development and validation of our two virtual reality labs. Next, we describe our current attempts at visualizing embodied interaction and the use of behavioral agents for simulating human-environment interaction. We conclude by discussing our current work and future directions, particularly our idea to integrate psycho-physiological tools for measuring cognitive and affective responses to these information rich environments.

Keywords: Architectural visualization · Virtual reality · Motion capture

1 Introduction

The built environment is increasingly integrated with information technology due to advances in wireless technology [1]. Progress has since been made in integrating geometry with information to simulate building performance. However, evaluating the ergonomic performance of the end user or their embodied experience while interacting with these pervasive systems remains a challenge. In this paper, we first describe the current challenges for design visualization when architecture is increasingly becoming pervasive. After identifying the challenges, we elaborate on the development of affordable immersive VR systems and their integration with off-the-shelf hardware and software to address these challenges.

© Springer International Publishing Switzerland 2015
N. Streitz and P. Markopoulos (Eds.): DAPI 2015, LNCS 9189, pp. 3–12, 2015.
DOI: 10.1007/978-3-319-20804-6_1

2 Challenge: Visualizing Designs and Human-Environment Interactions

Human interaction with architecture has dramatically changed in the last few decades. From static, non-responsive spaces, the façade and internal surfaces have become more interactive and responsive to stimuli from the environment (e.g. light, temperature, humidity etc.) and human behavior (e.g. movement sensors, auditory sensors, etc.). During the past decades, how humans interact with computers and information has significantly changed. The notion of interacting with traditional input devices such as a mouse or joystick is giving way to gesture-based and full body motion sensors. Visualizing architecture has evolved from exploring geometrical form to building information modeling, optimizing construction, responsive architecture and simulation of building performance with respect to material properties or energy among others. Recent efforts examining performance in architecture has given less attention to the notion of human agency compared to these trends. Visualizing interactions with the environment is a challenge whether it is simulating behavior of special needs populations (e.g. frail elderly) in ordinary settings or even that of normal adults within pervasive environments.

In this paper, we start by examining the development and validation of affordable virtual reality (VR) systems. This is the first step towards visualization technology that is experientially comparable (though it may not be functionally or representationally equivalent) to the corresponding real world. We then embraced the notion of human agency and attempted to simulate human behavior by integrating motion capture with virtual reality. Then we expand on this idea to develop intelligent agents to explore behavioral simulation in multi-actor and pervasive environments. We conclude by examining the use of psychophysiological measurement tools to assess empirically the quality of the human-environment interaction. In doing the above, we draw on theoretical ideas from architecture, HCI and media psychology. We also discuss technology implementation strategies using techniques borrowed from the entertainment industry and illustrate it through the development of affordable, accessible virtual reality technology and off the shelf hardware.

3 Immersive Virtual Environments for Simulation and Assessment of Human-Environment Interactions

Over the course of last 14 years and through the development of three virtual reality labs based on the VR-desktop approach, we have sought to represent as well as interactively explore architecture that is becoming increasingly pervasive. Design students have been using these labs to explore architecture as expressive elements focused on building form and the layers that comprise the form as identified by [2]: façade, interior and structure. These VR systems initially did not support embodied interaction, but interactions mediated through input devices like joysticks or a wireless mouse. Our labs have taken a distinctly human-centric approach focusing on human-environment interactions, instead of focusing on building information modeling

(BIM) and building performance with respect to materiality and energy. In this section, we describe our conceptualizations of these environments and give illustrative examples of our work. Our work in appropriating and integrating immersive virtual reality evolved in three broad stages with some overlap.

3.1   Context: Undergraduate Design Studio and Immersive Visualization

While teaching studio courses for beginning students of architecture, the authors have observed that students have difficulty visualizing space. They have difficulty imagining both the true volume of space as well as its experiential qualities. Envisioning the experiential aspects of a space under design is still a challenge despite improved photorealism now achievable through computer-generated renderings. We experience space while moving through it, i.e. from multiple points of view rather than a single static viewpoint. Most tools for architectural visualization are rarely at full scale and therefore necessitate a mental leap on the part of the designer to accurately capture the true extent and experience of the space. Virtual reality, which draws its spatial paradigm from architecture and the narrative and navigational models from film and multimedia technologies help overcome this challenge. It offers an entirely new way of seeing, inhabiting, and designing space. While virtual reality systems are very useful for visualizing the experiential aspects of architecture often, their prohibitive costs and operational complexity make them challenging to use. We addressed this challenge in the development of our virtual reality labs and integrated these solutions with the existing workflow. In doing so, we also drew on theories of representation and as well as that of media psychology.

3.2   Phase-1: Experiential Congruence for Architectural Representation

Development of the IEL and the iLab. We developed three iterations of the Immersive Environments Lab (IEL) at The Pennsylvania State University and more recently the Immersive Environments Lab (iLab) at the University of Missouri to bring immersive virtual reality within the reach of designers. While there are differences in technical implementation, we developed both the IEL and the iLab based on the desktop-VR approach [3]. The desktop-VR approach uses off-the shelf commodity computers and the familiar windows desktop environment. This lowers the bar for entry and extends the reach of these virtual reality systems. Both VR environments use a multi-projector, rear-projected display driven by graphics workstations running stereo-enabled applications on the Windows operating system. The IEL uses a passive stereo projection using three sets of dual projectors and the iLab uses active stereo projection using 3-D projectors. See [3–5] for technical details of the IEL implementation, [6] for that of the iLab. While affordability, accessibility and adaptability to existing workflows were important pragmatic considerations, we also drew on important theoretical considerations. Two important theoretical considerations are discussed below.

Spatial Presence as a Design Goal for Virtual Environments. We conceptualized these virtual reality environments as technologies that enable spatial presence [7]. Spatial presence is commonly defined as the subjective experience of "being there" in a mediated environment, forgetting one's immediate physical surroundings [8]. Presence enabling technology like virtual reality can help designers to immerse themselves in a virtual space under design and assess its experiential qualities. Spatial presence is a multi-dimensional concept and [9] have identified a number of factors that can influence a sense of presence. [10] pointed out the extent and fidelity of sensory information as a function of screen size, resolution and field of view are important variables that influence the sense of presence. The design goals of virtual reality systems also correspond to the self-location and action possibilities dimensions of the spatial presence experience as later explicated by [11]. Though not driven completely by empirical data, we were cognizant of variables that influenced spatial presence while developing our systems in addition to that of navigability. Early usability evaluations of the IEL received positive feedback from the students and they cited stereoscopic projection, large screen size and navigability as features that enhanced their design evaluation and communication [3] (Fig. 1).

Fig. 1. Design review using 3-D display on the right screen and drawings on the left in the first iteration of IEL development.

A Multi-Modal Approach to Virtual Reality Environments. During the installation of the first iteration of the IEL, we noticed an interesting phenomenon. We observed that students appreciated the immersive quality of the IEL experience but, often used at least one of the three screens to present orthographic drawings or other two dimensional images. This led us to refine our conceptualization of the role of virtual reality in architectural design. We also refined our approach by drawing from the literature on design cognition, particularly in the evaluative or critique phase of the design. The emphasis was no longer on the immersive experience, but rather focused on enhancing our understanding of architectural design for critique. We drew on the work of [12] and the need to facilitate drawing connections between different aspects of the design, which are often communicated through different representations and often via different modalities. We started approaching the lab as a multi-modal virtual environment where immersive virtual reality was seen as belonging to the larger milieu of interactive multimedia tools. Further development of the lab took into consideration the role of digital tools in each stage of the design process, its adaptability to the existing work-flow issues of representation and perception. We developed a multimodal virtual environment prototype using VRML and HTML and evaluated its viability in the IEL [13]. The development of the iLab was later informed by the positive feedback for this prototype and a more robust implementation was done there (Fig. 2).

Fig. 2. Design review at the iLab with 2-D and 3-D imagery

Validation of the VR-Desktop Taking a Media Effects Approach. The media effects approach to architectural visualization builds on Sundar's [14] approach to studying communication technology. Media effects research, for most part, takes a quantitative approach, identifying media characteristics as causal variables and cognitive, affective as well as behavioral responses as dependent variables. The media effects approach for architectural visualization has two important characteristics. The first is its variable-centered nature where visualization tools are conceptualized in terms of structural and content variables. The second characteristic is the emphasis on quanti-tative measurement of the dependent and mediating variables. We conducted system-atic evaluations of the various display and interaction affordances of these systems and, have been able to identify their relative contributions to spatial presence and spatial comprehension. These controlled experiments [15–17] found that display factors like stereoscopy, field of view and screen size had significant impact on spatial presence and comprehension. In addition, there were significant interactive effects between these variables showing the compensatory effect some of these variables have. Two of our recent studies [17, 18] also found significant effects for navigability. These findings have important implications for further development of VR systems whether for large-screen displays or for head-mounted displays like that of Oculus VR.

3.3   Phase-2: Embodiment and Improved Functional Isomorphism

Architects are primarily concerned with the design of static artifacts. Yet, the success of the designed environment depends on its affordance to facilitate human behavior.

Human behavior in a given environment is dictated by cognitive intent, environmental affordances for action and behavior of others. Predicting environment-behavior inter-actions in familiar environments and conditions are relatively easy. Predicting the behavior of users with physical (e.g. frail elderly) or cognitive disabilities (e.g. patients with dementia) is more difficult. After successfully implementing the immersive visualization features at the iLab, we focused on integrating motion capture technology with our VR environment. In addition to creating a greater sense of embodiment, our goal was to incorporate an ergonomically accurate integration of human behavior in real world with a virtual representation of design for evaluation. We chose healthcare settings and environments for the disabled as our research context given the complexity of human-human and human-environment interactions (Fig. 3).

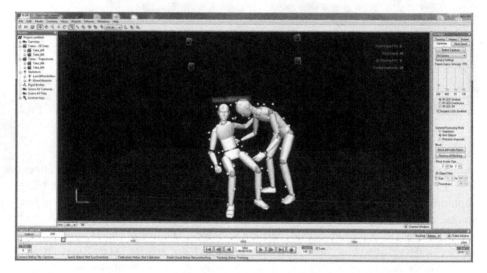

Fig. 3. Screenshot of motion capture data in the iLab for an assisted living scenario

We have developed our 3-D simulation approach building on the human factors framework proposed by [19] for improving patient safety. We started with an accurate 3-D depiction of the physical environment and human behavior in a given scenario (e.g. a medical procedure like intubation) using virtual reality. Using motion capture technology, human performance was captured and integrated with the virtual reality model of the physical setting. This will yield both precise quantitative data as well as accurate 3-D visual representations, which will help to analyze performance. We will then explore design improvements in the virtual prototype. Through motion-capture of interactions with environment, our work will go beyond recent work that use virtual reality mock-ups [20–22] or motion capture [23] independently in exploring healthcare designs. Our current work include scenarios of assisted living activities. Our goal is to develop detailed virtual reality environments as well as digital characters that can be used to test an environment under design.

3.4   Phase-3: Agent-Based Simulations

Predicting human behavioral dynamics during a crisis such as rioting crowds or a building fire is extremely difficult. Successful outcomes in a crisis depends on numerous factors including the adherence to building codes and quality of trained emergency response teams including EMT, fire and hazmat personnel. Studying human-environment interactions during crisis scenarios, predicting behavior and training personnel for dealing with such situations is a challenging task. These offer limited flexibility for new scenarios. Part of our ongoing efforts are directed at simulating these complex interactions between humans and the environment. We are tackling the challenge by creating behavioral agents using motion capture tools and artificial intelligence (AI) authoring software from the entertainment industry coupled with 3-D visualization techniques from architectural design. These virtual agents can then be used to evaluate the capabilities of a given space to accommodate specific behavior. In simple terms, we are currently evaluating a three-step workflow to achieve our goal of simulating behavior.

The first step is to capture movement from live subjects using a high fidelity, multi-actor motion capture toolkit and then to map the movement onto virtual characters using character animation tools. In a recently completed segment of this project, we successfully captured real world human movement and mapped it to a digital character model in an immersive virtual reality environment. This first attempt helped us evaluate ergonomic affordances of spaces under design.

Our ongoing project now uses a more sophisticated motion-capture infrastructure, Optitrack, with an 18-camera array that can capture: (1) more nuanced movement, (2) interaction between multiple actors, and (3) interaction between an actor and a given object. In addition to capturing full body movement, we are attempting to capture the nuances of hand movements and gestures by measuring figure flexure using a data glove. This will also allow us to capture nuances of interactive behavior (e.g. touching, grasping objects etc.). Through all this, we are developing a library of motion capture data. A wide array of human behavior simulation can then be generated using intelligent agent authoring software such as MassivePrime by drawing from this motion capture library. MassivePrime allows for the creation of AI enabled agents without the need for advanced programming languages. An integral component of these agents are their brain nodes that control their behavior. The agent's brain nodes also have 'senses' such as vision and sound. This allows an agent to interact with its environment in a human-like manner and adapt its behavior based on cues from the environment and other agents. We are mapping data from our motion capture into a set of actions for the programmable agent that can be triggered by its brain nodes. MassivePrime allows for multiple pass simulations where the results of one run can be used as an input for the next run, allowing development of richer behavioral simulations (Fig. 4).

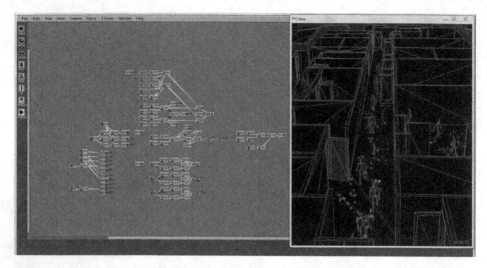

Fig. 4. MassivePrime simulation of crowd behavior during an emergency crisis scenario

4   Current Work and Future Directions

It is now common to integrate smart sensors and displays with building elements. We can now directly interact and manipulate information in various modalities as we navigate through space. This makes it necessary for us to look beyond established approaches for architectural visualization and representation. We need to develop new visualization approaches that help simulate embodied interaction not only with the built elements, but also with the accompanying multimodal information environment through a variety of interfaces. Therefore, the next step in the development of our labs is to further refine our visualization approach so as to conceptualize buildings, the embedded information technology and human-environment interactions holistically. We are adapting and enhancing our visualization tools to facilitate design and evaluation of pervasive environments. We are in the process of integrating our motion capture system with advanced virtual reality tools that can simulate the built environment as well as the information environment. We are also focusing our efforts on developing capabilities to evaluate interactions in these environments both from an ergonomic as well as psychological perspective. Design follows a propose-critique-modify cycle [24] and the critique or evaluation phase is equally important in enhancing the quality of the overall design. We are integrating psychophysiological and eye-tracking tools in addition to our motion capture tools building on strategies laid out in [25] to enhance our measurement capabilities for evaluation. We hope that our efforts will make an important contribution to visualization strategies for design and evaluation of pervasive environments.

References

1. Krogh, P.G., Grønbæk, K.: Architecture and pervasive computing - when buildings and design artifacts become computer interfaces. Nord. J. Archit. Res. **14**(3), 11–22 (2001)
2. Tomitsch, M., Vande Moere, A., Grechenig, T.: A framework for architecture as a medium for expression. In: Workshop on Pervasive Expression. Co-Located with International Conference on Pervasive Computing (Pervasive 2008), Sydney, Australia (2008)
3. Otto, G., Kalisperis, L., Gundrum, J., Muramoto, K., Burris, G., Masters, R., Slobounov, E., Heilman, J., Agarwala, V.: The VR desktop: an accessible approach to VR environments in teaching and research. Int. J. Archit. Comput. **1**(2), 233–246 (2003)
4. Kalisperis, L., Otto, G., Muramoto, K., Gundrum, J., Masters, R., Orland, B.: An affordable immersive environment in beginning design studio education. In: Proceedings of ACADIA, Thresholds - Design, Research, Education and Practice, in the Space Between the Physical and the Virtual, pp. 47–54 (2002)
5. Kalisperis, L., Otto, G., Muramoto, K., Gundrum, J., Masters, R., Orland, B.: Virtual reality/space visualization in design education: the VR-desktop initiative. In: Proceedings of eCAADe, Design E-ducation: Connecting the Real and the Virtual, pp. 64–71 (2002)
6. Balakrishnan, B., Kalisperis, L.N.: Me and my VE: demonstration 5 - building affordable VR environments for education and research. Hum. Factors Ergon. Soc. Annu. Meet. Proc. **56**, 2515–2516 (2012)
7. Balakrishnan, B., Kalisperis, L.N., Muramoto, K.: Spatial presence: explication from an architectural point of view. In: Lilley, B., Beesley, P. (eds.) Expanding Bodies: Art, Cities, Environment, Proceedings of the Annual Conference of ACADIA, pp. 120–127 (2007)
8. Witmer, B.G., Singer, M.J.: Measuring presence in virtual environments: a presence questionnaire. Presence Teleoper. Virtual Environ. **7**(3), 225–240 (1998)
9. Kalawsky, R., Bee, S.T., Nee, S.P.: Human factors evaluation to aid understanding of virtual interfaces. BT Technol. J. **17**(1), 128–141 (1999). Kluwer Academic Publishers
10. Ijsselsteijn, W.A., De Ridder, H., Freeman, J., Avons, S.E.: Presence: concept, determinants and measurement. In: Proceedings of SPIE - Human Vision and Electronic Imaging Conference, pp. 520–529 (2000)
11. Wirth, W., Hartmann, T., Böcking, S., Vorderer, P., Klimmt, C., Schramm, H., Saari, T., Laarni, J., Ravaja, N., Gouveia, F.R., Biocca, F., Sacau, A., Jäncke, L., Baumgartner, T., Jäncke, P.: A process model of the formation of spatial presence experiences. Media Psychol. **9**(3), 493–525 (2007). Taylor & Francis
12. Takala, T.: A neuropsychologically based approach to creativity. In: Gero, J.S., Maher, M.L. (eds.) Modeling Creativity and Knowledge Based Creative Design, pp. 91–108. Lawrence Erlbaum Associates Inc., Hillsdale (1993)
13. Balakrishnan, B., Kalisperis, L.N., Muramoto, K., Otto, G.H.: A multimodal approach towards virtual reality for architectural design [re]presentation. In: Kaga, A., Naka, R. (eds.) Rhythm and Harmony in the Bit-Sphere, Proceedings of CAADRIA 2006, pp. 513–519 (2006)
14. Sundar, S.S.: Media effects 2.0: social and psychological effects of communication technologies. In: Nabi, R.L., Oliver, M.B. (eds.) The SAGE Handbook of Media Processes and Effects, pp. 545–560. Sage Publications, Thousand Oaks (2009)
15. Kalisperis, L.N., Muramoto, K., Balakrishnan, B., Nikolic, D., Zikic, N.: Evaluating relative impact of virtual reality system variables on architectural design comprehension. In: Bourdakis, V., Charitos, D. (eds.) Communicating Space(s), Proceedings of eCAADe, pp. 66–73 (2006)

16. Balakrishnan, B., Oprean, D., Martin, B., Smith, M.: Virtual reality: factors determining spatial presence comprehension and memory. In: Lin, Y.-C., Kang, S.J. (eds.) Proceedings of the 12th International Conference on Construction Applications of Virtual Reality, pp. 451–459 (2012)

17. Oprean, D.: Understanding the immersive experience: examining the influence of visual immersiveness and interactivity on spatial experiences and understanding. Unpublished doctoral dissertation, University of Missouri (2014)

18. Balakrishnan, B., Sundar, S.S.: Where am I? How can I get there? Impact of navigability and narrative transportation on spatial presence. Hum. Comput. Interact. **26**(3), 161–204 (2011)

19. Parush, A., Campbell, C., Hunter, A., Ma, C., Calder, L., Worthington, J., Abbott, C., Frank, J.R.: Situational Awareness and Patient Safety. Royal College of Physicians and Surgeons of Canada, Ottawa (2011)

20. Dunston, P.S., Arns, L.L., Mcglothlin, J.D., Lasker, G.C., Kushner, A.G.: An immersive virtual reality mock-up for design review of hospital patient rooms. In: Wang, X., Tsai, J.J.-H. (eds.) Collaborative Design in Virtual Environments. ISCA, vol. 48, pp. 167–176. Springer, Heidelberg (2011)

21. Peavey, E.K., Zoss, J., Watkins, N.: Simulation and mock-up research methods to enhance design decision making. Health Environ. Res. Des. J. **5**(3), 133–143 (2012)

22. Kumar, S.: Experience-based design review of healthcare facilities using interactive virtual prototypes. Unpublished dissertation, The Pennsylvania State University (2013)

23. Carlson, J.N., Das, S., De la Torre, F., Callaway, C.W., Phrampus, P.E., Hodgins, J.: Motion capture measures variability in laryngoscopic movement during endotracheal intubation: a preliminary report. Simul. Healthc. J. Soc. Simul. Healthc. **7**(4), 255–260 (2012)

24. Chandrasekharan, B.: Design problem solving: a task analysis. AI Mag. **11**(4), 59–71 (1990)

25. Balakrishnan, B., Kalisperis, L.N.: Design visualization: a media effects approach. Int. J. Archit. Comput. **7**(3), 415–427 (2009)

Using the GQM Method to Evaluate Calmness in Ubiquitous Applications

Rainara M. Carvalho[1(✉)], Rossana M.C. Andrade[1],
and Káthia M. Oliveira[2]

[1] Group of Computer Networks, Software Engineering and Systems (GREat),
Federal University of Ceará (UFC), Fortaleza, Brazil
{rainaracarvalho,rossana}@great.ufc.br
[2] Laboratory of Automatic Control, Mechanics and Computer Science for
Industrial and Human-Machine Systems (LAMIH), CNRS UMR 8201, University of Valenciennes and Hainaut-Cambrésis (UVHC), Valenciennes, France
kathia.oliveira@univ-valenciennes.fr

Abstract. Ubiquitous systems change the way users interact with computers, because their services must be available everywhere at any time, supporting users in various everyday activities. An essential element for these systems is their calm interaction with users, which means the system should not disturb them unnecessarily. Literature currently lacks work focusing on how to evaluate calmness and case studies made in a real usage situation. The aim of this work is to propose a model, defined using the Goal-Question-Metric (GQM) method, for calmness evaluation in ubiquitous systems and to show our results from a case study with three ubiquitous applications.

Keywords: Ubiquitous applications · Calmness · Software measures · GQM

1 Introduction

With the improvement in miniaturization of computational devices and also in wireless communications, the last years have seen an increase in ubiquitous applications development [1]. Such applications completely change the way users interact with technology, once their services must be available everywhere at any time. They must support users in everyday activities and remain transparent with little or no need of attention. Thus, an essential characteristic for these applications acceptance is *calmness*, which was firstly cited by Weiser and Brown (1997) as a new approach to properly fit computing into people's lives [2].

As ubiquitous applications are embedded within everyday objects (*e.g.*, cell phones, watches) and environments (*e.g.*, home, office), there is a high risk of users

This work is a result of Maximum project supported by FUNCAP and CNRS under grant number INC-0064-00012.01.00/12.
R.M. Carvalho—PhD Scholarship (MDCC/DC/UFC) sponsored by CAPES.
R.M.C. Andrade—Researcher scholarship - DT Level 2, sponsored by CNPq.

© Springer International Publishing Switzerland 2015
N. Streitz and P. Markopoulos (Eds.): DAPI 2015, LNCS 9189, pp. 13–24, 2015.
DOI: 10.1007/978-3-319-20804-6_2

feeling annoyed and overwhelmed by them. A calm application must support user's activities at the right time and place, delivering the best service possible [3, 4]. We believe that calmness has a great impact on the user satisfaction, therefore, on the usability and acceptance of the ubiquitous application.

We propose in this paper to evaluate calmness by using software measurements. To perform these measurement, firstly, it is necessary to define what software measures should be collected. In this case, there is a well-known method in the Software Quality area called Goal-Question-Metric (GQM) [5]. GQM is a goal-oriented approach that follows a hierarchical structure model starting with the definition of a measurement goal, that is refined in several questions and, finally, into metrics[1], which will provide information to answer the questions. By answering these questions, it is possible to analyze if the goal is achieved.

This paper presents a model composed of a goal, questions and software measures, defined by the GQM method, for evaluating the calmness characteristic in ubiquitous applications. By applying this model, it is possible to verify if the application presents a good level of calmness and what could be improved within the application to improve calmness level. We also present results from a case study involving three mobile ubiquitous applications.

2   Calmness Evaluation in Ubiquitous Applications

Ubiquitous applications are those capable of monitoring environment and users in order to provide services as natural as possible. To achieve this goal, they have to comply with challenging requirements such as autonomy, heterogeneity, coordination of activities, mobility and context-awareness [6]. In the scope of Human-Computer Interaction (HCI), there is another indispensable characteristic for ubiquitous applications being used and accepted by users: *calmness*.

According to [2], a calm technology should move easily from the periphery of attention to the center, and back. Periphery is used to describe what we are attuned to without focusing on it explicitly. For example, when we are driving, we do not focus on sounds but rather on the road. However, when a specific sound related to an event occurs, this information comes to the center of attention. That means we can keep information in periphery and, only when necessary, we can attend to it.

Through a literature search, we found one study [3] that carefully defines *calmness* and how it can be evaluated. It proposes a conceptual framework for evaluating calmness in ubiquitous applications. The authors classify calmness from two statements: calm timing and calm interaction. Calm timing means that the ubiquitous application should interact with the user in the right situation. Calm interaction means that the application should remain out of the user's attention whenever possible. They propose a subject evaluation using values such as High, Medium, Low and Very Low. However, they do not apply the proposed framework to evaluate ubiquitous

---

[1] Metric was the term used previously, but currently, the standard ISO 25000 SQuaRE recommends the use of the term measure.

applications in a real usage situation. Also it does not define a measurement function or a collect method for the proposed values.

Other previous work that was found related to calmness were [4, 7]. They sate that calm technology should allow users to access new information peripherally, enabling them to decide whether to divert their attention and change their focus. These works aimed to create a model for evaluating if a technology is calm or not. Anthropology-Based Computing (ABC) and Peripheral Interaction (PI) are the objects of their studies. However, they still are testing fade-ups and calm ringtones.

We argue that an evaluation using software measurement is also needed for calmness in ubiquitous applications. According to [10], measurement is the process of defining, gathering and analyzing data about products, in order to provide meaningful information for the purpose of improving it. There are several papers in literature that use measures to evaluate ubiquitous applications [8–11], including a paper with measures to evaluate context-awareness [12]. However, the literature study did not encounter any papers with software measures to evaluate calmness.

3 A GQM Model to Evaluate Calmness in Ubiquitous Applications

Using the GQM method, we defined our goal as follows: "**Analyze** the ubiquitous application, **for the purpose** of evaluating, **with respect to** calmness, **from the viewpoints** of the user". Then, we derived three questions and eleven measures based on both literature review [3, 8–14] and interviews with five experts on ubiquity. The resulted GQM model is presented in Fig. 1.

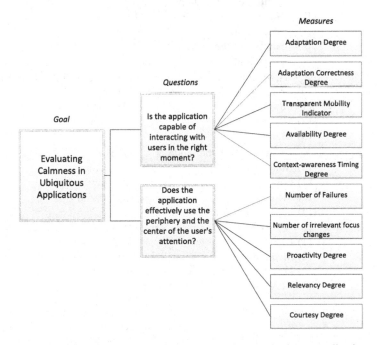

Fig. 1. The GQM model to evaluate calmness in ubiquitous applications

3.1   Question 1: Is the Application Capable of Interacting with Users in the Right Moment?

Users need to feel the ubiquitous application is available anytime and anywhere. This can be achieved by the following statements: (*i*) the context-awareness adaptation should happen when requested by a contextual change; (*ii*) this adaptation should be correct; and (*iii*) the application should have the characteristic mobility, which refers to a continuous or uninterrupted use of the systems as the user moves through several devices. Based on all these statements, we defined five measures showed in Table 1.

Table 1. Software measures for question 1

Name	Measurement function	Interpretation	Collect method
Adaptation degree	$X = \dfrac{\left(\sum_{j=1}^{N} \frac{Aj}{Bj}\right)*100}{N}$ N = Number of the different adaptations Aj = Number of times the system adapts Bj = Number of times an adaptation j was requested (the context changed)	Closer to 100 % is better	Automatic and observation
Adaptation correctness degree	$X = \dfrac{\left(\sum_{i=1}^{N} \frac{Ai}{Bi}\right)*100}{N}$ Ai = Number of correctly performed adaptations i Bi = Number of performed adaptations i N = Number of the different adaptations	The closer to 100 % is better	Automatic and observation
Indicator of transparent mobility	X = A, where A is (0) Nonexistent (1) Low (2) Medium (3) High	(0) Nonexistent (1) Low (2) Medium (3) High	Observation
Availability degree	X = B, where B is the mode of (0) Nonexistent (1) Low (2) Medium (3) High	(1) High (2) Medium (3) Low (4) Very low	User form
Context-awareness timing degree	X = C, where C is the mode of (1) High (2) Medium (3) Low (4) Very low	(1) High (2) Medium (3) Low (4) Very low	User form

The two first software measures are related to context-awareness adaptation. When the context changes (*e.g.*, location and activity) the application has to adapt to this new context, if this does not happen, the user probably will feel the application has not worked well. So, the measure *Adaptation Degree* counts how many times the system adapts when requested by a context change.

Adaptation Correctness Degree aims to identify if that adaptation happened in an expected way for the user, it means checking if the services and/or information were delivered in the right way with respect to what is expected for the user at that specific moment. To calculate this, it is necessary to identify which adaptations the system has that can be collected (N). Thus, it is possible to count how many times a particular identified adaptation occurred during a certain usage period of the application (Bi) and how many of times those adaptions have occurred correctly (Ai). As a system can have several adaptations happening, the measure shows a summation aiming to add up all the adaptations occurred, and then calculating an average by dividing by N.

Indicator of Transparent Mobility was based on the information about mobility from the work of [13]:

- **High** is when the application can move from one device to another, keeping the past interactions and adapting resources to the new device (*e.g.*, screen size), so the user can continue their tasks seamlessly.
- **Medium** is when the application can move from one device to another, keeping the past interactions and adapt to the new features. However, the user is likely to have to wait a long time to start interacting with the application on the new device.
- **Low** is when the application can move to another device. However, the application does not adapt to it. For example, the new screen size is not taken into account.
- **Nonexistent** is when the application cannot move from one device to another.

The two last measures (*Availability Degree and Context-awareness Timing Degree*) are qualitative and collected from the user after the use of the application.

3.2   Question 2: Does the Application Effectively Use the Periphery and the Center of the User's Attention?

This question is related to the first consideration Weiser wrote in his paper that a calm technology should move easily from the periphery of our attention to the center, and back. This leads to measure if the application is being proactive to reduce the decision-making time of the user, the number of times the user is unnecessarily harassed and the number of failures that occurred during use.

It is necessary to know if the application interacts with the user only when needed, delivering relevant information and requests. To answer this question, five measures were defined and presented in Table 2.

The first measure (*Number of irrelevant Focus Changes*) aims to identify the amount of time the user had to change focus due to the technology. This shift in focus happens when some user action has to be performed for the application to work

Table 2. Measures for question 2

Name	Measurement function	Interpretation	Collect method
Number of irrelevant focus changes	X = A, where A = Number of actions that changes user's focus during use of the application	The further away from 0 is better	Automatic and observation
Proactivity of the application	X = N - A where N = Number of total actions developed that can be supported by sensors A = Number of actions the application replaces	The closer to 0 is better	Developer form
Number of failures	X = N, where N = Total number of failures have occurred	The closer to 0 is better	Automatic and observation
Relevancy degree	X = B, where B is the mode of (1) High (2) Medium (3) Low (4) Very low	(1) High (2) Medium (3) Low (4) Very low	User form
Courtesy Degree	X = D, where D is the mode of (1) High (2) Medium (3) Low (4) Very low	(1) High (2) Medium (3) Low (4) Very low	User Form

correctly during use. For example, restart a particular sensor during use and/or restart the application are actions that change the user attention unnecessarily.

The second measure (*Proactivity of the application*) aims to identify what the degree of proactivity is by counting how many user actions the application is able to replace. This measure is calculated by counting how many actions were developed in the application that can be supported by sensors and which among these actions are replaced by the sensors. The closer to zero the better, as this means every action capable of being developed by the sensors was actually developed by them.

The third measure (*Number of failures*) aims to identify how many failures happened while the user was using the application. The more failures that occur, the more distractions the user will face.

Finally, the two last measures (*Relevancy Degree and Courtesy Timing Degree*) are qualitative and collected from the form the user has to answer after using the application.

3.3   Collection Methods

Each measure, as already presented above, is collected by one or more of the following collected methods:

- **User interaction Logs:** Generation of user interaction logs with the application through code instrumentation. These logs should be collected during the use of the application. Each application that will be evaluated need to be instrumented.
- **Questionnaires:** Two questionnaires were developed to collect some measures. One questionnaire[2] is composed of questions to the application developer and the other[3] to the user who answers after using the application, to collect the qualitative measures.
- **Observation by an Evaluator:** A form for manual observation by an evaluator is filled when following the user during the application use.

4   Case Studies

The collection of the proposed measures was performed through case studies with three ubiquitous applications developed for mobile devices on the Android platform as follows: GREatPrint, GREatMute and GREatTour.

4.1   GREatPrint

This application aims to print documents at the nearest printer from the user. The application works as follows: after choosing a file, the user clicks on the print button for a given document, then the application searches for the Wi-Fi network with the highest signal intensity, which signifies that it is probably the closest to the mobile device. With this information, the application checks which printer is in the range of that network. Thus, the application sends the document to be printed on that printer, and informs the user which printer was selected.

Twelve users participated on this application evaluation. The developer also participated by answering a form specific to the applications developers. The twelve users were divided in four groups of three people to execute the application in different floors and rooms. The task defined to be performed by the users was to print a pre-established document on the application. Users were asked to use the application in the GREat research lab, because GREatPrint are targeted for this environment.

An evaluator was present during the usage, noting, for example, if the captured context was correct, if the application failed, and other valid information. After usage, users were asked to answer the user questionnaire. Table 3 presents the results of the measures collected.

We can conclude that the application **must** be improved to better address context-awareness and mobility. An improvement suggestion is to add more context

---

[2] Details in http://www.great.ufc.br/maximum/images/arquivos/developerquestionnaire.pdf.

[3] Details in http://www.great.ufc.br/maximum/images/arquivos/userquestionnaire.pdf.

Table 3. Results from the GREatPrint evaluation

Question	Measure	Result	Interpretation
Is the application capable of interacting with users in the right moment?	Adaptation degree	79 %	The application is not able to recognize reliably how to interact with the user, because all the achieved results were under the appropriate. For example, the *Adaptation Correctness Degree* was very low; the application sends the document to the wrong printer almost half times
	Adaptation correctness degree	52 %	
	Indicator of transparent mobility	Nonexistent	
	Availability degree	Medium	
	Context-awareness timing degree	Medium	
Does the application effectively use the periphery and the center of the user's attention?	Number of focus changes	15 actions	Despite presenting a large number of failures and focus changing, the application implements all functions replaceable by sensors and also the users feel all information and service were relevant and the interaction was friendly
	Number of failures	33 failures	
	Proactivity degree	0	
	Relevancy degree	High	
	Courtesy degree	High	

information to infer more precisely the actual location of the user by utilizing more sensors such as the accelerometer or the magnetometer. Also an improvement would be to allow the use of the application on other device types, for example: desktops and notebooks.

4.2   GREatMute

GREatMute is a service that runs in the background of the user's mobile phone. It monitors the mobile user's Google Calendar for events during which the user cannot receive calls, *e.g.*, "meeting" or "class". By discovering such events, the application places the user's phone on silent mode during the event time, so user does not get disturbed.

Also, this application allows the user to specify which events they would like to the device to be on silent mode, this is performed by the registry of keywords to be monitored. When the application finds an event in which the title has one of the keywords registered, GREatMute schedules based on the information extracted from start time and end time of the event. During this time the phone uses the silent profile.

To execute the tests with GREatMute, users were asked to install the application on their own device and use it during a week. Thus, users experienced the use of the application in their actual day to day environments. The task for the user to perform was registering at least one event that would actually happen throughout the week on the calendar, as well as a corresponding keyword to the name of this event in the GREatMute application. A period of one week was selected because it was considered sufficient time for real events to happen that could be monitored.

For the testing of GREatMute, it was important to recruit people who knew how to use Google Calendar. If the users had previously used Google Calendar to schedule events, they would not have to also learn how to use it.

Only eight of the twelve invited users participated in the GREatMute evaluation. Table 4 presents the results.

Table 4. Results from the GREatMute evaluation

Question	Measure	Result	Interpretation
Is the application capable of interacting with users in the right moment?	Adaptation degree	92 %	The application has a very low degree of adaptation correctness. Almost always the application does not adapt properly (27 %). Also, the application is not able to move between several different devices when necessary and the users did not feel the application interact when was necessary
	Adaptation correctness degree	27 %	
	Indicator of transparent mobility	Nonexistent	
	Availability degree	High	
	Context-awareness timing degree	Very low	
Does the application effectively use the periphery and the center of the user's attention?	Number of focus changing	0 actions	All measures presented good results. The application can replace actions of users so they are not bothered to take many decisions
	Number Of failures	0 failures	
	Proactivity degree	0	
	Relevancy degree	High	
	Courtesy degree	High	

The application needs to improve in relation to the capability of interacting at the right moment. GREatMute could take into account two additional pieces of context information: the user's current location and the location of the event he/she registered on the calendar. Thus, it is possible to know if the user is at the event that they registered and thus change the mobile profile more reliably. If the user is not in an approximate radius of the registered venue, the application does not need to put the phone on silent mode.

4.3 GREatTour

GREatTour is a mobile guide for visiting the GREat Lab. It provides information about the environments of the laboratory that the user is visiting. The application works as follows: the user must scan a QR Code that is found on the door of the environment to update user location. Then, a map of the lab is displayed, highlighting the environment where the user is. So, the user can view media options related to this environment (texts, photos and videos). However, the rendering of this media depends on the battery level of the device. When battery is low (0–9 %), only text is displayed, when it is medium (10–20 %), text and images are displayed, and finally, when it is high (21–100 %), texts, images and videos are displayed.

Like with GREatPrint, the users were asked to use the applications in the GREat research lab, since this application is targeted for this environment. Also, an evaluator was present during the usage. In this case study, only six of the twelve users actually used the application, due to unavailability of the other users. Each user made three visits (tours) to the laboratory GREat, with different battery levels in order to test all application states. Each visit consisted of seeing three environments. In each environment, users updated the map and accessed all available media, according to battery of the phone. Table 5 presents the results.

Table 5. Results from GREatTour evaluation

Question	Measure	Result	Interpretation
Is the application capable of interacting with users in the right moment?	Adaptation degree	72 %	Although the degree of context correctness is high (100 %), the adaptation not always happens (72 %). Besides, users think the availability and timing need improvement
	Adaptation correctness degree	100 %	
	Indicator of transparent mobility	Nonexistent	
	Availability degree	Medium	
	Context-awareness timing degree	Medium	
Does the application effectively use the periphery and the center of the user's attention?	Number of focus changes	14 actions	Despite users feel the application shows only relevant requests and use effectively the periphery and the center of the attention, the degree of user attention requisition is very high and is completely far from acceptable value. GREatTour requests a lot of actions, including unnecessarily actions (14 actions), like restart the application and restart the connection with internet
	Number of failures	6 failures	
	Proactivity degree	14	
	Relevancy degree	High/Medium	
	Courtesy degree	High	

GREatTour provides a good degree of context-awareness correctness. However it **must** be improved to better address adaptation degree, mobility, availability, context-awareness timing, focus changing and proactivity. The following changes could improve GREatTour: (*i*) allow mobility between different devices (different phones and tablets) without loss of information in the new device screen and maintain the previous tour information; and (*ii*) use mobile sensors (*e.g.,* magnetometer, accelerometer and wi-fi) to detect the user location more transparently without the need for user intervention (QR code scans).

5   Conclusion and Future Work

By using the GQM method, it was possible to develop a model to evaluate calmness in ubiquitous applications. This model is composed of software measures that were applied in three ubiquitous applications developed for mobile devices: GREatPrint, GREatMute and GREatTour. As a result of these case studies, the measures indicate that these applications still need to improve to have good levels of calmness. This reveals an indication that the proposed model was able to assess Calmness.

However, due to the variety of application fields within ubiquitous computing, each application may require different test procedures. For instance, GREatMute required that the user use the application during the week on their mobile phones and after that the subjective measures were collected. On the other hand, GREatPrint and GREatTour were used inside the GREat Lab and an evaluator could observe the use. However, each one of them required different planning of scenarios, because the context is not the same between these applications.

Therefore, this proposed model does not exclude a plan for how an evaluation must be in different ubiquitous applications. The perspective for future work and improvement of this work is to create a methodology capable of systematically guiding an evaluator, so that they are able to assess calmness and investigate the influence of calmness on other characteristics of HCI, for example, Usability.

Acknowledgement. We would like to thank the Software Quality and Testing Cell (CTQS) of GREat for the technical support that they provided.

References

1. Weiser, M.: The computer for the 21st century. Sci. Am. **265**, 94–104 (1991)
2. Weiser, M., Brown, J.S.: The coming age of calm technology. In: Denning, P.J., Metcalfe, R.M. (eds.) Beyond Calculation. Copernicus, New York (1997)
3. Riekki, J., Isomursu, P., Isomursu, M.: Evaluating the calmness of ubiquitous applications. In: Bomarius, F., Iida, H. (eds.) PROFES 2004. LNCS, vol. 3009, pp. 105–119. Springer, Heidelberg (2004)
4. Brown, J.N.A., Leitner, G., Hitz, M., Mallofré, A.C.: A model of calm HCI. In: Peripheral Interaction: Shaping the Research and Design Space, Workshop at CHI (2014)

5. Basili, V., Rombach, H.: Goal question metric paradigm. In: Marciniak, J. (ed.) Encyclopedia of Software Engineering – 2, vol. 1, pp. 528–532. Wiley, Chichester (1994)
6. Rocha, L.S., Ferreira, J., Lima, F.F.P., Maia, M.E.F., Viana, W., Castro, M.F., Andrade, R. M.C.: Ubiquitous software engineering: achievements, challenges and beyond. In: Brazilian Symposium on Software Engineering (in portuguese) (2011)
7. Leitner, G.: A measure of calm. In: Conference on Human Factors in Computing Systems - Proceedings (2014)
8. Song, J., Park, K.R., Kwon, S., Lee, J.H., Yun, M.H.: The development of human-system interactivity metrics for ubiquitous service applying user-centered design methodology. In: World Congress on Services (2009)
9. Lee, J., Song, J., Kim, H., Choi, J., Yun, M.H.: A user-centered approach for ubiquitous service evaluation: an evaluation metrics focused on human-system interaction capability. In: Asia-Pacific Conference, APCHI (2008)
10. Ranganathan, A., Al-Muhtadi, J., Biehl, J., Ziebart, B., Campbell, R.H.H., Bailey, B.: Towards a pervasive computing benchmark. In: International Conference on Pervasive Computing and Communications Workshops (2005)
11. Scholtz, J., Consolvo, S.: Toward a framework for evaluating ubiquitous computing applications. IEEE Pervasive Comput. **3**, 82–88 (2004)
12. Santos, R.M., Oliveira, K.M., Andrade, R.M.C., Santos, I.S., Lima, E.R.R.: A quality model for human-computer interaction evaluation in ubiquitous systems. In: Latin American Conference on Human Computer Interaction, CLIHC (2013)
13. Yu, P., Ma, X., Cao, J., Lu, J.: Application mobility in pervasive computing: a survey. Pervasive Mob. Comput. **9**(1), 2–17 (2013)
14. Kourouthanassis, P.E., Giaglis, G.M., Karaiskos, D.C.: Delineating the degree of 'pervasiveness' in pervasive information systems: an assessment framework and design implications. In: Pan-Hellenic Conference on Informatics, PCI (2008)

Distributable Interface Design
for Web Applications

Gianni Fenu[✉] and Lucio Davide Spano

Dipartimento di Matematica e Informatica,
University of Cagliari, Via Ospedale 72, 09124 Cagliari, Italy
{fenu,davide.spano}@unica.it

Abstract. The increasing number of devices available for each person
allows to create unconventional interfaces that coordinate more than
one device for supporting the interaction. In this paper, we introduce a
framework for designing distributable web applications, which supports
moving and sharing the different parts of a user interface across different
devices. We depict the architectural solution and we introduce a set of
distribution patterns. In addition, we describe a concrete application of
the framework for a distributable video player application.

Keywords: Distributed interfaces · Web applications · User Interface
Engineering · Development tools

1 Introduction

The wide availability of different types of devices, both stationary and mobile,
is opening the opportunity for creating applications that go beyond a single
device. And this is not only limited to providing the same application in different
versions (e.g. one for desktop environments and one for mobiles), but also to
unconventional interfaces that coordinate more than one device for the same
user interface (UI).

As highlighted in [1], people is more and more developing a multi-screen
behaviour, which results in both the sequential and simultaneous usage of different screens at the same time. Therefore, creating applications that exploit such
new interaction habits effectively is an opportunity and a challenge for the HCI
community. On the one hand, applications able to exploit different devices at
once may be able to create experiences that go beyond the simple sum between
the capabilities of each considered device. On the other hand, the device coordination creates different technical challenges, and poor solutions may affect the
overall usability of the interface.

In this paper, we propose a framework for developing web applications allowing the interface to be distributed across the device we use everyday, for creating
a personal interactive space going beyond the single device. We first introduce a
distribution example scenario, identifying the users' needs, then we describe the
architecture of the proposed solution, and finally we discuss the implementation
of a first prototype supporting the proposed scenario.

© Springer International Publishing Switzerland 2015
N. Streitz and P. Markopoulos (Eds.): DAPI 2015, LNCS 9189, pp. 25–35, 2015.
DOI: 10.1007/978-3-319-20804-6_3

2   Related Work

Starting from the first applications of the ubiquitous computing concept, different techniques related to distributing parts of the user interface (UI) in different devices started to take place in research work: the user does not own a single device, but she is empowered with different computing platforms that are pervasive in the environment. The different efforts aimed for instance to the migration of the entire UI state from a device to another [2], or for the adaptation and configuration of a UI according to the actual device that renders it [3].

Demeure et al. [4] created a reference model for examining a distributed interface according to 4 dimensions: the computation (which part is distributed), communication (when the UI is distributed), coordination (who is distributed) and configuration (from which device to which device the distribution is operated). Such work opened the space for creating different engineering solutions and models for supporting the distribution.

In particular, the model-based approaches for user interfaces community produced different models supporting the distribution of user interfaces. In [5], the authors exploit a XML format for defining how an interactive application can be distributed across different dimensions: end user, display device, computing platform, and physical environment. Frosini and Paternò [6] introduce a framework and the associated runtime support for supporting dynamically the distribution across different devices, with a peer-to-peer architecture.

Another field where the distribution of user interface gained the attention of the research community is the creation of shared spaces. A first example is the collaboration in museum environments [7], where distributed interfaces were implemented for supporting the collaboration of museum visitors for solving didactic games through mobile devices.

The second example is related to the information visualization. VIGO [8] supports the distributed interaction in a multi-surface environment through four components: Views, Instruments, Governors and Objects. Hugin [9] ia a graphical framework for mixed-presence collaboration settings. In such environment, the information visualization application is shared between different tabletops, which should be coordinated over the network for both controlling the data and making the users aware of each other.

In this paper, we shift the emphasis from a self-contained model or architecture to a lightweight framework that exploits the usual structure of a web application for building the support for distributable interfaces. In this way, it would be possible to adapt existing applications for a distributed setting.

3   Example Scenario

In order to explain the framework concepts with a concrete example, we consider a simple on-demand video streaming application. We detail the envisioned interaction through a small scenario.

Robert is just back home from work and he decides to watch the last episode of his favourite TV series, Game of Phones, on DistrFlix. He just started watching the third episode on his laptop, when his wife Sarah interrupts him. She is a fan of Game of Phones too, and she would like to see the episode together with Robert. Therefore, Robert moves the video from the laptop to his Smart TV, while the information on the episode and the playback buttons are transferred to his smartphone, in order to be easily controlled from the sofa. While they are watching the episode, Robert receives different phone calls: one from his mother, one from his boss and one from the call center of his previous phone company, advertising discounts if he accepts to be their customer again. Sarah is annoyed since Robert never pauses the episode before answering the call, so she ask him to share the video control buttons on her smartwatch.

According to the scenario description, we have four involved devices: a laptop, a TV, a smartphone and a smartwatch. All these devices allow to control the access to the same application during the same session. During the interaction, the interface assumes three configurations across the four devices, which we summarize in Fig. 1. In the first one, the user accesses all the application functionalities on the laptop. In the second configuration, the UI is splitted between the TV (video) and the smartphone (playback controls and additional information). In the last one, the smartwatch and the smartphone provide a redundant control on the video playback.

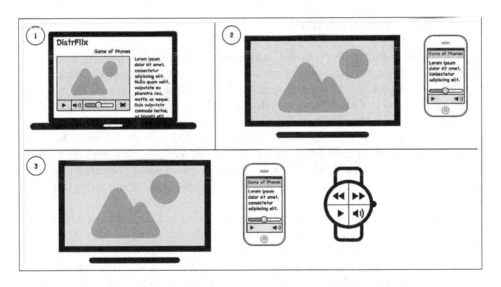

Fig. 1. Scenario interface mockup.

In Sects. 2, 5 and 6 we describe a framework for supporting the distribution of the UI components on the different devices and their state management. In Sect. 7 we show a concrete application of the framework for solving the situation described in the scenario.

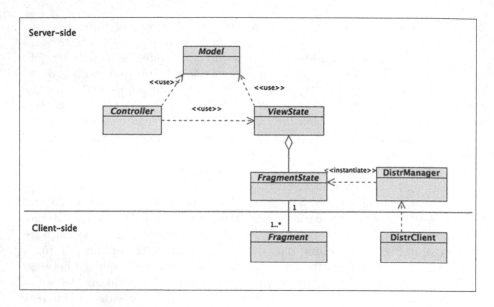

Fig. 2. Distribution framework reference architecture

4   Overall Architecture

The framework organisation is based on two main concepts. The first one is the definition of the UI parts that can be distributed across different devices. We started from the techniques for creating responsive layouts: the content of a single page is organised in a set of macro groups (that we call UI *Fragments*), which are positioned inside a grid. How such grid is displayed on a particular device screen (e.g. its rows and columns) depends on its width. In addition, each fragment has different associated styles according to viewport size. We push further this idea in order to support the distribution of web interfaces: the developer defines rules not only for positioning the fragments, but also for distributing them among different devices.

The second concept that grounds the distribution framework is the definition and the synchronization of the UI state, which must be shared among all the devices involved in the distribution process. We propose an abstraction mechanism for separating the UI element distribution aspect from the UI state management. Such mechanism is depicted in Fig. 2, which applies the separation concept inside the Model View Controller (MVC) pattern [10], since it is one of the most applied for organizing web applications. However, the separation concept we present in this paper is independent from the MVC, and it may be applied also to other variants (e.g. Presentation Model [11], Model View Presenter [12] or Model-View View Model [13]).

The component we modified for supporting the UI distribution is the *View*. The framework provides a view state abstraction (the *ViewState* class) for coordinating the dynamic changes to the state of a fragment. More precisely, the framework considers the rendering of a fragment on a particular device as a view on the UI state, which is instead the considered as the model of the fragment. The changes made by the user through a particular view modifies the values saved on the model (the UI state). They should be in turn reflected on the other fragments, which are rendered on different devices.

We detail both aspects in the following sections.

5   Fragment Management

A *Fragment* is a UI part that groups together interface elements that are logically related to each other. In our scenario, for instance, we have three different fragments: one related to the video, one related to the playback controls and one related to the TV show information. In order to establish how a UI can be distributed across two or more devices, the developer assigns a set of fragments to each of them. A fragment may be rendered in different ways according to the device type. However, it keeps the semantics of the UI controls: for instance a drop down list for a desktop interface may be rendered as a list view on mobile device, but the semantics of the action it supports (and therefore the reaction of the application back-end) is the selection of a value. The different rendering is supported through both CSS rules and/or different HTML code generation at server side.

The same fragment can be assigned to more than one client device. Therefore, its internal state must be synchronized across all the devices. Such synchronization is required at two levels: the UI and the application state. At the application level, the framework relies on the model component of the MVC pattern, which is shared by different views. In our case, such views are spread among the different devices. At the UI element level, the framework splits the state management in two parts. Such concept is similar to the distinction of abstract and concrete interactors in model-based approaches for user interfaces (i.e. as reported in [14]).

- The UI element *semantics*, which is independent from the actual widget exploited for supporting the user. A widget can support the *selection* or the *editing* of value (text, number, date etc.), it can *trigger* a specific command, or it can *display* information. This part of the state is maintained into the *ViewState* (see Fig. 1). The controller component of the MVC pattern accesses the *ViewState* for reading or updating the UI values, without relying on any information about their actual rendering.
- The UI element *implementation*, which depends on both the device type (e.g. laptop or smartphone) and the current state of the UI distribution among the devices. For instance, the control over the video stream position in our example can be implemented through a slider on the laptop and the smartphone, while on the smartwatch we decided to support it through a set of buttons. The widgets have semantically the same purpose (controlling the stream position value), but they are implemented differently. Therefore, there is a part of the state that depends on the actual implementation, which is maintained into the *FragmentState*.

At the code level, the framework provides the support for such coordination through a specific javascript object, which has a bidirectional binding with the UI elements and the server side part. This means that the fragment behaviour specifies (1) which fragment state variables change when the user interacts with a UI element, and (2) how the UI elements should be modified for reacting to a change on the fragment state object.

A fragment state object can be configured for containing different sets of variables according to the specific fragment. In addition, it includes different functions for getting and setting the variable values. In these functions, we encapsulated the synchronization protocol: the object manages a web socket communication with the application server for receiving and sending updates from and to other devices. The developer is not in charge of any synchronization, and he can specify the behaviour code as if the UI state was handled locally. The only requirement is managing it through a fragment state object extension.

The server side code reacts to the changes of all fragment states. The framework provides facilities for managing application and device level sessions. The application sessions are related to a single user that access an application through different devices. Therefore, an application session contains many devices sessions.

6 Distribution Management

Besides the classes for managing the view component state in the MVC pattern displayed in Fig. 1, the framework contains also the classes for managing the association between the fragments and the devices.

The first class, the *DistrClient* provides the user support for dynamically adding or removing a device from the distribution set. The user has a device management page where she can add all her personal devices. After this operation, the user can request to add one of her personal devices to the distribution set for each web application supporting the distribution. Optionally, the application developers may also request to specify which fragments they want to include on the different devices, providing a user-friendly name and description for them (e.g. playback controls).

Once the user requests to activate (or deactivate) the distribution towards a particular device, the *DistrManager* evaluates distribution strategy (in form of a set of rules coded by developers) and it creates (or destroys) the fragments related to the selected device, which in turn will receive an update message for displaying them.

In a given device, a fragment can be rendered in different modes: supporting the input, the output or both of them. In the input mode, the fragment contains only the interface elements that are devoted to collecting values from the user and those that depend on them (e.g. field labels etc.). In the output mode, the fragment renders only elements that have no interaction capabilities (texts, images, videos etc.). The mixed mode shows both types of interface elements, as usually happens in web interfaces. Such configuration allows developers to dynamically distribute fragments specifying an association between fragments and devices.

The mode is considered an attribute of such association by the fragment and its rendering is controlled accordingly.

Different patterns exist for defining such association. In our framework we considered the well-known CARE properties for the defining multimodal user interfaces [15]:

- *Complementarity:* two fragments are complementary if they are assigned to two different devices, but none of them is able to complete their corresponding task without the other. For instance, the video and the playback controls when split between the TV and the smartphone are complementary: the video is useless without the controls and the vice-versa.
- *Assignment:* a given fragment is assigned to only one device. In our scenario, the video fragment is assigned to the TV after the first device change.
- *Redundancy:* the same fragment is displayed in two (or more) devices and its functionalities should be confirmed in all of them for being executed.
- *Equivalence:* a fragment is displayed on more than one device. The user can activate its functionalities from anyone of them. In our scenario, the playback controls may be activated from both the smartphone and the smartwatch.

Developers may both select a single specific pattern for distributing the UI across the devices or require the users to select one of the patterns for a subset of fragments. In this case, the *DistrClient* allows two select among two or more distribution patterns, providing a user-friendly description for each choice.

7   Scenario Support

In this section we provide some technical details on the implementation of a Java prototype supporting the scenario described in Sect. 3 through the proposed framework. The starting point is the usual desktop interface for a video player, as shown in Fig. 3, which consists of three fragments: the larger part of the screen is dedicated to the video, with the controls displayed below it. The right bar contains the plot description.

The current state of this simple UI contains: the current position in the video stream, the player state (playing/paused), the volume level and the reading position in the description sidebar. All these variables are maintained in the *ViewState*, and they are valid independently from the UI elements we selected for interacting with the user. The *FragmentState* performs the mapping between such values and the UI elements in both directions. For instance, if the user changes the position of the slider knob for rewinding the video, the fragment state receives the new position of the knob and maps it to the correct time, notifying the *ViewState* object.

In our scenario, at a certain point Robert decides to continue watching the video on the TV, controlling its state from his smartphone. In order to do this, Robert needs a way for requesting the distribution, accessing the functionalities of the distribution client (*DistrClient*). The framework provides a reusable JSP which can be simply included into all the web application that require the support for the distribution.

Fig. 3. Laptop interface for the distributable video player.

In our example, we chose to insert a small arrow button at the bottom of the page (with a fixed positioning) that allows to access the distribution client UI. The button is visible in Fig. 3 in the bottom-left corner. Once pressed, the application shows the sidebar in Fig. 4 (left part), which displays the list of user's personal devices (after an authentication step). The panel contains a button for each one of them. In the example, we have four devices: the laptop (Davide Air), the smartphone (Nexus 5), the TV (Samsung TV) and the smartwatch (Gear S). Through these buttons, the user can select or deselect each device for the distribution: the green devices are currently active (they contain at least a fragment), while the other ones are not in use with the current web application.

In order to distribute the interface, the user presses the button of an inactive device. If the application has a configurable distribution policy for that kind of device (as in our example for smartphones), the user is requested to select the fragments to be included in the new device through the interface shown in Fig. 4 (right part): he simply clicks on a content, which is highlighted with a green box and a check icon on the top right corner. The user can de-select them clicking on the highlighted area again. In our scenario, we suppose that the user selects the smartphone, clicking on the video control and description fragments.

Once the selection is completed, the laptop *DistrClient* sends a request to the *DistrManager*, which in turn creates the new instances for the *FragmentState*, which registers for receiving updates from the *ViewState*. After that, the *DistrManager* notifies the smartphone *DistrClient*, which loads the web application interface. We implemented this push protocol in the prototype through a browser tab, which remains open as long as the device participates to the UI distribution

Fig. 4. Distribution client (left part) and fragment selection interface (right part).

Fig. 5. The web application UI distributed on a smartphone (left part) and a smartwatch (right part).

and receives the updates through a websocket. However, this step should be supported by the browser or by a dedicated application, in order to provide the user with a reliable and trustworthy mechanism. Finally, the smartphone shows the interface in Fig. 5 (left part).

Robert follows the same process for managing the devices when he wants to distribute the interface from the laptop to the TV (this time he selects only the video) and from the smartphone to the smartwatch. The interesting part in the final configuration is the equivalent video playback control from two devices. The application needs to coordinate the values entered by Robert through the smartphone and by Sarah from the smartwatch. The framework supports such combination as follows: when, for instance, Sarah presses the rewind button, the video control *Fragment* on the smartphone sends the update to the associated *FragmentState*, which writes the new value (e.g. the previous position minus five seconds) in the *ViewState*. The *ViewState* notifies the value change to all the other registered *FragmentState*s. One of them is associated to the phone that, again through a websocket, sends the notification to its associated *Fragment*, which is updated accordingly.

In addition, as shown in Fig. 5, the two interfaces provide different UI elements for the same action (same semantics, different implementation): the slider and the rewind and forward buttons allow the user to edit the same value (the video position) but the interaction is supported in different ways for different devices.

Finally, it is worth pointing out that the prototype implementation for the smartwatch interface is a native Android Wear application, which needs the support of an handheld for the network communication. The device limitations still does not allow to create web interfaces in such kind of devices, however we think that it will be possible soon.

8   Conclusion and Future Work

In this paper we introduced a framework for supporting the distribution of web-based user interfaces across different devices. We introduced the architecture of a device coordination solution that allows to separate the interface management aspect for the application logic. In addition, we described how it is possible to isolate the process of UI switching and splitting through a dedicated software component. Finally, we presented a distributed video player application as sample for the proposed framework.

In future work, we aim to provide a software library containing the reusable components for developing this type of applications. Our scope is to support the distribution as a specific aspect of UI development, which can be addressed injecting specific code even into existing applications. Moreover, we aim to merge the research in distribution with the solutions for developing multimodal interfaces, in order to go beyond the simple screen interaction for distributed UIs.

Acknoledgments. Lucio Davide Spano gratefully acknowledges Sardinia Regional Government for the financial support (P.O.R. Sardegna F.S.E. Operational Programme of the Autonomous Region of Sardinia, European Social Fund 2007–2013 - Axis IV Human Resources, Objective 1.3, Line of Activity 1.3.1 Avviso di chiamata per il finanziamento di Assegni di Ricerca.

References

1. Google: The new multi-screen world: Understanding cross-platform consumer behavior. Technical report (2012). Retrieved from: https://ssl.gstatic.com/think/docs/the-new-multi-screen-world-study_research-studies.pdf. Accessed 08 October 2014

2. Bandelloni, R., Paternò, F.: Flexible interface migration. In: Proceedings of the 9th International Conference on Intelligent User Interfaces, IUI 2004, pp. 148–155. ACM, New York (2004)
3. Calvary, G., Coutaz, J., Thevenin, D., Limbourg, Q., Bouillon, L., Vanderdonckt, J.: A unifying reference framework for multi-target user interfaces. Interact. Comput. **15**(3), 289–308 (2003)
4. Demeure, A., Sottet, J.S., Calvary, G., Coutaz, J., Ganneau, V., Vanderdonckt, J.: The 4C reference model for distributed user interfaces. In: Fourth International Conference on Autonomic and Autonomous Systems, ICAS 2008, pp. 61–69, March 2008
5. Melchior, J., Vanderdonckt, J., Van Roy, P.: A model-based approach for distributed user interfaces. In: Proceedings of the 3rd ACM SIGCHI Symposium on Engineering Interactive Computing Systems, EICS 2011, pp. 11–20. ACM, New York (2011)
6. Frosini, L., Paternò, F.: User interface distribution in multi-device and multi-user environments with dynamically migrating engines. In: Proceedings of the 2014 ACM SIGCHI Symposium on Engineering Interactive Computing Systems, EICS 2014, pp. 55–64. ACM, New York (2014)
7. Ghiani, G., Patern, F., Santoro, C., Spano, L.: A location-aware guide based on active rfids in multi-device environments. In: Lopez Jaquero, V., Montero Simarro, F., Molina Masso, J.P., Vanderdonckt, J. (eds.) Computer-Aided Design of User Interfaces VI, pp. 59–70. Springer, London (2009)
8. Klokmose, C.N., Beaudouin-Lafon, M.: Vigo: Instrumental interaction in multi-surface environments. In: Proceedings of the SIGCHI Conference on Human Factors in Computing Systems, CHI 2009, pp. 869–878. ACM, New York (2009)
9. Kim, K., Javed, W., Williams, C., Elmqvist, N., Irani, P.: Hugin: A framework for awareness and coordination in mixed-presence collaborative information visualization. In: ACM International Conference on Interactive Tabletops and Surfaces, ITS 2010, pp. 231–240. ACM, New York (2010)
10. Krasner, G.E., Pope, S.T., et al.: A description of the model-view-controller user interface paradigm in the smalltalk-80 system. J. Object Oriented Prog. **1**(3), 26–49 (1988)
11. Fowler, M.: Presentation model Retrieved from: http://martinfowler.com/eaaDev/PresentationModel.html. Accessed 08 October 2014
12. Potel, M.: Mvp: Model-view-presenter the taligent programming model for c++ and java (1996). Retrieved from: http://www.wildcrest.com/Potel/Portfolio/mvp.pdf. Accessed 08 February 2015
13. Smith, J.: Wpf apps with the model-view-viewmodel design pattern. Retrieved from: http://msdn.microsoft.com/en-us/magazine/dd419663.aspx. Accessed 08 October 2014
14. Paternò, F., Santoro, C., Spano, L.D.: MARIA: A universal, declarative, multiple abstraction-level language for service-oriented applications in ubiquitous environments. ACM Trans. Comput. Human Interact. **16**(4), 19:1–19:30 (2009)
15. Coutaz, J., Nigay, L., Salber, D., Blandford, A., May, J., Young, R.: Four easy pieces for assessing the usability of multimodal interaction: the CARE properties. In: Proceedings of INTERACT, vol. 95, pp. 115–120 (1995)

The Map as a Tool for Identifying Pervasive Interactions in Today's Home

Konstantinos Grivas[1] and Stelios Zerefos[2(✉)]

[1] Department of Architecture Engineering, University of Patras, University
Campus, 26500 Rion, Greece
kgrivas@upatras.gr
[2] Department of Applied Arts, Hellenic Open University, 18 Parodos Aristotelous St., 26335 Patras, Greece
zerefos@eap.gr

Abstract. The task of making the spectrum of home network connections visible in its entirety and details is a necessary first step towards a renewed understanding of home and domestic life as well as of the technical systems that underpin it. This paper proposes the categorization of pervasive interactions that take place in contemporary living spaces through certain criteria and tries to map them into the predefined spaces of today's home, by creating a basic visualization tool. The research concludes with an example of a "composite map" that shows all the interlinked interactions that take place in a contemporary home. This map can become a potential tool for further research in the fields of the structure, behaviour and countenance of home networks, of advances in intimate media, applications and networked devices, and of augmented architectural spaces that interact with complex and pervasive communication networks.

Keywords: Home mapping · Pervasive computing in architecture · Home automation · Automation control

1 The Networked Home

Home as a space – both the architectural envelope and the spatial configuration of objects or devices of daily use and personal value – is the material testimony of the identities and the habitual acts of its inhabitants. Modern home, was based on a functional division of internal space. Its roots date back to the 17th century rise of the bourgeois class in Europe, which signified a gradual evolution of a room-to-function correlation. Gradually, bourgeois homes became an agglomeration of rooms highly specific for their function (bed-room, living-room, play-room, bath-room, etc.). The specific function of each room was reflected in the furniture, equipment and decoration it had, as well as the engendering of it. The function of each room dictated a certain protocol of its usage (e.g. one can use it certain time of the day) and a certain behaviour (when in bedroom, wear robe) [1]. The division of home-space, primarily by function, is certainly a western practice. In different cultures, home-space is divided according to family hierarchy or structure or division between genders. The architectural space of

© Springer International Publishing Switzerland 2015
N. Streitz and P. Markopoulos (Eds.): DAPI 2015, LNCS 9189, pp. 36–48, 2015.
DOI: 10.1007/978-3-319-20804-6_4

home reflects the functional structure of it, and the relations of rooms reveal the structure and sequence of everyday life.

Current living trends however, augmented by wireless connectivity, suggest that the inhabitants of today's contemporary homes are largely investing personal time and value on the data connections taking place within and through their homes, a practice that can alter the "traditional" functions and rooms of "modern living". These connections become an increasingly important part of daily home-life routines catering for the inhabitants' "networked living demands" and contribute equally to the establishing of the person's or the household's social position within a larger but usually geographically distributed social circle. Yet most of these connections remain invisible – operating at the background – or difficult to trace or relate spatially in contrast to social and cultural theories that emphasize on mundane tasks as a means to understand everyday life [2].

Following previous work on mapping pervasive interactions in a home environment [3], this paper proposes the categorization of pervasive interactions that take place in contemporary living spaces applying certain criteria and tries to map them into the predefined spaces of today's home, by setting up a basic visualization tool according to current living trends. The interactions identified, based on wireless or conventional network communications within and through home-space, are categorized relatively to their basic attributes such as parties involved, purpose or goal, nature of data exchanged, exclusivity, result/effect, time/duration/reoccurrence, and others. These interactions include the documentation of trivialities of everyday life (e.g. monitoring of activities), the documentation of domestic based big data (e.g. monitoring and of household objects, data from sensing devices), the formation and presentation of identity (e.g. consciously projected data about home and inhabitants). Using this categorized list of network activities, we apply both quantitative and qualitative criteria in order to identify the most probable, common and important interconnections in a contemporary home. We regard that the task of making this spectrum of home network connections visible in its entirety and details is a necessary first step towards a renewed understanding of home and domestic life, as well as of the technical systems that underpin it. Of course the contemporary networked home is closely intertwined with parts not geographically linked to it. Communications between transport media and the house, between houses in a neighbourhood are a few connections that take place and influence domesticity. However, due to publication limitations we chose to present findings for home as a closed networked ecosystem, while all outgoing network activity is treated simply as a route to the internet to dens and gather information.

1.1 The Scenario

This paper is presenting the outlines and first findings of an ongoing speculative design experiment. The team's initial aim was to use a real living scenario, where activities and network functions would be mapped, and investigate methods of home network representations. For this purpose, we decided to involve only existing technologies, devices and today's living activities. Therefore we carried an initial research looking for networked appliances, devices, and objects as well as related applications for domestic use, that are commercially available.

We also decided to use as our testing environment a type of house that complies with the current European standards for average household (members and size). According to official statistics the average European household is 2.4 members [4], which means that families consisting of a couple alone, or with one child are considered typical of today's European societies. Moreover, the average European house occupies an area of approximately 120 sq.m., and has 4 main rooms (presumably: living-room with kitchen, 2 bedrooms, and bathroom).

This design experiment could have been based in an existing real household, and a real family, monitoring its life and environment, and visualising its networking activities. However, we deliberately chose to use for our scenario (as a background) a specific visionary architectural project of the 1950s, importing from it the architectural environment, and the explicit lifestyle of the (supposed) inhabitants, that could actually fit into the typical requirements set by the average European household. The project we used is "The House of the Future" [5], or HOF in short, by British architects Alison and Peter Smithson, designed and constructed in 1955-56 as a show-piece for the "Ideal Home Exhibition" organised by Daily Mail in Olympia, Kensington, London, UK (Fig. 1). This concept house was furnished and equipped with several innovative items and technologies (some existing as mock-ups). There are several aspects of the HOF that are of great interest today. It was a hypothetical arrangement of a house in 1980. The fluid architectural interiors and the lack of doors is quite reminiscent of today's homes or loft houses.

For the needs of our project we re-furnished this concept house with a new inventory consisting of networked items and several applications that would cater for the everyday life of a couple and renamed our project "House of Today" (HOT). This new inventory is superimposed to the existing household. Furthermore, we were inspired from the rich photographic material depicting casual activities inside the house in order to create simple narratives that would engage the pair of characters inhabiting the house into daily routines. Such narratives involve waking-up and breakfast, preparing dinner, or other activities.

In short, for our mapping experiment we created a hypothetical scenario based on real data. This enabled us to project a more complicated picture that would heighten the issues we would like to investigate. More than that, we found that the dialogue between the old concept-house with its retro-futuristic aesthetics and the visualizations of the new networked inventory, proved quite suggestive and at times ironic.

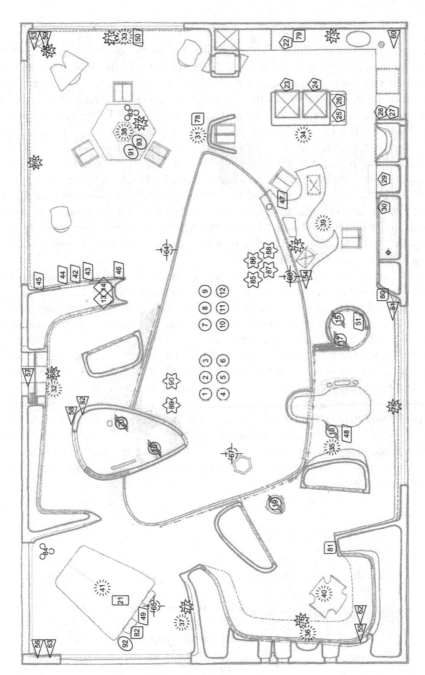

Fig. 1. Plan of the House of Today (HoT) with full inventory (No. 1-93). Each family of devices (e.g. wearable, kitchen, sleep, bath, surveillance, etc. is depicted with a dedicated symbol and a specific number, corresponding to the number in Table 1.

1.2   The Household Inventory

Home automation is receiving a renewed attention from companies producing net-worked devices and objects, mainly due to the rise of IoT, the evolution and wide-spread use of smart devices like smartphones and tablets as well as numerous applications developed for them [6, 7]. A quick survey showed that most of the available devices and applications relate to the automated and remote home control. John Thackara [8] back in 2001 has highlighted that "we are designing a world in which every object, every building—and nearly every human body—becomes part of a network service" which we will bequeath to next generations without having fore-thought the effects this will have on the quality of life. Thackara illustrates his critical vision with an example: "Ericsson and Electrolux are developing a refrigerator that will sense when it is low on milk. Imagine the scene. You'll be driving home from work in your car, and the phone will ring. "Your refrigerator is on the line," the car will say. "It wants you to pick up some milk on your way home." To which my response will be "tell the refrigerator I'm in a meeting."

Apart from home automation, connected devices available in the market tend to follow a few other trends, focusing around other areas concerning domestic and per-sonal life, such as health care, health monitoring, body caring, security and surveil-lance, connectivity, advice on cooking or other domestic tasks, energy consumption monitoring and generally environmental awareness.

In our hypothetical scenario we have selected a number of commercially available connected devices to make the inventory of the HOT. The couple of inhabitants – for the needs of our experiment we named them Anna (A) and Paul (P) – have (hypo-thetically) selected the devices described in Table 1. After having compiled the detailed, itemized list of the hypothetical household inventory of connected devices in the HOT, we assigned a unique identification number and a dedicated position for each item inside the plan. Each device is placed in its appropriate place on the house plan (Fig. 2) with an indication of its respective number distinction in the graphic sign for each device was made.

Table 1. List of connected devices in HOT

Id No.	Function	Device - description	Link
1	Wearable	Apple watch	https://www.apple.com
2		MC10 adhesive wearable	http://www.mc10inc.com
3		Ampstrip adhesive heart rate monitor	http://www.ampstrip.com/
4		UP24 Jawbone activity tracker	https://jawbone.com

(*Continued*)

Table 1. (*Continued*)

Id No.	Function	Device - description	Link
5–6		2 × WeMo keychain sensor (P + A)	http://www.belkin.com
7	Portable	Apple iPhone 6	https://www.apple.com
8		Apple iPad Air 2	
9		Apple MacBook Air	
10		Nokia Lumia 930	http://www.microsoft.com
11		Nokia tablet 2520	
12		Toshiba Tecra w50-a	http://www.toshiba.eu
13	Hubs	Smartthings hub	https://www.smartthings.com
14		D-Link Wireless N300 ADSL + 2 Gigabit Cloud Router	http://www.dlink.com
15	Bath	Eva showerhead	http://evasmartshower.com
16–19		4 × Dornbracht smart water (WC, shower, bath, washbasin)	http://www.dornbracht.com
20		Toto Intelligence Toilet II	http://www.toto.com
21	Sleep	Luna mattress	http://lunasleep.com/
22	Kitchen	LGThinQ refrigerator	http://www.lg.com
23–24		LGThinQ ovens	
25		iDevices kitchen thermometre	http://idevicesinc.com
26		Crock-Pot 6 Slow cooker (WeMo)	http://www.crock-pot.com
27		Mr. Coffee Smart optimal brew (WeMo)	http://www.mrcoffee.com
28		iKettle	http://www.firebox.com
29–30		LGThinQ Washer & Dryer	http://www.lg.com
31	Climate control	Nest thermostat	http://www.nest.com
32–37		6 × Sensibo A/C control (living, kitchen, bath, dressing, bedroom)	http://www.sensibo.com
38–41		4 × Haiku ceiling fan (living, bedroom, dressing, kitchen) with senseme connected to nest	http://www.bigassfans.com

(*Continued*)

Table 1. (*Continued*)

Id No.	Function	Device - description	Link
42	Electronics/media	Sony Bravia android TV	http://www.sony. com
43		Sony 4 K media player	
44		Sony HiRes Music Player	
45-49		5 × Sonos Play: wifi speaker (living, kitchen, bathroom, bedroom)	http://www.sonos. com
50		WD myCloud Mirror NAS	http://www.wdc. com
51		iShower	http://idevicesinc. com/ishower/
52–56	Surveillance/ security	5 × Withings Home camera (entrance, living, kitchen, dressing, bedroom)	http://www. withings.com
57		august smart lock at entrance	http://www. august.com
58-63		6 × WeMo room motion sensor (entrance, living, kitchen, bathroom, dressing, bedroom)	http://www.belkin. com
64–66	Sensing	3 × netatmo indoor weather station (living, bedroom, atrium)	https://www. netatmo.com
67		netatmo rain gauge (atrium)	
68–77	Lighting	10 × hue personal wireless lighting bulb (entrance, 4 × living, kitchen, bath, dressing, bedroom))	http://www2. meethue.com
78–82	Smart sockets	5 × WeMo smart socket (living, kitchen, laundry, dressing, bedroom)	http://www.belkin. com
83	Robots	irobot Roomba 880 vacuum cleaner	http://www.irobot. com
84		Karotz toy robot (living)	http://store.karotz. com
85–88	Plants	4 × Click&Grow smartpot (herbs)	http://www. clickandgrow. com
89–90		2 × Parrot flower power (atrium)	http://www.parrot. com
91–92	Miscellaneous	2 × Fireside smartframe (living, bedroom)	http://www. fireside.co
93		Nimbus dashboard (living)	http://www. quirky.com/ shop/596

1.3   Interactions and Connections

Normally, households comprise of people, animals (pets), objects (stuff) and territory (property land or space). Among those, humans tend to have the dominant role. Although inert things and the environment do have agency over the household, this is not active or purposeful. Augmented technologies provide composite things that are active and responsive and have a high or low reasoning. The current study is based on the idea that humans are among several quasi-equal parties within the as an eco-system. The parties involved into most augmented home interactions are the following:

- person: (PE) any human, owning, having access and agency over the household, occupying the home, or connected to it remotely or not.
- pet: (PET) autonomous real or virtual organism (other than human) belonging or connected to the household. Autonomous robots belong to pets.
- agent: (AG) software-based self-learning organism, physically or not manifested, that compliments home functions and environment. Remotely, or not, connected to the house. Agents can manage, facilitate, or even represent the house.
- node: (ND) mediating device, facilitating communication between parties.
- device: (DEV) complex machine/appliance/gadget with both a physical and an electronic component that performs specific tasks.
- application: (APP) software, with only an electronic component that performs specific tasks.
- object: (OB) physical object belonging to the household (this is not interactive unless it has a tag or becomes a device)
- tag: (TAG) electronic device attached to other parties (hosts) (persons/pets/nodes/ devices/objects) that performs specific tasks (identification, geo-location, etc.)

These individual parties can team together in order to form composite entities. Although most of the above parties can irrespectively conjoin in order to form composite entities, (PE + DEV, DV + ND, OB + TAG, PT + AG, DEV + APP + ND, etc.) some of the combinations seem to have specific relevance and can be named as distinct types. Some of these are analogous to traditional parts of a home. For example:

- house: (HOU) The complete list of parties comprising the household joined together forms the house. The house can interact as an entity with all parties.
- room: (RO) A portion of the house (not necessarily a spatially defined portion) that supports a person or a set of activities, or has specific access rules or ownership. This can interact independently to house.
- routine: (ROU) A cluster of entities that are normally interconnected in order to fulfill specific activities, tasks, rituals, e.g. "making breakfast".
- face: (FA) Face refers to clusters of entities working together in order to edit and project images of the house (or parts of it) to the outer world, social media, etc. (projecting identity). It is a public face and can deal with social communication.
- fence: (FC) A virtual structure comprising of several parties (objects, devices, agents, etc.) that limits access or cuts off specific connections. Example: "energy waste fence", "private data fence".

- vigilant: (VG) A composite party that monitors and warns about unwanted or potential threats, misbehaviours, ill-judgments, hazards, etc. Can be simply an agent, but in most cases is a combination of sensors, applications and devices.
- hearth: (HRT) More contrived and significant than a room, it is a place for the valuable(s) and a source of energy. Can be about safeguarding as much as for sustaining. Contains what makes sense to be bequeathed to next generations. Perhaps the entity which is about history, memories and traces of the past.
- depot: (DPT) less complicated than a room entity, with a specific function to store (and archive) data, archives, etc.
- other types of home entities may emerge.

2 Living Activities and Actions

Home, whatever form it takes, is the basis for fulfilling fundamental human needs for living, such as providing shelter, a place for rest and comfort, a place to store and protect possessions and, among others, a place to nurture oneself and family. Following Philip Agre's work [9] we have identified two different aspects of living and categorized them into activities and actions. To clarify this distinction, activities relate to the broad organization of human doings, such as sleeping or working, while actions explain specific procedures for doing things. Both of these concepts are dynamically interrelated to each other, meaning that any activity can be influenced by, as well as influence any action. For example, one can make food to eat, while her eating experience can modify her process of making food. Moreover, the relation between them can, over time, turn habitual, causing certain combinations of actions and activities to become the "unconscious" base for other, newer, more conscious activities [10, 11]. A behaviour can transform into a habit at any given time, as well as evolve and become more complex. Its identification is important for our work, as it has immediate effects on the visualization tools that we propose: new habitual series of actions can be represented and selected as a group.

By studying the interactions and connections that were described in the previous chapter (4), we have arrived at a set of activities and actions that can accommodate most of them and these are depicted in Table 2 and are used throughout our proposed visualizations at the following chapter. If we take the sleeping activity as an example, the following interrelations can occur between the actions in Table 2 and the list of devices in Table 1:

- We organize ourselves for sleep, through routines such as turning off the lights. This can be completed automatically through the WeMo motion sensor in the living room, when it does not sense anyone there, or the nest thermostat in conjunction with the Philips hue lights.
- We consume less energy when we to go to sleep. The nest thermostat learns our patterns and knows when we're sleeping to reduce heating and consequently energy consumption.
- We can make a hot milk to help us go to sleep and the iKettle can have it ready at the optimal time

- We reproduce sleeping patterns and the Luna mattress identifies them and informs us.
- We protect ourselves before we go to sleep (locking doors through the august smart lock and our phone).
- We can evolve our sleep by introducing white noise through an app in our smartphone and make it play through the Sonos wireless speakers
- We react to sleeping by waking up, preferably using the jawbone
- We can learn of sleep deficiencies and correct them via the www on any compatible device.
- We can buy (monetary exchange) a better pillow for a better sleep at any e-shop.

Table 2. Activities and actions in home living

Activities of home living	Actions for home living
Eating - Drinking	Organizing
Sleeping	Consuming
Hygiene	Making
Studying	Reproducing
Leisuring (oneself)	Maintaining/Protecting
Entertaining (others)	Evolving
Intercommunicating	Reacting
Extracommunicating	Learning
Working	Exchanging

3 Proposed Visualisations - Conclusions

Mapping activities inside the typical bourgeois western house, is almost like reading the plan, for each room is named and furnished according to its function as described before. In today's home, there are functions, aspects or activities superimposed onto the typical bourgeois-type functions. These functions, activities, actions, and several composite entities taking part in the home connections network, require a more complex and multilayered set of visualization and mapping techniques, as well as viewpoints. An initial survey on home network visualizations has been presented in previous work [3]. In this phase we initiated this design experiment and tried to create examples of how the specific home's network would be visually presented. Several views were considered: Dashboard view, Activity view, Action View, Immersive view, Accumulated view, and others. In the following Figs. 2, 3, 4, and 5 we present a few. This design experiment is in progress.

These initial visualizations were discussed among several people. This first evaluation revealed several basic issues:

1. Since the media that these will be probably shown in will be either smartphones or tablets, having relatively small screens, the density of information and of the graphics does affect the degree of comprehension of the home network. The more

Fig. 2. Dashboard View: Persons and Devices are shown. [07:32 am: Anna is waking up]. Active connections are shown in bright yellow lines, previous connections in orange and pending or anticipated connections in purple. To the right, there is information about current connections. Scrolling around with finger on screen, devices inform about their status. Map is shown in a tablet interface.

Fig. 3. Immersive View: Connections and devices are shown over the image of the real space. All other relevant information can be added to the layout. The image is shown in a smartphone interface.

Fig. 4. Action View: All available actions are displayed with icons. To the right the inhabitant can review details about current actions, as well as forthcoming ones. The network connections are shown in the style of recommendations between devices and actions, as well as details on near future actions.

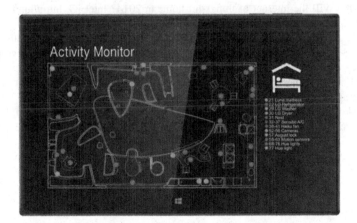

Fig. 5. Activity View: This view monitors specific living activities throughout the house by showing simple on/off functions of specific devices linked to the selected activity. For example for a sleeping activity the refrigerator goes into away mode, the washer and dryer start their operation, A/C units are shut down, along with lights, motion sensors and the door is locked.

dense the information and the graphics, the more difficult is to read and discern. On the contrary, less information and simpler graphics tend to result in fragmented concept of network.

2. A "technical" style of visualizing information about home activities, is evaluated as non-appealing to the more intimate nature of home everyday life. We were encouraged to consider more personified graphic layouts.
3. Reading information about network connections with the home plan makes it easier to localize spatially the events, but creates visual clutter. A simpler and more intuitive way is perhaps necessary.

References

1. Welter, V.M.: Ernst L. Freud. Architect. The Case of the Modern Bourgeois Home. Berghahn, New York (2011)
2. Galloway, A.: Intimations of everyday life. Ubiquitous computing and the city. Cult. Stud. **18**(2/3), 384–408 (2004)
3. Grivas, K., Zerefos, S., Mavrommati, I.: Mapping interactions in a pervasive home environment. In: Streitz, N., Markopoulos, P. (eds.) DAPI 2014. LNCS, vol. 8530, pp. 25–36. Springer, Heidelberg (2014)
4. Eurostat: Household composistion statistics (2011). http://ec.europa.eu/eurostat/statistics-explained/index.php/Household_composition_statistics#Further_Eurostat_information. Accessed 25 Feb 2015
5. Risselada, M. (ed.): Smithson Alison & Peter - from the House of the Future to a House for Today. 010 Uitgeverij, Netherlands (2004)
6. PSFK Labs: Why tablets are the key to making smart homes go mainstream. http://www.psfk.com/2014/06/tablets-smart-home-trend-intel.html. Accessed 27 June 2014
7. Kaplan, K.: Will the internet of things hit home in 2014? Intel iQ. http://iq.intel.com/will-the-internet-of-things-hit-home-in-2014. Accessed 31 Dec 2013
8. Thackara, J.: The design challenge of pervasive computing interactions. https://www.cs.cmu.edu/~jasonh/courses/ubicomp-sp2007/papers/08-thackara-design-challenge-pervasive.pdf. Accessed May 2001
9. Agre, P.E.: The dynamic structure of everyday life. Ph.D. thesis, Department of Electrical Engineering and Computer Science, MIT (1988)
10. Ehn, B., Lofgren, O.: Routines - made and unmade. In: Shove, E., Trentmann, F., Wilk, R. (eds.) Time, Consumption and Everyday Life. Practice, Materiality and Culture, pp. 99–112. Berg, Oxford (2009)
11. Ben, H.: Everyday Life and Cultural Theory: An Introduction. Routledge, London (2002)

Makers with a Cause: Fabrication, Reflection and Community Collaboration

Foad Hamidi[✉] and Melanie Baljko

Department of Electrical Engineering and Computer Science, Lassonde School
of Engineering, York University, Toronto, Canada
{fhamidi,mb}@cse.yorku.ca

Abstract. The potential of using maker and DIY approaches for collaborative learning is widely recognized. Maker techniques such as rapid prototyping are being increasingly adopted by schools, universities and colleges in order to effectively teach core design and science concepts. We describe our approach to facilitating a series of "MakeShops", maker workshops, for undergraduate engineering students, in which we used a *maker atelier* model to facilitate the design and implementation of self-directed maker projects that combined making and tinkering with reflection and community collaboration.

Keywords: Maker movement · Design facilitation · Pedagogy · Interdisciplinary collaboration · Self-directed learning

1 Introduction

In his seminal 1980 book on the potential of using computers for children's education, *Mindstorms*, Seymour Papert described the similarities he felt between Brazilian samba schools and his vision of a technological culture that "helps us not only to learn but to learn about learning" [1]. He envisioned a mode of learning that is "fully participatory" and is achieved through "real activity that can be shared by novices and experts" [1]. More than 30 years have passed since *Mindstorms* and, in recent years, the Maker Movement (or Do-It-Yourself (DIY) Movement) has emerged as a body of amateur and professional designers who often combine high-tech tools (e.g., 3D printers and embedded computers) with traditional manufacturing methods (e.g., glassblowing and woodworking) to create customized, small-batch designs [2]. The potential of this movement, especially in the light of the potentials of collaborative, self-directed and technology-mediated learning, is enormous [3, 4]. We believe the culture growing around the Maker Movement is serving in the technological/cultural role that Papert envisioned in his book and creates the conditions in which digital design and making can lead to genuine self-expression and empowerment.

Making is, of course, not new; the use of tools is associated with human evolution itself. A significant shift occurred in the Industrial Revolution, as modes of production,

© Springer International Publishing Switzerland 2015
N. Streitz and P. Markopoulos (Eds.): DAPI 2015, LNCS 9189, pp. 49–61, 2015.
DOI: 10.1007/978-3-319-20804-6_5

transitioning from industrial workshops into factory and assembly line contexts, became more complex and inaccessible; in the aftermath of this shift, consumers became increasingly distanced from modes of production. Making and tinkering, of course, continued, but the Maker Movement offers consumers the new possibilities for (taking up an active role in) the design of products that they use. We believe that the reason the Maker Movement is different from previous forms of making and tinkering are as follows: (a) a significant increase in the expressive potential of emerging technologies, at the same time as, a decrease in barriers to entry (in term of both affordability and expertise); and (b) a high degree of global and local community connectivity through the Internet, Maker Faires and emerging maker spaces. Making holds great potential for democratizing technology and provides valuable opportunities for learning and empowerment [5, 6]. However, for this to become reality, we believe that further critical reflection and socially aware motivation needs to be combined with prototyping and fabricating.

To explore the possibilities of making for education and empowerment, we designed and conducted a series of maker workshops, or "MakeShops", for undergraduate engineering students at our school. In these workshops, we combined the use of so-called "maker" tools and techniques, such as 3D printing, embedded electronics and wearable computers, and pedagogical elements, such as the facilitation, collaboration, and an "atelier" mode of engagement. We believe this approach has several aspects of potential use in similar, future workshops. First, we conducted the workshops through a facilitation model in which the workshop facilitator (first author of this paper) was also a participating maker (i.e., an *experienced* or *proficient maker*) working on a project simultaneously as the other participants. The sessions were conducted in what we term as a "maker atelier" approach, in which small teams worked on self-selected projects under the supervision of an *experienced maker*, rather than an instructor, and elements of performance and creative dialogue were encouraged. Second, we developed the workshop to elicit reflection around the values embedded in the design ideas that each team was working on and their social, political and economical implications. In this way, we aimed to combine the practice of making with reflection, aiming for more *informed action*, or *praxis,* which strives for a balance between theory and action [7]. Third, we encouraged the participants to collaborate with each other and other makers, both through face-to-face meeting and working sessions and through the making available of documentation and designs online. We describe these choices and their outcomes in more detail in the following sections.

2   MakeShops: Facilitating Creativity

We designed and conducted a series of maker workshops, MakeShops, to explore the possibilities of the maker approach in an experiential learning setting. We developed outreach and advertising materials, and an intake mechanism to receive applications from interested students. The workshops were offered as an extra-curricular activity (which would not result in additional academic credit). We applied for and received financial support for the workshop from the Technology Enhanced Active Learning

(TEAL) initiative, a special project that was launched in 2013 by the Lassonde School of Engineering at York University in Toronto. The venue for the workshop was the GaMaY research lab, which is a dedicated space for the research activities led by two faculty members and their graduate students in the department of Electrical Engineering and Computer Science. Due to the competing needs of multiple other projects, the lab space could only be used one day a week and all workshop materials would be stowed away in the interim. Of more than 30 applications, we accepted 10 undergraduate engineering student participants into the workshop, representing all levels of study (first-year to final-year). The workshop consisted of 10 3 h sessions, which took place every weekend over a 10 week-period. The first author (referred to as the *workshop facilitator* in the rest of the paper) facilitated the sessions.

In the first workshop meeting, we presented the participants with an overview of maker and DIY approaches, including a discussion of the tools and techniques available and a presentation of a series of maker projects curated for their creativity and thoughtfulness including, among others, the *Banana Piano* [9], *Botanicalls* [10] and 3D printed prosthetics [11]. This introduction was crucial, given our group of learners, who were engineering students. The participants were familiar with engineering design and requirements-based problem solving, and were not attuned to a mode of practice that is not centrally concerned with 'solving' a problem but rather is focused on creative expression, inventiveness, and exploration. The second session took the form of a "field trip", and was a visit to the Toronto Mini Maker Faire. In this session, the participants interacted with many example maker projects and met and spoke with local makers. In the third session, the participants divided into smaller teams (five teams of two members each) and undertook brainstorming sessions, which culminated in a project proposal (including budgets) for each team. These proposals were shared with fellow participants, who then provided critique and feedback. Once the project proposals were refined and approved by the workshop facilitator, the participants received material needed for their projects and started working on them. For sessions four onwards, project teams would discuss the work completed, the current state of their projects, and what they planned to accomplish in the next week. During these sessions, participants were encouraged to provide constructive feedback and help to one another. Additionally, a listing of student design competitions and showcases was created and shared with the participants, and each team was encouraged to submit their projects.

At the end of the workshops, in a collective brainstorming session, the participants discussed the learning and challenges around their projects and described steps forward. Additionally, the participants provided feedback about the workshops in a survey. Finally, we conducted free form interviews with eight of the participants, six months following the workshops to assess the efficacy and retention of the material learned during their projects.

In the rest of this section, we discuss our approach to the design and facilitation of the workshops.

2.1 Creating a Maker Atelier

The concept of "artist atelier"—as a shared work space in which novice artists work under the supervision of a master artist—has been a central notion in the artistic traditions of Western Europe [11]. When designing the workshops, we were inspired by this concept and incorporated elements of it in the instruction design. The following are some of the ideas we incorporated into the workshops:

Facilitation Rather than Teaching: In accord with recent research that shows great potential in self-directed and project-based learning [3, 4] the majority of the participants' time at the workshops were dedicated to the discussion and implementation of projects that they designed and conducted themselves. The workshop facilitator adopted an *experienced maker* role rather than an instructor. This role entails facilitation of collaboration and creativity through the creation of an atmosphere of trust and goodwill, where constructive feedback can be generated and exchanged between the participants. The workshop facilitator drew on his previous knowledge of existing maker projects, as well as hands-on previous experience with making to curate relevant and inspiring examples and ideas from the research literature and maker community. Another important role for the workshop facilitator was to provide structure (e.g., in terms of time and budget) on the projects, this was crucial so that the projects would be logistical constrained and feasible. As well, the set of constraints often fostered creativity in the participants; the importance of constraints is previously recognized, as they can structure creativity without being stifling [12].

The Use of Horizontal Teaching and Peer Support: During the workshops, the workshop facilitator also initiated and conducted a project with the same time and budget constraints as the participant projects. By doing so, he was also participating in the workshops directly by discussing and researching a project himself, asking for feedback and support from the other workshop participants. He purposely chose a project (i.e., wearable computing) in which he had a genuine interest, in order to engage in a genuine learning process at the same time with the other workshop participants. This approach helped foster a more horizontal teaching approach where participants engaged in more dialogue with the workshop facilitator and each other.

2.2 Making and Reflection

In recent years, the importance of exercising reflection and critical thinking when making is emphasized [6, 14, 15]. Reflection is a rather broad term; here we focus on value-oriented reflection, contextualization, and life-cycle thinking. Researchers have argued that maker methods have the potential to address social and economical problems if engaged with purposefully [16]. Value-sensitive design approaches, in combination with maker methods, provide a means to realize this potential. These approaches include Reflective Design [17] and Thoughtful Interaction Design [17], which emphasize the examination of unconscious values hidden in design decisions, and encourage the identification of side effects of a realized design, both positive and negative. In the workshops, we explicitly provisioned for the activity of reflection across multiple sessions, in which the participants considered and discussed the social, ethical and political implications of their projects. We strongly believed that the aim of the workshop should go beyond making projects that were merely "cool."

Reflection also includes contextualization, which requires knowledge and analysis of prior relevant work. For this, we pointed the teams to the research literature, and assisted them by recommending specific readings, both in terms of prior relevant projects and also in terms of relevant methodologies and theoretical approaches. For instance, we encouraged the team engaged in the Magic Wand project (described later), to read certain papers on tangible interfaces and embodied cognition.

Another aspect of design that we explicitly asked our participants to consider was to plan for the entire cycle of design, from ideation to deployment and disposal. For each project, the participants were required to come up with a detailed budget, to source their components by researching and investigating potential vendors and outlets, and to identify cost-benefit tradeoffs in their design. Additionally, they had to describe next steps for their project and investigate potential ways to turn their prototypes into products. This included a discussion of alternative deployment strategies, such as the open-source and creative commons approaches. Finally, they had to consider the recycling and reuse potential of their designs. Previous research has emphasized the importance of exploring these issues in maker initiatives [5].

2.3 Community Collaboration

An attractive and essential characteristic of the maker movement is the vibrant and diverse community of makers who are connected through a shared interest in creativity, inventiveness and the sharing of knowledge. This worldwide community is connected both through face-to-face meetings and events, such as various Maker Faires, and in online forums and virtual spaces, such as special interest Facebook groups, forums, etc. In the workshop sessions, we encouraged participants to get in contact with other makers and also to present their projects at maker events and design competitions. To support this goal, we organized a field trip to a local maker faire and introduced some of our maker community contacts to the participants.

As Dale Dougherty, the founder of both Make Magazine and Maker Faire, noted in a 2014 panel [19], a key motivation for makers is "to interact with other people" and have an audience that shares their interest in creativity and hands-on skills. This element of performance is apparent in the enthusiasm and range of presentation techniques manifest at Maker Faires worldwide. We built in possibilities for performance into the workshop via the weekly presentations, which required the teams to present their projects to one another every week. This provided a chance for them to get feedback and additionally acquire experience in presenting their ideas in a supportive environment.

3 Workshop Outcomes

Over the course of the workshops, five project teams emerged (five teams of two members each). One team opted out of the workshop after the 4th session, and the other four teams continued and worked on their projects to varying degrees of completion. The four project ideas were: an interactive 'Magic Wand', an open-source laptop, an affective wristband, and a voice-activated alarm clock. Of these four projects, the first two resulted in working prototypes and the other two projects were partially completed. Given the limited time and resources allocated to the projects, we believe the workshops were successful in motivating original projects and introducing participants to making in a hands-on experiential manner.

In the post-workshop brainstorming sessions and survey, the participants stated that they found the workshops useful and engaging. They identified the field trip to Mini Maker Faire as inspiring and they found the maker atelier approach useful in fostering creativity. They identified a lack of dedicated space and the short length of the workshops as elements that could be improved in the future. Three of the participants suggested that more hands-on programming and implementation instruction could be provided initially. Six of the participants identified the benefit of getting feedback from their peers during the design and implementation process. Two participants described the feedback as 'intimidating' and two described the feedback as unnecessary. All participants stated that they would recommend the workshops to friends and that they themselves would be interested in participating again.

Follow up interviews were conducted six months after the completion of the workshops with eight of the participants. In these interviews, participants still felt the workshops were useful and that they learned new concepts and techniques in them. One participant described it as "the best workshops I have attended". Several participants applied specific knowledge in coursework: one participant, who had learned how to analyze results from embedded accelerometers in the design of a customized controller and then applied this knowledge in order to incorporate an accelerometer into an e-health wearable course project. A second participant learned 3D modeling and fabrication and then consequently developed a customized 3D printed case for a course project; a third participant had learned how to use embedded speech recognition with the Raspberry Pi and then applied this knowledge to implement speech commands for a custom-made robot. These examples demonstrate the efficacy and retention of the learning acquired during the workshops. Beyond the learning of technical skills, participants also became motivated beyond coursework: two participants decided to start their own prototyping-based businesses using 3D printers as a main technology.

In the following subsections, we describe 3 projects connected to the workshop.

3.1 The Magic Wand

The Magic Wand is the outcome of a participant team project. The Magic Wand is a tangible, 3D printed, motion-detecting device that emits a laser light when moved in pre-defined patterns, simulating the casting of a spell. Inspired by the Harry Potter fantasy book and movie series, two of the workshop participants (Chitiiran Krishna

Moorthy and Sonal Ranjit, with subsequent participation by Kajendra Seevananthan) decided to develop their own customized, open-source version of the wand. The Magic Wand consists of a 3D printed shell that houses an Arduino microcontroller, motion detecting modules, a laser-emitting module and a battery. Figure 1 shows Magic Wand.

Fig. 1. The Magic Wand in the dark (top), with instructions (bottom left) and in use (bottom right).

The Magic Wand can be used individually to practice different movement patterns that correspond to spells or in pairs where two users, each with a wand, compete in a "light duel", to cast spells on each other. Currently, there are 4 movement patterns loaded into the wand's "firmware" (i.e., the Arduino software). After coming up with the design idea, the team investigated different approaches to embedded computing and examined code for motion detection components and laser emitting modules. This initial investigation included an examination of safety concerns of using lasers. Additionally, the team used 3D modeling to come up with several iterations of the wand design. Each week, the team presented their ongoing work at the workshop and got feedback from the other participants.

Members of the design team were also associated with a student Fantasy Fan Club at the university that regularly hosts events and gatherings. Throughout the time when the workshops were running, they consulted members of the Fan Club regularly about their ideas and got feedback from them on early prototypes. At the conclusion of the workshops they presented the wand at the Fan Club's annual show and tell. Thus, they engaged a community of potential users in their design process. Following the workshops, the participants submitted the Magic Wand to the Student Design Competition at the 2013 ACM Conference on Tangible, Embedded and Embodied Interaction (TEI), where it was accepted and showcased. The team also presented their project at the 2014 Toronto Mini Maker Faire. The team made the 3D model of their design available for download at the Thingiverse online 3D model repository, where, to date, it has been downloaded more than four hundred times (http://www.thingiverse.com/thing:248254).

3.2   HugBug

It consists of a large hat that is augmented with LED lights and a speaker system that plays music. The hat is activated by a microcontroller that detects touch (and thereby hugs). Figure 2 shows HugBug. It was designed in collaboration with a community partner (Natalie Comeau) who was experienced with designing clothing. Throughout the design process the workshop facilitator worked closely with her, as well as, with potential users at maker and wearable computing events.

Fig. 2. HugBug consists of a large hat augmented with lights and sound. It can be used as a performance or a teaching tool.

The idea behind HugBug is twofold: it is a wearable interface that augments hugs with digital media, and, it is an example of applying a simple Input-Output-Process model [21] to the design of a system to augment human capabilities (the sensors provide input, the lights and music provide output, and the microcontroller controls the process). In the latter context HugBug becomes a compelling teaching tool for children and adolescents. We used HugBug as a teaching tool in workshops for different populations, including marginalized children in Mexico, as well as, high school students in Canada [20].

3.3 TalkBox

TalkBox is a project that was initiated as a collaborative project between one of the workshop participants and a community partner. While not a participant project at the workshops, it serves as a demonstration of the benefits of supporting community collaboration. During the field trip to the local Mini Maker Faire participants met many makers. After the event, they reported their favorite projects and reflected on why they found them interesting. Several of the participants found a particular project presented by a local special education teacher and maker (Ray Feraday) most interesting. This project, an open-source communication board for non-verbal children, was made from a Makey Makey sensor board connected to a computer and a custom made chassis made from foam core and conductive tape that was connected to the sensor board, turning them, in effect, into touch sensitive keys. When the keys were touched, sound files were played back on the computer, making the system a low-cost, customizable communication board. The system was made to address the needs of children with disabilities who either could not use conventional assistive technology solutions or who were waiting for the delivery of new communication devices. The local maker and inventor had drawn on his first-hand experience of many years as a special education teacher to come up with the design.

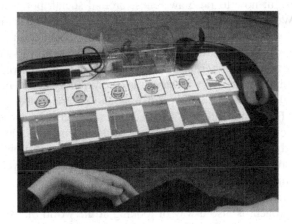

Fig. 3. TalkBox is an open-source customizable communication board for non-verbal children and adults.

Following the event, we contacted the inventor of the system and discussed possibilities of collaboration with him. One of the workshop participants in particular (Toni Kunic) became very interested in collaborating on the project. In the weeks that followed, we formed a team comprising of the inventor of the system, the interested workshop participant and both authors of this paper, to work on a new version of the system that was called TalkBox (Fig. 3). The new version of the system used the credit-card-sized Raspberry Pi computer (Model B+) and embedded touch sensors (MPR121 touch capacitive sensor) to make the system completely portable (e.g., so that it could be placed on a wheelchair tray). Additionally, new software was developed that allowed the easy loading of sound files and the customization of the system functionality [22].

The TalkBox project supported both the collaboration with community encouraged in the workshops (i.e., through collaboration with the local maker), and reflection on the social aspects of the design that aims to make technology more accessible to users who need it most. The system's design, along with all the software, was made open-source and placed on an online repository (https://github.com/tkunic/TalkBox). Since the workshops, the system has been further developed and a pilot user study is currently being planned to assess its usability. Additionally, the design has been presented at the International Conference on Computers Helping People with Special Needs [22] and has won the 2014 "Bridging the Gap" award, a design awarded at the 2014 Toronto Mini Maker Faire.

4 Discussion and Lessons Learned

In the introduction, we articulated the conjecture that maker culture is an instance of Papert's vision of a technological culture that is conductive to learning and to the emergence of creativity and inventiveness. We also fore fronted the key issue of value-sensitive design: how to raise awareness around social, political and economic issues in makers. We designed our workshops to provide not only a learning context for maker methods, but also a context for critical reflection. On the basis of evidence gathered from the workshop participants, we believe that our workshop design was successful, both in terms of fostering meaningful learning and in terms of supporting design outcomes that are community-based and community-oriented. Several teams deployed their results via open-source publishing and several maker projects, such as Magic Wand, HugBug, and TalkBox, focused on empowerment and expression. We believe explicit discussions around implications of design are important, and that such discourse is needed within the maker movement in order to move beyond the aim of merely making "cool" projects. There are myriad opportunities to develop projects that can potentially bring about positive change.

A key observation from the workshops was that making, in addition to being a method and an approach, is also a way of looking at the world that stands in contrast with 'canonical' problem-solving. The workshop participants were engineering students who were familiar with engineering design, specific computational technologies, and requirements-based problem solving. In contradistinction, maker projects are, oftentimes, not actually concerned with 'solving' a problem as opposed to being focused on creative expression, inventiveness, and exploration. Therefore, a first step in our approach was to introduce the workshop participants to this approach towards design. Presenting a series of seminal maker projects from around the world and organizing a field trip to the local Mini Maker Faire supported this introduction. In retrospect, we saw that some of the more junior participants would have benefited with a longer and more structured overview of maker methods and tools.

An important part of the workshops was creating opportunities for participants to meet makers outside of the workshops. This was achieved both through meeting local makers and, also, through presenting participant projects at maker events and design competitions. Thus, a second observation of the workshops was that getting involved in the external maker community, provided the participants with opportunities to experience maker culture first hand, and also to become participants and members of the community, rather than stay part of a passive audience.

A challenge was the limited time that was assigned to the workshops and a lack of dedicated space where more connections and meetings between the participants could happen in a less structured manner. As described previously, the venue for the workshop was a research lab, which could only be used one day a week. Workshop materials needed to be stowed away after each workshop session. This created barriers and inconvenience for the lab participants, and did not support very well our goal to foster serendipitous discovery. We affirm the importance of creating dedicated shared workspaces, similar to Fab Labs [23] and Maker Spaces [24].

5   Conclusion

We have presented results from a series of maker workshops, or MakeShops, conducted with undergraduate engineering students. During the workshops, we created a friendly, collaborative space for learning and sharing and encouraged the participants to provide feedback on each other's projects and present their work to one another. Additionally, we focused on the goal of fostering critical reflection by the participants, so that they would reflect on the impact of their design decisions and would recognize the importance of collaboration within their community. To facilitate the workshops, we used a maker atelier approach in which the workshop facilitator was developing a maker project simultaneously with the rest of the participant teams, taking on the role of experienced maker as opposed to instructor. The workshops were successful in teaching maker techniques to the participants, in building skills of critical reflection, and resulted in a series of working prototypes, several of which were presented at external venues outside of the workshops. What is particularly relevant is that participants were highly motivated to dedicate substantial amounts of their personal time to engage with this type of learning, even though they did not receive any type of formal credit for their project work. We believe in such projects, it is up to us, as facilitators and potential facilitators, to ensure that their learning is firmly rooted in critical reflection.

We believe our approach can be improved in the future by running the workshops over a longer period of time and organizing a dedicated workspace. Additionally, a more structured overview of maker methods and tools can provide scaffolding for participants with less experience.

Acknowledgments. We would like to thank all the workshop participants and our community partners. We are grateful for support received from the Technology Enhanced Active Learning (TEAL) initiative, which is a special project of the Lassonde School of Engineering, York University.

References

1. Papert, S.: Mindstorms: Children, Computers, and Powerful Ideas. Basic Books Inc., New York (1980)
2. Anderson, C.: Makers: The New Industrial Revolution. Crown Business, New York (2012)
3. Schneider, D.: Simon Hauger Revs Up High Schools with Car Projects. IEEE Spectrum. IEEE Press, New York (2013)
4. Davis, J.: How a radical new teaching method could unleash a generation of geniuses. Wired Business (2013). http://www.wired.com/2013/10/free-thinkers
5. Lindtner, S., Hertz, G.D., Dourish, P.: Emerging sites of HCI innovation: hackerspaces, hardware startups and incubators. In: Proceedings of CHI 2014, pp. 439–448. ACM Press, New York (2014)
6. Tanenbaum, J.G., Williams, A.M., Desjardins, A., Tanenbaum, K.: Democratizing technology: pleasure, utility and expressiveness in DIY and maker practice. In: Proceedings of CHI 2013, pp. 2603–2612. ACM Press, New York (2013)
7. Freire, P.: Pedagogy of the Oppressed. Bloomsbury Publishing, London (2000)
8. Resnick, M., Rosenbaum, E.: Designing for tinkerability. In: Honey, M., Kanter, D. (eds.) Design, Make, Play: Growing the Next Generation of STEM Innovators, pp. 163–181. Routledge, New York (2013)
9. Collective, B.S.M., Shaw, D.: Makey Makey: improvising tangible and nature-based user interfaces. In: Proceedings of TEI 2012, pp. 367–370. ACM Press, New York (2012)
10. Hartman, K.: Botanicalls: the plants have your number (2006). http://www.botanicalls.com/
11. Project Daniel (2014). www.notimpossiblelabs.com
12. Janson, H.W.: History of Art, 5th edn. Thames and Hudson, London (1995). Revised and expanded by Janson, A.F.
13. Stokes, P.D.: Creativity from Constraints: The Psychology of Breakthrough. Springer, New York (2005)
14. Hertz, G.: Critical making (2012). http://www.conceptlab.com/criticalmaking/
15. Ratto, M.: Critical making: conceptual and material studies in technology and social life. Inf. Soc. **27**(4), 252–260 (2011)
16. Hurst, A., Tobias, J.: Empowering individuals with do-it- yourself assistive technology. In: Proceedings of ASSETS 2011, pp. 11–18. ACM Press (2011)
17. Sengers, P., Boehner, K., David, S., Kaye, J.: Reflective design. In: Proceedings of the 4th Decennial Conference on Critical Computing (CC 2005), pp. 49–58 (2005)
18. Löwgren, J., Stolterman, E.: Thoughtful Interaction Design. MIT Press, Boston (2014)
19. Doughrty, D., Eidman-Aadahl, E., Resnick, M.: Making, coding, writing. Panel at Scratch@MIT Conference (2014)
20. Hamidi, F., Comeau, N., Saenz, K., Baljko, M.: A wearable interface for facilitating digital design for children. In: Proceedings of D&E 2014, pp. 706–709 (2014)
21. IBM Corporation: HIPO—a design aid and documentation technique. Publication number GC20-1851, IBM Corporation (1974)
22. Hamidi, F., Baljko, M., Kunic, T., Feraday, R.: Do-It-Yourself (DIY) assistive technology: a communication board case study. In: Miesenberger, K., Fels, D., Archambault, D., Peñáz, P., Zagler, W. (eds.) ICCHP 2012. LNCS, vol. 8548, pp. 287–294. Springer, New York (2012)

23. Gershenfeld, N.: Fab: The Coming Revolution on Your Desktop–From Personal Computers to Personal Fabrication. Basic Books, New York (2008)
24. Bowler, L.: Creativity through "Maker" experiences and design thinking in the education of librarians. Knowl. Quest **42**(5), 58–61 (2014)

Enabling Programmability of Smart Learning Environments by Teachers

Asterios Leonidis[1], Margherita Antona[1(✉)],
and Constantine Stephanidis[1,2]

[1] Institute of Computer Science, Foundation for Research and Technology –
Hellas (FORTH), N. Plastira 100, Vassilika Vouton, 700 13 Heraklion,
Crete, Greece
{leonidis, antona, cs}@ics.forth.gr
[2] Department of Computer Science, University of Crete, Crete, Greece

Abstract. The evolution of Information Technology (IT) and the emergence of the Ambient Intelligence paradigm have drastically affected the way users live and learn. Ambient Intelligence is a vision of the future that offers great opportunities to enrich everyday activities (e.g., on the road, at home, at work, etc.) and has been proven to play an important role in education. In smart learning environments, learning activities are enhanced with the use of pervasive and mobile computing. This paper presents an extensible software infrastructure that empowers teachers to design and program purposeful and engaging learning activities for formal and informal learning environments, by combining and orchestrating cloud-based, ambient and pervasive facilities and services.

Keywords: Visual programming · End-user development · Ubiquitous environments · Smart learning environments

1 Introduction

Ambient Intelligence is a vision of the future that offers great opportunities to enrich everyday activities (e.g., on the road, at home, at work, etc.) through the pervasive presence of a variety of objects – such as RFID tags, sensors, actuators, technologically enhanced artifacts, etc. – which are able to interact with each other and cooperate with their neighbors to reach common goals [17]. Such novel paradigm, also known as Internet of Things (IoT), is rapidly gaining ground [2] and aims to revolutionize the way people interact with computers, as smart environments will anticipate and react to human needs even without users' explicit commands [41].

In the meantime, people have also changed the way they learn due to the rapid pace of life and the strong dependence on technology for their daily activities. Transferring knowledge only through traditional classroom activities is considered obsolete, and new learning methodologies, which make use of technology, have emerged to improve the learning process by allowing learning in different locations. This sort of learning occurs anytime and anyplace, when and where the learner desires. Smart learning environments, rooted in intelligent tutoring and adaptive systems [10], context-aware

© Springer International Publishing Switzerland 2015
N. Streitz and P. Markopoulos (Eds.): DAPI 2015, LNCS 9189, pp. 62–73, 2015.
DOI: 10.1007/978-3-319-20804-6_6

ubiquitous learning [22], and mind tools [12], can be regarded as technology-supported learning environments that make adaptations and provide appropriate support (e.g., guidance, feedback, hints or tools) in the right places and at the right time, based on individual learners' needs, which might be determined via analyzing their learning behaviors, performance and the online and real-world contexts in which they are situated [23].

A key aspect for such environments to achieve their full potential is the ability to be open and extendable [16]. From an engineering perspective, these concepts outline the need for appropriate middleware frameworks and communication technologies that facilitate the introduction of new devices, services and software components [3]. On the other hand, from a user perspective, they rather emphasize the scarcity of programming methodologies and tools that could facilitate the construction of intelligent systems using existing technologies [45].

Operators of learning environments are not experienced programmers. They are teachers with limited, if not any, experience in computer programming, whereas the programmability of the environment is more complex than creating a rule that turns on the room's light when someone enters [29, 46]. This paper aims to demonstrate a prototype system that empowers teachers to create learning scenarios by reviewing and modifying the high-level "business logic" of a smart learning environment in a user-friendly manner through a visual programming platform.

2 Related Work

Within smart learning environments, various learning activities take place that make extensive use of ICT technology. Contrary to the past, where the e-learning paradigm dictated that digital technology was mainly used to gain access to learning content from a stationary device (e.g., portable or desktop computer) and interact in a sandboxed environment with it through specialized applications (e.g., e-learning portals), nowadays with the emergence of the Ambient Intelligence paradigm learners are able, and often required, to interact with multiple devices (either purely digital or augmented with technology) in order to accomplish predefined learning objectives, whereas in many cases learners are required to participate in kinesthetic learning activities, i.e., physically engaging classroom exercises such as moving to a certain place to accomplish a task [4].

For instance, [20] requires learners to use their mobile devices along with specialized equipment to analyze several poor quality power supply occurrences and then share and discuss their findings with their classmates; the latter requires sharing content with other devices in real time. In [14] the authors propose various learning activities that require collaboration among multiple applications and multiple users in real-time. Chang [9] taught recycling principles and [13] studied the effects of mobile blogging, both applied in the wild. Finally, [47] have implemented a system aiming to increase interactivity in the classroom by using mobile technologies. The emergence of this novel paradigm is also supported by the fact that various EU-funded projects aim at developing blended educational spaces where physical and digital artifacts are combined in learning activities, while digital and learning frameworks are developed to modernize and improve education by motivating learners' participation.

From the point of view of the learning experience, [43] identifies a set of requirements for smart learning environments which comprises effectiveness, efficiency, scalability, autonomy, engagement, flexibility, adaptiveness, personalization, conversation and reflection. Many of the above requirements however are closely related to the emerging paradigm of end-user development which dictates that at some point the end-user should be able to modify a software artifact [21, 31]. To that end, many alternatives have been proposed based on the visual programming paradigm, that has been proven to facilitate inexperienced users to quickly learn how to build simple programs [19]. Gray and Young [18] describes Virtuoso, a multi-user programming environment built using the Valve's Source engine that functions as a tool to allow non-professional users to create interactive educational video games. Maloney et al. [32] presents Scratch, a visual programming environment that allows users (primarily ages 8 to 16) to learn computer programming while working on personally meaningful projects such as animated stories and games. Chin et al. [11] reports a programming environment for customizing smart home environments where the user demonstrates the desired behavior and the system encodes it as a set of rules to be executed in real-time. Kubitza [28] argues that building environments with heterogeneous interconnected devices still remains a challenging task and proposes a toolkit to cover this technical complexity, so that designers and users of a smart environment can focus on the interaction design and the programming of intelligent and useful behavior. The majority of those systems employ a custom scripting language, embracing the concept, stemming from the gaming engineering community, that "smarter, more powerful scripting languages will improve game performance while making gameplay development more efficient" [48].

3 Framework Requirements to Support SLEs

The emerging trend of mobile and ubiquitous computing has attracted numerous researchers and vendors to build educational applications that benefit from innovative technological affordances. Nevertheless, the majority of those mobile and ubiquitous applications often do not meet their potentials due to the lack of tools that simplify their interplay with the environment [5] and the contained affordances. Therefore, to enhance the programmability of smart learning environments, a set of requirements were elaborated during the implementation of the overall framework.

Currently, the majority of educational applications targeting ambient and ubiquitous environments offer limited functionality as they operate within their own sandbox [1, 6, 36, 37, 49]. However, as intelligent environments blend into our daily activities and life-long learning becomes a necessity [42], the demand for federated educational services and applications is constantly increasing, and the need for appropriate facilities and tools becomes imperative. Thus, the proposed framework enables the development of complex learning scenarios in which educational applications cooperate with existing services/applications and benefit from ambient facilities (e.g., sensors, artifacts, etc.).

Fig. 1. High-level requirements for the AmIClass SDK

Composition and module reusability are desirable characteristics, which in the domain of software engineering partially determine the product quality. For that to be achieved, the communication channels through which applications can exchange information and the rules that mediate their interactions when forming complex federations are formally specified. Consequently, the proposed framework supports: (a) seamless integration of new learning applications and services, (b) reuse of existing facilities through composition & cooperation (based on semantic classification, compatibility checking, etc.), and (c) different degrees of openness [39] that will allow the dynamic discovery and use of semantically equivalent services (e.g., based on availability, QoS, preference, etc.) (Fig. 1).

Within the available learning infrastructures [5, 7, 34], teachers and learners cannot configure, let alone define, learning scenarios and activities. However, in the broader domains of Ambient Intelligent and agent-based computing, various solutions have been proposed [38] that facilitate the orchestration and dynamic adaptation of "execution scripts" that govern the entire process. Based on such well-known practices, the proposed framework provides: (i) a mechanism that facilitates the semantic classification of learning-oriented intelligent artifacts and services, and (ii) a "scripting" library that will support the orchestration and customization of the various learning facilities within ambient and ubiquitous learning environments. The library supports the definition of an appropriate context-sensitive decision-making logic, which can be dynamically modified either explicitly by the teacher or implicitly through activity monitoring (e.g., modification of the learning context, availability of available services and artifacts, recognition of undesirable situations, etc.).

The concept of Ambient Intelligence is built around the notion of multiple objects, embedded in the environment, being capable of recognizing and responding to the presence of different individuals; those entities (i.e., people, objects) and their current state of interaction are defined as contextual knowledge [15]. In order to design and apply suitable learning strategies in the context of ambient environments, the exploitation of contextual information is crucial. The proposed framework offers access to contextual knowledge to support context-aware decision- making. Within smart learning environments, the context of use includes [5, 15, 42]: (i) learner-related attributes (e.g., schedule, performance, skills, etc.), (ii) intelligent objects and their facilities, (iii) learning applications and services, and (iv) learning activities and their requirements. Contextual knowledge is used for appropriately adapting the learning process within various environments (e.g., benefit from technologically rich environments with multiple affordances, minimize interaction while on the move or when available time is limited, etc.).

4   Implementation Details

4.1   Overview

To satisfy the aforementioned requirements, the proposed work roots its core principles in the game scripting paradigm that has been successfully applied within the last decades and proposes a user-friendly scripting environment through which teachers can monitor and modify the "high-level" business logic of the learning environments they are in charge of through a visual programming language.

The AmIClass SDK offers a programming and a runtime environment that facilitates the definition, deployment, execution and monitoring of various learning activities that make use of ambient facilities within smart learning environments. Figure 2 provides an overview of the proposed software infrastructure.

AmIClass SDK aims to enable the design of purposeful and engaging learning activities for formal and informal learning environments, by combining and orchestrating cloud-based, ambient and pervasive facilities and services (Fig. 2). To that end, the following high-level components were implemented:

- **A Service Mediator Agent (SMA)** that integrates and provides access to ambient and pervasive services. It can resolve services offered by: (a) smart objects such as sensors, technologically augmented artifacts, interaction devices, etc., that expose their functionality in the form of software services, (b) Knowledge hubs that collect and provide personalized access to learning material from various content providers or learning management systems, (c) Context-sensitive observers that facilitate environmental monitoring and controllers that enable remote management, (d) Software-as-a-Service [44] Learning Applications that deliver their functionality over the network, (e) Profiling agents that simplify logging, enable personalization and promote social interaction, and (f) Security safeguards that implement access management policies.

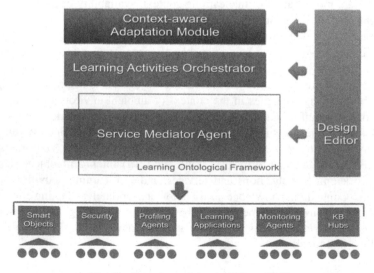

Fig. 2. Overview of the AmIClass SDK

- **A distributed Learning Activities Orchestrator (LAO)** that, through the SMA services, monitor and orchestrate the learning process by controlling the physical environment, as well as the learning services and applications. LAO facilitates: (i) dynamic service binding and use, (ii) conflict resolution, and (iii) adaptation of the activity workflow. Additionally, it supports the installation of external composite modules that extend existing functionality and offer new features. Finally, it supports the implementation of meta-services that can be integrated in the SMA to enable the realization of composite learning scenarios.
- **A Context-Aware Adaptation Module (CAAM)** that facilitates the decision-making process by evaluating rule sets that, based on the available contextual knowledge, determine which scenario alternatives should be applied or how active scenarios should be reconfigured.
- **An extensible Learning-Oriented Ontological Framework (LOF)** that: (a) Facilitates the classification of the environment and its smart objects, devices and services, (b) Allows semantic mapping of data and services extending existing knowledge, (c) Enables high-level semantic reasoning (e.g., is device X appropriate for displaying private content, etc., (d) Delivers a unified profiling model, (e) Simplifies services federation and reuse (including services dynamically added at run-time), and (f) Enables communication of heterogeneous systems.
- **A Design Environment (DE)** for defining and configuring learning activities' scripts.

4.2 Teacher-Friendly Features of the ClassScript Language

The ClassScript language aims to empower the definition of various learning scenarios in smart learning environments. Based on the Service Mediator Agent and the various distributed Orchestrators, any connected services are dynamically identified and using appropriate programming facilities (e.g., reflection) are exposed, via dynamic code generation, as external ClassScript modules that offer various functions. To support both professional and non-professional programmers, two different visibility levels are available, namely full access and teacher-friendly access, that aim to hide unnecessary complexity from novice end-users (Fig. 3).

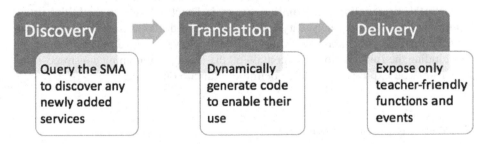

Fig. 3. Inspection process to export teacher-friendly functions and events

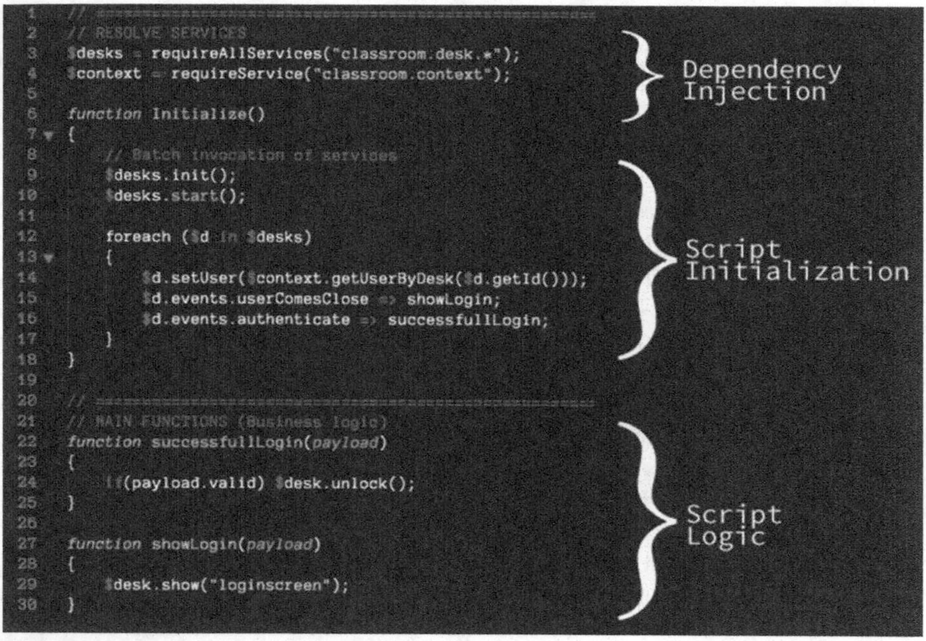

```
 1   //  =======================================================
 2   // RESOLVE SERVICES
 3   $desks = requireAllServices("classroom.desk.*");
 4   $context = requireService("classroom.context");
 5
 6   function Initialize()
 7   {
 8       // Batch invocation of services
 9       $desks.init();
10       $desks.start();
11
12       foreach ($d in $desks)
13       {
14           $d.setUser($context.getUserByDesk($d.getId()));
15           $d.events.userComesClose => showLogin;
16           $d.events.authenticate => successfullLogin;
17       }
18   }
19
20   //  =======================================================
21   // MAIN FUNCTIONS (Business logic)
22   function successfullLogin(payload)
23   {
24       if(payload.valid) $desk.unlock();
25   }
26
27   function showLogin(payload)
28   {
29       $desk.show("loginscreen");
30   }
```

} Dependency Injection

} Script Initialization

} Script Logic

Fig. 4. A sample ClassScript program

A valid program in ClassScript has a well-defined structure (depicted in the Fig. 4) which not only streamlines the parsing procedure, but most importantly facilitates its manipulation from the visual editor by the teachers acting as a master template that guides them. The structure is influenced by that of a program written in the C programming language [25] and requires import statements to precede function declaration that in turn precede the script's initialization function. In more details:

- **an import statement** defines the service dependencies and is equivalent to an include statement in C (e.g., find and resolve the necessary external services before executing a single line of code).
- **function declarations follow a C-like scope system.** Function are not hoisted, thus they can only be used if they have been declared beforehand [25]
- **a script's initialization function (i.e., the main function) defines the initial entry point** that prepares the necessary local structures and performs the registration of event handling functions for local and remote events. Finally, each function (including the **init** function) can contain all the usual programming constructs such as arithmetic expression, variable definition, function calls, etc.

4.3   Web-Based Management Suite

Teachers can control the smart environment through a web-based Management Suite by visually exploring the available programmable artifacts alongside with their scripts, while they can adapt their business logic either by modifying existing or by introducing new scripts. The teacher can browse through both stationary (e.g., Smart Desk [40], Educational Mini-games station [26], the Book of Elli [33]) and mobile artifacts that can be found in the environment. However, in such fluid environments, it is not only the physical manifestation that matters, but also the overall functionality offered. Therefore, teachers can browse through either physical instances (i.e., environment monitoring and management) or through conceptual "service containers" that could be instantiated anywhere at anytime (i.e., business logic manipulation).

For every artifact type, the teachers can explore: (i) the compatible services and (ii) the associated scripts, while for every artifact instance they can further examine the status of any deployed services as well (e.g., active, busy, idle, stopped). Similarly, for every service, teachers can explore the exposed functions and the events that could be triggered, alongside with the scripts that either consume any of the functions (i.e., direct use through dependency injection) or listen for any of the events to react accordingly [8].

To facilitate programming by non-professionals, a visual editor is provided through which teachers can view and modify the existing scripts or create new from scratch. Teachers combine graphical blocks [24] that correspond either to basic programming structures (e.g., loops, variable definitions, arithmetic expressions, etc.) or functions stemming from service containers, in order to define the script's sequential logic while event-based programming is supported by connecting the appropriate event handlers to the available hooks. Finally, upon script creation the teacher is able to immediately deploy it to a single artifact instance or a family/group of instances or schedule its later deployment.

An illustrative example is depicted in Figs. 4 and 5, which provide the textual and graphical equivalent of the same program. Its objective is to discover all the smart desks available within the current context of use, and for each one install the appropriate event handlers to be called when a person approaches the physical device or when that person successfully authenticates himself as the authorized student for that desk.

4.4 Distributed Runtime Environment

Smart learning environments inherently follow a distributed computing paradigm where the various software components are located on networked computers or smart artifacts that communicate and coordinate their actions by passing messages. Those devices expose a set of core learning services (e.g., Smart Desk services such the PUPIL [27] and the ClassMATE [30] frameworks) along with an instance of the AmIClass Runtime Environment that can host the orchestration scripts written in ClassScript and defining learning scenarios. Such orchestration scripts can be deployed either locally on multiple targets to balance the overall workload (e.g., a script that initializes every desk after a successful student authentication), or centrally in the AmIClass cloud (e.g., the script that orchestrates the entire lecture and communicates with the AmI-RIA subsystem [35]).

Therefore, the teacher can define at any time whether a script will be deployed on a single or on multiple targets. The system validates whether the appropriate

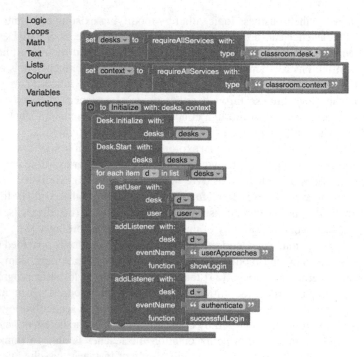

Fig. 5. The graphical equivalent of the above sample ClassScript program

requirements are met (e.g., the required services are available in that host). When the target of a script is defined, the main classroom orchestrator deploys an instance of that script by appropriately notifying the local runtimes to download, parse and execute the appropriate script. From that point on, the execution control is performed solely by the local(s) orchestrator(s), while the main classroom orchestrator can manage it if necessary by propagating the necessary commands (e.g., suspend the script that controls the assistant facility when a quiz test has been started).

In case of a script modification that is currently active, the runtime environment ensures that any pending activities are finalized before restarting all of its instances in order to deploy the latest version. Currently, the update policy defines that during restart any events emitted in between will be dropped, therefore scripts reinstate their last state based on what has been saved before termination without cascading intermediate effects. In a future extension, a more sophisticated cascading policy has been planned; any events transmitted between script restarts will be stored in appropriate buffers and will be propagated in a timely manner.

5   Conclusions and Future Work

The emerging trend of mobile and ubiquitous computing has attracted numerous researchers and vendors to build educational applications that take advantage of the innovative technological affordances. Nevertheless, the majority of the available educational applications often do not meet their potentials due to the lack of tools that simplify their interplay with the environment and the contained affordances. To this end, this paper has presented an extensible software infrastructure that enables the design of purposeful and engaging learning activities and speedups prototyping for formal and informal learning environments, by combining and orchestrating cloud-based, ambient and pervasive facilities and services.

The following high-level components have been implemented: (i) a Service Mediator Agent that will integrate and provide access to ambient and pervasive services, (ii) a distributed Learning Activities Orchestrator that will monitor and orchestrate the learning process, (iii) a Context-Aware Adaptation Module that will facilitate the decision-making process, and (iv) a Design Environment for defining and configuring learning activities' scripts, while interoperability will be facilitate through a common Learning-oriented Ontological Framework.

Future work includes: (i) the extension of the programming environment to make use of the available semantic description of the services to validate their compatibility and provide useful insights for the end-users, (ii) the extensive testing of the overall infrastructure, (iii) the enhancement of the scenario modification process to support on-the-fly updates that support cascading of events that happened during the update process and finally (iv) the evaluation of the entire environment by HCI experts and teachers in terms of usability and acceptance and by experienced developers of ubiquitous applications in terms of completeness.

References

1. Attewell, J., Carol, S.-S.: Mobile Learning Anytime Everywhere. Learning and Skills Development Agency, London (2004)
2. Atzori, L., Iera, A., Morabito, G.: The internet of things: a survey. Comput. Netw. **54**(15), 2787–2805 (2010)
3. Bandyopadhyay, S., et al.: Role of middleware for internet of things: a study. Int. J. Comput. Sci. Eng. Surv. (IJCSES) **2**(3), 94–105 (2011)
4. Begel, A., Garcia, D.D., Wolfman, S.A.: Kinesthetic learning in the classroom. ACM SIGCSE Bull. **36**(1), 183–184 (2004). ACM
5. Brown, E.: Education in the Wild – A Comprehensive Overview of Location-Based Contextual Learning. STELLAR Network of Excellence (2008)
6. Caballé, S., Lapedriza, À.: Enabling automatic just-in-time evaluation of in-class discussions in on-line collaborative learning practices. J. Digit. Inf. Manag. **7**(5), 290–297 (2009)
7. Caballé, S., et al.: Towards a generic platform for developing CSCL applications using grid infrastructure. In: IEEE International Symposium on Cluster Computing and the Grid, CCGrid 2004. IEEE (2004)
8. Cahill, V., Haahr, M.: Real + virtual = clever: thoughts on programming smart environments (1999)
9. Chang, C.-S.: WebQuest: M-learning for environmental education. In: Chen, T.-S., Hsu, W.-H. (eds.) IEEE International Conference on Wireless Mobile and Ubiquitous Technology in Education. IEEE (2010). doi:10.1109/WMUTE.2010.35

10. Chen, N.S., Graf, S., Hwang, G.J.: Adaptive learning systems. Knowledge management, organizational intelligence and learning and complexity. In: Encyclopedia of Life Support Systems (EOLSS), Developed under the Auspices of the UNESCO, Eolss Publishers, Oxford, UK (2012). http://www.eolss.net. Website eolss.net. Accessed 1 Feb 2013

11. Chin, J., Callaghan, V., Clarke, G.: End-user customisation of intelligent environments. In: Nakashima, H., Aghajan, H., Augusto, J.C. (eds.) Handbook of Ambient Intelligence and Smart Environments, pp. 371–407. Springer, New York (2010)

12. Chu, H.C., Hwang, G.J., Tsai, C.C.: A knowledge engineering approach to developing mind tools for context-aware ubiquitous learning. Comput. Educ. **54**(1), 289–297 (2010)

13. Cochrane, T.: Exploring mobile learning success factors. Alt-J **18**(2), 133–148 (2010). doi:10.1080/09687769.2010.494718. Routledge

14. Datta, D., Mitra, S.: M-learning: mobile - enabled educational technology. Innovating (2010)

15. Dey, A.K., Abowd, G.D., Salber, D.: A conceptual framework and a toolkit for supporting the rapid prototyping of context-aware applications. Hum. Comput. Interact. **16**(2), 97–166 (2001)

16. Dowling, C., Lai, K.-W. (eds.): Information and Communication Technology and the Teacher of the Future. LNCS (IFIP), vol. 132. Springer, New York (2003)

17. Giusto, D., et al. (eds.): The Internet of Things: 20th Tyrrhenian Workshop on Digital Communications. Springer, New York (2010)

18. Gray, O., Young, M.: Video games: a new interface for non-professional game developers. In: ACM International Conference on Computer-Human Interaction (CHI 2007) (2007)

19. Green, T.R.G., Petre, M.: Usability analysis of visual programming environments: a cognitive dimensions framework. J. Vis. Lang. Comput. **7**(2), 131–174 (1996)

20. Guerra, M.A., Francisco, C.M., Girão, P.S.: PortableLab: implementation of a mobile remote laboratory for the android platform. In: 2011 IEEE Global Engineering Education Conference (EDUCON). IEEE (2011)

21. Holloway, S., Julien, C.: The case for end-user programming of ubiquitous computing environments. In: Proceedings of the FSE/SDP Workshop on Future of Software Engineering Research. ACM (2010)

22. Hung, P.H., Hwang, G.J., Lin, Y.F., Wu, T.H., Su, I.H.: Seamless connection between learning and assessment- applying progressive learning tasks in mobile ecology inquiry. Educ. Technol. Soc. **16**(1), 194–205 (2013)

23. Hwang, G.J., Tsai, C.C., Yang, S.J.H.: Criteria, strategies and research issues of context-aware ubiquitous learning. Educ. Technol. Soc. **11**(2), 81–91 (2008)

24. Fraser, N.: Blockly: a visual programming editor (2013)

25. Kernighan, B.W., Ritchie, D.M.: The C Programming Language, vol. 2. Prentice-Hall, Englewood Cliffs (1988)

26. Korozi, M., et al.: Ambient educational mini-games. In: Proceedings of the International Working Conference on Advanced Visual Interfaces. ACM (2012)

27. Korozi, M., et al.: Towards building pervasive UIs for the intelligent classroom: the PUPIL approach. In: Proceedings of the International Working Conference on Advanced Visual Interfaces. ACM (2012)

28. Kubitza, T.: Towards a toolkit for the rapid creation and programming of smart environments. In: Workshop on End User Development in the Internet of Things Era. EUDITE (2015)

29. Leonidis, A., Korozi, M., Margetis, G., Grammenos, D., Stephanidis, C.: An intelligent hotel room. In: Augusto, J.C., Wichert, R., Collier, R., Keyson, D., Salah, A.A., Tan, A.-H. (eds.) AmI 2013. LNCS, vol. 8309, pp. 241–246. Springer, Heidelberg (2013)

30. Leonidis, A., et al.: ClassMATE: enabling ambient intelligence in the classroom. World Acad. Sci. Eng. Technol. **66**, 594–598 (2010)

31. Lieberman, H., et al.: End-user development: an emerging paradigm. In: Lieberman, H., Paternò, F., Wulf, V. (eds.) End User Development, vol. 9. Springer, Dordrecht (2006)
32. Maloney, J., et al.: The scratch programming language and environment. ACM Trans. Comput. Educ. (TOCE) 10(4), 16 (2010)
33. Margetis, G., et al.: Enhancing education through natural interaction with physical paper. Univ. Access Inf. Soc. 1–21 (2014). doi:10.1007/s10209-014-0365-0
34. Martin, S., et al.: M2Learn open framework: developing mobile collaborative and social applications. In: UBICOMM 2010, The Fourth International Conference on Mobile Ubiquitous Computing, Systems, Services and Technologies (2010)
35. Mathioudakis, G., et al.: Ami-ria: real-time teacher assistance tool for an ambient intelligence classroom. In: eLmL 2013, The 5th International Conference on Mobile, Hybrid, and On-line Learning (2013)
36. De Marcos Ortega, L., et al.: Using m-learning on nursing courses to improve learning. Comput. Inform. Nurs. 29(6), TC98–TC104 (2011). Topical Collection
37. Parsons, D.: Combining e-Learning and M-Learning: New Applications of Blended Educational Resources, vol. 154. Information Science Reference, Hershey (2011)
38. Peltz, C.: Web services orchestration and choreography. Computer 36(10), 46–52 (2003)
39. Poslad, S.: Ubiquitous Computing Smart Devices, Smart Environments and Smart Interaction. Wiley, Chippenham (2009)
40. Savvaki, C., Leonidis, A., Paparoulis, G., Antona, M., Stephanidis, C.: Designing a technology–augmented school desk for the future classroom. In: Stephanidis, C. (ed.) HCII 2013, Part II. CCIS, vol. 374, pp. 681–685. Springer, Heidelberg (2013)
41. Schmidt, A.: Implicit human computer interaction through context. Pers. Technol. 4(2–3), 191–199 (2000)
42. Sharples, M., Taylor, J., Vavoula, G.: Towards a theory of mobile learning. Proc. of mLearn 2005 1(1), 1–9 (2005)
43. Spector, J.M.: Conceptualizing the emerging field of smart learning environments. Smart Learn. Environ. 2014(1), 2 (2014)
44. Turner, M., Budgen, D., Brereton, P.: Turning software into a service. Computer 36(10), 38–44 (2003)
45. Uckelmann, D., Harrison, M., Michahelles, F.: Architecting the Internet of Things. Springer, Heidelberg (2011)
46. Ur, B., et al.: Practical trigger-action programming in the smart home. In: Proceedings of the 32nd Annual ACM Conference on Human Factors in Computing Systems. ACM (2014)
47. Wang, M.: Learning anytime, anywhere: using mobile. Learning 9, 1–7 (2008)
48. White, W., et al.: Better scripts, better games. Commun. ACM 52(3), 42–47 (2009)
49. Yau, J.Y.-K., Joy, M.S.: Designing and evaluating the mobile context-aware learning schedule framework: challenges and lessons learnt, pp. 85–92 (2010)

Co-creation in Context: The User as Co-creator Approach

Ingrid Mulder[1,2(✉)], Fenne Van Doorn[1], and Pieter Jan Stappers[1]

[1] ID-Studiolab, Faculty of Industrial Design Engineering, Delft University
of Technology, Landbergstraat 15, 2628 CE Delft, The Netherlands
[2] Creating 010, Rotterdam University of Applied Sciences, Wijnhaven 99-107,
3011 WN Rotterdam, The Netherlands
mulderi@acm.org

Abstract. By providing a platform for systemic innovation and co-creative partnerships, Living Labs open opportunities to get users involved early into the creative process of new ICT, product and services development. The concept leaves, however, much room on how to get users actually involved, and does not explain how to keep users engaged during the entire design process. The current work elaborates upon the user as co-creator approach and illustrates how current methods stressing participation and co-creation can be deployed to strengthen Living Lab practices. We present examples from the ProFit-lab Delft that demonstrate co-creation in context as well as the user as co-creator approach. We conclude with a discussion on the results and challenges to actively co-creating in context.

Keywords: Children · Co-creation · Context · Design methods · Empowerment · Living Labs · Systemic innovation

1 Introduction

Living Labs are welcomed as a way forward to stimulate new ICT product and services development by providing a platform for involving users in the various stages of innovation; these are amongst others, bringing the users early into the creative process in order to discover new and emerging behaviours and user patterns, bridging the innovation gap between technology development and the uptake of new products and services involving all relevant players, and allowing for early assessment of the socio-economic implications of new technological solutions by demonstrating the validity of innovative services [4, 19]. Living Labs have grown in popularity in the past years; Next to the increased interest and the growing numbers of self-defined Living Labs, there is also a palimpsest of perspectives of Living Labs and methods used. The variety and evolution of concepts, methodologies, tools as well as infrastructures challenge the scoping of the Living Lab phenomenon, and have resulted in a strong rise in publications aiming to position the Living Lab phenomenon much sharper by presenting landscapes, frameworks and acknowledged definitions [see for example 3, 5, 14].

© Springer International Publishing Switzerland 2015
N. Streitz and P. Markopoulos (Eds.): DAPI 2015, LNCS 9189, pp. 74–84, 2015.
DOI: 10.1007/978-3-319-20804-6_7

However, Living Labs are inherently complex by their systemic nature: the innovation process addressing societal challenges (*why*), the real-life environment (*where*), and the various multi-helix partners involved who are usually differently motivated and might benefit differently from the Living Lab concept (*who*), as well as the co-creation along the entire production cycle, from ideation to market deployment (*what*). Interestingly, the European Network of Living Labs has – since its inception – searched for ways to ensure the use of common methodologies and tools across Europe that support, stimulate, and accelerate the innovation process. See for example the Living Labs harmonization cube that addresses the systemic nature of Living Labs and contributed to the network's foundation [12, 13].

On top of that, the majority of Living lab experiences does not address this holistic perspective, but rather focuses on a particular perspective; making it harder to position Living Lab practices. Without doubt these discussions clearly facilitate common ground for sharing Living Labs practices, but might not necessarily contribute to a better understanding of the dynamics of innovation, the living part of the lab [12]. Living Labs are also a network of real people with everyday practices and experiences, a living network allowing partners to co-create in context [11, 12]. Living Labs employ specific methods and tools to interact with their users and stakeholders across the entire product and service development process, however, as concluded in our earlier work traditional methods for laboratory testing are emphasized over the use of co-creation techniques and participatory methods [11].

Differently put, the bigger part of user involvement remains merely reactive. Living Labs do, however, embrace the user as co-creator approach. The current work, therefore, addresses more intensive ways of engaging users, in more active roles, such as informing the design, or generating ideas and solutions themselves, and aim to contribute to a more elaborate user as co-creator approach.

2   User as Co-creator Approach

Over the past decades, the distance between designers and users has reduced. The by now traditional way is dominated by an 'expert' perspective in which trained researchers observe and/or interview largely passive users. The contribution of the users is to perform instructed tasks and/or to give their opinions about product concepts that were generated earlier by others without any input from them. Figure 1 shows this in the bottom-left corner. Increasingly, users appear in roles where they provide expertise and are given room for initiative, by participating in the informing, ideating, and conceptualizing activities in the early design phases. The participatory approach (i.e., 'user as partner', on the right in the diagram) has been led by Northern Europeans, originated in Scandinavia. A second dimension of development has been in the type of research that is conducted. The last two decades have shown a growth in research techniques, which have not only evaluative power (prove/disprove a hypothesis or idea), but also generative value (provide insights not yet known to the researchers). These latter developments are often supported by the inclusion of explorative actions using tools and techniques from design, such as making collages, diagrams, models, and other visualizations as a means to support self-observation and reflection. The two approaches are now beginning to influence one another.

Within this landscape, in the area of participatory design, the notions of co-creation and co-design have been growing. As can seen from the human centred design landscape illustrated in Fig. 1, the challenge to keep Living Labs living is to involve active users by making use of generative techniques, and so, practicing a 'user as co-creator' approach.

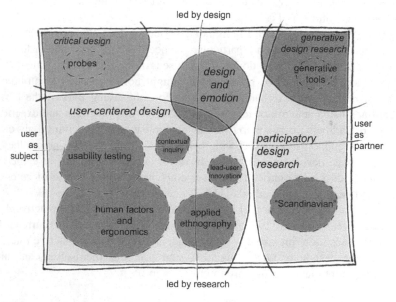

Fig. 1. The current landscape of human-centered design research as practiced in the design and development of products and services [from 17]

Living Labs do not use any of the Š, we see that the potential of the user as co-creator approach goes well beyond current practice of demonstration-and-reaction; both in the amount of time as well as in the commitment that is invested from all parties as well as in the depth and breadth of results that can be harvested from that.

2.1   Co-creation is About Participation and Context

Main forms of user participation in both industry and academia are after-the-fact testing. Users can react to a concept prototype in a demonstration, a focus group, or a usability test. The earlier phases in the process are mostly conducted within the lab or company, often based on literature study and market and segmentation studies. This is reflected in the emphasis put on 'demonstrators' as deliverables of projects. Involving users in earlier phases is important to ensure that the concepts of products and services that are developed fit into the lives of the target groups.

For that, the development team, including researchers, designers, engineers, and others involved, must build an understanding of the context of product use, i.e., the full ramifications of who, where, what, when, how, and why which surrounds the product. This fuller understanding of the context is the more necessary as current ICT product and service design increasingly address complex interactions between users, products, services, and infrastructure, with increasing opportunities for mistakes due to 'blind spots' in the development team.

Sleeswijk Visser and colleagues [20] describe how such information can be gathered from users in a structured way, and point to two important factors: (1) generative activity (having people create artefacts as a way to stimulate observation, reflection, and discussion), and (2) sensitizing (letting participants go through a process of reflection over several days or weeks, in order to deepen their knowledge. Both tools of expression, and time for reflection are needed to work the participating user into the 'expert of their experience' to contribute with own initiative and input based on their experiences in Living Labs practices.

3   Context – ProFit-lab Delft

ProFit Delft is a Living Lab environment where companies in the area of sports and exercise can install product prototypes or production models to have them tested by citizens. The context is an actual playground, a real-life environment, where interactions take place during everyday use by the local community. This makes the lab very relevant for companies as well as knowledge institutes. Researchers use the ProFit-lab to collect data on the end-user interaction with the installed products in a real-life setting. However, the upcoming users were already involved before the first constructions of the Living Lab environment have been started. Their needs are investigated and form the basis for creating inviting concepts and environments.

Next, an observation system and different sensors are placed throughout the Living Lab environment to measure intensity of use, the user activity levels, as well as other use parameters. This provides relevant scientific feedback on the effects of the prototypes/products that are placed in the ProFit-lab; facilitating accelerated product development in this way. One of the first steps in the creation of the ProFit-lab was the organisation of an innovation competition, in which companies were challenged to develop new products that would fit within the lab. Submitted concepts are evaluated by a small representation of the user group and their advice was given to the jury who decided on predetermined criteria which concept wins. The winning team received an award voucher and support to develop their design into a prototype that can be placed in the ProFit-lab.

3.1   Contextmapping

In order to place innovative concepts in the ProFit-lab that support the specific target group and focus, user needs are explored through a "contextmapping" approach [20]. Contextmapping is a procedure for conducting contextual research with users, aiming to inform and inspire designers in the fuzzy front end of the design process. In these contextmapping sessions, participants receive creative assignments in which they make something that is related to their experiences and then discuss it. Through this procedure they are provided with the means to access deep levels of knowledge. By actively involving users, a fit between the design and use of a product is ensured. The insights from contextmapping-research are given to contestants in the innovation competition, as input for their submissions.

As an example, the ProFit-lab in Delft is further discussed. A traditional playground in Delft, located next to an elderly home and near to schools and family houses, is transformed into the new ProFit-lab. This ProFit-lab is targeted at children and elderly, with a focus on "being active together". In order to reveal the needs and wishes of the two specific target groups and their interaction with each other, a contextmapping study was conducted [see [24] for details]. Both children and elderly started with a sensitizing booklet, in which they observed their own activities and reflected on themselves over a period of time. After the sensitizing the participants came together in a group session. There were three different kinds of sessions: children only, elderly only, and a mixed session. All the data from the booklets and sessions (such as the creative outings and recorded discussions) were analysed, clustered and transformed into "Insight Cards" describing behavioural patterns, wishes, needs and experiences as voiced by the

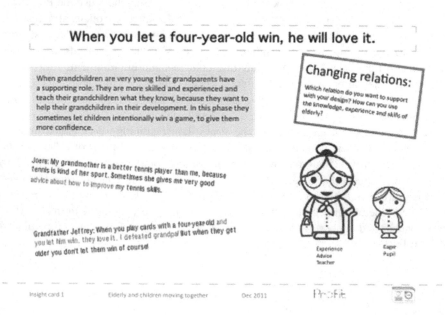

Fig. 2. Example of an Insight Card

participants (see Fig. 2). These cards are presented to the contestants in the innovation competition.

Next to future users, many other stakeholders actively participated in the ProFit-lab. For example sports associations, a school for sports-management, several elderly associations, and a housing cooperative. They all are eager to work together within the ProFit-lab once it is realised. Their contribution could be for example to bond future users and organise activities and programmes related to the innovations tested in the ProFit-lab. Through their early contribution, the ProFit-lab that is currently under construction can also be designed and organised to reflect the concerns of these stakeholders.

3.2 Children as Researchers

In order to enhance the expert role of the users, a second case was conducted in which twenty children, aged 9 to 12, from a primary school in Delft took on the role of researcher themselves, doing interviews with peers and grandparents. Getting this responsible role motivated the children and listening to peers made them developing a more grounded opinion of their own [25]. The overall assignment for the children was to generate ideas for a new playground in which children and elderly can be active together. In order to create these ideas they had to research their target group by interviewing peers and grandparents. This project consisted of 3 meetings with small groups of children (4–5) and a researcher, the individual conduction of 2 interviews by each child and a final creative session. An overview of the activities per meeting:

Meeting 1. All children sketched ideas for new playground equipment, to be used by children and elderly together, and found out that it is hard to think of other people's needs and wishes. Subsequently, they thought of questions to ask their target group as input for a research booklet. This booklet was further developed by the researcher to help children conduct their interviews.

Fig. 3. Children practicing interviewing on each other

Meeting 2. During the second meeting with the researcher, each small group of children was briefly trained in interviewing skills and practiced the use of the research booklet by interviewing each other (see Fig. 3).

Conduction of Interviews. Individually the children interviewed either their peers or grandparents. The interviews were audio-recorded and notes were written down in the research booklet. They had two weeks to perform this task.

Meeting 3. The groups of children came together with the researcher for a feedback session in which their results were discussed. They explained and compared their research booklets and shared their experiences. After this discussion the children filled in templates of personas as a summary of different kinds of participants they had encountered.

Creative Session. The whole class participated in this session at the same time and new groups were formed to generate ideas together, each group included children with knowledge from the two different target groups. In their new groups, the children thought again of ideas to place in the new playground, but now with the use of their personas and their gained knowledge about the target group.

This case study showed that children are able to work as collaborators in contextual user research. The design of playground equipment is a motivating and understandable goal for them. The training was a necessary step to improve their interview skills and to get to know the children and their points of view. The most important aspect of this collaboration process was the way the children adopted the role of researcher. They felt ownership and developed a serious and focused attitude. In their role of researcher, the children discovered similarities and differences between themselves and others. Besides gaining valuable insights from their participants, they accessed and shared their own experiences, resulting into personal insights in the target group to be used by designers. See van [25] for more details.

Concept Evaluation. Next to user needs research, the Profit-Lab Delft also involved users as co-researchers to evaluate the submitted concepts in the innovation competition [23]. Two elderly and two children interviewed peers about their opinions on the five competition entries. After that, they reported their findings in a feedback session to the lead researcher. They explained the answers they gained with their research booklets and expressed their own opinion as well. Subsequently, they ranked the competition entries in order of attractiveness and discussed in what way the original user insights from the contextmapping research were traceable in these new designs. There was not much time for this evaluative research with users, so by recruiting four co-researchers, we included the opinion of twelve people.

3.3   Meaningful Relationship with Users

Until now, the input from users in the Profit-Lab was on demand; when a research question popped up users were involved. In the future we strive for a more meaningful and beneficial relationship for all parties. Getting a more sustainable relationship with users and binding them to the Profit-Lab is important. It turned out that giving users the role of co-researcher is motivating, it gives them ownership and responsibility. Binding a group of co-researchers to a Living Lab and giving them the role of ambassadors might be an important step in the development of a sustainable relationship with users.

4 Discussion and Conclusions

Different types of stakeholders involved in user-driven innovation benefit differently from the Living Lab concept. Users are empowered to influencing the development of ICT services and products. For industry innovation processes can be more effective by partnering with other companies as well as end-users. Even for Small and Medium Enterprises (SMEs), the development, validation, and integration of new ideas and rapidly scaling-up their local ICT services and products to other markets becomes an opportunity by joining a Living Lab consortium. Participating in a Living Lab is a way to deal with the complexity of product development, which is growing rapidly on many fronts: new technologies, global competition, merging of products, services, and infrastructure, sustainability issues, and speeding up the innovation process.

4.1 Smart Industry Goes Community-Driven Innovation

Especially at large US industries such as Microsoft, new methods have found their way into industrial organizations. Moreover, co-creation techniques are rapidly finding their way into education, and – through the new generation of designers – into practice. But actual long-term or deep involvement of users in product development is limited. In industry, product- and concept-testing (after these have been finalized and implemented) are commonplace. However, techniques to involve users in the idea generation, information, and strategy-defining phases are not often applied in practice. In part this is because of the enduring technology push, in part because existing methods such as (design) ethnography are expensive and require changes in the way product development processes are conducted in the company. On the other hand, in Europe a range of (mainly academic) projects have shown the viability and value of user-inspired approaches, and have delivered new, appropriate methods.

Theories of innovation commonly distinguish two forces: technology push and market pull [18]. If product development relies exclusively on the former, this leads to 'technological tricks in boxes, with a button added to start their use'. The latter, taken alone, caters only to the needs of which people are explicitly aware. The competition on user qualities has created a third force, which has been called the 'contextual push' or the 'people insights' [21]. By this way, new products addressing tacit and latent needs come about, not through a new technical possibility or a visible demand from buyers, but through increased insight in the needs and dreams of possible future users. The most telling outcomes of these approaches are new products for which no buyers existed yet, however, these approaches can also be applied to existing products and markets. Key lesson in this area is that everyday people, if involved in an appropriate way [see 20], are a rich source of experiential knowledge, and are eager to participate in a design project if their expertise receives appropriate recognition. The participation not only of everyday people as potential customers, but also of all other stakeholders along the value-chain can be seen as the foremost required element for the successful operation of a Living Lab.

Co-creation requires an open mindset towards sharing and collaboration. This is not trivial. Although, board members preach open innovation in pre-competitive collaboration with all possible stakeholders, including users, companies seem not eager to share with their competitors. Even within companies, employees are not always keen in sharing ideas. Involving users and incorporating the user's context helps companies to get deeper insights in the end-users' needs and values.

Although participatory design has its roots in the Scandinavian democratic movements, viewing participants as equal, as partners, current participatory practices are not always addressing these equal grounds. Arnstein [1] already criticized many participatory practices as not really giving the users a substantial influence in the process. Living Labs can provide such a space for co-creative partnerships [10].

4.2   Living Methodologies

The true value of getting deeper insights in user values and needs as well as discovering product or services ideas might be in the fuzzy front end, the early stages of strategy and alliance formation, and concept development. Whereas the Living Lab approach has been introduced as a methodology for experimentation and co-creation in real-life environments, where users together with other stakeholders such as researchers, industry partners, and designers look for new ideas, solutions, new products and services, current Living Labs practices, however, demonstrate too often reactive users rather than users as active co-creators. These practices show insights that are for the most part based on the usage of traditional methods, and are consequently, not exemplary in demonstrating the added value of a Living Lab over other user-centric methodologies. In order to have the Living Lab – and its methodology – growing to maturity, it is crucial to awaken the living part by making use of its infrastructure, and by continuously evaluating in all phases, thus before, during and after use and in-situ.

In addition, the use of living methodologies [9, 12] to come close to the user and his rich experiences as well as giving attention to the fuzzy front end as a phase advancing the product/service idea is a first step to embrace Living Labs' potential. For this, generative techniques and contextmapping [20] proved to be successful. In addition, by capturing rich experiences and social dynamics of everyday life, Living Labs make far better use of the promised ecological validity of the presented systemic innovation approach.

4.3   Empowerment Though Co-creation

In keeping with an increasing number of researchers, for example in the platform 'Researching Children International', children should be enabled to participate in research and design concerning their lives and surroundings. They are supported and driven by article 12 of the UN convention of the rights of the child [22], which states that children have the right to form and express their views in all matters affecting them. Also amongst design researchers [for example 6, 16], there is also a growing believe that it is important to include children in the development of technology that influences their lives and they want to empower children to have a say about the environment in which they live.

Next to that, there are indications that active participation in research contributes to cognitive, social and identity development of children [7] and of young adults [15]. According to Dedding and colleagues [2] participation strengthens the involvement in society and understanding of democracy, which leads to a healthy and strong community, and especially in case of children it adds to their personal development as well. As nicely put forward by Kellett [8]: 'the concept of children as active researchers is rapidly gaining credence in response to changing perspectives on children's status in society'.

Acknowledgements. This work has been mainly based on the authors' experiences gained in our research on Contextmapping and European projects such as CoreLabs and ProFit. Feedback on presented work at ICE 2009 [11] encouraged us to elaborate on the respective paper with examples from our user as co-creator practices. The IST Project CoreLabs: Co-creative Living Labs (No. IST-035065) has been partly funded by the European Commission (www.corelabs.eu). ProFit is an Interreg IVB funded project (www.profitproject.org) in which various cities in North-West Europe (Delft, Eindhoven, Kortrijk and Sheffield) participate. The Contextmapping project is part of TU Delft's ID-StudioLab, at the Faculty of Industrial Design Engineering.

References

1. Arnstein, S.R.: A ladder of citizen participation. JAIP **35**(4), 216–224 (1969)
2. Dedding, C., Jurrius, K., Moonen, X., Rutjes, L.: Kinderen en jongeren actief in wetenschappelijk onderzoek: ethiek, methoden en resultaten van onderzoek met en door jeugd [Children and Youngster actively engaged in scientific research: ethics, methods, and results on research with and by youth]. LannooCampus (2013)
3. Dell'Era, C., Landoni, P.: Living lab: a methodology between user-centred design and participatory design. Creativity Innov. Manage. **23**, 137–154 (2014)
4. European Commission: Living Labs for user-driven open innovation, an overview of the living labs methodology, activities and achievements, January 2009
5. Følstad, A.: Living Labs for innovation and development of communication technology: a literature review. EJOV Electron. J. Virtual Organ. Netw. **10**, 99–131 (2008)
6. Guha, M.L., Druin, A., Chipman, G., Fails, J.A., Simms, S., Farber, A.: Working with young children as technology design partners. Commun. ACM **48**(1), 39–42 (2005)
7. Hart, R.A.: Stepping Back from 'The Ladder': Reflections on a Model of Participatory Work with Children. Springer, dordrecht (2008)
8. Kellett, M.: Children as active researchers: a new research paradigm for the 21st century? ESRC, UK (2005)
9. Mulder, I.: Living labbing the rotterdam way: co-creation as an enabler for urban innovation. Technol. Innov. Manage. Rev. **2**(9), 39–43 (2012)

10. Mulder, I.: Sociable smart cities: rethinking our future through co-creative partnerships. In: Streitz, N., Markopoulos, P. (eds.) DAPI 2014. LNCS, vol. 8530, pp. 566–574. Springer, Heidelberg (2014)
11. Mulder, I., Stappers, P.J.: Co-creating in practice: results and challenges. In: Thoben, K.D., Pawar, K.S., Katzy, B., Bierwolf, R. (eds.) Collaborative Innovation: Emerging Technologies. Environments and Communities. Centre for Concurrent Enterprise, Nottingham (2009)
12. Mulder, I., Velthausz, D., Kriens, M.: Living methodologies: understanding the dynamics of innovation. In: Schumacher, J., Niitano, V.-P. (eds.) European Living Labs – A New Approach for Human Centric Regional Innovation, pp. 31–38. Wissenschaftlicher Verlag Berlin, Berlin (2008)
13. Mulder, I., Velthausz, D., Kriens, M.: The Living Labs harmonization cube: communicating living lab's essentials. EJOV, Electron. J. Virtual Organ. Netw. 10, 1–14 (2008)
14. Pallot, M., Trousse, B., Senach, B., Scapin, D.: Living Lab research landscape: from user centred design and user experience towards user cocreation. In: Proceedings of the Living Lab Summer School, Paris August 2010
15. Pucci, E.L., Mulder, I.: Star(t) to shine: unlocking hidden talents through sharing and making. In: Streitz N., Markopoulos, P. (eds.) DAPI 2015. LNCS, vol. 9189, pp. 85–96. Springer, Heidelberg (2015)
16. Read, J.C.: Validating the fun toolkit: an instrument for measuring children opinions of technology. Cogn. Technol. Work 10(2), 119–128 (2008)
17. Sanders, E.B.-N., Stappers, P.J.: Co-creation and the new landscapes of design. CoDesign 4(1), 5–18 (2008)
18. Scherer, F.M.: Demand-pull and technological opportunity: scmookler revisited. J. Ind. Econ. 30, 225–237 (1982)
19. Schumacher, J., Niitano, V.-P. (eds.): European Living Labs – A New Approach for Human Centric Regional Innovation. Wissenschaftlicher Verlag Berlin, Berlin (2008)
20. Sleeswijk Visser, F., Stappers, P.J., van der Lugt, R., Sanders, E.B.-N.: Contextmapping: experiences from practice. Codesign 1(2), 119–149 (2005)
21. Stappers, P.J., van Rijn, H., Kistemaker, S., Hennink, A., Sleeswijk Visser, F.: Designing for other people's strengths and motivations. Adv. Eng. Inform. 23, 174–183 (2008)
22. UN convention on the rights of the child, (1990)
23. van Doorn, F., Gielen, M., Stappers, P.J.: Friends sharing opinions: users become co-researchers to evaluate design concepts. In: Proceedings of IASDR 2013 (2013)
24. van Doorn, F., Gielen, M., Stappers, P.J.: Involving children and elderly in the development of new design concepts to become active together. Interact. Des. Archit. 20, 86–100 (2014)
25. van Doorn, F., Stappers, P.J., Gielen, M.A.: Design research by proxy: using children as researchers to gain contextual knowledge about user experience. In: Proceedings. of the ACM Conference on Human Factors in Computing Systems (CHI 2013), Paris, France, 27 Apr–2 May 2013

Star(t) to Shine: Unlocking Hidden Talents Through Sharing and Making

Emilia Louisa Pucci[1(✉)] and Ingrid Mulder[2,3]

[1] Round Feather LLC, 947 Tingley Ln, San Diego, USA
emilia.louisa.pucci@gmail.com
[2] Creating 010, Rotterdam University of Applied Sciences, Wijnhaven 99-107,
3011 WN Rotterdam, The Netherlands
mulderi@acm.org
[3] ID-Studiolab, Faculty of Industrial Design Engineering, Delft University
of Technology, Landbergstraat 15, 2628 CE Delft, The Netherlands

Abstract. The current article embraces the transformational role digital fabrication has to empower people doing things previously unthinkable while making it accessible to a larger audience. Using a research-through-design approach, we have co-designed a six-step workshop series to activate young adults' hidden talents through sharing and making. The division in steps was meant to empower the students gradually and from within their own interests and qualities. The resulting workshop platform serves as a best practice in learning 21st century skills, lowering the threshold of access to digital fabrication in education. The students were active co-creators and obviously learnt new skills. Some students even had a mind-shifting experience, and demonstrated that it is indeed possible to transform dropouts into engaged and successful individuals, who are role models for their peers: *"stars shining bright in their local community"*.

Keywords: 21st century skills · Empowerment · FabLabs · Maker Movement · Transforming society

1 Introduction

The Maker Movement is providing all kinds of people around the world with the tools and infrastructures to unleash their intrinsic ability to create, make, and innovate. This spreading trend of learning-by-doing has the potential to empower people in doing things previously unthinkable, through the potential of 3D printing, laser cutting, Internet of Things, electronics, and so on. The unleashing of creative processes can be coined as 21st century skills, which refer to amongst others digital literacy, creativity, critical thinking, problem solving, as well as collaboration and communication skills. It is commonly accepted that these higher-order skills are essential for successful participation in society. As the OECD concluded in its report 'Towards an OECD Skills Strategy': "Numerous efforts have been made to identify 'key competencies' and 'employability skills' over the past decades. However, apart from the universally acknowledged importance of basic literacy and numerical skills, there is little hard

© Springer International Publishing Switzerland 2015
N. Streitz and P. Markopoulos (Eds.): DAPI 2015, LNCS 9189, pp. 85–96, 2015.
DOI: 10.1007/978-3-319-20804-6_8

evidence of what other skills are required for workers to obtain better labour outcomes and cope with a more fluid labour market" [6].

In keeping with recent trends in STEM (Science, Technology, Engineering, Mathematics) and STEAM (including Arts and Design) education, we elaborate upon the capabilities that FabLabs bring to a broader audience, which have until recently been reserved only to a few professionals and embrace the value of making and prototyping as a way to provide deeper, richer learning experiences [4]. Without doubt, the Maker Movement has impacted the design profession in terms of skills required as well as design methodologies and practices, by making tools and infrastructures easily accessible to a wider spectrum of people. Actually, the FabLab itself provides an excellent framework to facilitate the ignition of practice-based education, as demonstrated by the Fab@School project [3]. We, therefore, have explored what role FabLabs can play in design education by experimenting with these 21st century skills. In this way, we aimed to prepare upcoming design professionals for the changes in design practice [5]. More specifically, we have implemented the power of the FabLab approach to attract people, to get their hands "dirty" with digital manufacturing in Stadslab Rotterdam. Initiated from the educational need to prepare students in the field of Communication and Media Design, Media Technology, and Computer Science in the digital revolution in making and prototyping, the lab bridges the gap between production design and the integration of microelectronics and programming. Stadslab Rotterdam can be best classified as a FabLab+, which emphasizes electronic as well as sensor devices, Internet of Things, and Open Data. In the current work, we elaborate on the educational role of FabLabs, and address how digital fabrication technologies can be made more accessible to uninitiated and underprivileged communities, so as to provide them with a broader skillset than just the ability to use a tool or machine to re-create predefined templates, thus enhancing their participation in society.

2   Context

Afrikaanderwijk is a highly multicultural neighborhood in Rotterdam South, the Netherlands, where the generally low level of education of the inhabitants and their ethnic background relegate them to a lower level of society. In our earlier work young adults from Afrikaanderwijk were interviewed to gain insights on their lifestyle, needs, and passions [8] The interviewed young adults were for the most part of non-European descent and second-generation immigrants. All displayed a few common traits: they attended low level schools, struggled to find a job and are frequently stigmatized as problematic. When asked about their dreams, the answers tended to be vague: some young adults wanted to become star soccer players like Lionel Messi, but the common answer was that they did not have anything specific they liked to do or wanted to improve their ability in. From their answers and behaviors, it seemed as though they did not feel allowed to have dreams, ambitions and to cultivate their talents or interests. Interestingly, they all showed that they were tech savvy, digitally social, and full of passions, yet with no engagement in their neighborhood and little means to achieve their dreams for the future. As we identified a strong unexpressed, inherent potential in the young adults, who actually belong to the first generation of digital natives [7], we decided to trigger the natural fluency in their relationship with new technologies to unlock their hidden talents while co-creating with them a workshop on 3D printing.

3   Approach

"A constellation of stars.

Each star shines of its own light, yet together they create a beautiful image. Invisible connections allow the creation of the pattern in the blue sky."

The above interaction vision has been used to guide a series of co-design activities with the "hidden stars", the often 'neglected' young adults in the age group of 16–24 years. Using a research-through-design approach, the present project aims at strengthening the young adults' awareness of their individual passions and talents, motivating them to share them with their peers in order to develop them together, empowering them both as individuals and as a cohesive community, in order to obtain respect and recognition in a process of mutual benefit towards and from the social ecology of the Afrikaanderwijk.

3.1   Searching for the Right Co-creative Partnerships

The first engagement strategy attempted with the youth of Afrikaanderwijk was to involve the founder of an independent youth association in the project, who was involved in the previous study and was the main gatekeeper to the young adults at that stage of the project. As a trigger to spark the young adults' interest in 3D printing, personalized key chains of their local football team were 3D printed and given to them. The outcome of this strategy was not positive: the founder of the association, who had initially displayed interest in collaborating to empower his young adults, dropped out of the project without any explanation. This unpleasant experience showed that a mismatch in agendas between designer and stakeholders undermines the design process. It also showed that designing "for" someone is not the way to go. Although the key chains were designed as a sensitizing prototype and the choice of the design was selected after analyzing the adolescents' answers to the interviews, the design was made "for" them and not "with" them. The element of active involvement and personal empowerment of the adolescents needed more careful consideration.

The second engagement strategy, therefore, stressed partnering with a local school to co-create a project of youth self-empowerment through 3D printing. In our search for local high schools in the neighborhood, we were more sensitive towards engaging with a committed partner with a compatible agenda in achieving the goal of empowering their students. Two schools were regarded as potential partners: one regular high school and a "Wijkschool", which is a local initiative that offers alternative education to students who dropped out of the national educational system. In this way students can get a basic certificate equivalent to the lowest level of education, which enables them to enter the labour market. In the residents' view, the Wijkschool is a "last chance school to participate in society." The director of the regular high school expressed his doubts about his students' capability to carry out a workshop on 3D printing due to their low educational level, and was unwilling to explore collaboration. Nevertheless, the first meeting with a coach and her students at the Wijkschool opened up chances to collaborate. The coach showed a proactive and open attitude towards the proposal, and displayed no doubt about her students' ability to learn how to 3D print. Interestingly, the two educators displayed quite opposite views of their students: the former seemed to underestimate their potential while the latter educator was actively involved in promoting their talents.

3.2   Co-creating a Plan for Empowerment

Obviously, the Wijkschool became our partner in co-designing a workshop series on talent empowerment. A tight collaboration with Sophie, the coach of the Wijkschool, enabled an effective co-design to activate young adults' talents through 3D printing; the resulting workshop proposal consists of 6 iterative steps. The division in steps was meant to empower the students gradually and from within their own interests and qualities. The following steps were carried out once a week during the student's workshop hours:

Step 1.   *Share your passions:* students were introduced to the FabLab and invited to share their passions and interests;

Step 2.   *Share your ideas:* the students sketched an initial product idea through brainstorming;

Step 3.   *Share your designs:* at the FabLab, the students transformed their design into a 3D model with Tinkercad and 3D printed it;

Step 4.   *Share your knowledge:* students made an Instructable (tutorial) to share their knowledge with global community;

Step 5.   *Share your opinion:* students were invited to evaluate the workshop, learning how to provide feedback;

Step 6.   *Share your experience:* the students presented their work to their own local community, becoming an inspiring force to their peers.

In the next section we elaborate on how we carried out the workshop steps through learning-by-doing and evaluated its influence on self-empowerment with the students of the Wijkschool.

4   Unlocking Young Adults' Talents

Planning a workshop needs to take into account many practical aspects that might seem futile, yet are crucial to make it feasible. For example, various time and location constraints motivated the extensive number of steps: the Wijkschool has two hours per week available for workshops, and the FabLab has its own schedule. Moreover, Sophie remarked that the students tend to lose concentration fast, so each step must be engaging, fun, and straightforward.

The workshop steps were carried out for the most part at the Wijkschool or in other locations in the Afrikaanderwijk, with the exception of the day at the FabLab, for which the students needed to cross the bridge to go to the FabLab to 3D print. The flow of the workshop was planned in progressive steps to empower the students incrementally, allowing them to have the time to accept a new workshop concept, a new technology, and a new view of themselves as inspiring role models for the others. Valuable insights emerged in each step, informing the following one in an iterative process of collaborative learning.

4.1 Share Your Passions

Setup. The first step, *share your passions*, was carried out at the Wijkschool. This was also the first contact with the students. They were asked to share their passions through an online questionnaire. Then, with an interactive presentation in Dutch, the students were sensitized to the value of sharing their passions, 3D printing, the FabLab, and the following steps of the workshop.

Outcomes. The first encounter with the Wijkschool students was marked by initial distrust: they displayed strong group cohesion and a proud homologation to a "street culture" attitude, slightly opposing the first author -the facilitator- as the "outsider."

Engaging with the students with an informal attitude and openly speaking poor Dutch[1] lowered the threshold of distrust in them. Furthermore, sharing her passions and weaknesses facilitated empathy and building trust with the students, in a process of mutual discovery. Initially, the students did not show any particular excitement for 3D printing, and manifested suspicion towards its utility and purpose. Seeing pictures of the FabLab and a video showing the 3D printing process helped greatly to stimulate anticipation towards the experience. Yet, the students' interest really arose when the benefits of 3D printing were highlighted to them: they could use it to make their own business ideas become tangible, and it could also be a good skill to show in their portfolio. This way it became relevant for them, and worthy of their attention.

4.2 Share Your Ideas

Setup. The goal of the *share your ideas*-step was to engage the students of the Wijk-school in using their passions as an inspiration to sketch an object. The sketch was the first part of a creative process leading to the design of a 3D model, which would be 3D printed at FabLab in the following step. Students were given technical constraints in order for their designs to be feasible on the 3D printers, though they were asked to design something that was meaningful for them: either a personal project or a present for someone important for them.

Outcomes. Despite some chaos at the beginning of the workshop, having a structured presentation helped to bring order. The students, later, immersed themselves in a productive workflow, with very interesting results. Some students struggled with the

---

[1] The first author is originally Italian, studying in the Netherlands.

technical limitations to their designs: one student was very disappointed when invited to simplify his design to be feasible with the current technology, but continued trying.

Other students found the limitations fun and challenging, such as one who took very accurate measurements for his drawing of an iPhone stand, ending up with a fully designed product. Others made the project very personal, such as a student who sketched a medallion with his name and Thai-box champion, or another student, who designed her own logo for her future career as a fashion designer. Overall, the students engaged in the sketching activity in a fluid and spontaneous way, and at the end all those who participated had sketched something meaningful for them (Fig. 1).

Fig. 1. Students sketching during step 2 – share your ideas

4.3 Share Your Designs

Setup. The goal of the third step, *share your designs*, was to stimulate the Wijkschool students to exit the boundaries of their neighborhood and experience a new learning environment at FabLab Rotterdam. A research aim of this step was to gain insights into the effect of changing context on the students' level of engagement. The workshop activities were planned carefully, in order to keep the students' engagement on a high level throughout the entire day. At first, they were introduced to the FabLab facilities and philosophy. Second, they were invited to revise their sketches from the previous workshop, and in case they did not have one, they could make one. After that, the students were introduced to Tinkercad, an open source, 3D modeling software for 3D modeling their sketch. Following this activity, the students would finally 3D print their designs, seeing their idea transformed into a tangible 3D prototype. In this way, problem-solving skills were challenged: iterating by making (as opposed to only drawing) was encouraged and enabled by the 3D printers.

Outcomes. A group of 6 students came to 3D print at FabLab Rotterdam: without previous experience, the students learned how to 3D model on Tinkercad and to use the 3D printers in just a few hours. Through learning by doing, they quickly iterated their designs when they saw they did not print as expected. Their level of engagement was high throughout the whole activity: one student, who had joined only for this step of the workshop, managed to 3D print her keychain immediately and was very proud. "Look I made it by myself! I want to show it to my father" she said.

Some of 3D printers had technical issues, so at a certain point the general level of frustration rose. One student became very emotional after his prototype failed for the third time, and left before his fourth attempt was finished. The girl, who had designed her fashion designer logo in the previous step, could not make her design simple enough to print it as she wanted it. The student, who had designed an iPhone stand, also had to go through many failed prototypes, before he could get his prototype right, yet he relentlessly kept trying until he finally made it.

The peer-to-peer learning environment facilitated bonding between FabLab staff, students, and coach, resulting in a fun and successful experience for everyone (see Fig. 2). Furthermore, their empowerment experienced by making their idea into a tangible artifact had an "addicting" effect on the students, who expressed their desire to come back. The current experience demonstrated that a change in context could positively influence the students' personal commitment. Interestingly, any passerby observing the interaction in the FabLab would not have noticed a difference between university students and the students from the Wijkschool, demonstrating an inclusive community. Everyone was solving problems, designing, prototyping, and sharing tips.

Fig. 2. Wijkschool students 3D printing at the FabLab during step 3 – share your designs.

4.4 Share Your Knowledge

Setup. In step 4, *share your knowledge*, the students were back at the Wijkschool. They collected and structured the main insights gained during their experience with 3D printing by creating a step-by-step tutorial on the website Instructables.

Outcomes. Sharing knowledge was the most painful part for the students, and had the highest drop-out rate during the project. Hardly any of the students present at the FabLab participated in this step, which made it rather difficult to create an Instructable on 3D printing. Step 4 showed very clearly how the local context contributes to shaping the students' attitude towards learning, in this case in a negative way. As Sophie remarked, it was a welcome back to the daily reality at the Wijkschool, demonstrating how a disorganized school system creates discontinuity in the participation in the workshop activities.

Almost towards the end of the workshop, the student who 3D printed the iPhone stand at FabLab, showed up to finalize the Instructable, which was a very surprising event. He had displayed a very high level of engagement at the FabLab, demonstrating to be a bright student passionate about learning, yet as the coach had announced, with very discontinuous levels of concentration and commitment. Peer pressure kept him from seriously trying to achieve his goals in life, which was a pity, since he demonstrated that he was quite talented. While making the Instructable he managed to resist his peers' pressure, showing that his motivation could be triggered beyond the need of approval from his group, with the promise of recognition for his skills both at school as well as in the Instructables community. Eventually, the desire to impress an external person who was willing to invest time in his development contributed to his motivation.

4.5 Share Your Opinion

Setup. In step 5, *share your opinion*, the students were summoned to express their opinion on the workshop, providing feedback for future improvements through a discussion and a mindmap exercise.

Outcomes. Seven students participated in this step of the workshop. Clara, Zaha, and Yussef were the three who had followed nearly all the workshop steps, and were therefore, the most informed in the overall process. Moreover, the other students had participated in at least three steps, and could also contribute in a valuable way. The discussion about the workshop steps was insightful, especially in view of using it as material to create the platform in the next stage of the project. When appropriately facilitated, the students managed to give voice to their true opinions, yet they did not display a proactive attitude in proposing new approaches, limiting their input to evaluating what happened during the workshop steps. The mind map activity showed that the students were able to follow the rules of the assignments, yet also showed that they do not go beyond the strict requirements. However, it proved to be a useful tool to sensitize them to the work behind the organization of a workshop, and all the elements required engaging participants effectively.

4.6 Share Your Experience

Setup. Step 6, *share your experience*, is the last step of the workshop; the students were encouraged to share their experience on 3D printing with the rest of their peers from the Wijkschool during "Be Inspired Day". The goal was twofold: on one hand, allow the students who joined the workshop to become positive role models for their peers. On the other hand, inspire the students to dare to step out of their comfort zone and be open to learning new skills in different environments, in order to have a chance to develop their talents and empower themselves.

Outcomes. For the occasion, a keynote presentation was designed with the title: "Share your experience. How technologies, design, and open minds bring people together." The slides were meant as a support for the different speakers of the day: the two authors, Sophie the coach, as well as Clara and Yussef, the two students who participated in most of the workshop. The reaction of the audience was a bit chaotic: the students were quite undisciplined during the presentation, until Clara and Yussef, their

Fig. 3. Yussef on stage, sharing his experience on 3D printing towards the audience at the Klooster (Theater) during the "Be Inspired Day".

peers who had participated in the workshop came on stage; they showed the audience what they had made and how it was meaningful to them, as it addressed their own passion. The students were sensibly more silent during their presentation, and a general state of curiosity and excitement rose when the medallion made by Yussef was passed around for them to see it (Fig. 3).

The "Be Inspired Day" was obviously "the moment of truth"; the unique experience created with a group of students of the Wijkschool was presented to the wider student community. The audience's response was, understandably, quite defensive, yet it was evident that the presentations had inspired positively more than one student, crucially bridged by Yussef and Clara, who became new role models.

5 A Platform for Stars to Shine

The experiences of the workshop series clearly stressed the synthesis of the most valuable interactions for a peer-to-peer workshop platform aimed at activating the students of the Wijkschool to self-empowerment. Differently put, the outcomes informed the design of a workshop platform for empowerment, which employs online social media, FabLabs, and ubiquitous technologies to foster community participation and peer-to-peer learning. The platform aims at allowing a community of students to share and develop their portfolio of skills through a series of hands-on workshops within their school or youth center, where they can become active co-creators according to their level of participation. Figure 4 shows how the "ladder of student participation," inspired by Arnstein's model [1], assigns different roles to the students, according to their engagement in the workshop activities. The hierarchical structure depicted in the model is not static; on the contrary, social mobility is encouraged, allowing the students to move up and down the ladder throughout the different workshop cycles.

Fig. 4. Ladder of student participation.

The workshop platform is launched within a school or youth center, facilitated by a local coach. The first step is *Join the Group*, where the coach introduces the new workshop platform to the students and invites them to join the dedicated Facebook group. The second step is *Design your Badge*: here students personalize their membership badge. Each badge has a unique RFID tag connected to a personal FB profile. After the launch, the workshop runs in cycles, which are sustained by the student community. In the third step the coach launches a *Call for Themes* for the next workshop. Students propose their idea and vote for the best one. In the fourth step, the

Winner is announced: the idea with the most votes wins. The winner receives a "relay stick" with an active RFID, and is entrusted with authority and central communication functions to become the chief in charge. In the fifth step, *Invite*, the chief in charge has a week to organize a workshop, and invites peers by connecting with the relay stick. The sixth step consists in the *Workshop and Instructable*, at the FabLab, where students make their own real 3D printed or laser cut product. Then they create an Instructable to share their knowledge. After the workshop the students *Rate the workshop*: by tilting the relay stick, the students give their rate, which appears on the Facebook group. A week later, during the Be Inspired Day, the Chief in Charge and the Crew Members inspire their peers by sharing their workshop experience Fig. 5.

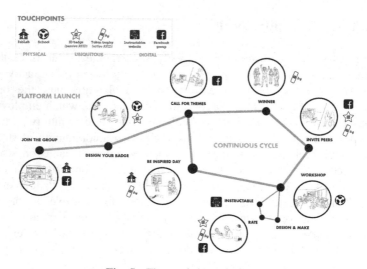

Fig. 5. The workshop platform.

The platform has been evaluated with the participation of students from two different Wijkschools during two workshops on laser cutting. The outcomes confirmed the results on students' empowerment and exceeded expectations [see 8, 9].

6 Discussion and Conclusions

The platform as well as the intended interactions have been evaluated, and it can be concluded that they lowered not only the threshold of access to digital fabrication in education, but also the students became active co-creators in the workshops while collaboratively learning new skills. Key to the project's success lies in leveraging the students' technological fluency by making digital fabrication accessible and engaging them in an open co-design process. By making and sharing, they quickly acquired the so-called 21st century skills. The current project also showed the potential to build a thriving community of empowered individuals, serving as a "best practice" for future interventions not only in similar socio-cultural conditions [10]. More specifically, the gained insights contribute to how 21st century skills can be embedded in STEAM educational programs, as well as how they contribute to successful participation in society, see also [2]. By connecting the people to a network where the FabLab is one of the nodes, a learning community can spread beyond the physical environment of a school. On the one hand, the school is alleviated from the cost of implementing an internal FabLab, on the other hand, students are entrusted with the tools to shape their own learning curriculum, inspiring others to do so. FabLabs all over the world can use this process in a very cost-effective way in order to create new co-learning processes that can reach out to underprivileged and uninitiated communities in a more inclusive way, empowering individuals to contribute to open social innovation.

Differently put, one reason why the Wijkschool students have failed in the current education system might be that traditional educational models are not appropriate to teach new generations of digitally savvy youngsters. Traditional silo mentality is the biggest obstacle to change, as it perpetuates a top-down approach where the teacher is the owner of the knowledge while the students are seen as passive receivers. In order to promote 21st century skills, we embrace and advocate for a participatory bottom-up approach to learning by making, where:

1. By identifying the inherent learning potential of digital natives, reluctant students are transformed into empowered individuals;
2. By giving students ownership of their creative process, the learning experience is more effective and lasting;
3. By entrusting the students with the tools to shape their own learning curriculum, they become co-learners and co-creators of knowledge.

It can be concluded that harnessing the most valuable assets in the local community, which are the young adults' passions and digital literacy, and sharing these assets by rules of trust and reciprocity, enables a community to become cohesive and to empower its members. More specifically, the two presenting students at the "Be Inspired Day" demonstrated in a convincing way, that it is indeed possible to transform from dropouts into engaged and successful individuals, who can become role models for their peers: "*stars shining bright in the local community*".

It was striking to see how Yussef, the student who made the medallion, was convinced that participating in the workshop was a mind-shifting activity for him. He clearly understood that he too could have a key role in this transformational change, by becoming an ambassador of the project. Clara, on the other hand, got accepted in a highly selective fashion design school. Her dream of becoming a fashion designer had always seemed far fetched, but through participating in the workshop activities, she was able to design and make her own logo tangible, motivating her to create her own portfolio and apply for admission to the fashion design school. Breaking the autopilot of the status quo in the Wijkschool also proved to be an empowering experience for Sophie, the students' coach. Her passion for participatory educational approaches was not encouraged, and even hindered, by the school's management. Yet, she has been empowered by the collaboration with FabLab, since by facilitating her students' learning process with digital technologies, she could remain a relevant role model for them while learning new skills herself. Today, change goes faster than one can cope with, so it is not easy to remain relevant as an expert in a rapidly changing environment. Teachers need to learn how to teach in a different way. The current project empowers teachers to rapidly scale up their knowledge, allowing them to develop new skills so they can stay relevant for their students. By flipping the classroom, we can break the traditional divide between teacher/expert and student/recipient to create communities of co-learners, subverting a mistake-averse teaching model into an environment that allows for experimentation and dynamic lifelong learning. In their new role of facilitators, teachers can become meaningful role models for their students, while at the same time training the students to become facilitators themselves. In this way, they can create a ripple effect on a wider societal scale.

If we have the teachers and their colleagues on board, and they feel empowered to be ambassadors, we likely can scale the current practices, repeat them, and have them embedded in the educational system, as well as making the platform self-sustaining.

Acknowledgments. The current project was part of a Master of Science graduation project in Design for Interaction at Delft University of Technology carried out in Creating 010's program Meaningful Design in the Connected City in collaboration with Wijkschool Feijenoord and FabLab Rotterdam. The project has been nominated for the Dutch Design Awards 2013 as well as shortlisted for the Interaction 14 Awards. As a cherry on top, the TU Delft Student Inspiration Award 2014 was presented to Emilia Louisa Pucci, for making an inspiring contribution to our community.

References

1. Arnstein, S.R.: A ladder of citizen participation. JAIP **35**(4), 216–224 (1969)
2. Blevis, E., Chow, K., Koskinen, I., Poggenpohl, S., Tsin, S.: Billions of interaction designers. Interactions **21**(6), 34–41 (2014)
3. Blikstein, P.: Digital fabrication and making in education: the democratization of invention. In: Walter-Herrmann, J., Büching, C. (eds.) FabLabs: of Machines, Makers and Inventors. Transcript Publishers, Bielefeld (2013)
4. Honey, M., Kanter, D.E.: Design, Make, Play: Growing the Next Generation of STEM Innovators. Routledge, New York (2013)
5. Mostert-van der Sar, M., Mulder, I., Remijn, L., Troxler, P.: FabLabs in design education. In: Proceedings of E&PDE 2013, International Conference on Engineering and Product Design Education, Dublin Institute of Technology (DIT), 5–6 September, pp. 629–634, Ireland (2013)
6. OECD: Towards an OECD Skills Strategy. OECD Publishing, Paris (2011)
7. Prensky, M.: Digital natives, digital immigrants. Horizon **9**(5), 1–6 (2001)
8. Pucci, E.L.: IK BEN STER(K). A peer-to-peer talent development platform empowering young adults. Master Thesis Design for Interaction, Faculty of Industrial Design Engineering, Delft University of Technology. Delft, The Netherlands (2013)
9. Pucci, E.L.: IK BEN STER(K). A peer-to-peer talent development platform empowering young adults (video) (2013) http://t.co/0u1vGyP7KE
10. Sanders, L., Stappers, P.J.: From designing to co-designing to collective dreaming: three slices in time. Interactions **21**(6), 24–33 (2014)

A Framework for Navigating Human Behavior Through Gameful Digital Rhetoric

Mizuki Sakamoto and Tatsuo Nakajima[✉]

Department of Computer Science and Engineering, Waseda University,
Tokyo, Japan
{mizuki, tatsuo}@dcl.cs.waseda.ac.jp

Abstract. The use of gameful digital rhetoric presented in this paper becomes a bridge between the areas of behavior science and cultural studies, and a promising tool to enhance the real world to enable people to realize human well-being. In this paper, we propose two models to enhance meaning in the real world based on the concepts typically used in digital games to assist in the analysis and design of gameful digital rhetoric. The models offer appropriate abstractions to enhance the real world with gameful digital rhetoric. We also show results of experiments to incorporate gameful digital rhetoric in the real world.

Keywords: Gameful digital rhetoric · Games · Persuasive technologies · Human well-being

1 Introduction

Our aim is to enhance the real world surrounding people to enable them to realize human well-being. *Seligman* defines the well-being theory [10] as a theme of positive psychology. He defines five factors needed for humans to flourish: *positive emotion, engagement, meaning, relationships* and *achievement*. The factor of human well-being contributes to steering people toward desirable behavior. For example, positive emotions reduce the risk of catching a cold or an infectious disease. Additionally, a husband and wife who have positive images of one another can create a fruitful married life. *Seligman* notes that people without positivity tend to think there is no way to improve their lives by themselves, while people with high positivity can act to have productive lives [10]. Therefore, it is important to focus on achieving human well-being to guide human behavior.

Persuasive technology uses information technology to move people. This concept has the power to affect people's behavior [6]. Persuasive technology emphasizes the strengths of computers, such as toughness, processing capacity, extensibility and ubiquity. It focuses on changing behavior, attitude and thinking as a result of interaction with computers. Although persuasive technology works for temporary behavior change, many people have difficulty changing their current behavior to more desirable behavior. Behavioral economics asserts that people have a status quo bias, defined as a strong tendency to remain at the status quo. Behavioral economics explains that status quo bias occurs because the disadvantages of altering the status quo loom larger than

© Springer International Publishing Switzerland 2015
N. Streitz and P. Markopoulos (Eds.): DAPI 2015, LNCS 9189, pp. 97–108, 2015.
DOI: 10.1007/978-3-319-20804-6_9

the advantages. However, we believe that navigation succeeds if people can achieve human well-being as a result of their behavior change. From the viewpoint of realizing human well-being, we must improve the method of navigation by using information technology, including persuasive technology.

Recently, *Calvo* argues *positive computing*, where technologies are used to flourish us [3]; this compliment persuasive technology to enhance human well-being with information technologies because pervasive technology does not take into account whether navigated human behavior is virtuous or not. On the other hand, positive computing aims to lead human towards well-being. However, it's design is based on highly abstracted concepts; thus, it is not easy to use the concepts without more concrete concepts.

Using games' power can make the navigation process meaningful and valuable to connect positive computing with persuasive technology. Using games' power can make the navigation process meaningful and valuable. A digital game, which is produced by the assembly of information technology, has the power to provide all of the above factors to realize human well-being. *Edward Castranova* identified positive emotions as the single most important motivation for game playing [4]. *Seligman* argues that engagement is a concept related to flow [10]. During flow, people typically experience deep enjoyment, creativity, and complete involvement with life. *Csikszentmihalyi* notes that the flow experience has all the building blocks of flow, such as clear goals each step of the way, immediate feedback on one's actions, and balance between challenges and skills [5]. Almost all digital games include immediate feedback under players' control, and well-designed digital games provide clear goals and appropriate challenges based on each player's skill. Regarding meaning, games have various rhetorical aspects, and many people discuss their rhetoric; currently, the rhetorical power is being reinvestigated to understand the powerful effects of games [1]. Additionally, games create positive relationships. Digital games explicitly provide meaningful and valuable benefits for taking part in collective behavior. In fictional game worlds, players frequently tend to collaborate to achieve a common goal because they reap individual benefits by achieving the goal. In MMORPG, like in World of Warcraft[1], multiple players must cooperate to perform a complex mission. *McGonigal* argues that gamers form bonds with other gamers quickly. She represents the relationship created through collective activities in games' social fabric [7]. Achievement is often used in games, and it is a useful incentive to motivate people. Games clarify the process of achievement by using points, badges, leaderboards and other similar features.

More recently, digital designers have begun to adopt ideas from game design to incentivize desirable user behaviors. The idea of taking entertaining and engaging elements from video games and using them to incentivize participation in other contexts has been studied in a variety of fields. In education, this approach is known as serious gaming, and in human computing, it is sometimes referred to as games with a purpose. *Newsgames* [11] contain ideological messages represented through the interactive form. Recently, digital marketing and social media practitioners have adopted this approach under the term *gamification*. The idea is to use game mechanics,

---

[1] http://us.battle.net/wow/en/.

such as online games, to make a task entertaining, thus encouraging people to conscientiously complete tasks. *Serious games* focus on the aspects of games as simulation, and *newsgames* use games' power to make arguments. As for gamification, it uses games' power to motivate people. The roles of these games vary widely; however, all use games' rhetorical aspects to influence real-world behavior.

We can use games' power to achieve clear purposes, such as improving education, inspiring people, and increasing business engagement; however, a mere entertainment game is itself valuable for many game fans. The value provided by playing games also has great power to influence people's emotions. It is necessary to focus on two different aspects of games' power, the a rhetorical aspect and a value-related aspect objective and subjective parts. By combining these two aspects, we can discuss the full power of games, which contributes to enhancing the real world.

In this paper, we consider games' power in terms of both rhetoric and the value. We propose two models, one including the rhetoric and the other including the value. The former is named the *GamiRhetoric* model, and the latter is the *GamiValue* model. The concept of dividing games' power into two aspects is useful to designing and analyzing digital games or gamified services. However, the rhetoric and value usually overlap in a digital game. Some digital games or gamified services focus mainly on the rhetorical intent, such as educating or inspiring users, while others focus on the emotional value, such as providing fun or pleasure. Our two models can cover both cases. Regarding the former, it is appropriate to focus on considering which rhetoric suits the intent of the game or gamified services based mainly on the *GamiRhetoric* model. With the latter, it is useful to add a variety of values by utilizing the *GamiValue* model. Figure 1 presents an overview of both the rhetoric-focused and the value-focused designs.

Combining the rhetorical aspect and emotional values by playing digital games is useful to enhancing our real world. In games, various virtual objects are embedded in the game worlds to influence players' behavior. Digital games consist of various digital rhetorical elements. In this paper, we call the digital rhetoric gameful digital rhetoric. Typical virtual objects are virtual currency, virtual humans, virtual goods and virtual clothes. Gameful digital rhetoric are as expressions that inform, persuade and inspire

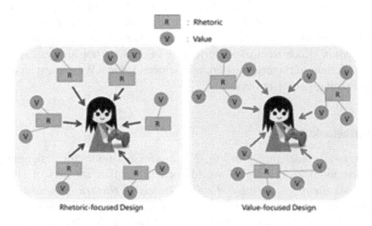

Fig. 1. Rhetoric-focused design and value-focused design

human behavior through digitally mediated virtual objects incorporated into the real world using digital technologies. Digital rhetoric in video games often plays a role of manipulating a player's actions to advance the game. It also becomes a sign that encourages a particular type of human behavior when it is embedded in the real world through the ubiquitous computing technology. Incorporating gameful digital rhetoric into the real world contributes to enhancing the meaning of the real world if the gameful digital rhetoric is meaningful to people. Thus, virtual objects can be useful tools to influence human behavior, thinking, and feeling in the real world. The enhanced meaning through gameful digital rhetoric makes explicit the desirable goal achieved through activities and encourages people by offering many attractive imaginary and artificial benefits.

A digital game offers a virtual world that contains various virtual objects and missions to influence a player's behavior in the fictional world. Well-designed video games offer players many attractive imaginary and artificial benefits through meaningful and valuable experiences. When designing an attractive digital game, a game developer defines its meaning through how a player perceives virtual objects and events in the virtual world. If the player feels that the world is meaningful, he or she will enjoy the game. We believe that the same applies in our real world. If we perceive that objects and events in our real lives are meaningful and valuable, we can enjoy our lives.

2 Frameworks for Analyzing Games' Power

We must discuss the tool set to analyze and design the information service that enhances meaning in our real world. In this section, we propose two new models to enhance meaning in our real world based on the concepts typically used in digital games to facilitate the analysis and design of gameful digital rhetoric by focusing on both structured meaning and emotional meaning aspects. The first model is the *GamiRhetoric* model, which defines six frames to examine how to enhance meaning in the real world. The second is the *GamiValue* model, which defines eight frames to attach value to virtual objects. The former is more related to the structured meaning aspects, while the latter mainly depends on the emotional meaning aspects. The *GamiRhetoric* model defines a rough frame, and the *GamiValue* model allows for more detailed discussion. Each item of rhetoric and value does not always exist independently, and each item of rhetoric may contain various values. We present an example to analyze the existing games in Sect. 3.

2.1 GamiRhetoric Model

The *GamiRhetoric* model shown in Fig. 2 is a semiotic model for designing gameful digital rhetoric to make the digital world meaningful that consists of six types of rhetoric: *curious rhetoric, narrative rhetoric, collective rhetoric, procedural rhetoric, social rhetoric* and *economic rhetoric*, where these are extracted from the experiences with building several community-based mobile crowdsourcing services [9].

Curious rhetoric influences people through our five senses, such as visual and auditory, which offer us emotional engagement, such as interest, happiness or comfort, and increase our curiosity, motivating our activities. Narrative rhetoric contains an argument specified into a narrative. A typical narrative teaches people what they should do in their ideal daily lives and has two types of aspects. The first aspect is describing ideological messages in the narrative, and the second aspect concerns goal setting in the narrative. Collective rhetoric presents participants' accumulated efforts, and is one of essential motivations for participants to continue their efforts. Procedural rhetoric was presented by *Bogost*, who stated that it involves the practice of using processes persuasively [1]. This type of rhetoric is peculiar to digital games, which work based on interaction with a player. Finally, economic and social rhetoric offers norms, rules and mechanisms for interactions among people that are typically used to coordinate collective action in the real world. This rhetoric includes various social mechanisms, such as market economy, gift economy, altruistic society, battle and role-playing mechanisms, which are also typical underlying mechanisms used in popular video games.

As for using the frame of the *GamiRhetoric* model, enhancing the meaningfulness added to each frame is important. The agency and immersion properties are useful concepts that are used in video games to make objects more meaningful. The agency property relates to whether participants can control the effects in their activities, and the immersion property to whether the effects reflect the players' real activities without violating reality.

2.2 GamiValue Model

There is research that focuses on the concept of value to design attractive products. Using values has recently been recognized as an important design approach to developing desirable information services [2]. In analyzing digital games, it is useful to summarize systematically what values players feel toward digital games.

The values in the *GamiValue* model are extracted from a semiotic point of view [8], and the model defines eight frames to attach the following values to virtual objects: *informative, aesthetic, empathetic, stimulative, serene, common, rare* and *ideological values.*

Informative value is the utility of the information in helping users make better decisions. Aesthetic value is an important concept in making artifacts more attractive. Aesthetics is a branch of philosophy addressing the nature of art, beauty, and taste and the creation and appreciation of beauty. Empathetic value is effectiveness in evoking a user's emotions. Empathy engages the user, making him/her feel close to the empathetic form, regardless of whether it is a living being. Stimulative value arouses people's senses through feelings such as excitement, surprise, thrill, and enthusiasm. Serene value is also related to players' feelings; however, the value is serene, containing calmness, warmth, comfort and relaxation. Common value and rare value are generated in social community. Objects with common value are considered to be valuable by and available to many. Objects with popularity, such as fashionable and famous brands, have common value. In contrast, objects with rare value are unique and difficult to obtain. Some objects with high rarity enable their owners to feel self-esteem by showing their status. What is here referred to as ideological value is the notion of influencing users' thinking and behavior through influencing their attitudes and values—in other words, educating users on a deeper level.

3 Analyzing the Rhetorical Aspects of the Existing Game

In this section, we analyze the Nintendo game *Pokémon* using the *GamiRhetoric* and *GamiValue* models. We can observe the types of rhetoric and values that exist in *Pokémon*-related media. The basic concepts of *Pokémon* are battling and obtaining *Pokémon* throughout the game story. Having sold more than two hundred million and sixty million copies[2], the *Pokémon* video game software provides much value for players all over the world. Some players place value on the battles, while others value collecting and amassing *Pokémon*. Additionally, *Pokémon* is an open game, which means that enjoyment can be felt even outside of the game. The *Pokémon* world contains multiple media channels through which the details of the world are defined using a transmedia storytelling concept, including *Pokémon*-related comics, animated cartoons, movies, card games, festivals, amusement parks, and character goods. Each medium is synergized with the game, and much of the rhetoric and value exist in each medium in addition to the game itself.

3.1 Rhetoric in the Pokémon Game

The *Pokémon* game contains all six types of rhetoric of the *GamiRhetoric* model presented in Sect. 2.1. The visuals of various *Pokémon*, the visuals and sounds of each city that the player visits and the battle scenes become parts of the curious rhetoric. Because there are over seven hundred *Pokémon*[3] in the game, the possibility that there are some *Pokémon* fitting a player's preferences is high. These characteristics enhance agency and immersion. Additionally, for a player, obtaining his/her favorite *Pokémon* and exploring his/her favorite city strengthen the bond between the player's interest and the game world. They also increase the agency property.

Collective rhetoric is added by the elements of badges, experience points and an illustrated *Pokémon* guide. The guide heightens the agency property because the recorded *Pokémon* are only those that players have obtained or met. Additionally, the entire game relies on the mechanisms of incremental achievement following the player's level. The strong relationship between the game and the players' activities contributes to increasing the agency and immersion properties.

The narrative of the *Pokémon* world contains ideological messages, such as friendship between or at least coexistence of players, who are called *Pokémon* trainers, and Pokémon. These themes containing reality and the agency property are generated by the story progressing based on the player's control.

---

[2] http://www.pokemon.co.jp/corporate/business/.
[3] This figure is based on Pokémon data of 2014/10/12.

Pokémon game has basic mechanisms, such as the elements of obtaining, battling and exchanging *Pokémon*. These elements have the characteristics of procedural rhetoric. Players obtain *Pokémon* by throwing a *Poké Ball* to *Pokémon*, which means that the player and *Pokémon* become friends; this feature is one of the main themes of Pokémon world. We can only execute these types of activities in the digital world. Procedural rhetoric adds agency and immersion with immediate feedback through the interactions between the player and the digital world.

Player undertake the basic actions of battle and exchanging *Pokémon* as a *Pokémon* trainer with non-player characters in digital world; however, they can perform these activities with actual people. This dynamic is a part of social rhetoric. Economic rhetoric, such as virtual economy and the rarity of *Pokémon*, also exists in the game's world. The social rhetoric and the economic rhetoric provide a strong relationship to the real world. This rhetoric gives digital games reality, which is crucial in increasing agency and immersion.

3.2 Value in the Pokémon Game

In this section, we discuss the value in each type of rhetoric as described in the above section. Regarding curious rhetoric, players can derive aesthetic value from the graphics of cities and landscapes in the game and empathetic value from the *Pokémon*, which look similar to players. Empathetic value is also generated by the *Pokémon* that the player obtains and raises. This effect is related to collective rhetoric and narrative rhetoric. The sources of value differ depending on the situation. If the source that generates empathy concerns only *Pokémon*'s visual appearance, then only curious rhetoric influences players. However, players can also empathize with Pokémon because they have spent substantial time together and had dramatic interactions with the *Pokémon*. In that case, a player's *Pokémon* cannot be replaced by other *Pokémon*, although they share an identical visual appearance. The key factors are the collective rhetoric and narrative rhetoric. A description of brave and thoughtful characters or a story containing the coexistence of people and *Pokémon* includes the ideological factors and conveys ideological value through narrative rhetoric. Procedural rhetoric can provide various values. The variations among *Pokémon* and their moves during battle enable players to consider infinite strategies. This variation relates to the informative value by enhancing the possibility that the players will make decisions through their preferred methods. During the blistering battle, players can feel stimulative value. Interaction with *Pokémon* is part of procedural rhetoric and provides significant serene value for *Pokémon* fans. Economic rhetoric generates value among social communities. Obtaining particularly popular *Pokémon* is connected to common value; in contrast, acquiring rare *Pokémon* generates rare value.

3.3 Enhanced Meaning and Value Through Other Media

Pokémon is an open game with which many media are synergized. The analysis in this section explains how the original game derives additional meaning and value through other media, such as animation, toys and other goods and festival events.

Animation is strongly related to narrative rhetoric. Although the actor who performs the actions of obtaining *Pokémon*, fighting, and exploring is the player himself/herself in the digital game, the performer of these actions is an animated character in animation. A translation of the narrative rhetoric, then, occurs. This process encourages audiences to think deeply about ideological value in animation, such as the importance of bravery, friendship and challenge. As for the *Pokémon*-related events, curious rhetoric is incorporated into them. Curious rhetoric from participating in the real-world events enhances agency and immersion, which is leads the participants to feel great interest in the game and empathy for the characters. Additionally, *Pokémon* events often contain collective rhetoric and economic rhetoric because there are some rare *Pokémon* that can only be obtained at the events. The experience of participating in the events becomes visible in the form of collecting rare *Pokémon* in the digital world. The *Pokémon* movie is screened every year, and players can obtain rare *Pokémon* related to the movie. The main *Pokémon* in the movie often have background stories in which the narrative rhetoric defines the meaning of the *Pokémon*'s existence. This type of story enhances the empathetic value of the *Pokémon*. In the real world, collection of *Pokémon* goods alters the collection of digital *Pokémon*. It is also collective rhetoric, which can generate rare, empathetic and serene value.

In *Pokémon,* the combination of many types of rhetoric immerses players in the *Pokémon* world. One of *Pokémon*'s main themes, collection is comparatively easy to incorporate into the real world while maintaining consistency. Manufacturing goods relating to many types of *Pokémon* provokes empathy in many people. Another main theme, battle, is also easy to realize in the real world because there are many physical games involving battle between people using objects, such as chess and poker and other card games. Various media can support realizing aspects such as collection and battle, which make the contents of *Pokémon* more attractive. In these ways, the narrative of the virtual *Pokémon* world, whose leading character is the player himself/herself, enters the real world.

4   Incorporating Gameful Digital Rhetoric into the Real World

In this section, we discuss incorporating gameful digital rhetoric into the real world to make the real world meaningful and valuable. Through the analysis of the existing game with the *GamiRhetoric* and *GamiValue* models in Sect. 3, we found that there are both appropriate and inappropriate cases in which to incorporate gameful digital rhetoric into the real world.

Incorporating economic and social rhetoric into the real world tends to succeed because these factors exist in the real world by nature. Collective rhetoric is also easy to use. For example, the collection of cards, seals or other goods prevails among many people. If the theme of collection is consistent in the game world, then many fans consider collection meaningful and valuable. In particular, the collection of tangible things in the real world increases agency and immersion. As for curious rhetoric, we must consider the boundary between the digital fictional world and the real world. Embodying the virtual characters in the real world using the ubiquitous computing technology is a relatively easy method by which to enhance the real world; however, the degree of the influence depends on the target individual. People who think that there is a strong boundary between the digital fictional world and the real world consider the embodied object meaningless. Therefore, curious rhetoric loses its power as rhetoric. However, whether the fusion of gameful digital rhetoric and the real world succeeds is influenced by the game's theme. In cases in which the main theme in the digital world is also universal in the real world, such as the theme of "love" or "music", we can blur the boundary because we can feel reality in the theme. We must be sure to incorporate narrative rhetoric. When incorporating a fictional narrative into the real world, it is possible to enhance the agency property. Role-playing by playing a fictional role in the real world without losing one's grasp on reality is effective in incorporating fictional gameful digital rhetoric into the real world. However, when the audience of a narrative loses their sense of reality, they cannot play a fictional role because they are aware that the narrative remains inside the fictional world, which has no direct relationship to the real world. Then, the rhetoric can exist only in the fictional world, and it merely influences the audience's behavior and thinking in the real world. Although the audience of a realistic narrative may understand the meaning in the narrative, giving only a realistic narrative becomes less valuable. We must consider the tradeoff between the degree of reality and fictionality when we use the narrative.

To evaluate the influence of rhetoric described in the above section in the real world, we conducted some experiments. These experiments are a first step in considering how to incorporate gameful digital rhetoric into the real world. In the experiments, we discuss the following three aspects, which are often found in games: storytelling, gift economy, and feedback. The types of rhetoric and value do not always exist independently, and a scene will include a few different types of rhetoric/value. Consequently, it is useful to consider the influence of rhetoric/value based on a general scene.

Six people (five male and one female) participated in the experiment, and their ages ranged from 21 to 28. We created some situations based on each scene, and the participants completed questionnaires under various configurations. This discussion is useful for influencing human behavior by incorporating games' power as a form of gameful digital rhetoric into the real world.

4.1 Storytelling for Collective Action

The experiment investigated a style of a narrative. The aim of the experiment was to investigate whether a narrative in a game has a greater effect than a narrative in traditional media, such as a book or movie.

In this experiment, each participant was presented with two types of narratives that were used in the two configurations. Both narratives represented the necessity of participating in collective action to achieve a sustainable society; however, the manners of presenting the narratives differed. The first narrative was written from a third-person perspective that contained many general sentences (e.g., *"Recently, the environmental problem has become serious"* or *"To solve the environmental problem, it is important for many people to co-operate."*). Conversely, the second narrative contained sentences from a first-person perspective, as if the reader were a person who was concerned about the problem and performed concrete activities to protect nature, with a style typically used in video games. Additionally, the second narrative expressed the influences of collective activities with concrete roles or numbers (e.g., *"You are the chosen person with the special power to save the world"* or *"If you set the temperature of your air-conditioner even one degree higher, you can reduce your use of CO_2 by 33 kg and save 1,800 yen in a year."*).

After the experiment, we asked the participants' opinions about the two configurations. The participants answered the following questionnaire on a 5-point Likert scale (5 = strongly agree, 4 = agree, 3 = don't know, 2 = disagree, 1 = strongly disagree) after reading the above two narratives.

Q1 Can you understand the importance of taking some action to contribute to solving the environmental problems?

Q2 Do you intend to take some action to contribute to solving the environmental problems?

In Q1, the acceptability of the first narrative was 4.00, and that of the second narrative was 4.17. In Q2, the acceptability of the first narrative was 2.83 and of second narrative 4.00. The score of the second narrative exceeded that of the first narrative in both Q1 and Q2. All of the participants responded that the experiment with the second narrative motivated them more than the first narrative. In the first narrative, participants answered *"I can understand that environmental problems are important issues, but I cannot understand how the problem is related to me"* and *"I cannot imagine what I can do to help solve the problems or what the effect of my current behavior is on our society."* Conversely, with the second narrative, one participant stated *"It is easy to understand the importance because there were some examples of concrete activities and concrete numbers"* and *"I feel a sense of closeness with the narrative"*. From the results of the experiments, we argue that the second narrative provided more of the agency property than the first narrative; then, the narrative rhetoric became more powerful as rhetoric in the second narrative. The style of narratives significantly affects human behavior, and some ideas from video games are useful in creating better narrative. Specifically, a video game typically uses narrative from the first-person perspective, and both curious and collective rhetoric can augment the narrative to present concrete information to complement the information presented in the narratives. Incorporating strong narrative rhetoric through games' power, such as providing the first-person perspective, visualizing concrete numbers with scores or points, and procedural representation based on players' control contribute to increasing the informative value, allowing better decision making. It is a promising way to provide the agency property to encourage participants to take desirable actions. It can also enhance the ideological value, leading people to think at a deeper level.

4.2 Gift Economy

In this experiment, we compare the effects of a favorite person/character and a human stranger, and each participant experiences two configurations with a favorite person/character and a human stranger. In the experiment, we also investigate how a participant feels the rarity of a gift from one of those favorite figures. After the experiment with a favorite person/character or stranger, we asked the following questions to each participant, similar to those in Sect. 4.1.

Q3 Under the condition that "you are given a gift by your favorite person/character", please answer the following questions I–III.

Q4 Under the condition that "you are given a gift by a stranger", please answer the following questions I–III.

I: How much happiness do you feel?
II: How much rarity do you feel about the gift?
III: How much reciprocity do you feel when you are asked for a favor?

In Q3-I and Q3-III, all of the participants' answers were 5.00, and in Q3 II, the average was also high, 4.50. In contrast, the results related to the gift from the stranger recorded low scores. The average degree of happiness was 2.33, rarity was 2.50, and reciprocity was also 2.33. For all of the questions, all of the participants responded that the experiment with a favorite person/character gave them more delight than an interaction with a stranger. With a favorite person/character, one participant answered "*I want to cherish and reciprocate a gift if I was given a gift by my favorite*", and another participant said "*I think I cherish the gift more than had I bought it by myself*". Conversely, a participant who received a gift from a stranger said "*It [the degree of happiness] depends on whether the gift is pleasant or useful for me*". There were some negative opinions, such as "*I have doubts when a stranger gives me a gift*" or "*The gift from a stranger is terrible.*" This result shows that the curious rhetoric did not work well in the case of a stranger. Gifts from strangers are not sufficiently meaningful to generate emotional benefits, especially empathetic value and economic value. Although being 'given a gift' is the same in both configurations, the attitude of participants was largely different. The important factor to motivate people appears not to be a mechanism, such as a 'gift', but rather the meaning attached to the mechanism. Focusing exclusively on the mechanism may create a danger of rendering a service meaningless. Additionally, we suggest that building relationships among friendly community members results in better influences on participants' attitudes and behavior because the empathetic human—even if virtual—evokes a positive feeling about the experience among participants.

5 Conclusion

Our aim is to enhance the real world to enable people to realize human well-being. As a first step toward achieving this aim, we provide the tool, rhetoric and value defined by the *GamiRhetoric* and *GamiValue* models. We believe that the gameful digital rhetoric provided by information technology is a bridge between the areas of behavior science and cultural studies. Our research contributes to enhancing the real world to enable realization of human well-being.

References

1. Bogost, I.: Persuasive Games: The Expressive Power of Video Games. The MIT Press, Cambridge (2007)
2. Boztepe, S.: User value: competing theories and models. Int. J. Des. **1**(2), 55–63 (2007)
3. Calvo, R.A., Peters, D.: Positive Computing: Technology for Wellbeing and Human Potential. The MIT Press, Cambridge (2014)
4. Castranova, E.: Exodus to the Virtual World: How Online Fun is Changing Reality, pp. 7–111. Palgrave Macmillan, New York (2007)
5. Csikszentmihalyi, Mihaly: Flow and the Psychology of Discovery and Invention. HarperPerennial, New York (1997)
6. Fogg, B.J.: Persuasive technology: using computers to change what we think and do. Ubiquity (2002). doi:10.1145/764008.763957. Article ID: 5
7. McGonigal, J.: Reality is Broken: Why Games Make Us Better and How They Can Change the World. Penguin Press, New York (2011)
8. Sakamoto, M., Nakajima, T., Alexandrova, T.: Enhancing values through virtuality for intelligent artifacts that influence human attitude and behavior. Multimed. Tools Appl. (2014). doi:10.1007/s11042-014-2250-5
9. Sakamoto, M., Nakajima, T., Akioka, S.: Gamifying human behaviour in crowdsourcing for co-ordinating people collectively. Waseda University Technical Report (2014)
10. Seligman, M.E.P.: Flourish: A Visionary New Understanding of Happiness and Well-Being. Free Press, Washington, DC (2011)
11. Treanor, M., Mates, M.: Newsgames: procedural rhetoric meets political cartoons. In: Proceedings of DIGRA 2009 (2009)

Evaluating Ubiquitous Computing Environments Using 3D Simulation

Arlindo Santos and Helena Rodrigues[(✉)]

Centro Algoritmi, Escola de Engenharia, Universidade do Minho,
Campus de Azurém, 4800-058 Guimaraes, Portugal
acsantos@ipb.pt, helena@dsi.uminho.pt

Abstract. Human activity is very dynamic and subtle, and most physical environments are also highly dynamic and support a vast range of social practices that do not map directly into any immediate ubiquitous computing functionally. Identifying what is valuable to people is very hard and obviously leads to great uncertainty regarding the type of support needed and the type of resources needed to create such support. We have addressed the issues of system development through the adoption of a Crowdsourced software development model [13]. We have designed and developed Anywhere places, an open and flexible system support infrastructure for Ubiquitous Computing that is based on a balanced combination between global services and applications and situated devices. Evaluation, however, is still an open problem. The characteristics of ubiquitous computing environments make their evaluation very complex: there are no globally accepted metrics and it is very difficult to evaluate large-scale and long-term environments in real contexts. In this paper, we describe a first proposal of an hybrid 3D simulated prototype of Anywhere places that combines simulated and real components to generate a mixed reality which can be used to assess the envisaged ubiquitous computing environments [17].

1 Introduction

The creation of smart environments that are adaptive and responsive to the context in which they are being used, and mainly characterised by the fusion between physical and virtual environments, has been one of the strongest ideas in the field of Ubiquitous Computing. According to this view, physical environments will be equipped with visual, audio and many other types of sensing systems, pervasive devices and networks, allowing users to interact with such environments in a more efficient, more informed, or simply more enticing manner [8,15].

The ability to build sophisticated smart environments that respond and react to users mainly depends on the ability of the underlying infrastructure to provide the appropriate system support to create applications and bring together the entities in the environment that are needed to create that support. This has lead to the development of generic infrastructures that aim to support the transparent

© Springer International Publishing Switzerland 2015
N. Streitz and P. Markopoulos (Eds.): DAPI 2015, LNCS 9189, pp. 109–118, 2015.
DOI: 10.1007/978-3-319-20804-6_10

management of the relevant resources in the physical and virtual environments, while providing application developers with an integrated execution environment and programming abstractions that enable them to create new applications without having to consider the details of the underlying infrastructure [20].

Despite the significant advances in areas such as wireless communications, personal devices, global computing, sensors technology, computation and storage power, we have not yet reached this vision [6]. There seems to be two prevailing problems that cut across existent approaches for system support for Ubiquitous Computing. The first one is concerned with the exact definition of the appropriate type of system support to be offered to applications. Without well-established applications and reference scenarios, it is very difficult to identify and prioritise requirements for system support for Ubiquitous Computing. Without a rich and operational infrastructure it is very hard to create an integrated environment where meaningful applications may emerge [21]. The second problem is concerned with the inherent challenges posed by evaluating systems that are designed to be seamlessly integrated into our everyday lives [7]. Human activity is very dynamic and subtle, and most physical environments are also highly dynamic and support a vast range of social practices that do not map directly into any immediate service needs. In those cases, identifying what is valuable to people is very hard and obviously leads to great uncertainty regarding the type of support needed and the type of resources needed to create such support [21].

We have addressed the issues of Ubiquitous Computing systems development through the adoption of a Crowdsourced software development model [13]. We have design and developed Anywhere places, an open and flexible system support infrastructure for Ubiquitous Computing that is based on a balanced combination between global services and applications and situated devices: global services and applications provide functionality that can be relevant anywhere, thus obviating the need to create dedicated services on a case-by-case basis; situated devices, such as displays, networks, and mobile phones, provide context and enable meaningful links between global services and the physical environment. Additionally, it also offers users a more active role in handling the connections of the system and the consequent ambiguities that may arise, with the most important example being the association of users, users interactions, services and applications with particular situations [21].

The second problem, however, remains an open one. The evaluation of system support for Ubiquitous Computing environments is very difficult because we cannot find globally accepted metrics and because it is very difficult to evaluate large-scale and long-term environments in real contexts [23]. Moreover, traditional evaluation techniques such as laboratory studies allow researchers to study specific aspects of the system, but are not satisfactory to evaluate the use of technology in real contexts over time [7].

Simulated 3D environments offer an interesting solution to immersive prototyping as they can provide an alternative for an initial evaluation of the system, enabling people to experience the functionality of different Ubiquitous Computing environments, and provide a fast track to develop virtual worlds that replicate the type of environments that needs to be prototyped [17,19,24]. Moreover, as stated in [5], *"The similarities between virtual worlds and ubiquitous computing environments warrant extrapolating issues from virtual worlds to a world of ubiquitous computing. This extrapolation is particularly useful because virtual worlds are both presently observable and populous enough to allow for the observation of potential emergent behaviour[1] "*.

In this paper, we describe a first proposal of an hybrid prototype of Anywhere places that combines simulated and real components to generate a mixed reality which can be used to assess the envisaged ubiquitous computing environment [17]. We will focus on the definition of the main characteristics of the Anywhere places prototype and the evaluation goals.

2   Prototypes of Ubiquitous Computing Environments

As stated above, the evaluation of system support for Ubiquitous Computing is very difficult because we cannot find globally accepted metrics and because it is very difficult to evaluate large-scale and long-term Ubiquitous Computing environments in real contexts.

The prototyping and evaluation of ubiquitous computing environments may be said to have followed three main approaches. One that is focused in the development of real world controlled prototypes, mainly performed in the laboratory, a second that is focused on rapid iterative prototyping platforms and toolkits, and a third that is focused in the use of simulation platforms for prototyping Ubiquitous Computing environments.

In the first category, the most influent works on system support for Ubiquitous Computing environments have focused the evaluation on the functionality offered by the middleware [3,4,11,12,14,22,25]. The main objectives were focused on uncovering the main middleware services and components that should support the design and development of specific Ubiquitous Computing settings, e.g. at home, at work, at a shopping environment, or at hospitals. Researchers have not been particularly well succeed in porting the solutions outside the laboratory, mainly because of the lack of support to accomplish diverse physical boundaries of any functionality and, in that way, accommodate for various notions of smart environments on the same physical environment [20].

In the second category, graphical toolkits allow for end-users to build Ubiquitous Computing applications for a particular instrumented environment, without requiring them to write any code. Although not as expressive as existing programming systems, such platforms allow end-users to define application behaviour exerting control over sensing systems [9,10].

In the third category, immersive prototypes within simulated 3D environments allow for rapid development and evaluation of Ubiquitous Computing environments in the early stages of the development life cycle [1,17–19,24]. This

---

[1] Emergent behaviour is the process by which a number of simple entities "operate in an environment, forming more complex behaviours as a collective.", Wikipedia, Emergence, http://en.wikipedia.org/wiki/Emergence (last visited Jan. 2, 2015).

category has produce important knowledge on the definition of the design space of immersive prototyping for ubiquitous computing and its alignment with specific evaluation goals [17].

In our approach we intend to integrate a Ubiquitous Computing platform (the Anywhere places platform) with a 3D simulator, providing the functionally to create 3D simulations of Ubiquitous Computing environments. Our prototype will accommodate for various notions of Ubiquitous Computing environments on the same physical environment, equipped with a diverse set of physical resources that will be shared cross multiple environments.

3   The Anywhere Places Platform

Currently, Anywhere places is a web platform that coordinates, under the unifying concept of Place, interaction from local resources and application logic from applications. The concept of Place mainly focuses on defining the execution context for applications and interactions. A place generates content, such as place sessions, resources and active applications. Additionally, we also include common content types, which may be found in classical Ubiquitous Computing environments, such as documents, photos, messages, presences, location and interaction information obtained through a wide set of resources with different characteristics and providing different stimulus. This focus on data provides the main path towards interoperability between the functionality offered by multiple applications.

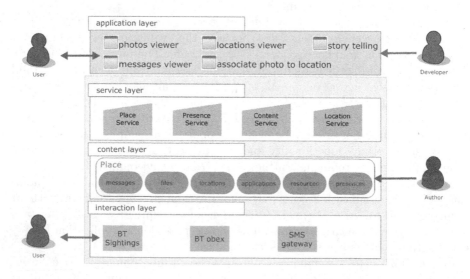

Fig. 1. Anywhere places Platform.

Figure 1 provides an overview of the Anywhere places platform. This architecture supports the adoption of a *Crowdsourced* system software development model. This model brings together system architects, physical resources owners, application developers, place owners and end-users into an open collaboration that is able to generate new added value for all the parties involved. These actors operate in the different constructs of the software development model that are explained below: Kernel services and Peripheral services [13].

Kernel Services: Kernel services, instantiated in the Service and Content layers, are responsible for managing all the information about places and the associated applications, and they are the element that glues the other elements into an integrated execution. Kernel services handle sensing and interaction information associated with places and enable the development of situated applications based on that data space. Place creators, or Ubiquitous Computing authors, can attach an open-ended set of applications to places, enabling a broad range of place-centric content to be generated and exchanged as part of the usage in that place. The nature of requirements for Kernel services are not so related with end-user perceived functions, but are normally determined by the system architects who are proposing the system and its abstractions.

Peripheral Services: Peripheral services deliver the majority of end-users value. In Ubiquitous Computing, examples may include sending a SMS to the environment or being detected by a Bluetooth scanner, and visualising the context of that particular Ubiquitous Computing environment. There are two types of peripheral services: the local resources and the place-based applications. A local resource (Interaction Layer) is any type of device or service that is associated within the place setting and supports some form of sensing or interaction within the place. Place-based applications (Application Layer) offer functionality directly to end-users within the context of a particular place by leveraging on the respective content and local resources. The process of selecting the mix of applications that will be associated with any particular place provides a flexible mechanism for bringing into a place the most appropriate combination of functionality, possibly without having to create any new applications. Anywhere places' applications are developed by third-party developers and hosted somewhere on the web. They use the Anywhere places API to consume and generate place-sensitive content.

For example, consider a physical space, such as the city, including different facilities, equipped with sensors and other resources such as displays, location systems and other types of ubiquitous resources. We may envisage a model that would allow the creation of particular places, integrating a subset of available resources and globally available applications, that would adapt their behaviour to situated user interactions within the place: a check-in application that would discover available places and allow for user presence registration into a specific place; an advertisement application that adapts content to the place's environment (number of users, type of place, for example) [16] or a digital public notice application that collects information from local users [2].

3.1 Anywhere Places Evaluation Goals and 3D Simulation Prototype Characteristics

Our objective is to conduct a developer-centric evaluation of the Anywhere places platform as we intend to evaluate how easy it is for place creators to create a specific Ubiquitous Computing environment, and a user-centric evaluation as we intend to evaluate the degree with which users perceive the concept of Place as a high-level representation of physical space that accommodates diverse Ubiquitous Computing environments functionality and user interactions. Our evaluation goals are thus the following:

- To which extent the concept of Place allows for the definition of high-level space representations that accommodate the diversity of possible Ubiquitous Computing environments.
- To which extent physical resources may be explicitly associated to a place and be shared by diverse Ubiquitous Computing functionality in the physical environment.
- To which extent the appropriation and recombination of simple applications created for places, in different ways in a Place, may offer more meaningful and diverse functionality to users in the physical space.
- To which extent the concept of Place accommodates applications that span several places, building on local resources but offering a wider functionality.
- To which extent the concept of Place frames the interpretation of implicit or explicit user interactions with physical resources offering the adequate execution environment for user actions in a particular situation.

Building on the work in [17], where analysis dimensions for immersive prototyping are introduced, we present a first characterisation of the Anywhere places and envisaged ubiquitous environments simulation prototypes. Considering that currently our main goals are to evaluate the main Anywhere places system concepts for supporting the creation of diverse Ubiquitous Computing functionality, the most relevant dimensions are 3D modelling and simulation, Hybrid prototyping, Controlled environment manipulation and Multi-user support.

3D Modelling and Simulation. We intent to provide a mean for space owners to construct ubiquitous environments that provide functionality to the environment visitants. However the establishment of different types of ubiquitous environments at large scale for evaluation purposes represents a significant cost both at monetary and logistic levels. The capability to build virtual spaces enhanced with virtual sensors, public displays and personal devices is then essential to our work. The complexity of physical resources and their communication properties, such as communication models, availability or communication protocols, are not the main characteristics to be considered in our prototypes. A realistic simulation should mainly consider the type of user interactions with the available devices and the type of data they provide to the ubiquitous environment.

Hybrid Prototyping. Our prototype should combine simulated and real components to generated a mixed reality which can be used to assess the Anywhere places system and the ubiquitous environments created on top of it. In particular, we intent to integrate in the simulated environments the Anywhere places platform functionality as well as external Web applications that execute somewhere in the Web. Virtual personal devices and sensors in the simulated environment will react to users interactions and communicate interactions data with the Anywhere places platform. On the other hand, Web applications and services will use that data to produce information to users in the simulated environment.

Controlled Environment Manipulation. We need to attach behaviour to the main system objects such as a variety of sensors and other hardware devices such as bluetooth devices, personal devices, printers or displays. In particular, we should be able to define the behaviour of system objects in the perspective of the type of data generated by user interactions and sent to the Anywhere places platform. The most common method for expressing behaviour is programming it through the use of scripts [17].

Multi-user Support and User Driven Interactions. An important feature to be addressed in our prototype is the ability for multiple users to explore the ubiquitous environments, creating the conditions for ubiquitous environments and ubiquitous platforms testing and evaluation. Supporting multiple place owners that share resources and simulated or real components for reuse in the construction of different ubiquitous environments, enables evaluation of their behaviour and mental models, but also evaluation of the Anywhere places platform. Supporting multiple place users enables evaluation of their interactions with the physical environment and of the overall ubiquitous environment's behaviour.

3.2 Simulation the Anywhere Places Framework with the OpenSimulator Environment

The OpenSimulator environment has already been explored for creating 3D simulations of Ubiquitous Computing environments [1,17,24]. We have undertaken the first steps towards the integration of OpenSimulator, an open source multiplatform, multi-user, 3D application server, with the Anywhere places platform. The OpenSimulator environment supports the connection of multiple real users and enables the evaluation of user driven behaviour and user driven interactions within the environment, supports the use of programming scripts to express the behaviour of different objects such as ubiquitous computing resources, and combines simulated and real components.

We have created a very simple ubiquitous environment 3D simulation in OpenSimulator, as shown in Fig. 2. The physical environment was augmented with three resources that consist of a public display, a bluetooth presence detector and a person's mobile phone (every avatar can pick a mobile phone). The ubiquitous environment corresponds to a set of ubiquitous functionality within

Fig. 2. Simulation of an ubiquitous environment.

the boundary defined by a place in the Anywhere places platform. The place aggregates physical resources, user interactions and functionality.

Resources correspond to OpenSimulator objects, which behaviour is programmed by LSL (Linden Scripting Language[2]) scripts. These scripts detect users interactions with the environment, such as an avatar arrival or mobile phone interactions, and send user interaction descriptions to the Anywhere places platform. We have associated with the place two applications which provide the ubiquitous environment functionally: a Web application that shows place-based relevant content (displaying presence information, as an example), and a mobile application that displays placed-based content to the avatar according to user requests. Applications are global and run on specific servers, but executing in the place's context. Users correspond to OpenSimulator avatars which behave according to the corresponding real user actions such as entering in the place's boundary.

4   Conclusions

In this paper we have addressed the problem of evaluating ubiquitous computing environments. We described Anywhere places, an open and flexible system support infrastructure for Ubiquitous Computing that is based on a balanced combination between global services and applications and situated devices, and defined our evaluation goals for the platform. We advocated that Simulated 3D environments offer an interesting solution to immersive prototyping as they can provide an alternative for an initial evaluation of the system. We then discussed the main characteristics of the Anywhere places and the main characteristics of the envisaged simulation prototypes of Ubiquitous environments. Based on these characteristics, we have undertaken the first steps towards the integration

---

[2] http://en.wikipedia.org/wiki/Linden_Scripting_Language (Last visited Jan 15, 2015).

of OpenSimulator, an open source multi-platform, multi-user 3D application server, with the Anywhere places platform, which will be the basis for the construction and evaluation of different ubiquitous environments.

Acknowledgment. Research group supported by FEDER Funds through the COMPETE and National Funds through *Fundação para a Ciência e a Tecnologia* under the Project UID/CEC/00319/2013.

References

1. Abade, T., Gomes, T., Silva, J.L., Campos, J.C.: Design and evaluation of a smart library using the APEX framework. In: Streitz, N., Markopoulos, P. (eds.) DAPI 2014. LNCS, vol. 8530, pp. 307–318. Springer, Heidelberg (2014)
2. Alt, F., Shirazi, A.S., Kubitza, T., Schmidt A.: Interaction techniques for creating and exchanging content with public displays. In: Proceedings of the SIGCHI Conference on Human Factors in Computing Systems, CHI 2013, pp. 1709–1718. ACM, New York (2013)
3. Bardram, J.E., Christensen, H.B.: Pervasive computing support for hospitals: An overview of the activity-based computing project. IEEE Pervasive Comput. **6**(1), 44–51 (2007)
4. Blackstock, M., Lea, R., Krasic, C.: Evaluation and analysis of a common model for ubiquitous systems interoperability. In: Indulska, J., Patterson, D.J., Rodden, T., Ott, M. (eds.) PERVASIVE 2008. LNCS, vol. 5013, pp. 180–196. Springer, Heidelberg (2008)
5. Boone, M.S.: Ubiquitous computing, virtual worlds, and the displacement of property rights. ISJLP **4**, 91 (2008)
6. Caceres, R., Friday, A.: Ubicomp systems at 20: Progress, opportunities, and challenges. IEEE Pervasive Comput. **11**(1), 14–21 (2012)
7. Connelly, K.: On developing a technology acceptance model for pervasive computing. In: UbiComp 2007 - Proceedings of the 2007 ACM Conference on Ubiquitous Computing (2007)
8. Cook, D.J., Augusto, J.C., Jakkula, V.R.: Ambient intelligence: Technologies, applications, and opportunities. Pervasive Mob. Comput. **5**(4), 277–298 (2009)
9. Dey, A.K., Sohn, T., Streng, S., Kodama, J.: iCAP: interactive prototyping of context-aware applications. In: Fishkin, K.P., Schiele, B., Nixon, P., Quigley, A. (eds.) PERVASIVE 2006. LNCS, vol. 3968, pp. 254–271. Springer, Heidelberg (2006)
10. Greenhalgh, C., Izadi, S., Mathrick, J., Humble, J., Taylor, I.: ECT: a toolkit to support rapid construction of ubicomp environments. In: Proceedings of UbiComp 2004 Demonstration, pp. 207–234. Springer (2004). www.crg.cs.nott.ac.uk/jym/ect/ect.php
11. Grimm, R., Davis, J., Lemar, E., Macbeth, A., Swanson, S., Anderson, T., Bershad, B., Borriello, G., Gribble, S., Wetherall, D.: System support for pervasive applications. ACM Trans. Comput. Syst. **22**(4), 421–486 (2004)
12. Johanson, B., Fox, A., Winograd, T.: The interactive workspaces project: Experiences with ubiquitous computing rooms. IEEE Pervasive Comput. **1**(2), 67–74 (2002)
13. Kazman, R., Chen, H.-M.: The metropolis model a new logic for development of crowdsourced systems. Commun. ACM **52**, 76–84 (2009)

14. Kindberg, T., Barton, J., Morgan, J., Becker, G., Caswell, D., Debaty, P., Gopal, G., Frid, M., Krishnan, V., Morris, H., Schettino, J., Serra, B., Spasojevic, M.: People, places, things: web presence for the real world. Mob. Netw. Appl. **7**(5), 365–376 (2002)

15. Kindberg, T., Fox, A.: System software for ubiquitous computing. IEEE Pervasive Comput. **1**(1), 70–81 (2002)

16. Kubitza, T., Clinch, S., Davies, N., Langheinrich, M.: Using mobile devices to personalize pervasive displays. SIGMOBILE Mob. Comput. Commun. Rev. **16**(4), 26–27 (2013)

17. Moreira, S., José, R., Campos, J.C.: An empirical study on immersive prototyping dimensions. In: Kurosu, M. (ed.) HCII/HCI 2013, Part I. LNCS, vol. 8004, pp. 421–430. Springer, Heidelberg (2013)

18. Nishikawa, H., Yamamoto, S., Tamai, M., Nishigaki, K., Kitani, T., Shibata, N., Yasumoto, K., Ito, M.: UbiREAL: realistic smartspace simulator for systematic testing. In: Dourish, P., Friday, A. (eds.) UbiComp 2006. LNCS, vol. 4206, pp. 459–476. Springer, Heidelberg (2006)

19. O'Neill, E., Lewis, D., Conlan, O.: A simulation-based approach to highly iterative prototyping of ubiquitous computing systems. In: Proceedings of the 2nd International Conference on Simulation Tools and Techniques, Simutools 2009, ICST (Institute for Computer Sciences, Social-Informatics and Telecommunications Engineering), pp. 56:1–56:10. ICST, Brussels, Belgium, Belgium, 2009. ICST (Institute for Computer Sciences, Social-Informatics and Telecommunications Engineering) (2009)

20. Rodrigues, H., José, R.: System implications of context-driven interaction in smart environments. Interact. Comput. **26**(2), 105–117 (2014)

21. Rodrigues, H., José, R., Santos, A., Silva, B.: New directions for system support in pervasive computing. In: Proceedings of PerCom Workshops IEEE Computer Society (2012)

22. Roman, M., Hess, C., Cerqueira, R., Campbell, R.H., Nahrstedt, K.: Gaia: A middleware infrastructure to enable active spaces. IEEE Pervasive Comput. **1**, 74–83 (2002)

23. Santos, A., Rodrigues, H., José, R.: Evaluating a *crowdsourced* system development model for ambient intelligence. In: Bravo, J., López-de-Ipiña, D., Moya, F. (eds.) UCAmI 2012. LNCS, vol. 7656, pp. 145–152. Springer, Heidelberg (2012)

24. Silva, J.L., Campos, J.C., Harrison, M.D.: An infrastructure for experience centered agile prototyping of ambient intelligence. In: Proceedings of the 1st ACM SIGCHI Symposium on Engineering Interactive Computing Systems, EICS 2009, pp. 79–84. ACM, New York (2009)

25. Sousa, J.P., Garlan, D.: Aura: an architectural framework for user mobility in ubiquitous computing environments. In: WICSA 3: Proceedings of the IFIP 17th World Computer Congress - TC2 Stream/3rd IEEE/IFIP Conference on Software Architecture, pp. 29–43. Kluwer, B.V, Deventer (2002)

The Transformative Potential of Making in Teacher Education: A Case Study on Teacher Training Through Making and Prototyping

Susanna Tesconi[1(✉)] and Lucía Arias[2]

[1] Universitat Autónoma Barcelona, Barcelona, Spain
susanna.tesconi@e-campus.uab.cat
[2] LABoral Centro de Arte y Creación Industrial, Gijón, Spain
larias@laboralcentrodearte.org

Abstract. The paper describes an ongoing research on teacher education for the implementation of making and digital fabrication in educational settings taking part at LABoral Art Centre, Spain. It aims to define key points and indications for the design of learning environments for teachers through making and prototyping in the context of an art centre as an open education lab. We present a qualitative instrumental case study articulated around two dimensions: the analysis of the context of the art centre, and the design of two teaching education programs. The analysis of LABoral context aims to explore the potentiality of an open lab and its related community as a learning environment for teacher education. The study of the teaching education programs is set to define the principles in order to put forward a proposal for the design of a learning environment for teacher education in making.

Keywords: Making · Teacher training · Prototyping · Empowerment · Art · Design

1 Introduction

In the past 10 years, we assisted to the growth of several grassroots movements for the democratization of technology and invention, such as the diffusion of open-hardware rapid prototyping tools like Arduino, the development of the fab lab network and the 'explosion' of the maker culture. The diffusion of these tools and their use in communities are inspiring several sectors of the society for a switch from a user mentality to a creator one through the democratization of manufacturing.

If we look at maker culture as learning model we can say that it is an example of self-organized social learning that emphasizes informal, networked, peer-led and shared learning motivated by fun and self-fulfilment [1]. A growing number of practitioners and researchers belonging to the educational community see in maker-centred activities the potential for a pedagogical and methodological change in education based on empowerment of student through the creative use of technology and the access to tasks, such as programming and fabrication, previously reserved to experts [2–5].

© Springer International Publishing Switzerland 2015
N. Streitz and P. Markopoulos (Eds.): DAPI 2015, LNCS 9189, pp. 119–128, 2015.
DOI: 10.1007/978-3-319-20804-6_11

As Paulo Blikstein [3] argues the learning model of the emergent maker movement is based on three theoretical and pedagogical pillars: experiential education, constructionism and critical pedagogy. The ideas of Dewey [6], Fröbel [7], Montessori [8], Freire [9] and Papert [10, 14] are the 'bricks' of the theoretical framework of making as constructionist, experiential, emancipatory view of learning.

In the past five years, hundreds of papers and articles on making and the maker movement have been published. There is a general consensus in literature about the transforming potential of making-centred pedagogies and practices on learning. Mostly, the studies refer to the beneficial effects of implementing maker-centred education in STEM (science, technology, engineering, mathematics) subjects, but, also, several studies underline the potential of making experiences for personal empowerment, cognitive development and community building [4, 5, 11–13].

Maker-centred, constructionist learning environments have, of course, a tremendous potential for innovating educational practices, but, in order to make it real, we need to foster a constructionist culture in teacher education.

In a typical constructionist learning environment, children use technology to build projects that are significant for them. Constructionist teachers rarely follow a fixed curriculum, they act as facilitators of the individual learning process, not as instructors [3]. Also they understand learning as an active process in which the learner, constructs meaning through the interiorization of actions and sensory input in a social context where motivation is a key component.

We believe that in order to spread along the teacher community a maker-centred, constructionist approach we need to promote a methodological, political and epistemological change in teaching practice. We think we need to build a culture based on experimentation, design, invention, inquiry as key points in order to promote significant, situated learning with the students.

Due to the fact that implementation of making activities in education is quite recent, majority of studies focus on the effects it has on students learning. At the moment, there is still a lack of studies on teachers training in making. We decide to address our research to the design of a teacher training model.

We focus on making as an emergent inquiry-based educative practice that has the potential to make a change in traditional teaching practices of public school educators. We see making as an empowering opportunity for teachers in order to foster experimentation skills, encourage intellectual risk taking and improve agency and authorship. Making activities also foster the change of traditional social roles in class by establishing an equal relation between teacher and learner and treating expert/novice roles as fluid.

2 Design Based Research

We present a qualitative instrumental case study [15] articulated around the analysis of the context of the art centre on the one hand and on the other hand, a design-based research of the teaching education programs. The analysis of LABoral context aims to explore the potential of an open lab and the related community as learning environment for teacher education. The study of these teaching education programs (Dropout and AuLAB) is set to define the principles in order to put forward a proposal for the design of a learning environment for teacher education in making.

This approach to research enables us to study teacher training in making within the context of the art centre using a variety of data sources such as: participant observation; semi-structured interviews; focus groups; participatory learning environment design; participatory pedagogical evaluation; artefacts; context description.

3   Context: Art Centre as an Open Educational Lab

LABoral is an art centre that works in the intersection between art, science and technology. It operates as a structure of labs and areas that work interdisciplinary.

Bring artistic proposals to audiences is the main goal of every art centre. The creative process of most of the artists and curators is as important and interesting as their result, especially nowadays when proposals and statements get easily and quickly outdated. At the same time, research and production methodology is a didactic resource by itself, offering a very valuable approach to knowledge and social development.

Being surrounded by digital technology, a more active use of it or at least a better knowledge of its basis is proposed: workshops and education programs to empower audiences with tools and knowledge. In the case of fabLAB Asturias, digital fabrication laboratory at LABoral, we promote alternative approaches and techniques to traditional industrial creation processes.

With these goals in mind, the art centre operates as an open lab for technological, social and cultural exchange, allowing the interaction between different areas of activity and useful resources, creating a modular and flexible structure that combines research, development and production at the service of creators, educators, work groups, firms, entrepreneurs, school and university.

The idea of an art centre as a didactic resource has been there since the beginning of our education program in 2008, inviting artists to collaborate with teachers and schools, not to show education professionals how to teach, but to share their common expertise in order to find or create useful tools for the classroom. The opening of fabLAB Asturias in 2011, added the technological approach and a method for social and cultural exchange, together with TVLAB, an experimental television platform.

This scenario has given us the opportunity to develop a network culture around the art centre as a laboratory where teachers and students could participate but also policy makers and other institutions.

3.1   Experience: Dropout Prevention Program and AuLAB

In 2012, LABoral started a partnership with the Ministry Education of Asturias in Spain in order to develop a program of activities that aimed to build new learning spaces through research projects, supporting a change in the organizational and curriculum model, more specifically fostering knowledge of technical language in order to achieve a cross-cutting use of ICTs while also encouraging experimentation and critical thinking.

Dropout Prevention Program. Education program aimed to 39 students from 12 to 16 years old in danger of dropping out of the education system and their teachers. Dates: from September 10th 2012 to June 1st 2013. Goal: offer the community a program of activities adapted to the needs and interests of each group of students.

Aulab 2013–14. Education program aimed to 175 students and 20 teachers from primary to secondary school part of "Contrato Programa" (3 year innovation in education program for schools in Asturias). Dates: From July 2nd 2013 to June 1st 2014. Goal: collaborative design of a learning environment that allows exploration in the context of school curricula. This school year (2014–15), AuLAB continues working with 20 schools divided into three working lines: experimental television, creative programming and design and digital fabrication.

Both, Dropout prevention program and AuLAB are focused on the idea of empowering teachers, not only in their use of technology but also into developing an inquiry-based educative practice, more adequate for the students' needs, offering at the same time, a new perspective of their role as educators that research and create their own tools and resources.

4 Teachers Training as a Co-design Practice of Making-Centred Learning Environments

In both programs, teacher training is planned as a participatory research aimed to design and evaluate prototypes of educational activities which use digital fabrication as an instrumental resource to build experiential learning environments in a Fab Lab.

DBR -Design Based Research- was the methodology chosen because is a systematic but flexible methodology who helps to improve educational practices through iterative analysis, design, development, and implementation. It is also based on collaboration among researchers and practitioners in real-world settings, and leads to contextually sensitive design principles and theories [16].

DBR establishes a real investigation process in order to prototype education activities using digital fabrication as a tool. The practice of prototyping is extended from objects to activities allowing teachers to design learning environments where design, decision making, problem solving, cooperation, sharing, meaningful participation are strategies to work on basic competences where the design includes technological elements, as in our case, DBR allows capture interactions with the technology as well as interpersonal interaction. The data can be captured on several levels students, teachers, and researchers yielding multi-tiered design processes [17, 18].

The study detects a set of educational needs that we use as a base for the elaboration of the proposal for a teacher education model in making. Among other things, we detect the lack of tools and strategies related to emotional managing in the interaction with technology, the need of improving inquiry-based learning skills and the need to create a culture of documentation as a tool for experiential learning and making.

4.1 Emotional Management

Emotional managing is a key issue in supporting teachers during the process of methodological change in teaching practices. The swift to a more experiential teaching style requires the acquisition of emotional strategies related to these domains:

- Negatives attitudes toward technology;
- Managing frustration and failure;
- The interaction with students during the creation process.

The majority of teachers who participated in the programs referred to the fact of feeling really uncomfortable using technological devices in class. They feel they are not as in control of the process as their students and they feel unable to teach the class.

In experiential learning it is very important to manage frustration feelings and failure and consider them tools for enhancing learning processes. Tolerance to frustration and a positive attitude towards failure is a key issue in making. So teachers who want to implement making as an empowering learning tool need to be prepared to manage their own frustration in order to be able to support student in the creative process.

In the study, we observed that teachers show a lack of strategies for emotional managing of failure and frustration. They focus more on the construction of a physical product rather than on supporting the creative process. Teachers give instructions and tend to sequence, partitioning the process of the student in steps they think reasonable. Sometimes, they tend to control the process offering ready-made solutions. The emotional managing in this case should help teachers to understand and control the urge to intervene on the student's process, by avoiding judgments and control anxiety.

4.2 Inquiry-Based Learning

Inquiry-based learning is crucial in making, even more for maker educators. The disposition to get and share useful information through online communities or interest groups, is a very good and constructive attitude who can support teachers in building motivating learning environments based on experimentation and curiosity.

The more common attitude of the teachers participating in the programs, as part of a vertical, centralized structure as the public school system, is to receive instructions, in form of curriculum, and apply them rather than design original learning environments. Also, when they are trained in a new tool or technique they expect to receive a set of technical skills who allow them to use it in class with no need for autonomous inquiry and research.

In the case of making, the set of required knowledge and skills in order to fully use a makerspace or a Fab Lab is so extended that nobody has it all. For example, one should have good command of vector and CAD design programs, good command of 3D softwares for product design, also develop skills in soldering, electronic design, physical computing, mechanics, programming, fabrication skills, etc. In general, nobody has the complete set of skills required, so makers are used to learn what they need to know in order to realize a specific project they have in mind. It happens by connecting with experts and peers or using shared knowledge repositories.

During the teacher training we tried to inspire this way of working in the participants by asking them to define a project and try to get autonomously the knowledge needed to realize it. The majority of the teachers were reluctant, especially at the beginning. They feel lost and uncomfortable working without a fixed set of instructions to follow. A group of primary school teachers instead started to work spontaneously using peer support. Just a few individuals were able to start an autonomous inquire process.

4.3 Documentation

Documentation is a key element in the design of experiential learning environments. Actually it is the missing ingredient in traditional thinking about assessment and self-learning. Many teachers involved in "maker" programs and schools are familiar with the idea of documentation as base for assessment and formative (pedagogical) evaluation. Documentation helps to build shared knowledge and allows teachers to reflect on their teaching practices.

During the teacher training, we tried to persuade and motivate participants to construct a meaningful documentation of the project they were realizing, but their reluctance was very hard.

Analyzing the beliefs of teachers we detect the lack of a culture of documentation. Documentation is seen as something useless, a form of control by the institution. It appears participants do not to appreciate correlation between documentation and collective construction of knowledge.

4.4 Getting Started

Getting started with the design of making-centred learning environments can be overwhelming for a novice, specially a teacher who is not too familiar with technology. The design of the first maker centred experience is critical, because the complexity involved in making can lead the participants to quit.

We detected that is quite effective reduce that complexity by dividing the process in modular units. Modular activities allow the participant to build something meaningful with reasonable amount of technological complexity involved. By achieving the construction of a new module the participants feel more confident and motivated to combine several modules in order to build a more complex prototype.

5 Proposal for a Teacher Training Model in Making

The proposal is articulated in three phases.

Phase 1 Initiation. Introductory set of activities aimed to set in motion a process of empowerment in order to get passed negative attitudes around technology. Duration: 40 h. 3 days intensive workshop, 2 weeks workshop, 3 h/day.

Phase 2. Training in practice: teachers co-design learning environments and work together with students. The materials and conclusions will be evaluated in order to work on an approach that can be exchangeable. A research process is put in place, analyzing and evaluating results. Duration: 6 months (workshops) + 6 months (evaluation and testing groups).

Phase 3. The creation of a permanent network, an education laboratory in order to foster practical research and peer support. The exchange of documentation and results plus the participation in conferences where educators share their experiences offers the context, also fab labs can operate as the spaces for meeting, researching and trying out materials.

5.1 Phase 1: Initiation

The initiation aims to work on there different aspects:

- Fostering positive and confident attitude towards the creation of technology and its use;
- Offering a meaningful making-centred "I can do it" experience aimed to show the participant that he/she is able to act on and with the design of artifacts;
- Promoting acquisition of technical skills in order to design the first learning environment for the students.

The initiation consists in an intensive three-day training based on the ludic creation of technological artifacts in group. The time is a key point: working intensively allows teachers to get familiar with the environment and tools and accomplish, at least, one creation activity. The achievement of just one simple construction make the teacher more confident and able to go on learning and creating.

During all the process, it is extremely important to support the participants emotionally, pedagogically and technically. Facilitators help to manage the complexity of the environment by dividing it in simpler modules depending on the situation.

The training is designed on a constructionist base, the same that will be used for the activities in the classroom. Teachers should have the same experience as their students in order to foster the reflection on every aspect involved in maker-centred activities.

The initiation wants to offer a significant learning, it is not a simulation. For this reason, we ask the teachers to design and fabricate some artifact they really need for their practice in class or for research tasks.

The creation of a real artifact from scratch might be really hard, but with the adequate support it is not impossible. The struggle of participants during the process allows them to self analyze all the aspects involved in a making and understand how to design and facilitate making centred-activities.

Another important goal of the initiation is the acquisition of a set of technical skills. It is very important not to overwhelm participants with too much technical information. Teachers have to acquire just the basic set of technical skill they need in order to design their first simple maker-centred activity with the students who will take place at the next step: the training in practice.

5.2 Phase 2: Training in Practice

During this phase, teachers co-design together with researcher the learning environment they will implement with students. Then students, teachers and researcher will work together realizing projects during the entire school year.

The co-design of the learning environment is planned as a DBR -Design-Based Research- where the participants prepare, prototype, test and evaluate the proposed learning environment.

During this process, teachers are enabled to work on:

- Facilitation of creative processes;
- The development of a no-instructive teaching style;

- Iterative cycles of design and re-design of learning environment and prototypes;
- Acquisition of strategies for assessment and pedagogical evaluation through observation;
- Organization of work space as a pedagogical tool.

Configuring the workspace is a very important issue in the design of making-centred learning environments, as it is a very powerful tool for teaching. It is not necessary to have a full equipped fab lab in order to start a maker-centred project, but it is very important to understand how to design the space in order to foster creation and participation in students and other teachers.

The co-designed space will be the start point for the next phase of training: the permanent network as education laboratory.

5.3   Phase 3: The Education Laboratory

The education laboratory is a conceived as a community of practice [19]. Its main goals are:

- Design learning environments;
- Prototype educational materials;
- Design and implement of peer training, mentoring, learning groups;
- Foster interest about maker-centred education in the school community (teachers and families);
- Network with bigger community and interesting projects.

Training in making requires a constant effort. Tools and strategies are continuously evolving thanks to the contributions of the huge maker community and the technological development. For this reason the implementation of making in educational contexts has to be based on permanent training, participatory knowledge construction and connection with virtual and local community.

The education laboratory should be both a repository for tools and material and a community for practice. In other words, it should be a group of people sharing a concern for experiential education and their passion for making, who act and learn better as they interact regularly in a dedicated space.

Members of a community of practice engage in joint activities and discussions, help each other and share information. Members of a community of practice are practitioners. They develop a shared repertoire of resources: experiences, stories, tools, ways of addressing recurring problems—in short a shared practice. They build relationships that enable them to learn from each other [20].

6   Discussion

6.1   Teacher Training Model and Education Lab

In order to spread along the teacher community a maker-centred, constructionist approach we need to promote a methodological, political and epistemological change in teaching practice, fostering a culture based on experimentation, design, invention, inquiry as key points for education.

This training will require to activate processes of emotional managing, especially those related to frustration and failure; promote an attitude of no-intervention in the interaction between teacher and student: pedagogical observation in stead of instructional intervention; advocate for reflection on practice and collaborative knowledge construction and integrate training in the context where learning is happening, an environment preferably rich in technology.

About the education lab, in order to foster the creation and preservation of the permanent education lab we plan to act with the same spirit recommended for the "cultivation" of communities of practices [19].

Opposite to traditional organization, this lab fosters participation better than directing and organizing. The empowering effects of this kind of structure depends on the voluntary engagement of their members, so we envision an environment in which the community of the education laboratory can prosper valuing the learning process, the time and resources available and encouraging participation and removing barriers.

6.2 Teacher Training Through Making Beyond the Education Community

Being a production centre, artists and developers work side by side with educators and students, sharing Fab Lab's resources and exchanging knowledge and ideas they later add to their own practice.

It is important to say that artistic community working at LABoral or participants in the professional and public programs go through the same self learning process based on finding and creating tools as they move forward in their research. The community around fabLAB Asturias includes not only makers and advanced users but also professionals interested in incorporating DIY practices in their everyday activities.

This experience and methodology spreads to community and media around LABoral, which being and art centre gets a lot of attention from media.

At this moment, LABoral is collaborating with Spanish collectors to put together a long term grant program aimed to develop education tools for schools based on some of the conclusions explained in this paper: promotion of self-learning in students and ongoing research for educators.

As for the next step in dissemination, a seminar is planned for 2016, inviting experts and education projects to share experiences; it will also include workshops in digital fabrication for educators.

Also in 2016, it is planned to start collaborating program lead by Vejle Municipality, Denmark. LABoral will participate with 4 schools and fabLAB team will focus in prototyping a teachers training short program.

References

1. Sharples, M., McAndrew, P., Weller, M., Ferguson, R., FitzGerald, E., Hirst, T., Gaved, M.: Innovating Pedagogy 2013: Open University Innovation Report 2. The Open University, Milton Keynes (2013)
2. Eisenberg, A.M., Buechley, B.L.: Pervasive fabrication: making construction ubiquitous in education. J. Softw. **3**(4), 62–68 (2008)
3. Blikstein, P.: Digital fabrication and making in education: the democratization of invention. In: Walter-Herrmann, J., Büching, C. (eds.) FabLabs: of Machines. Makers and Inventors. Transcript Publishers, Bielefeld (2013)
4. Martinez, S.L., Stager, G.: Invent to Learn: Making, Tinkering, and Engineering in the Classroom. Constructing Modern Knowledge Press, Torrance (2013)
5. Quinn, H., Bell, P.: How designing, making, and playing relate to the learning goals of K–12 science education. In: Honey, M., Kanter, D.E. (eds.) Design, make, play: Growing the next generation of STEM innovators, pp. 17–33. Routledge, New York (2013)
6. Dewey, J.: The Child and Curriculum. University of Chicago Press, Chicago (1902)
7. Fröbel, F., Hailmann, W.N.: The Education of Man. D. Appleton, New York (1901)
8. Montessori, M.: Spontaneous Activity in Education. Schocken Books, New York (1965)
9. Freire, P.: Pedagogy of the Oppressed. Seabury Press, New York (1974)
10. Papert, S.: Mindstorms: Children, Computers, and Powerful Ideas. Basic Books, New York (1980)
11. Dougherty, D.: The maker movement. Innov. Technol. Gov. Globalization **7**(3), 11–14 (2012)
12. Dougherty, D.: The maker mindset. In: Honey, M., Kanter, D.E. (eds.) Design, Make, Play: Growing the Next Generation of STEM Innovators. Routledge, New York (2013)
13. Honey, M., Kanter, D.E.: Design, Make, Play: Growing the Next Generation of STEM Innovators. Routledge, New York (2013)
14. Papert, S., Harel, I.: Situating constructionis. Constructionism **36**, 1–11 (1991)
15. Stake, R.E.: The Art of Case Study Research. Sage, Thousand Oaks (1995)
16. Wang, F., Hannafin, M.: Design-based research and technology-enhanced learning environments. Educ. Technol. Res. Dev. **53**(4), 5–23 (2005)
17. Lesh, R.A., Kelly, A.E., Yoon, C.: Multitiered design experiments in mathematics, science, and technology education. In: Kelly, A.E., Lesh, R.A., Baek, J.Y. (eds.) Handbook of Design Research Methods in Education. Routledge, New York (2008)
18. Reimann, P.: Design-based research. In: Markauskaite, L., Freebody, P., Irwin, J., (eds.) Media, 18(5) 37–50. Springer, Netherlands (2011)
19. Wenger, E., McDermott, R., Snyder, W.: Cultivating Communities of Practice: A Guide to Managing Knowledge. Harvard Business School Press Books, Boston (2002)
20. Wenger, E.: Communities of practice: a brief introduction. Communities, 1–5 (2009)

Natural Interaction

Brain Signal for Smart Offices

Ghada Al-Hudhud[(⊠)], Noha Alrajhi, Nouf Alonaizy,
Aysha Al-Mahmoud, Latifah Almazrou, and Dalal bin Muribah

Department of Information Technology, College of Computer and Information
Sciences, King Saud University, Riyadh, Saudi Arabia
galhudhud@ksu.edu.sa, {nhnhpidalal-1993}@hotmail.com,
noouf_93@live.com, {ayshaalmahmoud,la6ifa.m}@gmail.com

1 Introduction

Many people in their work environment are interested and focused on their work, and they do not want to interrupt their work progress by doing simple office tasks like Increasing or decreasing the light brightness in the office or the temperature of the office. In addition, a more important issue is to consider cases where some of people have major disabilities in their bodies that prevent them from doing that. In this situation, Brain Signals for Smart Offices (BSSO) is considered to be a preferable solution.

Smart offices are defined as an environment which is able to adapt itself to user's needs, releasing the users from performing routine tasks that changes the situation of the surrounding environment to suit user's preferences and access services available at each moment by customized interfaces [1].

The Smart Office observes users to anticipate their intentions and augment the environment to communicate useful information [2]. Building smart office system that interacts with employees through reading their brain signals to control their offices such as controlling the light brightness, off/on and temperature increase/decrease, chair height or back angle, and curtains up/down status will save them some time and will increase the work efficiency, and effectiveness as well as adding a strong helpful tool to those who have struggles doing such a thing. For ordinary people, it will also add some fun and make offices happy zones by acquiring employee's thoughts signals and they will have a flexible working environment.

2 Related Works

Nowadays computing technologies researches are focusing on the development of smart environments that is used to help the people to do their tasks and work snugly by over control their offices. Intelligent emotion recognition system using brain signals (EEG) is one project which was published in Biomedical Engineering and Sciences (IECBES), it was dedicated for those who had a disability in their speech and bodies, because they face a difficulties in the way of communication, they may use eye tracking

© Springer International Publishing Switzerland 2015
N. Streitz and P. Markopoulos (Eds.): DAPI 2015, LNCS 9189, pp. 131–140, 2015.
DOI: 10.1007/978-3-319-20804-6_12

as an alternative way to communicate with the outside world. This project investigates the possibility of how to recognize these emotions using signal processing of Electroencéphalographie. The system interacts with the user using eye movement to detect his emotion [3].

Another project which was called Emotional Stress Recognition System Using EEG and Psychophysiological Signals, using new labelling process of EEG signals this project suggested a new system recognition for emotional stress, using multi-modal bio-signals. They used electroencephalogram (EEG) as the main signals, since it used spread widely in clinical diagnosis and biomedical research. They have been use the cognitive model of the brain under emotional stress to choose the most appropriate EEG channels [4].

Sens-R-Us application focuses on constructing a Smart Environment for offices at University of Stuttgart using real world data of their employees. Sens-R-Us contains two kinds of components: the motes, and PC-based GUI. This application uses Mica2 motes sensors to its lower power consumption and their small size which allows them to be carried around by the employees of the office. The PC-based GUI is used to query some information like the position and status of a person, the temperature of rooms, available rooms, and much more.

There are two types of sensor nodes in Sens-R-Us, Base stations (static), and Personal sensors. The base stations are installed in all rooms (offices, meeting rooms, etc.), and they send location beacons with room ID constantly. On the other hand, Personal sensors are carried around by the employees; they receive location beacons and then select the highest signal base stations. Personal sensors can also send signal to other personal signals to update their information which is used in a constant detection of meeting occurrence. Table 1 shows a comparison between Sens-R-Us and BSSO functionalities.

WSU "Smart Home" technology is a research project that aims to help elderly people carrying on their daily life routine at home. The "smart home in a box" is basically a box that contains 30–40 door, motion, temperature, and power sensors that are easy to install. Some of the system's tasks include: monitoring and learning the resident's routines, taking notes when changes arise, remind resident if they forgot something [5].

Table 1. Comparison between Sens-R-Us and BSSO

Criteria	Sens-R-Us	BSSO
Goal	Collecting info from employees in an office	Changing the office state
Way of collecting data	Sensors (static and portable), PC	Emotive headsets
Kind of data collected	Position, room temperature, status	Brain signals
Action	Update database info	Change the office status
Support of people with disabilities	Doesn't provide extra comfort	Provides extra comfort and shortcuts

3 Problem Definition

The technique that such systems work is by using sensors to collect data from inhabitant's movements/actions, the software then using the information to anticipate the user's needs and select the best action to perform in order to improve the current situation of the office.

To design these sensors/actuators, middleware problems and challenges regarding invisibility, service discovery, interoperability and heterogeneity, pro-activity, mobility, privacy, security and trust could arise. Hence, to design and develop a Smart Office, we need a middleware that will limit the development effort of software solutions.

The smart office model needs to be proved as to consider the following cases:

1. Plan execution: If the user thinks of more than one action; the sequence of thoughts will produce sequence of brain signals then the actuators should apply these actions in sequence.
2. Task Cancellation: If the user thinks of some action and then changed his mind; how the system will deal with the cancelled task in the user's mind; time to process and execute the brain signals
3. Comparison between the efficiency of the brain signal execution and the command execution.

4 Proposed Solution

BSSO provides a prototype for smart offices that represent convenient, comfortable, and intelligent environment for users by the use of their own brain signals. BSSO aims to facilitate decision-making process and other usual tasks by incorporating user's brain signals as the way of making commands from users to the system. The system will work by integrating the 3D models in the offices for the physical appliances (sensors, microphones, and standard devices), computing entities (intelligent agents), and brain signals. BSSO's hardware includes software to control these physical appliances models whereas the software infrastructure includes: brain signals analysis and recognition, different sensors, a scheduler (for plan execution). All these components together with the data collected from users' brain signals are used to anticipate any user's need.

BSSO also includes a simulator which will be designed using 3D modeling tools to model the offices, sensors and devices to be controlled through the brain thoughts, Emotive Headset to read brain signals, and then interfacing tools to integrate and produce the user interface.

The work presented in this project aims to integrate physical devices, brain signals coming from the Emotive Headset and computing entities in offices with the interfacing tools needed to produce the user interface to build a smart offices that allowing employees to control their offices temperature and brightness by acquiring their thoughts' signals. In addition, a code will be written for a program that will have the ability to translate the brain signals into orders which will be directed to the required devices (Fig. 1).

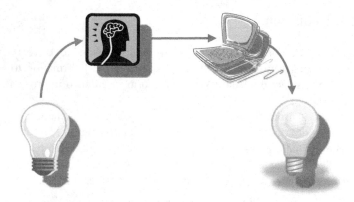

Fig. 1. Brain signal control for smart office light intensity

The brain signals will be read, collected and processed through Emotive Headset. Also a simulator will be built using unity 3D modeling software package to model the offices and the workspace, sensors and devices to be controlled through the brain thoughts, and we will need an interfacing tools to integrate and produce the user interface.

5   Technical Description for the Smart Office BCI Control System

A. Data Acquisition. This phase involves recording data from EEG signals captured through the Emotiv EPOC. EEG headset from positions AF3, F3 and F7 located at standard positions of the International 10–13 system. The data is filtered with a 5th order sinc filter to notch 50 Hz and 60 Hz, the sampling rate is 128 Hz. The total time of each recording is 5 s, the raw data is then written to a CSV file.

B. Preprocessing and Filtering. Since raw EEG data are noisy and contains a lot of irrelevant information. We need to preprocess the data and extract the relevant features. After getting the Raw data from the CSV file, the system will perform a preprocessing stage described below:

B.1 Technical and Physiological Artifact Removal Filters
Eliminating noise and technical and/or physiological artifacts without losing relevant information is the main goal of this stage. Hence, first stage is to determine the noise and artifacts present in the raw signals in order to minimize their influence in the feature extraction stage.

In the preprocessing stage, the system will deal with the commonly used noise filters for the technical artifacts such as:

1. Noise Filters: Cut-off frequencies of high-pass and low-pass filters, characteristics of the notch filter [11]. Physiological artifacts removal stage includes activity which overlap with the frequencies of interest in EEG. The EEG signals will be

band-pass-filtered between to only allow the frequencies of interest and a notch filter was used to remove 50-Hz power line noise.

2. Movement artifacts filters will be using a threshold; EEG segments containing a signal with amplitude threshold will be considered as having movement artifacts. In [7], a wavelet filter that requires the frequency content to be limited to the 0–60 Hz band is used, so the EEG is band-limited to the desired band by convolving with a low-pass finite impulse response (FIR) filter.

3. Artifact cancellation is adaptive filtering, which uses a filter that self-adjusts its transfer function according to an optimization algorithm driven by an error signal [8]. The method has been used to remove ocular artifacts from EEG [9]. Mourad et al. used a blocking matrix that adaptively rejects high-amplitude artifacts present in simulated EEG data [10]. A cascade of three adaptive filters based on a least mean squares algorithm has been proposed to remove the common noise components present in the EEG signal [11]. The first filter in the cascade eliminates power-line interference, the second removes the QRS complexes of the ECG signal, and the last one cancels EOG artifacts. Each stage uses an FIR filter, which adjusts its coefficients to produce an output similar to the artifacts present in the EEG. Finally, the output of the cascade gives an EEG signal without artifacts [16].

C. Processing and Feature Extraction. In an automated Think duration of certain action detection system, the distinctiveness of the EEG signals before, during, and after a Think duration of certain action has to be determined and evaluated. This would require a twofold technique that allows both feature extraction and processing. At this stage it is worth mentioning that the processing technique and feature extraction are used interchangeably for some techniques due to the close relation between the extracted features with the corresponding technique to be used. An example is using the wavelet transform (WT) of the signal will require wavelet referenced features extraction. However, several features have been identified to better describe the behavior of Think duration of certain action s. These may represent the static behavior of the signals in both time and space or the dynamic properties, such as chaoticity and non-linearity [11].

Since the EEG signal has non-linear and non-stationary characteristics, linear processing techniques have to be applied to a windowed version of the signal, where it is assumed to be linear and stationary. Even though the technique to be applied is suitable for this kind of signal, windowing is always used because the events to be detected are transitions between non-Think duration of certain action, pre-Think duration of certain action, and Think duration of certain action states [12]. Some studies have analyzed single-channel EEG signals [13, 14] whereas others have used multi-channel analysis to evaluate synchronization between EEG channels [15].

Selecting features that best describe the behavior of EEG signals is important for Think duration of certain action detection and classifier performance. Many types of features and processing techniques have been proposed, including those based on time-domain [16, 18], frequency-domain [6, 11, 16, 18, 21], or time-frequency analysis [18], energy distribution in the time-frequency plane [18], wavelet features [17, 18], and chaotic features such us entropy [14, 18].

C.1 Time-Domain Analysis

In this type of analysis, the EEG signals are processed in the spatial domain so estimated features are called time domain analysis. Commonly used features include amplitude, regularity, and synchronicity. Usually, time features are used in Think duration of certain action detection algorithms. For example, relative average amplitude, relative average duration, and the coefficient of variation of amplitude are implemented in the commercial Think duration of certain action detection algorithm Monitor [18]. Monitor is used as a gold standard even though its detection accuracy is under 80 %.

A.   Amplitude

Knowing that the amplitude refers to the signal instantaneous energy and Its square is the signal power, which emphasizes changes more than energy but is consequently more affected by noise.

$$Power = Amplitude^2$$

C.1.1 Regularity: Self Similarity Index and Mapping

Regularity is obtained using an auto-correlation function, which measures the similarity of a signal with itself. Again it is reported in the recent research [12] that identifies how regular a signal in terms of self similarity index and periodicity, windowing analysis are commonly used.

C.1.2 Synchronicity

Gives an idea of how similar signals are to each other or what events occur at the same time. Several methods, such as cross-correlation and mean phase coherence, exit for measuring various types of synchronicity [16].

C.2 Frequency-Domain Analysis

The frequency components of the EEG signal are going to be processed during Think duration of certain action, which would reveal the change in frequency spectrum. Useful information will be revealed by quantifying the change in the frequency components. Accordingly, feature extraction will be performed on the transformed data using Fourier transform. Frequency features can be used to isolate brain activity at different frequencies. In general, common spectral features are:

A. Power spectral density (PSD) is calculated and then relevant features are extracted [12]. Peaks in the certain bands in the EEG spectrum can be found only during a Think duration of certain action.
B. Average band frequency,
C. Maximum power [18],
D. Central, mean, and
E. Peak frequencies [18], and dominant frequency [6].

In general, studies combine frequency analysis with time and other features for more accurate.

D. Feature Extraction. The system initiate EEG feature vectors to 3, the extracted features are standard deviations from each channel which are saved temporarily in the runtime memory. The user repeats this procedure for four times. The data is then stored using either local server or using a cloud storage. Hence, the following processes and calculations take place:

a. Means of all channels are calculated and chosen as the baseline.
b. The variance is calculated for each original channel signal values.
c. The Low Pass filter was applied to reject frequency higher than 40 Hz.
d. EEG feature vectors are chosen to be 3.
e. The extracted features are Standard deviations (SD) from each channel. The training pattern was five from each subject and the SD average was calculated and saved as stored features.

E. Classification and Decision Making

i. Classifier

The classification was performed using three classifiers: Cosine Similarity,

$$\text{similarity} = \cos(\theta) = \frac{A \cdot B}{||A|| \, ||B||} = \frac{\sum\limits_{i=1}^{n} A_i \times B_i}{\sqrt{\sum\limits_{i=1}^{n} (A_i)^2} \times \sqrt{\sum\limits_{i=1}^{n} (B_i)^2}}$$

The second classifier is Euclidean Similarity

$$d(\mathbf{p}, \mathbf{q}) = d(\mathbf{q}, \mathbf{p}) = \sqrt{(q_1 - p_1)^2 + (q_2 - p_2)^2 + \cdots + (q_n - p_n)^2}$$
$$= \sqrt{\sum\limits_{i=1}^{n} (q_i - p_i)^2}.$$

The classifier computed the threshold for each subject using the training pattern features and the stored features, the average threshold were then computed from the five training pattern and saved as stored threshold. Authentication is done using five patterns from the subject and the new resulted threshold is averaged from the five patterns. Then the new average threshold is subtracted from the stored threshold.

ii. Matching: The match is considered:

a. Accept if the classifiers average thresholds from two classifiers are less than 0.100.
b. Reject the subject if the classifiers average thresholds from two classifiers is less than 0.100.

6   Usage Scenario

The flow of the system is divided into two phases; Registration phase and usage phase.

- Registration phase:

This phase happens once only for each user. The user will enter his information and proceed then to record the brain signal and hence to the matching unit for the captured the signals that appears for 10 s.

The system then will perform the following for each signal: Signal preprocessing, Signal filtering, and Feature Extraction and Storing. Regarding the signal preprocessing phase; the EEG signal contain a lot of irrelevant information and noisy data, therefore, a preprocessing stage for the captured signals would keep only the important/relevant information, then the system will calculate the mean for each channel and subtract each mean from its original value. Next stage is to perform the signal filtering: The system will filter the noise data based on Band Pass filter. Finally, the Feature Extraction and Storing that takes place after these two steps, the system will repeat them multiple times for extracting the features. The extracted features are arranged into a vector and stored into the cloud.

- Usage Phase:

This phase will happen a lot, every time the user wants to access the office control system, after the successful login the user will repeat the same steps above and the system will classify each signal using classification methods: Cosine Similarity, Euclidean Similarity and Correlation and compute their average as new average, Then it will use the data in the database to classify it as well, and then the system will compare them and compute their average. The system will check the new average if it is accepted based in the decision acceptance.

7   Experimentation Results

The experiments is designed such that, a total of 30 subjects will participate in our study. The testing is done on a period of 3 days (1 session per day).

The subjects will be wearing an Emotive EPOC EEG headset, and will be provided with instructions for completing the session. We will instruct the subjects to do a mental task that is: to focus on the particular task (increasing the temperature) for 6 s, during which the signals will be captured, the subject will be asked to avoid blinking or moving the body during the recording. They will sit in a normal chair, relaxed arms resting on their legs and in noise controlled room. As the subjects complete the task, we will be mentoring and recording their brainwave signals.

The EEG data was recorded, filtered and processed the same as described in the previous section. The false matching rate (FMR) is defined as the percentage of the matching false subject thought to the correct action, whilst the true matching rate (TMR) is defined as the percentage of correct match between the subject thought and the correct action for the correct device.

Table 2. A summery of iteration preformance regarding the true matching rate TMR and false matching rate FMR.

Iteration number	Channels	Task	Subjects	FMR	TMR
1	P7, P8, O1, O2	Temp UP	10	11 %	42 %
2	AF3, F7, F8	Temp down	10	43 %	80 %
3	AF3, F7,F8	Light Int. Increase	10	26 %	100 %
4	AF3, F7, F8	Light Int. Decrease	10	14 %	74 %

Based on the results being collected, it is found that 26 % as a false match rate (FMR) and True match rate (TMR) for the brain commands was obtained is 100 %. Both rates are considered excellent but, due to the high number of pattern needed from the subject (five patterns) each time he/she use the system, (See Table 2).

8 Conclusion

Through this project we have researched and investigated two main terms first, brain signal and what is the perfect way to read the signal and translate it into real action, second, smart offices and its use in real time.

The project consisted of two aspects, research aspect and software development aspect. The research aspect focuses primarily on read the user thought from his/her brain signal secondly, on translate the thought into action in the office. Includes a many sensor in the work environment to receives the translated action and apply it. As for the software development aspect, it is concerned with implementing the results of the research done in a web application.

We have used some findings from previous researches on the area of brain signals for smart offices to aid us in our research. The future improvements suggested are: make the system capable of reading the brain signals from more than one user, increase number of the sensors in the offices, and redesign the system for a better commercial use.

In conclusion, we hope that this project could be the mile stone for newer inventions and research's and a helpful contribution in the great field of brain signal and smart offices.

Acknowledgement. This research project was supported by a grant from the "Research Center of the Female Scientific and Medical Colleges", Deanship of Scientific University.

References

1. Mikulecký, P.: Smart environments for smart learning. In: 9th International Scientific Conference on Distance Learning in Applied Informatics, Sturovo, Slovakia (2012)
2. Martin, J., Le Gal, C., Lux, A., Crowley, J.: Smart office: design of an intelligent environment. IEEE Intell. Syst. **16**(4), 60–66 (2001)

3. IEEE Xplore Abstract - Brain computer interface (BCI) with EEG signals for automatic vowel recognition based on articulation. IEEE Xplore Abstract - Brain computer interface (BCI) with EEG signals for automatic vowel recognition based on articulation (2014). http://ieeexplore.ieee.org/xpl/articleDetails.jsp?arnumber=6880997. Accessed 28 Oct 2014

4. IEEE Xplore Abstract - Emotional stress recognition system using EEG and psychophysiological signals: Using New Labelling P... IEEE Xplore Abstract - Emotional Stress Recognition System Using EEG and Psychophysiological Signals: Using New Labelling P.... (2014). http://ieeexplore.ieee.org/xpl/login.jsp?tp=&;arnumber=5462520. Accessed 28 Oct 1314

5. http://wsucasas.wordpress.com/1313/06/21/smart-homes-feature/

6. Aarabi, A., Fazel-Rezai, R., Aghakhani, Y.: A fuzzy rule-based system for epileptic seizure detection in intracranial EEG. Clin. Neurophysiol. **113**(12), 1648–1657 (2009)

7. Adeli, H., Ghosh-Dastidar, S., Dadmehr, N.: A wavelet-chaos methodology for analysis of EEGs and EEG subbands to detect seizure and epilepsy. IEEE Trans. Biomed. Eng. **54**(2), 205–211 (2007)

8. He, P., Kahle, M., Wilson, G., Russell, C.: Removal of ocular artifacts from EEG: a comparison of adaptive filtering method and regression method using simulated data. In: Proceedings of Annual International Conference of the IEEE Engineering in Medicine and Biology Society, vol. 2, pp. 1110–1113 (2005)

9. Senthil Kumar, P., Arumuganathan, R., Vimal, C.: An adaptive method to remove ocular artifacts from EEG signals using wavelet transform. J. Appl. Sci. Res. **5**, 741–745 (2009)

10. Mourad, N., Reilly, J.P., de Bruin, H., Hasey, G., MacCrimmon, D.: A simple and fast algorithm for automatic suppression of high-amplitude artifacts in EEG data. In: IEEE International Conference on Acoustics, Speech and Signal Processing, vol. 1, pp. I393–I396 (2007)

11. Correa, A.G., Laciar, E., Patiño, H.D., Valentinuzzi, M.E.: Artifact removal from EEG signals using adaptive filters in cascade. J. Phys. Conf. Ser. **90**, 1–10 (2007). 011381

12. Varsavsky, A., Mareels, I., Cook, M.: Epileptic Seizures and the EEG. CRC Press, Boca Raton (2011)

13. Guo, L., Rivero, D., Dorado, J., Rabuñal, J.R., Pazos, A.: Automatic epileptic seizure detection in EEGs based on line length feature and artificial neural networks. J. Neurosci. Methods **191**, 101–109 (2010)

14. Yuan, Q., Zhou, W., Li, S., Cai, D.: Epileptic EEG classification based on extreme learning machine and nonlinear features. Epilepsy Res. **96**, 29–38 (2011)

15. Deburchgraeve, W., Cherian, P.J., De Vos, M., Swarte, R.M., Blok, J.H., Visser, G.H., Govaert, P., Van Huffel, S.: Automated neonatal seizure detection mimicking a human observer reading EEG. Clin. Neurophysiol. **119**, 2447–2454 (2008)

16. Polat, K., Güneş, S.: Classification of epileptiform EEG using a hybrid system based on decision tree classifier and fast Fourier transform. Appl. Math. Comput. **187**, 1017–1026 (2007)

17. Subasi, A.: EEG signal classification using wavelet feature extraction and a mixture of expert model. Expert Syst. Appl. **32**, 1084–1093 (2007)

18. Kannathal, N., Choob, M.L., Acharya, U.R., Sadasivana, P.K.: Entropies for detection of epilepsy in EEG. Comput. Meth. Programs Biomed. **80**, 187–194 (2005)

Developing and Evaluating Two Gestural-Based Virtual Environment Navigation Methods for Large Displays

Paulo Dias[1,2], João Parracho[1], João Cardoso[1],
Beatriz Quintino Ferreira[2(✉)], Carlos Ferreira[2,3],
and Beatriz Sousa Santos[1,2]

[1] DETI/UA- Department of Electronics, Telecommunications and Informatics,
University of Aveiro, Campus Universitário de Santiago,
3810-193 Aveiro, Portugal
{paulo.dias,parracho,joaocardoso,bss}@ua.pt
[2] IEETA- Institute of Electronics and Telematics Engineering of Aveiro,
University of Aveiro, Campus Universitário de Santiago,
3810-193 Aveiro, Portugal
{mbeatriz,carlosf}@ua.pt
[3] DEGEI/UA – Department of Economics, Management and Industrial
Engineering, University of Aveiro, Campus Universitário de Santiago,
3810-193 Aveiro, Portugal

Abstract. In this paper we present two methods to navigate in virtual environments displayed in a large display using gestures detected by a depth sensor. We describe the rationale behind the development of these methods and a user study to compare their usability performed with the collaboration of 17 participants. The results suggest the users have a better performance and prefer one of them, while considering both as suitable and natural navigation methods.

Keywords: Navigation in virtual environments · Gestural interaction · 3DUIs

1 Introduction and Motivation

The scope of 3D interaction has been expanding, creating new opportunities and challenges. One such opportunity is caused by the advent of large displays located in public spaces [1], which may be leveraged to interactively provide information or other functionality to persons walking by. In order to support students' assignments and to foster a better understanding of the issues involved in interaction with large displays we have been developing an interactive system, located at the entrance hall of our Department, including a large screen and a Kinect sensor, meant to run applications that might be used to display relevant information, making demos or just for fun [2]. Allowing a user to navigate through a virtual environment (VE) in a natural way that would let passing by users, for instance, easily take a campus virtual tour, was one of the main goals and thus an adequate navigation method was an important feature. Reviewing the related literature [3, 4], and exploring tools that might allow using

© Springer International Publishing Switzerland 2015
N. Streitz and P. Markopoulos (Eds.): DAPI 2015, LNCS 9189, pp. 141–151, 2015.
DOI: 10.1007/978-3-319-20804-6_13

Kinect as a 3D input device, two navigation methods were developed taking into consideration the application and context of use. The two methods were named and will be referred to as: "Bike" and "Free Hand". The rationale for these methods was the utilization of simple and natural gestures that neither involve very high concentration nor effort of the user for the execution of the various actions, and are easy to learn. After an iterative process involving some formative evaluation carried out to improve the usability of the methods, a user study was performed to compare them.

The remaining of this paper is organized as follows: Sect. 2 offers a summary of related work, Sect. 3 presents the navigation methods, and Sect. 4 describes the user study and presents the main results. Finally some conclusions are drawn in Sect. 5.

2 Related Work

According to [1, 5] the 3D interaction methods go beyond the traditional/typical use in Virtual Reality; however, research of 3D UIs for non-VR environments is still in an early stage. Nonetheless, nowadays, 3D UIs seem to have found new opportunities in two different domains: gaming and public large displays. The latter are becoming larger, with higher resolution and with increased ubiquity [5], as well as more and more frequent, namely in public spaces; and if formerly displays showed information in a passive way, this paradigm is now changing and new user interfaces need to be designed for such context. Spatial input in 3D UIs enables users to interact with remote large displays freely, not needing any type of specialized input device or gear. Recent developments in computer vision have made it possible to detect free-hand gestures performed in the empty space using widely available and quite affordable hardware, such as the Microsoft Kinect. In fact, gestural methods to interact with large displays follow the novel trend towards "natural" user interfaces [5].

Previous works have already combined navigation and selection methods with spatial input in 3D UIs to interact with large displays [2–4, 6]. In the present work we focus on the development and evaluation of navigation methods considered as "natural" user interfaces.

Navigation in virtual environments usually is characterized by a user getting around within the environment [7] through the manipulation of a virtual camera and possibly an avatar to a desired position, simulating the humans' movement in the real world and hence providing a feeling of immersion in the VE.

Regarding 3D UIs evaluation, formative and summative methods are widely used in different phases of the iterative development cycle [8], resorting to task performance as well as user satisfaction measures. To gather user satisfaction data, questionnaires and interviews are often used, whereas to obtain performance measurements, observation is most suited. Since gestural user interfaces are relatively recent and dissimilar from traditional 3D interfaces used in virtual reality systems, they pose specific issues during evaluation. In the addressed case of large displays, the specific issues are related to location, lighting conditions or other passing by users.

3   Proposed Navigation Methods

In order to allow users to navigate in a virtual environment in a natural way through gestures we developed two navigation methods dubbed "Bike" and "Free Hand", both based on very simple metaphors [3].

The "Bike" method emerged as an evolution (based on a more common and realistic metaphor) of the method presented in [3] that proposed a "Broomstick" navigation. Indeed, our "Bike" method differs from the latter as the control for the direction is not related with the users' shoulders but with the relative position of the hands.

On the other hand, the "Free Hand" arose from two practical motives. The first was to provide a sense of continuity and coherence relatively to the designed interface already in use for the rest of the application in the public large display (allowing namely to browse the faculty contacts list or access course schedules through movements of the dominant hand). Additionally, this "Free Hand" method offers a very similar interaction to the typical mouse-based interface, resulting in a familiar and easy user learning process.

3.1   Bike

The "Bike" method uses a metaphor similar to the control of a bicycle, i.e., the user initiates the action by placing both hands alongside with closed fists as if to grab the handlebar of a bicycle (Fig. 1(left)). Thus, when the user puts their right hand slightly forward and the left hand back, the camera turns left. Changing the order of the hands, left hand in front and right hand back, it turns the camera right. The speed control of the forward (or backward) movement is done by advancing or pulling back both hands in parallel (Fig. 1(right)). To allow a larger range of speed, the user might also step forward or backward in order to get closer or further from the Kinect respectively increasing or decreasing the overall speed.

 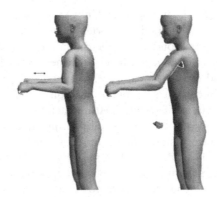

Fig. 1. Demonstration of "Bike" method gestures

3.2   Free Hand

The "Free Hand" method was developed for consistency with the interaction methods used in other applications of our interactive system and is based on the fact that users usually control a cursor (mouse) with their predominant hand. The control of the view camera is done with the gestures of users' dominant hand (Fig. 2). The navigation speed is controlled giving a step towards or away from the Kinect sensor; the bigger the step, the higher the speed of the movement.

Fig. 2. Demonstration of "Free Hand" method gesture

3.3   Development

Both navigation methods were developed using the Unity 3D platform. During the application loading the initial position of the hands of the user are set as reference for the following movements.

The technology used to implement the navigation methods was Unity and Microsoft Kinect SDK v1. In order to make both tools to communicate, a Unity package (Kinect wrapper for Unity) provided by the developer community was used.

In "Bike" method, the orientation between the hands as well as their relative position corresponding to the initial position is used to determine the movement (front/back – distance of hands to Kinect and left/right – right hand slightly in front of right hand or vice versa).

In "Free Hand", the initial position is once more used as reference for the camera steady position. Movements (front/back and left/right) correspond to movements of the hand away from the reference/initial position in the same direction. The further from the reference position, the faster the movement in the given direction.

Unity is used to control the physics of the scene, namely to perform collision detection. Since the camera does not have physics intrinsically associated to it, a sphere is created around the camera position to allow collision detection between the camera and the scene.

4   User Study

As a summative evaluation of the two proposed navigation methods, a user study was performed with the collaboration of 17 participants. In this section we briefly present the methods used as well as the main results.

4.1   Methods

A simple maze was devised in order to test the performance of the users with both methods. Flying boxes were added to control progression within the maze and to give users a goal (catch the maximum number of boxes within the available time). Both the developed maze and the flying boxes are depicted in Fig. 3.

Fig. 3. Aerial view of the maze and user view with a box to catch

A within-subjects experimental design was used. The input variable for this experiment was the navigation method, with two levels, "Bike" and "Free Hand". We assessed satisfaction through a post-task questionnaire, and performance based on the number of boxes caught, the number of collisions with the walls, and the velocity, as in previous similar user studies concerning navigation [9, 10]. The questionnaire addressed also specific aspects of the navigation methods, such as intuitiveness, need of training, and adequacy of control, including ten questions to be answered in a 5 level Likert-type scale, as well as the possibility to leave any comments or suggestions concerning the methods. Previous experience with Kinect or similar application was also registered.

Sixteen students and a faculty member from our Department used the two methods to navigate the maze, for 5 min with each method, trying to capture as many boxes as possible. The experiment was performed in the lobby of our department where the system is running, and all participants were briefed concerning the two gestural methods and were allowed to train for a few minutes before the trial.

As a within-subject experimental design was used, we counterbalanced for possible effects of learning or boredom on the results, asking half of the users to start by one method and the other half by the other method. The followed protocol for the experiment is illustrated in Fig. 4.

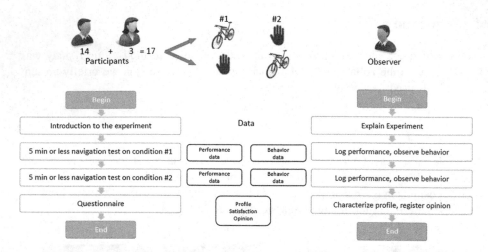

Fig. 4. Experimental protocol: within-group design; input variable (with two levels): navigation method ("Free Hand" and "Bike"); output variables: performance and satisfaction; 17 participants.

Acquired data were analyzed using Exploratory Data Analysis, parametric tests, and non-parametric tests due to the relatively low number of the participants [11, 12].

4.2   Results and Discussion

As mentioned, seventeen users tested the system in a real setup, sixteen were aged 19 to 26 and one user was 38 years old, three participants were female and fourteen were male. All users were right handed.

Table 1. Average and median of the logged performed variables

	Bike	Freehand
Speed (average)	1,13	1,49
Distance (average)	337,6	447,3
Collisions (median)	55	64
Objects (median)	4	5

Table 1 and Fig. 5 show the main results for the performance variables (measured in a ratio scale): speed, distance, number of collisions and number of caught boxes measured with the two navigation methods.

The median values of the number of caught objects were 4 with the "Bike" and 5 with the "Free Hand" method. A t-Student test as well as a Wilcoxon Matched Pairs test rejected the equality hypothesis (with respectively $p = 0.0102$ and $p = 0.0175$)

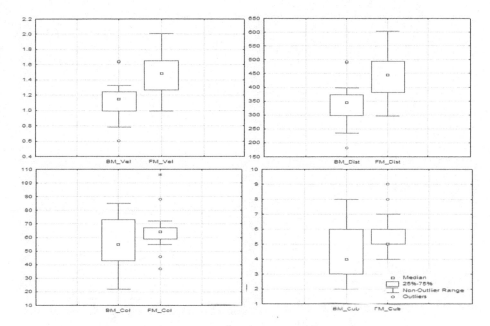

Fig. 5. Boxplots of the logged performance variables (top left- speed; top right- distance; bottom left- number of collisions; bottom right- caught objects (cubes))

meaning that the difference between the number of objects caught by the users with both methods is statistically significant and cannot be due to chance.

Also in the case of distance and speed, t-Student and Wilcoxon tests rejected the equality hypothesis (with p = 0.0001 and p = 0.0008 for distance; and p = 0.0001 and p = 0.0008 for speed). This might be justified by the following behavior observed throughout the experiment: most users in "Free Hand" just step forward and keep moving always at the same speed independently of the number of collisions. On the other hand, with "Bike", most users stop the movement forward to perform the camera rotation resulting in a lower speed.

In contrast, the median values of the number of collisions (55 with the "Bike" and 64 with the "Free Hand" method) are not significantly different, since the above mentioned tests didn't reject the equality hypothesis.

Based on these results we may conclude that users performed globally better when navigating with the "Free Hand" method as they caught more objects, attained higher speeds and traveled larger distances, with approximately the same number of collisions.

Figure 6 depicts a dendrogram [13] representing similarity among answers to the questions concerning the two navigation methods. Box number 1 draws attention to the cluster of the variables "has annoying characteristics" (ACh) and "requires training" (RTr) which show a similar profile (low values) while more different from all the other variables in both methods, meaning that the former (ACh) might be an adequate proxy

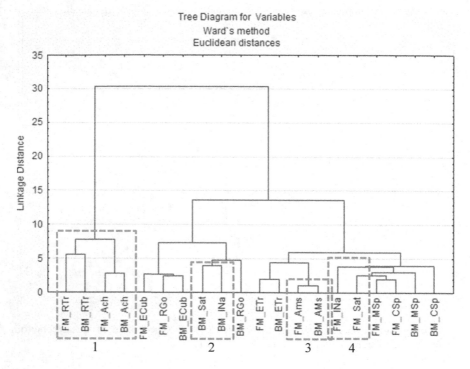

Fig. 6. Dendrogram showing similarity among answers to the questions concerning the two navigation methods: "Bike" (BM) and "Free Hand" (FM). Boxes show noticeable cases.

for the need of training (RTr). Moreover, their low values suggest that these aspects are considered suitable by users in both cases.

Boxes number 2 and 4 highlight the clusters formed by variables "intuitive navigation" (INa) and satisfaction (Sat) for "Bike" and "Free Hand" methods, respectively, suggesting a high correlation between the two variables, which might imply that intuitiveness is a fundamental characteristic of a navigation method.

Box number 3 points out that the users' answers concerning application messages (variable AMs) were almost identical for both methods, meaning that there is virtually no difference between the feedback provided by the application in both cases.

Figure 7 shows the main results of the post-experiment questionnaire concerning the two navigation methods: "Bike" (BM) (blue) and "Free Hand" (FM) (red). It depicts the bar charts of the users' answers to the questions (in a 5 level Likert-type scale) that were significantly different for both methods, from left to right and from top to bottom: CSp - camera speed is adequate, RGo – easy to reach goal, ACh – has annoying characteristics, RTr - requires training, Sat - overall satisfaction. These ordinal variables were tested using Wilcoxon Matched Pairs test which rejected for all these five cases the equality hypothesis with the corresponding p values: CSp: p = 0.0431; RGo: p = 0.0015; ACh: p = 0.0382; RTr: p = 0.0367; Sat: p = 0.0010.

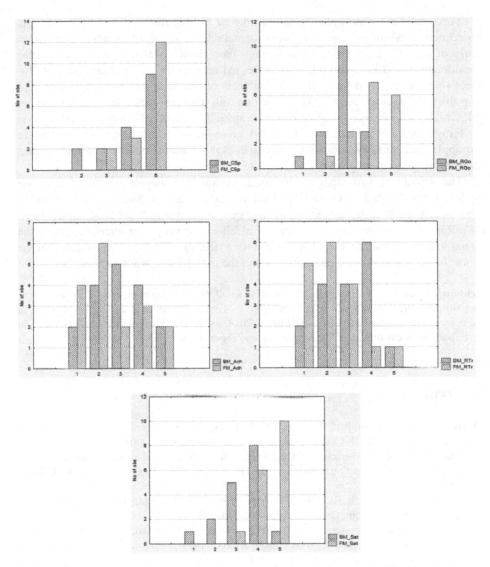

Fig. 7. Questionnaire results concerning the two navigation methods: "Bike" (BM) (blue) and "Free Hand" (FM) (red) for the questions that where significantly different for both methods (in a 5 level like-type scale from 1- totally disagree to 5- totally agree) (from top-left to bottom-right CSp- camera speed is adequate, RGo- easy to reach goal, ACh- has annoying characteristics, RTr- requires training, Sat- overall satisfaction (1- not at all satisfied to 5 – very much satisfied).

5   Conclusions

In this work we address the development and evaluation processes of two gesture-based virtual environment navigation methods designed for interaction with a large display.

Throughout the experiment, a similar interest in both methods was noticed by the experimenter. While the users' performance and satisfaction were significantly better in some of the measured variables with the "Free Hand", we believe that users also considered the "Bike" method as suitable and natural for navigation, and in retrospective we understood that the main constraint of the latter was that users could not stop the interaction efficiently. This is in line with the "non-parkable" issue pointed in [5], which hampers increasing precision in spatial/free-hand 3D interfaces.

Fatigue was not considered in this work given the limited duration of interaction in our application. However for longer interactions this factor should be considered since more tiring gestures might be less adequate.

The affordance provided by the used metaphor, a bicycle handlebar, may be explored visually and is an envisaged future work direction. Such discoverability of possible actions is of the utmost importance since these methods are to be implemented on public displays applications, requiring a self-explanatory user interface, where the visual representation of a bicycle handlebar or a steering wheel or even an avatar of the users' hands, may indicate passing-by users the initial form of interaction.

Acknowledgements. The authors are grateful to all volunteer participants. This work was partially founded by National Funds through FCT - Foundation for Science and Technology, in the context of the project PEst-OE/EEI/UI0127/2014, and by the Program "Partilha e Divulgação de Experiências em Inovação Didática no Ensino Superior Português" (84/ID/2014).

References

1. Bowman, D.A., Coquillart, S., Froehlich, B., Hirose, M.: 3D user interfaces: new directions and perspectives. IEEE Comput. Graphics Appl. **28**(6), 20–36 (2008)
2. Dias, P., Sousa, T., Parracho, J., Cardoso, I., Monteiro, A., Santos, B.S.: Student projects involving novel interaction with large displays. IEEE Comput. Graphics Appl. **34**(2), 80–86 (2014)
3. Ren, G., Li, C., O'Neill, E., Willis, P.: 3D freehand gestural navigation for interactive public displays. IEEE Comput. Graphics Appl. **33**(2), 47–55 (2013)
4. Boulos, M.N.K., Blanchard, B.J., Walker, C., Montero, J., Tripathy, A., Gutierrez-Osuna, R.: Web GIS in practice X: a Microsoft Kinect natural user interface for Google earth navigation. Int. J. Health Geographics **10**(1), 45 (2011)
5. Bowman, D.A.: 3D user interfaces. In: Soegaard, M., Dam, R.F. (eds.) The Encyclopedia of Human-Computer Interaction, 2nd edn. The Interaction Design Foundation, Aarhus (2014). chapter 32, https://www.interaction-design.org/encyclopedia/3d_user_interfaces.html
6. Ren, G., O'Neill, E.: 3D selection with freehand gesture. Comput. Graphics **37**(3), 101–120 (2013)
7. Jankowski, J., Hachet, M.: Advances in interaction with 3D environments. In: Computer Graphics Forum (to appear)
8. Bowman, D.A., Kruijff, E., Poupyrev, I., LaViola, J.: 3D User Interfaces: Theory and Practice. Addison Wesley, Boston (2005)
9. Santos, B.S., Dias, P., Pimentel, A., Baggerman, J.W., Ferreira, C., Silva, S., Madeira, J.: Head-mounted display versus desktop for 3D navigation in virtual reality: a user study. Multimedia Tools Appl. **41**(1), 161–181 (2009)

10. Lapointe, J., Savard, P., Vinson, N.G.: A comparative study of four input devices for desktop virtual walkthroughs. Comput. Hum. Behav. **27**(6), 2186–2191 (2011)
11. Hoaglin, D., Mosteller, F., Tukey, J.: Understanding Robust and Exploratory Data Analysis. Wiley, New York (1983)
12. Hettmansperger, T., McKean, J.: Robust Nonparametric Statistical Methods (Kendall's Library of Statistics), vol. 5, p. 467. Arnold, London (1998)
13. Hair Jr, J., Black, W.C., Babin, B.J., Anderson, R.E.: Multivariate Data Analysis – A global Perspective, 7th edn. Pearson Education, Upper Saddle River (2008)

Immersing Users in Landscapes Using Large Scale Displays in Public Spaces

Giannis Drossis[1(✉)], Antonios Ntelidakis[1], Dimitris Grammenos[1],
Xenophon Zabulis[1], and Constantine Stephanidis[1,2]

[1] Institute of Computer Science, Foundation for Research
and Technology – Hellas (FORTH), N. Plastira 100, Vassilika Vouton,
700 13 Heraklion, Crete, Greece
{drossis,ntelidak,gramenos,zabulis,cs}@ics.forth.gr
[2] Department of Computer Science, University of Crete, Crete, Greece

Abstract. This paper reports on the design and implementation of BeThere-Now, a public interactive information system where users are depicted immersed in various sceneries. The work is focused on the domain of info-tainment in public spaces using large displays and aims on short-time usage. The implemented system employs a mixed reality application through which users are informed about different sceneries and also create personalized digital postcards. This process is accomplished using computer vision algorithms in order to depict users and objects, while removing the background of the scene. Finally, the lessons learned from the long-term deployment of the system out-in-the-wild are presented, providing an insight on the users' actions and reactions and feedback on future research directions.

Keywords: Large scale displays · Interactive public spaces · Immersive user experience · Background segmentation · Green screen · Interactive postal cards

1 Introduction

Public spaces form an important part of our everyday life – they create a sense of belonging, provide a place where we can socialize, relax, and learn something new [3]. A public space is a social space that is generally open and accessible to people, involving necessary, optional and social activities [5].

Public displays are for anyone to interact in a walk-up-and-use [10] manner. In public displays, a large proportion of users are passers-by and thus first-time users. Most of the research on public displays has been carried out by running installations in local communities, yet this research has only recently started. Public spaces such as the bus stop or the cafe can act as 'encounter stages' on which people negotiate boundaries of a social and cultural nature.

Info-tainment [13] is a growing domain which applies to public spaces. Apart from approaches that rely on handheld displays, such as [11, 16], large-scale displays are widely applied for immersive user experience in public displays [12]. Postcards are a widely adopted approach for visitors to state their presence in a specific location.

© Springer International Publishing Switzerland 2015
N. Streitz and P. Markopoulos (Eds.): DAPI 2015, LNCS 9189, pp. 152–162, 2015.
DOI: 10.1007/978-3-319-20804-6_14

Nevertheless, they are passive and fail to natively incorporate the users' presence in a scenery. On the contrary, an interactive system that could mix the real world (the users) with the virtual (the sceneries) could act as an informative system which is more pleasurable and desirable to use.

In this context, this paper describes the design and implementation of a mixed reality system employed in large public displays, in which users are immersed in numerous sceneries. By employing computer vision algorithms, users are depicted standing before the various sceneries, within the landscapes and the vistas projected, as if they were at that place. The system aims to inform and entertain multiple visitors or passers-by in a straightforward manner, while being personal: users see themselves in a large display and are able to seamlessly switch between different landscapes.

2 Related Work

Mixed reality (MR), sometimes referred to as Hybrid reality (encompassing both augmented reality and augmented virtuality) refers to the merging of real and virtual worlds to produce new environments and visualizations, where physical and digital objects co-exist and interact in real time. Mixed reality encompasses augmented reality and augmented virtuality as it does not take place in the physical or the virtual world, but in a combination of the two. Mixed and Augmented Reality is applied in various contexts, including:

- Games: augmented reality is applied to augment tabletop games [19] in order to preserve the physical artifacts of the game, but also enrich the user experience.
- Advertisement: advertising employs Augmented Reality to impress and attract users. Such an early example is MINI's advertisement [6], where users may show a magazine to their webcam in order to view a 3D model of MINI. Furthermore, [7] create an advertisement game in order to promote traditional products in a large scale wall display.
- Cultural Heritage: Mixed reality is applied to augment physical exhibits and allow users to retrieve additional information regarding exhibits of their interest. Grammenos et al. [8] use pieces of paper that host additional information upon placement over areas of interest. Furthermore, Barry et al. [1] use mobile devices to augment a museum's physical world with 3D representations of ancient livings, bridging nowadays with the prehistoric times.

Large scale displays are a common approach for visualizing information in public spaces [2, 9, 17]. A common approach for the display of users within landscapes is the adoption of the green screen [4] (such as in television weather reports). This tactic, however, holds two major drawbacks: firstly, user intervention is required in order to achieve satisfactory results – especially in scenes with lightning variations - but more importantly holds color limitations, as any green objects in the actual world will not be displayed in the final result.

Most of the times users enjoy a personal user experience. Moreover, information sharing and more specifically photographs are a widely used practice [14, 15] which users appreciate. Furthermore, photographs act as keepsakes and allow users to take home the presented information or share them with their friends or relatives (person-to-person information sharing).

3 Be There Now!

3.1 The Concept

The concept of BeThereNow is based on the idea of creating an immersive application, where users are depicted standing in various sceneries as if they were there. The objectives of our work can be summarized as follows:

- The system should work like a **magic mirror**, where users watch themselves in the display, as if they were standing in various sceneries.
- Users (**Foreground**) should be depicted in front of various landscapes (**Background**).
- Straightforward usage.
- Apply meaningful, elegant and aesthetically pleasing means of changing the displayed sceneries.
- Effective and precise background subtraction.
- Users should be able to capture digital photographs and send them by email.
- The system should not be static, but provide a demonstration mode which intrigues the users to engage with it.

Fig. 1. The setup as designed in a 3D model prototype (a depth sensor is located at the top, a touch screen at the left, an interactive cube at the right and the projection in the middle)

The system is used in a walk up and use manner while also offering users the ability to browse through different sceneries. Therefore, once the users step in front of the display they are instantly shown. Meanwhile, a physical cube (Figs. 1 and 4) resides next to the display, which can be rotated in order to switch through the various sceneries. When the cube is rotated, a synchronized virtual cube - having the different landscapes at its sides - is also rotated, creating a one to one mapping of the actual with the virtual object. This metaphor is also applied when the demonstration mode is applied, where the virtual cube starts rotating and the landscapes are therefore switched after a short interval (30 s). The demonstration mode is enabled when no users are near the system and disabled upon any user entering the effective area in front of it. Users can use a secondary touch display, residing at the side of the display, in order to either change the language of the displayed image description or take a snapshot of themselves in the currently displayed scenery. The system's overall rendering process is separated in two primary sections: **Background** and **Foreground**. Background refers to the pictures of the sceneries used to immerse the users into, while foreground contains the users or objects that stand in front of the display. The background is in essence the virtual cube, while the foreground is estimated using a background removal process.

An additional optional capability of the system is the addition of **Foreground Mask** to sceneries: some areas of the background can appear in front of the users (e.g. objects such as a desk). This option enhances the reality of the settings as users can be immersed in a room, standing, for instance, in front of a desk and appear as if they are studying. Additionally, another usage example involves showing theatrical costumes (Fig. 5), which the visitors can virtually 'wear' by standing in such a position that their bodies are completely hidden and only some of their parts are visible. The overall rendering process is illustrated in Fig. 2 below.

Fig. 2. Rendering order of different application layers: **Background** contains the pictures of the background sceneries, **Foreground** refers to the picture of the users and **Foreground Mask** includes all the parts of the background that appear in front of the users

3.2 Implementation

Computer Vision Algorithm

Silhouette extractor. The vision module employs a typical RGB-D sensor (i.e. Microsoft Kinect or an Asus Xtion camera). RGB-D sensors provide two images: a conventional RGB image and a depth image registered to the former one. Through the depth image, the 3D coordinates of surfaces in the RGB image are measured.

In case that the RGB sensor is judged insufficient in terms of quality or resolution, an additional high resolution RGB camera is employed, which is rigidly mounted on top of the RGB-D sensor. Then, color images are provided by the additional camera, while color images from the RGB-D sensor are disregarded. The aforementioned was mainly the case for early RGB-D sensors but is not required for more modern ones (i.e. Kinect 2) as they also provide a high end color camera.

The sensor is placed so that covers the scene including the ground plane (see Fig. 1) and thereafter calibrated so as to estimate its relative posture to the scene. A computer vision component is responsible for two things. First it detects objects (persons) in the depth image, finds their outlying contours, and maps these contours to the color image. Then, these contours determine the portion of the color images to be displayed as foreground in the large scale display.

Calibration. Calibration is a two-step process. The first is conventional intrinsic and extrinsic, grid-based calibration [18]. If an additional color camera is employed, it is this one that is calibrated instead of that of the RGB-D sensor. Using this calibration, the location of an imaged 3D point in the depth image, is found in the color image.

The second determines a cuboidal volume in the scene, aligned with the ground plane, which we call out "working volume". Only within this volume objects (persons) are considered by the system. To achieve this, the ground plane is estimated first, by imaging an empty scene and extracting the 3D points of the ground plane. By least-squares fitting of a plane to these points, the ground plane is approximated. The two lateral to the camera planes of the cuboid are perpendicular to the camera axis. The remainder cuboid faces are defined from the aforementioned planes, so that they limit the working space according to the sensor's range so that very distal surfaces are not considered.

Foreground segmentation. The method finds the foreground in the color image, using the 3D information that the depth image avails. At each frame, input to the method is the depth and color images. The system finds surface points within the working volume in 3D, as well as, the regions where these surfaces occur in the depth image as silhouettes. These silhouettes are mapped to the color image to the foreground.

Due to sensor limitations, the depth image often exhibits pixels with missing values. This hinders foreground detection because the effect is intensely pronounced upon outlines, due to the depth discontinuity that they image; and, in our application, also due to human hair.

To reduce missing depth values, we apply nearest neighbour NN filling for such missing values. That is for an invalid pixel we assign the depth value of the nearest valid depth pixel with a neighborhood, if any, to the invalid pixel we currently evaluate. The output is the processed depth image which is henceforth called D.

We use image D to compute the 3D points of the scene within the working volume. These are foreground 3D points. The 2D pixels corresponding to these points define foreground mask M upon D. Next, a connected component procedure is employed on M in order to isolate the blobs corresponding to humans. Thus the blobs are filtered according to their size, excluding minute blobs that occur due to sensor noise. For each resultant blob we extract the external contours as well as the internal contours. Minute internal contours are attributed to sensor noise and are filled.

Using the calibration between the depth and color camera, the 3D counterparts of the contour pixels in the depth image are predicted in the color image. In this way, the contours from the depth image are transferred to the color image. Note that due to the aforementioned NN preprocessing all such pixels have a depth value. We apply a 2D

Gaussian smoothing on the transferred contours to account for possible inaccuracies. Areas in the color image encapsulated by the smoothed contours C map of the foreground in the depth image (see Figs. 1 and 6).

The final step of the algorithm is to encode the result by creating an RGBA image. The RGB channels of this image are copied from the color image. The alpha channel contains the, aforementioned, mask of the foreground. Channel A is created by filling the external contours in C, but not the internal ones. In practice, the alpha channel is employed to restrict the color RGBA image so that only the foreground appears in it.

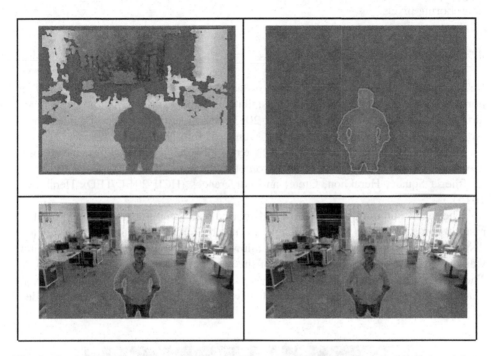

Fig. 3. Overview of the proposed approach. The processed depth image (top left) is used to compute 3D points of the scene and keep those within the working volume and above the floor plane. We apply a connected component procedure on the corresponding depth pixels and we extract the contours of the size-dominant blobs (top right). Since cameras are calibrated, contours from the depth image can be mapped to the color image, projecting upon it their 3D counterparts (bottom left). Contours are finally smoothed to account for inaccuracies (bottom right).

Technologies used. The system was developed using Microsoft's XNA framework in combination with Windows Presentation Foundation (WPF). XNA is used for the rendering of the users in the various landscapes, while the user interface is implemented using WPF. The computer vision component was developed using C ++. Finally, an Arduino board equipped with a light sensor was used for the identification of the cube's orientation.

An optimization that was needed involved smoothing the persons' outline. Due to the sensor's inefficiency in accurately discriminating the foreground (the people's shapes) from the background (what lays behind the users in the real world), a custom smoothing algorithm was needed in order to fade out the boundaries of the foreground. An early implementation was developed in CPU but was later replaced by an HLSL shader, running in GPU, due to performance drop. The computer vision component provides the users' contours slightly inflated and thus containing a few pixels of the background as an outline. At rendering stage, the outline is faded out, using a neighbor-based algorithm, where each pixel's alpha value is the average of all its neighboring pixels.

4   Deployment in Public Spaces

BeThereNow is currently permanently installed in several public spaces, including ports, airports and museums. These installations include the Heraklion and Chania airports (since July 2013 and November 2013 respectively), Telloglion Foundation of Art (since January 2014) and Heraklion Municipal Info-point (since January 2015).

Additionally, it has been deployed in temporary public installations, including a travel trade show (ITB Berlin, 2014), promotional events (World Tourism Day 2013, Eleftheria Square, Heraklion, Crete) and conferences (HCII 2014, TEDx Heraklion, 2015).

The visual output of the system was displayed using an ultra-short-throw projector, resulting in a projection 2.7 m wide and 1.6 m tall. Furthermore, a 12" touch monitor displaying a camera graphic was used to allow taking photographs. The touch monitor was also used to change the language of the descriptions presented at the projection. The displays are accompanied by a physical cube, equipped with a rotation sensor, placed at the opposite side of the touch display (Figs. 1 and 3). The cube also included

Fig. 4. Heraklion airport installation

Fig. 5. Users interacting with the setup at Telloglion Foundation of art. Users are virtually wearing theatrical costumes (left) and sitting on chairs (right)

magnets so as to provide a physical constraint and stabilize the rotations that the cube would end up to.

Sometimes people used their own cameras or smartphones in order to acquire a photograph, not noticing the system's related functionality. When more than one user was approaching the system concurrently the extra functionality was noticed by the users that were not distracted by having a camera in hand. In general, users in groups tended to focus on the entertaining part of the system, rather than exploring different sceneries. For example in Fig. 6, a girl is grabbing her friend to approach the system and take a photo together.

Fig. 6. A girl is insisting on taking a group photo, grabbing her friend by the arm and laughing after taking it.

In total, more than **21000 photographs** have been taken up to now using the system in permanent installations. The photographs provided extensive feedback on the ways that people used the system. The following points summarize the ways that they used the system, sorted according to how often they were noticed. People:

- Tried to take a serious posture while looking as appealing as possible.
- Made comical expressions or postures.
- Pretended to interact with elements of the scenery (e.g. Fig. 5 - objects, animals, etc.)
- Stood still and serious, keeping a more disciplined posture.
- Walked away from the system, hesitating to appear inside a photograph and resulting into an empty scenery.

It is worth mentioning that children that interacted with the system always took more than one photograph, thus underlining the entertaining nature of the system. The same pattern was also noticed in the case of multiple users concurrently using the system, where not only they were photographed more than once, but also in different backgrounds.

5 Lessons Learned

On-site observation was used to gain an insight on people's actions and reactions using the system. The system was in general met with excitement by the users. People of all ages, ranging from young children to elderly, appeared to enjoy interacting with it. The vast majority of users could straightforwardly understand how to take photographs and manipulate the sceneries using the physical cube.

The main conclusions can be summarized as follows:

- Make interactive parts distinct and differentiate them from the system's physical setup, so that they are clearly noticeable.
- Allow people to interact both with the system and with each other.
- Users in groups tend to focus more on the entertaining and fun aspects of the system, rather than on information provision.
- People share their personal information without second thoughts (e.g. email address) when they are going to receive something that includes their own image.
- Keepsakes aid in creating a feeling of being personally engaged with the system.

6 Conclusions

The response to the system by people of all ages was unanimously positive. The concept of immersing users in various landscapes created a positive emotion to both the people who used the system, but also to bystanders. Users were intrigued by the displayed sceneries to approach the system and were able to interact instantaneously, usually being surprised in a positive manner when seeing themselves on the large display.

The system's permanent installations served their purpose by both informing passers-by and entertaining them in various contexts, such as the airports' arrivals hall and museums. Users explored various local sightseeing locations and exhibited elements respectively, offering them the ability to become a part of the displayed vistas that would be otherwise unattainable, as if they were there. The system succeeded in drawing people's attention, both for urging them to engage with the system and for the bystanders, who watched other users being immersed in the projected landscapes.

Acknowledgements. The work reported in this paper has been conducted in the context of the AmI Programme of the Institute of Computer Science of the Foundation for Research and Technology-Hellas (FORTH). The authors would like to express their gratitude to Thanasis Toutountzis for his aid in manufacturing the rotating cube, as well as Manolis Apostolakis and Manolis Stamatakis who shaped the artistic concept and helped in the creation of the permanent installations.

References

1. Barry, A., Trout, J., Debenham, P., Thomas, G.: Augmented reality in a public space: the natural history museum. London Comput. **7**, 42–47 (2012)
2. Brignull, H., Rogers, Y.: Enticing people to interact with large public displays in public spaces. In: Proceedings of INTERACT, vol. 3, pp. 17–24 (2003)
3. Carr, S., Francis, M., Rivlin, L.G., Stone, A.M.: Public Space. Cambridge University Press, Cambridge (1992)
4. Foster, J.: The Green Screen Handbook: Real-World Production Techniques. CRC Press, Boca Raton (2014)
5. Jan, G.: Life Between Buildings: Using Public Space. Island Press, Washington (2011)
6. Geekology. Cool: Augmented Reality Advertisements, http://www.geekologie.com/2008/12/14-week, 19 December 2008. 19 (Accessed 20 April 2015)
7. Grammenos, D., Margetis, G., Koutlemanis, P., Zabulis, X.: Paximadaki, the game: creating an advergame for promoting traditional food products. In: Proceeding of the 16th International Academic MindTrek Conference, pp. 287–290. ACM (October, 2012)
8. Grammenos, D., Zabulis, X., Michel, D., Padeleris, P., Sarmis, T., Georgalis, G., Koutlemanis, P., Tzevanidis, K., Argyros, A.A., Sifakis, M., Adam-Veleni, P., Stephanidis, C.: Macedonia from Fragments to Pixels: a permanent exhibition of interactive systems at the archaeological museum of Thessaloniki. In: Ioannides, M., Fritsch, D., Leissner, J., Davies, R., Remondino, F., Caffo, R. (eds.) EuroMed 2012. LNCS, vol. 7616, pp. 602–609. Springer, Heidelberg (2012)
9. Hornecker, E.: "I don't understand it either, but it is cool"-visitor interactions with a multi-touch table in a museum. In: 3rd IEEE International Workshop on Horizontal Interactive Human Computer Systems, TABLETOP 2008, pp. 113–120. IEEE (October, 2008)
10. Shahram, I., et al.: Dynamo: a public interactive surface supporting the cooperative sharing and exchange of media. In: Proceedings of the 16th annual ACM Symposium on User Interface Software and Technology. ACM (2003)
11. Keil, J., Pujol, L., Roussou, M., Engelke, T., Schmitt, M., Bockholt, U., Eleftheratou, S.: A digital look at physical museum exhibits. In: Proceedings of the Digital Heritage (2013)
12. Lantz, E.: A survey of large-scale immersive displays. In: Proceedings of the 2007 Workshop on Emerging Displays Technologies: Images and Beyond: The Future of Displays and Interaction, p. 1. ACM (August, 2007)
13. Lucas, A.M.: 'Info-tainment' and informal sources for learning science. Int. J. Sci. Educ. **13** (5), 495–504 (1991)

14. Neustaedter, C., Fedorovskaya, E.: Capturing and sharing memories in a virtual world. In: Proceedings of the SIGCHI Conference on Human Factors in Computing Systems, pp. 1161–1170. ACM (April, 2009)

15. Nunes, M., Greenberg, S., Neustaedter, C.: Sharing digital photographs in the home through physical mementos, souvenirs, and keepsakes. In: Proceedings of the 7th ACM Conference on Designing Interactive Systems, pp. 250–260. ACM (February, 2008)

16. Madsen, C.B., Madsen, J.B., Morrison, A.: Aspects of what makes or breaks a museum ar experience. In: 2012 IEEE International Symposium on Mixed and Augmented Reality (ISMAR-AMH), pp. 91–92. IEEE (November, 2012)

17. Russell, D.M., Trimble, J.P., Dieberger, A.: The use patterns of large, interactive display surfaces: case studies of media design and use for BlueBoard and MERBoard. In: Proceedings of the 37th Annual Hawaii International Conference on System Sciences 2004, p. 10. IEEE (January, 2004)

18. Tsai, R.Y.: An efficient and accurate camera calibration technique for 3D machine vision. In: Proceedings of IEEE Conference on Computer Vision and Pattern Recognition, Miami Beach, FL, pp. 364–374 (1986)

19. Zidianakis, E., Antona, M., Paparoulis, G., Stephanidis, C.: An augmented interactive table supporting preschool children development through playing. In: Proceedings of the AHFE International 2012, pp. 21–25 (2012)

A Gesture Recognition Method
for Proximity-Sensing Surfaces in Smart
Environments

Biying Fu[1]([✉]), Tobias Grosse-Puppendahl[1], and Arjan Kuijper[1,2]

[1] Fraunhofer IGD, Fraunhoferstr. 5, 64283 Darmstadt, Germany
{biying.fu,tobias.grosse-puppendahl}@igd.fraunhofer.de
[2] Technische Universität Darmstadt, Hochschulstr. 10, 64289 Darmstadt, Germany
arjan.kuijper@gris.tu-darmstadt.de

Abstract. In order to ease the daily activities in life, a growing number of sophisticated embedded systems is integrated into a users environment. People are in need to communicate with the machines embedded in the surroundings via interfaces which should be as natural as possible. A very natural way of interaction can be implemented via gestures. Gestures should be intuitive, easy to interpret and to learn. In this paper, we propose a method for in-the-air gesture recognition within smart environments. The algorithm used to determine the performed gesture is based on dynamic time warping. We apply 12 capacitive proximity sensors as sensing area to collect gestures. The hand positions within a gesture are converted into features which will be matched with dynamic time warping. The gesture carried out above the sensing area are interpreted in realtime. Gestures supported can be used to control various applications like entertainment systems or other home automation systems.

Keywords: Gesture recognition · Dynamic time warping · Capacitive proximity sensing

1 Introduction

In-the-air gesture recognition within smart environments offers a number of highly promising application scenarios. They range from increasing hygiene in public restrooms to touchless interactions with infrastructure, such as doors. In this paper, we investigate the use of a proximity-sensing surface in smart environments. Being based on capacitive sensing, it can detect human interactions within distances of up to 30 cm [4]. The surface can be attached to walls, placed within doors, or integrated underneath tables. A particular challenge is the design of computationally-cheap algorithms for recognizing gestures. In this work, we identify relevant gestures based on a number of potential use-cases and propose a generic method for gesture recognition. It employs computationally inexpensive algorithms that can be implemented on low-cost embedded systems.

© Springer International Publishing Switzerland 2015
N. Streitz and P. Markopoulos (Eds.): DAPI 2015, LNCS 9189, pp. 163–173, 2015.
DOI: 10.1007/978-3-319-20804-6_15

Latest developments in our society lead to the use of smart technologies that simplify everyday activities in life. More and more applications in the areas of human machine interfaces are demanded, all having the same goal of sensing human interactions in a more or less natural manner. Capacitive gesture-recognition systems are able to fulfill this need while offering highly interactive system designs at low cost. A great benefit of capacitive sensing is the ability of being installed unobtrusively under any non-conductive surface.

Fig. 1. A proximity-sensing surface acting as a door opener from [5]. Users are able to open and close the door based on swipe-gestures.

In order to specify the requirements for our proposed gesture-recognition method, we identified a number of use-cases.

1. *Interaction with a smart door* (shown in Fig. 1): Due to hygiene consideration in a public restroom, it will be practical to open, lock, unlock and close the door without touching the doorknob. The state of the door (e.g. locking it) can be easily changed using simple hand gestures, as introduced in [5].
2. *Controlling roller blinds:* A proximity-sensing surfaces can be used to open and close the roller. Here, vertical swipe gestures offer a natural way of controlling the appliance.
3. *Controlling Entertainment Systems:* Those supported gestures can be used to control a music player or other entertainment applications.
4. *Soft authentication in restricted areas:* By carrying out an authentication gesture, doors can be locked or unlocked. Moreover, alarms can be switched off in combination with occupancy detection.
5. *Controlling lights and illumination:* Gestures in front of a proximity-sensing surface can be employed to turn lights on and off. Moreover, circular gestures allow to dim the lights to ones needs.

2   Related Work

Providing means for natural interaction is an important goals when designing smart environments. For example, the user could switch on a standing lamp just with a simple hand gesture when she or he enters the room. It is also possible to use the whole body for interaction, for example by analyzing postures on furniture [6]. However, in this paper we aim at recognizing gestures carried out by a human hand. Many different modalities have been applied for gesture recognition, many of them based on cameras like the Microsoft Kinect [9]. Other modalities include capacitive approaches, for example by using body-attached electric field sensors [3], or ultrasound [7].

Camera based gesture recognition uses image processing and statistical methods like HMMs or DTW to perform gestures recognition. However, computer vision approaches are computationally expensive, as the bandwidth of information is very large. Here, the challenge is to efficiently extract information needed in a short time, in order to perform live gesture recognition. Capacitive sensing on the other hand is low power and efficient. Using this modality, several gesture recognition methods have been investigate, like [2] or the Swiss-Cheese Extended Algorithm presented in [4]. In the latter work, the authors use models to eliminate areas, in which no object may exists. Object tracking is performed with a particle filter to measure which predicts the new user's hand position above the sensing area. The algorithm is able to recognize and track multiple hands in real time. As this approach may not be executed on a microcontroller, we will present an approach based on Dynamic Time Warping (DTW).

DTW is a widely used method to perform gesture recognition. In [10], the authors developed a microcontroller-optimized implementation to warp a long common subsequence with a reference sequence and feedback the spotted subsequence in real time. This implementation can also be used to detect the QRS complex in a long ECG time signal as well as to detect a predefined gestures within a time sequence. Very similarly, we will use DTW as a basis for our gesture recognition method in this paper. In the next chapter, the chosen method for gesture recognition above a capacitive sensing area will be explained in detail.

3   Proposed Gesture Recognition Model

As we intend the proximity-sensing surface to be low-cost and installed ubiquitously in a user's environment, our focus lies on computationally inexpensive algorithms. The implementation was realized based on the Rainbowfish platform [4], which is depicted in Fig. 1. It consists of 12 transparent electrodes each serving as a capacitive proximity sensor. The overall proximity sensing surface of the Rainbwofish has a dimension of 40 cm × 25 cm containing 12 rectangular transparent electrodes used for determining the position of a human hand. It is also possible to feedback live performed user actions using LED lights integrated beneath the transparent platform, which can also be seen in the depicted figure. Object localization above the sensing surface is performed using a straightforward weighted averaging method developed by [1], which offers a fast way of position calculation. To provide a smoother localization, a 2D position estimation Kalman Filter is also implemented. The estimated position by Kalman Filter is further improved by the measurement.

The next major step is the gesture recognition and thus its interpretation, in order to make interaction between user and their environment possible. With our proposed method we can quickly and almost confidently detect a set of simple hand gestures based on the traditional dynamic time warping method. All recognizable gestures so far using single hand is listed in the Fig. 2. In the following sections the implementation will be further explained in detail aiming to give you an better impression of how gesture recognition is done.

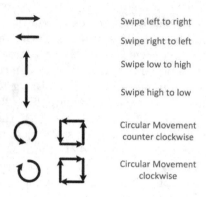

Fig. 2. Figure illustrates all confidently recognizable simple hand gestures using dynamic time warping method.

3.1 Dynamic Time Warping

The method of dynamic time warping presented in [8] is used to compare two time series, while one of them is usually based on a template database of reference hand gestures. In order to find the best match of a given time series compared to a template database, a cost function is calculated for two sequences prepared. The best match with the highest score, or the lowest cost, will be the intended hand gesture out of the predefined database. The mapping is performed in a nonlinear fashion, since the length of a performed gesture can be varied which depend on the gesture's speed. Therefore, the two time series could be non-linearly scaled in order to optimally match each other.

Following this approach brings in one constraint: the first element and the last elements of both time series should be mapped together, which is the so called boundary condition. Suppose we have two time series $A = (a_i)$ with Index $i = 1..N$ and $B = (b_j)$ with Index $j = 1..M$, whereas the length of both sequences could be different. We are looking for an optimal path between these two sequences with the smallest score, whereat (a_1, b_1) and (a_N, b_M) should be mapped together. The concept is illustrated in Fig. 3. The score matrix of dimension NxM can be built comparing elements of both time series with each other. The path through the score matrix will always be the sum of the smallest score differences. Possible scores can be built using the Euclidean distance, some error measures or other self-defined scores adapted to the individual need.

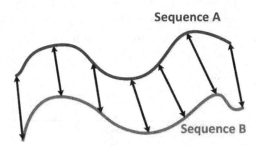

Fig. 3. Figure illustrates the method of dynamic time warping. Two different sequences A and B are aligned to each other in an optimum path using minimum score.

3.2   Implementation

As described in the introduction, a time series of hand positions will be sampled in time into a discrete sequence. Depending on the duration above the sensing area, the gesture can be of different lengths. Each short sequence within the gesture is converted into features, which is used to conduct the time warping method in order to interpret the performed gesture. In the following paragraph, the feature extraction will be explained in detail. The feature representation is illustrated in Fig. 4 with a simple circular chart diagram. The radial component of this circular chart represents the velocity component of the consisting part of a gesture. One single gesture is sampled in consisting hand positions above the sensing area. From one sample point to the successive sample point the velocity component will be calculated. If it is below a certain threshold, it will be interpreted as an indecisive slow movement and will be represented with the character Z. Otherwise, the angular movement of the velocity component will be calculated and mapped adequately to the appropriate angular character. The start of the gesture is set, if the user's hand is above the sensing area and thus the starting command will be filled with a character S symbolizing the start of this gesture. The ongoing gesture is evaluated as long as the gesture can be recognized and the final termination of the determined gesture can be set by leaving the sensing area. As soon as the user's hand leaves the sensing area, the end character E will be added to the command stream. An E can also be generated when the hand remains above a certain point for a longer time. This ensures that there is no obligation of leaving the surface with the hand. The definition of the used character can be found in Table 1.

Table 1. The meaning of the characters used in the dynamic time warping method.

Character	Definition
S	Start of a gesture
Z	Slow velocity component between two successive parts of a gesture
D	Angular component indicating horizontal movement from left to right
B	Angular component indicating horizontal movement from right to left
C	Angular component indicating vertical movement from high to low
A	Angular component indicating vertical movement from low to high
E	End of a gesture

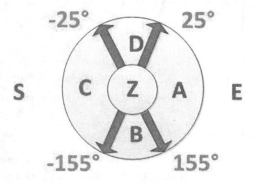

Fig. 4. The figure illustrates the way how the tangent of relative movement is mapped to the respective string character. A character S will be added, when the user's hand is detected on the sensing area for the first time and the character E will be added when no object is above the sensing plane. As long as the relative movement is small, the character Z is added, otherwise the other characters in the circle chart will be added accordingly.

The graphical interpretation of the angular distribution with respect to their corresponding string characters can be seen in Fig. 4. Due to the geometric property of the sensing area, where the length is broader than the width, it is reasonable to chose the angular distribution such that it is in favor of the horizontal movement. Caused by the larger x-axis with respect to the y-axis, the user has more freedom and precision by performing horizontal swipes.

An exemplary template for horizontal gesture moves from left to the right can be represented by a sequence like $SDDDE$, whereas real-world may also contain noise such as $SDDDZZDDDE$. Therefore, the temporally stretched real-world strings will be compared with all possible reference command strings. The reference gesture with the lowest score and thus the highest matching score is the intended user gesture. One special cost function and it's distance function can be seen in the Figs. 5 and 6.

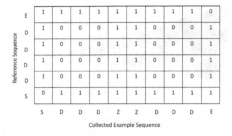 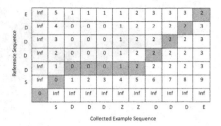

Fig. 5. The cost function for the collected performed gesture on the x-axis with the reference string on the y-axis is depicted. The cost is 1, if the character is mismatched.

Fig. 6. The dist function is depicted in the figure. The yellow path follows the best alignment from the end of the sequence backwards to the beginning of the sequence (Color figure online).

With following assumptions, I used two additional weighting functions to further improve the cost of the dynamic time warping method, which are both of temporary and spatially natures. Since the sensing area is large, the gesture performed in the middle of the sensing area should be more intended and precise as on the border of the sensing area. Therefore the spatial weighting function will be given by the Eq. 1.

$$w(x, y) = 1 - A \cdot exp\left(-\frac{\left(x - \frac{L}{2}\right)^2}{2} - \frac{\left(y - \frac{W}{2}\right)^2}{2 \cdot \sigma_y^2} \right) \tag{1}$$

The uncertainty in the y direction is larger, since as mentioned previously the geometric dimension of the x direction is larger than the y direction. In Eq. (1) L means the length

$$L = x_{max} - x_{min}$$

and W means the width

$$W = y_{max} - y_{min}$$

of the sensing area and A is a constant factor. The penalty is the smallest in the middle of the sensing area and enlarged at both sides as can be seen from Fig. 7. Furthermore I presume that the gesture in the middle of the time sequence is more intended and precise than at the beginning or at the end of a gesture. Suppose the length of the command sequence is L, then the weighting function can be give by Eq. 2.

$$w(n) = 1 - \frac{1}{\sqrt{2\pi}} \cdot exp\left(-\frac{\left(n - \frac{L}{2}\right)^2}{2} \right) \tag{2}$$

In Eq. 2 the index n stands for the index of character collected in time and L is the number of the overall gesture collected so far. The penalty is larger at

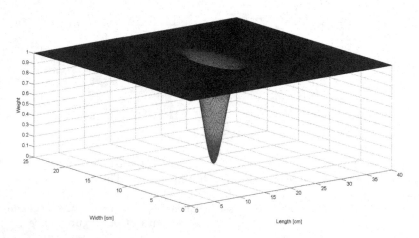

Fig. 7. The spatial weighting function in Eq. 1 with $W = 25\,\mathrm{cm}$, $L = 40\,\mathrm{cm}$ and $\sigma_y = 1.6$.

the beginning and the end of a sequence, while the penalty is zero exactly in the middle of the sequence.

The software realization can be found in the flow chart in Fig. 8. The capacitive sensors keep actively measuring the activities above the sensing area. Once it detects the presence of a user's hand, the start character S will be added to the command sequence. Afterward it keeps reading sensor values to update the gesture. The corresponding string command keeps adding to the existing command sequence. The algorithm keeps detecting the gesture performed by the user in realtime, as long as the user's hand does not leave the sensing area. As soon as the user's hand leaves the sensing area, the last gesture will be analyzed and afterward the command sequence will be cleared, such that the system will be ready for a new gesture.

4   Validation and Interpretation

Based on a user study conducted with 10 different test persons, we evaluated the feasibility of our proposed method. Each test person was supposed to execute the presented gestures given in Fig. 2. Each gesture was performed ten times above the sensing area. The result is evaluated and summarized in the confusion matrix, which is shown in Table 2.

From the confusion matrix given in Table 2, we can seen that the circular movements can be detected with a true positive rate of more than 98 %, while the other simple linear gestures can be assigned a true positive rate of more than 90 % as well. It is quite apparent, that the performed circular movements clockwise or anticlockwise are recognized with very high accuracy, while the simple linear movements are less accurate, but still with a detection rate of over 90 %. Simple linear movements is less error prone, since the capacitive sensing

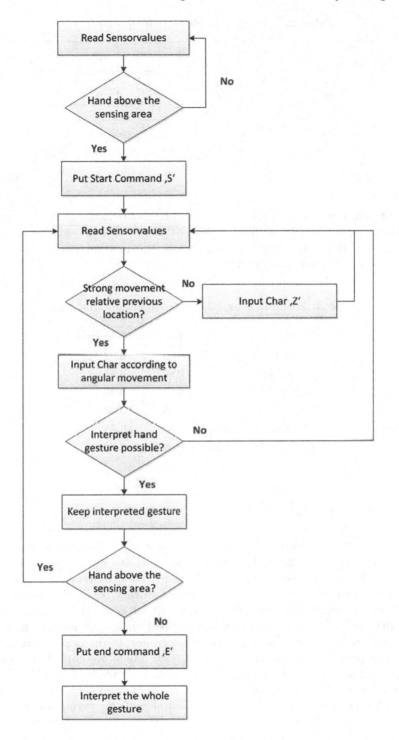

Fig. 8. Figure illustrates the flow chart of the software implementation.

Table 2. The table shows the confusion matrix.

classified \ True	⇒	⇐	⇑	⇓	↻	↺
⇒	92		5	6		
⇐		96			1	1
⇑	4	3	95	3		
⇓	4	1		90		
↻				1	98	1
↺					1	98

area is too sensitive, that it measures every tiny movements above the sensing area. The recoginition rate is high, if the gesture are clearly performed.

To have a more precise expression of how the method works, we use the precision and recall matrix (Table 3).

Table 3. The table shows the precision and recall matrix.

Gestures	Precision	Recall
Swipe Right	0.89	0.92
Swipe Left	0.98	0.96
Swipe Upward	0.91	0.95
Swipe Down	0.95	0.90
Circular Clockwise	0.98	0.98
Circular Anticlockwise	0.99	0.98

5   Conclusion and Outlook

In this paper, the proposed gesture recognition was successfully realized using dynamic time warping method. A user study is conveyed and the results are evaluated and summarized. It showed that the circular movements clockwise or anticlockwise can be detected with very high accuracy, while the simple linear movements are somehow not so error prone. But all in all, the allowed gestures can be detected with quite high certainty in real time. The implementation is simple and can be coded on a simple micro-controller. In the near future, further goal is to expand gesture recognition with both hands accomplishing different more complicated gestures on the left and right side of the sensor board. We hope to allow more complex interactions with the environment, such as turning a virtual key gestures, and further more natural gestures performed with both hands.

References

1. Braun, A., Hamisu, P.: Using the human body field as a medium for natural interaction. In: Proceedings of the 2Nd International Conference on PErvasive Technologies Related to Assistive Environments, PETRA 2009, pp. 50:1–50:7. ACM, New York (2009). http://doi.acm.org/10.1145/1579114.1579164
2. Braun, A., Hamisu, P.: Designing a multi-purpose capacitive proximity sensing input device. In: PETRA 2011, pp. 151–158 (2011). http://dl.acm.org/citation.cfm?doid=2141622.2141641
3. Cohn, G., Morris, D., Patel, S., Tan, D.: Humantenna: Using the body as an antenna for real-time whole-body interaction. In: Proceedings of the SIGCHI Conference on Human Factors in Computing Systems, CHI 2012, pp. 1901–1910. ACM, New York (2012). http://doi.acm.org/10.1145/2207676.2208330
4. Grosse-Puppendahl, T., Beck, S., Wilbers, D.: Rainbowfish: Visual feedback on gesture-recognizing surfaces. In: CHI 2014 Extended Abstracts on Human Factors in Computing Systems, CHI EA 2014, pp. 427–430. ACM, New York (2014). http://www.opencapsense.org/fileadmin/opencapsense-org/publications/chi2014.pdf
5. Grosse-Puppendahl, T., Beck, S., Wilbers, D., Zeiß, S., von Wilmsdorff, J., Kuijper, A.: Ambient gesture-recognizing surfaces with visual feedback. In: Streitz, N., Markopoulos, P. (eds.) DAPI 2014. LNCS, vol. 8530, pp. 97–108. Springer, Heidelberg (2014). http://dx.doi.org/10.1007/978-3-319-07788-8_10
6. Große-Puppendahl, T.A., Marinc, A., Braun, A.: Classification of user postures with capacitive proximity sensors in AAL-environments. In: Keyson, D.V., Maher, M.L., Streitz, N., Cheok, A., Augusto, J.C., Wichert, R., Englebienne, G., Aghajan, H., Kröse, B.J.A. (eds.) AmI 2011. LNCS, vol. 7040, pp. 314–323. Springer, Heidelberg (2011). http://dx.doi.org/10.1007/978-3-642-25167-2_43
7. Gupta, S., Morris, D., Patel, S., Tan, D.: Soundwave: Using the doppler effect to sense gestures. In: Proceedings of the SIGCHI Conference on Human Factors in Computing Systems, CHI 2012, pp. 1911–1914. ACM, New York (2012). http://doi.acm.org/10.1145/2207676.2208331
8. Kruskal, J.B., Liberman, M.: The symmetric time-warping problem: from continuous to discrete. In: Sankoff, D., Kruskal, J.B. (eds.) Time Warps, String Edits, and Macromolecules - The Theory and Practice of Sequence Comparison, chap. 4. CSLI Publications, Stanford (1999)
9. Pheatt, C., Wayman, A.: Using the xbox kinect™ sensor for gesture recognition. J. Comput. Sci. Coll. 28(5), 226–227 (2013). http://dl.acm.org/citation.cfm?id=2458569.2458617
10. Roggen, D., Cuspinera, L.P., Pombo, G., Ali, F., Nguyen-Dinh, L.-V.: Limited-memory warping LCSS for real-time low-power pattern recognition in wireless nodes. In: Abdelzaher, T., Pereira, N., Tovar, E. (eds.) EWSN 2015. LNCS, vol. 8965, pp. 151–167. Springer, Heidelberg (2015)

Developing Intuitive Gestures for Spatial Interaction with Large Public Displays

Yubo Kou[1(✉)], Yong Ming Kow[2], and Kelvin Cheng[3]

[1] Department of Informatics, University of California, Irvine, CA, USA
yubok@uci.edu
[2] School of Creative Media, City University of Hong Kong, Hong Kong, China
yongmkow@cityu.edu.hk
[3] Keio-NUS CUTE Center, National University of Singapore,
Singapore, Singapore
idmkksc@nus.edu.sg

Abstract. Freehand gestures used in gestural-based interactive systems are often designed around technical limitations of gesture capturing technologies, resulting in gestures that may not be intuitive to users. In this paper, we investigated freehand gestures that are intuitive to users with common technical knowledge. We conducted a gesture solicitation study with 30 participants, who were asked to complete 21 tasks on a large display using freehand gestures. All gestures in the study were video-recorded. We conducted in-depth interviews with each participant to ask about the gestures they had chosen and why they had chosen them. We found that a large proportion of intuitive freehand gestures had metaphoric origins from daily uses of two-dimensional surface displays, such as smart phones and tablets. However, participants may develop new gestures, particularly when objects they are manipulating deviated from those commonly seen in surface technologies. In this paper, we discuss when and why participants developed new gestures rather than reusing gestures of similar tasks on two-dimension surface displays. We suggest design implications for gestures for large public displays.

Keywords: Large displays · Gestures · Freehand · Spatial interaction

1 Introduction

In recent years, the popularization of more robust and affordable depth-sensing cameras, such as the Microsoft Kinect, has made it easier for large display developers to include freehand gestures as user-interaction options. While significant progress has been made in hardware technologies for tracking and capturing human and their gestures [1], few research studies had been done to identify interactions that would be intuitive to ordinary users [2–4]. In addition, the gestures chosen by system designers are often restricted by technical implementation limitations such as freehand recognition ability.

Intuitiveness of gestural-based and interactive systems is particularly important in the contexts of public displays. Here, system users are very likely to have chanced upon the system, are interacting with the system for the first time, and for a relative short

© Springer International Publishing Switzerland 2015
N. Streitz and P. Markopoulos (Eds.): DAPI 2015, LNCS 9189, pp. 174–181, 2015.
DOI: 10.1007/978-3-319-20804-6_16

period of time. This is a challenging situation since these users would quickly lose interest if interaction with the system proves difficult. Adding to this is the fact that performing freehand gestures requires more effort when compared to computing devices like mouse and keyboard [5]. Thus, users would want to complete their tasks as efficiently as possible.

In this study, we elicited freehand gestures from 30 participants who were asked to complete 21 gestural tasks in front of a large display. All gestures were video-recorded and analyzed. In addition, we conducted in-depth interviews to understand how participants derived their gestures in relation to the given tasks.

2   Related Work

Freehand gestures studies to-date have tended to begin by designing a set of gestures, and then conduct experiments to elicit performance measures, such as the accuracy of those gestures [5–8]. However, in these studies, factors such as intuitiveness of the gestures to users themselves have been taken for granted.

In studies around gestures of two-dimensional surface devices, Wobbrock et al. [9] coined the term *guessability*, to refer to "quality of symbols which allows a user to access intended referents via those symbols despite a lack of knowledge of those symbols." They argued that in many contexts, it is unrealistic to assume that users are willing to learn the system. And therefore, systems must be designed such that users will be encouraged by early "success despite the user's lack of knowledge of the [design intents]" [4, 9].

In Wobbrock et al's [4] study, users were first presented with the intended effects of gestures. They were then asked to perform gestures that would lead to these effects. By repeating this among many users, an intuitive gesture set can be derived. Other studies had utilized this approach to design gesture sets for web browser commands on large televisions [10], multi-display environments involving large surfaces and tablet devices [11], as well as motion gestures with mobile phones [12].

Recently, researchers have begun to adopt the approach to examine natural and intuitive gestures in other contexts. For example, Grandhi et al. [3] asked users to manipulate physical objects without physically touching them (freehand), such as coins, papers, and cups, to identify how users may interact with embodied systems. While our research interest is also on freehand gestures, we are more interested in their uses with large public displays.

3   Method

We adopted the guessability methodology for our user study. In each study session, we asked each of our participants to conduct a randomized series of 21 tasks using freehand gestures (Fig. 1). To generate the study tasks on large display, we adopted simple tasks from Wobbrock et al. [4] that are commonly used on the large display, and included additional map-related operations. We then extended the task set after a pilot test of five colleagues in our lab.

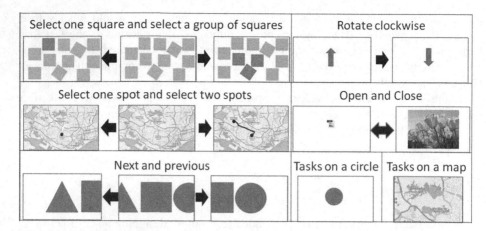

Fig. 1. 21 tasks (tasks on a circle include enlarge/shrink and move up/down/left/right and; tasks on a map include zoom in/out and pan up/down/left/right).

We recruited 30 university students to participate in the actual study. The participants aged between 18 and 31 years old, with an average age of 22.3. Among the participants, 19 were females and 11 were male. 28 participants were social science students, whereas 2 were from computer sciences. All participants were right handed. All participants, except one, owned a multi-touch smart-phone. Eleven participants also owned a tablet.

At the start of each session, we asked the participant to stand 3.5 m, or 11.5 ft, away from the projection screen. The projection screen was 2 m × 1.5 m, or 6.6 × 4.9 ft, in size with a resolution of 1024 × 768. For each task, we presented the participant a Microsoft PowerPoint animation on the screen. We asked the participant to use their hands and arms in any way they like to make that animation happen again. This process was repeated until each participant had completed all 21 tasks. All of these gestures were video-recorded. At the end of each session, we conducted in-depth interviews to ask users how they came up with each gesture. If they mentioned gestures on surface technology, we further asked them what the differences or similarities were between their own gestures and those used on surface technology. All interviews were voice-recorded, transcribed, and analyzed to identify common themes.

The video-recordings include a total of 630 video-recorded gestural sequences. We analyzed all the gestures using the taxonomy of spatial gestures developed by Wobbrock et al. [4], see Table 1.

In this taxonomy, gestures may be classified based on three dimensions: hand pose, hand path, and hand number. Hand pose is defined by the physical appearance of each finger and the orientation of the hand. Static hand pose means that the hand pose does not change even when the hand moves. For example, when people use one index finger to tap, their hand pose does not change but their hand moves. Dynamic hand pose means hand pose changes while the user is performing a gesture, for example, index finger and thumb on one hand moves while closing the gap between the two fingers. Hand path refers to the trajectory and the direction of hand's movement. Hand number refers to whether participants used one or two hands to perform the tasks.

Table 1. Taxonomy of spatial gestures

Hand pose	Static hand pose	Hand pose does not change.
	Dynamic hand pose	Hand pose changes.
Hand path	Still hand	Hand stays still in the space, hand pose may change.
	Moving hand	Hand moves from one place to another in the space.
Hand Number	One hand	Using only one hand.
	Two Hands	Using two hands.

4 Findings

Our findings are presented in two sections. The first reports how these participants tried to build connections between large displays and surface technologies. The second describes the moments when our participants realized that they must create new gestures that are different from surface gestures.

4.1 Learning from Surface Technologies

In the interviews, the participants often refer to surface technologies in their daily life when they were asked to explain why they had used a gesture. For example, a 20-years-old female participant, who had only used one-index-finger in every task, told us: "*I think [the large display] is the same as my iPhone so one finger is enough.*" Another example was how some participants used one finger to do the task move the circle right because it was what they commonly do on their smart phones. We correlated this finding with our video-recorded data, and found that in our user-generated gestures, 400 or 63.5 % of these gestures were learnt from those used on multi-touch smart phones and tablets.

4.2 Diverging from Surface Technologies

We identified several factors that influence participants' choices of gestures on large displays.

Size Matters. Our study included six tasks that involved manipulating a circle (*move the circle right/left/up/down and zoom in/out the circle*), and six tasks that involved manipulating a map. When participants were asked to manipulate maps, they used less finger-based gestures when compared to circles, from 67.8 % to 48.3 %, and more palm-based gestures, from 30 % to 51.1 %.

In our interview, a 25-years-old male participant explained that he needed two palms to *move the map* because, "*the map looks much heavier than the circle.*" Many participants who held similar opinion and explained that the circle was small, and thus one finger was enough to manipulate it. However, the map was so large that they believed they would need to use one palm to move it. Due to the perceived "size" and "weight" of the map, participants used palms, rather than fingers, as pointers to manipulate these objects. The larger the object was, the more often that hands appeared to be preferred, as a 22-years-old male participant said "*I will use two hands if the display is huge, like panorama.*"

Despite palms being seen as more appropriate for manipulating large objects, our participants expressed concerns about the perceived "accuracy." For example, when a female participant was asked to *select one spot on a map*, she said, "*the spot is too small on the map, I'm afraid I will miss it if I don't zoom in.*" Many participants expressed the desire to alternate between palm and finger (i.e., a finger to select spots on a map while using the palm to pan the map), e.g. "*one finger is more accurate than a whole hand!*" said a 20-year-old female participant.

With the use of palms on large objects like maps, we observed that participants interesting ways in which they would indicate direction to which they wanted to move them. When a palm was held up to the map, participants perceived that a friction existed between the palm and the map. This perceived friction guided their subsequent actions, thus deviating from their experience with surface technologies. For example, when participants were asked to move a map left, right, or down, seven (23.3 %) participants also turned their palm facing the same direction—as if this would help to slide the object in the right direction. However, this only happened twice (6.7 %) in the "pan the map up" task. One 30-year-old male participant explained, "*It is [an unnatural posture for] my palm [to] face up. I don't usually do that [in daily life].*"

Mapping Tasks to Actions in Daily Life. Participants frequently mapped tasks to actions they often did in their daily life. For example, the task *rotate clockwise* asked participants to operate an arrow on the display, so that the arrow would rotate around its center by 180 degrees and stop when pointing towards the bottom. Ten participants (33.3 %) posed their hands in a way that looked like they were holding on to an object - they rotated their hands to perform the task. We asked them why they used their whole hand rather than merely using one finger. A 23-year-old male participant explained, "*It is similar to rotating a knob on a door. One finger is not strong enough to move the knob.*" Another participant said, "*I can't remember I have ever done this [rotate] on my phone, so I pick [the gesture of] opening a door.*" When participants faced tasks which they did not find correspondences on surface technologies, they mapped them to what they did during their daily life.

Simplified and Complex Mental Models. Participants had varying understandings of the given tasks. Some participants made simplified assumptions. For example, they considered *close* the same as *zoom out*. This finding is consistent with Wobbrock et al.'s findings [4] where participants tended to use one simple gesture to accomplish two different tasks, such as *zoom in* and *enlarge*. However, we also observed complex mental model from other participants where they considered the tasks complex. They devised two-steps gestures for those tasks. For example, when they were asked to pick a spot on a map, they feared that they might pick a wrong spot if they were to simply point their fingers at it. Therefore, they would first zoom-out the map, and then pick the right spot. The explanation given by the participants suggested one important characteristic of large displays – *untouchability*. People cannot touch any physical objects when they are operating on public large displays. Because participants could not touch the objects on large displays as they would usually do on their touchscreen devices, they believed that tasks on large displays were more difficult and they must devise multiple steps to achieve certain goals.

5   Discussion

Our findings point to prior user experience with surface technologies as being the provider for the tacit skills transfer to the context of spatial interaction with large displays. While surface technologies were widely used, and provided convenient analogies to freehand gestures, users are able to innovate where objects to be manipulated appeared to be dissimilar to those found in previous technologies. In particular, when it comes to manipulating *small objects* on screen (e.g., a spot), designers can draw analogies from surface technology use. In fact, previous studies have also shown that this type of *one-index-finger gesture* was originally a mouse gesture that had transferred from desktops into surface technology use [4, 13, 14]. Fikkert et al. found that simple gestures based on the act of pressing buttons, a common everyday action, was the most intuitive [15]. This legacy interaction method had remained highly relevant even for spatial interactions.

For actions that were analogous to those found in surface technologies, most of our participants had opted to use one-index-finger gestures; but for large objects like maps, the same participants had opted for palm-based gestures, as these objects were perceived to be "heavier." While one-index-finger gestures were borrowed from analogies that could be traced to the mouse pointer, and thus more *guessable*, palm-based manipulation may be a new interaction approach for computing systems utilizing spatial interactions. In this case, analogies for palm-based manipulation had not come from technology use, but instead from ordinary notions such as weight, size, and the ways such objects are used in daily life. Another example that derived from daily experience was when completing the task *rotate*, our participants mapped the arrow to a door knob and acted as if they were holding the knob. In both cases, they drew these gestures from their daily experience of interacting with objects they were familiar with. This suggests that designers should be aware of varying referents which users are likely to draw to give meanings to their freehand gestures.

When interacting with large displays at a distance, our participants were seeking a sense of physically touching the objects. They frequently derived gestures from their physical experience with surface technologies or their daily life, in which they could either touch the screen or manipulate the physical objects. Some participants realized that they could not actually touch the objects shown in large displays, as oppose to how they would interact with touchscreen devices and daily physical objects. This untouchability caused uncertainty to our participants, who were sometimes unsure whether they had successfully selected the operable objects. Therefore, they felt they must create ways to select the objects, which sometimes resulted in complicating some steps, especially in the task *next*. This suggests that designers should devise mechanisms that can provide users certainty and confidence in manipulating objects. For example, many users mentioned that they expected there would be a cursor on the large display, which followed their hands' movement.

6 Limitations and Future Work

In this study, we have varied a few object variables including object number, size, and movement. However, other object variables may have influenced their choices, such as higher granularity of object's size, trajectory, and movement speed. In future work, we will consider more of these variables and see how they affect participants' choices.

Our current experiment setup asked participants to define one gesture for each task. Therefore, when some participants designed multiple gestures, we asked them to pick only one gesture for one task. In future study, we should consider multiple gestures and see how these can influence development of intuitive freehand gestures.

Acknowledgement. This research is supported by the National Research Foundation, Prime Minister's Office, Singapore under its International Research Centre @ Singapore Funding Initiative and administered by the Interactive and Digital Media Programme Office.

References

1. Williamson, J., Murray-Smith, R.: Rewarding the original: explorations in joint user-sensor motion spaces. In: Proceedings of the 2012 ACM Annual Conference on Human Factors in Computing Systems - CHI 2012, pp. 1717–1726. ACM Press (2012)
2. Lee, J.C.: In search of a natural gesture XRDS Crossroads. ACM Mag. Students **16**, 9 (2010)
3. Grandhi, S.A., Joue, G., Mittelberg, I.: Understanding naturalness and intuitiveness in gesture production. In: Proceedings of the 2011 Annual Conference on Human Factors in Computing Systems - CHI 2011, pp. 821–824. ACM Press, New York (2011)
4. Wobbrock, J.O., Morris, M.R., Wilson, A.D.: User-defined gestures for surface computing. In: Proceedings of the 27th International Conference on Human Factors in Computing Systems - CHI 2009, pp. 1083–1092. ACM Press, New York (2009)
5. Nancel, M., Wagner, J., Pietriga, E., Chapuis, O., Mackay, W.: Mid-air pan-and-zoom on wall-sized displays. In: Proceedings of the 2011 Annual Conference on Human Factors in Computing Systems - CHI 2011, pp. 177–186. ACM Press, New York (2011)
6. Malik, S., Ranjan, A., Balakrishnan, R.: Interacting with large displays from a distance with vision-tracked multi-finger gestural input. In: Proceedings of the 18th Annual ACM Symposium on User Interface Software and Technology - UIST 2005, pp. 43–52. ACM Press, New York (2005)
7. Vogel, D., Balakrishnan, R.: Distant freehand pointing and clicking on very large, high resolution displays. In: Proceedings of the 18th Annual ACM Symposium on User Interface Software and Technology - UIST 2005, pp. 33–42. ACM Press, New York (2005)
8. Fikkert, W., van der Vet, P., Nijholt, A.: Gestures in an intelligent user interface. In: Shao, L., Shan, C., Luo, J., Etoh, M. (eds.) Multimedia Interaction and Intelligent User Interfaces, pp. 215–242. Springer, London (2010)
9. Wobbrock, J.O., Aung, H.H., Rothrock, B., Myers, B.A.: Maximizing the guessability of symbolic input. In: CHI 2005 Extended Abstracts on Human Factors in Computing Systems - CHI 2005, pp. 1869–1872. ACM Press, New York (2005)
10. Morris, M.R.: Web on the wall: insights from a multimodal interaction elicitation study. In: Proceedings of the 2012 ACM International Conference on Interactive Tabletops and Surfaces - ITS 2012, pp. 95–104. ACM Press, New York (2012)

11. Kurdyukova, E., Redlin, M., André, E.: Studying user-defined iPad gestures for interaction in multi-display environment. In: Proceedings of the 2012 ACM International Conference on Intelligent User Interfaces - IUI 2012, pp. 93–96. ACM Press, New York (2012)

12. Ruiz, J., Li, Y., Lank, E.: User-defined motion gestures for mobile interaction. In: Proceedings of the 2011 Annual Conference on Human Factors in Computing Systems - CHI 2011, pp. 197–206. ACM Press, New York (2011)

13. Fikkert, W., van der Vet, P., van der Veer, G., Nijholt, A.: Gestures for large display control. In: Kopp, S., Wachsmuth, I. (eds.) Gesture in Embodied Communication and Human-Computer Interaction, pp. 245–256. Springer, Heidelberg (2010)

14. Cheng, K., Pulo, K.: Direct interaction with large-scale display systems using infrared laser tracking devices. In: Proceedings of the Asia-Pacific Symposium on Information Visualization - APVis 2003, pp. 67–74. Australian Computer Society, Darlinghurst (2003)

15. Fikkert, W., van der Vet, P., Nijholt, A.: User-evaluated gestures for touchless interactions from a distance. In: 2010 IEEE International Symposium on Multimedia, pp. 153–160. IEEE (2010)

AR Coloring Jigsaw Puzzles with Texture Extraction and Auto-UV Mapping Algorithm

Youngho Lee[⊠]

Department of Computer Engineering, Mokpo National University,
Jeonnam, Korea
youngho@mokpo.ac.kr

Abstract. There have been many applications with AR technology such as advertisement, education, etc. Books with AR technology are the most interesting application area. In this paper, we propose an AR coloring jigsaw puzzles which provides users with puzzle pieces for coloring and AR/VR worlds for colored 3D animations. The proposed puzzle is composed of a jigsaw puzzle with unpainted pieces and a smart phone application. The jigsaw puzzle with unpainted pieces is designed large pieces of puzzle and several uncolored pieces. The smart phone application has an AR scene for extracting color from puzzle and a VR world for user interaction with colored animals.

Keywords: Augmented reality · Virtual reality · Coloring book · Vuforia SDK

1 Introduction

With the popularization of mobile display devices, augmented reality has grown up nowadays. Although many researchers still try to find out killer applications, many interesting commercial applications apply the concept of augmented reality. Augmented Reality (AR) is a concept of computer applications which augment virtual objects on objects in real world [1, 2].

There have been many research activities of AR books not only on 3D visualization but also on readers' interaction. Magic book is a famous augmented reality book developed by HITlab at Newzland [3]. When a user looks magic book through hand-held displays with camera, the user can see 3D animated object over the paper book in real world through the display devices. Early magic book utilized marker-based tracking technique which use black rectangular shape markers.

ARToolkit is a marker-based tracking library for augmented reality applications [4]. It was originally developed by one of developers of Magic book. Later, with the enhancement of computer vision algorithm, natural feature tracking (markerless tracking) technology is applied to AR books. So, pictures on the paper book can be used for tracking instead of black rectangular shape markers. Virtual pop-up book was AR book with natural feature tracking [6]. Digilog Book provided several interaction ways to users [7, 8]. ARtalet was authoring tools with full 3D AR UI for digilog book [8].

However, even previous AR books show the fusion of real and virtual scene successfully, it is hard to find concrete relationship between pictures or markers on a paper book and 3D animated objects. ColAR is an interactive AR coloring book for

© Springer International Publishing Switzerland 2015
N. Streitz and P. Markopoulos (Eds.): DAPI 2015, LNCS 9189, pp. 182–187, 2015.
DOI: 10.1007/978-3-319-20804-6_17

children [5]. Even though many AR books focused on visualization and direct user interaction, ColAR presents not only 3D models on a book but also colored 3D models with painted textures by uses. ColorPopUp Sketch Book was also one of AR coloring book [11, 12]. However, when children read this book, they need to hold smart devices with their hands. It could be hard work for little children.

In this paper, we propose an AR coloring jigsaw puzzles which provides users with puzzle pieces for coloring and AR/VR worlds for colored 3D animations. The puzzle is designed in three worlds: (1) putting and coloring a puzzle in real world, (2) taking a picture in AR scene, (3) moving to VR world and enjoying it. Thus children would enjoy coloring jigsaw puzzle, and painting 3D animated model. They also spend a lot of times with playing 3D animated models in VR world.

To realize this idea, we made jigsaw puzzle which have unpainted pieces. Then we implemented a smart phone application for painting 3D models in AR and for putting them in VR worlds. So, we design algorithm to extract specific rectangular area on a puzzle from video in real-time, and then transforms the image of area into rectangular for texture mapping. To get specific rectangular area on a jigsaw puzzle, we calculate transform matrix from local coordinates to world coordinates, and world coordinates to screen coordinates. To warp trapezoid into rectangular shape, we calculate projection matrix for image warping and apply interpolation method. Finally eliminating blur effect caused by image processing, we apply histogram equalization to the texture.

This paper is organized as follows. In Sect. 2, we explain augmented reality and its SDKs briefly. In Sect. 3, the proposed AR coloring jigsaw puzzle are explained. Implementation of whole application is in Sect. 4. Finally we conclude our paper in Sect. 5.

2 Related Works

Many researchers have interest in book with AR technology. Normally, books with AR technology are composed of a paper book, a display such as HMD with camera, and a computer for image processing and graphic rendering. Magic book is one of first book with AR technology. When users look at the pages of a real book through a hand held display they can see virtual content superimposed over the real pages. It also provides user interaction and navigation methods. Virtual pop-up book shows 3D animated models with similar approach with magic book. It use natural feature tracking algorithm so that there are no markers on a real paper book. Digilog book integrated visual and haptic feedback into AR book. It also provides authoring tool with 3D UI for author, so users can rotate and translate virtual object with hand-held manipulation tools. ColAR allows users to paint in the book pages and then see them 3D models with the painted color.

The main function of AR SDKs are visual tracking with camera in real time. ARToolkit is the well-known sdk for the desktop applications. It uses black square markers. After that there have been many researches to design shape of AR marker. ARToolkit Plus provides ID-assigned markers. Instead of image pattern in rectangular, it use visually coded pattern inside marker. OsgART combines computer vision based tracking libraries with the OpenSceneGraph library. Vuforia SDK is mobile AR development kit which supports both android and IOS. It also supports unity3D

Table 1. Comparison of AR SDKs [13–19]

	Type	Mobile platform
ARToolkit	Free + commercial SDK option	iOS/Android
D'Fusion	Free + commercial SDK option	iOS/Android
Metaio SDK	Free + commercial SDK option	iOS/Android
AndAR	Free	Android
BazAR	Open source	–
FLARToolkit	Open source	Web
OsgART	Open source	–
vuforia	Free + commercial SDK option	iOS/Android

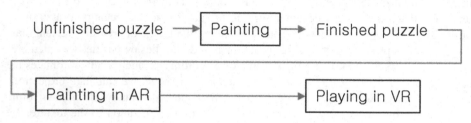

Fig. 1. Process of AR coloring jigsaw puzzle

extension. Not only simple plain image tracking, it also provides cylinder and cube shape objects tracking API, extended tracking, text recognition etc. So we select vuforia sdk for our implementation because it provides powerful mobile AR API and it is free to use (Table 1).

3   Design of AR Coloring Jigsaw Puzzle

Jigsaw puzzle is a game that makes a whole picture with several small pieces of blocks. The reason why people play with jigsaw puzzle is that they want to see the full picture when they put all pieces together. So people have interesting in making something and looking the final funny results. To make this puzzle more interesting, we allow users to paint pieces of puzzle and to watch the results in 3D virtual worlds. Figure 1 shows the procedure.

Generally, vision based tracking algorithm includes image registration, frame capture, calculations such as pose estimation and calibration, and 3D model augmentation. We integrate vision based tracking algorithm with texture extraction of marker from screen image for coloring. To extract the image area we calculate four-corner points of marker shown in mobile device screen.

With perspective matrix and image from camera, the four-point of marker shown in screen is found. The four corner points of marker is calculated in the form of 3D coordinates in virtual world. Then it converts 2D screen coordinates by applying perspective matrix. With this points we process image warping with homogeneous matrix because points in 3D is projected onto 2D screen. This calculation performs by calculating inverse of homogeneous matrix. Then we get a rectangular image only shown marker area. After that, we expand the extracted trapezoid shape-image into rectangular shape. Finally we apply uv- mapping on 3D model with the image.

4 Implementation

We implemented our product for children age from 3 to 7. So jigsaw puzzle was designed small number and big size of pieces. As shown in Fig. 2(a), the puzzle has 16 pieces. There are unpainted dragons. We selected dragons because children have interest in dragons usually. Text and other parts of figures are important clues for visual tracking.

We used Unity3D 4.5 and vuforia 3.0.8 and target device is a smart phone and a tablet [10]. The puzzle was registered on target manager in the vuforia development web site, so that we downloaded dataset for image tracking. The two algorithms were implemented with C# language in unity project. Figure 2(b) shows 3D animated dragon on smart phone screen. The border of pieces mapped to black line in dragon. To enhance color, we applied color histogram equalization. Histogram equalization is a method in image processing of contrast adjustment using the image's histogram.

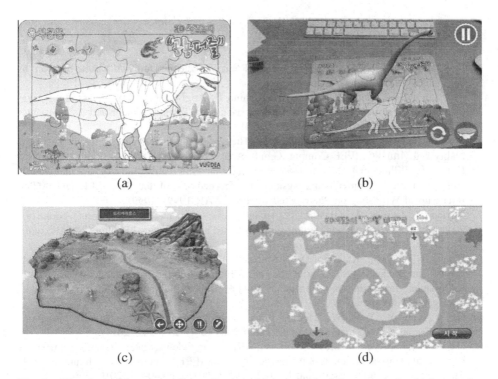

(a)   (b)

(c)   (d)

Fig. 2. AR coloring jigsaw puzzle application. (a) is unpainted jigsaw puzzle, (b) is painting process by taking picture with camera, (c) is dragon world. Dragons live there. (d) is mini game. The painted dragons appears in there.

After coloring 3D animated models, it moved to virtual world (dragon world) in Fig. 2(c). There are 20 different dragons, so children could make 20 painted dragons. The dragons are saved in dragon worlds and children can enjoy playing with them. In dragon world, children can move and feed the dragons. Finally there are mini games. In mini games, the painted dragon appeared as game characters as shown in Fig. 2(d).

5   Conclusion and Future Works

We proposed an AR coloring jigsaw puzzles which provided users with puzzle pieces for coloring and AR/VR worlds for colored 3D animations. The puzzle is designed in three worlds: (1) putting and coloring a puzzle in real world, (2) taking a picture in AR scene, (3) moving to VR world and enjoying it.

During demonstration to children, we found that children have interesting in drawing and watching the painted 3D models. Children spend long time to put the puzzle together and to play dragons in a virtual world while they spend short time in an AR world. When children use this puzzle, they have to hold a smart device with their two hands. However it is difficult to hold a smart device with hands in long time. It was a problem of most mobile AR system.

References

1. Ronald, A.: A survey of augmented reality. Presence: Teleoperators and Virtual Environ. **6** (4), 355–385 (1997)
2. Milgram, P., Takemura, H., Utsumi, A., Kishino, F.: Augmented reality: a class of displays on the reality-virtuality continuum. In: Proceedings of Telemanipulator and Telepresence Technologies, vol. 2351, pp. 282–292 (1994)
3. Billinghurst, M., Kato, H., Poupyrev, I.: The magicbook—moving seamlessly between reality and virtuality. IEEE Comput. Graph. Appl. **21**(3), 6–8 (2001)
4. Kato, H., Billinghurst, M.: Marker tracking and hmd calibration for a video-based augmented reality conferencing system. In: Proceedings of the 2nd IEEE and ACM International Workshop on Augmented Reality (IWAR 1999) (1999)
5. Adrian, C., Dunser, A., Grasset, R.: An interactive augmented reality coloring book. In: 2011 10th IEEE International Symposium on Mixed and Augmented Reality (ISMAR), vol. 26–29, pp. 259–260 (2011)
6. Taketa, N., Hayashi, K., Kato, H., Noshida, S.: Virtual pop-up book based on augmented reality. In: Michael, J.S., Gavriel, S. (eds.) Human Interface and the Management of Information. Interacting in Information Environments. LNCS, vol. 4558, pp. 475–484. Springer, Heidelberg (2007)
7. Ha, T., Lee, Y., Woo, W.: Digilog book for temple bell tolling experience based on interactive augmented reality. Virtual Reality (VR) **15**(4), 295–309 (2011)
8. Ha, T., Lee, Y., Ryu, J., Lee, K., Woo, W.: ARtalet: tangible user interface based immersive augmented reality authoring tool for Digilog book. In: IEEE Proceedings of 5th International Symposium on Ubiquitous Virtual Reality (ISUVR 2010), pp.40–43 (2010)
9. Ha, T., Woo, W.: Design considerations for implementing an interactive DigiLog book. EuroMed 2014 **8740**, 732–739 (2014)

10. Vuforia SDK. https://developer.vuforia.com/
11. Lee, Y., Choi, J.: Texture extraction from video and image warping for AR coloring book. Comput. Sci. Appl. Lect. Notes Electr. Eng. **330**, 361–365 (2015)
12. Lee, Y., Choi, J.: Design of AR coloring book with Vuforia SDK. Int. Conf. Embed. Syst. Intell. Technol. **9**, 69–70 (2014)
13. ARToolkit. http://www.hitl.washington.edu/artoolkit/ (Accessed March 2015)
14. Total Immersion. http://www.t-immersion.com/
15. Metaio. http://www.metaio.com/
16. bazAR. http://cvlab.epfl.ch/software/bazar
17. osgART. https://www.artoolworks.com/community/osgart/
18. FLARToolkit. http://www.libspark.org/wiki/saqoosha/FLARToolKit/en
19. AndAR. https://code.google.com/p/andar/

Smart Kiosk with Gait-Based Continuous Authentication

Duong-Tien Phan[(⊠)], Nhan Nguyen-Trong Dam,
Minh-Phuc Nguyen, Minh-Triet Tran, and Toan-Thinh Truong

Faculty of Information Technology, University of Science VNU-HCM,
Ho Chi Minh City, Vietnam
dntnhan@apcs.vn, {1112328,1112224}@student.hcmus.
edu.vn, {tmtriet,ttthinh}@fit.hcmus.edu.vn

Abstract. The authors propose to develop a smart kiosk that plays the role of an identity selector activated implicitly when a user is approaching that kiosk. The identity of a user is recognized implicitly in background by a mobile/wearable device based on his or her gait features. Upon arriving at a smart kiosk, the authentication process is performed automatically with the current available user identity in his or her portable device. To realize our system, we propose a new secure authentication scheme compatible with gait-based continuous authentication that can resist against known attacks, including three-factor attacks. Furthermore, we also propose a method to recognize users from their moving patterns using multiple SVM classifiers. Experiments with a dataset with 38 people show that this method can achieve the accuracy up to 92.028 %.

Keywords: Gait-based recognition · Continuous authentication · Smart kiosk · Mobile device · Wearable device

1 Introduction

Ambient intelligence allows the creation of smart interactive environments in which users can access useful data and services fitting their own demand at anytime and anywhere. Upon recognizing a user's identity, a computing system can provide appropriate features and services. Therefore, authentication is one of the essential steps for smart interactive environments.

In this paper, we propose an architecture for a Smart Kiosk system. A smart kiosk plays the role of an identity selector activated implicitly when a user is approaching that kiosk. By this way, when a user arrives at an available kiosk in idle state, i.e. there is no active user using that kiosk, the kiosk allows that user to access various online services, such as Facebook, Gmail, Flickr, etc. with appropriate identities associated with his or her registered account in Smart Kiosk system. With a flexible architecture, new types of services can be integrated into a smart kiosk.

We choose gait feature as a biometric factor and design a compatible scheme for our proposed Smart Kiosk system. Our system exploits gait features, body movement patterns of a user, for implicitly continuous user identification and authentication.

© Springer International Publishing Switzerland 2015
N. Streitz and P. Markopoulos (Eds.): DAPI 2015, LNCS 9189, pp. 188–200, 2015.
DOI: 10.1007/978-3-319-20804-6_18

By this way, a user can access not only utilities in a kiosk but also other online services, such as Facebook, Gmail, Flickr, etc. at kiosks available in public areas.

User's gait dominates the security of the system. Using gait-based authentication allows us to avoid the vulnerability when traditional authentication tokens, such as active badge with infrared signal, RFID tags, or NFC-enable tokens are lost or stolen. Furthermore, as the authentication process is carried out in background continuously, it would be more natural for users to access their data and services immediately without performing an explicit authentication step, such as pushing fingers into a fingerprint scanner, or speaking to a microphone.

There are two main components in our proposed Smart Kiosk system: (i) gait-based continuous authentication module in a wearable device/mobile device, and (ii) interactive kiosk to provide users with services corresponding to their identities.

The main contributions of our papers are as follows:

- We study and analyze the security of biometric-based scheme by Khan et al. [5] and show that the scheme still cannot resist three-factor attacks. We then propose a new scheme to fix this vulnerability. By this way, we stress the importance of biometric factor, which does not have a discernible interest.
- We propose a new method for implicitly continuous gait-based authentication embedded in a wearable/mobile device. In our proposed method, we use multiple SVM classifiers to boost the accuracy for user identity classification from gait data captured from motion sensors of a wearable/mobile device.

The structure of our paper is as follows. In Sect. 2, we first introduce the notations used for authentication schemes in this paper and present the advantages and vulnerability of existing secured authentication schemes, especially against three-factor attacks. We then present the trend to apply biometric features for authentication to replace traditional approaches and several existing methods for gait-based identity recognition. In Sect. 3, we present our proposed Smart Kiosk system with continuous implicit gait-based authentication via mobile/wearable devices. The details of our proposed authentication scheme using biometric features (i.e. gait features) and our method to recognize a user based on his or her gait feature using multiple SVM classifiers are presented in Sect. 4. Section 5 focuses on security analysis of our proposed authentication scheme as well as experimental results to evaluate the accuracy of gait-based identity recognition. Conclusions and discussion on future work are in Sect. 5.

2   Background and Related Work

2.1   Secured Authentication Scheme

Traditional authentication is based on passwords [1] and is susceptible to dictionary attacks. To improve security, two-factor [2, 3] and three-factor [4–7] authentication schemes have been proposed. In 2012, An proposed an enhancement of an efficient biometrics-based remote user authentication scheme using smart cards [4], and claimed that the scheme was secure against many kinds of attack, such as user impersonation attack, server masquerading attack. In 2013, Khan et al. [5] showed that An's scheme was vulnerable to several attacks and could not provide mutual authentication between the user and the server. In order to fix the flaws, Khan et al. proposed their improved scheme and claimed that the new scheme was secure even if the secret information stored in the smart card was revealed to an attacker. With this concern, Khan et al. have a further step in the right direction that is protecting user even though more and more information is leaked. In 2014, Sarvabhatla et al. [6] and Wen et al. [7] respectively analyzed the weakness of Khan et al.'s scheme, such as off-line password guessing attack, impersonation attack, server masquerading attack, malicious user, stolen smart card, leakage of password, parallel session attack. They both proposed new biometrics-based scheme and claimed that the schemes was secure and resisted all major cryptographic attacks.

However, Sarvabhatla et al. and Wen et al. do not consider the use of biometric factor in Khan et al.'s scheme. We point out that Khan et al.'s scheme cannot take the advantage of biometric factor. As a result, this scheme is vulnerable to three-factor attacks. This kind of attack implies that attacker has two of the three factors: password, shared information, and biometric [8]. In biometrics-based scheme, users should be safe even when password and shared information are leaked. Moreover, user's identity should be kept secret in the scheme, but it can still protect a user when ID is leaked.

Our new scheme utilizes biometrics as the main security factor to fix the vulnerability in Khan et al.'s scheme. We also employ the strategy in our previous work [9, 10] to use random numbers and hash functions to establish a secure authentication process with multi servers using mobile or wearable devices.This strategy requires less computation cost than methods with bi-linear pairing.

2.2   Cryptanalysis Khan et al.'s Scheme

For simplicity of presentation, we introduce the main notations used in authentication schemes presented in this paper. We inherit these notations from the scheme by Khan et al. [5] (Table 1).

In Khan et al.'s scheme, the value $g_i = (ID_i \| PW_i) \oplus f_i$ is stored in the smart card. Note that, the value $f_i = h(B_i \oplus K_i)$ is biometric factor in this scheme. An attacker can retrieve f_i easily by computing $(ID_i \| PW_i) \oplus g_i$. Therefore, the security of this scheme is downgraded by perform three-factor attack and biometric factor have no advanced.

Table 1. Notations with their descriptions

Notations	Description	Notations	Description
R	Trusted registration center	K_i	Random number chosen by U_i
S_i	Server	R_c	Random number generated by SC_i
U_i	i^{th} user	R_s	Random number generated by S_i
ID_i	Identity of U_i	x_s and y_s	Secret keys maintained by S_i
PW_i	Password of U_i	$h(.)$	One-way hash function
B_i	Biometric template of U_i	$\oplus$	Bitwise XOR operator
SC_i	Smart card of U_i	$\|$	Concatenation operator

In order to perform three-factor attack, we assume attacker have the shared information $\{c_i, e_i, g_i, j_i, h(.)\}$, password PW_i and identity ID_i. This scenario still can happen in the real life. Therefore, authentication scheme should take the advantage of biometric factor to protect users.

An attacker can do the following steps to impersonate legitimate user U_i:

- Attacker U_A computes $f_i = (ID_i||PW_i) \oplus g_i$, $K_i = (ID_i||PW_i) \oplus j_i$. U_A generates a random number R_c and computes the following equations: $r_i = h(PW_i \oplus K_i) \oplus f_i$, $M_1 = c_i \oplus f_i$, $M_2 = e_i \oplus r_i$, $M_3 = M_1 \oplus R_c$, $M_4 = h(M_1||R_c) \oplus ID_i$, $M_5 = h(M_2||R_c)$. U_A sends the login request $\{M_3, M_4, M_5\}$ to S_i.
- On receiving login request $\{M_3, M_4, M_5\}$ from U_A, the server S_i firstly computes $M_6 - h(x_s||y_s)$, $M_7 = M_3 \oplus M_6$, $M_8 = h(ID_i||x_s)$, $ID_i = M_4 \oplus (M_6||M_7)$.
- S_i checks the format of ID_i. Obviously, ID_i is valid, S_i then checks if $M_5 = h(M_8||M_7)$. Of course, both are equal, S_i generates a random number R_s and computes the following equations: $M_9 = M_8 \oplus R_s$, $M_{10} = h(M_8||R_s)$. Then, S_i sends the reply message $\{M_9, M_{10}\}$ for its authentication to U_A.
- Receiving $\{M_9, M_{10}\}$ from S_i, the attacker U_A computes $M_{11} = M_9 \oplus M_2$ and checks if $M_{10} = h(M_2||M_{11})$ or not. If both are equal, U_A computes $M_{12} = h(M_2R_c||M_{11})$ and sends the reply message $\{M_{12}\}$ to S_i.
- Receiving $\{M_{12}\}$ from U_A, the server checks if $M_{12} = h(M_8M_7||R_s)$. Obviously, both are equal, S_i accepts the login request $\{M_3, M_4, M_5\}$ of U_A with U_i's identity.

Attacker U_A successfully impersonates the user U_i without U_i's biometric.

2.3 Authentication with Biometric Features

Using biometric data, a source of high-entropy information, for authentication and identity management has the following advantages: (i) not to be lost or forgotten; (ii) difficult to copy or share; (iii) hard to forge; and (iv) not to be guessed easily [7].

Together with authentication methods based on traditional biometric data, such as fingerprint, iris, voice, etc., there is a new trend to exploit body movement patterns of a user, a.k.a gait features, for identity recognition. Pan et al. use k-nearest neighbors method for gait recognition with data captured from an accelerometer [11]. Nickel and Busch propose to use Hidden Markov Model to authenticate users when they walk [14].

Among existing methods for gait recognition, Support Vector Machine is one common approach to classify users from their gait features [12, 13, 15]. Therefore, in this paper, we also follow this common trend to devise own method based on SVM for user identification based on gait feature. However, we do not use a single SVM classifier as in existing methods [12, 13, 15] but take advantages of multiple weak SVM classifiers to boost the overall accuracy.

3   Proposed Architecture and Methods for Smart Kiosk Using Gait-Based Authentication

3.1   Proposed Architecture of Smart Kiosk Using Gait-Based Authentication

Figure 1 illustrates the idea of continuous implicit authentication with gait data collected from wearable or mobile devices, such as smart watches, activity trackers, or smart phones. Gait-based user authentication has two main properties. First, it is a continuous authentication process, not a one-time operation. Therefore, it is more secure than one-time authentication schemes, such as methods with PIN or password, because the system can continuously monitor a user to ensure that the user is still a legal one. When an abnormal phenonmenon occurs, such as when a user is knocked out or falls, the current session is terminated and the authentication is restarted. Second, gait-based authentication process is performed implicitly. A user does not need to pay attention to this background process. When the user needs to prove his or her identity to a system, the current identity is available for use.

Fig. 1. Continuous implicit authentication with gait data using wearable device/mobile device

Figure 2 illustrates a typical scenario of usage at a smart kiosk using gait-based authentication. When a user arrives at a free kiosk, his or her wearable/mobile device establishes a secure communication channel with the kiosk to perform the

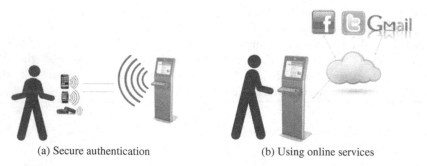

(a) Secure authentication   (b) Using online services

Fig. 2. Secure authentication (a) and using online services (b) at Smart Kiosk with wearable device/mobile device

authentication process to the centralized Cloud Service of Smart Kiosk system using the current active user ID recognized from the device. Depending on the particular implementation, a user may be required to tap his/her device to the NFC module of a kiosk to activate the authentication process, or the process is automatically performed when the user is in the proximity of the kiosk using Bluetooth Low Energy.

Figure 3 demonstrates the architecture of the Smart Kiosk system to use biometric gait data as means of single-sign-on. The current active user ID recognized in a wearable/mobile device is transmitted via secure channel to the kiosk. Upon receiving a service request with a user ID from a kiosk, Smart Kiosk service translates the user ID into a collection of digital identities of that user, such as his or her username and password to login to the requested online service. Smart Kiosk service plays the role of an identity provider to supply appropriate digital identities to different services, relying parties. In Smart Kiosk service, we propose a mechanism to manage different online service wrappers as plugins so that new service can be added into Smart Kiosk service in the future.

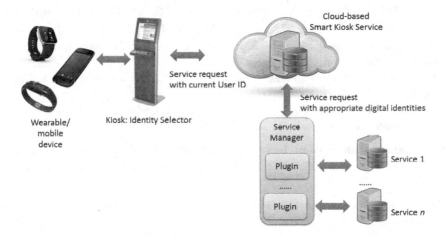

Fig. 3. Overview of the architecture to map a current user ID into appropriate digital identities for different online services

3.2 Proposed Scheme and Gait-Based Method

Our scheme includes four phases: registration, login, and mutual authentication and password-change phases. The phases are describe in detail as follow.

Registration Phase: When U_i registers with R, U_i chooses ID_i, PW_i, random nonce K_i, K_i' and input biometric template B_i. Then, U_i sends $\{ID_i, PW_i \oplus B_i \oplus K_i\}$ to R via secure channel.

- Step 1: When receiving registration message from U_i, R generates random value n to make different secret key at different time.
- Step 2: R computes

$$C_i = h(x_s||y_s||h(n)) \oplus h(ID_i||(PW_i \oplus B_i \oplus K_i))$$
$$e_i = h(x_s||y_s||ID_i||h(n)) \oplus h((PW_i \oplus B_i \oplus K_i)||ID_i)$$
$$f_i = h(h(x_s||y_s||h(n))||h(x_s||y_s||ID_i||h(n)))$$

Then, R sends $\{C_i, e_i, f_i, n, h(.)\}$ to U_i via secure channel

- Step 3: The user's device computes: $g_i = (ID_i||PW_i||B_i) \oplus n_j j_i = (ID_i||PW_i) \oplus K_i$

The user hide his/her ID_i and PW_i by computes: $hID_i = ID_i \oplus h(B_i||K_i')$, $hPW_i = PW_i \oplus h(K_i'||B_i)$.

The user stores $\{C_i, e_i, f_i, g_i, j_i, hID_i, hPW_i, K_i', h(.)\}$ in the device.

Login Phase: To perform login phase, user's device compute the biometric B_i of U_i and flow the following steps:

- Step 1: Retrieves ID_i and PW_i by compute: $ID_i^* = hID_i \oplus h(B_i||K_i')$, $PW_i^* = hPW_i \oplus h(K_i'||B_i)$, $K_i^* = (ID_i^*||PW_i^*) \oplus j_i$, $n = g_i \oplus (ID_i^*||PW_i^*||B_i)$.
- Step 2: User's device compute: $M_1 = C_i \oplus h(ID_i^*||(PW_i^* \oplus B_i \oplus K_i^*))$, $M_2 = e_i \oplus h((PW_i^* \oplus B_i \oplus K_i^*)||ID_i^*)$, and check if $f_i = h(M_1||M_2)$. If this information matches, user passes the biometrics verification; otherwise user's device terminates the session.
- Step 3: User's device generate random value R_c and compute the following equation:
  $M_3 = M_1 \oplus R_C$, $M_4 = h(R_C) \oplus ID_i$, $M_5 = h(M_2||R_c)$, $n = (ID_i||PW_i||B_i) \oplus g_i$
- Step 4: User's device sends the login request $\{h(n), M_3, M_4, M_5\}$ to S_i

Authentication with Session Key Agreement Phase: When receiving the login message, server S_i and the user's device perform the following steps to mutual authenticate:

- Step 1: S_i computes the following values: $M_6 = h(x_s||y_s||h(n))$, $M_7 = M_3 \oplus M_6$, $ID_i = M_4 \oplus h(M_7)$
- Step 2: S_i checks the format of ID_i. If ID_i is valid, S_i computes $M_8 = h(x_s||y_s||ID_i||h(n))$, and then check if $M_5 = h(M_8||M_7)$. If both equal, S_i generates a random number R_s and computes: $M_9 = M_8 \oplus R_s$, $M_{10} = h(M_8||R_s||M_7)$. Then, S_i sends the reply message $\{M_9, M_{10}\}$ for its authentication to user's device
- Step 3: On receiving $\{M_9, M_{10}\}$ from S_i the user's device computes $M_{11} = M_9 \oplus M_2$. Then, it checks if $M_{10} = h(M_2||M_{11}||R_c)$ or not. If both are equal, the device computes $M_{12} = h(M_2||R_c||M_{11})$. Then, it sends the reply message $\{M_{12}\}$ for its authentication to S_i
- Step 4: On receiving $\{M_{12}\}$, server checks if $M_{12} = h(M_8||M_7||R_s)$ or not. If both are equal, S_i accepts the login request of the user U_i.
- Step 5: U_i and S_i compute session key to encrypt exchange information after mutual authenticaion. U_i computes session key $SK = h(R_c||M_1||M_2||M_{11})$, S_i computes session key $SK = h(M_7||M_6||M_8||R_s)$.

Password Change Phase: When the user wishes to change his/her old password PW_i, the user and user's device invole folloing steps:

- Step 1: user's device compute the biometric B_i of U_i and Retrieves ID_i and PW_i by compute: $ID_i = hID_i \oplus h(B_i||K_i')$, $PW_i = hPW_i \oplus h(K_i'||B_i)$, $K_i = (ID_i||PW_i) \oplus j_i$. Then, user's device compute: $M_1 = C_i \oplus h(ID_i||(PW_i \oplus B_i \oplus K_i))$, $M_2 = e_i \oplus h((PW_i \oplus B_i \oplus K_i)||ID_i)$, and check if $f_i = h(M_1||M_2)$. If this information matches, user passes the biometrics verification; otherwise user's device terminates the session.
- Step 2: User input new password PW_i^*
- Step 3: User's device update the following values:

$$C_i = C_i \oplus h(ID_i||(PW_i \oplus B_i \oplus K_i)) \oplus h(ID_i||(PW_i^* \oplus B_i \oplus K_i))$$
$$e_i = e_i \oplus h((PW_i \oplus B_i \oplus K_i)||ID_i) \oplus h((PW_i^* \oplus B_i \oplus K_i)||ID_i)$$
$$g_i = g_i \oplus (ID_i||PW_i||B_i) \oplus (ID_i||PW_i^*||B_i)$$
$$j_i = j_i \oplus (ID_i||PW_i) \oplus (ID_i||PW_i^*)$$
$$hPW_i = PW_i^* \oplus h(K_i'||B_i)$$

3.3 Proposed Method for Gait-Based Authentication Using Ensemble Support Vector Machine

In traditional Support Vector Machine (SVM) learning models, all samples in the training set are used to build the model. In this paper, the authors propose a modified form of SVM, which can be considered as ensembling multiple SVM classifiers to boost the overall accuracy.

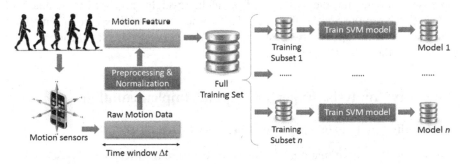

Fig. 4. Train multiple SVM classifiers with different subsets of the training set

Figure 4 demonstrates the process to train multiple SVM classifiers with different subsets of training data. Raw motion data captured from motion sensors within a pre-defined time window Δt is normalized into gait motion features. From the full training set, we randomly create n training subsets, each of which contains P % samples from the training set. Then n lightweight SVM classifiers are trained with these training subsets. Although each of these lightweight classifiers may not be as robust as a strong classifer trained with the whole training set, ensembling all n lightweight classifiers with an appropriate voting scheme is promising to achieve higher accuracy in classification than using a single strong classifier.

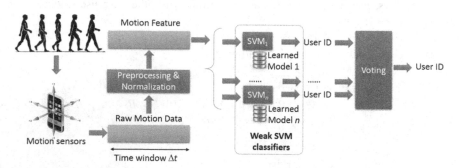

Fig. 5. User authentication with biometric gait data using multiple SVM classifiers

Figure 5 shows the main steps in our proposed SVM-based method for user identification based on his or her gait features with multiple SVM classifiers. Raw motion data is collected continuously in background mode and the process to recognize a user is activated periodically. After the preprocessing step to normalize raw motion data, motion feature is fed as an input into multiple weak SVM classifers, each of which uses a different learned model. Outputs of all these SVM classifiers are fused in the voting scheme to determine the user ID.

There are numerous measures to consolidate lightweight classifiers and voting is chosen in our proposed method. Within voting method, the predicted class of each sample is the one that has the most votes from all lightweight classifiers. If the output of classifier C_i for sample S is L_p, then class L_p has one vote from classifier C_i. Finally, if the number of votes upon class C_j exceeds the rest classes, our classification model predicts C_j as the class of sample S.

4   Security Analysis, Experiments, and Implementation

4.1   Security Analysis of Proposed Scheme and Method

In this section, we prove that our scheme is more secure than Khan et al.'s scheme by exploiting the advantage of biometric factor and can resist many kinds of attacks.

User Impersonation Attack: If an attacker wants to impersonate as a legitimate user to login the server, he/she must correctly forge the values: $h(n), M_3, M_4, M_5, M_{12}$. However, the attacker cannot do this even if he/she can extract the shared values stored in the user's device, because the attacker cannot get the value ID_i, PW_i which can only be computed based on the knowledge B_i, which is very difficult to copy or share and extremely hard to forge. Hence, our proposed scheme can resist against the user impersonation attack.

Server Masquerading Attack: If an attacker wants to impersonate as the legitimate server S_i, he/she must forge the correct message $\{M_9, M_{10}\}$. However, since the attacker does not have the value x_s and y_s, she cannot obtain the value of M_6, M_7, M_8, and therefore cannot compute the correct M_9, M_{10}. Hence, the attacker cannot perform server masquerading attacks to fool the user.

Password Guessing Attack: Suppose the attacker can extract the secret values $\{C_i, e_i, f_i, g_i, j_i, hID_i, hPW_i, K'_i, h(.)\}$ stored in the user's device, and try to derive the user's password PW_i based on some protocol transcripts. In our proposed protocol, we hide user's password by using biometric factor: $hPW_i = PW_i \oplus h(K'_i \| B_i)$. An attacker cannot get PW_i since the attacker does not know the user's biometrics information B_i. Moreover, our scheme does not send information contained user's password in the login and authentication scheme. Therefore, attacker cannot get any clue to guess user's password.

Replay Attack: In this kind of attack, the adversary first eavesdrops the communication flows of U_i, and later tries to imitate U_i to login S_i by replaying the eavesdropped messages. The proposed scheme using random nonce in both user and server side. These random values change randomly in each session. Therefore, the replayed message can be easily detected and dropped by S_i or U_i. Thus, the proposed scheme is capable of detecting and resisting the replay attack.

Insider Attack: In our proposed scheme, the user submits $PW_i \oplus B_i \oplus K_i$ instead of PW_i, B_i to the registration center R in the registration phase. Even though the registration server can obtain the value of K_i stored in user's device, the registration center cannot get PW_i and/or B_i, which may also be used by the user in other applications. Hence, our proposed scheme is secure against the insider attack.

Stolen Shared Information Attacks: If an attacker know the shared information $\{C_i, e_i, f_i, g_i, j_i, hID_i, hPW_i, K'_i, h(.)\}$ of user U_i and wants to use this information to login to the server, he/she has to input the correct information B_i. However, B_i is very difficult to copy or share and extremely hard to forge. Therefore, the attacker cannot successfully be authenticated by the server.

Three-Factor Attack: In this kind of attack, we assume an attacker has the shared information $\{C_i, e_i, f_i, g_i, j_i, hID_i, hPW_i, K'_i, h(.)\}$, password PW_i and identity ID_i of user U_i. The attacker now have to get random values n, K_i and biometric B_i to compute $h(n), M_3, M_4, M_5, M_{12}$ to authenticate with server S_i. This means the attacker have to guess three values n, K_i and biometric B_i in the same time. This can not be done in the real-time. Thus, our scheme can resist three-factor attack.

Security Comparison: In Table 2, we present the security comparison of our method with three existing schemes by Khan et al. [5], Sarvabhatla et al. [6], and Wen et al. [7]. Besides common types of attacks, our method can also resist three-factor attack which has not been considered by Sarvabhatla [6] and Wen [7].

Table 2. Comparison of ability to resist various kinds of attacks

Feature	Khan et al. [5]	Sarvabhatla et al. [6]	Wen et al. [7]	Ours
Prevent user impersonation attack	No	Yes	Yes	Yes
Prevent server masquerading attack	No	Yes	Yes	Yes
Prevent password guessing attack	No	Yes	Yes	Yes
Prevent stolen smart cards attacks	No	Yes	Yes	Yes
Mutual authentication	No	Yes	Yes	Yes
Strong replay resistance	Yes	Yes	Yes	Yes
Prevent insider attack	Yes	Yes	Yes	Yes
Three-factor attack	No	Not Consider	Not Consider	Yes

4.2   Experiment on User Recognition with Gait Data

In this experiment, we use the dataset containing 38 classes corresponding to 38 different users labeled from 1 to 38. There are 4329 samples in the training set and 4453 samples in the test set. Each feature has 288 sampling values collected from the accelerometer. The proportion ($P\%$) of training set that SVM model uses to build lightweight classifiers and the number of classifiers are two parameters in our experiment. Setting the value of P in the set {50, 60, 70, 80, 90} and the number of classifiers in the range 1 to 15, the authors probe the accuracy when using the fused model on test set. Figure 6 illustrates the result of our experiment.

As Fig. 6 shows, at the starting point (i.e. the number of classifiers is 1), using 80 % of training set results in the highest accuracy of 91.444 % while the lowest accuracy (88.996 %) is recorded when only half of the data are put into the training process. As we double the number of models, a sharp plunge is witnessed at 3 lines "80 % Training Set", "90 % Training Set", and "70 % Training Set". The other 2 lines, which is "60 % Training Set" and "50 % Training Set", experience a slight drop but the trough of accuracy (88.951 %) in our experiment is hit by the line corresponding to lower proportion of data set. When the number of models reaches 3, all lines soar

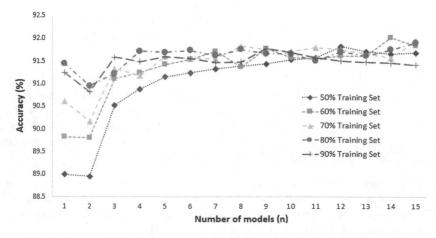

Fig. 6. Accuracy of gait-based user identification with multiple SVM classifiers

dramatically and fluctuate between 91.000 % and 92.000 % as we use more than 5 models in building the integrated classifier. By experiment, we choose the best combination of parameters as 60 % training set and 14 lightweight classifiers. In our experiment, this combination yields to 92.028 % in accuracy.

5 Conclusion

We propose Smart Kiosk system to allow users to access data and online services associated with their personal identities using implicitly continuous gait-based authentication. To realize our proposed system, we propose a user classification method based on gait data using multiple SVM classifiers and a secure authentication scheme with biometric data. In the prototype implementation of Smart Kiosk system, we use Android mobile devices for real time authentication. Currently the Smart Kiosk service can interact with Facebook, Gmail, and Flickr.

In fact, different methods to recognize users from their gait features and other schemes for user authentication can be applied into our proposed system to create different implementations. Currently, we are studying deep learning approach to learn higher-level representation of motion data captured from sensors of mobile/wearable devices for better accuracy of user identification. We also consider different strategies to devise new authentication schemes with biometric data to enhance the security for users in smart interactive environments.

Acknowledgement. This research is funded by Vietnam National University HoChiMinh City (VNU-HCM) under grant number B2015-18-01.

References

1. Lamport, L.: Password authentication with insecure communication. Commun. ACM **24**(11), 770–772 (1981)
2. Lee, C.C., Hwang, M.S., Liao, I.E.: Security enhancement on a new authentication scheme with anonymity for wireless environments. IEEE Trans. Industr. Electron. **53**(5), 1683–1686 (2006)
3. Yang, G., Wong, D.S., Wang, H., Deng, X.: Two-factor mutual authentication based on smart cards and passwords. J. Comput. Syst. Sci. **74**(7), 1160–1172 (2008)
4. An, Y.: Security analysis and enhancements of an effective biometric-based remote user authentication scheme using smart cards. J. Biomed. Biotechnol. **2012**(519723), 6 (2012)
5. Khan, M.K., Kumari, S.: (An improved biometrics-based remote user authentication scheme with user anonymity. J. Biomed. Biotechnol. **2013**(491289), 9 (2013)
6. Sarvabhatla, M., Giri, M., Vorugunti, C.S.: A secure biometrics-based remote user authentication scheme for secure data exchange. Embed. Syst. **2014**, 110–115 (2014)
7. Wen, F., Susilo, W., Yang, G.: Analysis and improvement on a biometric-based remote user authentication scheme using smart cards. J. Wireless Pers. Commun. **80**(4), 1747–1760 (2014)
8. Fan, C.I., Lin, Y.H.: Provably secure remote truly three-factor authentication scheme with privacy protection on biometrics. IEEE Trans. Inf. Forensics Secur. **4**(4), 933–945 (2009)

9. Thinh, T-T., Tran, M-T., Duong, A-D.: Robust mobile device integration of a fingerprint biometric remote authentication scheme. In: 26th IEEE International Conference on Advanced Information Networking and Applications (AINA 2012), pp. 678–685 (2012)

10. Thinh, T-T., Tran, M-T., Duong, A-D.: Robust secure dynamic ID based remote user authentication scheme for multi-server environment. In: 13th International Conference on Computational Science and Its Applications (ICCSA 2013). LNCS, vol. 7975, pp. 502–515 (2013)

11. Pan, G., Zhang, Y., Wu, Z.: Accelerometer-based gait recognition via voting by signature points. IET Electron. Lett. **45**(22), 1116–1118 (2009)

12. Frank, F., Mannor, S., Precup, D.: Activity and gait recognition with time-delay embeddings. In: The 24th AAAI Conference on Artificial Intelligence 2010, pp. 1581–1586 (2010)

13. Dandachi, G., Hassan, B.E., Hussein, A.E.: A novel identification/verification model using smartphone's sensors and user behavior. In: 2nd International Conference on Advances in Biomedical Engineering (ICABME 2013), pp. 235–238 (2013)

14. Nickel, C., Busch, C.: Classifying accelerometer data via hidden Markov models to authenticate people by the way they walk. IEEE Aerosp. Electron. Syst. Mag. **28**(10), 29–35 (2013)

15. Hoang, T., Choi, D., Vo, V., Nguyen, A., Nguyen, T.: A lightweight gait authentication on mobile phone regardless of installation error. In: The 28th IFIP TC 11 International Conference (SEC 2013), pp. 83–101 (2013)

Gesture-Based Configuration of Location Information in Smart Environments with Visual Feedback

Carsten Stocklöw[(✉)] and Martin Majewski

Fraunhofer Institute for Computer Graphics Research IGD,
Fraunhoferstr. 5, 64283 Darmstadt, Germany
{carsten.stockloew,martin.majewski}@igd.fraunhofer.de

Abstract. The location of objects and devices in a smart environment is a very important piece of information to enable advanced and sophisticated use cases for interaction and for supporting the user in daily activities and emergency situations. To acquire this information, we propose a semi-automatic approach to configure the location, size, and orientation of objects in the environment together with their semantic meaning. This configuration is typically done with graphical user interfaces showing either a list of objects or a representation of objects in form of 2D or 3D virtual representations.

However, there is a gap between the real physical world and the abstract virtual representation that needs to be bridged by the user himself. Therefore, we propose a visual feedback directly in the physical world using a robotic laser pointing system.

Keywords: Smart environments · Configuration · Personalization

1 Introduction

Technologies that realize the paradigm of Ambient Assisted Living (AAL) and Smart Environments have found an increasing interest in the scientific community and on the market. Most notably, sensors and actuators for Home Automation, smart entertainment systems like TV and Hifi sets as well as devices such as smartphones or tablet computers. Simple scenarios allow the user to directly interact with and to control the devices in the intelligent environment. More sophisticated applications try to analyze the context of the user, e.g. the location of the user and the location of objects in the surrounding. This can be used for a variety of scenarios. For example, a fall detection application could be enhanced to determine if the user has fallen down on the ground or is simply lying down on a sofa, if the location of the sofa is known; a burglar could be detected by a smart floor if activity is detected near a window and no activity was detected before from a user that could have gone inside the room to the window; a user interface is following the user from one room to the next, thus presenting the

© Springer International Publishing Switzerland 2015
N. Streitz and P. Markopoulos (Eds.): DAPI 2015, LNCS 9189, pp. 201–211, 2015.
DOI: 10.1007/978-3-319-20804-6_19

information on the device that is closest to the user; or for multimodal interaction (e.g. pointing at an object to control its parameters). Therefore, location of users and objects in the environment can be considered a very important piece of information for the system to enable high-level applications.

Consequently, there is a need to acquire location information of objects in the surrounding. This can be done online via camera-based systems that continuously monitor the area of interest. However, there may be multiple cameras needed to monitor a whole appartement, thus increasing the costs of such a system, and there are justified privacy concerns of constantly monitoring a private home. Another possibility would be to use active tags on each object and exploit the Received Signal Strength, but those mechanisms need the tags on each object. Some of those technologies have been investigated in the EvAAL competition [1].

Most of the bigger objects can be considered to be stationary. This includes some devices (like TV, refrigerator), furniture (like sofa, table), as well as built-in objects (like windows). Therefore, we use a one-time configuration that needs to be repeated if bigger changes in the environment occur. This configuration can make use of camera-based systems to gather the information needed without privacy concerns. However, the algorithms to detect and identify objects from a camera image are not yet fully reliable, and objects that are not in the visible range cannot be recognized. Thus, we propose a semi-automatic approach to detect objects that can be enhanced with detailed information from a user, e.g. by selecting a specific model for the detected TV. In this case, the user would be a technician that performs the one-time configuration.

This configuration is typically supported by the system with visual feedback in form of graphical user interfaces showing either a list of objects or a representation of each object in form of 2D or 3D virtual representations. However, there is a gap between the real physical world and the abstract virtual representation that *needs to be bridged by the user himself*. Therefore, we provide a visual feedback directly in the physical world using a robotic laser pointing system that is able to show where the user is pointing to. This can be used to reliably select elements in the environment as it has been shown that a direct visual feedback is an important aspect to increase the accuracy of pointing gestures.

2   Related Work

Bridging the gap between the physical world and a virtual representation of it was subject of many scientific publications and areas. The term *Mixed Reality* is often used to describe technologies that "involve the merging of real and virtual worlds somewhere along the 'virtuality continuum' which connects completely real environments to completely virtual ones" [11]. As part of this continuum, Augmented Reality "refers to all cases in which the display of an otherwise real environment is augmented by means of virtual (computer graphic) objects". This is often realized by smartphones or tablet computers that need to be directed towards the real object, making it cumbersome for devices with large displays or impose restrictions related to the interaction in case of devices with small displays. Another class of devices are specialized glasses or head-mounted displays that are out of the scope of this work.

The MirageTable [2] uses a curved screen; an image is shown on that screen with a stereoscopic projector. Interaction with hand gestures can be done directly on that screen, but the interaction area is restricted to the screen.

Hossain et al. [5] present a system that combines the home automation system of the real world with the virtual world of Second Life[1]. Events from one representation is reflected in the other. The system has been found to be "appealing and useful to the user". However, there is no mixture of the two representations; the user interacts either in the real or in the virtual world.

The XWand, part of the WorldCursor [15] project by Microsoft Research in 2003 is a signal-processing pointing device, that can be seen as an indirect predecessor of the very popular Nintendo Wii Remote controller shipped with the same-named Wii video games console. The XWand is equipped with a three-axis magnetoresistive permalloy magnetometer that measures its yaw angle relating to the Earths magnetic field and a two-axis accelerometer to sense the acceleration relative to the gravity vector. Its purpose is to determine the pitch and roll angle of the device so it can be used as a spatial pointing device. The Nintendo Wii Remote[2], released three years after Microsoft's publication, uses a more advanced technology featuring a single three-axis accelerometer chipset. The Sensor Bar, a kind of visual homing system, completes it. The Sensor Bar includes a couple of spatial separated infrared LEDs that are tracked by the Wii Remote's image sensor providing additional orientation information.

The second part of the WorldCurser project is a small laser robot arm that projects a small red light-spot into the pointing direction of the XWand device. This way a direct environmental feedback system is created that tries to close the gab between the users and the systems interpretation of the performed action. There are two main limitations within the WorldCursor project. First, it is mandatory for the user to carry a pointing device to perform the action and is therefore not meeting the paradigm of unobtrusiveness in terms of Ambient Intelligence. Second, the system is not aware of any location-based information, like the spatial distribution and dimensions of walls and furniture. Therefore just mimicking the movement of the XWand, either absolute or relative, results in the feedback projection.

Majewski et al. proposed a more advanced solution to solve these two concerns with the Visual support system for selecting reactive elements in intelligent environments [7] that is also part of the technical realization of this paper. The Environmental Aware Gesture Leading Equipment recognizes marker free pointing gestures performed by the user with the Kinect RGB-D camera, calculates the intersection point of the pointing direction with the internal virtual representation of the environment and provides a direct absolute cue-projection onto that physical location. Majewski et al. [8] presented an extension to this system

---

[1] http://secondlife.com.
[2] http://us.wii.com/ (visited on 05/03/2015).

that combines different location technologies, like the CapFloor [4] system, to dynamically determine forbidden areas where projection could cause harm and should therefore not be performed at all, e.g. when projected directly onto the eye-area of another person.

The Beamatron project of Wilson et al. [14] shows an even more advanced marker free interaction approach in terms of information projection using several Kinect cameras, a microphone array setup, as well as a high definition projector mounted on a stage-light robot arm. While the usage of the mentioned sensing system provides direct user-to-machine interaction, the projector enables a high detail information feedback of the performed interaction directly into the users environment such as menus and 3D graphics. This bidirectional interaction paradigm makes it also possible to use the projected information for interaction like grabbing a projected document and dragging it to different locations.

Stahl et al. [12] introduced the concept of 'synchronized realities' and created a 3D virtual representation of a real living lab. Actions in either representation are synchronized and reflected in the other one. However, this system is used only to control elements of the environment, not for configuration or to change the location of an element.

3   System Overview

This chapter describes the main components that are needed to realize our interaction concept - a vision based reconstruction of the environment, a visual feedback system with a robotic laser pointing system, and a semantic model to classify and describe the objects and their properties. We use Microsoft Kinect as RGB-D sensor for the reconstruction, to track the user, and to recognize free-air gestures from the skeleton data.

3.1   Vision-Based Reconstruction

The reconstruction of the environment is performed using a RGB-D camera that provides a 2D camera image with additional depth information (Microsoft Kinect One). We first analyse the scene as a whole by detecting the floor, ceiling, and walls with a plane recognition method. With this information the recognition of objects can be enhanced using this contextual information. Similar approaches have been reported by Koppula et al. [6] who used visual appearance, local shape and geometry, and geometrical context (e.g. a monitor is always on-top-of a table); the micro precision in home scenes increased by 16,88 % with this additional reasoning on geometrical context. Xiong et al. [16] used Conditional Random Field to model geometrical relationships (orthogonal, parallel, adjacent, and coplanar) between planar patches to classify walls, floors, ceilings, and clutter. The recognition rate increased from 84 % to 90 % when using certain contextual information in combination with local features.

As the reconstruction is not the main part of this contribution, we used a simple approach as shown in Fig. 1. We first use RANSAC to detect planes in the

Fig. 1. Reconstruction of the environment: camera image (left), detected objects (right) (Color figure online)

3D point cloud. The normal vector of these planes then determines whether the plane belongs to a wall (vertical plane, shown in red in the figure). The lowest horizontal plane is considered the floor (gray), and planes parallel to the floor plane are further evaluated according to their distance to the floor plane, their shape and size. That way, we can recognize, for example, a table (green) or a sofa in the environment.

3.2 Visual Feedback System

Visual feedback in the physical world is provided by the E.A.G.L.E. Eye, a robotic laser pointing system, introduced by Majewski et al. [7]. The system is shown in Fig. 2. The E.A.G.L.E. Eye is based on an Arduino microcontroller board that is operating a laser mounted on two servo motors that allow free and precise positioning of a laser dot in the room.

Fig. 2. Visual Feedback Robot (left) and mounted on living room ceiling (right)

By showing a laser dot in the room it is possible to provide feedback about where the user is pointing at. The framework tracks the skeleton data of the user and can calculate the intersection of the pointing ray with the environment. The laser pointing system can show the laser dot at exactly this intersection point, thereby following the user's pointing direction and giving direkt feedback in the physical world.

If the location, size, and orientation of an object is known, it can also be used to highlight a selected object by showing the laser dot at the center of that object. Optionally, the laser is able to go into a blinking mode, indicating that a selection has been completed. Additionally, the laser can also indicate the location, size, and orientation of an object by moving along the silhouette of that object, as described in Sect. 4.

3.3 Semantic Model

The semantic model to describe objects and their properties is realized as a set of ontologies with each ontology representing a certain application domain. The ontologies are taken from universAAL[3].

A basic ontology models physical things and their location. This ontology is described in detail by Marinc et al. [10]; an excerpt is depicted in Fig. 3. Each physical thing has a location that can be a room with a certain function. Additionally, each PhysicalThing has a shape and each location can be contained in or adjacent to another location (not shown here).

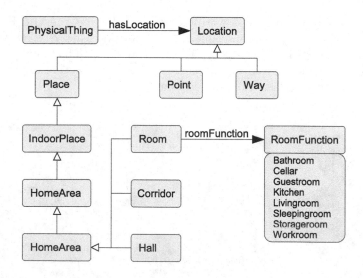

Fig. 3. Location ontology (excerpt)

Other ontologies model different types of devices, e.g. a LightSource (from device ontology), a TV, or a Stereoset (from multimedia ontology), as shown in Fig. 4. Each device has appropriate properties, e.g. a light source has a brightness

---

[3] http://depot.universaal.org.

value. As subclasses of the class PhysicalThing they inherit also the location property. Other devices are, for example, blinds, curtain, heater, humidity sensor, smoke sensor etc.

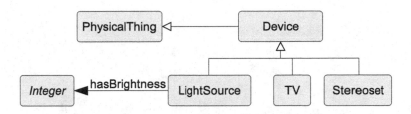

Fig. 4. Device ontology (excerpt) and multimedia ontology

The furniture ontology represents different kinds of furniture. These ontology classes have no additional properties except the ones that are inherited from the super class, PhysicalThing (Fig. 5).

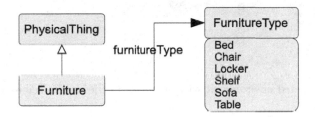

Fig. 5. Furniture ontology

4   Interaction Between Physical and Virtual World

In this section we describe our concept of bridging between the physical and the virtual world. Basically, we can distinguish between the two directions of (1) interacting in the physical world with reactions in the virtual and (2) interacting with the virtual representation with reactions in the physical world.

We assume that the reconstruction of the environment has already segmented and annotated different objects. However, this annotation can only be done according to a certain recognition rate and may be incorrect or not precise enough. For example, a TV could be recognized by the system automatically, but to actually use this device in a smart environment we may need the specific model to interoperate with the right protocol. Hence, it is needed to modify existing annotations. Additionally, the location, size, and orientation of objects may be incorrect and needs to be adjusted. Therefore, the system should be able to select and to modify information in a unified way that synchronizes the virtual representation with the physical world.

Figure 6 shows an example of a reconstructed environment. The objects are shown with their bounding box, which is highlighted when the object is selected.

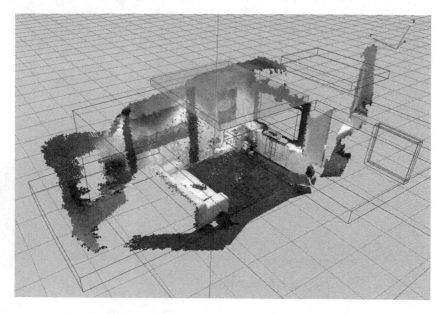

Fig. 6. Reconstructed environment with segmented objects; the ceiling lamp is highlighted

One way of interaction is the selection of elements. Using a graphical user interface (GUI), this method is well-known utilizing a mouse or a touchpad. For the real world, existing work often uses pointing gestures, e.g. by exploiting the skeleton data coming from RGB-D sensors. When synchronizing the two worlds, this can lead to an additional selection in the GUI. However, if an object is selected in the GUI, there is normally no visual feedback in the real world. This is enabled in our system with the robotic laser pointing system that can visually support the selection by showing where the user is pointing to and by pointing at the center of an object if that object is selected. To verify the location, size, and orientation of that object the laser pointing system can also move along its projected bounding box, or along the shape, if the shape could be reconstructed. For solid objects, the bounding box may need to be shrinked so that the laser pointer is always visible on the object. For non-solid objects, the bounding box may need to be expanded. For example, for a window the bounding box is expanded so that the laser pointer is moving around the object and is always visible on the wall surrounding the window.

When an object is selected the metadata, e.g. the type of the object, can be modified. This can also be done with gestures, for example by selecting a type from a list of elements as shown by Stocklöw et al. [13]. However, as there may be many options to choose from this interaction method may be too cumbersome. Therefore, the usual method of selection in a GUI should be preferred. The location, size, and orientation could also be modified in the real world. A possible method is descibed by Marinc et al. [9]

5   Individual Evaluations

We evaluated our concept with different prototypes for the different tasks of the configuration process.

The robotic laser pointing system was evaluated by Majewski et al. [7] with 20 subjects between 22 and 65 years and a median age of 27 years. Each subject had to aim and select a sequence of eight different targets of different size that were placed in a room. It was shown that the visual feedback system has significantly improved the pointing accuracy.

The method ef modifying the bounding box of existing objects was evaluated by Marinc et al. [9] with eleven users, measuring the time they needed to create three boxes for Couch, TV, and Light. It was concluded that this method is well suited to allow common users to build up a virtual environment.

Braun et al. [3] have evaluated the selection and control of objects in the environment with multimodal input using gesture and speech. The test was performed by nine subjects between 21 and 29 years. The subjects considered the interaction to be intuitive and easy to master and particularly liked how pointing can simplify the complexity of speech commands. There was a noticeable learning effect from the first to the last tasks, reducing the number of wrong attempts and increasing the interaction time.

6   Conclusion

Bridging the gap between the virtual and the physical world is a task that often needs to be performed by the user. Several approaches exist for various use cases and technologies to support the user regarding this task. In this work we have proposed a method to use free-air hand gestures for interaction and a robotic laser pointing system for visual feedback in the real world; synchronizing the information in the two realms. This method was applied to the domain of configuration of location information in smart environments as this is an important piece of information to enable advanced and sophisticated use cases for interaction and for supporting the user in daily activities and emergency situations.

Future work includes improvement of the vision-based reconstruction and the integration into an overall system.

Acknowledgements. This work is partially financed by the European Commission under the FP7-ICT-Project Miraculous Life (grant agreement no. 611421).

References

1. Barsocchi, P., Potort, F., Furfari, F., Gil, A.: Comparing AAL indoor localization systems. In: Chessa, S., Knauth, S. (eds.) EvAAL 2011. CCIS, vol. 309, pp. 1–13. Springer, Heidelberg (2012)
2. Benko, H., Jota, R., Wilson, A.: Miragetable: freehand interaction on a projected augmented reality tabletop. In: Proceedings of the SIGCHI Conference on Human Factors in Computing Systems, CHI 2012, pp. 199–208. ACM, New York (2012)
3. Braun, A., Fischer, A., Marinc, A., Stocklöw, C., Majewski, M.: Context-based bounding volume morphing in pointing gesture application. In: Kurosu, M. (ed.) HCII/HCI 2013, Part IV. LNCS, vol. 8007, pp. 147–156. Springer, Heidelberg (2013)
4. Braun, A., Heggen, H., Wichert, R.: CapFloor – a flexible capacitive indoor localization system. In: Chessa, S., Knauth, S. (eds.) EvAAL 2011. CCIS, vol. 309, pp. 26–35. Springer, Heidelberg (2012)
5. Hossain, S., Rahman, A., El Saddik, A.: Bridging the gap between virtual and real with second life client in a virtual home automation system. In: 2011 24th Canadian Conference on Electrical and Computer Engineering (CCECE), pp. 001212–001217, May 2011
6. Koppula, H., Anand, A., Joachims, T., Saxena, A.: Semantic labeling of 3D point clouds for indoor scenes. In: NIPS (2011)
7. Majewski, M., Braun, A., Marinc, A., Kuijper, A.: Visual support system for selecting reactive elements in intelligent environments. In: Proceedings of 2012 International Conference on Cyberworlds, Fraunhofer-Institut für Graphische Datenverarbeitung (IGD) and Technische Universität Darmstadt (TUD) and European Association for Computer Graphics (Eurographics) and IFIP Working Group 5.10 on Computer Graphics and Virtual Worlds, pp. 251–255. IEEE Computer Society Conference Publishing Services (CPS), Los Alamitos (2012)
8. Majewski, M., Dutz, T., Wichert, R.: An optical guiding system for gesture based interactions in smart environments. In: Streitz, N., Markopoulos, P. (eds.) DAPI 2014. LNCS, vol. 8530, pp. 154–163. Springer, Heidelberg (2014)
9. Marinc, A., Stocklöw, C., Braun, A.: Building up virtual environments using gestures. In: Stephanidis, C., Antona, M. (eds.) UAHCI 2013, Part III. LNCS, vol. 8011, pp. 70–78. Springer, Heidelberg (2013)
10. Marinc, A., Stocklöw, C., Tazari, S.: 3D interaction in AAL environments based on ontologies. In: Wichert, R., Eberhardt, B. (eds.) Ambient Assisted Living. ATSC, vol. 2, pp. 289–302. Springer, Heidelberg (2012)
11. Milgram, P., Kishino, F.: A taxonomy of mixed reality visual displays. IEICE Trans. Inf. Syst. **E77–D**(12), 1321–1329 (1994)
12. Stahl, C., Frey, J., Alexandersson, J., Brandherm, B.: Synchronized realities. J. Ambient Intell. Smart Environ. (JAISE) **3**(1), 13–25 (2011)
13. Stocklöw, C., Wichert, R.: Gesture based semantic service invocation for human environment interaction. In: Patern, F., de Ruyter, B., Markopoulos, P., Santoro, C., van Loenen, E., Luyten, K. (eds.) AmI 2012. LNCS, vol. 7683, pp. 304–311. Springer, Heidelberg (2012)
14. Wilson, A., Benko, H., Izadi, S., Hilliges, O.: Steerable augmented reality with the beamatron. In: Proceedings of the 25th Annual ACM Symposium on User Interface Software and Technology, UIST 2012, pp. 413–422. ACM, New York (2012)

15. Wilson, A., Pham, H.: Pointing in intelligent environments with the world cursor. In: Proceedings of Interact 2003 (2003)
16. Xiong, X., Huber, D.: Using context to create semantic 3D models of indoor environments. In: Proceedings of the British Machine Vision Conference, pp. 45.1–45.11. BMVA Press (2010). doi:10.5244/C.24.45

Subjective User Experience and Performance with Active Tangibles on a Tabletop Interface

Jan B.F. van Erp[1,2(✉)], Alexander Toet[1], Koos Meijer[1],
Joris Janssen[1], and Arnoud de Jong[1]

[1] TNO Human Factors, Kampweg 5, Soesterberg, The Netherlands
{jan.vanerp,lex.toet,joris.janssen,arnoud.dejong}
@tno.nl
[2] Human Media Interaction, University of Twente, Drienerlolaan 5,
Enschede, The Netherlands

Abstract. We developed active tangibles (Sensators) that can be used in combination with multitouch tabletops and that can provide multisensory (visual, auditory, and vibrotactile) feedback. For spatial alignment and rotation tasks we measured subjective user experience and objective performance with these Sensators. We found that active feedback increased accuracy in both tasks, for all feedback modalities. Active visual feedback yielded the highest overall subjective user experience and preference scores. Our contribution is that active feedback improves subjectively perceived performance and reduces perceived mental workload. Additionally, our findings indicate that users prefer to be guided by visual signs over auditory and vibrotactile signs.

Keywords: Tangible interfaces · User experience · Tabletop · Multimodal · Active feedback

1 Introduction

Tangible user interfaces (TUIs) provide an intuitive way to interact with digital information through manipulating physical objects. They combine the dynamic qualities typical of digital information with physical affordances. In combination with multi-touch tables TUIs provide passive haptic feedback and visual feedback. Users can handle TUIs similar to everyday objects, which simplifies system interaction and reduces cognitive load. The power of this concept is for instance effectively illustrated by Urp [1], an application for working with architectural elements in the context of urban planning and design, which allows users to move physical models of houses around on a tabletop surface to observe changes in sunlight and shadows.

Frequently quoted benefits of TUIs include eyes-free interaction, spatial multi-plexing and bimanualism [2] and the natural affordances of tangible objects [3, 4]. In addition, they can be acquired faster and manipulated more accurately than for instance multi-touch widgets or a mouse in simple control tasks [5, 6].

Active feedback refers to the ability to actively influence the interaction, e.g. by changing the object's position or orientation, or multimodal feedback via the haptic,

© Springer International Publishing Switzerland 2015
N. Streitz and P. Markopoulos (Eds.): DAPI 2015, LNCS 9189, pp. 212–223, 2015.
DOI: 10.1007/978-3-319-20804-6_20

auditory or visual modality. Most TUIs currently used with multitouch tabletops are passive objects that offer no active feedback. If active feedback is provided at all, it is usually only in the visual modality and on the tabletop surface (e.g. in the form of halos or virtual knobs around the tangibles), forcing users to look at the table to see the effect of a manipulation. Actuated TUIs can convey task relevant information through multiple or alternative sensory channels, thus facilitating information processing by simplifying information and guiding user attention. In addition, multimodal feedback has the ability to enhance both objective and subjective performance measures in tasks with high perceptual and cognitive load [7]. Vibrotactile cues can effectively replace visual progress information [8, 9] and visual alerts [10], although they are not effective when replacing visual direction or spatial orientation cues [10]. Audio cues have been found to speed up task performance [11], and can attract attention to tangibles that are outside the field of view. Hence, distributing feedback over different modalities may reduce workload and enable multitasking by reducing within- channel interference [12–14]. In addition, actuated TUIs that are linked to and dynamically represent digital information afford bidirectional interaction while maintaining consistency between the physical interfaces and their representations [15], between remotely coupled TUIs [16, 17], or between TUIs and their underlying digital model [18].

We developed active tangibles (Sensators, Fig. 1) that can wirelessly communicate with for instance a tabletop surface and provide direct visual, auditory, vibrotactile, or multimodal feedback while taking haptic input, thereby allowing an intuitive interaction that stretches even beyond the boundaries of the tabletop surface. In addition, wireless connectivity allows to store information in these objects and reuse them on another tabletop or to superimpose different objects, thus enabling distributed interaction between different users on different tables [19, 20].

Fig. 1. The Sensators. The grey areas are coated with conductive paint and are connected with touch sensors. Left: activated Sensator emitting red light. Right: numbers on top serve to identify the Sensators. Arrows serve to indicate their orientation.

In contrast to passive tangibles, Sensators can actively guide the user and confirm when they have reached a given location and orientation through multisensory feedback. Hence, Sensators have the potential to enhance and intensify the interaction and collaboration experience between users (e.g. on multitouch surfaces) by supporting new interaction styles and techniques. In this study we investigated user performance with Sensators in two spatial tasks: a Movement and a Rotation task. Our first hypothesis (H1) is that both tasks will be performed faster and with higher accuracy (i.e. a lower error rate) when receiving active feedback compared to receiving only passive visual feedback. Our second hypothesis (H2) is that visual feedforward cues signaling which of the Sensators have to be moved will lower task completion timed by reducing search time. Thirdly, we hypothesize (H3) that any form of active feedback will improve subjective user experience by reducing the amount of cognitive effort required to determine the state of the system and the effects of one's actions. Finally, (H4) we expect that active visual feedback will enhance user experience to a larger extent than auditory and tactile feedback, because people are less experienced at being guided by vibrotactile [21] and auditory signs [10, 22, 23], and because vision dominates the auditory and haptic sense in spatial tasks [22, 24].

2   Related Work

Active tangibles have been introduced before in the context of tabletop systems. The Haptic Wheel [25] is a mobile rotary controller providing haptic feedback for eyes-free interaction to reduce cognitive load and visual attention in visually demanding tasks. The SmartPuck [26] is a multimodal tangible interface providing visual, auditory and tactile feedback which has been used to navigate geographical information in Google Earth. Touchbugs [27] are autonomously moving TUIs that can provide haptic feedback and accept haptic input. Tangibles that move autonomously [18] or provide vibrotactile collision feedback [28] have been demonstrated in furniture arrangement scenarios. Active tangibles have also been used for auditory and haptic rendering of scatter plots [29].

However, there are only a few studies on user experience and performance with active tangibles [30, 31]. It appears that active tangibles can effectively support users in solving complex spatial layout problems [30] and in fine-grained manipulation tasks [31] by providing haptic feedback. In this study we further investigate the experience and performance with active TUIs providing multisensory feedback in two spatial tasks.

3   Methods

3.1   Participants

21 adults (10 females, 11 males, mean age = 36.7 years, age range: 20–48 years) were recruited for this experiment. 17 participants were right-handed. None of the participants had any physical disabilities. Participants were compensated €30, - for their participation. All participants used a computer on a weekly basis (M = 30 h per week). 12 participants played computer games on a weekly basis (M = 6 h per week). 20 participants had previous experience with multi-touch technology on mobile phones. One participant had previous experience using a multi-touch tabletop interface.

3.2   Material

A Samsung Surface 40 (SUR 40: www.samsung.com) was used as a multi-touch tabletop computing device. The SUR 40 allows users to directly manipulate digital content using both multi-touch hand gestures and through the manipulation of tangibles. The SUR 40 features a 40 inch Full HD (1080p) display and multiple Bluetooth connections. The active tangibles (referred to as 'Sensators' in the rest of this study) used in this experiment were specially developed to be used in combination with an interactive multi-touch tabletop. Each Sensator (6.5 × 6.5 × 5.0 cm) includes an Arduino mini micro-controller and a Bluetooth communication module which enables communication with the SUR 40. The Sensators can convey vibrotactile, visual and auditory feedback through various functional parts. Embedded in their translucent 3D printed housing are two small electronic motorized actuators or tactors. Each tactor can independently produce nine levels of vibrotactile signals. An RGB LED centered on top underneath the housing enables a Sensator to display different colors. An embedded mp3 audio processing shield enables a Sensator to play mp3 audio output signals. A Sensator also contains two independent touch sensors connected to the top of its four sides. See [32] for more details.

In this study each Sensator was marked both with its number (1, 2 or 3) and an arrow symbol (2D orientation), while a fiducial marker was attached to its bottom. This enabled the SUR40 to track both the location and orientation of each Sensator independently. The experiment was performed in a brightly lit room with white walls. The participant stood directly behind the SUR 40. A side table was placed next to the SUR 40 on its right side. A blue A4 paper sheet, attached to the surface of this side table within reaching distance of the participant's right arm, functioned as a target location during some phases of the experiment. The experimenter stood about 3 m from the participant, and operated a tripod mounted video camera to record the experiments.

3.3   User Tasks

Participants performed two task: a *Movement Task* which involved the displacement of the Sensators to different designated target positions, and a *Rotation Task* which involved adjustment of the orientation of the Sensators to a single designated target site. During the experiments the display of the SUR40 showed an abstract map with a realistic appearance but without any cues that might interfere with the task. A map was used as background since it likely that Sensators will ultimately be applied in the context of geographical information displays.

The three Sensators were placed on their corresponding icons on the SUR40. Prior to the start of each trial the screen showed two buttons: one on left side labeled 'Start 1' and one on the right side labeled 'Start 2'. To ensure that the participant's hands were in the same starting position for each trial these two buttons had to be pressed simultaneously for 200 ms. After starting a trial a grey button labelled 'Finish' appeared in the bottom center of the screen. By pressing this button the participant could finish the trial. White circles labeled H1, H2 and H3 served as a passive visual cues during the experiment, indicating target locations for the Sensators with corresponding labels.

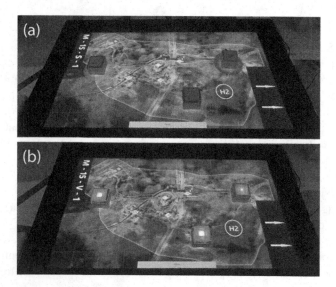

Fig. 2. Tabletop mode (upper) and visual feedback (lower) modes used in the Movement Task. The two Sensators on the left are in their correct positions.

Movement Task. At the start of each experiment the Sensators were placed on icons with corresponding numbers (H1, H2, and H3) shown in the lower part of the SUR40 map display. On each trial up to three target icon positions were updated on the screen, and the participant 's task was to move the Sensators with updated target locations to their new positions as accurately and quickly as possible. Participants were asked not to lift the Sensators from the table surface, since the SUR40 needs direct contact with a Sensators' fiducial marker to track its location and pointing angle. They were allowed to use both hands. Each trial that ended with one or more Sensators not in the correct position was labeled as incorrect.

Performance in the Movement Task was tested for six different feedback techniques, which served to quickly guide the users to the correct target location in a stepwise fashion. Four feedback modes were actively provided by the Sensators: Vibrotactile, Auditory, Visual and Multimodal (= Visual + Auditory + Vibrotactile). In addition, the Tabletop provided visual feedback, and we included no feedback or Baseline condition. In the Vibrotactile feedback mode, the Sensators started vibrating when they came within 300 p (22 p = 1.0 cm) of the target location. At a distance of 200, 100 and 50 p the vibration intensity increased stepwise. Vibration stopped when the Sensator came within 8 pixels (the error margin) of the target location, indicating the correct location had been reached. In the Auditory, Vibrotactile, and Multimodal modes the intensity of the feedback signal increased stepwise while approaching the target and stopped when the Sensator had reached its target position. The Auditory feedback technique was similar to the Tactile technique, but instead of a vibration the Sensator produced a tone that increased in pitch when it approached the target location. In the Visual feedback mode Sensators with an updated target location turned blue. When a Sensator came within the error margin of its target location the Sensator turned green indicating the correct position had been reached (see Fig. 2). The Multimodal feedback technique was a combination of the individual Vibrotactile, Auditory and Visual feedback techniques. In the Tabletop visual feedback mode Sensators with an updated target position were surrounded by a blue disc (R = 140 p) with an opacity of 50 %. This disc (which served as a feedforward cue) remained underneath a Sensator while it was being moved to its new location, and it turned green when the target position was reached (Fig. 2). In the Baseline mode, no feedback was provided and the Sensators acted as passive tangibles. In this case, the users only had the target icons on the tabletop surface as passive visual cues. Participants performed 15 trials per feedback technique.

Rotation Task. Throughout this experiment the Sensators were at fixed locations, indicated on the SUR40 display by icons labeled with their corresponding numbers (white discs with R = 3.5 cm, labeled H1, H2, and H3). On each trial of the Rotation Task a single red disc (R = 1.5 cm) appeared at a different location on the SUR40 display, and the participants had to rotate all three Sensators to orient their pointing angles to this target as accurately and quickly as possible. They were allowed to use both hands. Each trial that ended with one or more Sensators not correctly oriented was labeled as incorrect.

Performance in the Rotation Task was tested for six different feedback techniques, which served to quickly point the users to the correct target orientation in a stepwise fashion. In the Vibrotactile feedback mode a Sensator started vibrating when the pointing angle of the Sensator came within 50 degrees of the angular direction of the target. At angles of 40, 30 and 20 degrees the vibrating intensity increased until it came within 10 degrees (the error margin), when it stopped vibrating indicating it pointed in the correct direction. Auditory feedback was similar to Vibrotactile feedback, but instead of vibrating the Sensator produced a tone which increased in pitch until it pointed in the correct direction. In the Visual feedback mode all Sensators became blue at the start of each trial and they turned green when the Sensators were correctly oriented. A Sensator that was displaced for more than 5 cm from its start position would turn red. The Multimodal feedback technique was a combination of the Vibrotactile, Auditory and Visual feedback techniques. In the Tabletop visual feedback mode a Sensator that needed to be reoriented was surrounded by a blue disc (R = 140 p) with an opacity of 50 %, which turned green when the Sensator was turned in the correct direction. In the Baseline mode, no feedback was provided and the Sensators acted as passive tangibles. In this case, the participants could only use the target icons on the tabletop surface as passive visual cues. Participants performed 15 trials per feedback technique.

3.4 Experimental Design

The experiment was performed according to a 2 × 6 within-subject design with **Task type** (*Movement Task, Rotation Task*) and **Feedback modality** (*Vibrotactile, Auditory, Visual, Multimodal, Tabletop, Baseline*) as independent variables. Each of the six feedback levels was tested in a separate block of trials. Each participant performed six blocks of 25 trials (150 trials in total). Each block started with 15 trials of the Movement Task (of which the first three were practice trials), followed by 10 trials of the Rotation Task (of which the first two were practice trials).

For each trial in the experiment we logged accuracy and task completion time. Accuracy was defined as the fraction of trials that was correctly performed. Task completion time was the time that elapsed between the start of a trial and the moment the finish button was pressed. To measure perceived workload participants scored two items from the NASA Task Load Index (NASA TLX: "How mentally demanding was the task?" and "How successful were you in accomplishing what you were asked to do?") on a 20 point scale [33]. Participants also rated their overall experience of the different feedback techniques on two nine point bipolar semantic rating scales from the Questionnaire for User Interaction Satisfaction (or QUIS: respectively item 3.1: ranging from 'terrible' to 'wonderful', and item 3.4: ranging from 'difficult' to 'easy' [34–36]). Finally, at the end of the experiment the participants were asked rank order the six feedback modalities for both tasks from 'most preferred' to 'least preferred'. Analysis of variance (ANOVA) was used to test the relationships between the main variables, Bonferroni correction was applied where appropirate. The statistical analyses were performed with IBM SPSS 20.0 for Windows (www.ibm.com).

3.5   Procedures

At the start of the experiment the participants read and signed an informed consent. Then the experimenter explained the multi-touch system and the Sensators and he demonstrated the Movement Task and the Rotation Task. Then six experimental blocks were presented in a randomized order. After each block the participants rated the applied feedback technique for each task using the UEQ. At the end of all six experimental blocks the participants rank ordered the six feedback techniques according to their subjective preference. The experimental protocol was reviewed and approved by TNO internal review board on experiments with human participants, and was in accordance with the Helsinki Declaration of 1975, as revised in 2000 [37].

4   Results

One participant was excluded because of an incomplete dataset. Nine participants reported a lag in the multimodal feedback condition for both tasks, which probably resulted from a software error. Analysis of the videos showed that the lag reached up to 300 ms. Since a lag of this magnitude will significantly affect the results [38] the Multimodal condition was not further analyzed in this study.

The ANOVA showed that for both tasks the mean accuracy scores were significantly lower for Baseline feedback ($p < .001$), while they did not differ significantly between the other feedback techniques. Feedback resulted in an average of 92.5 % accuracy, in contrast to a Baseline accuracy of 70 % (Table 1).

Table 1. Mean (SD) accuracy per feedback condition (N = 20)

Feedback modality	Movement task	Rotation task
Auditory	0.96 (0.07)	0.96 (0.07)
Tabletop	0.93 (0.06)	0.96 (0.08)
Vibrotactile	0.89 (0.07)	0.86 (0.11)
Visual	0.92 (0.08)	0.95 (0.06)
Baseline	0.70 (0.21)	0.66 (0.21)

Incorrect scores were excluded in the calculation of the task completion time and the scores were cutoff at 15.000 ms. For the Movement Task, one-way repeated measures ANOVA revealed no significant difference between mean task completion time in all five feedback conditions. For the Rotation Task, the ANOVA showed that Tabletop feedback resulted in significantly faster task performance than both Vibrotactile and Baseline feedback (p < .001), while Visual feedback was also faster than Vibrotactile feedback (p < .05). The means for both tasks are given in Table 2.

Table 2. Mean (SD) task completion time (ms) per feedback condition (N = 20

Feedback modality	Movement task	Rotation task
Auditory	8153 (1021)	8388 (1358)
Tabletop	8202 (1241)	7869 (1204)
Vibrotactile	7935 (1139)	9232 (1461)
Visual	8005 (1343)	8183 (1104)
Baseline	7462 (1781)	9324 (1740)

The NASA TLX measured perceived performance and mental workload on two 20 point scales. A Wilcoxon signed-rank test showed that for both tasks participants rated their performance significantly higher in both the Visual and Tabletop feedback modes than in the other modes (Z − 3.078, p < .005), while performance in the Baseline mode was perceived as worse compared to all other feedback modes. A similar analysis showed that both Visual and Tabletop feedback yielded significantly less perceived mental workload than Vibrotactile and Baseline feedback, while Auditory feedback did not differ significantly from all other feedback techniques. Since there were no interaction effects both scores were combined in Table 3.

Table 3. Mean (SD) NASA TLX scores per feedback condition (N = 20)

Feedback modality	Movement task	Rotation task
Auditory	5.1 (3.2)	6.3 (4.4)
Tabletop	3.9 (2.9)	4.6 (2.9)
Vibrotactile	5.7 (2.7)	7.6 (4.0)
Visual	3.4 (2.3)	4.3 (2.3)
Baseline	9.2 (4.9)	9.0 (5.1)

The QUIS was used to measure user experience on two nine point scales labeled terrible-wonderful and difficult-easy. A Wilcoxon signed-rank test showed that for both tasks participants rated both the Visual and Tabletop feedback as significantly more wonderful than the Auditory, Vibrotactile and Baseline feedback techniques ($Z = -3.467$, $p = .001$). A similar analysis showed that participants found both Visual and Tabletop feedback significantly easier to use than Vibrotactile and Baseline feedback, while there was no significant difference between Visual and Tabletop feedback. Since there were no interaction effects both scores were combined in Table 4.

Table 4. Mean (SD) QUIS scores per feedback condition (N = 20)

Auditory	4.9 (2.0)	6.3 (1.7)
Tabletop	7.2 (1.2)	7.3 (1.6)
Vibrotactile	5.4 (1.7)	5.2 (1.6)
Visual	7.5 (0.9)	7.6 (1.0)
Baseline	4.3 (2.1)	3.8 (2.0)

Since there were no interaction effects between both tasks, we combined their raking scores for the different feedback techniques (Table 5). Wilcoxon signed-rank tests showed that Visual feedback was rated significantly higher than Auditory, Vibrotactile and Baseline feedback ($p < .001$), while Tabletop feedback was rated significantly higher than both Auditory and Baseline feedback ($p < .005$). There was no significant difference (at the Bonferroni corrected alpha level of .005) between Auditory, Baseline and Vibrotactile feedback ($p = .04$).

Table 5. Mean (SD) rank scores per feedback condition (N = 20)

Feedback modality	Rank
Auditory	4.0 (1.2)
Tabletop	2.1 (1.4)
Vibrotactile	3.9 (1.4)
Visual	1.9 (0.9)
Baseline	5.0 (1.1)

5 Conclusions and Discussion

Hypothesis H1 (both - Movement and Rotation- tasks will be performed faster and with higher accuracy with active feedback) was only partly confirmed. Active feedback had no effect on task completion time for the Movement Task. For the Rotation Task however, both Visual and Tabletop feedback yielded significantly faster task performance than Vibrotactile feedback, while Tabletop feedback also resulted in shorter task completion times than Vibrotactile feedback. Also, all active feedback modes significantly increased accuracy for both tasks, while there was no significant difference between the accuracy in the different active feedback modes.

Hypothesis H2 (visual feedforward cues signaling which Sensators have to be moved reduce search time and thereby task completion time) could not be tested due to software errors.

Hypothesis H3 (active feedback improves subjective user experience) only holds for the Visual and Tabletop feedback modes. Participants rated their performance significantly higher in these feedback modes than in the other feedback modes while performance in the baseline mode was perceived as worse compared to all other feedback modes. Visual and Tabletop feedback also significantly reduced perceived mental workload compared to Vibrotactile and Baseline feedback, while Auditory feedback did not differ significantly from all other feedback modes in this respect.

Finally, hypothesis H4 (active visual feedback enhances user experience more than auditory and tactile feedback) was also partly confirmed. Visual feedback was rated significantly higher than Auditory, Vibrotactile and Baseline feedback, while Tabletop feedback was rated significantly higher than both Auditory and Baseline feedback. There was no significant difference between Auditory, Baseline and Vibrotactile feedback.

Summarizing, we found that all active feedback techniques increased accuracy in both tasks. Active visual (Visual and Tabletop) feedback yielded the highest accuracy in both tasks, fastest performance in the Rotation task, and overall highest subjective user experience and preference scores. Without active feedback (Baseline condition) subjectively perceived performance was lowest and perceived mental workload was highest. Although Visual and Tabletop feedback performed equally well in most cases, Visual may be preferable, since visual feedback from the tangible itself reduces clutter and occlusion on the display surface, and the signal remains visible when the tangible is used beyond the boundaries of the tabletop. Future work should investigate the potential added value of auditory or visual feedback in attracting attention to Sensators that are outside the SUR40 surface, and further investigate optimal combinations of multimodal feedback (in bi- and tri-modal combinations) and the effects of feedforward cues on task completion time.

References

1. Underkoffler, J., Ishii, H.: Urp: a luminous-tangible workbench for urban planning and design. In: Proceedings of the CHI 1999, pp. 386–393. ACM Press (1999)
2. Fitzmaurice, G.W., Buxton, W.A.S.: An empirical evaluation of graspable user interfaces: towards specialized, space-multiplexed input. In: Proceedings of the CHI 1997, pp. 43–50. ACM Press (1997)
3. Fitzmaurice, G.W., Ishii, H., Buxton, W.A.S.: Bricks: laying the foundations for graspable user interfaces. In: Proceedings of the CHI 1995, pp. 442–449. ACM Press (1995)
4. Hurtienne, J., Stößel, C., Weber, K.: Sad is heavy and happy is light: population stereotypes of tangible object attributes. In: Proceedings of the TEI 2009, pp. 61–68. ACM Press (2009)
5. Tuddenham, P., Kirk, D., Izadi, S.: Graspables revisited: multitouch vs. tangible input for tabletop displays in acquisition and manipulation tasks. In: Proceedings of the CHI 2010, pp. 2223–2232. ACM Press (2010)

6. Weiss, M., Hollan, J.D., Borchers, J.: Augmenting interactive tabletops with translucent tangible controls. In: Müller-Tomfelde, C. (ed.) Tabletops – Horizontal Interactive Displays, pp. 149–170. Springer, London (2010)

7. Lee, J.-H., Spence, C.: Assessing the benefits of multimodal feedback on dual-task performance under demanding conditions. In: Proceedings of the BCS-HCI 2008, vol. 1, pp. 185–192. British Computer Society (2008)

8. Brewster, S., King, A.: An investigation into the use of tactons to present progress information. In: Costabile, M.F., Paternó, F. (eds.) INTERACT 2005. LNCS, vol. 3585, pp. 6–17. Springer, Heidelberg (2005)

9. van Veen, H.A.H.C., van Erp, J.B.: Tactile information presentation in the cockpit. In: Brewster, S., Murray-Smith, R. (eds.) Haptic HCI 2000. LNCS, vol. 2058, pp. 174–181. Springer, Heidelberg (2001)

10. Prewett, M.S., Elliott, L.R., Walvoord, A.G., Coovert, M.D.: A meta-analysis of vibrotactile and visual information displays for improving task performance. IEEE Trans. SMC-C 42(1), 123–132 (2012)

11. Huang, Y.Y., Moll, J., Sallnäs, E.L., Sundblad, Y.: Auditory feedback in haptic collaborative interfaces. Int. J. Hum. -Comp. Stud. 70(4), 257–270 (2012)

12. Wickens, C.D.: Multiple resources and performance prediction. Theor. Issues Ergon. Sci. 3, 159–177 (2002)

13. van Erp, J.B.F., Werkhoven, P.: Validation of principles for tactile navigation displays. In: Proceedings of the Human Factors and Ergonomics Society Annual Meeting, pp. 1687–1691. SAGE Publications (2006)

14. Elliott, L.R., Van Erp, J.B.F., Redden, E.S., Duistermaat, M.: Field based validation of a tactile navigation device. IEEE Trans. Haptics 3(2), 78–87 (2010)

15. Ressler, S., Antonishek, B., Wang, Q., Godil, A.: Integrating active tangible devices with a synthetic environment for collaborative engineering. In: Proceedings of the Web3D 2001, pp. 93–100. ACM Press (2001)

16. Richter, J., Thomas, B.H., Sugimoto, M., Inami, M.: Remote active tangible interactions. In: Proceedings of the TEI 2007, pp. 39–42. ACM Press (2007)

17. Brave, S., Ishii, H., Dahley, A.: Tangible interfaces for remote collaboration and communication. In: Proceedings of the CSCW 1998, pp. 169–178. ACM Press (1998)

18. Rosenfeld, D., Zawadzki, M., Sudol, J., Perlin, K.: Physical objects as bidirectional user interface elements. IEEE CGA 24(1), 44–49 (2004)

19. Kubicki, S., Lebrun, Y., Lepreux, S., Adam, E., Kolski, C., Mandiau, R.: Simulation in contexts involving an interactive table and tangible objects. Sim. Mod. Pract. Theory 31, 116–131 (2013)

20. Lepreux, S., Kubicki, S., Kolski, C., Caelen, J.: From centralized interactive tabletops to distributed surfaces: The Tangiget concept. Int. J. Hum. -Comp. Interact. 28(11), 709–721 (2012)

21. Van Erp, J.B.F.: Guidelines for the use of vibro-tactile displays in human computer interaction. In: Proceedings of Eurohaptics, pp. 18–22 (2002)

22. Nesbitt, K.: Designing multi-sensory displays for abstract data (Ph.D. Thesis). 2003. Sydney, Australia, School of Information Technologies, University of Sydney (2003)

23. Sigrist, R., Rauter, G., Riener, R., Wolf, P.: Augmented visual, auditory, haptic, and multimodal feedback in motor learning: A review. Psychon. Bull. Rev. 20(1), 21–53 (2013)

24. van Erp, J.B.F., Kooi, F.L., Bronkhorst, A.W., van Leeuwen, D.L., van Esch, M.P., van Wijngaarden, S.J.: Multimodal interfaces: a framework based on modality appropriateness. In: Proceedings of the Human Factors and Ergonomics Society Annual Meeting, pp. 1542–1546. SAGE Publications (2006)

25. Bianchi, A., Oakley, I., Lee, J.K., Kwon, D.S., Kostakos, V.: Haptics for tangible interaction: a vibro-tactile prototype. In: Proceedings of the TEI 2011, pp. 283–284. ACM Press (2011)
26. Kim, L., Cho, H., Park, S., Han, M.: A tangible user interface with multimodal feedback. In: Jacko, J.A. (ed.) HCI 2007. LNCS, vol. 4552, pp. 94–103. Springer, Heidelberg (2007)
27. Nowacka, D., Ladha, K., Hammerla, N.Y., Jackson, D., Ladha, C., Rukzio, E., Olivier, P.: Touchbugs: actuated tangibles on multitouch tables. In: Proceedings of the CHI 2013, pp. 759–762. ACM Press, (2013)
28. Riedenklau, E., Hermann, T., Ritter, H.: An integrated multi-modal actuated tangible user interface for distributed collaborative planning. In: Proceedings of the TEI 2012, pp. 169–174. ACM Press (2012)
29. Riedenklau, E., Hermann, T., Ritter, H.: Tangible active objects and interactive sonification as a scatter plot alternative for the visually impaired. In: Proceedings of the ICAD-2010, pp. 1–7. ACM Press (2010)
30. Patten, J., Ishii, H.: Mechanical constraints as computational constraints in tabletop tangible interfaces. In: Proceedings of the CHI 2007, pp. 809–818. ACM Press (2007)
31. Pedersen, E.W., Hornbæk,K.: Tangible bots: Interaction with active tangibles in tabletop interfaces. In: Proceedings of the CHI 2011, pp. 2975–2984. ACM Press (2011)
32. van Erp, J.B.F., Toet, A., Janssen, J.: Uni-, bi- and tri-modal warning signals: effects of temporal parameters and sensory modality on perceived urgency. Saf. Sci. 72, 1–8 (2015). doi:10.1016/j.ssci.2014.07.022
33. Hart, S.G.: Nasa-Task Load Index (Nasa-TLX); 20 Years Later. In: Proceedings of the Human Factors Ergonomics Society. Annual Meeting, HFES, pp. 904–908 (2006)
34. Chin, J.P., Diehl, V.A., Norman, K.L.: Development of an instrument measuring user satisfaction of the human-computer interface. In: Proceedings of the CHI 1988, pp. 213–218. ACM Press (1988)
35. Harper, B.D., Norman, K.L.: Improving user satisfaction: The questionnaire for user interaction satisfaction version 5.5. In: Proceedings of the First Annual Mid-Atlantic Human Factors Conference, pp. 224–228 (1993)
36. Slaughter, L.A., Harper, B.D., Norman, K.L.: Assessing the equivalence of paper and on-line versions of the QUIS 5.5. In: Proceedings of the 2nd Annual Mid-Atlantic Human Factors Conference, pp. 87–91 (1994)
37. World Medical Association. World Medical Association Declaration of Helsinki: Ethical principles for medical research involving human subjects. J. Am. Med. Assoc. 284(23), 3043–3045 (2000)
38. Wickens, C.D., Hollands, J.G.: Engineering psychology and human performance, 3rd edn. Prentice-Hall, Upper Saddle River (2000)

Auditory Browsing Interface of Ambient and Parallel Sound Expression for Supporting One-to-many Communication

Tomoko Yonezawa[(✉)]

Kansai University, Ryozenji, Takatsuki, Osaka 5691095, Japan
yone@kansai-u.ac.jp
http://res.kutc.kansai-u.ac.jp/~yone/

Abstract. In this paper, we introduce an auditory browsing system for supporting one-to-many communication in parallel with an ongoing discourse, lecture, or presentation. The live reactions of audiences should reflect the main speech from the viewpoint of active participation. In order to browse numerous live comments from audiences, the speaker stretches her/his neck toward a particular section of the virtual audience group. We adopt the metaphor of "looking inside" toward the direction of the seating position with repositioned and overlaid audiences' voices corresponding to the length of the voice regardless of the seating of real audiences. As a result, the speaker could browse the comments of the audience and show the communicative behaviors when she/he was interested in a particular group of the audience's utterances.

Keywords: Auditory space · One-to-many parallel communication · Browsing interface · Audience interaction

1 Introduction

Recent online communications have been developed based on multiple participants in the same thread. Especially in unofficial and online communities, there are various discussions among numerous participants without hesitation. Thus the methods of knowledge creation and communication are growing and wide-ranging.

On the other hand, our face-to-face and real-space communication provides rich expressions in each modality; however, there are several limitations of face-to-face communications: psychological burdens, number of simultaneous participants, and the total understanding of the communication modality. The number of participants is limited because of our recognition ability. In a university lecture or presentation in academic societies, comprehensive understanding of the audience's perspective and reactions is one of the important factors for interactive communication, although the number of participants makes understanding more difficult. In this way, potential speakers of the comments made by the audiences hesitate to speak their statements in the main communication.

© Springer International Publishing Switzerland 2015
N. Streitz and P. Markopoulos (Eds.): DAPI 2015, LNCS 9189, pp. 224–233, 2015.
DOI: 10.1007/978-3-319-20804-6_21

From the speaker's standpoint, the reactions from the audiences are important resources for the talk. Comprehensive understanding of the reactions' tendency becomes more difficult with a larger number of participants, although the talk without reactions may cause a disjunction of needs among members of the audience and the speaker.

To solve these problems, there have been trials for parallel communication during the discourse, lecture, or presentation. There have been several researches on chat-based communication using text-based communication tools, such as Twitter [1,2]. Twitter[1] is a social communication tool called "micro blogs." The silent texts do not directly disturb the contents of the main talk. Although the audiences can communicate in the chat system on the screen at the side of the speaker, the speaker cannot look at and read the contents of the chat during her/his talk at the same time. Moreover, linguistic information is difficult to process in our brains during our speech. Even if the speaker can look at the screen of the chat, the simultaneous checking for content causes confusion during the talk.

In this research, we introduce an auditory browsing interface for supporting one-to-many communication that is parallel with ongoing lectures or presentations. Our proposed system enables one to control spatially auditory browsing that expresses participants' reactions through a web-audio-based sound network. As a result, the speaker could show communicative behaviors when she/he was interested in the audience's utterances.

We adopted musical sounds as feedback media to the audiences' reaction contrary to the linguistic information. In order to represent the total tendency of the reaction, musical sound with tonic, dominant, or subdominant harmony is audialized corresponding to the reaction types: positive, negative, or wondering reactions. For browsing individual reactions, the audience members are categorized into six groups by their reactions and the length of the reaction.

Each component sound of the harmony is assigned to a particular place in virtual space. We adopt a metaphor of a "looking inside" gesture for the browsing interface of individual reactions. The speaker browses the auditory sources of the audiences' reactions during her/his speech by moving her/his head.

2   Related Works

There are several research-fields related to our proposal. We mention both audience communication and auditory browsing systems as follows.

2.1   Audience Communication

There have been various efforts to overcome the problems in audience communication. Audience participation [3] is a simple interactive system for summarizing audience reactions.

---

[1] http://twitter.com/.

Audiences originally do not make active messages for the speaker or other audience members, except with nonverbal and passive gestures such as eye-gazes [4]. In contrast to passive approaches, bidirectional communication using a "clicker" [5] has been proposed for audience communication. Special equipment with a keypad for audience communication was introduced [6] for a virtual theater. Coded signals for each member of the audience have thus been created as a media component of audience communication; however these systems do not consider natural interaction and freedom of expression for audience members.

There were chat-based communication trials using Twitter in parallel with the main presentation [1,2]. Although the trials enriched discussions among participants, it was not possible for the contents of the discussions to be reflected in the main presentation. The speaker cannot concentrate on the conversation among the participants at the same time as giving the speech. The verbal contents of the chat-based communication would disturb the main talk.

As Baird proposed an audience for participation in music notation [7], we adopted an auditory browsing method of musical sound during the main talk for understanding the overall reaction and selective listening of audience groups separated by reaction type.

2.2   Auditory Browsing Systems

There have been researches of interfaces for auditory browsing systems in the research field of auditory display. The idea of sonic browsing [8,9] is an idea for managing and browsing among numerous auditory sound sources. Especially for information retrieval [9], the hyperbolic tree is an important key to browsing in numerous sounds. Consequently, browsing in groups divided by similarity seems to be understandable for auditory systems.

There is also an aural browsing system based on 3D auditory space with consideration for hypermedia interfaces [10]. The idea of the 3D auditory space was also adopted for the personal voice memo systems [11,12]. We have adopted the virtual 3D auditory space overlaying a real space in an auditorium or lecture hall. The spatial sound is produced in real space for understanding and sharing the audience's reaction.

3   System Structure

3.1   System Concept

In this system, we propose a one-to-many parallel communication based on overlaid musical sound reflecting audiences' reactions in the real space. The purpose of the system is to make smoother the browsing of audience reactions by a speaker, in order to perform an effective presentation while engaging the members of the audience at the same time. In order to enable one-to-many communication in real space, we propose an expressive method for reactions of enormous participants to a presentation speaker by adopting ambient sound stimuli. Compared to vocal

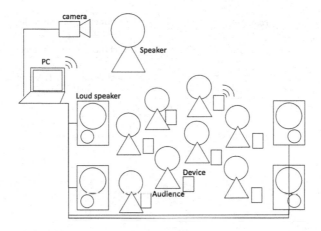

Fig. 1. System overview

sounds containing continuous pitches, musical sounds do not disturb speech or conversation.

In one-to-many communication such as discourses, lectures, and presentations, the seating position of the audience is related to the attitude and interest in the content [13]. We accordingly adopted a virtual arrangement of the seating position corresponding to the reaction type of the audience regardless of the real position, for ambient communication.

3.2   System Overview

The proposed system of the reaction-browsing interaction is implemented by (1) an auditory browsing interface for the speaker and (2) the system that captures the audiences' reactions.

The browsing interface consists of 1-(i) an image-based detection of the direction of the speaker's face using a web camera; 1-(ii) the levels of interactive browsing structured with overall, partial, and individual reactions; and 1-(iii) spatial and musical auditory designs for each reaction level.

For capturing audiences' reactions, we propose using two types of input from the audiences: 2-(i) text inputs, such as chat-based communication using Twitter, and 2-(ii) vocal inputs, such as murmured voices from each audience.

As the 3D spatial audio environment for both the presenter and the enormous participants, the feedback sound of the audiences' reactions is generated by four loud speakers and the individual smart devices of the participants (Figs. 1 and 2) by adopting a web-audio framework.

3.3   Spatial Arrangement of the Audiences' Reactions

The first step in auditory browsing, and overall browsing of reactions, uses the harmonic sound structure corresponding to the six reaction types. Figure 3 shows

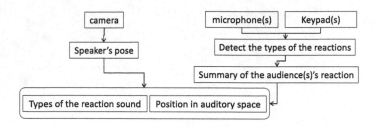

Fig. 2. System flow

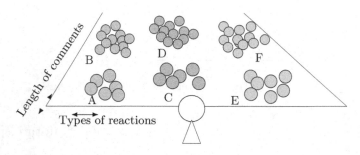

Fig. 3. Individual utterances grouped by types of reactions

the arrangement of virtual groups by reaction type. The overlaid sound sources in the real space express virtual groups by each type of reaction.

The distance from the speaker expresses the intent of the audience. Based on this metaphor of seating position, we first prepared two levels of the distance between the speaker and the audience members. The groups A, C, and E are assigned to the reactive participants. We thus adopt the metaphor of seating position to the repositioning of the audience voices corresponding to the length of the voice regardless of the seating of real audience members.

Next, the system assigns groups by reaction type: (1) positive, (2) negative, and (3) not understood. The groups are assigned to the horizontally spreading groups; (1) the positive reaction group is assigned to C and D; (2) the negative reaction group is assigned to E and F; and (3) the reaction group of wondering feedbacks is assigned to A and B.

3.4   Background-Musical Mappings for Browsing

For a comprehensive design of the audialization of the audiences' reactions, we focused on the level of the reaction volume, that is total, group, or individual. In order to produce musical feedback as an audialization of the audiences' reactions, the system used the software MIDI[2] instrument in the PC with Pd-extended[3].

---

[2] Musical Instrument Digital Interface.

[3] Pure Data (aka Pd) is an open source visual programming language. http://puredata.info/.

Table 1. Musical sound mappings for gradually integrated audialization

Steps in audialization	Sound localization	Type of sound	Instruments
Total reaction	Virtual position of the group	Harmonic chord	Strings
Sound for reaction numbers	Real position of each seat	Stepwise melody	Keyboard instrument

Table 2. Mappings of harmonic structure for reaction types

Reaction type	Negative		Positive		Wondering	
Reaction length	long	short	long	short	long	short
Reaction group	A	B	C	D	E	F
Mapped key	B	A	C	G	D	F

Corresponding to the selected level of the reaction volume, the system switches the sound for ambient communication, as shown in Table 1.

Audialization of Overall Reactions. As an overall reaction, the system makes musical harmony by the reactions with positive, negative, and confused nuances. The virtual positions of the reaction sounds are set as shown in Fig. 3, and the musical note of the reaction is assigned by the reaction type and length as same as the virtual position of the reaction group as shown in Table 2.

The musical notes are considered for the combination effects of the harmony. The harmonic structure is prepared based on C5. A stable impression by tonic harmony is caused by the positive reactions with C and G. An unstable impression by sub-dominant harmony is caused by the wondering reactions with F and D. An inharmonic impression is caused by the negative reactions with G and E.

The number of the reacting audiences is reflected to the number of multiple octaves from 0 to 5. Thus the different nuance of the harmony is expressed by the combination of the reaction rate. For expressing a continuous state of the total reaction, the musical notes use "strings" in MIDI software instruments.

Audialization of Group Reactions. The second step, partial browsing, enables one to focus on a particular type of reaction. In this step, the individuals in the speaker's selected group are audialized using melodic notes while a harmony of the total reaction is played at a lower volume. Musical notes in the harmonic scale, which correspond to the number of the participants in the reaction group, are played back in a stepwise loop sequence based on the real seat-position of the reacted participants in the group.

In this step, the harmonic code of stringed instruments is changed by adjusting the base sound; that is, the assigned key to the group in Table 2. A major or minor code is selected by the circle of fifths, one of modulatory spaces.

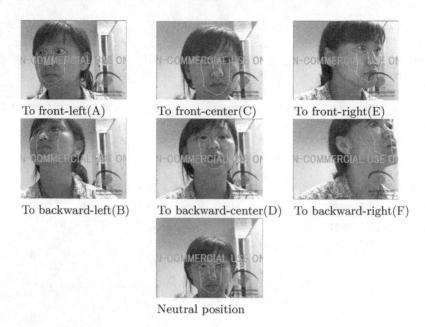

To front-left(A)   To front-center(C)   To front-right(E)

To backward-left(B)   To backward-center(D)   To backward-right(F)

Neutral position

Fig. 4. Head gesture for directions of audiences' groups

The melodic sound is generated by the number of the reacted audience members within 16 steps and 240 [bpm], with looping. Each note indicates each reacted audience with sound localization by her/his real seat. The musical notes for the loop melody are selected from constituent members of the harmony using "piano" in MIDI software instruments.

When the speaker faces the direction of a particular audience with a reactive melody, the speaker can finally access each murmured voice and asynchronously communicate with the participants.

3.5   Auditory Browsing Interface

The system adopts an image-based face-tracking method using FaceAPI[4] and a simple detection of speech intervals for a browsing interface of the presenter. The stepwise browsing of detailed reactions enables the presenter to make unconfused speech with appropriate communication with the audience.

The harmonic sounds expressing overall reactions are heard when the presenter speaks with her/his head at the neutral position (the first step).

In order to browse and select a particular reaction group, the speaker inclines her/his head as though she/he were looking into a particular section of the group, as shown in Fig. 4. When a duration of the gesture continues more than two seconds within a segment of the speech, the browsing mode of the sound feedback changes into the selected group (the second step).

---

[4] Seeing Machines, FaceAPI, http://www.seeingmachines.com/product/faceapi/.

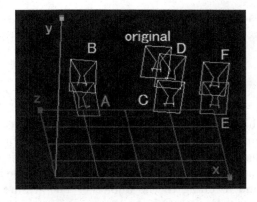

Fig. 5. Means of 3D coordinates for eyes, nose, and mouth

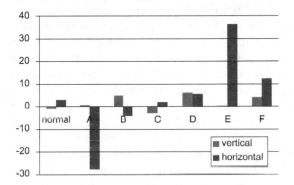

Fig. 6. Horizontal and vertical angles of the head for each direction

When the presenter gazes at a particular participant in connection with a musical note in the second step, she/he can listen to the raw reactions of individuals (the third step). In this step, the speaker inclines her/his head toward the real seating position of the audience members who have made some comments.

Figures 5 and 6 show the mean positions and directions of the speaker's head toward each reaction group. Support vector machine (SVM) is used for automatic estimation of the speaker's gesture. The narrower range of features in looking into a particular group makes it more difficult to select the group; a wider range makes it more difficult to recognize the speaker's gesture.

3.6   Separation of the Reaction Types

To capture the reactions of the audiences, we focused on their murmured voices. Prosodic analyses show effective results [14, etc.] and there have been trials to make systems with automatic recognition [15, etc.]. We focused on the prosodic patterns of the ending of words [16] in order to classify them into (a) positive, (b) negative, or (c) confused reactions. The sources of the voice data are captured through each individual's devices such as note PCs, smartphones, or smart tablet, through their microphones and are sent to an auditory reaction server.

4 Discussion

The proposed method aimed to enable speaker-audience communication by ambient musical sound. The speaker's interface for auditory browsing seemed to be similar to offer the same easy control as using a joy-stick with the upper body. At the same time, the gesture of the speaker performs the role as though she/he were looking into and listening to the audience. The gesture of the speaker's attention is expected to draw tension and consciousness of the participation of the audience. On the other hand, the gesture sometimes appears without the intention of hearing it. To treat the gesture separately from the non-intentional one, we should consider the appropriate duration of the stable pose.

The audience's intention of a comment added to the main talk should be carefully considered from the viewpoint of consensus between the user and the system with automatic collection/recognition of her/his utterance.

The present implementation is limited to sitting speakers; however the speaker may move and walk around in the front space of the lecture hall or auditorium. In order to correspond to the normal talks, the system should be considered to be attached to the speaker's clothes as a wearable system or to adopt a wide-range of image processing to capture similar gestures. With further detection of the speaker's attention and intention, it is possible to adopt gaze direction in order to capture the natural signs of face-to-face communication.

5 Conclusion

In this research, we introduce an auditory browsing interface for supporting one-to-many communication in parallel with ongoing lectures or presentations. Our proposed system enables us to spatially control auditory browsing, that expresses participants' reactions by overlaying 3D sound using loud speakers and individuals' smart devices for a web-audio based sound network. As a result, the speaker could show the attentive behaviors when she/he was interested in the audiences' reactions. As future works, we should develop a stable gestural interface for the speaker walking around the lecture hall or auditorium. The evaluation from the viewpoint of both the audiences and the speaker should be also discussed as further possibility of the auditory and ambient communication in parallel with the main talk.

Acknowledgement. This research was supported in part by KAKENHI 24300047 and KAKENHI 25700021. The authors would like to thank the participants in the experiment.

References

1. Rekimoto, J., Ayatsuka, Y., Uoi, H., Arai, T.: Adding another communication channel to reality: an experience with a chataugmented conference. In: ACM CHI 98 Cconference Summary on Human Factors in Computing Systems, pp. 271–272 (1998)
2. Nishida, T., Igarashi, T.: Lock-on-Chat: boosting anchored conversation and its operation at a technical conference. In: Costabile, M.F., Paternó, F. (eds.) INTER-ACT 2005. LNCS, vol. 3585, pp. 970–973. Springer, Heidelberg (2005)
3. Maynes-Aminzade, D., Pausch, R., Seitz, S.: Techniques for interactive audience participation. In: Proceedings of the 4th IEEE International Conference on Multimodal Interfaces, p. 1520. IEEE Computer Society (2002)
4. Streeck, J.: Gesture as communication II: the audience as co-author. Res. Lang. Soc. Interact. **27**(3), 239–267 (1994)
5. Trees, A.R., Jackson, M.H.: The learning environment in clicker classrooms: student processes of learning and involvement in large university-level courses using student response systems. Learn. Media Technol. **32**(1), 21–40 (2007)
6. Ahn, S.C., Kim, I.-J., Kim, H.-G., Kwon, Y.-M., Ko, H.: Audience interaction for virtual reality theater and its implementation. In: Proceedings of VRST, pp. 41–45 (2001)
7. Kevin, C.: Baird, real-time generation of music notation via audience interaction using python and gnu lilypond. In: Proceedings of NIME 2005, pp. 240–241 (2005)
8. Fernstrom, M., Brazil, E.: Sonic Browsing: an auditory tool for multimedia asset management. In: Proceedings of the International Conference on Auditory Display (ICAD) (2001)
9. Brazil, E., Fernstrm, M., Tzanetakis, G., Cook, P.: Enhancing sonic browsing using audio information retrieval. In: Proceedings of the International Conference on Auditory Display (ICAD) (2002)
10. Lumbreras, M., Rossi, G.: A metaphor for the visually impaired: browsing information in a 3D auditory environment. In: Conference Companion on Human factors in Computing Systems, pp. 216–217 (1995)
11. Yonezawa, T., Yamazoe, H., Terasawa, H.: Portable recording/browsing system of voice memos allocated to user-relative directions. In: Pervasive 2009 Adjunct Proceedings, pp. 241–244 (2009)
12. Yonezawa, T., Yamazoe, H., Terasawa, H.: Voisticky: sharable and portable auditory balloon with voice sticky posted and browsed by user's head direction. In: IEEE ICSPCC 2011, pp. 118–123 (2011)
13. Montello, D.R.: Classroom seating location and its effect on course achievement, participation, and attitudes. J. Environ. Psychol. **8**(2), 149–157 (1988)
14. Shriberg, E., Stolcke, A., Jurafsky, D., Coccaro, N., Meteer, M., Bates, R., Taylor, P., Ries, K., Martin, R., Van Ess-Dykema, C.: Can prosody aid the automatic classification of dialog acts in conversational speech? Lang. Speech **41**(3–4), 443–492 (1998)
15. Grimm, M., Kroschel, K., Narayanan, S.: Support vector regression for automatic recognition of spontaneous emotions in speech. In: Proceedings of IEEE ICASSP, vol. 4, p. IV-1085 (2007)
16. Ishi, C.T.: Perceptually-related F0 parameters for automatic classification of phrase final tones. IEICE Trans. Inf. Syst. **E88–D**(3), 481–488 (2005)

Design and Development of Distributed, Ambient and Pervasive Interactions

Immersiveness of Ubiquitous Computing Environments Prototypes: A Case Study

Tiago Abade[1,2], José C. Campos[1,2], Rui Moreira[1,2], Carlos C.L. Silva[1,2],
and José Luís Silva[3(✉)]

[1] Departamento de Informática, Universidade do Minho, Braga, Portugal
[2] HASLab/INESC TEC, Braga, Portugal
{pg20691,a49401}@alunos.uminho.pt
jose.campos@di.uminho.pt, carlos.l.silva@inesctec.pt
[3] Madeira-ITI/Universidade da Madeira, Funchal, Portugal
jose.l.silva@m-iti.org

Abstract. The development of ubiquitous computing (ubicomp) environments raises several challenges in terms of their evaluation. Ubicomp virtual reality prototyping tools enable users to experience the system to be developed and are of great help to face those challenges, as they support developers in assessing the consequences of a design decision in the early phases of development. Given the situated nature of ubicomp environments, a particular issue to consider is the level of realism provided by the prototypes. This work presents a case study where two ubicomp prototypes, featuring different levels of immersion (desktop-based versus CAVE-based), were developed and compared. The goal was to determine the cost/benefits relation of both solutions, which provided better user experience results, and whether or not simpler solutions provide the same user experience results as more elaborate one.

Keywords: Ubiquitous computing · Virtual environments · Prototyping · Evaluation · Immersiveness · APEX

1 Introduction

In ubiquitous computing, a variety of computer devices are commonly used to assist and automate human tasks and activities in the physical world [13]. Due to the constant growth of information technologies, there has been a tendency to equip places of our daily life with ubiquitous computing devices. Currently, the main issue of developing such environments is that developers have to "rely on either low-fidelity techniques (such as paper prototypes and mental walk-throughs) or simply wait for a full scale deployment" [18] for testing and validation. This makes it inconvenient and costly to actually develop the systems. In many cases, it is not possible to install prototypes for testing purposes as that would be disruptive of ongoing activities. Hence, it is of utmost importance to find means of prototyping ubiquitous environments in a rapid fashion without disrupting key services of human society.

© Springer International Publishing Switzerland 2015
N. Streitz and P. Markopoulos (Eds.): DAPI 2015, LNCS 9189, pp. 237–248, 2015.
DOI: 10.1007/978-3-319-20804-6_22

Even though prototypes are not intended as final products, they must be both robust and refined for a fair evaluation [6]. The more detailed and realistic a prototype is, the more a user is able to discern the future utility of the prototyped system. The usefulness of an ubiquitous computing application will be determined by the developers' skills in identifying users' requirements and expectations. It is important that these requirements and expectations are met. By designing prototypes and letting users test them, a developer can better assess the potential impact and relevance that the system may have on a real scenario [6, 18].

The use of immersive Virtual Reality (VR) environments has been demonstrated to support accomplishing these goals [17]. We have created the APEX framework [17], that relies on a three-dimensional (3D) application server to create simulations for ubiquitous environments. This framework was successfully used in the prototyping of ubiquitous computing environments, enabling the detection of potential user problems (functional [16] or non-functional [1]) in the early phases of development, while reducing the cost of redesign.

One of the goals of the work is that the framework must provide prototypes that feel real enough, allowing users to interact with the virtual environment in a way that feels natural. This can be accomplished through different levels of immersion, from simple desktops to more immersive and complex setups. For example, by taking advantage of the functionality of a CAVE (Cave Automatic Virtual Environment) [3], a virtual reality theater where a user can be immersed with stereoscopic 3D imaging.

On one hand, desktop-based prototypes provide a less immersive experience but are simpler and cheaper to develop and deploy. On the other hand, CAVE-based prototypes provide an more immersive user experience, but their are more complex to develop and interact with as well as more expensive to deploy. There is a need to compare and determine which solutions provide better user experience results and to which extent the added cost of a CAVE is justified. The goal of this paper is exactly to present one such comparison. The long term goal is to support developers evaluate the cost/benefits of each approach.

The paper is structured as follow: Sect. 2 presents related work. Section 3 describes the case study used (i.e. a smart library). The two user studies (Desktop-based versus CAVE-based) are presented in Sect. 4. Section 5 describes the results, and Sect. 6 discusses the results and summarizes with conclusions and future work.

2   State of the Art

Prototypes provide designers with a way of checking proposed solutions with low investment. However there is a tension between the quality of the results provided by the prototypes and the effort needed to make them close enough representations of the final systems once implemented. Prototypes should provide results which adequately reflect the experience of the physical implementation of the system on location.

The prototyping of ubiquitous computing (ubicomp) systems can be approached from multiple perspectives, from prototypes of specific devices to prototypes of spaces equipped with such devices (see [4] for a good overview). We are specifically interested in the latter case.

Several approaches to the prototyping of ubicomp environments have been proposed [9–11,17,19]. Most of the approaches use virtual reality, some use Augmented Reality (e.g. the VARU framework [19]), and the work of Singh et al. [18] presents an initial approach to using immersive video. APEX [17] is unique in that, through a multi layer prototyping approach, it enables analysis at different levels of abstraction, from models of the system's behaviour to immersive virtual reality simulations.

Research results stated that User Experience (UX) evaluations can benefit from using virtual reality [14]. The veracity of evaluations in virtual environments (their ecological validity) has been addressed in many contexts. For example, Orland et al. [12] considered virtual worlds as representations of landscape realities and as tools for landscape planning suggesting their ecological validity. Scott [15] addresses it in the medical context and claims that virtual reality has promising ecological validity.

Solutions to improve different aspects of the immersion experience include, stereoscopic 3D, multi-display support and the use of external physical devices by providing a more natural style of interaction. How much immersion is enough and when simpler solutions provides the same user experience results has been discussed by Bowman and McMahan [2] in the general context of VR. A very recent work [5] compared three evaluation methods for mobile interactive systems: field-based studies, classical lab-based studies and evaluation using Immersive Video Environments (IVE). They claim that using IVE lead to identifying nearly the same number of major usability problems, similar effectiveness and task efficiency as the field-based study. The results suggest that in some areas IVE-based evaluations and field-based studies lead to similar results, while IVE exhibits most of the lab-based study benefits (e.g. repeatability and control). The authors present some initial insights into the benefits/drawbacks of the three evaluation methods, but state that further research is needed to fully understand which method is more appropriate for a particular situation.

While the evaluation using IVE seems to be an adequate method for some areas,VR simulations seem a more promising approach in the case of ubicomp environments.

3   A Smart Library Prototype

In order to compare the experience of using APEX-based prototypes at different levels of immersion, an exiting prototype of a smart library was used (see [1]). The user visible component of the prototype consists of a virtual world developed in OpenSimulator[1] (an open source multi-platform, multi-user 3D application server) and accessed through an appropriate viewer.

---

[1] http://opensimulator.org (last accessed February 20, 2015).

The physical library on which the prototype is based, is located in the Gualtar campus of the Minho University in Braga, Portugal (see Fig. 1a). The building has 3 floors, including a ground-floor where the main reception is located. The other two floors are identical and have reading and study rooms (see Fig. 1b). Each of these two floors is composed of a reception (on the right in the figure) flanked by doors that give access to the reading/study rooms. These rooms have 6 table sections (marked with circles in Fig. 1b).

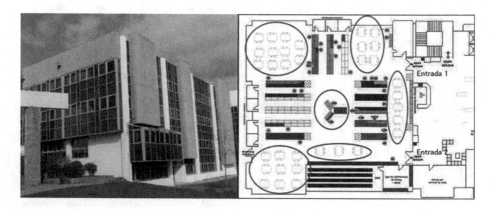

Fig. 1. a - Library of the University of Minho; b - Table sections of the library

The prototype used represented the enhancement of the library with ubicomp technology providing indication of seat availability within each floor. Two types of information panels were simulated to provide information about seats in the library. The first type (the alphanumeric panel – see Fig. 2c) shows information on seat availability in a textual format. Two alphanumeric panels were placed on every floor, at the main entrance and in the center of every reading/studying room. The second type of information panel presents a depiction of the floor plan of the library, and indicates the availability of seats using red and green LEDs lights (see Fig. 2d). LED panels were located at the entrance of each floor.

Virtual presence sensors were placed in the environment. Every time a sensor is triggered, this information is sent to every screen present in the building to refresh the data displayed.

4   User Studies: Desktop Versus Cave

The prototype described in the previous section was evaluated through two user studies. More than evaluating the actual system being prototyped, the main focus of the studies was in understanding whether the prototype could be useful in performing such evaluation. And, in particular, to compare different levels of immersion in the deployment of the prototypes. Hence the users studies used different deployment setups. In one case the prototype was presented to users

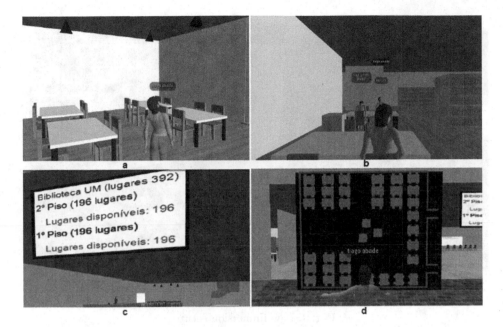

Fig. 2. OpenSimulator representation of the Library: a - ceiling movement sensors (highlighted with triangular markers); b - sitting at a table triggers pressure sensors; c - alphanumeric panel; d - LED panel (Color figure online).

on a desktop machine, to create what we consider a low immersion condition. In the other case, the high immersion condition, the prototype was deployed in a CAVE environment, using stereoscopic projection.

4.1 Low Immersion Setup

In the low immersion condition the prototype was presented to users on a 22" Samsung SyncMaster 3D 2233RZ screen. In effect, the machine used to run APEX (a Intel Core i5-2400 machine with two Asus GeForce GTX460 1 GB DirectCU 2DI GDDR5 PCI-E GPUs) featured 3 such screens, but for this setup only one screen was being used to present the virtual world (see Fig. 3).

Interaction with the environment was achieved, in typical fashion, via keyboard and mouse. The viewer used was the CoolVLViewer.

4.2 High Immersion Setup

In the high immersion condition, a CAVE available at the Laboratory of Perception and Vision from CCG (The Computer Graphics Center) in Guimarães, Portugal was used. The CAVE in question was composed of three rear projection screens set as a single flat screen, which means that they were lined up on a single plane right next to each other. As represented in Fig. 4, the system is a

Fig. 3. Low immersion setup

cluster with three machines (lvp-node0, lvp-node1 and lvp-node2), one for each projector.

The CAVE had support for NVIDIA 3D Vision technology. Each machine of the cluster had a NVIDIA Quadro 4500 graphics card. The projectors (Christie Mirage S+4k) had active stereo support. Deploying APEX on the CAVE, however, presented some problems. The first was identifying a viewer able to produce a stereoscopic view of the virtual world. The second, projecting views of the world through the three projectors in the CAVE. Remember that typical viewers for OpenSimulator are designed for a desktop use on a single screen.

In [7] an analysis of the alternatives was carried out. In short, the conclusion was that, while it was possible to have a stereoscopic view of the virtual world (through the Dale's SL Viewer) and to have three (or more) coordinated views of the world projected in different screens, with currently available viewers having three coordinated stereoscopic views was not feasible. The Dale's SL Viewer can only be used to generate one view into the world. Because each machine is directly connected to one projector only, we were restricted to using a single projector. Although a single projector setup did not actually surround a user in a cubic fashion, it does provide a larger image that results in a more immersive experience than obtained with the desktop screen. Additionally, the use of 3D enhanced the experience.

Testing Dale's SL Viewer's stereoscopic 3D modes, inside the CAVE, resulted in the following:

– Anaglyph stereo: since this mode is compatible with almost any kind of system, no problems happened when using it. With the appropriate 3D red/cyan

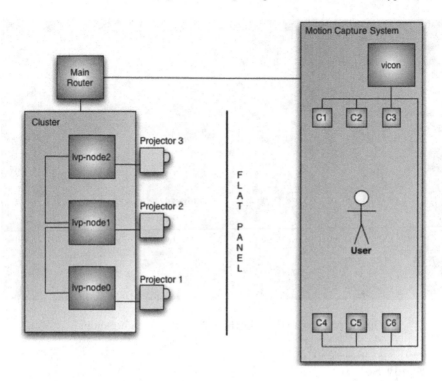

Fig. 4. CAVE in the LVP

glasses, the user can see a three-dimensional scene as a result of the binocular disparity depth cue provided by the anaglyph. Figure 5 shows Dale's SL Viewer running in anaglyph stereo mode inside the CAVE;

- Active stereo: taking into account the hardware used for the CAVE, i.e. the graphics cards have 3-pin din output that can be used to connect to the projectors via GPIO, and the NVIDIA Quadro graphics cards have OpenGL quad-buffered stereo support for NVIDIA 3D Vision, it is possible to obtain stereoscopic 3D using this mode. However, testing did not show adequate results. This may be due to abnormal configuration of the projectors and graphics drivers;
- Passive stereo: considering that the projectors do not have polarized filters, this mode was not supported.

Given the above, anaglyph stereo was used in the user tests. Note that since running the user studies, the CAVE has suffered and extensive overhaul and the use of Active stereo is now feasible.

Interaction was achieved through the use of a Wiimote controller, programmed to act as and input device to the virtual world. Test subjects could wither use the Wiimote's movement or keys to control the avatar representing them in the virtual world.

Fig. 5. Anaglyth stereo in the CAVE (Color figure online)

4.3 Study Setup

As described earlier one goal of the study was to assess whether significant differences could be found in the experience of using the prototype under different immersion conditions. Considering that students are the largest group of users of the library, test subjects were recruited from the student population. In total 21 students participated in the study. A between subjects setup was used with 12 students integrating the low immersion condition and 9 integrating the high immersion condition.

The students were briefed with a short introduction about the purpose of the prototype and the information they would find in the simulation. During this phase they had also the opportunity of exploring the environment in the relevant immersion condition.

After that initial phase, they were asked to enter the library and find an available seat, using the screen panels' assistance if they so wished. Each student used the simulation individually but bots were introduced in several seats to improve the realism of the experience. Students were free to explore the environment without being disturbed. No time restrictions were placed in relation to accomplishing the designated task of finding a place to seat.

While in the virtual environment students were observed, their movements and the steps they took to find a place to sit noted. After completing the tasks, students were asked to answer a questionnaire. Besides related to the characterization of the test subjects, the questionnaire was composed of 30 questions, addressing topics related to the screen panels and to the use of the virtual

Table 1. Comparison of some results

		Low immersion					High immersion				
		1	2	3	4	5	1	2	3	4	5
1	Able to recognize the environment			1	**9**	2			2	**7**	
2	Helps analysis of alternatives			1	3	**8**	1		2	**5**	1
3	Advantageous to create prototypes				2	**10**				3	**6**
4	Advantageous to introduce panels				1	**11**				**5**	4
5	Panels are well located		3	**5**	4		1	1	**4**	2	1
6	Would only use LED panels		**5**	4		3	1	**3**		3	2
7	I would recommend the approach				2	**10**			1	**5**	3
8	I would use the approach				4	**8**				4	**5**

environment as a prototype. Answers were given in a 5 points Likert scale. The
questionnaire was divided into the following sections:

- Profile of the students, including their experience of games using controls
  similar to those used in this user study.
- Evaluation of the prototype as a tool for evaluation. Here, aspects such as
  immersion, utility and user satisfaction were measured.
- Evaluation of the prototyped solution, including questions concerned with the
  location, design and behaviour of the screen panels.

Twelve students, with an average age of 23 years, participated in the low immersion condition of the study. Of the 12 students that participated in the study,
10 declared they were familiar with third-person gaming.

Nine test subjects, with an average age of 28 years, participated in the high
immersion condition of the study. Of the 9 students, 5 declared they were familiar
with third-person gaming.

5 Results

The two main aspects addressed in the study will now be discussed. To simplify
presentation, only the more relevant/illustrative questions are addressed.

Table 1 presents a summary of the result discussed below. For each of the
questions, the number of times a particular value in the Likert scale was chosen
is indicated. Modes are highlighted in boldface. We run a Mann-Whitney test for
differences across two independent samples, and we found significant differences
across groups (low vs high immersion) in three of the items in Table 1:

- Question 2: The approach helps analysis of alternatives ($p = 0,013$)
- Question 4: The introduction of panels would be advantageous ($p = 0,021$)
- Question 7: I would recommend the approach ($p = 0.020$).

In all cases the low immersion condition had an higher score than the high immersion condition. However, looking at Table 1 responses to these three questions
all have a mode on the positive side of the scale (totally agree vs. agree).

5.1   The Prototype as an Evaluation Artifact

In both cases test subjects were able to identify the environment (mode of 4). Results in the first condition were slightly more positive (answers were in the range 3 to 5; against 3 to 4 in the second condition) but that can be attributable to the test subjects in the first study being more familiarized with the library as the test subjects in the second study were on a different campus of the University.

Also in both cases there was agreement that the approach helps in the design process. For example the question regarding support for identifying alternative solutions had a mode of 5 in the first condition and 4 in the second. Interestingly the answers were more positive in the low immersion scenario, when compared to the high immersion scenario. We posit that this might be due to the more 'intimidating' setup of the CAVE, but this is something that needs further research. In both conditions there was a mode of 5 in the answer to the question regarding whether the subjects saw an advantage in building a virtual reality representation of the system before actual physical deployment. Similarly, the answers to the questions regarding whether the test subjects would use or recommend the approach all had positive results, with a mode of five in all cases, except for the question about recommending the approach, which in the high fidelity condition had a mode of 4. Again, we believe that the fact that a CAVE was used might have made the test subjects less confident that it would be feasible to use the approach on a regular basis but more research is needed in this case.

5.2   Screen Panels' Evaluation

Regarding consistency of the results, it can be observed that in both conditions there was agreement that the introduction of the panels in the library would be beneficial. The mode was 5 in the first condition and 4 in the second, but answers in that second case were almost equally distributed between 4 and 5 (5 votes against 4). A mode of 3 was obtained in both cases in the question regarding whether the panels' location was adequate.

Regarding the question of whether using the LED panels only would be enough, the answer was negative in the low immersion condition (mode of 2), while the observation of the test subjects' behavior showed that they resorted mainly to these panels. Hence there was some contradiction between observed behavior and the results of the questionnaire. In the high immersion condition this discrepancy was less obvious as the result was bi-modal (split between disagree and agree). However, again in this case observation of the test subjects showed a clear preference for the LED panels. Determining whether this is representative of actual usage will require physical installation of the system. However, in previous work we were able to observe that the user's behavior in the virtual world was consistent with their behavior in the physical world [8].

6   Discussion and Conclusions

In this paper we have addressed the issue of how immersive ubicomp prototypes need to be. A virtual reality based prototype of a ubicomp system was tested on both a desktop computer and in a CAVE. Overall there was no major significant differences in the results of the two conditions. This indicates that for the particular needs of the prototyping approach used, the added cost of deploying the prototypes in a CAVE environment does not seem to pay off.

Whether the results of the tests adequately reflect the behavior and experience of users in the actual system once fielded was not the issue in this case. In previous work we have addressed this issue [8], and the ecological validity of virtual worlds has also been argued for in the literature [12,15].

A limiting factor of the study that was carried out is the fact that we were not able to use a fully immersive setup in the CAVE. The setup used did represent, at the time, the best that could be achieved with the APEX framework in the available CAVE. In this sense the study faithfully represents the available alternatives. Since then, the CAVE has been subject to a major overhaul and a more immersive setup is now possible. We plan to repeat the study in this setup, and also add, as an intermediate condition, a 3D desktop setup.

Acknowledgments. This work is funded by Fundação para a Ciência e a Tecnologia (FCT) through Projecto Estratégico – LA 9 – 2014-2015 (PEst-OE/EEI/LA0009/2015).

References

1. Abade, T., Gomes, T., Silva, J.L., Campos, J.C.: Design and evaluation of a smart library using the APEX framework. In: Streitz, N., Markopoulos, P. (eds.) DAPI 2014. LNCS, vol. 8530, pp. 307–318. Springer, Heidelberg (2014)
2. Bowman, D.A., McMahan, R.P.: Virtual reality: how much immersion is enough? Computer 40(7), 36–43 (2007)
3. Cruz-Neira, C., Sandin, D.J., DeFanti, T.A., Kenyon, R.V., Hart, J.C.: The CAVE: audio visual experience automatic virtual environment. Commun. ACM 35(6), 64–72 (1992)
4. Davies, N., Landay, J., Hudson, S., Schmidt, A.: Guest editors' introduction: rapid prototyping for ubiquitous computing. IEEE Pervasive Comput. 4(4), 15–17 (2005)
5. Delikostidis, I., Fritze, H., Fechner, T., Kray, C.: Bridging the gap between field- and lab-based user studies for location-based services. In: Gartner, G., Huang, H. (eds.) Progress in Location-Based Services 2014. Lecture Notes in Geoinformation and Cartography, pp. 257–271. Springer, Switzerland (2015)
6. Hodges, S., Izadi, S., Han, S.: wasp: a platform for prototyping ubiquitous computing devices. In: Proceedings of the 1st International Workshop on Software Engineering Challenges for Ubiquitous Computing (SEUC 2006) (2006)
7. Moreira, R.: Integrating a 3D application server with a CAVE. MSc thesis, University of Minho (2011)
8. Moreira, S.: Simulating Ubiquitous Computing Environments. MSc thesis, University of Minho (2013)
9. Nazari Shirehjini, A.A., Klar, F.: 3dsim: rapid prototyping ambient intelligence. In: Proceedings of the 2005 Joint Conference on Smart Objects and Ambient Intelligence: Innovative Context-Aware Services: Usages and Technologies, pp. 303–307. ACM (2005)

10. Oh, Y., Kang, C., Woo, W.: U-vr simulator linking real and virtual environments based on context-awareness. In: Proceedings of the International Workshop on Ubiquitous Virtual Reality (ISUVR 2009), pp. 052–055 (2009)

11. O'Neill, E., Lewis, D., Conlan, O.: A simulation-based approach to highly iterative prototyping of ubiquitous computing systems. In: Proceedings of the 2nd International Conference on Simulation Tools and Techniques, p. 56. ICST (Institute for Computer Sciences, Social-Informatics and Telecommunications Engineering) (2009)

12. Orland, B., Budthimedhee, K., Uusitalo, J.: Considering virtual worlds as representations of landscape realities and as tools for landscape planning. Landscape Urban Plann. **54**(1), 139–148 (2001)

13. Poslad, S.: Ubiquitous Computing: Smart Devices, Environments and Interactions. Wiley, Chichester (2009)

14. Rebelo, F., Noriega, P., Duarte, E., Soares, M.: Using virtual reality to assess user experience. Hum. Factors: J. Hum. Factors Ergonomics Soc. **54**(6), 964–982 (2012)

15. Scott, F.: An Investigation into the Ecological Validity of Virtual Reality Measures of Planning and Prospective Memory in Adults with Acquired Brain Injury and Clinical Research Portfolio. Ph.D. thesis, University of Glasgow (2011)

16. Silva, J.L., Campos, J.C., Harrison, M.D.: Formal analysis of ubiquitous computing environments through the APEX framework. In: Symposium on Engineering interactive computing systems, ACM SIGCHI, pp. 131–140 (2012)

17. Silva, J.L., Campos, J.C., Harrison, M.D.: Prototyping and analysing ubiquitous computing environments using multiple layers. Int. J. Hum. Comput. Stud. **72**(5), 488–506 (2014)

18. Singh, P., Ha, H.N., Olivier, P., Kray, C., Kuang, Z., Guo, A.W., Blythe, P., James, P.: Rapid prototyping and evaluation of intelligent environments using immersive video. In: 8th International Conference on Human Computer Interaction with Mobile Devices and Services (Mobile HCI 2016), pp. 264–264. ACM (2006)

19. Vanacken, L., De Boeck, J., Raymaekers, C., Coninx, K.: Designing context-aware multimodal virtual environments. In: Proceedings of the 10th International Conference on Multimodal Interfaces, pp. 129–136. ACM (2008)

Employing Virtual Humans for Interaction, Assistance and Information Provision in Ambient Intelligence Environments

Chryssi Birliraki[1,2(✉)], Dimitris Grammenos[1(✉)], and Constantine Stephanidis[1,2]

[1] Institute of Computer Science, Foundation for Research and Technology - Hellas (FORTH), N. Plastira 100, Vassilika Vouton, 70013 Heraklion, Crete, Greece
{birlirak,gramenos,cs}@ics.forth.gr
[2] Computer Science Department, University of Crete, Heraklion, Crete, Greece

Abstract. This paper reports on the design, development and evaluation of a framework which implements virtual humans for information provision. The framework can be used to create interactive multimedia information visualizations (e.g., images, text, audio, videos, 3D models) and provides a dynamic data modeling mechanism for storage and retrieval and implements communication through multimodal interaction techniques. The interaction may involve human-to-agent, agent-to-environment or agent-to-agent communication. The framework supports alternative roles for the virtual agents who may act as assistants for existing systems, standalone "applications" or even as integral parts of emerging smart environments. Finally, an evaluation study was conducted with the participation of 10 people to study the developed system in terms of usability and effectiveness, when it is employed as an assisting mechanism for another application. The evaluation results were highly positive and promising, confirming the system's usability and encouraging further research in this area.

Keywords: Virtual humans · Virtual agents · Virtual assistants · Embodied agents · Multimodal interaction · User-agent interaction · Usability evaluation

1 Introduction

Virtual humans are embodied agents that exist in virtual environments that look and act like humans and users can interact with them. They are employed as user interfaces and can serve various needs for human-computer interaction, including guidance, assistance, information provision and user training. Virtual humans exhibit human-like qualities and can communicate with humans, or even with each other, using natural human modalities and are capable of real-time perception, cognition and action.

Ambient Intelligence (AmI) environments are characterized by the ubiquitous and unobtrusive presence of electronic equipment in the users' environment that allows sensing the users' actions and react accordingly in order to help them achieve their

© Springer International Publishing Switzerland 2015
N. Streitz and P. Markopoulos (Eds.): DAPI 2015, LNCS 9189, pp. 249–261, 2015.
DOI: 10.1007/978-3-319-20804-6_23

goals. In AmI environments the interface is indistinguishable from the physical setting, as the real world assumes the role of the interface.

The incorporation of virtual humans in AmI environments can enhance the social aspects of interaction offering human-like anthropocentric communication. This work presents the design, development and evaluation of a framework which employs virtual humans able to provide multimodal interaction, assistance and information provision in AmI environments. In general, the framework:

- Is dynamic and flexible so as to fit diverse needs of other systems and the environment.
- Allows virtual humans to act as assistants to other systems offering real-time help, tutorials and user training on interaction techniques.
- Offers the ability to use virtual humans as standalone "applications".
- Uses the virtual human's body gestures and speech so as to provide information.
- Is able to visualize information in different forms, such as images, videos, 3D models, text and audio.
- Uses a data model for information storage and retrieval.
- Supports natural multimodal interaction using a variety of means, including verbal interaction and gestures.
- Integrates techniques regarding user interaction in three dimensions and mobile devices.

2   Related Work

2.1   Ambient Intelligence Environments and Interaction Techniques

Ambient intelligence (AmI) is an emerging discipline that brings intelligence to our everyday environments and makes those environments sensitive to us. The features that are expected in Ami environments and technologies: sensitivity, adaptation, transparency, ubiquity and intelligence. According to Weiser [1], "the most profound technologies are those that disappear. They weave themselves into the fabric of everyday life until they are indistinguishable from it".

In Ambient Intelligence environments, the interaction is different from the typical interaction techniques due to the fact that the environments should be "transparent" from the technological point of view and their interaction techniques are human-centric. Multimodality is the "key" for AmI to provide systems that can be easily manipulated from different groups of people who operate in many different ways individually. Multimodality is the mixture of textual, audio, and visual modes in combination with media and materiality to create meaning [2].

In computer science, speech recognition is the translation of spoken words into text. Some systems use speaker independent speech recognition, while others use a training procedure, where an individual speaker reads sections of text into the system, like Hindi or Kaldi Speech Recognition System both using HTK [3–5]. The feature of invisibility in speech is vital because in AmI environments the transparency is important. This makes the technique challenging to voice-based interfaces in the design and use, but simultaneously helps them to provide an alternative way of interaction with impaired users or in environments where other techniques are difficult to be used or cannot be used at all.

Gestures can be defined as a form of non-verbal communication in which visible body actions communicate particular messages. The recognition of gestures is an issue on which much work is found in literature [6, 7]. There is a diversity of gesture types, including hand gestures [8] and body gestures [9]. Gestures can also be used for manipulating "smart humans" [10], like robots, and controlling their movements.

Context aware systems generally track users and through that offer a large range of information on demand. Context awareness may be used as a mean to provide navigation in 3D space. Another form in which context awareness appears in literature is the progressive information visualization. When the user is far away from the system then the information displayed is more like an overview and when the user come closer the system displays more details of information [11].

Nowadays, many people have smartphones and it is reasonable to expect that they carry them even when they are playing games. Researchers have proposed the use of motion gestures for a variety of input tasks, e.g., to navigate maps or images, to input text, to control a cursor and to verify user identity [12]. Users generally enjoy gestures as a way to use their mobile phones to intuitively interact with other devices [13].

2.2 Existing Approaches for Virtual Humans

Virtual environments can become useful training tools if used properly and for the appropriate training application. Training systems of the future need to simulate all aspects of a virtual world, from the physics of the scene objects to realistic human behavior. Therefore, projects, like Virtual Humans [14, 15] are concentrating on high fidelity embodied agents that are integrated into these environments.

Embodied conversational agents (ECA) [16] are a form of intelligent user interface. Graphically embodied agents aim to unite gesture, facial expression and speech to enable face-to-face communication with users, providing a powerful means of human-computer interaction. A virtual human can itself serve as an exhibit of technology. Consolidating this idea InterFaces project has created virtual museum guides that are in use at the Museum of Science in Boston [17].

Virtual humans can be powerful tools in a wide range of areas. The ICT Virtual Human Toolkit [14] was designed to support researchers with the creation of embodied conversational agents. It offers a collection of modules, tools, libraries, a framework and an open architecture that integrates these components. Apart from virtual agents, the Toolkit services full coverage of subareas such as speech recognition, audio-visual sensing, natural language processing, dialogue management, nonverbal behavior generation and realization, text to speech and rendering. Another powerful animation engine is Maxine [18], which allows management of scenes and virtual characters and focuses on multimodal and emotional interaction in order to establish more effective communication with the user.

Multimodal interaction seems straightforward in everyday life, but a closer look exposes that such interaction is indeed complex and contains a variety of coordination levels. For a better understanding of how multimodal behaviors are coordinated, Zhang at [19] proposes a real-time multimodal human-agent interaction system in which human contributors interact with a virtual agent in a virtual environment.

3 Motivation and Rationale

Various systems already exist that offer diverse features related to virtual humans including conversational abilities, user training, adaptive behavior and virtual human creation, but they constitute limited, "monolithic" attempts that do not provide a comprehensive solution that can cater for broader needs, such as the ones imposed by AmI environments. In this context, the aim of the work described in this paper is the design, development and evaluation of a generic and adaptable framework that combines all the aforementioned features and employs virtual humans in order to provide interaction, assistance and information provision in ambient intelligence environments. Towards this end, the envisioned framework needs to be highly dynamic and flexible so as to be independent of its context of use. Since the information flow among the three fundamental components of AmI environments – i.e., the users, the individual systems and the integrated "smart" environment - is omnidirectional, the system should also be able to communicate with all of them.

There are three distinct roles that virtual humans must be able to support by acting as: (a) assistants for third-party systems; (b) standalone applications and (c) integral parts of emerging smart environments. When acting as an assistant, the framework should provide the tools needed for presenting information in the form of tutorials and real-time help. Furthermore, the virtual humans should support the users' training on interaction techniques applied for the assisted system. As a standalone application, the framework should provide categorized information visualization and interactive help about the interaction techniques and information presented. Finally, when the virtual humans are embedded in smart environments, the framework should be able to support all the aforementioned functionalities individually or even in combination.

In addition to the above, virtual humans created using the framework should be expressive in order to be as realistic as possible and enhance the human-oriented character of the system. Therefore, the information provided by the virtual human should be accompanied by body animations and synthesized speech. Additional information may be offered in various forms, including text, images, audio, videos and 3D models. These means of information visualization should be dynamic, adaptable and interactive so that different users can manipulate them in different ways.

Finally, a fundamental characteristic of systems embedded in AmI environments is the adoption of natural user interaction techniques. As interaction with virtual humans in ambient intelligence environments presented in related literature mainly focuses on conversational interaction and user tracking in space, the suggested framework should support but also enhance and extend these techniques by including verbal communication, kinesthetic interaction and mobile devices.

4   System Overview

4.1   Basic Components and System Visualization

The Virtual Human (Bryan). Bryan (below) is an animated human-like virtual assistant aiming to provide assistance to every application using it as well as to every user handling the application. In the framework, applications can modulate the assistance they wish to be given. The assistance obtained from Bryan comes through hand and body gestures and speech. The system allows the description to be dynamic and adaptive at any point. Furthermore, Bryan responds to the users' wishes and obeys to real time system commands that may come and performs them at once.

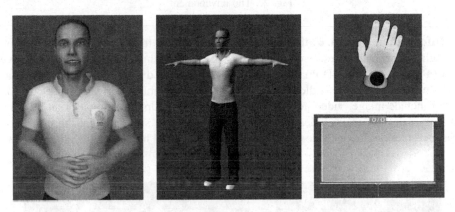

Fig. 1. (Left) Bryan, (middle) T-pose of Bryan, (right) hand cursor - projection screen

Projection Screen. The projection screen (Fig. 1) is another important design component, as a large proportion of the information visualization is displayed on it, e.g., images, videos and text. As the entire system needs to give the impression of an informative, helpful and training environment, the information is displayed on a projection screen as a typical presentation.

Virtual Hand Cursor. The user employs a virtual hand cursor (Fig. 1) to communicate with the system and select items. This hand cursor moves along the user's hand and follows precisely the movements of the user's hand. The goal is to give the user the impression that they actually position their real hand on the scene and that they are in control of the interaction in every way.

Button Components. A number of ready to use interactive buttons are available that contain animations on their idle, hover and click states and provide actions that affect the entire environment, such as the mute, show subtitles, previous stage, next/previous, play/pause and others.

Environment. The environment (Fig. 2) that encloses all the visual components is represented as an ordinary room with walls and pictures on them. Lights surround the scene to give a more realistic graphical environment with shadows on the objects. The user's viewpoint and field of view can dynamically change depending on the current information provision needs.

Fig. 2. The environment

Information Categorization. This subsystem allows the provision of information through distinct categories. Each category is visualized using a title and a representative item (a 3D model or a 2D image). Each category item is dynamic, interactive and has its own animation states (idle, hover, click). The available information presentation media include image, video, text, 3D object and audio. Upon selection of an item the category selection menu hides and the camera moves in space so that the projection screen resides on the one side of the screen and the virtual human on the other (Fig. 3).

Fig. 3. (Left) selection of presentation type, (right) image gallery presentation

User Interaction Training Tool. This tool employs the virtual human in order to teach to the user the interaction techniques supported by the respective application. In this case, the scene is divided in two areas: (a) the assistant area and (b) the interaction techniques area. In the assistant area, the virtual human is presented in full body view and can perform any interaction technique employing hand/full body gestures or speech commands. In the training technique area, a list comprising all the available interaction techniques to be taught is presented. Users can select a technique to practice and the assistant gives the respective instructions.

Structured Tutorial. This component can provide structured instructions regarding the target application, its functions and how one can interact with it. The presentation of the tutorial is divided into three areas. The assistant stands on the left side of the scene and presents information through speech (in the user's preferred language) accompanied by body, hand and face animations. In the central part of the scene visual information is rendered on a projection screen through images, videos and written text. Appropriate control buttons are provided for each distinct medium. Finally, a list of the chapters in which information is divided is displayed on the right side of the scene.

Real Time Assistance. The virtual human subsystem allows applications to send explicit commands directly to the assistant in order to help the users when needed. These commands vary in complexity and can range from overly simple, such as "speak X", to very complex ones, as for example "speak X and show Y image/video while you animate Z motion for E time". To this end, a communication system has been developed in order for the application and the assistant to collaborate.

4.2 Existing Installations

Up to now, the presented system has been used in various environments supporting diverse applications. For instance, in the context of a smart hotel room, it was employed to provide assistance to the users regarding the room's functionality. In this case, a virtual assistant is displayed in the room's television. In another setup, the virtual human is projected at the entrance door of a building and is used to welcome visitors and provide access to it via voice recognition and speaker identity verification. Finally, in a third case three distinct agents are used to provide assistance in different rooms of a building. In this case, agents can also communicate with each other, while users can also act as intermediaries, passing messages of one agent to another, as a means of personalization (e.g., a phrase like "Bryan sent me" can be said to another virtual agent as a means of user identification evoking all the related context and adaptation that Bryan has already instantiated for the specific user).

4.3 Implementation

The system is developed in C# programming language on the Unity Platform[1]. The system is represented by Unity Game Objects which contain two main parts that manipulate different aspects of an element: the component part, which contains the necessary information for each element and implements all the needed functions in order to handle it at a higher level. Each component may be part of a hierarchy, but is able to render itself and contains values for: transformation, rendering and physics and the script part, which defines the behavior of each element and controls every component associated with. The scripts are attached as components to other components or Game Objects in Unity. Scripting architecture is adopted aiming at keeping each element's distinct implementation from its behavior. This way, code reusability and the system extendibility are supported.

---

[1] Unity, http://unity3d.com/.

5   Evaluation

5.1   Set-up and Participants

The evaluation session took place at FORTH's Ambient Intelligence Facility. The system was set up in a room with a 55" display. A total of 10 users participated in the evaluation, 5 females and 5 males. The age of the participants varied from 20 to 35 years old. Six of the users had intermediate or high computer expertise whereas the other participants had limited expertise. Even though the majority of the users were familiar with computers and touch screen systems, they did not have familiarity with hand gesturing or speech recognition as a mode of interaction.

5.2   The Evaluation Scenario

The scenario of the evaluation involves a virtual human, Bryan, being used as an assistive system to an interactive exhibit in a museum. The interactive exhibit that was assisted was TimeViewer [9, 20] a system with complex interaction involving hand and leg gesturing and therefore requiring user guidance. Therefore, assistance and gesture training was imperative for the users to be able to interact with the system, regardless of how natural the gestures were.

5.3   The Evaluation Process

The evaluation process started with the users being informed about the goals of the evaluation process. A series of tasks were assigned to the participants in order to measure the usability of the system. The tasks covered all the primary functionalities of the system in order to assess both the system's design and interaction techniques.

Furthermore, an additional series of tasks were given for the usage of TimeViewer so as to measure the effectiveness of the assistance provided by the virtual human. During the evaluation process, the evaluators provided assistance only when asked for, in order to examine whether users were able to manipulate the system and utterly depict the effectiveness of the virtual assistant.

In addition to the tasks, the participants filled in questionnaires in order to assess the opinion of the users and retrieve qualitative results in a formal way (Table 1.). Furthermore, the participants were encouraged to express their thoughts throughout the evaluation process, which were written down using notes. Finally, a system usability scale (SUS) questionnaire was assigned in order measure the usability of the system in terms of design, interaction and effectiveness as an assistive tool.

5.4   Results

Usability and Interaction. The users found the virtual human very helpful and pleasurable to interact with. The information displayed by the system was clear and users did not face difficulties in perceiving any aspect of the system. Although there were a few comments regarding some design decisions, the users found the user interface self-explaining and intuitive.

The System Usability Scale [21] provides a reliable tool for measuring usability. It consists of a 10 item questionnaire with five response options for the participants; from strongly agree to strongly disagree.

A SUS score above a 68 would be considered above average and anything below 68 is below average. The results of System Usability Scale were very encouraging with a final score of 84. The graph above displays the SUS score per participant (ranging from 70 to 92.5 – Graph 1).

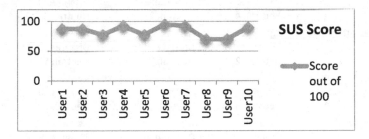

Graph 1: (Left) selection of presentation type, (right) image gallery presentation

Gestural interaction involved hand movement in any direction and the manipulation of a virtual cursor. The users performed the supported gestures without difficulty and found them intuitive for specific tasks, such as displaying the next image in a slide-show. Furthermore, they were able to control the virtual cursor in order to select items shown at the display. Four of the users (40 %) initially faced difficulties using the cursor when moving it to the lower part of the display. However, once they got familiar to it they could manipulate the system without problem.

The participants were provided with the list of all the available voice commands in order to assess the responsiveness, the exactness and the usefulness of speech recognition. Despite not being accurate at all times, users generally managed to manipulate the system using voice commands with a maximum of three tries. Despite the fact that the system did not focus on human-assistant conversation, voice recognition proved to be pleasing and successful, motivating future research in this area.

A smartphone was given to the participants of the evaluation and the available gestures were described. The users enjoyed interacting using mobile devices but preferred the other interaction techniques (hand gestures and speech recognition) which were considered more natural.

Table 1. The users' answers to the evaluation questionnaire regarding the three supplied means of interaction: gestures, voice commands and smartphone gestures

Questions	Gestures	Voice commands	Smartphone interaction
I like interacting with this method	Agree: 10 Disagree: 0 Neutral: 0	Agree: 9 Disagree: 0 Neutral: 1	Agree: 8 Disagree: 1 Neutral: 1
No special training is needed to learn	Agree: 9 Disagree: 0 Neutral: 1	Agree: 9 Disagree: 0 Neutral: 1	Agree: 6 Disagree: 0 Neutral: 4
Corresponding precisely to my actions	Agree: 6 Disagree: 0 Neutral: 4	Agree: 6 Disagree: 2 Neutral: 2	Agree: 6 Disagree: 0 Neutral: 4
It was awkward to use	Agree: 3 Disagree: 5 Neutral: 2	Agree: 6 Disagree: 4 Neutral: 0	Agree: 0 Disagree: 5 Neutral: 5
Responded promptly to my actions	Agree: 7 Disagree: 0 Neutral: 3	Agree: 3 Disagree: 2 Neutral: 5	Agree: 3 Disagree: 0 Neutral: 7
It was tiring to use	Agree: 0 Disagree: 9 Neutral: 1	Agree: 2 Disagree: 6 Neutral: 2	Agree: 2 Disagree: 5 Neutral: 3
I would prefer another method of interaction	Agree: 0 Disagree: 7 Neutral: 3	Agree: 1 Disagree: 8 Neutral: 1	Agree: 0 Disagree: 6 Neutral: 4

Effectiveness in Manipulating TimeViewer. The users were able to start interacting with TimeViewer immediately after they were informed by Bryan. They were aware of the supported gestures and knew what to expect to see. Especially after training, users were confident and able to perform the gestures right ahead.

Indicatively, 30 % of the users stated (without being asked) that the training was very helpful and considered themselves experienced users after experimenting using the virtual assistant as they had "tried it in action before". The confidence was so apparent that one of the users stated his belief that "gesture tracking is more precise in TimeViewer", although the same software and hardware was used in both cases.

Supplementary to the assigned tasks, the users were given extra questions in order to extract additional information and urge them to express their opinion regarding the efficiency and the helpfulness of the virtual assistant. The users believed that Time-Viewer would be difficult to use without interactive guidance, as other methods such as leaflets would be insufficient. Moreover, Bryan as an assistant was described as sufficient, comprehensive and did not display redundant information.

6   Conclusion and Future Work

This paper reports on the design, development and evaluation of a framework which implements virtual humans supporting body gestures and speech synthesis that can be used for information provision. The framework can be used to create interactive multimedia information visualizations (e.g., images, text, audio, videos, 3D models) and provides a dynamic data modeling mechanism for storage and retrieval and implements communication through multimodal interaction techniques. The interaction may involve human-to-agent, agent-to-environment or agent-to-agent communication. The generated virtual agents can have diverse roles, as they can be used as assistive tools for existing systems, standalone "applications" or even as vital parts of smart environments.

When acting as an assistant, the framework provides the tools needed for presenting information in the form of tutorials and real-time help. Furthermore, the virtual humans support the users' training on interaction techniques applied for the assisted system. As standalone application, the framework provides categorized information visualization and interactive help about the interaction techniques and information presented. Finally, when the virtual humans are embedded in other environments the framework is be able to create hybrid mode that supports all the aforementioned functionalities individually or even in combination.

The developed framework supports multiple multimodal techniques in order to fit to various ambient intelligence environments and offer natural interaction, such as gestural, verbal and tangible interaction, in a wide range of setups.

A preliminary evaluation has already been conducted in order to assess the framework in terms of usability, effectiveness and likeability. Additional, more extensive assessments, with a larger number of participants covering a broader age range, are planned in order to further validate and improve the current implementation.

Based on the encouraging evaluation results, further research work is already underway in regarding the use of virtual humans in ambient intelligence environments. Improvements in the system's design are also foreseen based on observation results and specific user comments. Since speech recognition proved to be very popular among the users, the conversational abilities of the supported virtual humans will also be extended and improved.

A key drawback of the framework when used in practice was that lack of an interactive means for providing all the required digital content to the system. This will be addressed by the development of a visual tool for content insertion and editing. Finally, since the framework is built using an engine that supports interoperability with mobile devices future work will seek to port and adapt the current implementation to address the needs imposed by user mobility, as well, as small and multi-touch displays and sensor-enabled interaction.

Acknowledgements. The work reported in this paper has been conducted in the context of the AmI Programme of the Institute of Computer Science (ICS) of the Foundation for Research and Technology-Hellas (FORTH). The authors would like to express their gratitude to Anthony Katzourakis for the artistic work and 3D modelling and to the Signal Processing Laboratory (SPL) of ICS-FORTH and especially Elena Karamichali for creating the speech recognition system.

References

1. Weiser, M.: The Computer for the twenty-first century. Sci. Am. **265**, 94–104 (1991)
2. Murray, J.: Composing multimodality. In: Lutkewitte, C. (ed.) Multimodal Composition: A Critical Sourcebook. Bedford/St. Martin's, Boston (2013)
3. Povey, D., Ghoshal, A., Boulianne, G., Burget, L., Glembek, O., Goel, N., Hannemann, M., Motlicek, P., Qian, Y., Schwarz, P., Silovsky, J., Stemmer, G., Vesely, K.: The Kaldi speech recognition toolkit. In: IEEE 2011 Workshop on Automatic Speech Recognition and Understanding. IEEE Signal processing Society (2011)
4. Kumar, K.: Hindi speech recognition system using HTK. Int. J. Comput. Bus. Res. **2**, 2229–6166 (2011)
5. Hidden Markov Model Toolkit (HTK) speech Recognition. http://htk.eng.cam.ac.uk/develop/atk.shtml
6. Suarez, J., Murphy, R.: Hand gesture recognition with depth images: a review. In: 2012 IEEE RO-MAN, pp. 411–417. IEEE (2012)
7. Biswas, K.K., Basu, S.K.: Gesture recognition using Microsoft Kinect. In: 2011 5th International Conference on Automation, Robotics and Applications (ICARA), pp. 100–103 (2011)
8. Drossis, G., Grammenos, D., Birliraki, C., Stephanidis, C.: MAGIC: developing a multimedia gallery supporting mid-air gesture-based interaction and control. In: Stephanidis, C. (ed.) HCI International 2013 - Posters' Extended Abstracts. Springer, Heidelberg (2013)
9. Drossis, G., Grammenos, D., Adami, I., Stephanidis, C.: 3D visualization and multimodal interaction with temporal information using timelines. In: Kotzé, P., Marsden, G., Lindgaard, G., Wesson, J., Winckler, M. (eds.) INTERACT 2013, Part III. LNCS, vol. 8119, pp. 214–231. Springer, Heidelberg (2013)
10. Grzejszczak, T., Mikulski, M., Szkodny, T., Jędrasiak, K.: Gesture based robot control. In: Bolc, L., Tadeusiewicz, R., Chmielewski, L.J., Wojciechowski, K. (eds.) ICCVG 2012. LNCS, vol. 7594, pp. 407–413. Springer, Heidelberg (2012)
11. Grammenos, D., Zabulis, X., Michel, D., Sarmis, T., Georgalis, G., Tzevanidis, K., Argyros, A., Stephanidis, C.: Design and development of four prototype interactive edutainment exhibits for museums. In: Stephanidis, C. (ed.) Universal Access in HCI, Part III, HCII 2011. LNCS, vol. 6767, pp. 173–182. Springer, Heidelberg (2011)
12. Ruiz, J., Li, Y., Lank, E.: User-defined motion gestures for mobile interaction. In: Proceedings of the SIGCHI Conference on Human Factors in Computing Systems, pp. 197–206. ACM, 2011
13. Kray C., Nesbitt D., Dawson J., Rohs M.: User-defined gestures for connecting mobile phones, public displays, and tabletops. In: Proceedings of the 12th International Conference on Human Computer Interaction with Mobile Devices and Services, pp. 239–248. ACM (2010)
14. Hartholt, A., Traum, D., Marsella, S.C., Shapiro, A., Stratou, G., Leuski, A., Morency, L.-P., Gratch, J.: All together now, introducing the virtual human toolkit. In: Aylett, R., Krenn, B., Pelachaud, C., Shimodaira, H. (eds.) IVA 2013. LNCS, vol. 8108, pp. 368–381. Springer, Heidelberg (2013)
15. Virtual Human Toolkit. https://vhtoolkit.ict.usc.edu
16. Cassell, J., Prevost, S., Sullivan, J., Churchill, E.: Embodied Conversational Agents. MIT Press, Cambridge (2000)

17. Swartout, W., et al.: Ada and Grace: toward realistic and engaging virtual museum guides. In: Allbeck, J., Badler, N., Bickmore, T., Pelachaud, C., Safonova, A. (eds.) IVA 2010. LNCS, vol. 6536, pp. 286–300. Springer, Heidelberg (2010)
18. Baldassarri, S., Cerezo, E., Seron, F.J.: Maxine: a platform for embodied animated agents. Comput. Graph. **32**(4), 430–437 (2008)
19. Zhang, H., Fricker, D., Smith, T.G., Yu, C.: Real-time adaptive behaviors in multimodal human-avatar interactions. In: International Conference on Multimodal Interfaces and the Workshop on Machine Learning for Multimodal Interaction, p. 4. ACM (2010)
20. Drossis, G., Grammenos, D., Bouhli, M., Adami, I., Stephanidis, C.: Comparative evaluation among diverse interaction techniques in three dimensional environments. In: Streitz, N., Stephanidis, C. (eds.) DAPI 2013. LNCS, vol. 8028, pp. 3–12. Springer, Heidelberg (2013)
21. Brooke, J.: SUS-a quick and dirty usability scale. Usability Eval. Ind. **189**, 4–7 (1996)

From Collaborative Scenario Recording
to Smart Room Assistance Models

Gregor Buchholz$^{(\boxtimes)}$ and Peter Forbrig

Department of Computer Science, University of Rostock,
Albert Einstein Street 21, Rostock 18055, Germany
{gregor.buchholz,peter.forbrig}@uni-rostock.de

Abstract. There is still much to be done in implementing assistance systems for Intelligent Environments. Different approaches exist that aim at providing the user with useful and pleasant functionality. One group of methods uses behavioral models to derive supportive actions from the observation by sensors. This is a promising approach but creating such models is a laborious and error-prone task. Examples of the behavior of persons in intelligent environments and their interactions with the devices are a starting point for the (partial) generation of such models. In this paper we present an approach to record user behavior without the need of real users performing in the real environment. As a special thematic priority we will focus on the preparation phase of collaborative scenario recording and the used notation. Additionally, the paper will explain the generation of models from the recorded traces.

Keywords: Intelligent environments · Ubiquitous computing · Task models

1 Introduction

Numerous engineering techniques for interactive systems use the application of models as their basis. Among those, task model based approaches focus on the tasks users want to accomplish while interacting with the system. One main characteristic of such approaches is the application of models not only in the requirements analysis and development phases but also during run time. Ambient Intelligent Systems like Smart Environments can profit from these models, too. Such systems need to be aware of the users' movements, positions, their interaction with devices, the states of those devices and so on. With the help of models, the system tries to anticipate appropriate actions to support the users.

The interplay of different things around us like wearable computers and stationary devices is known as Ubiquitous Computing and considered to be part of our near future [10]. Environmental monitoring through sensors of all kinds enables them to gather information about many aspects including, beside their own current state (e.g. "position"), the amount, states and history of neighboring devices. In addition, the

The work of the first author is supported by DFG graduate school 1424 *Multimodal Smart Appliance Ensembles for Mobile Applications* (MuSAMA) at the University of Rostock, Germany

N. Streitz and P. Markopoulos (Eds.): DAPI 2015, LNCS 9189, 262–273, 2015.
DOI: 10.1007/978-3-319-20804-6_24

availability of information about the context (e.g. "temperature" and "brightness") and persons acting therein (e.g. "number", "position", movement data) opens up perspectives for new software systems. The vision tied to networked devices of diverse types is that of an invisible but omnipresent computer that assists the users (or at least offers them support) in their activities based on its knowledge about the context and the current situation. The goal is to provide the best assistance possible with the currently connected devices.

In this paper we focus on scenarios in closed rooms with different kinds of sensors (e.g. real-time location systems like UbiSense[1], cameras, radio tomography), stationary actuators (lights, projectors, screens) and personal devices like users' laptops that join and leave the ensemble dynamically [9] ("Smart Meeting Rooms"). Depending on the number and type of devices that are available at a specific time the system can offer more or less functionality as each single device as well as device combinations contribute some functions.

Fig. 1. Smart appliance lab

Figure 1 shows an example application of a Smart Appliance Lab: The room, equipped with presentation devices and sensors, distributes slides and other information over the available screens in a way that every person's needs, interests and preferences are matched. Persons acting as a presenter play a special role in this use case: Depending on their position within the presentation zones the content is rearranged. Other use cases beyond the depicted presentation scenario, e.g. working in two or more

---

[1] UbiSense real-time location systems: http://www.ubisense.net/ .

groups, discussions or collaborative activities (parts of the content are contributed by different users) have to be supported, too.

1.1 Providing Assistance in Intelligent Rooms

Several competing methodological approaches are dedicated to provide assistance in Smart Environments. One group of methods uses concepts of artificial intelligence in order to adapt to changing behavior of users, to infer intentions from the observed activities and to provide assistance in reaching a predicted target state, defined as a set of variable assignments describing aspects of the environment [1, 6]. The increasing diversity of user activities and growing number of users, however, are accompanied with a higher demand for training data in order to ensure the recognition of user activities with sufficient accuracy. Moreover, during run time the calculations required to identify possible successor states and their probabilities place even greater demands on processing power and memory which, while reducible by certain state space compression methods, nevertheless are substantial.

A second group of approaches attaches much more importance to the mainly manual design of behavior models. Intertwined activities of different users fulfilling different roles can be described in separate models. Interdependencies between the models are described by special notations [14]. The application of such models significantly reduces the search space for possible pro-active assistance, lowering the resource requirements and promoting and fostering more targeted user assistance.

The models' adequacy and appropriateness is of vital importance for the system's utility value and thus the acceptance level among users. Model based development methods take account of this core requirement by giving much weight to the role of models during all development phases from requirements analysis and system design through to usability testing. The creation and discussion of models of varying degree of formality are a main concern during the discourse between user and analyst. Nevertheless, with increasing level of detail and decreasing level of abstraction (which is the most laborious part of such hierarchical models as the task tree progressively broadens downwards) more and more use is made of recorded scenario protocols [12] whose obtaining is an elaborating and expensively task too.

1.2 Model Construction from Scenarios

As shown in [4], the construction of task models as formalization of requirements analysis results can be combined with a partly automatic generation of model fragments. Two activities directed towards each other are combined: The expert-driven top-down-modeling forms the basic structure of the hierarchical model and a bottom up-generation completes it and derives temporal relations from the recorded scenario traces. Thus, the labor-intensive construction of widely branched model trees is considerably simplified and has experienced a noticeable acceleration. Figure 2 gives an overview of the entire process.

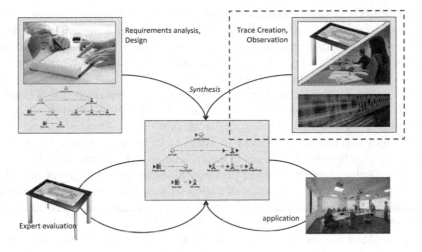

Fig. 2. Model creation process overview

However, the recording of scenario traces in the physical Smart Meeting Room is quite resource intensive. That motivates the development of a more efficient method to generate scenario traces in a virtualized environment. This paper describes an approach to the creation of behavioral models in the context of Smart Meeting Rooms combining the manual modeling of user activities on more abstract levels with the semi-automated generating of detailed model fragments. It especially highlights the recording of example traces in a simulated, virtual Smart Environment and the planning of those scenarios.

2   Related Work

Several approaches address the scenario-based formalization of human behavior, many of which fall into the field of process mining. A comprehensive collection of such algorithms is implemented in the ProM framework[2] [13]. Some of the numerous applications beyond the "basic" mining of processes are the identification of bottle-necks, verification of business rules, and creation of social network graphs. Importing from a number of different sources is possible and many plug-ins for import formats and functionality are available. In common with the majority of process mining approaches the focus lies in the extraction, visualization and optimization (in terms of resource usage) of processes. Here, it is taken less concern for requirements like human readability and understandability, support for a strong orientation towards a hierarchy reflecting different levels of abstractions from the viewpoint of a user and the suitability of the resulting models for discussions between modeling experts and untrained persons.

---

[2] http://www.promtools.org/prom6 .

Reference [11] presents an ontology-based approach to define and recognize event patterns in sensor streams of Smart Environments using an EL^{++} description logic, see [2]. Their results regarding recognition rate, run-time performance and "ease of design" seem to be promising, although the system does not integrate direct interaction between users and the system's underlying models.

In [5] a method for automatic work flow induction is presented that is based on First-Order Logic representations and learns behavior models in Smart Environments from scratch by increasingly refining the work flow model (starting with an empty model). It uses two predicates (*activity* to assign tasks to steps and *next* to describe a following relation between two steps) to describe cases and two predicates to describe work flows. During learning, pre- and post-conditions are generated, too. Currently, it does not include distinct consideration of multi-user scenarios. The presented approach by itself in fact does allow for more than one person's "sensor trace" to be considered, but parallel and interlaced activities are not addressed explicitly.

An example of a system generating task models is *ActionStream*, introduced in [8], that records user activities for a long period of time while all interactions are interpreted as terminals of a grammar. By continuously adapting the grammar's production rules, *ActionStream* learns a formal model of the user's behavior. Such approaches are likely to produce quite precise models successfully covering the learned scenarios, lacking however a semantic meaning of the non-terminals. The resulting models, as "correct" as they may be, are of limited use in the communication between stakeholders during the development phase of a system.

3 Creation of Scenario Traces

Deriving task models from the traces is the purpose of capturing example scenarios. User behavior in this context covers all aspects of movements and interactions that are detectable by the environments sensors: walking, standing, sitting, talking, pointing, bringing devices into the ensemble, connecting devices (e.g. a laptop and a projector), using devices, and more. The traces describe a sequence of such events as captured and extracted from the sensor data streams. Recording a scenario demands for a thorough planning in order to create a set of examples that cover main use cases as well as exceptions and variations. In the following section we describe how to prepare efficient play-throughs.

3.1 . Planning the Scenario Recording

For each use case a set of scenarios is developed that describes possible variations of actions sequences. In preparation for each cooperative recording of a scenario a graphical description of the planned interaction sequence is created. The purpose of these paper plans is to serve as handling instruction during the recording of scenarios. Such a plan should represent all important aspects of the envisioned users' behavior in the Smart Environment during the considered situation. To describe such a scenario we use the *ActionSketch* notation with the extended adaption for interactive environments [3].

The basic set of *ActionSketch* notation elements is designed for WIMP and Multi-touch interaction. The principle remains the same: Each frame depicts the initial state (black), user actions (green), and system actions (orange). While the first frame should show the complete initial state of the system all of the following frames only show the changes between frames. These rules (i.e. color coding and the notation of changes) also apply for the sketching of behavior in Interactive Environments. Here, the set of interaction icons is further extended by some symbols: a circle inside an ellipse to represent a person's position and representations from architectural sketches for common objects like tables and walls. In order to distinguish between different persons in the room, we changed the notation of persons to "a letter inside an ellipse". Additionally, we use a simple notation of timestamps: Each frame is labeled with the time difference in respect to the first frame with the initial state.

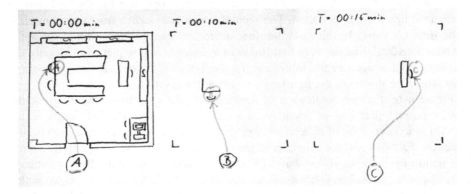

Fig. 3. ActionSketch example sequence

In Fig. 3 a simple example for the beginning of a frame sequence describing a multi user scenario is given. The first frame (timestamp 00:00) shows the room with the projector screens ("S"), the tables, chairs, the door, and a workstation in the lower right corner. At the beginning, Person "A" is outside the room. Beginning at the timestamp 00:00 that person moves to a chair. This arrow is drawn in green to mark it as user action, as movements in a Smart Room with sensors can be interpreted as interaction. The user action does not cause any system actions, so there is nothing to be drawn in orange. The second frame (timestamp 00:10) only shows the differences to the last state of the actions in the preceding frame: Now, person "B" moves from outside the room to another chair. That specific chair and a little part of the table are repeated again for easier orientation. In the third frame (timestamp 00:15) person "C" enters the room and moves to the presenter table. Again, only some little parts of the room are drawn for orientation purposes. More frames are added for a complete description of a scenario which can be used as guidance during the simulation.

In practical use, we make certain simplifications and modifications to reduce the number of frames and increase legibility. Two exemplary adaptations are described in the following:

- If the actions of two consecutive frames can be drawn without overlapping, we combine them to one picture. The action of the original first frame is annotated with a roman 1 ("I"), the second frame's action with "II" and the timestamps are labeled as "T_I" and "T_{II}".
- In order to distinguish more clearly between actions of different users we use colors (besides green and orange) that mark each person in a unique manner. If so, the person "B" is referred to as person "blue", for example.

Interactions between users and a device in the room can be noted in two ways: One possibility is to draw the device interface "inline", i.e. the UI is drawn in a dotted rectangle within the room frame. That option is exclusively suitable for very simple interactions like pressing a button. The second option is to switch from the room view to the device's view. In this case, the first device interaction frame would show the complete interface (like the very first frame of a *ActionSketch* sequence) with only the differences and actions in the following frames. Leaving the device view, the whole room would be shown in the first frame showing the room again.

Please note that our application of *ActionSketch* does not allow the usage of the "OR" construct that can be found in the original specification. The usage of the notation as a description of a scenario as described here is meant to define one specific sequence of actions and not a number of possibilities. The latter would be seen as a use case within the context of our work. On the other hand, constraints like timestamps cannot be seen as absolute certainty, as a simulation by hand is inherently tainted with a certain degree of inaccuracy. So the minimum requirement of a scenario definition is to describe the actions that are performed by the users and their temporal order.

In the following sections we describe the system to simulate the scenarios defined by such frame sequences. The next section discusses the infrastructural setting followed by a characterization of the used hardware and the recording software.

3.2   Protocols from Observations in the Physical Environment

During the usage of the Smart Environment (as depicted in Fig. 1) the middleware Helferlein[3] provides the different application modules with the event streams produced by the sensors. The modules can feed their own events into the common event storage. Every module can use the publish/subscribe-mechanism to get notified as soon as a new event of the specified type is detected.

For the purpose of scenario recording additional modules have been developed. They collect and store the events produced by the table computer while moving the tagged objects over the room plan (See paragraph "software" in Sect. 3.3 for more details). The extraction of semantically meaningful events from the sensor streams can

---

[3] The middleware Helferlein: https://code.google.com/p/helferlein/.

be achieved in different ways. One way is to use sliding window techniques [7]. Such an algorithm is implemented as a module on the middleware. The occurrences of previously defined event patterns in the incoming data streams from different sensors are detected that are characteristic for certain user activities. The definition of these patterns has to be adjusted for different room setups, e.g. for changing sets of sensors.

The output of that module is a new event stream: the "basic action stream" that contains user-related events abstracted from sensor data. Such higher level events can be used as execution trigger for the models during run time. To enable an efficient binding between events and the models, the events are further aggregated in two ways.

1. Spatial Aggregation - As not every single change of position of every user in the room has a direct influence on the model execution progress we introduce a more abstract event category. Therefore, previously defined zones in the room with distinct meanings serve as references, e.g. presentation zones in front of the displays, the entrance area around the door, the seating accommodations and so on. The basic movement events are no longer the only possible triggers for the model execution but events raised when users enter or leave such a zone can be used, too.
2. Temporal Aggregation - Movement information inside and outside the defined zones are not always interesting to focus on in the highest level of detail. Therefore, key frames are calculated that represent users' movements as a discrete set of data points.

Both forms of aggregation produce new events that are made accessible by other modules through the middleware's publish/subscribe mechanism.

The recording of scenarios in the Smart Environment always entails a lot of work. In the following, a method is described to significantly reduce the costs of producing such protocols.

3.3 Generation of Protocols in the Virtualized Environment

Hardware. For the implementation of a system for producing protocols exemplifying use cases a Samsung SUR40 has been selected. The SUR40 is a computer in the form of a table running *Microsoft PixelSense 4* (formerly known as *Microsoft Surface*). Its 40" display features multi-touch interaction and object recognition by attaching Identity Tags to things. Figure 4 shows (a) a SUR40 table computer and (b) two cubes with

Fig. 4. (a) Samsung SUR40 table computer, (b) Cubes with identity tags

three Identity Tags each. During the recording of a scenario each cube represents the position of one person within the room. Three sides of each cube are labeled as SIT, STAND, and INTERACT, respectively. The opposite sides have a corresponding Identity Tag printed on. The recognition of a tag is interpreted as the label on the top side of the cube. Of course, each cube has its own set of tags. A position change in the state STAND is interpreted as normal walking and via INTERACT the interaction with a device nearby can be initiated.

Software. The middleware of the Smart Environment (*Helferlein*) is complemented by modules encapsulating the room's devices and sensors. A common interface enables other modules to request and use the public properties and methods of each object. For a large part of the devices emulations have been implemented providing an idealized (i.e. fault free) virtual device functionality via the same interface as the corresponding real device. Each module encapsulating a device or a sensor can be requested to deliver a GUI specification with property visualizations and method activators.

The recording of scenario protocols as described here uses these modules to emulate the devices in the Smart Environment and Surface2TUIO and TUIO4j[4] for the processing of multi-touch and object recognition events.

A schematic view of the room's setup is the core element of the GUI visualizing the furnishings and devices. The defined zones are highlighted in different colors. Personal devices can be integrated as separate objects with their own Identity Tag or as attached to a user.

The GUI features four main elements:

1. Room Plan - The interaction space with a schematic room view is the biggest part of the interface. Visual feedback shows the recognized position of tagged objects. Interaction elements for devices are displayed as soon as the INTERACT function of a person is selected.
2. Property Panel - Here the properties and methods of the currently selected object are visible. In the case of sensors (e.g. brightness sensor or thermometer) the behavior of the emulation object can be controlled. Thus, environmental conditions like strong incidence of light can be integrated into the scenario.
3. Status Panel with Timeline Display - This area shows meta data of the current recording, the timeline and its controls. To successively record parallel activities the user can jump to an earlier point in time and then record a second activity etc.
4. Protocol View - This view replaces the Room Plan and shows the recorded protocols. Here, protocol events can be assigned to tasks in the behavioral model as needed for further processing during model generation. Multiple protocols can be assigned to a use case in preparation of the succeeding steps.

Figure 5 shows a situation during a scenario recording: The defined zones are highlighted in red (A, entrance zone), green (B, presentation zone), and blue (C, seat regions. The current positions of the two simulated persons are circled in yellow. On the right-hand side the Property and Status Panel are visible. Thus, scenario traces for different use cases can be recorded.

---

[4] TUIO2j: https://code.google.com/p/tuio4j/ .

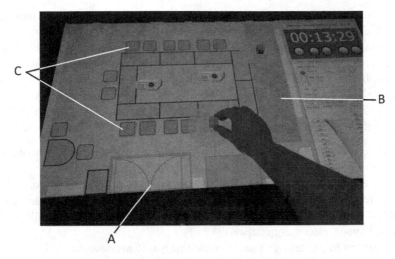

Fig. 5. Recording a Scenario on the touch table

Classification. The system described in this paper aims at the design of user assistance in smart environments at an early development stage. It is a significant advantage that no physical hardware in the room has to be installed. In fact, the specific configuration and layout of the room's equipment may be even unclear or may be subject to change and it is not the objective of this system to explore and compare different room designs, although that would be possible to a certain degree, too. It is for this reason that we decided to use a quite simple 2D layout at a certain abstraction level as a room representation. Of course it would be possible to use a more detailed graphical (e.g. 3D) design but that would disguise the development status of the system and anticipate decisions that have not been taken yet. However, our tool can be complimented by a 3D tool in the later development phases.

3.4 Limits of the Protocol Creation

Not all aspects of usage observable in the real environment can be included in the recording on a table computer. This is especially true for unexpected behavior and events like the opening of a window, leaving the room for a short time, interruptions through external factors and some more. Such situations have to be considered during the planning of a scenario recording and during the later steps of model generation and evaluation.

4 Conclusion and Future Work

In this paper we presented an approach to plan and produce scenario traces as examples for the usage of Intelligent Environments. The application of the *ActionSketch* notation allows an efficient and intuitive way to prepare and describe the sequence of actions that form a scenario. Multiple scenarios demonstrate different possible variations of use cases. They can be used to support the modeling of task trees in such a way, that the essential structure of the models is created manually based on the collected domain knowledge and the scenario traces are used to extract more detailed information about the process. In this context, the use of devices with multi-touch and object recognition capabilities allows an intuitive scenario recording by experts and users.

Multiple users can interact in the scenario and assume roles dynamically. The application of the proposed system can be summarized in the following steps:

1. Identify requirements with conventional methods (interviews, questionnaires etc.).
2. Formalize knowledge from step 1 as task model as far as possible.
3. Define scenarios by developing stories using the *ActionSketch* notation.
4. Use the recording software to produce scenario traces for a specific use case.
5. Combine the result of step 2 with generated model fragments using results of step 4 (semi-automatic model completion).
6. Check generated model by simulation and revise, if necessary.

The resulting models can then be used as the basic for the environment's supportive actions. So far, the tool chain from scenario recording (implemented in the Helferlein framework) and the model construction implementation are only loosely coupled. In order to support a fluent transition between recording, modeling and generating, the different parts should be integrated into the framework. Beyond this, expert evaluation of the task models in the virtual environment will be possible by integrating the run time environment for the instantiating and processing of task models into the system. Thus, several phases of the assistance development process for Smart Environments will be able to benefit from the virtualization of the room including devices, sensors, and the users' behavior.

References

1. Armentano, M.G., Amandi, A.A.: Recognition of user intentions for interface agents with variable order Markov models. In: Houben, G.-J., McCalla, G., Pianesi, F., Zancanaro, M. (eds.) UMAP 2009. LNCS, vol. 5535, pp. 173–184. Springer, Heidelberg (2009)
2. Baader, F., Brandt, S., Lutz, C.: Pushing the EL envelope. In: Proceedings of the IJCAI 2005, pp. 364–369. Morgan Kaufmann, San Francisco (2005)
3. Barros, G.: Extending ActionSketch for new interaction styles: gestural interfaces and interactive environments. In: Marcus, A. (ed.) DUXU 2014, Part II. LNCS, vol. 8518, pp. 509–520. Springer, Heidelberg (2014)
4. Buchholz, G., Forbrig, P.: Combining design of models for smart environments with pattern-based extraction. In: Kurosu, M. (ed.) HCI 2014, Part I. LNCS, vol. 8510, pp. 285–294. Springer, Heidelberg (2014)
5. Ferilli, S., De Carolis, B., Redavid, D.: Logic-based incremental process mining in smart environments. In: Ali, M., Bosse, T., Hindriks, K.V., Hoogendoorn, M., Jonker, C.M., Treur, J. (eds.) IEA/AIE 2013. LNCS, vol. 7906, pp. 392–401. Springer, Heidelberg (2013)
6. Kiefer, P.: Mobile intention recognition. In: Kiefer, P. (ed.) Mobile intention recognition, pp. 11–53. Springer, New York (2012)

7. Krämer, J., Seeger, B.: Semantics and implementation of continuous sliding window queries over data streams. ACM Trans. Database Syst. **34**, 4:1–4:49 (2009)

8. Maulsby, D.: Inductive task modeling for user interface customization. In: Proceedings of the IUI 1997, pp. 233–236. ACM, New York (1997)

9. Ramos, C., Marreiros, G., Santos, R., Freitas, C.F.: Smart offices and intelligent decision rooms. In: Nakashima, H., Aghajan, H., Augusto, J.C. (eds.) Handbook of Ambient Intelligence and Smart Environments, pp. 851–880. Springer, New York (2010)

10. Robles, R.J., Kim, T.-h.: Context aware systems, methods and trends in smart home technology. In: Kim, T.-h., Stoica, A., Chang, R.-S. (eds.) Security-Enriched Urban Computing and Smart Grid. Communications in Computer and Information Science, pp. 149–158. Springer, Heidelberg (2010)

11. Scalmato, A., Sgorbissa, A., Zaccaria, R.: Describing and recognizing patterns of events in smart environments with description logic. IEEE Trans. Cybern. **43**, 1882–1897 (2013). IEEE

12. Seyff, N., Maiden, N., Karlsen, K., Lockerbie, J., Grünbacher, P., Graf, F., Ncube, C.: Exploring how to use scenarios to discover requirements. Requirements Eng. **14**(2), 91–111 (2009). Springer, Heidelberg

13. van der Aalst, W.M.: Process mining in the large: a tutorial. In: Zimányi, E. (ed.) eBISS 2013. LNBIP, vol. 172, pp. 33–76. Springer, Heidelberg (2014)

14. Wurdel, M., Sinnig, D., Forbrig, P.: CTML: Domain and task modeling for collaborative environments. J. Univ. Comput. Sci. **14**(19), 3188–3201 (2008). (Special Issue on Human-Computer Interaction)

Hierarchical Narrowcasting

Michael Cohen$^{(\boxtimes)}$

Spatial Media Group, University of Aizu, Aizu-Wakamatsu,
Fukushima 965-8580, Japan
mcohen@u-aizu.ac.jp

Abstract. Narrowcasting, in analogy to uni-, broad-, and multicasting, is a formalization of media control functions that can be used to adjust exposure and receptiveness. Its idioms have been deployed in spatial sound diffusion interfaces, internet telephony, immersive chatspaces, and collaborative music audition systems. Here, we consider its application to desk-top music composition systems, using Pure Data ("Pd"), a dataflow language for audio and multimedia, to develop a proof-of-concept. A hierarchical model of a drum kit is deployed, applying narrowcasting at various levels of aggregation to drum machine sequences. These ideas can also be extended to audio augmented reality situations.

1 Introduction

Generally, we are deluged with stimuli, and must devise and deploy strategies for focusing attention or maintaining privacy. There are many techniques for hiding information. For particular instance, hierarchical data structures, presentable as outlines or trees, allow branches to be hidden (collapsed) or revealed (expanded).

Narrowcasting (Cohen, 1998, Cohen, 2000, Cohen and Villegas, 2015)— by way of analogy with broad-, uni-, any-, and multicasting— is an idiom for limiting media streams, formalized by the expressions shown in Fig. 1, to distribute, ration, and control privacy, attention, and presence, as illustrated by Table 1. One could call such deliberate filtering "interinactivity," "disattention," or a "cold spot" (opposite of "hot spot").

"Privacy" has two interpretations, the first association being that of avoiding "leaks" of confidential information, protecting secrets. But a second interpretation means "freedom from disturbance," in the sense of not being bothered by irrelevance or interruption. Narrowcasting operations manage privacy in both senses, filtering duplex information flow through an articulated communication model. Sources and sinks are symmetric duals in virtual spaces, respectively representing media emitters and collectors. Sources can be explicitly "turned off" by muting, or implicitly ignored by deliberately selecting some others. Similarly, sinks can be explicitly deafened or implicitly desensitized if other sinks are "attended."

Previous research explored the power of two-level hierarchies for narrowcasting mixing control. For such arrangements, the terminal tier can be usefully called "sinks," adjustable with **attend** and **deafen** narrowcasting commands, in

© Springer International Publishing Switzerland 2015
N. Streitz and P. Markopoulos (Eds.): DAPI 2015, LNCS 9189, pp. 274–286, 2015.
DOI: 10.1007/978-3-319-20804-6_25

The general, simplified expression of inclusive activation is

$$\text{active}(x) \ = \ \neg\text{exclude}(x) \land (\exists \, y \ \text{include}(y) \Rightarrow \text{include}(x)). \tag{1a}$$

A channel is active unless it has been explicitly disabled or a peer has been focused upon to the exclusion of the respective channel under consideration. So, for mute and select (or solo), the source relation is

$$\text{active}(\text{source}_x) \ = \ \neg\text{mute}(\text{source}_x) \land (\exists \, y \ \text{select}(\text{source}_y) \Rightarrow \text{select}(\text{source}_x)), \tag{1b}$$

mute explicitly turning off a source, and select disabling the collocated complement of the selection (in the spirit of "anything not mandatory is forbidden"). For deafen and attend, the sink relation is

$$\text{active}(\text{sink}_x) \ = \ \neg\text{deafen}(\text{sink}_x) \land (\exists \, y \ \text{attend}(\text{sink}_y) \Rightarrow \text{attend}(\text{sink}_x)). \tag{1c}$$

Fig. 1. Simplified formalization of two-level narrowcasting and selection functions in predicate calculus notation, where '$\neg$' means "not," '$\land$' means conjunction (logical "and"), '$\exists$' means "there exists," '$\Rightarrow$' means "implies," and '$\Leftrightarrow$' means mutual implication (equivalence). The suite of inclusion and exclusion narrowcast commands for sources and sinks are like analogs of burning and dodging (shading) in photographic processing. The duality between source and sink operations is strong, and the semantics are analogous: an object is inclusively enabled by default unless, (a) it explicitly excluded with **mute** (for sources) or **deafen** (for sinks), or, (b) peers are explicitly included with **select** (**solo**) (for sources) or **attend** (for sinks) when the respective object is not. Because a source or sink is active by default, invoking **exclude** and **include** operations simultaneously on an object results in its being disabled.

The general expression of two-tier activation is

$$\text{active}(object_x) \ = \ \neg\text{exclude}(object_x) \land \tag{2a}$$
$$(\exists \, y \ (\text{include}(object_y) \land (\text{self}(object_y) \Leftrightarrow \text{self}(object_x))) \Rightarrow \text{include}(object_x)).$$

A channel is active unless it has been explicitly disabled or a relevant peer has been focused upon to the exclusion of the respective source under consideration. So, for mute and select (solo), the source relation is

$$\text{active}(source_x) \ = \ \neg\text{mute}(source_x) \land \tag{2b}$$
$$(\exists \, y \ (\text{select}(source_y) \land (\text{self}(source_y) \Leftrightarrow \text{self}(source_x))) \Rightarrow \text{select}(source_x)).$$

For deafen and attend, the sink relation is

$$\text{active}(sink_x) \ = \ \neg\text{deafen}(sink_x) \land \tag{2c}$$
$$(\exists \, y \ \text{attend}(sink_y) \land (\text{self}(sink_y) \Leftrightarrow \text{self}(sink_x))) \Rightarrow \text{attend}(sink_x)).$$

Fig. 2. Formalization of two-tier narrowcasting and selection functions with **self** attribute in predicate calculus notation, where symbols are as above in Fig. 1 and '$\Leftrightarrow$' means mutual implication (equivalence).

contrast to the start tier labeled "sources," with **select** (or **solo**) and **attend** narrowcasting commands. **Select**ion is like plugging headphones into consumer electronic devices that automatically disable loudspeakers: explicitly enabling a sink (the headphones display) implicitly disables other sinks (the speakers display). In graphical applications, the usual "object .. operation" idiom is that enforcedly singleton objects are selected with "radio button" conventions, and that multiple objects can be toggled in and out of the selection set (as with Shift+click). In narrowcasting interfaces, the respective narrowcasting attributes are independent, so "solo" is rather a misnomer, and "**select**" is preferred.

Audio windowing (Cohen and Ludwig, 1991), in analogy to graphical windowing user interfaces, treats soundscapes as articulated elements in a composite display (Begault, 1994). In GUIs (graphical user interfaces), application windows can be rearranged on a desktop, minimized, maximized, and reordered. Audio windowing similarly allows configuration of auditory sources. Soundscapes, analogous to layers in graphical applications, can be combined simply by summing, although in practice some scaling (amplification & attenuation), normalization, equalization, or other conditioning can yield more articulate results.

Having applied narrowcasting to mobile voice communication (Fernando et al., 2009), internet telephony (Alam et al., 2009a, 2009b), and virtual & mixed reality (Ranaweera et al., 2013, Cohen and Villegas, 2015), we now apply it to computer music, deploying it in Pure Data ("Pd") (Matsumura, 2012, Chikashi, 2013), a multimedia dataflow programming environment. There are many digital audio workstation (DAW) and music sequencing & composition applications— such as Audacity,[1] Adobe Audition (formerly Brothersoft Cool Edit),[2] AudioTool,[3] PG Music Band-in-a-Box,[4] Steinberg Cubase,[5] MakeMusic Finale,[6] Apple GarageBand,[7] Abelton Live,[8] Apple Logic,[9] Propellerheads Reason,[10] Avid Sibelius,[11] and SuperCollider[12]— but Pd has an advantage of generality and programability. Almost all such applications feature single-level mute and solo operations, but only mixing groups resemble anything like multilevel narrowcasting.

By simulating existential quantifiers as list traversal operations (Cohen and Saito, 2008), Pd can implement mute and select (solo) functions on, for instance, a synthesizer. For example, a sample-based drum kit might have its own "sink," collecting the sounds from each of the kick (bass) drum, snare drum, tom-toms, closed and open hi-hats and other cymbals, whereas the bass, rhythm, and lead guitars might be separately miked. However, for nesting depths greater than two, such simple taxonomy is no longer sufficient. With no explicit representation of sinks in such environments, attend and deafen functions are subsumed by layers of select and mute controls. A second-level node, which as a sink would have been subject to deafen and attend for two-level architectures, is a composite source in multilevel topologies (Fig. 3).

2   Use Case: Drum Kit

A contemporary drum kit serves as a realistic domain for narrowcasting experiments, since it is multitimbral (different sounds for its components), polyphonic (separable channels so an audio manager can treat atomic sources as layers in

---

[1] http://audacity.sourceforge.net.
[2] http://creative.adobe.com/products/audition.
[3] http://audiotool.com.
[4] http://www.pgmusic.com.
[5] http://www.steinberg.net/en/products/cubase.
[6] http://www.finalemusic.com.
[7] http://www.apple.com/mac/garageband.
[8] http://www.ableton.com/en/live.
[9] http://www.apple.com/logic-pro.
[10] http://www.propellerheads.jp/products/reason.
[11] http://www.sibelius.com.
[12] http://supercollider.sourceforge.net.

The general expression of multitier activation is

$$\texttt{active}(object_x) = \neg \texttt{exclude}(object_x) \wedge \tag{3a}$$
$$(\exists \, y \, (\texttt{include}(object_y) \wedge (\texttt{group}(object_y) = \texttt{group}(object_x))) \Rightarrow \texttt{include}(object_x)).$$

The function of the self flag used above in Figure 2 is replaced by testing for shared membership in groups defined by various separated flags. The multilevel relation becomes

$$\texttt{active}(source_x) = \neg \texttt{mute}(source_x) \wedge \tag{3b}$$
$$(\exists \, y \, (\texttt{select}(source_y) \wedge (\texttt{group}(source_y) = \texttt{group}(source_x))) \Rightarrow \texttt{select}(source_x)).$$

Fig. 3. Formalization of multilevel narrowcasting and selection functions, where symbols are as above in Fig. 1.

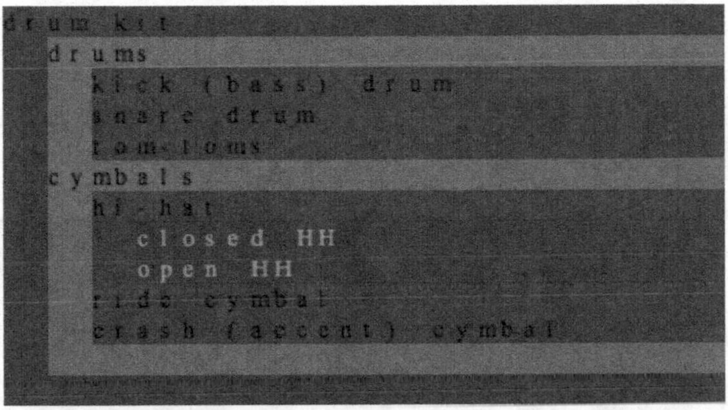

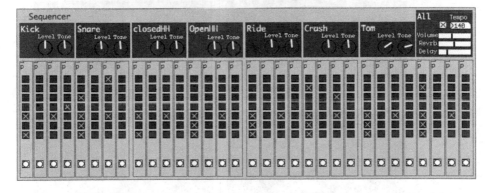

Fig. 4. Drum kit used for prototype

Fig. 5. Drum machine sequencer (originally developed by Nobuo Koizumi and Julián Villegas)

a compositable soundscape), and multilevel (modelable as a hierarchical structure). This drum kit is presented in outline form in Fig. 4.

Alternatively and equivalently, such a hierarchy can be expressed as nested lists: $[drumkit[drums[\underline{kick}, \underline{snare}, \underline{tom}], cymbals[hi - hat[\underline{closed}, \underline{open}], \underline{ride}, \underline{crash}]]]$.

Such organization is different from taxonomies such as the Hornbostel-Sachs

Table 1. Narrowcasting for $^{s}\text{OU}^{\text{rce}}_{\text{Tput}}$ and $^{s}\text{IN}^{k}_{\text{put}}$. (Figures by Julián Villegas with support of Shun Shiratori.)

	Source	Sink
Function	Radiation	Reception
Level	Amplification, Attenuation	Sensitivity
Direction	OUTput (display)	INput (control)
Presence Locus	Nimbus (projection, exposure)	Focus (attention)
Instance	Speaker	Listener
Transducer	Loudspeaker	Microphone or dummy-head
Organ	Mouth	Ear
Express	Megaphone	Ear trumpet
Include	Select (Solo)	Attend
Suppress	Muzzle	Muffle
Exclude	Mute	Deafen
own		
reflexive	(Thumb up)	(Thumbs down)
other		
transitive	(Thumb down)	(Thumbs up)

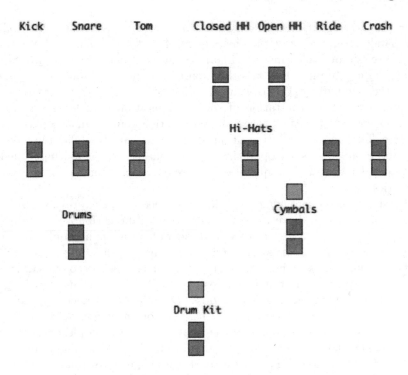

Fig. 6. Drum kit narrowcasting interface prototype

classification system since it reflects the practical deployment of the instruments, rather than the "family tree" relation. Henceforth in this description, drum kit components are underlined according to their logical depth in this hierarchical organization.

A drum machine sequencer, originally developed by Nobuo Koizumi and Julián Villegas and the graphical interface of which is shown in Fig. 5, is used for the base of a proof-of-concept prototype, as seen in Fig. 6. The `Interface.pd` module contains a `Sequencer.pd` module, which in turn contains a `Playback.pd` module, which was extended with a newly developed `narrowcasting.pd` controller to enable or disable respective streams. Such a sequencer can be programmed with drum patterns, suggested (Bardet, 1987) or original.

3   Multilevel Narrowcasting Hierarchies

A two-level hierarchy is receptive to the source-sink narrowcasting expressions in Fig. 1. In such an organization, `selection` is across all sources so presence or absence of another sink as organizational branch doesn't affect policy. Extension to more than two levels introduces complications, including some considerations that motivate careful definitions of control semantics.

Multilevel `mute` is as straight-forward as its two-level instance: the channel or aggregate is disabled. However, multilevel `select` introduces some subtleties. For instance, should `selection` of a source be considered across an entire hierarchical level of parallel sources, or just in the context of that source's immediate group? For instance, should selecting a <u>cymbal</u> implicitly deactivate a <u>drum</u>? Should `selecting` <u>hi-hat</u> implicitly `mute` other source channels (not only the <u>cymbals</u>, but also the other <u>drums</u>)? They are in different branches of the taxonomical tree, but the usual interpretation of such an operation is to focus on just the selected source, even if there are otherwise active sources in a separate part of the tree. That is, introduction of higher-level organization shouldn't disrupt usual interpretation of such operations. A reasonable case could be argued for either policy. Ultimately, the question is more of a user interface issue than one of semantics.

In two-level teleconferencing scenarios, described by the expressions in Fig. 2, avatars iconifying users have Boolean "self" state, indicating association with each respective user. Implicit `mute` due to `selection` is applied only to objects with the same `self` or non-`self` attribute as the object being `selected`. So `selecting` a source unassociated with oneself, such as a remote conversant, would `mute` other conversants but not sources associated with the user making the selection. Likewise, `selecting` one of possibly multiple instances of one's own sources would stifle other `self`-projections, but not affect non-`self` sources.

The same scoping technique can be applied to the example musical application, parameterizing application of implicit `mute` via `selection` by optionally separating related sources. For instance, if a user chose to isolate the <u>hi-hats</u>, `selecting` either <u>open</u> or <u>closed</u> hi-hat would `mute` the other, but not affect other <u>cymbals</u>, let alone the <u>drums</u>. If a user chose not to bundle the <u>hi-hats</u> for the `select` operation, `selecting` one of them would `mute` all the other <u>cymbals</u>.

Likewise, <u>drums</u> and <u>cymbals</u> can also be optionally encapsulated. If, for example, the <u>drums</u> (<u>kick</u>, <u>snare</u>, <u>tom</u>) were so bundled, `selecting` any would `mute` unselected drums, but not affect audibility of the <u>cymbals</u>. If the bundling were disabled, `selecting` <u>any drum</u> would have the effect of muting any instrumental source channel, <u>drum</u> or not.

Almost always a human mixer will want at least optional access to the finest (smallest granularity) selection available. That is, one reserves the right to configure a mixing console such that, for example, `selecting` <u>open hi-hat</u> would `mute` the <u>kick drum</u> unless the <u>kick drum</u> were also `selected`.

In the prototype user interface, shown in Fig. 7, `mute` toggles are shaded red and `select` toggles are green, according to usual "traffic signal" conventions. "Separate" flags, shown in yellow in the GUI, override the default behavior, asserting separate consideration for the bracket with which it's associated. Any grandparent node can have such an associated `separate` attribute.

Such yellow-colored isolation flags establish a containment. That is, choosing the <u>kick drum</u> will `mute` the <u>ride cymbal</u> unless the <u>drums</u> & <u>cymbals</u> are distinguished, since that separation flag articulates the drum kit, but `selecting` hi-hat containment distinguishes <u>HHs</u> and non-<u>HHs</u>.

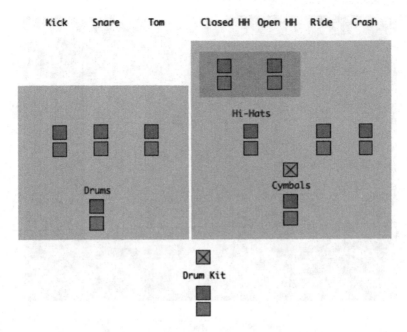

Fig. 7. Drum kit narrowcasting interface with separation flags asserted, distinguishing drums vs. cymbals and also hi-hats vs. non-hi-hat cymbals (Color figure online)

If separated, selecting closed or open HH would not affect the other cymbals— ride and crash— but selecting either of those would deactivate the HHs (unless, of course, they were themselves selected, individually or collectively).

A track is active if there is a path on the notional tree from the track's leaf to the root of the hierarchy unimpeded by explicit exclusion or implicit exclusion caused by selection of any unseparated branches. Such atomic track-based modulations are only the beginning of a cascade of stages in the delivery of the composite signal. For audio mixing, the audibility chain also includes other track and mix effects (such as equalization), sequencer intensity, OS gain, and headphone or speaker volume.

As a "thought experiment" (not yet implemented), it's possible that one might, as in Fig. 8, articulate toms = lo ∪ mid ∪ hi. If the toms separate flag were not asserted, lo tom would be active (audible) unless toms (low, mid, & high) were muted, drums (kick, snare, & toms) were muted, drum kit (drums & cymbals) was muted, or mid or hi tom were selected but low tom wasn't, or kick or snare were selected but toms weren't, or cymbal was selected but drums wasn't. If the toms separate flag were asserted, then low tom would be active unless any of its ancestors were muted or mid or hi tom were selected but low tom wasn't. Selection of other tracks outside the separated toms group wouldn't affect activation of any of the toms, including the low tom.

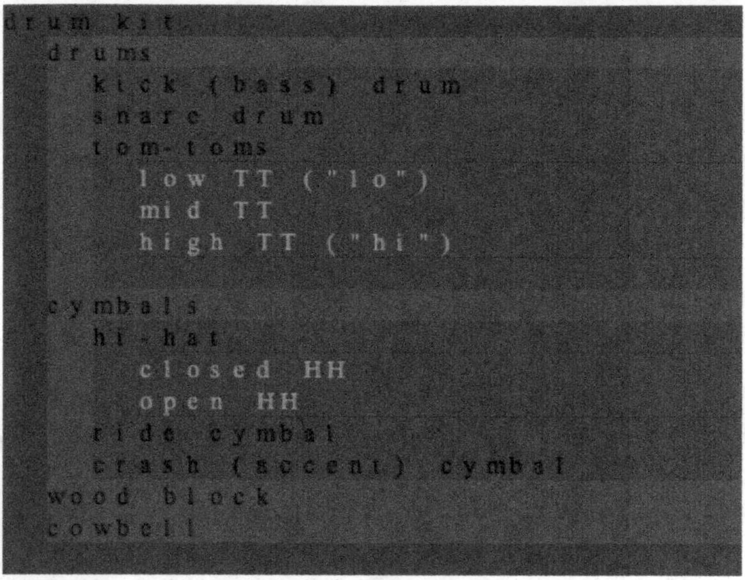

Fig. 8. Extended drum kit

If, for another example, another component such as <u>wood block</u> were added to the drum kit (on the same level as the <u>drums</u> and <u>cymbals</u>), then asserting drum kit separation would prevent both the <u>cymbals</u> and the <u>drums</u> from being implicitly muted if the <u>wood block</u> were selected. Containment in this situation works in both directions: selection of an element within such a separated group doesn't affect (implicitly mute) channels outside the group, and vice versa.

Ultimately such policies are a user interface issue: Mathematical or logical elegance would be no consolation if ordinary operation were awkward or confusing. So the real question is, how will people actually use such controls? The test case explored is not contrived, but small-sized, and proper validation requires a larger domain, such as a 32- or 64-track input situation. The goal is not concision of such narrowcasting expression, but intuitiveness of operation.

4   Audio Augmented Reality (AAR) Scenario

Augmented reality (also known, variously, as mixed or enhanced) refers to overlaying synthetic information in displays upon naturally apprehended stimuli. In visual domains, AR composites computer graphics (CG) on top of optical scenes. In auditory domains, AR composites virtual audio signals into natural soundscapes for AAR, audio augmented reality.

As illustrated by Fig. 9, a use-case scenario of an errand-running pedestrian illustrates application of hierarchical narrowcasting to AAR (Cohen and Villegas, 2015). An imagined subject dons an AAR display, *wearware*, perhaps headphones

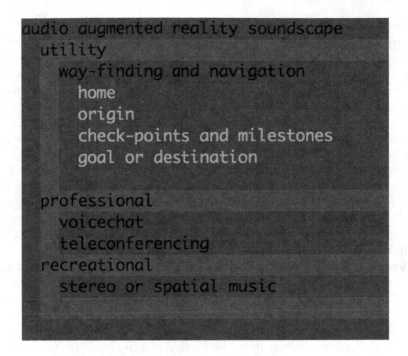

Fig. 9. Hierarchical audio augmented reality soundscape

or nearphones attached to eyewear, or enjoys some blended combination of personal and public display, ubicomp *everyware*. His or her presence is forked, so the subject inhabits multiple scenes simultaneously, *anyware*, with automatic prioritization of soundscape layers, *awareware*. Following a hierarchical taxonomy for virtual perspectives (Cohen, 1998), these layers can be sorted into proximal, medial, and distal classes, described here in decreasing order of intimacy and self-identification, corresponding to utility–professional–recreational classifications.

- **A first-person, utility soundscape:** A proximal "reality browser" layer comprises way-showing, navigation cues: directionalized sounds signifying north, home or origin, intermediate checkpoints, destinations... Populating this layer are auditory icons, recorded everyday sounds with direct associations (such as swooshing of outgoing mail), and earcons, more abstract sounds signifying scene objects (such as ringtone themes associated with particular callers). For instance, the traveler might hear a snippet of a recording of a relative's voice from home, or a tone from a milestone marker. Except for nonliteral distance effects, the soundscape corresponds to a what is sometimes imprecisely called a "PoV" (point-of-view) visual perspective, tightly bound to the position of the listener's head. The rendering is responsive to translation (location) as well as rotation (orientation) of a human user. This intimate perspective can be described as egocentric, centered inside a subject.

- **A second-person, professional soundscape:** At the same time, the user monitors intermittent voicechat among colleagues, whose respective channels are directionalized to suggest arrangement of desks at their office. Relaxing the tight correspondence of a 1st-person perspective, an endocentric soundscape allows a displaced or telepresent experience, analogous to that often used in games in which players may view their own avatar from over-the-shoulder or behind-the-back. Such medial rendering is sensitive to orientation of the "meatspace" pilot but not location: as a subject physically moves about, the soundscape twists but does not shift. Surrounding voices neither recede nor approach; there is no "parallax." This perspective can be described as egocentric, centered on (but not within) each subject, a kind of metaphorical tethering. Like a 1st-person soundscape, it is idiocentric, centered upon oneself. Respective sinks are still self-identifiable and personal, but the sensation is more like an out-of-body experience, an "auto-empathic" sensation of being aware that, for example, one's ears are displaced.
- **A third-person, recreational soundscape.** Our subject also enjoys music rendered with respect to his or her head, such as a conventional stereo mix. This distal perspective, perhaps shared with others, can be described as exocentric, centered outside a subject, as it is oblivious or indifferent to the position of the listener. Unlike 1st- and 2nd-person aural perspectives, it is allocentric, egalitarian and non-individualized. An entire audience might share a sweet spot.

These layers are combined, basically by adding them, since their perceptual spaces are coextensive, overlaid on the actual environment of the user. Such a composite soundscape is over-crowded, but narrowcasting provides a user interface strategy for data reduction, selectively managing and culling hypermedia. Within each soundscape, sources are individually controllable, either explicitly (via mute) or implicitly (by selecting others). Narrowcasting sinks fuse multiple layers while preserving their individual activatability (via deafen and attend), like a "visible/invisible" toggle switch in a graphical application, or an "ignore" sender or thread function in e·mail and web-forum browsers. Sinks are designated monitors of respective composited soundscapes; sources are sound effects, distributed voices, and music populating those layers.

5   Conclusion and Future Work

Narrowcasting attributes can also be crossed with spatialization and used for "polite calling" or "awareware," reflecting a sensitivity to one's availability, like the "online"–"offline" status switch of a conferencing service. An incoming call might automatically muzzle or attenuate sources in a music layer by deafening or muffling its associated sink. Focusing on an office conference (by attending its sink) could stifle other soundscapes. Awareware exemplifies intelligent interfaces that maintain a model of user state, adjusting multimodal I/O to accommodate context and circumstances besides position.

Despite the elegance of the predicate calculus notation, the actual prototype uses explicit expressions to evaluate the active status of the respective tracks. I would like to use such formal expressions as [$\underline{drumkit}[\underline{drums}[\underline{kick}, \underline{snare}, \underline{toms}$ [$\underline{lo}, \underline{mid}, \underline{hi}$], $\underline{woodblock}$], $\underline{cymbals}[\underline{hi} - \underline{hats}[\underline{closed}, \underline{open}], \underline{ride}, \underline{crash}], \underline{cowbell}]$] to automatically specify and compile narrowcasting policy. Now, the rules are inelegantly encoded manually, in an ad hoc manner, but it should be possible to completely generate both GUI layout and underlying policy automatically just from such a specification of the connectivity graph.

Modulation of source exposure or sink attention (Benford et al., 1995, Greenhalgh and Benford, 1995) need not be "all or nothing": nimbus (source exposure) and focus (sink sensitivity) can be respectively partially softened with muzzling and muffling (Cohen, 1993). More subtly, frequency-based processing such as LPF (low-pass filtering) can be applied for `muzzle` and `muffle` effects. We plan to extend the Pd prototype to include such signal processing. There are many possible idioms for such controls. For the audio domain used here, such interfaces will be used by sound mixing engineers, not computer scientists, so ease-of-use is more important than mathematical or conceptual flourishes (Cohen et al., 2013).

References

Alam, M.S., Cohen, M., Villegas, J., Ahmed, A.: Narrowcasting for articulated privacy and attention in SIP audio conferencing. JMM. J. Mob. Multimedia. 5(1), 12–28 (2009a). www.rintonpress.com/journals/jmmonline.html, www.rintonpress.com/xjmm5/jmm-5-1/012-028.pdf

Alam, S., Cohen, M., Villegas, J., Ashir, A.: Narrowcasting in SIP: articulated privacy control. In: Ahson, S.A., Ilyas, M. (eds.) SIP Handbook: Services, Technologies, and Security of Session Initiation Protocol, Chap. 14, pp. 323–345. CRC Press: Taylor and Francis, Boca Raton (2009b). ISBN-10 1–4200-6603-X, ISBN-13 978-1-4200-6603-6, www.crcpress.com/product/isbn/9781420066036

Bardet, R.-P.: 200 Drum Machine Patterns. Hal Leonard Publishing Corporation, USA (1987)

Begault, D.R.: 3-D Sound for Virtual Reality and Multimedia. Academic Press, Cambridge (1994). ISBN 0-12-084735-3

Benford, S., Bowers, J., Fahlén, L., Greenhalgh, C., Mariani, J., Rodde, T.: Networked virtual reality and cooperative work. Presence: Teleoperators Virtual Environ. 4(4), 364–386 (1995). ISSN 1054–7460

Chikashi, M.: Pure Data Tutorial and Reference, Works Corporation (2013) (in Japanese). ISBN 486267142-X, ISBN-13 978-4862671424

Cohen, M.: Throwing, pitching, and catching sound: audio windowing models and modes. IJMMS: J. Person-Comput. Interac. 39(2), 269–304 (1993). ISSN 0020–7373, www.u-aizu.ac.jp/mcohen/welcome/publications/tpc.pdf

Cohen, M.: Quantity of presence: Beyond person, number, and pronouns. In: Kunii, T.L., Luciani, A. (eds.) Cyberworlds, Chap. 19, pp. 289–308. Springer, Tokyo (1998). ISBN 4-431-70207-5

Cohen, M.: Exclude and include for audio sources and sinks: analogs of mute & solo are deafen & attend. Presence: Teleoperators Virtual Environ. 9(1), 84–96 (2000). ISSN 1054–7460, www.mitpressjournals.org/doi/pdf/10.1162/105474600566637

Cohen, M., Haralambous, Y., and Veytsman, B.: The multibibliography package. In: TUG: The 34th Annual Meeting of the TEX Users Group, pp. 83–89 (2013). tug.org/tug2013/, www.ctan.org/pkg/multibibliography

Cohen, M., Ludwig, L.F.: Multidimensional audio window management. In: Greenberg, S. (ed.) Computer Supported Cooperative Work and Groupware, Chap. 10, pp. 193–210. Academic Press, London (1991). ISBN-10 0–12-299220-2

Cohen, M., Saito, H.: Existential quantifiers in Mathematica for narrowcasting predicate calculus. 3D Forum: J. Three Dimensional Images **22**(2), 55–58 (2008). ISSN 1342–2189, jglobal.jst.go.jp/public/20090422/200902289181169720

Cohen, M. and Villegas, J.: Applications of audio augmented reality: wearware, everyware, anyware, & awareware. In: Barfield, W., Caudell, T. (eds.) Fundamentals of Wearable Computers and Augmented Reality, 2nd edn., Chap. 13, pp. 309–330. Lawrence Erlbaum Associates, Mahwah (2015, In press). ISBN 0-8058-2902-4

Fernando, O.N.N., Cohen, M., Dumindawardana, U.C., Kawaguchi, M.: Duplex narrowcasting operations for multipresent groupware avatars on mobile devices. IJWMC: Int. J. of Wireless and Mobile Computing **3**(4), 280–287 (2009). ISSN 1741–1084, 1741–1092, www.inderscience.com/info/inarticle.php?artid=29348

Greenhalgh, C., Benford, S.: Massive: a collaborative virtual environment for teleconferencing. ACM Trans. Comput. Hum. Interac. **2**(3), 239–261 (1995)

Matsumura, S.: Pd Recipe Book– Introduction to Sound Programming with Pure Data. BNN (2012) (in Japanese). ISBN 4861007801

Ranaweera, R., Cohen, M., and Frishkopf, M.: Narrowcasting enabled immersive music browser for folkways world music collection. In: Capin, T., Balcisoy, S., Thalmann, D. (eds.) CASA: Proceedings International Conference on Computer Animation and Social Agents, Istanbul (2013). www.cs.bilkent.edu.tr/~casa2013, ISBN 978-605-4348-53-4

Development of a User-Oriented IoT Middleware Architecture Based on Users' Context Data

Taehyun Ha, Sangwon Lee$^{(\boxtimes)}$, and Narae Kim

Department of Interaction Science, Sungkyunkwan University, Seoul, Korea
ontophilla@gmail.com, narae0113@naver.com,
upcircle@skku.edu

Abstract. How to manage the connections of things efficiently with heterogeneous things is one of the important issues for IoT middleware development.
Many researches have been focused on this issue but still no one accepted as the
common model in the IoT environment. In this sense, we aim to develop a new
IoT middleware architecture containing simple key-value model based and
no-model based context-awareness function. The suggested middleware represents the context data without strictly defined data structure. Rather, it processes
the context more focusing on the other technical aspects. We build the middleware architecture based on the basic structure of GSN (Global Sensor Networks). Also, by adapting no-model based context representation method
suggested by Habit, we added the context-awareness function to the GSN.
Through the middleware, many heterogeneous things not integrated on the
standard structure can be managed effectively. We expect the suggested middleware can provide a flexible solution in current IoT development situation.

Keywords: IoT middleware architecture · GSN · Context-awareness

1 Introduction

Through the evolution of Internet, the concept of IoT (Internet of Things) that everyday
objects are connected to the Internet has been newly devised. Ashton (2009) [2] firstly
coined the definition in a presentation in 1998, and through the MIT Auto-ID centre,
ITU(International Telecommunication Union), and other researchers, the IoT researches have been widely discussed [8]. Nowadays, over the range from household to
industry, many IoT applications are being developed by researchers and engineers.

The IoT bundles many technology together and needs to be supported by middleware solutions. Many kinds of the middleware solutions have been suggested (e.g.,
GSN [1], Hydra [9], Ubiroad [10]), but not yet any of these solutions are not accepted
as the standard solution. Especially, as Perera et al. (2014) [8] mentioned, even the
context-awareness function is important in the IoT paradigm, many of these solutions
have been not focused on the context-awareness. In this sense, it can be the meaningful
research that developing IoT middleware architecture containing effective
context-awareness functions.

© Springer International Publishing Switzerland 2015
N. Streitz and P. Markopoulos (Eds.): DAPI 2015, LNCS 9189, pp. 287–295, 2015.
DOI: 10.1007/978-3-319-20804-6_26

Besides, several researchers have been studied for the context-awareness. Especially, it is important that how to represent these complex users' context. Bellavista, et al. (2012) [4] categorized the context representation models into the three models: general models (e.g., key-value, markup scheme, and object oriented models), domain-specific models, and no model. We focused on the no model based methods because it can covers wide scopes of user context despite its some limitations.

In this paper, we introduce a user-oriented middleware architecture based on the users' context data. The basic middleware architecture is based on the GSN. Also we adapt the context awareness function which is not supported by the GSN devised by Habit [6]. The suggested middleware analyze the users' context data and utilizes it to manage the connections of things (relationship management), find the optimal path of the nodes (service management), and decide where the new things are added to the sensor network (service discovery).

2   Backgrounds

2.1   IoT Middleware Architecture

Middleware is the software that facilitates communication by connecting heterogeneous devices, hardware, and protocols in various environments. Among the several studies reviewing different kinds of IoT middleware, Bandyopadhyay, et al. [3] presented the overall features of the existing middleware in the IoT domain. In their study, functional components of IoT-middleware were discussed in the five sections: interoperation, context detection, device discovery and management, security and privacy, and managing data volumes. Based on these functional aspects, they classified the some existing middleware. Table 1 shows the results.

As shown in Table 1, Hydra [9] and Ubiroad [10] cover the all functional components of IoT-middleware. The Hydra (Officially, the Hydra project was ended in 2010, and now its name has been changed as "LinkSmart" because of the problem of intellectual rights to the name "Hydra") adapted a context-awareness function based on SWRL (Semantic Web Rule Language) and OWL (Web Ontology Language). Thus it can process the users' contexts with more expressive power [11]. On the other hand, the Ubiroad's solution is basically based on the concept of GUN (Global Understanding Environment). Its layers consist of semantic adapters, behavioral, coordination layer, and based on the users' scenario, the middleware manages the connections of things. However, still not enough cases of these applications have been reported, and more precisely no one covers the full set of the functionalities to meet the requirement of IoT-middleware [3].

Meanwhile, GSN (Global Sensor Networks) [1] has been developed to address the sensor networks in general. Thus, it can be adapted to the various situations. Also, as the connections of things are depicted as a network, we can catch the connections intuitively and apply some network analysis techniques to the network (e.g., complex network analysis). Figure 1 shows the overall structure of GSN.

Table 1. IoT-middleware comparison

IoT middleware	Features of middleware				
	Device management	Interoperation	Platform portability	Context awareness	Security and privacy
HYDRA	✓	✓	✓	✓	✓
ISMB	✓	✗	✓	✗	✗
ASPIRE	✓	✗	✓	✗	✗
UBIWARE	✓	✗	✓	✓	✗
UBISOAP	✓	✓	✓	✗	✗
UBIROAD	✓	✓	✓	✓	✓
GSN	✓	✗	✓	✗	✓
SMEPP	✓	✗	✓	✓	✓
SOCRADES	✓	✓	✓	✗	✓
SIRENA	✓	✓	✓	✗	✓
WHEREX	✓	✓	✓	✗	✗

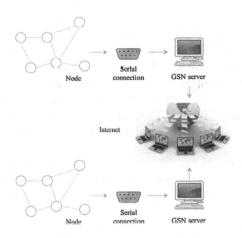

Fig. 1. Overall structure of GSN

The GSN covers several interface protocols such as Zigbee, RFID, WiFi, and Bluetooth. It uses basic unit named virtual sensor (node) and communicates with them using the wrappers. The official project website (https://github.com/LSIR/gsn) provides the packages and users can set up the environment easily.

However, as already shown in Table 1, the GSN does not cover the interoperation and context awareness functions. Also, as Perera, et al. (2013) [7] mentioned, when more and more sensors get connected to the Internet, the sensor search functionality becomes critical. Nevertheless, if we develop a model addressing these limitations, the middleware can be used as a basis for designing user-centered middleware. In other words, by adapting context awareness methods to the GSN, we would be able to gather the users' context information and utilize it for setting the network connections between users and things based on the GSN concept.

2.2   No Model Based Context Representation

To apply the context awareness function to the GSN, we need to consider how represent, process, and deliver the context, and support it in runtime. This is the concept of context data distribution. Bellavista et al. (2012) [4] have progressed the surveys of the context data distribution for mobile ubiquitous systems. As a part of the research, they classified the context data representation models as like Fig. 2.

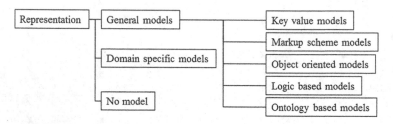

Fig. 2. The classification of the context data representation

As each of the data representation model has some limitations, some hybrid models based on two or even more have been suggested to overcome the limitations. Among the context representation models in Fig. 2, we need to focus on the no model based methods. The methods do not represent the data structure. Rather, it more focuses on the other technical aspects. As the no model based representation methods are not limited by data structures, it can describe more extensive context than the other methods. In other words, this method allows covering heterogeneous things in middleware more easily.

Among the related researches for the no model based methods, Habit [6] uses the user's context data to create data distribution routes. Figure 3 shows the example of content dissemination network configuration, and detail process descriptions for the Habit are below.

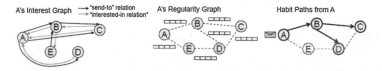

Fig. 3. Content dissemination networks from A's viewpoint

Building a Content Dissemination Networks: In Fig. 3, *A* is the one of the nodes in Habit. *A* maintains a list of nodes interested in receiving contents of *A*. The other nodes that encounter node *A* are called *familiar strangers* (*FS*). *A* maintains the *familiar strangers* in a certain number of hops (*maxHops*) and the number of *familiar strangers* is limited by the maximum number (*maxFS*). Every node in Habit maintains the interest graph. Besides, *A* also configures the *regularity graph* (i.e., regularity table). *A*'s *regularity graph* consists of *regularity weights* between *A* and *familiar strangers*. The *regularity weights* mean the number of times specific node (*A*) meets another node in given regularity interval of the week. For example, if *A* meets the *B* three times in the hour slot Monday 10AM-11AM (this day/time slot can be adjusted to the human-meaningful time slot such as commute item slot, working time slot) in last five weeks, the *regularity weight* is 0.6. Each node can build the content dissemination networks by: (1) changing the direction of each edge in the *interest graph* (transforming the relation "interest in" into the relation "send content to"), and (2) overlaying it onto the *regularity graph*.

Reasoning on the Content Dissemination Network: After Habit builds the content dissemination network, Habit finds the optimal route for node *A*. This is the reasoning of the content dissemination network, and consists of four steps as follows.

(1) **Determine Recipients:** the reverted *interest graph* is consulted to determine what nodes *R* are interested in receiving content from *A* ($R = \{B, C, D\}$).

(2) **Find Cheapest Paths:** Find the paths that can reach the node of destination. In Fig. 3, if *A* try to reach node *D*, there are three routes that *A-B-D*, *A-B-C-D*, and *A-E-D*. In this case, the first and second routes are chosen because their costs are 0. On the other hand, the third route's cost is 1 because of *E* (not the member of *R*), and this route will be not chosen. Besides, the Habit also calculates the regular weights (i.e., delivery probabilities) of the chosen routes. To avoid the computational complexity, Habit uses simple heuristic method: only the first non-zero regularity weight between a pair of nodes is considered before moving on to the next edge, and set the minimum *regularity weight* as the delivery probability of the route. Let assume the *regularity weight* between *A* and *B* is 0.7, and *B* and *D* is 0.3. Then the delivery probability of the route *A-B-D* is 0.3 ($min\{0.7, 0.3\}$).

(3) **Select Paths:** If more than one route is chosen, the route has the maximum delivery probability is selected.

(4) **Optimizations:** As *A* covers nodes within *maxFS* and *maxHops* range, *A* may not always be aware of all nodes interested in receiving *A*'s messages. In this case, the intermediary may then follow the same steps that *A* did, and discover the new paths.

To describe sensor networks as an intuitive model and make a basis for applying network analysis techniques into the sensor network, we develop a new IoT middleware architecture basically based on GSN architecture. Also, to address the GSN's limitation for context awareness functions, we additionally adapt simple key-value context model and the Habit's content dissemination method. Similar approach has been studied by Perera et al. (2013) [7]. They developed IoT middleware architecture containing context awareness function. Their middleware aimed to search the sensors more efficiently in huge networks environment by using the ontology based context awareness function. In this model, the context property consists of such as accuracy, reliability, latency. As this model aims to reduce the sensor networks size, it is more appropriate to the users who have to deal with tremendous items. On the other hand, we aim to develop the user-centered middleware identifying the context in individual dimension (e.g., user preferences) [5]. Our approach more actively utilizes the users' usage patterns into the middleware, and thus can provide the practical solutions.

3 Development of a User-Oriented IoT Middleware Architecture

In this section, we describe the user-oriented IoT middleware architecture. As the middleware is basically based on the GSN, basic structure of our middleware follows the GSN structure. We describe our middleware architecture by the three conceptual parts of modules. Generally, the middleware architecture consists of some other sub modules, but we would more focus on the three parts of our model originally suggested. Figure 4 shows the overall architecture of our middleware.

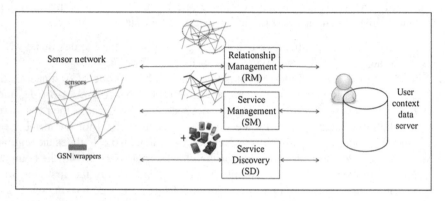

Fig. 4. The IoT middleware architecture based on users' context data

3.1 Relationship Management Module

To manage the connections of things efficiently, clustering methods can be used as a useful solution in aspect of it reduces the computational complexity. In our middleware, the relationship management module clusters the things by either local first strategy or content (thing's usage) first strategy. For example, let assume the situation there are four things in the sensor network: A (television located in house 1), B (air heater located in house 2), C (television located in house 3), and D (robot vacuum cleaner located in house 1), and house 1 and 2 are placed in near distance. In this situation, the relationship management module makes the two clusters of the things: {A, B, D} and {C} if the module uses local first strategy. On the other hand, if the relationship management module uses content first strategy, the module makes the three clusters of things: {A, C}, {B}, and {D}. These clustering strategies are decided referring the user's pattern, and refreshed at the defined time interval. Thus it is related to the service management module below (the relationship management module checks what types of the contextual properties (i.e., location or usage) are in close relationship between the things in optimal paths configured by the service management module). Figure 5 shows the relationship management strategies.

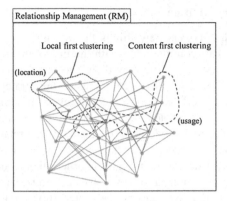

Fig. 5. Relationship management strategies

3.2 Service Management Module

Based on the concept of content dissemination network in Habit, the service management module analyzes the user's pattern and selects the optimal path. In other words, based on the user's transaction history for the things in networks, the service management module configure the content dissemination network containing send to- and interested in- graphs, and regularity weights. In this content dissemination network, routes from start node (things) to destination node are listed and calculated their costs. After the calculations, the module chooses cheapest routes. If the more than one route is chosen, then select the route which has the maximum delivery probability. Figure 6 shows the example for how the service management module selects the optimal path.

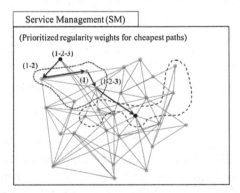

Fig. 6. Example of selecting processes in service management module

3.3 Service Discovery Module

Service discovery module covers new things that are not added to the middleware. When a new thing tried to communicate with the things in the sensor network, the service discovery module requests the new thing's location and usage. Then add it to the network by using GSN wrapper. According to the strategy currently used by relationship management module, the service discovery module decides a position where the new thing should be added, and what nodes would be prepared to the communications with the new node. For example, if the relationship management module uses the location first strategy, the new node is placed based on its location. At the same time, the service discovery module informs other nodes placed nearby the new node to prepare the communications with the new node. On the other hand, if the relationship management module follows the content first strategy, the new node is placed nearby the nodes which have similar usages. Figure 7 shows the process in service discovery module.

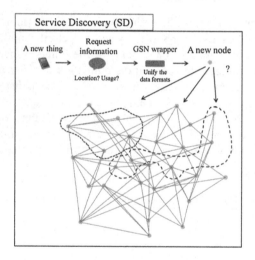

Fig. 7. Process in service discovery module

4 Conclusion

In this study, we proposed a user-oriented IoT middleware architecture based on the GSN and Habit. The middleware adds the things in the sensor network using the GSN wrapper, and each module in the middleware manages the connection of things using the users' context. As the architecture does not define the strict context structures, it is relatively free to analyze context, and thus can cover more wide range of the context. Even the middleware requires context information of things that location and usage, it is quite little things comparing other middleware requires.

However, in aspect of accuracy, it can be pointed out that other context representation models such as ontology based models, logic based models can be better to distribute and analyze the user's context. Moreover, it is another matter to pick the specific method in the context representation methods. It requires many times and costs for making the systems based on various context distribution methods. We need to provide a practical solution for combining heterogeneous things into the IoT environment. In this sense, our study tried to develop the middleware architecture which can be used more broadly with less effort.

In future study, we will conduct the validation test for the suggested middleware in user scenario based environments. Some validation criterions can be used such as accuracy and latency. Also, comparative analyses for the other types of context distribution methods can be considered. Through these validation tests, some limitations of the suggested user-oriented middleware architecture would be supplemented.

Acknowledgements. This research was supported by the Ministry of Education, South Korea, under the Brain Korea 21 Plus Project (No. 10Z20130000013) and Basic Science Research Program (No. NRF-2014R 1A 1A2054531).

References

1. Aberer, K., Hauswirth, M., Salehi, A.: Global sensor networks. Technical report (2006)
2. Ashton, K.: That 'internet of things' thing. RFiD J. **22**(7), 97–114 (2009)
3. Bandyopadhyay, S., Sengupta, M., Maiti, S., Dutta, S.: Role of middleware for internet of things: a study. Int. J. Comput. Sci. Eng. Surv. 2(3), 94–105 (2011)
4. Bellavista, P., Corradi, A., Fanelli, M., Foschini, L.: A survey of context data distribution for mobile ubiquitous systems. ACM Comput. Surv. (CSUR) **44**(4), 24 (2012)
5. Eugster, P.T., Garbinato, B., Holzer, A.: Middleware support for context-aware applications. In: Garbinato, B., Miranda, H., Rodrigues, L. (eds.) Middleware for Network Eccentric and Mobile Applications, pp. 305–322. Springer, Heidelberg (2009)
6. Mashhadi, A.J., Ben Mokhtar, S., Capra, L.: Habit: leveraging human mobility and social network for efficient content dissemination in delay tolerant networks. In: World of Wireless, Mobile and Multimedia Networks & Workshops (WoWMoM), pp. 1–6. IEEE (2009)
7. Perera, C., Zaslavsky, A., Christen, P., Compton, M., Georgakopoulos, D.: Context-aware sensor search, selection and ranking model for internet of things middleware. In: IEEE 14th International Conference on Mobile Data Management (MDM), pp. 314–322. IEEE (2013)
8. Perera, C., Zaslavsky, A., Christen, P., Georgakopoulos, D.: Context aware computing for the internet of things: a survey. Commun. Surv. Tutorials **16**(1), 414–454 (2014)
9. Sarnovský, M., Kostelník, P., Butka, P., Hreňo, J., Lacková, D.: First demonstrator of hydra middleware architecture for building automation. In: Proceedings of the Scientific Conference Znalosti (2008)
10. Terziyan, V., Kaykova, O., Zhovtobryukh, D.: Ubiroad: semantic middleware for context-aware smart road environments. In: Fifth International Conference on Internet and Web Applications and Services (ICIW), pp. 295–302. IEEE (2010)
11. Zhang, W., Hansen, K.M.: Towards self-managed pervasive middleware using owl/swrl ontologies. In Fifth International Workshop on Modelling and Reasoning in Context (MRC), pp. 1–12. TELECOM Bretagne (2008)

Measuring the Arrangement of Multiple Information Devices by Observing Their User's Face

Saori Kikutani[1], Koh Kakusho[1(✉)], Takeshi Okadome[1],
Masaaki Iiyama[2], and Satoshi Nishiguchi[3]

[1] School of Science and Technology, Kwansei Gakuin University, Sanda, Japan
{kiku,kakusho,houmi}@kwansei.ac.jp
[2] Academic Center for Computing and Media Studies, Kyoto University,
Kyoto, Japan
iiyama@mm.media.kyoto-u.ac.jp
[3] Faculty of Information Science and Technology, Osaka Institute
of Technology, Hirakata, Japan
satoshi.nishiguchi@oit.ac.jp

Abstract. We propose to measure the 3D arrangement of multiple portable information devices operated by a single user from his/her facial images captured by the cameras installed on those devices. Since it becomes quite usual for us to use multiple information devices at the same time, previous works have proposed various styles of cooperation among the devices for data transmission and so on. Other previous works propose to coordinate the screens so that they share the role of displaying contents larger than each screen. Those previous works obtain the 2D tiled arrangement of the screens by detecting their contacts with each other using sensing hardware equipped on their edges. Our method estimates the arrangement among the devices in various 3D positions and orientations in relation to the user's face from its appearance in the image captured by the camera on each device.

Keywords: Multiple portable devices · Device coordination · Screen arrangement · Facial image processing · Camera calibration

1 Introduction

It becomes quite usual for us to use multiple information devices such as mobile or tablet PCs, smartphones, PDAs at the same time. Aiming to take full advantage of those devices, many previous works have proposed various styles of cooperation among those devices for transmission and sharing of selected data among the devices [1–4], operation of the contents displayed on the screens [5, 6], and so on. Some other previous works propose to coordinate the screens so that they share the role of displaying contents, which, for example, are larger each screen.

In order to make several screens coordinated with each other for this purpose, we need to measure their arrangement in advance. The previous works described above obtain the tiled 2D arrangement among the screens based on their adjacency detected

© Springer International Publishing Switzerland 2015
N. Streitz and P. Markopoulos (Eds.): DAPI 2015, LNCS 9189, pp. 296–304, 2015.
DOI: 10.1007/978-3-319-20804-6_27

by their physical contact with each other using sensing hardware equipped on their edges [7, 8]. However, as we experience in setting the screen arrangement of a PC and its external display manually, we often prefer more various arrangements such as those of screens placed a little bit apart or in contact with each other just at their corners. It is also useful to display a 3D virtual space by specifying a 3D screen arrangement where we are surrounded by the screens.

In this article, we discuss how to measure those various arrangements of multiple screens. Since recent information devices are usually equipped with cameras, we measure the screen arrangement of the devices using the images of the user captured by those cameras on the devices. In the field of computer vision, the 3D geometric arrangement of multiple cameras is conventionally measured by the method for so-called *strong camera calibration*, in which the same set of markers whose 3D positions have already known is observed by each camera. We employ the feature points on the user's face for those markers. When a user is operating some information devices, the user should keep gazing at their screens and thus his/her face can be observed from the camera on each device. The facial feature points of the user appearing in the camera image can be extracted by facial image processing, although those facial feature points may sometimes fail to be extracted depending on their appearance in the image. The positions of the facial feature points on the face are approximately available because they are similar for any persons, although some amount of personal differences are included in those positions.

By considering these properties of facial feature points, we discuss how to measure the arrangement of information devices with their cameras from the images of the user's face. In the discussion, we also try to cope with the failure in extracting facial feature points by introducing the continuity of the change in the arrangement of the devices as a geometric constraint.

2   Measuring Arrangement of Devices

Measuring Geometric Arrangement of Each Device and the User's Face. As we described above, we measure the arrangement of portable information devices at each moment of their operation by the same user at the same time by employing the feature points of the user's face as the markers for the strong calibration of the cameras on the devices. The 3D position of the k-th feature point on the face is denoted by $p_k(k = 1, \cdots, K)$, where K is the number of the feature points that we employ for the calibration. These 3D positions of the facial feature points are represented by the face-centered coordinate system with its origin at the center between the two eyes, the x axis passing through the eyes from left to right on the face, the y axis directed downward on the face and the z axis set forward from the face. The 2D positions where the k-th facial feature point appears in the image captured by the camera on the i-th information device is denoted by $q_k^i(i = 1, \cdots, N)$, where N is the number of the devices. This 2D position is represented by the camera-centered coordinate system with its origin at the optical center of the camera, the x, y axes set rightward and upward to the image plane, and the z axis forward along the optical axis of the camera. The geometric relation among these face-centered coordinate system and camera-centered coordinate systems for the i-th device and the j-th device in the situation where the user is gazing at the screens of those devices is illustrated in Fig. 1.

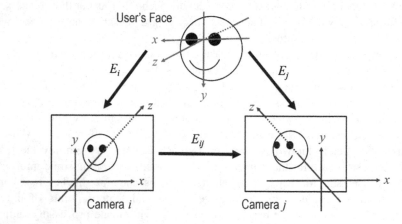

Fig. 1. Geometric relation among the cameras on different devices and the user's face

The geometric relation between p_k and q_k^i can be described as follows:

$$q_k^i = \lambda A_i E_i p_k \tag{1}$$

Where A_i is the matrix of the internal parameters of the camera on the i-th device. This matrix mathematically represents the process of optical projection from each point in the 3D space onto the 2D image plane of the camera with scaling parameter λ. The matrix E_i includes the external camera parameters that consist of rotation matrix R_i and translation vector t_i, which represent the orientation and the position of the user's face relative to the camera on the i-th device, as follows:

$$E_i = \left[\begin{array}{ccc|c} & R_i & & t_i \\ \hline 0 & 0 & 0 & 1 \end{array} \right] \tag{2}$$

In Eq. (1), q_k^i is given as the 2D position of the k-th facial feature point extracted from the image obtained by the camera on the i-th device by facial feature processing, whereas p_k can be specified from the 3D position of the k-th facial feature point of the standard human face if we ignore its personal difference. Matrix A_i of the camera on the i-th device can be obtained by preliminary internal camera calibration using usual markers.

Since E_i includes 12 variables, this matrix can be determined by solving the equations above, if p_k and q_k^i are obtained for not less than six facial feature points out of K. When the user is gazing at the screen of the i-th device, it is expected to be possible to obtain q_k^i for more facial feature points from his/her facial image captured by the camera on the device by facial image processing. Thus, by solving Eq. (1) for all the variables in E_i, we can measure the geometric arrangement of the user's face and the camera on the i-th device. Since the camera installed on an information device is usually fixed around the edge of the screen with its optical axis perpendicular to the screen, we can estimate the geometric arrangement of the user's face and the screen of the device by measuring the position of the camera on the i-th device relative to its screen in advance.

After $E_1, \cdots, E_N$ for all the cameras on all the devices are obtained, the geometric arrangement of the i-th device and the j-th device $(i \neq j)$ can be calculated from E_i and E_j as follows:

$$E_{ij} = E_j E_i^{-1} \tag{3}$$

Where E_{ij} is the matrix that represents the orientation and the position of the camera on the i-th device relative to that on the j-th device $(j = 1, \cdots, N; \ j \neq i)$.

Continuity in the Geometric Arrangements. When a user is operating multiple information devices, the user is usually not gazing at the screens of all the devices at the same time, but gazing at only one of those screens depending on his/her interest. In that situation, facial feature point extraction is successful for the image obtained by the camera on the device gazed by the user because his/her face is captured by the camera from the very front, whereas extraction of facial feature points often fails for the images obtained by the cameras on the devices that are not currently gazed by the user, depending on his/her facial orientation to the cameras. Failure in extracting facial feature points is also caused by occlusion of those points due to the user's unconscious behavior such as putting a hand over the mouth and so on.

Since the geometric arrangement of different devices are indirectly obtained from the arrangement of each device and the user's face, the information about the arrangement related to the devices with the camera images at the moments when the failure in facial feature point extraction occurs for those images is completely lost during the user's operation of the devices. Moreover, even when the geometric arrangement is estimated for a device and the user's face after facial feature point extraction is successful for the camera image of the device; the estimated geometric arrangement inevitably includes a certain amount of error.

In order to cope with the problems above, we introduce the continuity in the estimated arrangement. The geometric arrangement of the devices and the user's face does not change drastically as far as the user keeps operating those devices at the same time in a similar manner. By considering it, we estimate the geometric arrangement under the constraint that the difference between the estimated arrangements at adjacent moments should be small as much as possible. This constraint smooth's the geometric arrangements estimated for each device and the user at different moments when those arrangements can be measured after successful feature point extraction, as well as extrapolates the arrangements at the moments when those arrangements cannot be measured due to the failure in facial feature point extraction by simply duplicating the arrangements estimated at previous moments.

Let us represent E_i at any moment τ of the user's operation of multiple devices by $E_i(\tau)$. When the facial feature points are successfully extracted from the image obtained by the camera on the i-th device, $E_i(\tau)$ can be directly measured by the procedure described in 2.1, but includes a certain amount of error. When those facial feature points cannot be extracted from the camera image, $E_i(\tau)$ cannot be measured. Thus, we estimate the correct value of $E_i(\tau)$, regardless of the possibility of its measurement. The estimated value of $E_i(\tau)$ is denoted by $\hat{E}_i(\tau)$. In order to make $\hat{E}_i(\tau)$ coincide with $E_i(\tau)$ when it is measure from the camera image, and to make $\hat{E}_i(\tau)$ close to $\hat{E}_i(\tau - 1)$ at the previous moment $\tau - 1$, $\hat{E}_i(\tau)$ is determined so that the following function $\mathcal{E}$ is minimized at each possible moment τ:

$$\mathcal{E}\big(\hat{E}_i(\tau)\big) = \sum_{\tau}\Big\{f_i(\tau)\,\big\|\hat{E}_i(\tau) - E_i(\tau)\big\|_F^2 + \big\|\hat{E}_i(\tau) - \hat{E}_i(\tau - 1)\big\|_F^2\Big\} \tag{4}$$

Where $f_i(\tau)$ is the variable that takes the value 1 at the moment τ when facial feature point extraction is successful for the camera image of the i-th device, and becomes zero otherwise. This function evaluates the difference of $\hat{E}_i(\tau)$ from $E_i(\tau)$ and $\hat{E}_i(\tau - 1)$ using Frobenius norm denoted by $\|.\|_F$.

3   Experimental Results

Comparing Results from Facial Feature Points and Corners of a Grid. We have implemented the procedure described above by employing OKAO Vision of OMRON Corporation for facial image processing and OpenCV for other image processing including camera calibration.

We first compared the results of estimating the geometric arrangement between a camera and the user's face from facial feature points and markers used by the traditional camera calibration method. We employed six facial feature points, which include the inner corners and the outer corners of the eyes and the wings of the nose because they are comparatively stable for extraction by facial image processing and distributed widely over the face. We specified the positions of these facial feature points on the face-centered coordinate system based on the data of the standard human face [10], neglecting the personal difference. For the markers used for the traditional camera calibration method for comparison, we employed six corners around the center of a grid pattern on a checkerboard.

The results are shown in Fig. 2. Virtual 3D objects are drawn on the face and the checkerboard using the estimated arrangement. In spite that the actual positions of the facial feature points in the face-centered coordinate system are neither the same as the positions specified from the standard human face nor located on a flat plane such as a chessboard, the error in the appearance of the virtual object drawn based on the arrangement estimated from those facial feature points is comparable to the result from the corners of the grid patterns. This result shows that the facial feature points are sufficiently available for estimating the arrangement of an information device and its user's face.

(a) Result from the six facial feature points.   (b) Results from six corers of a grid.

Fig. 2. Comparison between the results of camera calibration using the facial feature points and corners of a grid pattern.

Estimating the Arrangement of Two Devices and the User's Face. For evaluating the error in estimating the geometric arrangement of the information devices and the user's face by our method, we compared the estimated arrangement of the devices with their actual arrangement observed by a camera at the viewpoint of the user. In the experiment, two tablet PCs were gazed by the same user. At the top of each PC, we installed a web camera. The user wore eyeglasses equipped with a camera at their bridge as shown in Fig. 3, in order to obtain the images of the devices from the viewpoint of the user. The thick black frame of the eyeglasses was covered by a fabric tape in a skin color in case facial feature point extraction was interfered by the frame.

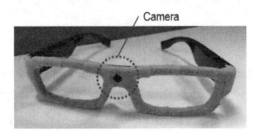

Fig. 3. Eyeglasses with a camera at their bridge

Figures 4(a) and (b) are the images obtained by the cameras on the two devices, where the points in each image are the facial feature points extracted by facial image processing. Figure 4(c) illustrates the result of drawing the appearances of the devices from the viewpoint of the user based on the geometric arrangement estimated by our method on the image observed by the camera on the eyeglasses. The difference of the estimated arrangement from the actual arrangement seems to be acceptable for the purpose of coordinating the contents to be displayed on the screens of the devices.

(a) User image by the left camera.   (b) User image by the right camera.

(c) Actual image taken by the camera on the eyeglass superimposed by the estimated appearances of the devices.

Fig. 4. Resultant images without failures of facial feature point extraction occlusion

We also estimated the arrangement of the same devices in the situation where the facial feature points fail to be extracted. Figures 5(a) and (b) are the images obtained by the cameras on the two devices in the situation. Since the user places a hand on the face, no facial feature point is extracted. Figure 4(c) illustrates the result of drawing the appearances of the devices from the viewpoint of the user based on the geometric arrangement estimated by our method in this situation. By extrapolation of the geometric arrangement at this moment from that estimated at the previous moment, the appearances of the devices are still be able to be obtained. Although the geometric arrangement of the devices and the user's face are slightly changed due to the motion of the user for placing the hand on the face, the amount of the error between the estimated appearance and the actual one is similar to that in the result of Fig. 3(c). This result shows that the extrapolation of the arrangement in our method is effective when the motion of the user is small. However, we need more sophisticated method for the extrapolation to cope with more various situations with the failure of facial feature point extraction.

(a) User image by the left camera.   (b) User image by the right camera.

(c) Actual image taken by the camera on the eyeglass superimposed by the estimated appearances of the devices.

Fig. 5. Resultant images with occlusion of the face

4 Conclusions

We proposed to measure the 3D geometric arrangement of multiple portable information devices using the facial images of the user captured by the cameras on the devices. In our method, facial feature points are extracted from the images taken by the camera on the devices and the geometric arrangement of each device and the user's face by using the camera calibration technique. To cope with the errors of estimating the geometric arrangement from facial feature points as well as the failure in extracting those facial feature points, we introduce the process of smoothing and extrapolation for the geometric arrangements estimated at different moments. From some experimental results, we confirmed that our method can estimate the arrangement of the devices and the user's face with the amount of error acceptable for coordination of contents to be displayed on the screens of those devices even at the moment when the facial feature points fail to be extracted due to occlusions as far as the change in the arrangement is small.

For one of the future steps, we need to introduce more sophisticated methods for extrapolating the geometric arrangement of the devices and the user's face to cope with more various and large amounts of changes in the arrangement by analyzing the patterns of the change during operation of multiple information devices by users. It is also useful to employ the data of the orientations, accelerations and so on of the devices obtained by various kinds of sensors usually installed in recent information devices to further reduce the error in estimating of the geometric arrangement.

References

1. Yatani, K., Tamura, K., Hiroki, K., Sugimoto, M., Hashizume, H.: Toss-it: intuitive information transfer techniques for mobile devices using toss and swing actions. IEICE Trans. Inf. Syst. **E89-D**(1), 150–157 (2006)
2. Dippon, A., Widermann, N., Klinker, G.: Seamless integration of mobile devices into interactive surface environments. In: ACM International Conference on Interactive Tabletops and Surfaces (ITS 2012), pp. 331–334 (2012)
3. Schmidt, D., Seifert, J., Rukzio, E., Gellersen, H.: A cross-device interaction style for mobiles and surfaces. In: Designing Inteactive Systems Conferece (DIS 2012), pp. 318–327 (2012)
4. Seifert, J., Dobbelstein, D., Schmidt, D., Holleis, P., Rukzio, E.: From the private into the public: privacy-respecting mobile interaction techniques for sharing data on surfaces. Pers. Ubiquit. Comput. **18**(4), 1013–1026 (2013)
5. Hahne, J., Schild, J., Elstner, S., Alexa, M.: Multi-touch focus+context sketch-based interaction. In: EUROGRAPHICS Symposium on Sketch-Based Interfaces and Modeling, pp. 77–83 (2009)
6. Baur, D., Boring, S., Feinter, S.: Virtual projection: exploring optical projection as a metaphor for multi-device interaction. In: ACM SIGCHI Conference on Human Factors in Computing Systems (CHI 2012), pp. 1693–1702 (2012)
7. Hinckley, K.: Synchronous gestures for multiple persons and computers. In: ACM Symposium on User Interface Software and Technology (UIST 2003), pp. 149–158 (2003)
8. Schneider, D., Rukzio, J.J.E.: MobIES: extending mobile interfaces using external screens. In: International Conference on Mobile and Ubiquitous Multimedia (MUM 2012), pp. 59:1–59:2 (2012)
9. https://www.dh.aist.go.jp/database/91-92/data/list.html

SpreadView: A Multi-touch Based Multiple Contents Visualization Method Composed of Aligned Layers

Joong Ho Lee, Hyoyoung Kim, and Ji-Hyung Park[(✉)]

Korea Institute of Science and Technology, Hwarangno 14-gil 5, Seoul,
Seongbuk-gu 136-791, Korea
yapl53@gmail.com, {090752, jhpark}@kist.re.kr

Abstract. There have been many studies concerning development of large scalable interactive displays employing multi-touch interfaces, which is rapidly replacing conventional static methods of presenting information to the public. Interactive large displays are used in various fields, such as in the education sector as interactive whiteboards, way-finding screens in retail and hospital environments and so on. We propose the SpreadView, a new method for displaying digital contents on public large display, which generates pages corresponding to the traditional content files included in the traditional folder in PC, and generates an information display layer including a folder display portion corresponding to the traditional folder and giving output the aligned information display layers. The SpreadView senses multi-touch events to change an output format of the information display layer according to various user manipulation patterns such as one point touch or one point drag on a page, two point touches or pinch on a page, multiple touches on multiple pages in the information. Through these various touch manipulations the SpreadView rearrange information display so as to correspond the user's expectations. The SpreadView may provide a design motivation to improve the usability in manipulating big amount of digital contents under the other forms of computing environment such as tabletop computing, virtual reality and augmented reality.

Keywords: Multi-touch · Interactive large display · Contents visualization

1 Introduction

Digital immersion is moving into public spaces. Interactive screens and public displays are deployed in urban environments, malls, and shop windows. Inner city areas, airports, train stations and stadiums are experiencing a transformation from traditional to digital displays enabling new forms of multimedia presentation and new user experiences. The market sees digital signage as more beneficial compared to static signage because content that updates frequently can be digitally updated, saving the cost of printing [12]. Digital signage also has the ability to be interactive with imbedded touch screens, movement detection and image capture devices. Czerwinski et al. [4] showed that larger displays improved recognition memory and peripheral awareness. This finding implies that people can more easily be made aware of instant information

© Springer International Publishing Switzerland 2015
N. Streitz and P. Markopoulos (Eds.): DAPI 2015, LNCS 9189, pp. 305–316, 2015.
DOI: 10.1007/978-3-319-20804-6_28

in public spaces as well, which will lead to effective provision of various content, such as advertisements, promotions, notices and so on. Tan et al. [13] reported a series of studies demonstrating the advantages of large displays on 3D navigation in virtual worlds. It is certain that large-scale display, in providing a wide field of view, helps users understand complex context in the view more easily. Furthermore, even if the visual angle is maintained, simply having a physically larger display improves performance on spatial tasks. Large displays naturally lend themselves to collaboration research as well based on their size, cost, and privacy concerns. Various papers have dealt with the use of large displays for collaboration. There is both a clear trend toward larger displays and mounting evidence that they increase user productivity and aid user recognition memory. However, G. Robertson et al. [10] showed that numerous usability problems inhibit the potential for even greater user productivity. P. Peltonen et al. [9] investigated a large multi-touch display installed in a central location in Helsinki, Finland. They analyzed how public availability is achieved through social learning and negotiation, and how the display restructures the public space. They found that the multi-touch feature, gesture-based interaction, and the physical display size contributed differentially to these uses. Furthermore, hedonic aspects are increasingly considered an important factor in user acceptance of information systems, especially for activities with high self-fulfilling value for users. J. Novak and S. Schmidt [8] demonstrated a higher hedonic stimulation quality of a touch-based large-display cooperative travel consultancy workspace than that of a traditional advisory setting. Coupled with qualitative user feedback highlighting visual qualities and touch-based interaction, these findings suggest the importance of intrinsic hedonic stimulation qualities in large-display visual workspaces.

In line with the previous researches, we propose novel contents visualization method composed of aligned layers, which supports multi user manipulation of large number of digital contents with multi-touch interaction. Figure 1 shows the Spread-View operating on 246-inch multi-touch integrated large display. The SpreadView is directed to maximize the number of pieces of digital contents displayed on a restricted screen. This method is composed of five steps of process – generating a page corresponding to a content file included in a folder; generating a folder display portion corresponding to the folder and an information display layer including the page; outputting the information display layer on a content display apparatus; sensing touch of the content display apparatus; and changing an output format of the information display layer based on the sensed touch. The generating the information display layer step includes aligning the folder display portion and the page of the information display layer in one direction. Owing to the distinctive features described above the Spread-View provides fast and easy interaction for searching and indexing among various types of digital contents without loss of space on display. This interaction concept may give designers a variety of inspirations such as intuitive user interaction with a number of virtual objects in 3D space or new user interface design to point, designate and select an object among big amount of candidates on large size of space or surface.

Fig. 1. The SpreadView provides multiple contents display view controlled by user's instant touch manipulation.

2 Related Work

Interactive large displays are deployed increasingly in a variety of settings, including exhibitions, events, museums, and other public places [8]. As situated media technology is rapidly maturing, it is likely that the trend will accelerate, so that people will become more accustomed to the large interactive walls. There are various researches about use of public displays situated in indoor and public environment. Morales-Arnada and Mayora-Ibarra introduced Dymo [11], a situated large interactive display outside of the workplace, within shared and sociable spaces such as common areas at universities and conferences, cafes, and hotel foyers designed to enable the sharing and exchange of a wide variety of digital media. Similarly, Fass et al. designed MessyBoard [6], an large, projected, shared bulletin board that is decorated collaboratively by a small group of users. Santa and Barra[16] proposed semi-public displays as a universal way for publicizing internal information and collaborative working in an office environment without other traditional means. Hinrichs and Carpendale [7] described findings from a field study that was conducted at the Vancouver Aquarium to investigate how visitors interact with a large table exhibit using multi-touch gestures. Visualizing contents of public display is one of the main research topics in this area. EMDialog [8] proposed by Hinrichs et al. provides a visual exploration environment for an artist's work in a museum that offers interplay between two integrated visualizations along temporal and contextual dimensions. Similarly, Bohemian Bookshelf [19] aims to support serendipitous discoveries in the context of digital book collections which can be facilitated through visualization. Clases and Moere [3] present Street Infographics, an urban intervention that visually represent data that is contextually related to local issues, and is visualized through situated displays that are placed within the social and public context of an urban environment.

Interaction for browsing is also a matter of concern to many researchers in designing interactive public display field. Coutrix et al. [4] suggested FIZZYVis, a walk-up-and-use interface that displays information through bubbles reacting to touches, and its design goals. Peltonen et al. [14] examined interaction with the system, CityWall, a large multi-touch display installed in public space in various social configuration. Alt et al. present a digital public notice area Digifieds [1] which is built to understand emerging practices and provide easy and straight forward interaction techniques to be used for creating and exchanging content. They demonstrate that some challenges have to be confronted when designing interactive public displays: attention needs to be attracted; interactivity needs to be communicated [12]; the user need to be motivated to interact [2, 9]; suitable interaction techniques need to be provide. This work focuses on second and fourth challenges.

3   SpreadView: Design

3.1   System Structure

The SpreadView is composed of three main devices and two databases. The Fig. 2 is a diagram showing an internal configuration of the SpreadView for displaying content. The system includes a touch sensor, a conversion controller, a display unit, a file database and a conversion information DB.

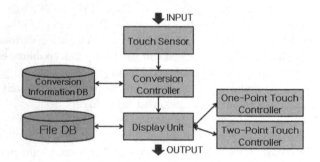

Fig. 2. An internal configuration of the SpreadView

The contents are multimedia contents including image, video, animated picture and so on. All or part of content can be displayed according to content types. For example, if content is an image the entire image or a part of the image can be displayed on the screen. If content is a video, a captured scene of a representative screen may be used as a part of content displayed on the content display apparatus and the reproduced video may be displayed on the content display apparatus. Content is displayed in correspondence with actual content and an object corresponding to (selected or extracted from) content is referred to as a "page". The touch sensor detects or senses touch of the display. The touch sensor receives user input based on haptic or tactile touch. The touch sensor includes various software components for performing various operations such as an operation for determining whether the content display apparatus is touched, an operation for determining whether a touch point is moved and an operation for tracking movement of a touch point. The movement of a touch point is divided into one-point touch and two-point touch. One-point touch is defined as instantaneous touch if a touch property is less than a predetermined touch property threshold and is defined as continuous touch if a touch property is greater than the threshold value.

The conversion controller serves to change an output format of an information display layer based on touch information sensed by the touch sensor. The display unit serves to output a folder display portion corresponding to a folder and an information display layer including a page corresponding to a content file in a folder. That is, the display unit visually displays the page to the user. The display unit combines with the touch sensor. The file DB serves to store content, which DB stores content in a tree structure of folders. That is, since files are stored in a hierarchical structure, content of a single folder may be displayed and higher folders of content files may be represented in an information display layer. The conversion information DB serves to store output information changed by the conversion controller. The conversion controller includes a one-point touch controller and a two-point touch controller. The one-point touch controller changes the output format of the display unit if one point is touched. The two-point touch controller changes the output format of the display unit if two points are touched. The two-point touch is applied to only the case where two points are included in the same information display layer. If two points are respectively included in different information display layers, each of the two points may be perceived as one point touched in each information display layer. In case of two-point touch, a determination as to whether two points are touched in a single page is first made. If two points are touched in the single page, the screen output format is changed depending on whether the touched two points are moved at the same velocity or at different velocities. If the two points are not touched in the single page, that is, if the two points are touched in different pages, a screen output format is separately changed.

3.2 Operation Process

The Fig. 3 is a flowchart illustrating the operation process. The system loads and checks file data from the file DB, where the folder information and the file information stored in the file DB is checked. The system generates a folder display portion corresponding to a folder and generates a page corresponding to a file using all or part of the loaded file information. The folder display portion and the page of the information display layer may be aligned in one direction, that is, in a horizontal direction or a vertical direction. And system loads the existing conversion information stored in the conversion information DB and outputs an information display layer including the folder display portion and the page on the screen. If the existing conversion information is not present, initialization is performed, that is, the information display layer is equally or randomly divided so as to output the folder display portion and the page. The system always waits for a touch operation, maintains the existing screen if a touch operation is not performed, and determines a screen display method of the page according to touch velocity.

If a one-point touch operation is performed, it is determined whether or not touch is instantaneous touch. If touch is instantaneous touch, one page is maximally enlarged and displayed on the entire screen and, if touch is not instantaneous touch, that is, if touch is continuous touch, the size of the page adjacent to the page corresponding to one point is changed and the output position of the page corresponding to one point is moved. On the other hand, if the one-point touch operation is not performed,

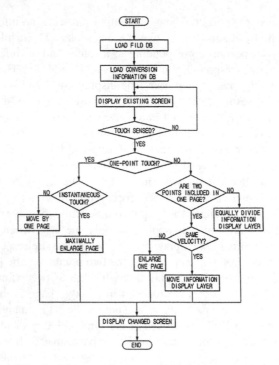

Fig. 3. The operation process of the SpreadView

a two-point touch operation is performed. If two points included in a single page are touched, the screen display method of the page differs according to movement velocities of two touch points represented two-dimensionaliy. The velocity includes the size and direction of the movement. If the two points represented two-dimensionally are moved at different velocities, the touched page is enlarged based on a movement path. If the velocities of the two points represented two-dimensionally are the same, the page including the touch points are moved along the information display layer. If the two touch points are moved at the same velocity in a direction perpendicular to the information display layer direction, the display position of the layer is changed. If two points included in different pages are touched, the sizes of the pages are equally divided and displayed on the screen.

3.3   Interaction

Figure 4(a) is a diagram showing an output screen of displaying multiple contents such as an image, a video, digital document by dividing the screen of the display area in a horizontal direction. The information display layer may be referred to as a page set including a plurality of pages. Figure 4(b) and (c) show three information display layers. A plurality of pages included in a folder based on an internal tree structure of a file system is represented on one information display layer. If another folder among folders represented in the folder display portion is selected, the page of the selected folder may be represented on a content display unit. Since all the internal angles between the edges of a rectangle are 90°, if the positions of two diagonally facing points are defined, a unique rectangle may be defined, the screen output method can be described using coordinates of a left upper end and coordinates of a right lower end of a page.

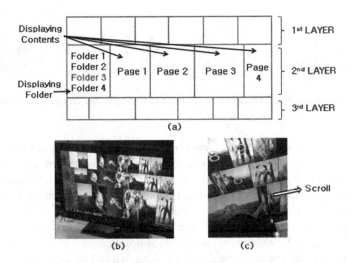

(a)

(b)   (c)

Fig. 4. A layout pattern of the multiple digital contents on the SpreadView

One-Point Instantaneous Touch Interaction. In case of one-point instantaneous touch, as shown in Fig. 5, it is assumed that left upper end coordinates of the page before touch are $(x1, y1)$ and right lower end coordinates of the page before touch are $(x2, y2)$ and that left upper end coordinates of the page after touch are $(x1', y1')$ and right lower end coordinates of the page after touch are $(x2', y2')$. The touch page is output on the entire screen based on the maximum width and length of the display. It is possible to prevent the page from being cut by adjusting the length of the page to the length of the screen. Thus, the coordinates of the page may be represented according to the length of the page.

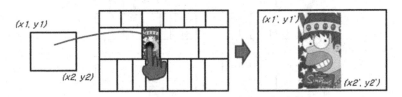

Fig. 5. The page is enlarged after one-point instantaneous touch

One-Point Continuous Touch Interaction. Figure 6 is a diagram showing a screen output method upon one-point continuous touch. If a middle page "4" is touched and the touch point is continuously moved to the right, the width of a left page "3" is increased without changing the size of the page "4". If the touch point of the page "4" is further moved to the right, a right page "5" is overlapped and is not displayed meaning that the page "4" is folded.

Fig. 6. The adjacent pages are changing their width according to the one-point continuous touch on the page.

Two-Points Continuous Touch Interaction. If two touch points are moved at different velocities in one page, a screen is output while the page is enlarged or reduced and the left and right pages and the upper and lower information layers are increased or decreased. As shown in Fig. 7(a), two touch points are selected in one page, which are moved by different sizes in different directions. The size of the page, the sizes of the left and right pages, and the sizes of the upper and lower information display layers are changed according to the movement of the touch points.

In case of two points in the same direction, as shown in Fig. 7(b) and (c), if the two touch points are moved along the information display layer at the same velocity, all the pages of the corresponding information layer may be moved regardless of the change in size of individual page. For example, if the two touch points are moved in the vertical direction of the information display layer at the same velocity, the corresponding information layer may be vertically moved regardless of change in size of the individual page.

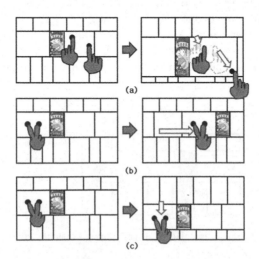

Fig. 7. Two-points continuous touch interaction

Two-Points of Individual Pages Interaction. Figure 8 shows a screen output method upon touch of two points of individual pages. If two points of different pages are touched, the sizes of the pages interposed between both pages are equally divided and output on the screen.

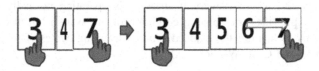

Fig. 8. Two-points interaction of individual pages; the sizes of the pages interposed between both pages are equally divided

4   Implementation

We developed 246 inch interactive large display which consists of an multi-touch sensor array comprised of LED components (emitters and receivers), a signal controller, PC interface software, and an application driver program. ARM 7 was used for detecting sensor signals and serializing and interfacing a LAN connection between the sensor frame and the computer. The test software for the prototype was developed using Visual C in the Win XP environment.

4.1   Hardware

Figure 9 shows the overall construction of our multi-touch system. The frame possesses a PCB, Printed Circuit Board and IR arrays of transmitters and receivers which are mounted around the frame. Each LED modules consist of a transmitter and receiver pair. When the left side of the array is activated as a transmitter, MCU switches the right side of the array as a receiver to detect IR light from the left side. Light detection information is transferred into MCU, which analyzes and converts the information into a data table where a 1 indicates that light was successfully received and a 0 indicates detection failure. The size of the data table depends on the number of LED modules. The data table is converted to serialized TCP/IP protocol and LAN Port transfers the data to PC via LAN RJ45.

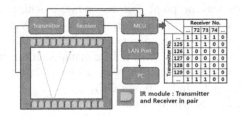

Fig. 9. Overall construction of our multi-touch system.

4.2   Software

To verify the data from hardware, raw data monitoring software is necessary. The left side of Fig. 10 shows the screen shot of raw data monitor program. The raw data from the data table is represented as shown where a red mark in the matrix means successful detection of light. By using this program, we could monitor how large the transmitter emission angle is and whether every IR module is operating normally or not. This software not only provides the sensing condition of the system but also provides its operating speed by indicating the elapsed time of scanning cycles. This program was developed with Visual C on Windows XP.

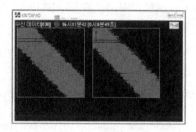

Fig. 10. Multi-touch detection to generate touch information for application programs.

5   Conclusion

We have presented a design for displaying digital content on interactive large display. The method for displaying content includes: generating a page corresponding to a content file included in a folder; generating a folder display portion corresponding to the folder and an information display layer including the page; outputting the information display layer on a content display apparatus; sensing touch of the content display apparatus; and changing an output format of the information display layer based on the sensed touch. The key feature of the SpreadView is 'space effectiveness' that is 'no waste of space between pages' regardless of page layout pattern and 'intuitive and easy to control' such as zoom, move, alinement and reconfiguration through simple touch gestures. The information display layer includes aligning the folder display portion and the page layers in one direction so that user scroll each layers parallel to others without deterioration of page alignment. And SpreadView provides effective control interaction for rearrangement of size of layers and pages. To change the size of the information display layers, user touches one point and drag while touching and holding another layer, which makes the size of layer sets rearranged equally. With same manner, when user touches two pages which belongs to same layer, the SpreadView equally resized the pages placed among two selections. These unique manipulation methods are the special design for the large display composed of large numbers of information, which has not been applied in conventional window based GUI.

We believe that designers will be well served in considering the issues we have presented and applying the tools we have provided in this study. The provision of effective contents visualization with intuitive manipulation could lead to in-depth engagement in display content, which may successfully deliver such information as ads, notices, campaigns, and so on. And we expect the SpreadView would elevate the recognition degree of digital contents arranged on 2D or 3D information space, which leads users to in-depth understanding to the contents, providing a more attractive experience, which results in effective transfer of information with intuitive operation of large number of digital contents, which is beneficial not only to public large display but also to other computing environments such as tabletop computing, virtual reality and augmented reality display etc.

References

1. Alt, F., Shirazi, A.S., Kubitza, T., Schnidt, A.: Interaction techniques for creating and exchanging content with public displays. In: 2013 SIGGHI Conference on Human Factors in Computing Systems, pp. 1709–1718. ACM (2013)
2. Claes, S., Moere, A.V.: Street infographics: raising awareness of local issues through a situated urban visualization. In: 2013 ACM International Symposium on Pervasive Displays, pp. 133–138. ACM (2013)
3. Coutrix, C., Kuikkaniemi, K., Kurvinen, E., Jaccuci, G., Avdouevski, I., Makela, R.: FizzyVis: Designing for playful information browsing on a multitouch public display. In: 2011 ACM Symposium on Designing Pleasurable Products and Interfaces. ACM (2011)
4. Czerwinski, M., Robertson, G., Meyers, B., Smith, G., Tan, D.: Large display research overview. In: 2006 SIGGHI Conference on Human Factors in Computing Systems. ACM (2006)
5. Fass, A.M., Forlizzi, J., Pausch, R.: MessyDesk and MessyBoard: two designs inspired by the goal of improving human memory. In: 2002 ACM Conference on Designing Interactive Systems. pp. 303–311. ACM (2002)
6. Hinrichs, U., Carpendale, S.: Gestures in the wild: studying multi-touch gesture sequences on interactive tabletop exhibits. In: 2011 SIGGHI Conference on Human Factors in Computing Systems, pp. 3023–3032. ACM (2011)
7. Hinrichs, U., Schmidt, H., Carpendale, S.: EMDialog: bringing information visualization into the museum. In: IEEE Transactions on Visualization and Computer Graphics, vol. **14**, no. 6, pp. 1181–1188. IEEE (2008)
8. Novak, J., Schmidt, S.: When Joy Matters: The Importance of Hedonic Stimulation in Collocated Collaboration with Large-Displays. In: Gross, T., Gulliksen, J., Kotzé, P., Oestreicher, L., Palanque, P., Prates, R.O., Winckler, M. (eds.) INTERACT 2009. LNCS, vol. 5727, pp. 618–629. Springer, Heidelberg (2009)
9. Peltonen, P., Kurvinen, E., Salovaara, A., Jacucci, G., Ilmonen, T., Evans, J., Oulasvirta, A., Saarikko, P.: "It's Mine, Don't Touch!": interactions at a large multi-touch display in a city centre. In: 2008 SIGGHI Conference on Human Factors in Computing Systems. ACM (2008)
10. Robertson, G., Czerwinski, M., Baudisch, P., Meyers, B., Robbins, D., Smith, G., Tan, D.: The large-display user experience. J. IEEE Comput. Graph. Appl. 25(4), 44–51 (2005)
11. Santa, P.C., Barra, O.M.: Interactive semi-public displays to support local mobility in working environments. In: 1st Mexican Workshop on Human Computer Interaction (2006)

12. Satoh, I.: An agent-based framework for context-aware digital signage. In: Ambient Intelligence and Future Trends - International Symposium on Ambient Intelligence. vol. 72, pp. 105–112. Springer, Berlin (2010)
13. Tan, D.S., Gergle, D., Scupelli, P., Pausch, R.: With similar visual angles, larger displays improve spatial performance. In: 2003 SIGGHI Conference on Human Factors in Computing Systems. ACM (2003)
14. Thudt, A., Hinrichs, U., Carpendale, S.: The Bohemian bookshelf: supporting serendipitous book discoveries through information visualization. In: 2012 SIGGHI Conference on Human Factors in Computing Systems, pp. 1461–1470. ACM (2012)
15. Valkanova, N., Walter, R., Moere, A.V., Muller, J.: MyPosition: sparking civic discourse by a public interactive poll visualization. In: 18th ACM Conference on Computer-Supported Cooperative Work and Social Computing. pp. 1323–1332. ACM (2014)

Bandage Man: A Spatial Interaction Design in a Sensible Space for Connecting Family

Min-Nan Liao and Teng-Wen Chang[✉]

National Yunlin University of Science and Technology, Douliu City, Taiwan
{M10234002, tengwen}@yuntech.edu.tw

Abstract. The alienation between family members is mainly caused by the descendant's work and study, which causes that the elderly live in the countryside lonely and cannot be actually concerned and cared by the descendants. Gradually, the relation between family members is alienated. In this paper, the life information of the elderly is recorded with sensing network through furniture. The physical object on the child end can receive the emotional information of the elderly. Through the interaction mode of feeling transmission between the sensing network and Bandage Man, it is to synchronize the inter-generational family affection contact, so as to increase the interaction opportunity between family members and form a feeling concern network between families.

Keywords: Elderly living alone · Feeling network · Man-machine interaction · Family concern

1 Introduction

The difference between the elderly living alone and the ordinary old people is that the elderly living alone must take are of themselves in life, and their difficulties in psychology and life also increase accordingly. Although many elderly satisfied with the way they live, loneliness is still one of the most serious problems mentally. While desire to have some accompany, the asynchronous living patterns with their descendant's time creates inconvenient for both parties. While their psychological demand can be met only with the high concern and assistance of relatives, they need a way of time synchronous design to connect with their descendants.

1.1 Feeling Communication of Asynchronous Life

Due to demand for life currently, most of the descendants are busy with work and seldom contact with their parents actively, while the elderly living alone also dare not disturb the life of their descendants, but they are always willing to help their descendants actively. Because of being strange to science and technology and insufficient economic ability, they do not know how to help their descendants, and the gradual worsening of health causes less action capability of elderly loving alone, and their range of motion is also shrunk gradually. For a long time, the psychological levels of sense of loneliness, sense of existence, wanting to be concerned and accompanied of

© Springer International Publishing Switzerland 2015
N. Streitz and P. Markopoulos (Eds.): DAPI 2015, LNCS 9189, pp. 317–324, 2015.
DOI: 10.1007/978-3-319-20804-6_29

the elderly living alone increase continuously. When communicating with others, most of the elderly living alone think that their ideas are correct, and cannot trust the other side, so it is easy to cause problem in the intergenerational communication; on the other hand, because of transnational information fall, there is no common topic. Most of the elderly think their ideas are correct and often cannot accept their descendant's words, and it is felt that it is unable to trust the other sides between two generations, so problem will occur between two generations, and on the other hand, no common topic may promote the further interaction.

1.2 Intergenerational Family Role Influence

Lee [1] Mentioned 3 types of research that can further develop the intergenerational family role: (1) influence of social structure on the family interaction; (2) interactive influence on subjective factor and self-motivation; (3) influence on communication and interaction of self-feeling with the aged parents. The intergenerational family role expands the idea of blending and communication symbolizing the interaction and provides a condition for the interaction and communication between the elderly and their descendants, in which the behavior, hobby, feeling and faith of the elderly are the influential factors. The factors influencing the interaction mechanism between the elderly and the society include education degree, income condition, age and health condition [1, 2].

1.3 Purpose and Method: Find Out the Daily Behaviors of the Elderly Living Alone, Solve the Asynchronous Living Mode with the Family Members

Through the observation method and interview, this paper intends to analyze the interactive relation between the activity range and daily behavior of the elderly living alone, and understand the daily activity behavior of the elderly. Moreover, it aims to analyze the interaction between the actual idea and demand of the elderly and their family members. The methods and steps are as follows:

1. Observe the activity range and daily behavior of the elderly and understand the demand and purpose of daily life
2. Determine the interaction mode with the descendants through the analysis on the daily behaviors
3. Establish the feeling network between the elderly living along and family members through the sensing network between the physical objects
4. Ask parents to actively concern the life condition of parents

2 Literature Review

2.1 Family Concern and Feeling Contact

The intimacy influencing the family relation is the emotional influence of the elderly, and trust and confidence in the family members are the factors to increase the inter-generational interaction between families. While encouraging the elderly to actively concern with the descendants might increase interaction relation between the descendants and the elderly. The elderly provide many resources, while obtain less return, and the elderly are in poor health and the descendants seldom give concern and assistance, which are the main reasons to reduce the interaction between the elderly and descendants.

Ying et al. [3] Proposed a far-distance emotional interaction design to solve the problem of "Empty Nest". The existence of the family members is known through two lamps. Knowing about the life condition of the descendants or parents through simple interaction can also help to concern the other side. Most of the feeling networks need time to cultivate and establish, but because of far distance and the inconsistency in time, the feelings between each other are lost, causing less and less interaction between the family members.

2.2 Sensing Network and Cloud Computing

For the development of physical computing and embedded computing, it is to use computer computing to control the physical subject. The interaction mode is to sense the behaviors of people in contact type and non-contact type; the computer computes and analyzes the data. The result is known from the information processed by the computer, and such model is to transmit the information through input end, output end and the man-machine communication [4] (as shown in Fig. 1). The user steps on the device to transmit the body weight data to the micro-control electronic circuit in the middle; various data are transmitted into the digital signal, which can be read by the computer via the controller. Through the communication of sequence, the signal is transmitted to the computer for computing processing. The computer-processed data are transmitted back to the microcontroller in the middle and then fed back to the users through the electronic subject [5].

Through the concept of distributed computing, the sensed elements are embedded into the furniture and environment in the daily life. Various computing and sensing and display devices are integrated in our living environment, and the daily schedule of the residents and users will not be disturbed. The computed information is feedback, and the information is transmitted to the residents and users in environment, without sensing the existence of technology. The computer communicates with the users to form an interactive space.

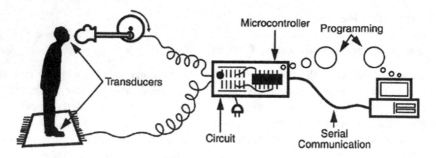

Fig. 1. Physical calculation system mechanism [4]

2.3   C-HANS Model

The Contextual-Human Ambient Network S-C-HANS Model is proposed in [6]. The concept of C-HANS Model respectively includes Network Sever, Ambient Agent, and Human.

Human is the user of activity and behavior of the interaction space. In the space, there is the event of single person and more persons, and different feedbacks will be given according to different conditions. The concept of Ambient Agente is that a communication bridge is established between the computer and sensor in the virtual environment, which is classified into 3 modes, "sensing agent", "event agent" and "response agent". The three models transmit the information sensed by the people in the living environment to the cloud end, through the computing judgment. Based on different information, or the excessive standard, different feedbacks will be made. Network Sever is the hub of the system, which can store the information from different environments, such as the sensing data, user activity, multi-space communication. The collected information is used to know about the environmental condition and the information transmitted by various sensors through the computing analysis, judge the interaction event and make a feedback action. When the data is transmitted to the server in wireless manner in a living environment, the information is written into the data library, while the system records the user habit as the judgment and feedback next time, and the loop interaction continues (as shown in Fig. 2).

3   Contextual Analysis

In this research, 15 elderly living alone above 65 years old are interviewed and their daily lifestyle is observed. Their common behavior and range of daily activity, behaviors and events and the furniture used are sorted out. All the 15 old patients have descendants and they live independently and manage themselves, their descendants work or study in other places. And understand the daily lifestyle of the elderly living alone, and the furniture they usually contact, like chair, bed, TV set, gate, room door kitchen (gas stove), tableware, outdoor vegetable garden and flower watering tool is listed. In this research, the current behaviors and life conditions are known through environment, event, furniture and event, the three situational assumed in this research are as follows:

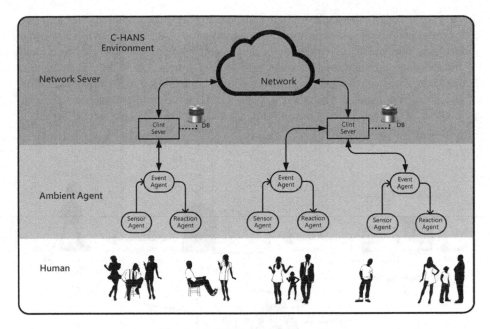

Fig. 2. C-HANS Environment [6]

Scene 1: when the environment is the vegetable garden, the gate and flower watering tools must be contacted, respectively the human infrared detects and temperature sensor detects vegetable garden and flower watering tool. Through the judgment whether it is morning or afternoon, it is able to clearly know that the elderly event is watering in the vegetable garden. Through the time spent in the vegetable garden, it is to judge whether the elderly is happy or worried.

Scene 2: when the environment is the sitting room, the chair and TV set must be contacted. Respectively the pressure sensor detects sitting, the indicative sound sensor detects whether the TV set is turned on, so as to judge that the elderly event is watching TV in the sitting room. Through the force of the sitting chair and the volume of TV set, it is to understand the emotion of the old people.

Scene 3: when the environment is the bedroom, the room door, bed must be contacted, respectively the human infrared detects the going in and out of the room, pressure sensor detects whether it is getting up or going to bed, whether it is morning or evening. Through the time of getting up and going to bed, it is to judge whether the condition of the elderly living alone is good or bad.

4 Experiment and System Design

The digital technology is used to help the interaction between family members, and an emotional network is established. This research analyzes the data about the daily life of 15 old people living alone. The furniture and environmental installation sensors contacted by them are divided into chair with micro switch, bed with pressure sensor, gate with human infrared, vegetable garden and watering tool with humidity sensor. The sensor transmits the signal according to the activity time of the elderly living alone, the system judges the current event/behavior and whether the emotion is good or not, and the information is transmitted to the cloud system timely via WIFI for judgment. Through the score information, the information is transmitted to the physical entity device. The descendants can see their parents' condition according to the device color, and make a call to their parents, or go home for visit. In the following, scene 2 is taken as an example (as shown in Fig. 3).

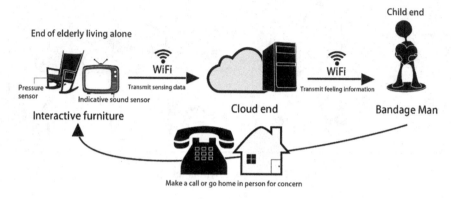

Fig. 3. System architecture diagram of scene 2

Four emotions, including happiness be yellow (50–75), anger be red (75–100), sadness be blue (0–25) and joy be green (25–50) are divided based on the scores (0–100) as the basis for the color of Bandage Man LED in the descendants end, so as to understand the daily condition of the elderly living alone and increase the contact between the old people and family members (as shown in Fig. 4).

Fig. 4. Display of four emotions with colors (Color figure online)

The context of our Bandage Man is mainly located in either the living room of our decent, or the office. According to the observation of living conditions of elderly people living alone, the behaviors are often through furniture sensors to compute behavior that can detect some guessing on the emotional attitudes or changes. Four kinds of emotions, as the displayed in Fig. 4 are divided into four colors representing elderly current mood. As shown in Fig. 5, the Bandage Man is in red, angry or higher temper will trigger decent to concern and contact their elderly to find out what happen and further activate the communication desired by the elderly. These settle reflection will not disturb the current working process and patterns of family members but to amplify the emotion communication as designed.

Fig. 5. Office situational

5 Conclusion

The daily life behavior of the elderly living alone is computed with sensing network through furniture, the daily data are transmitted to the system for computing and judgment, and the life information of the elderly is recorded everyday. The physical subject in the descendants end can receive the emotional information of the elderly. The information between the physical subjects is transmitted to the Bandage Man on the descendants end, and through the color feedback. The descendants can see the life condition of the elderly, and actively concern their parents, so that the asynchronous lifestyle between the generations can synchronize the intergenerational affection connection through the transmission of emotional interaction mode between the sensor and Bandage Man. Hence, the interaction opportunity of family members can be enhanced to form an affection concern network between families. Based on the proposed Bandage Man, further experiments will be conducted on actual users for verification of the design.

References

1. Lee, G.R.: Children and the elderly interaction and morale. Res. Aging **1**, 335–360 (1979)
2. Wood, V., Robertson, J.F.: Friendship and kinship interaction: Differential effect on the morale of the elderly. J. Marriage Fam. **40**, 367–375 (1978)
3. Ying, F., Li, B., Li, Z., Li, X., Tao, J., Gao, S.: Telepathy lamp: remote affective interaction based on ambient metaphor for emotional caring of the elderly. In: System Science, Engineering Design and Manufacturing Informatization (ICSEM), 2010 International Conference on, pp. 129–132 IEEE (2010)
4. O'Sullivan, D., Igoe, T.: Physical computing: sensing and controlling the physical world with computers. Thomson Course Technology, Boston (2004)
5. Yu, G.-J., Chang, T.-W.: Reacting with care: the hybrid interaction types in a sensible space. In: Jacko, J.A. (ed.) Human-Computer Interaction, Part III, HCII 2011. LNCS, vol. 6763, pp. 250–258. Springer, Heidelberg (2011)
6. Chang, T.-W. , Jiang H., Chen S.-H., Datta S.: Dynamic skin: interacting with space. In: The 17th International Conference on Computer Aided Architectural Design Research in Asia, pp. 89–98. CAADRIA, Chennai (2012)

Learning Instead of Markers: Flexible Recognition of Mobile Devices on Interactive Surfaces

Philipp Mock[1](✉), Jörg Edelmann[2], and Wolfgang Rosenstiel[1]

[1] University of Tübingen, Sand 13, 72076 Tübingen, Germany
{philipp.mock,wolfgang.rosenstiel}@uni-tuebingen.de
[2] Knowledge Media Research Center, Schleichstr. 6, 72076 Tübingen, Germany
j.edelmann@iwm-kmrc.de

Abstract. We propose an approach for recognition of mobile devices on interactive surfaces that do not support optical markers. Our system only requires an axis aligned bounding box of the object placed on the touchscreen in combination with position data from the mobile devices integrated inertia measurement unit (IMU). We put special emphasis on maximum flexibility in terms of compatibility with varying multi-touch sensor techniques and different kinds of mobile devices. A new device can be added to the system with a short training phase, during which the device is moved across the interactive surface. A device model is automatically created from the recorded data using support vector machines. Different devices of the same size are identified by analyzing their IMU data streams for transitions into a horizontally resting state. The system has been tested in a museum environment.

Keywords: Human computer interaction · Tabletop interaction · Markerless object tracking · Machine learning

1 Introduction

Large interactive tabletop installations are frequently used in museums or other kinds of exhibitions as a visitor information system. In many cases, a visitors guide for mobile devices accompanies these installations. Using mobile devices and a tabletop in conjunction offers several opportunities for the design of information systems. For example, such a combination can be used to allow visitors to create a selection of favorite artworks on their smart phone while visiting the exhibition. This individual selection can later be transferred to the tabletop in order to access further information that cannot be presented adequately on the small screen of a mobile device. The other way round, a visitor can select an individual tour on a tabletop at the entrance of a museum or trade show and then transfer it to an app on a smart phone that will guide him or her through the exhibition. To realize this, the devices need to communicate with each other.

© Springer International Publishing Switzerland 2015
N. Streitz and P. Markopoulos (Eds.): DAPI 2015, LNCS 9189, pp. 325–336, 2015.
DOI: 10.1007/978-3-319-20804-6_30

While the data can simply be sent via UDP socket connection or Bluetooth, the problem of assigning individual data streams to a specific device is not trivial.

The easiest way of achieving a correct assignment is to use the tabletop's touch sensor for the recognition. That way, the device can simply be placed on the interactive surface to establish the communication. If an optical sensor is used, optical markers attached to mobile devices are a fast and reliable way to realize this (e.g., camera based [5], Microsoft PixelSense). However, many sensor types do not support these markers. Particularly touch frames, which sense active fingers from the side and which are frequently used for large screen diagonals, do not support this kind of interaction (e.g., PQ Labs G4 [11]). As a consequence, another way of sensing mobile devices has to be found for these cases.

In this work, we present a recognition system that does not rely on optical markers and has minimum requirements regarding the touch sensor. Our tracking software is designed to simply be run in the background to provide object recognition for any given application.

As the amount of information that an interactive screen provides for a touch interaction varies heavily depending on the actual sensor configuration, we focus on using only the most basic features (x- and y-position and size in the form of an axis aligned bounding box) in conjunction with accelerometer data from the mobile device.

2   Related Work

The most common way of enabling object recognition on an optical screen are fiducial markers: An optically individual marker (similar to a QR code) is placed on an object and the optical sensor uses computer vision and object recognition algorithms to detect and track an active marker (e.g., [3,5,7,10]). This is possible for installations that sense interactions from below the screen with sufficient resolution.

When optical markers are impractical or the sensing technique does not support markers, the communication between mobile devices and a large screen installation has to established in other ways. One way to do this is to use the built-in flashlight of a mobile device [2,13]: combined with an optical touch sensor, short messages can be encoded with a series of automatically generated short light pulses. These can be used as an authentication scheme to establish bidirectional communication between a large screen device and a mobile phone or tablet.

Miyaoku et al. [8] proposed a light signal marker method called "C-Blink". Here, the LCD of a mobile device is used to emit so called hue-difference-blinks that a large screen installation can detect using a screen-side sensor.

Built-in IMUs have also been successfully used to implement communication between mobile and tabletop devices. For instance, Schmidt et al. enable pick-and-drop-style transfer of objects between a mobile phone and an interactive surface using a combination of accelerometer and multi-touch sensor data [12]. Phone touch events are discriminated from finger touch events by the surface and device identities are determined using data from an external accelerometer attached to the mobile device.

Albarelli et al. recognize appear and stop gestures of mobile devices on an interactive screen by using supervised machine learning methods [1]. For each gesture, a model is trained with a large data set containing positive and negative examples optical touchscreen combined with acceleration and velocity measurements obtained from mobile devices. The authors could show that using such an approach can be a robust alternative to using optical markers.

3 Contribution

The main contribution of this work is a lightweight tracking software for marker-less detection of mobile devices, which can be used with any type of interactive surface that can detect the size of an object on the screen. Similar to [1], we use a machine learning approach to discriminate objects on the screen (e.g., a mobile phone or a tablet) from regular finger touch interactions. A trained object is described with the axis aligned bounding box only to ensure compatibility with all common touch sensing hardware. The identity of mobile devices is eventually determined with IMU data: a device is assigned to a touch event with correct dimensions, if a simultaneous transition to a horizontally resting state is detected with the integrated IMU.

For our tracking software, we put special emphasis on ease of use and maximum flexibility. Accordingly, we describe how a new device can be added to the system by moving it across the screen's surface for a short period of time. A model is then automatically created from recorded interaction data. The resulting device model inherently reflects characteristics like sensor noise, since real observations from the touch sensor are used as training data. Our software was designed to be run in the background and distribute touch and object events via TUIO protocol [6].

The proposed system was developed to enable an intuitive way of establishing the communication between two devices for a visitor information system in a

Fig. 1. Practical evaluation of the system in an art museum environment: Users can select artworks on their mobile while visiting the exhibition. The mobile device can be placed on the tabletop to access more detailed information about an artwork.

museum environment. The visitor information system uses mobile devices in conjunction with a large touchscreen. Tablets and mobile phones can be used within the exhibition as a multimedia guide. During the visit, artworks can be tagged to create a collection of personal favorites on the mobile device. Later on, visitors can access additional information for these favorites on the tabletop after exiting the exhibition. The object recognition system was evaluated in an experimental exhibition that uses reproductions of the original artworks and which is used for several museum and visitor research studies (see Fig. 1).

4 Detecting Object Shapes

The possibilities of recognizing objects on the surface of an interactive screen largely depend on the used multi-touch technology. Regarding optical touch sensing, most technologies can be separated into approaches that detect fingers and objects from below the screen (e.g., with a camera) and approaches that use senders and emitters which are placed around the screen and thus detect the visual hull of an object from the sides (e.g., [4,9]). Depending on the hardware, a system of the latter kind provides the convex hull, an object aligned bounding box or just an axis aligned bounding box for an active object.

We are using an 80" tabletop device equipped with a PQ Labs G4 multi-touch screen [11], which is another example for the visual hull technique, for a visitor information system in an art museum. Apart from position on the screen, the G4 touch frame provides an axis aligned bounding box that correlates to the number of sender/emitter-pairs that have been blocked by an object.

As the number of features that describe an object is very low (width and height of the axis aligned bounding box) and we know the dimensions of the original device, simple trigonometry can be used to verify whether the size of a bounding box matches the dimensions of a mobile device. However, if we assume that the mobile device is a perfect rectangle, we potentially induce errors due to device characteristics like rounded corners. If the sensor furthermore suffers from noise, this also has to be modeled separately. In order to avoid the parameter tuning that would be necessary to fit a parametrized model to the exact shape of a device while considering the sensor noise of the interactive surface, we chose a machine learning approach instead. That is, recording real measurements of a device on the tabletop and using this data to train a support vector machine (SVM).

SVM classifiers are binary large margin classifiers that optimize the decision boundary between data samples of two categories so that the distance between the separating hyperplane and all data points is maximized. This generally reduces the generalization error of the classifier. The objective of distinguishing a certain active mobile device from any other input can be considered an anomaly detection problem. We implemented this by using a one-class SVM, which determines the hyperplane that separates samples from one class from the origin with maximum margin. A one-class SVM is trained with data from a single class. The necessary labeled data can be obtained with a dedicated training phase during which the

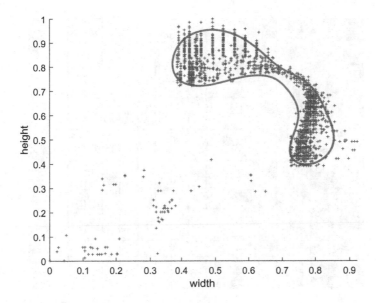

Fig. 2. Normalized measurements of width and height of an iPod on the screen's surface. The decision boundary of the one-class SVM classifier is depicted in red. Note that the data set contains highly noisy measurements and unintentional input.

mobile device is moved across the screen's surface. Figure 2 illustrates a data set that was obtained from such a training phase. As the number of features (width and height) is low compared to the number of samples (several thousand), we use a radial basis function (RBF) kernel for our one-class SVM classifiers. The SVM parameters ν and γ, which control the number of outliers in the training data and the standard deviation of the RBF, have to be optimized per training data set using grid search. Figure 3 shows the results for an example data set. In this case, $\nu = 0.04$ and $\gamma = 28$ gave the best results.

Using this approach, a new device can be added as follows: Apart from the default tracking mode, our object recognition application can also be operated in training mode. To add his or her device, a user switches to training and is then requested to place the device on the screen. After moving the mobile device around for 30 s, a device model is automatically created from the recorded data, which can be henceforth used for tracking. In order to avoid having multiple models for nearly identical sized devices, a combined model can be created, if the performances of two models show comparable classification performance for samples of the respective other class. Still, having multiple models for similar sized objects is not a problem, because device identity is ultimately determined using accelerometer data.

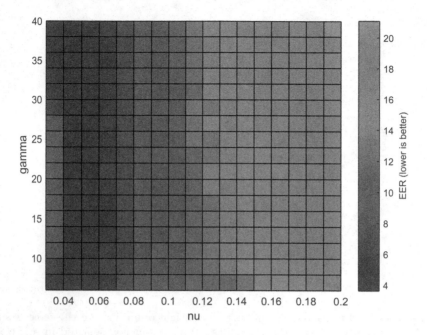

Fig. 3. Grid search results for an example training data set of iPod Touches including a significant number of noisy samples. The EER values apply to recorded regular finger touches.

5 Communication with Mobile Devices

When regarding only the sizes of objects, two devices with equal dimensions cannot be kept apart. Furthermore, a palm or multiple fingers can randomly cause patterns that are falsely classified as a trained object. To identify a particular device and to avoid false positives from unintentional input, the IMU of a mobile device is included into the decision process. Transitions from any inclination to a horizontally resting state can be observed directly from the accelerometer signal.

One way to integrate IMU data into the system is to model appear and stop gestures of mobile devices with combined data from the touch sensor and the IMU, as described in [1]. That is, synchronizing the clock of all involved devices and modeling causalities of observed touches and measurements from the position sensors. The resulting models reflect mutual relations between IMU and touch data for each of the modeled gestures. While this can result in very good detection rates, it requires a relatively high amount of samples for each of the modeled gestures, so that overfitting of the training data is avoided. For example, a model that matches the behavioral patterns of only a few users perfectly could produce substantial errors for unknown users who use the system in a different manner.

As our software was designed to be used in various different museum and visitor research application scenarios with a broad variety of devices, it is rather inconvenient to retrain gestures whenever a new device is added to the system.

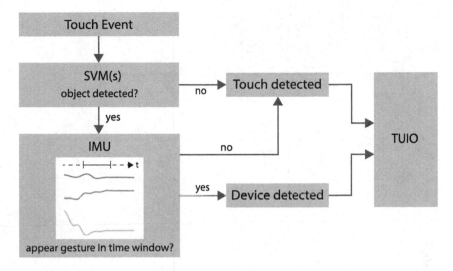

Fig. 4. The device recognition process including SVM classifiers trained with objects sizes and a subsequent analysis of accelerometer data. Figure 5 shows a more detailed example of accelerometer data during an appear event including the applied time windows.

This is why we opted for a simpler yet more flexible approach instead: Device dimensions are determined with the above object detection based on one-class SVM classifiers. Whenever a device SVM gives a positive result (i.e., an object of the expected size has been detected), the IMU data of all nearby mobile devices (sent via UDP) is analyzed for transitions to a resting state. The overall classification process is illustrated in Fig. 4.

A transition is characterized by a predetermined number of measurements corresponding to motion followed by a number of measurements that correspond to a resting device. To be more precise, we require all acceleration values to be within a threshold of 0.05 around the expected values (Ax and $Ay \approx 0$, $Az \approx -1$) at the end of the action and at least of them to be out of the range beforehand (compare Fig. 5). Eventually, a detected touch is associated to a specific device, if such a transition is detected within a short time window after a positive result of the corresponding SVM.

The timespan between a positive SVM classification and a detected IMU gesture depends on several factors: network latency, refresh rate of the accelerometer data and the way a device is placed on the surface. The first two factors add up to a overall system latency. For an IMU refresh rate of 10 Hz every measurement that is read before a device is accepted adds 100 ms to the system latency that is induced by the UDP network. We got the best results using a window of five consecutive measurements (2 in motion, 3 horizontally resting).

Lastly, the actual gesture influences the required duration because the velocity and direction of motion determine the time it takes before the IMU values level out at the expected resting state. Recorded data revealed that the difference

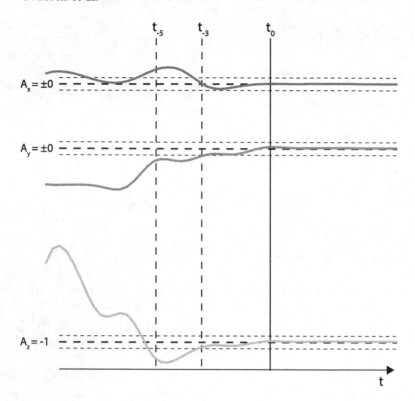

Fig. 5. Visualization of the accelerometer data of a device when being placed on the tabletop. The device is recognized at t_0. The time window starts at t_{-5}, a resting state is detected from t_{-3} on.

between a slow and a very fast gesture can be up to 200 ms. This interval also has to be added to the overall time window. Taking these factors into account, we found that a time window of 700 ms yielded the best results.

A contact area that has been associated with a certain device remains linked to it until it disappears. This means, that the SVM does not need to correctly identify a device on a permanent basis. Still, a problem of most touch sensors is that finger and object tracking is not perfect especially for rapid movements. As a consequence, a recognized touch can disappear for one or more consecutive frames. When it reappears, it usually receives a new identifier, resulting in sequential *TOUCH UP* end *TOUCH DOWN* events.

A stability timer for disappearing objects can fix this issue. That is, whenever a touch, which is associated with a mobile device, disappears and a new touch appears at the approximate same position, the system analyzes the IMU data of the respective device: If the device remained on the surface, the IMU data will not show an appear gesture. Consequently, if A_z remains within a threshold of 0.05 around -1, the new touch is assigned to the device. This induces a short delay for remove events as we have to wait for IMU data, but depending on the used touch sensor it potentially increases the object tracking stability significantly.

6   Results

In order to evaluate the object shape SVM classifiers, we recorded size measurements of iPod Touches and iPad Minis that were moved on the screen's surface and regular finger interactions during normal use of the visitor information application. Each of the resulting data sets contains between 1500 to 2000 samples. The device models where trained with samples from a 30 s training phase.

We found that the optimal model parameters vary for different training data sets. The determining factor is how clean the initial data sets are. That is, how many unintentional touches are included in the recorded data. The more noisy samples are included, the more samples have to be considered as outliers. This can directly be adjusted with the ν parameter. In our evaluations, the average equal error rate (EER) for different iPod models is 6.11 compared to regular finger touches. iPad Minis are easier to distinguish from iPods due to the major difference in terms of screen diagonals. Accordingly, average EER is 2.9 for this case. Performance of the iPad Mini models was uniformly good: averaged EER values are 0.41 for fingers and 0.89 for iPods. Figure 6 illustrates the performance of an iPod model compared to finger and iPad interactions in a receiver operating characteristic (ROC) curve for $\gamma = 20$ and $\gamma = 10$. We advise against using devices that are much smaller than an iPod Touch or a regular smart phone. This is because small objects are likely to be confused with fingers, which drastically increases the likelihood of false positive classifications.

The recognition rates of the IMU based device identification are harder to evaluate during real-world usage, because studies in the experimental exhibition usually require participants to put their mobile device on the tabletop only once or twice. As we could not create any meaningful statistics from this sparse data, we asked members of our department to place mobile devices on the tabletop in close succession to create a large number of samples within a short period of time. That way, we recorded a total of 440 appear events from 7 participants. Altogether, 99.09 % of these gestures were recognized correctly from the IMU data streams.

In order to estimate the system's robustness with regard to IMU data from other devices, we furthermore evaluated data streams from normal usage of a mobile visitor information application. The critical factor for misclassifications due to collisions with other data streams are false positive recognitions of devices that are currently not interacting with the tabletop. Accordingly, the test persons were asked to visit the experimental exhibition and use their mobile devices to retrieve information about the exhibits in form of audio, text and illustrations.

For one device, an average of 1.05 transitions into a resting state were detected per minute. The probability p of a collision can be calculated using a hypergeometric distribution as $p = \binom{N-n_{active}}{k} / \binom{N}{k}$. N is the total number of time steps and n_{active} is the number of time steps during which transitions are accepted due to a positive result of an SVM. k is the number of detected transitions during the considered time frame. When assuming one device being placed on the tabletop per minute, a time window of 700 ms and the above 1.05 transitions per minute, this gives a collision likelihood of 1.17 %. The value increases with additional devices or more frequent device interactions.

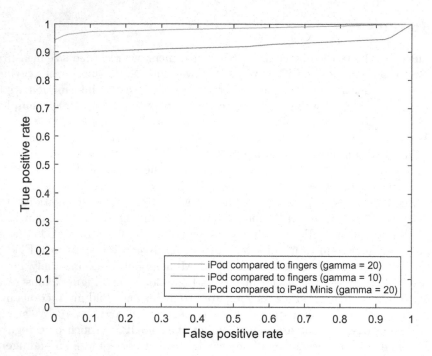

Fig. 6. ROC curve of an iPod model compared to finger interactions and iPad Minis with different kernel parameters. For $\gamma = 20$, EER is below 5 compared to both categories.

7 Discussion and Future Work

Our results reveal that basic sensor data (axis aligned bounding box and position) is sufficient to implement recognition of mobile devices on an interactive surface. By keeping sensor requirements at a minimum, we ensure compatibility with a broad range of touch sensors. We could show that data from a 30 s training phase is enough to add a new device model to the recognition system. As a proof of concept, the approach was applied to a visitor information system in a museum environment.

We identify devices with similar dimensions by incorporating position data from the mobile's integrated IMU. The gesture models for appear events have been simplified in order to achieve high flexibility in terms of using different types of mobile devices. The achieved classification accuracies qualify our approach for a variety of application scenarios where infrequent misclassifications are tolerable (e.g., a visitor information system or a multi-media presentation platform for meeting rooms).

Although we got satisfactory results in our testings, there are some limitations to the system's performance. First, the number of simultaneously used mobile devices has a strong impact on the reliability of the tracking, as the approach we propose is probabilistic. We found that misclassifications are unlikely for a small number of devices. Still, the likelihood of confusing two devices increases with every additional data stream that is transmitted to the tabletop. This means that the approach will perform poorly in application scenarios with a large amount of simultaneously active mobile devices. In this case, a proximity sensor could reduce the number of devices that communicate with the tabletop at a time. If the facility, for example, provides an indoor positioning system, the communication could be disabled for all units that are not in direct proximity to the interactive surface.

Apart from that, it is possible to intentionally evoke tracking errors by laying down the mobile at a very slow pace or by exactly timing two gestures with different devices to one another. However, we do not see this as a major drawback, as we did not observe any occasions where this happened by accident.

It should also be noted that a user has to pick up his or her device and place it down again in case the tabletop did not recognize it in the first place. This is a problem of all gesture based solutions for object recognition.

In the future, we intend to explore the possibilities of using an approach similar to the one presented in this work to reduce the amount of unintentional input on a touchscreen. More precisely, we want to validate whether an interaction model trained from a large data set of regular finger touches can be used to make a tabletop more robust against clothes or other objects accidentally touching the screen.

Acknowledgements. Philipp Mock was a doctoral student of the LEAD Graduate School [GSC1028], funded by the Excellence Initiative of the German federal and state governments.

References

1. Albarelli, A., Bergamasco, F., Celentano, A., Cosmo, L., Torsello, A.: Using multiple sensors for reliable markerless identification through supervised learning. Mach. Vision Appl. **24**(7), 1539–1554 (2013)
2. Hesselmann, T., Henze, N., Boll, S.: Flashlight: Optical communication between mobile phones and interactive tabletops. In: Proceedings of the ITS 2010, pp. 135–138. ACM (2010)
3. Hodges, S., Izadi, S., Butler, A., Rrustemi, A., Buxton, B.: Thinsight: Versatile multi-touch sensing for thin form-factor displays. In: Proceedings of the UIST 2007, pp. 259–268. ACM (2007)
4. Jovanovic, N., Korst, J., Pronk, V.: Object detection in flatland. In: Proceedings of the ADVCOMP 2009, pp. 95–100. IEEE Computer Society (2009)
5. Kaltenbrunner, M., Bencina, R.: Reactivision: a computer-vision framework for table-based tangible interaction. In: Proceedings of the TEI 2007, pp. 69–74. ACM (2007)
6. Kaltenbrunner, M., Bovermann, T., Bencina, R., Costanza, E.: Tuio: a protocol for table-top tangible user interfaces. In: Proceedings of the 2nd Interactive Sonification Workshop (2005)

7. Marquardt, N., Kiemer, J., Greenberg, S.: What caused that touch?: Expressive interaction with a surface through fiduciary-tagged gloves. In: Proceedings of the ITS 2010, pp. 139–142. ACM (2010)
8. Miyaoku, K., Higashino, S., Tonomura, Y.: C-blink: a hue-difference-based light signal marker for large screen interaction via any mobile terminal. In: Proceedings of the UIST 2004, pp. 147–156. ACM (2004)
9. Moeller, J., Kerne, A.: Zerotouch: an optical multi-touch and free-air interaction architecture. In: Proceedings of the CHI 2012, pp. 2165–2174. ACM (2012)
10. MultiTouch Ltd., Multitaction codice. http://www.multitaction.com/products/software/codice/
11. PQ Labs. G4 multi-touch screen. http://multitouch.com/product_g4.html
12. Schmidt, D., Chehimi, F., Rukzio, E., Gellersen, H.: Phonetouch: a technique for direct phone interaction on surfaces. In: Proceedings of the UIST 2010, pp. 13–16. ACM (2010)
13. Schöning, J., Rohs, M., Krüger, A.: Using mobile phones to spontaneously authenticate and interact with multi-touch surfaces. In: Proceedings of the Workshop on Designing Multitouch Interaction Techniques for Coupled Public and Private Displays (2008)

GlassNage: Layout Recognition for Dynamic Content Retrieval in Multi-Section Digital Signage

Adiyan Mujibiya[✉]

Rakuten Institute of Technology, Rakuten Inc., 4-13-9 Higashi-Shinagawa,
Shinagawa-Ku, Tokyo, Japan
adiyan@acm.org

Abstract. We report our approach to support dynamic content transfer from publicly available large display digital signage to users' private display, specifically Glass-like wearable devices. We aim to address issues concerning dynamic multimedia signage where the content are divided into several sections. This type of signage has become increasingly popular due to optimal content exposures. In contrast to prior research, our approach excludes computer vision based object recognition, and instead took an approach to identify how contents are being laid-out in a digital signage. We incorporate techniques to recognize basic layout features including corners, lines, edges, and line segments; which are obtained from the camera frame taken by the user using their own device. Consequently, these layout features are combined to generate *signage layout map*, which is then compared to pre-learned layout map for position detection and perspective correction using homography estimation. To grab a specific content, users are able to choose a section within the captured layout using the device's interface, which in turn creates a request to *contents server* to send respective content information based on a timestamp and a unique section ID. In this paper, we describe implementation details, report user study results, and conclude with discussion of our experiences in implementation as well as highlighting future work.

Keywords: Digital signage · Public display · Public-to-private · Multi section · Layout recognition · Computer vision · Visual features · Line segment · User study

1 Introduction

Due to the increasing availability and adoption of mobile smart devices, users can enjoy online shopping from any location reachable within a network. Users generally access applications that can record a significant amount of individual information; thus, users can engage in convenient and personalized shopping experiences relative to their context and preference. However, despite efforts to optimize visualization for small screens, visual representation to support marketing engagement of e-commerce items on mobile devices remains limited.

© Springer International Publishing Switzerland 2015
N. Streitz and P. Markopoulos (Eds.): DAPI 2015, LNCS 9189, pp. 337–348, 2015.
DOI: 10.1007/978-3-319-20804-6_31

Fig. 1. We report our approach to realize contents transfer from multi-section digital signage to users' private display, such as Glass-like wearable system. We use computer vision approach that includes corner, line, edge, and line segment detection to identify signage layout within user's camera view.

In recent years digital signage has penetrated significant numbers of indoors and outdoors public spaces and gradually replacing traditional printed or electric (bulbs/LED) billboards in train or bus stations, department stores, office entrances, on building walls, and many city streets. This trend is mainly driven by the decreasing cost to deploy large LCD displays that are practically suitable to visualize dynamic information, which can be customized and scheduled based on marketers' preference. These displays offer attractive visualizations of various types of content that can easily attract pedestrians' attention, thereby serving as strategic entry points for advertising and e-commerce. Interactive digital signage with large displays is suitable for dynamically presenting extensive information to a large number of users. The common practice to maximize content exposure in digital signage is to divide the screen canvas into several sections respective to content's type or genre. This multi-section signage offers clean layout design for supporting simultaneous multi-channel content delivery.

Significant numbers of users are hesitant to interact with public digital signage due to privacy concerns. Other people near the display can easily see private activities and content, which makes users reluctant to input personal information such as names, passwords, credit card numbers, and addresses. Marketers also observed that depending on the digital signage's location and content, users are hesitant to even show interest to publicly visible signage; therefore limiting the strategic effectiveness of deploying advertisements in digital signage. We believe that an effective solution to maximize limited resources and obtain maximum user experience is the sharing of a large display to visualize extensive information and displaying personalized content on the users' private display.

Research aiming to close the gap between public signage and user's private mobile devices has been conducted very actively in Human-Computer Interaction (HCI) field [1–8]. In this work, we specifically address content bridging for multi-section digital signage. Search query keywords, URLs, QR codes as well as other 1D/2D barcodes are still widely used to provide users with an affordance to access a specific content's detailed information. However, excessive usage of texts, visual codes, and URLs are incompatible for multi-section signage due to spatial and design constraints.

In this paper, we report *GlassNage*, an approach to address aforementioned issues by implementing *signage layout recognition* based on computer vision techniques, which includes corner, lines, edges, and line segment detection of images captured on the user's device. The aforementioned 2D features are used to generate *signage layout map*, which is then matched with pre-learned layout map to define which layout is being used, and further, to detect corrected perspective using homography calculation. To grab a specific content, users are able to choose a section within the captured layout using the device's interface, which in turn creates a request to *content server* to send respective info based on a timestamp and a unique section ID. Actual usage scenario is depicted in Fig. 1.

Using this approach, we mitigate requirement to pre-learn content for section-specific object recognition, thus allowing dynamic changes of content in each section. In real-world practices, these dynamic content include seasonal scheduling, real-time updates, changing contents source/channel, and so on. Moreover, our layout recognition performs in real-time at up to 8 fps for 720 p resolution (1280 × 720), deployed in a Glass-like wearable device with OMAP4430 2 GB RAM dual-core System-on-Chip (SoC), on the Android 4.4.2 operating system.

In this paper, we contribute to HCI community by presenting *GlassNage* prototype design and implementation, as well as user study evaluation results. In addition, we also discuss limitations, insights, and design principles for future work and for other researchers with similar interests to bridge public content for private consumption.

2   Related Work

Various research and development in online-to-offline (and vice versa) shopping approaches using signage have been undertaken. TESCO deployed a trial advertising campaign that leverages static QR codes for product displays in a subway station [7]. Users could access product websites by scanning the QR codes with their devices. However, despite recent advancements in QR codes as well as other 1D/2D barcodes technology [9], these codes remain visually perceivable cues that potentially clutter signage design. Moreover, in multi-section dynamically scheduled content signage, putting visual codes on each section of signage layout is not a feasible solution.

A recent survey has highlighted the need for research in interactive digital signage that utilizes both public and private screens [1]. Turner [2] proposed cross-device eye-based interaction, which is a content-sharing mechanism that combines user gaze information with mobile input modalities to enable content transfer between public and personal displays in close proximity. However, this system requires special devices to detect public display and map user gaze information to a screen. SWINGNAGE [8] is a gesture-based mobile interaction system for a distant public display that focuses on item search and comparison on the public display. Users interact with content on the display using private devices. However, users are required to perform device pairing, which is based on the detection of user gesture information with a mobile device using a depth-camera. Due to camera line-of-sight issues and vision-based user-tracking limitations, this pairing mechanism is not feasible when multiple users simultaneously connect to the display from a relatively distant location.

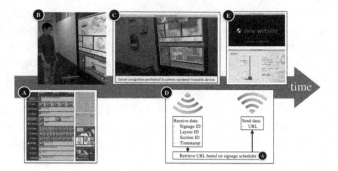

Fig. 2. Workflow of our proposed approach involves: (a) signage display is managed by a content scheduling server, and when (b) a user has interest to the content in a specific section of the signage, s/he uses *GlassNage* app installed in a wearable Glass device to perform layout recognition and section selection (c). Selected signage section ID paired with a timestamp is (d) sent to the server to obtain relevant info of the selected content (e). Consequently, user is able to perform follow-up actions within his/her private display.

Touch-Projector [4, 6] and Shoot & Copy [5] highlight a method to leverage camera equipped mobile device to recognize content that are being visualized in larger public screen, this method is referred as *mobile interaction through video*. Although partially sharing common concept of the underlined computer vision methodology, *GlassNage* focuses on applicability and deployment scaling in commercial signage, hence we extend the system design and implementation to omit the requirement of a *central processing server*, i.e., layout recognition is being performed in users' private device. *GlassNage*'s target is commercial or marketing digital signage; therefore, we focus on user's privacy protection and enhance the system to provide detailed information of a specific content on users' private display.

3   GlassNage Implementation

3.1   Interaction Scenario Using GlassNage Framework

We highlight the framework of our proposed approach in Fig. 2. The signage content is developed on the top of Adobe Integration Runtime (Adobe AIR) platform. We construct a signage content scheduler server to control visualization for multiple displays, as well as to handle requests sent from *GlassNage* app.

When a user is interested in a specific content of the digital signage, s/he uses *GlassNage* app to take an image that captures a large part of the signage. The application subsequently performs signage layout recognition, and then overlays recognized layout in the users' private display. User is then able to select which section does s/he wish to obtain more detailed information. User's selected section ID paired with a timestamp will be sent to the server for obtaining a URL, which is a link to a web page containing detailed information of its respective content. *GlassNage* app will visualize the received URL to give users a notification to view this information.

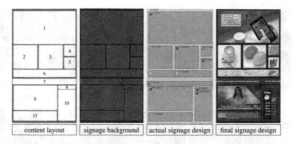

Fig. 3. We describe signage layout design process that is necessary to be compatible with *GlassNage* framework. First, we define a static *content layout* that serves as a ground truth for our layout recognition. Second, we fill the layout with a background design that preserves visual characteristics of the content layout. Third, we assign content source for each section of the signage using server side application. The contents in each section can be dynamically scheduled. Lastly, we fill the frame with actual content

3.2 Digital Signage Layout Design Approach

We describe our layout design approach in Fig. 3. We define a static layout consisting multiple sections, and assign a unique ID for each section. For visual enhancement, we create signage frame that functions as a placeholder for each section, as well as to increase visual affordance of the multi-section design. We select background design that largely preserves visual characteristics of the predefined static layout. Based on this layout, we assign content source for each section. Lastly, we fill the layout with assigned content for final visualization. Our prototype incorporates 11 sections (Fig. 3, left), which includes content such as café interior and exterior image slideshow, food and beverage menu image slideshow, special offer image slideshow, news (text and video), as well as weather forecast. We chose this layout mainly to represent typical model of multi-section signage deployed in cafés. Additionally, we intended to create more challenging recognition problem for testing purposes.

3.3 Layout Recognition

We implement client-server protocol to realize layout recognition and content distribution. Our layout recognition software was implemented within the *GlassNage* mobile application, which was mostly written in Java, with some parts in C ++ for computationally resource consuming functions. We utilize camera equipped Glass-like wearable as target device, considering that the device is equipped with a see-through optical head-mount display that will enhance user experience on public-to-private content retrieval.

We aggregate visual features such as corners, lines, edges, and line segments; to obtain computational model of the signage layout based on relative positioning of the aforementioned visual features. We use these 2D features due to the low computation time that is crucial for deploying the algorithm to mobile device with limited computing resources. Firstly, we apply this approach to the base content layout (Fig. 3, left)

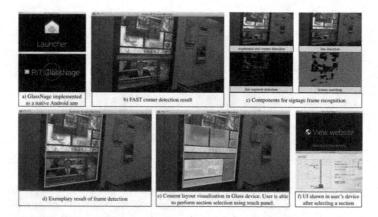

Fig. 4. We developed a mobile app, namely *GlassNage*, to perform the following functions: (1) layout recognition from an image captured using camera equipped device, (2) perform perspective correction, (3) let a user selects a section which s/he wants to receive further information from, and (4) visualize a website containing content's detailed information. We describe our layout recognition approach in (b)–(e).

to form ground truth content layout map, which is utilized to match with features aggregated from the same approach that is applied to the camera frame. We implemented our matching using FLANN [10]. We describe the overview of our layout recognition approach in Fig. 4(b)–(d).

3.4   User's Selection Method and Visualizing the Result

An exemplary figure of user's view after successful layout recognition is depicted in Fig. 4(e). The green outline visualizes the detected signage layout, and sections are highlighted in colored shades. To select a section, user can browse through sections using the Glass device's touch interface by flick gestures. For other mobile device such as smartphones, users can simply tap on the desired color-shaded section.

After user selection has been confirmed, the *GlassNage* mobile application creates a request to the content distribution server to send back a URL that refers to details or further information related to selected section (depicted in Fig. 2(d)). This request contains data such as signage ID, layout ID, section ID, and a timestamp (obtained when user's selection is confirmed). The server side of our system also manages contents scheduling, therefore pairing between a specific timestamp to layout section ID and its' respective content is straightforward. After receiving and process this request, the server will then send a URL to the client *GlassNage* mobile application. The user is then presented with the URL on their private heads-up display, and has the choice to browse detailed content using the browser.

4   Evaluation

4.1   GlassNage Application Statistics

To evaluate *GlassNage* mobile application performance, we used Android application analysis tools available in the Android SDK. We deployed *GlassNage* in a Glass-like wearable device with OMAP4430 2 GB RAM dual-core System-on-Chip (SoC), on Android 4.4.2 operating system. Our layout recognition performs in real-time at up to 8 fps for 1280 × 720 (720 p) resolution. The camera of this device had 54.8 degrees horizontal and 42.5 degrees vertical Angle-of-View. A series of quantitative and qualitative user study were conducted to test the feasibility of *GlassNage* approach. The results are presented in the following subsections.

4.2   Focus of the User Study

In our experiments, we used *GlassNage* mobile application that was deployed in a Glass-like wearable device. We identified a usability issue when a user is trying to frame the content that they are actually seeing with the camera frame. I.e., natural users' Field-of-Vision (FoV) do not align well with the camera's Angle-of-View (AoV). This is mainly caused by:

1. There is only a single camera, i.e. not stereoscopic, which does not compensate 3D gaze.
2. The position of the camera is in the front-right part of the frame, which does not match with human FoV's centroid.
3. The camera only has a relatively narrow AoV (54.8 degrees horizontal and 42.5 degrees vertical), compared to in total of 124 degrees FoV of the human.

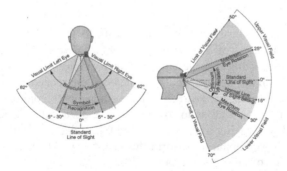

Fig. 5. We identify an issue in framing a user's Field-of-Vision (FoV, shown in blue shade) against the Glass device camera's Angle-of-View (AoV, shown in red shade). In this figure, we illustrate where these two viewing angles overlaps to each other. From this illustration, we can observe that when a user is looking horizontally straight, a part of the camera's AoV is actually outside the user's typical paracentral and near-peripheral FoV area. In vertical scenario, we can observe that some parts of user's near-peripheral FoV (when considering eye rotation) are not covered by the static camera AoV.

We illustrate our finding in Fig. 5. Based on this finding, we first focused in indicative factors of users targeting behaviour and also their accuracy. The second focus of our study was to assess users' perceptual workload when using *GlassNage*.

4.3   Quantitative User Study

We conduct a series quantitative user study to test users behaviour as well as their accuracy when trying to align their perceptual FoV and Glass device's camera AoV.

Participants. We recruited six participants for this study. The participants were all from outside of our research organization. They were 4 male and 2 female, age 25.4 ± 4.21 years old. All of the participants were familiar with the Glass-like wearable device, and were confident of wearing, seeing the display, and interact with the side-mounted touch panel.

Table 1. The absolute deviations (mean ± std) of gazing towards a target

Sect#	Absolute deviations (pixels) per-participant						Mean
	1	2	3	4	5	6	
1	32.61 ± 14.12	23.1 ± 9.18	31.21 ± 8.36	53.47 ± 16.85	46.1 ± 23.42	33.63 ± 16.28	36.68 ± 14.7
2	21.8 ± 6.31	18.17 ± 8.22	24.15 ± 12.56	19.1 ± 13.17	27.42 ± 10.41	23.32 ± 10.86	22.32 ± 10.26
3	34.21 ± 12.68	26.21 ± 8.54	23.2 ± 8.43	34.74 ± 14.29	41.12 ± 12.56	38.32 ± 15.91	32.97 ± 12.06
4	15.56 ± 12.23	24.14 ± 8.62	31.93 ± 10.12	28.24 ± 12.86	22.48 ± 8.41	31.43 ± 15.35	25.63 ± 11.27
5	20.72 ± 12.12	17.45 ± 9.32	19.33 ± 16.51	23.4 ± 18.35	27.14 ± 11.23	16.55 ± 13.84	20.77 ± 13.56
6	57.42 ± 23.72	48.04 ± 21.61	32.12 ± 16.35	43.63 ± 12.11	39.55 ± 23.2	53.32 ± 21.61	45.68 ± 19.79
7	64.13 ± 18.44	54.56 ± 21.85	32.94 ± 12.66	45.34 ± 23.56	35.46 ± 17.87	44.71 ± 13.94	46.19 ± 18.05
8	28.13 ± 8.24	32.65 ± 12.43	23.55 ± 14.82	62.04 ± 34.7	18.76 ± 6.76	34.96 ± 18.21	33.35 ± 15.86
9	16.84 ± 6.33	24.85 ± 10.57	19.49 ± 8.8	22.43 ± 10.04	33.14 ± 13.19	17.56 ± 8.21	22.39 ± 9.52
10	24.12 ± 9.28	18.43 ± 5.86	23.17 ± 12.18	17.45 ± 4.88	25.37 ± 8.12	16.13 ± 9.36	31.73 ± 8.28
11	32.11 ± 13.61	27.34 ± 16.51	34.73 ± 16.44	23.49 ± 12.03	37.26 ± 9.43	31.2 ± 10.22	31.02 ± 13.04

Procedures. Firstly, we instructed the participants to stand 2 meters in front of a 60-inch monitor that was pivoted vertically (resembles the setup depicted in Fig. 1 left). The monitor was displaying signage content that previously described in Fig. 3. We assigned 11 sections in the signage, and presented content related to coffee shop menu, news, weather, etc. Second, we instructed the participants to comfortably center their head posture and FoV, as well as to focus their eye gaze onto a designated section, promptly followed with taking a picture with the Glass-like wearable device's camera app. We asked each participant to perform this task for all 11 sections of the signage, and repeat this series of tasks for 5 times.

Data Statistics. For each signage section, we obtained 5 images from each participant; i.e., in total we have 30 images capturing the same signage section. The images were taken using the 5MP camera of the Glass-like wearable device, which translates to 2528×1856 pixel resolution. We imported the images from the internal storage of the Glass-like wearable device into a desktop PC to perform further analysis. We did not change the size or aspect ratio of the images.

Processing and Analysis. Firstly, we locate the centroid of each image (xc, yc) = (1129, 928). We then locate the target signage section in the image, extract the centroid (xs, ys), and calculate the Euclidean distance between image centroid (xc, yc) = (1129, 928) and captured section centroid (xs, ys).

Results. We compile the results in Table 1. Table 1 shows a comprehensive comparison of how users targeting behaviour and accuracy are affected by the size and position of the signage sections. Section number 1, 2, 3, 8, and 10 represent larger signage section area. In these sections, users' center targeting absolute deviations were relatively high. Section 6, 7, 9, and 11 represents horizontally wide sections. Notably for section number 6 and 7, absolute deviations were the highest of all sections. Interestingly, sections with small area such as 4, 5, and 9 have relatively lower absolute deviations.

Insights and Design Implications. We observe participants' behavior during the signage section targeting study, as an addition to the assessment of participants' accuracy when trying to align their perceptual FoV and Glass device's camera AoV. We compile our insights as listed below:

1. Participants tended to perform fine-adjustment to their framing when targeting at sections that have small area (e.g. section number 4, 5, 9). Therefore, we can conclude that users are more cautious during targeting (hence their overall absolute deviations are lower), when compared to targeting sections with larger area.
2. Sections with larger area give users more instant confidence in targeting task. However, the absolute deviations are relatively high. Therefore, we need to incorporate more deviation permissive framing procedure to the GlassNage app, or any other system that relies on Glass-mounted camera capture.
3. Sections with horizontally wide area are quite difficult for users to target, when we compare users targeting with section's centroid. This is mainly due to spatial perception of users when framing such sections, where users are more likely to be satisfied with their framing although it's not horizontally centered.
4. Overall, using our Glass-like wearable device, we learned that more sophisticated alignment method is desirable to support users' perceptual matching between their FoV and Glass device's camera AoV. In current *GlassNage* implementation, we mitigate this issue with allowing the user to firstly capture an image, and then perform layout recognition. By doing so, we allow users to capture image that consists their section-of-interest, as well as other important landmark features.

4.4 Qualitative User Study

A qualitative user satisfaction study was conducted to test the usability of *GlassNage*. We recruited the same participants as the previous Quantitative User Study.

Procedures. Each participant was provided with a Glass-like wearable device that was pre-installed with *GlassNage* application. S/he was then given a brief introduction followed by a set of instructions on how to use *GlassNage*. This was immediately followed by asking each participant to interact with the app and digital signage. The experimenter intervened when specific questions were asked, or when the instructions were misunderstood. After the exercise, the participants were asked questions related to the perceived workload from the NASA-TLX assessment [11].

In addition, "Was *GlassNage* hard to learn?" was always added into the questionnaire to gain insight on learning curve of *GlassNage*. This was followed by several general questions about *GlassNage* that are shown below:

1. Did *GlassNage* make the content browsing experience more enjoyable?
2. Did you feel that fetching content items through *GlassNage* is more effective than previously available methods?
3. Do you have any additional comments?

All the questions above were rated using the Likert scale (1: strongly agree – 5: strongly disagree).

Results. Table 2 shows the participants' rating on the perceived workload (NASA-TLX) of the user study.

Table 2. The ratings (mean ± std) of the NASA-TLX questions

Subscale	Question	Rating
Mental demand	Did *GlassNage* require a lot of mental demand?	3.61 ± 1.52
Physical demand	Did *GlassNage* require a lot of physical activity?	4.60 ± 1.32
Temporal demand	Did you feel time pressure why using *GlassNage*?	4.52 ± 0.21
Effort	Did *GlassNage* require a lot of effort to use?	3.24 ± 1.42
Frustration	Was *GlassNage* frustrating to use?	3.64 ± 1.25
Learning	Was *GlassNage* hard to learn?	4.23 ± 1.52
Overall performance	Overall did *GlassNage* perform well?	1.21 ± 1.51

The results from Table 2 show that participants felt positive while using *Glass-Nage*. The average rating for the subscale "mental demand", "effort", and "frustration" was the lowest at 3.61 ± 1.52, 3.24 ± 1.42, and 3.64 ± 1.25, respectively. On the other hand, the participants showed positive feelings that *GlassNage* was not difficult to learn (4.23 ± 1.52). Finally, the participants felt that overall *GlassNage* did perform well (1.21 ± 1.51).

The general questions suggested that subjects agree that *GlassNage* did make the content browsing experience more enjoyable (1.02 ± 0.24) and also felt that *GlassNage* is more effective (1.43 ± 0.84) than previous methods of content fetching.

Many comments were given regarding technical issues in the application such as:

1. Implement finger pointing gesture recognition to select content rather than using touch panel.
2. Implement faster signage section recognition framework.
3. Include a function to "push" information to public signage

In addition to the user obtained feedbacks, we observed that some participants initially had difficulties to grab a frame capture of their desired section. This is coherent with the issue we raise in Quantitative User Study subsection. This motivates us to explore ways to mitigate this problem.

5 Discussion

With *GlassNage* we explored a simplistic design to incorporate signage layout recognition to assist users in selecting the specific part of dynamic signage content. We realize that our simplistic design may only work for very particular interface designs that consist of different tiles with clear contours. However, we believe that this work contributes in highlighting the maximal result using minimal computational strategy, and discuss limitation of this particular strategy.

A limitation remains that borders between content must remain visible; to be recognizable as line or line segments. We argue that visible borders can be incorporated within the signage design itself; hence mitigate the visual sense of a *frame*. In the case of content appearing as 2D features, our layout features incorporate correlation between lines, corners, and line segments, hence mitigate the false negatives. Temporal comparison between multiple frames can also be implemented to filter non-static lines, corners, and line segments.

6 Conclusion and Future Work

We presented *GlassNage*, an approach to support dynamic content transfer from publicly available large display digital signage that has multiple sections, to users' private display. We implemented a series of computer vision techniques to detect and recognize content layout. We have conducted quantitative and qualitative user study to evaluate users' targeting behavior, users' perceived workload, and *GlassNage* framework usability. We also highlighted insights and interface design implications which were aggregated from the user study results and observation of participants' behavior. In future iteration of this research, we plan to explore non-distractive layout frame visualization, and finding appropriate interface design to accommodate smoother user's section selection.

References

1. She, J., Crowcroft, J., Fu, H., Li, F.: Convergence of interactive displays with smart mobile devices for effective advertising: a survey. ACM Trans. Multimedia Comput. Commun. Appl. **10**(2), Article 17, 16 pp. (2014) doi:10.1145/2557450
2. Turner, J.: Cross-device eye-based interaction. In: Proceedings of the Adjunct Publication of the 26th Annual ACM Symposium on User Interface Software and Technology (UIST 2013 Adjunct), pp. 37–40. ACM, New York, NY, USA (2013). doi:10.1145/2508468.2508471
3. von Gioi, R.G., Jakubowicz, J., Morel, J.-M., Randall, G.: LSD: a line segment detector. Image Process. Line **2**(2012), 35–55 (2012). http://dx.doi.org/10.5201/ipol.2012.gjmr-lsd
4. Boring, S., Baur, D., Butz, A., Gustafson, S., Baudisch, P.: Touch projector: mobile interaction through video. In: Proceedings of the SIGCHI Conference on Human Factors in Computing Systems (CHI 2010), pp. 2287–2296. ACM, New York, NY, USA (2010). doi:10.1145/1753326.1753671

5. Boring, S., Altendorfer, M., Broll, G., Hilliges, O., Butz, A.: Shoot and copy: phonecam-based information transfer from public displays onto mobile phones. In: Proceedings of the 4th International Conference on Mobile Technology, Applications, and Systems and the 1st International Symposium on Computer Human Interaction in Mobile Technology (Mobility 2007), pp. 24–31. ACM, New York, NY, USA (2007). doi:10.1145/1378063.1378068

6. Boring, S., Gehring, S., Wiethoff, A., Blöckner, A.M., Schöning, J., Butz, A.: Multi-user interaction on media facades through live video on mobile devices. In: Proceedings of the SIGCHI Conference on Human Factors in Computing Systems (CHI 2011), pp. 2721–2724. ACM, New York, NY, USA (2011). doi:10.1145/1978942.1979342

7. The QR Code Tesco Store: From Concept to Reality. http://2d-code.co.uk/tesco-qr-code-store/. Accessed 20 Feb 2015

8. Yamaguchi, T., Fukushima, H., Tatsuzawa, S., Nonaka, M., Takashima, K., Kitamura, Y.: SWINGNAGE: gesture-based mobile interactions on distant public displays. In: Proceedings of the 2013 ACM International Conference on Interactive Tabletops and Surfaces (ITS 2013), pp. 329–332 (2013). ACM, New York, NY, USA. doi:10.1145/2512349.2514596

9. Chu, H.-K., Chang, C.-S., Lee, R.-R., Mitra, N.J.: Halftone QR codes. ACM Trans. Graph. Article 217 32(6), 8 pp. (2013). doi:10.1145/2508363.2508408

10. Muja, M., Lowe, D.: Fast approximate nearest neighbors with automatic algorithm configuration. In: Proceedings of the International Conference on Computer Vision Theory and Applications, pp. 331–340 (2009)

11. Hart, S.G., Staveland, L.E.: Development of NASA-TLX (Task Load Index): results of empirical and theoretical research. Adv. Psychol. 52, 139–183 (1988). North-Holland, ISSN 0166-4115, ISBN 9780444703880

Manseibashi Reminiscent Window: On-Site AR Exhibition System Using Mobile Devices

Naoya Okada$^{(\boxtimes)}$, Jun Imura, Takuji Narumi, Tomohiro Tanikawa,
and Michitaka Hirose

Graduate School of Information Science and Technology, The University of Tokyo,
Hongo 7-3-1, Bunkyo-ku, Tokyo 113-8656, Japan
{m_okada,imura,narumi,tani,hirose}@cyber.t.u-tokyo.ac.jp

Abstract. In this research, we propose the design of a sustainable on-site past-scene experience system applied in a public location using personal mobile user devices. Through our system, to experience an AR exhibition, users simply download an AR application onto their personal mobile device. By superimposing a past-scene image of an actual site onto the present scene, users can appreciate the past scene on-site through their own device without the need for any special AR device or support staff. We held both attended and unattended on-site exhibitions to evaluate the social acceptableness and effectiveness of the proposed unattended exhibition system. The results show that, using the personal mobile devices of the users, the proposed system is deemed socially acceptable, and that our unattended exhibition system can evoke and maintain user interest as much as an attended exhibition. In addition, we have been distributing this system as an iPad/iPhone application through the Internet, and the number of users is continuously increasing, thereby proving the sustainability of our proposed exhibition system.

Keywords: Augmented reality · Digital museum · Mobile device · Public exhibition

1 Introduction

Museums have attempted to effectively convey their exhibits in various ways. It is important that not only the exhibit itself but also its background information be conveyed to viewers [1]. However, museum exhibitions cannot sufficiently convey background information because the materials are not in the related locations. In addition, certain types of materials such as architectural constructions or civil structures cannot be exhibited inside a museum because of their size. Therefore, a new type of exhibition system is needed to show on-site exhibits outside a museum. On the other hand, to realize a more effective exhibition than that achievable through existing methods, which use panels or displays, researches regarding an interactive exhibition system using augmented reality (AR) technology have been recently reported [2]. Arakawa affirmed that users can feel a sense of immersion more deeply, and can understand a geometric

© Springer International Publishing Switzerland 2015
N. Streitz and P. Markopoulos (Eds.): DAPI 2015, LNCS 9189, pp. 349–361, 2015.
DOI: 10.1007/978-3-319-20804-6_32

space, the exhibition itself, and the intention of the camera operators by actively moving their bodies according to video sequences recording the motion of the exhibit [3]. Moreover, an outside exhibition using AR was developed, the results of which show that exhibiting historical materials superimposed onto an actual space is very effective at motivating users to learn history and have a greater understanding of a particular exhibit [4].

However, field exhibitions using AR are still temporary or limited experiments, and a system for creating exhibitions in a public space that can fulfill the functions of a real museum has yet to be designed. In order to realize a continuous exhibition on site, various limitations for operation in public space need to be taken into account. One of the biggest limitations is that docents required for the exhibition or terminals cannot be set up in an actual location. Therefore, in this research, we aim to establish a new type of outside exhibition in a public space of an urban district that is sustainable even without the use of a docent. We designed an on-site past-scene experience system for use in a public space by applying mobile user devices, and published our system as a mobile application. Users simply have to download our application onto their own device when they visit an exhibit. By holding their device toward the present scene, they can see a past version of the scene and learn how historical architecture or civil structures change over time. We held both attended and unattended on-site exhibitions to evaluate the social acceptableness and effectiveness of our proposed system.

2   Related Works

In this section, we first introduce previous researches regarding outside exhibition systems. We then describe some methods used to generate panoramic images from real photography or video materials, which we make use of in this research. Finally, we describe a guidance method we developed on our own to induce the users to react to and appreciate the image materials provided as they were intended.

Many exhibition systems for use outside of a museum have been developed to convey background information on an architectural environment that cannot be saved inside a museum and is closely related to a real location. On-site virtual time machine [5] is an AR exhibition system that superimposes past-scene photographs onto a current scene through a PC display. It associates past images with the current state using Bundler [6], and estimates the position and attitude of the camera using PTAM [7], which realizes a geometrically natural overlay. This study shows that users can understand the history of an exhibit more deeply by seeing images superimposed through a PC display than by simply viewing printed images on-site. Archeoguide [8] and OutdoorGallery [9] are examples of outside AR exhibition systems, which construct 3D models of the Olympia and Asuka-kyo ruins and superimpose them over a real location. However, these models are quite different from the real ruins. If real photograms of the subject are available, they can help users learn the history of the exhibit better than 3D models because users can see the surrounding area around the main exhibit as well as the real images, thereby better matching the actual scene. These systems use a Head Mounted Display (HMD) for a video presentation, and GPS, DGPS,

(Differential Global Positioning System), and an MR system [10] with a magnetometric sensor for position measurements. Therefore, assistants to hand out an HMD to users and transmitters used for sensing need to be available on-site. However, for users to be able to visit and appreciate an outside exhibition any time they like, it is essential that the exhibition be manageable without the use of any assistants. In addition, placing transmitters or AR markers at the location prevents the sustainability of an exhibition owing to their maintenance requirements, and devices that emit electric waves or magnetism can have an adverse effect on the location itself. Therefore, the personnel distribution or installation of special devices should be avoided in a sustainable exhibition in the public space of an urban district. In this research, we developed an unattended system without the installation of any special devices. Users can visit and appreciate an exhibit using their own personal mobile device such as an iPhone or iPad.

To take images from all perspectives and take advantage of the high reality of photographs and video sequences, a technique called Image Based Rendering (IBR) can be used. One of the most basic methods of IBR is reconstructing the image corresponding to any visual line direction using a panoramic image. QuicktimeVR (QTVR) [11] can be used to render and present an image clipped from a panoramic image according to the visual line direction of the user. Although it is generally not easy to take a panoramic image directly, panoramic stitching technologies, which are used to generate a panoramic image automatically from images taken by normal cameras, have been developed. We can easily access such features using Microsoft's Image Composite Editor [12].

In AR systems used for educational purposes, it is effective for users to freely and actively appreciate an exhibit. However, users are liable to overlook some important aspects of the content or continually view unimportant points, which can harm the educational effect. Therefore, a method to induce the users attention is needed. Indicating words or symbols explicitly in certain regions of a video sequence to attract the user's attention can prevent viewers from discovering features in non-indicated regions. Research has shown that users tend to remember the points they discover voluntarily for a longer period of time than those points explicitly indicated by the applied system [5]. Therefore, in this research, we induce the users attention by adding ambient effects to the displayed image. We developed a method to notify the user regarding a specific region of the image and attract their attention in an AR system using a rotation with a degree of freedom [13]. In our method, we induce the user's gaze by changing the brightness of the area around the point of attention according to a specific pattern based on Saliency-guided Enhancement (SGE) [14].

3   Design of Proposed System

3.1   Summary of Proposed System

The outline of our proposed system is as follows:

1. Users visit the exhibition location. They install the appropriate application onto their own mobile device either on-site or in advance.

2. They look for the point where a photograph of a past scene was taken by holding their mobile device toward the present scene.
3. The application compares the device camera image to the reference scene image taken in advance, and calculates the device position and orientation.
4. If the application determines that the user is standing at the correct point and facing the proper direction, it renders the whole-sky image area of the past scene generated using photographic materials.
5. By moving their devices around, users can see the past scene in the direction they are facing through the screen of the device. They can also easily compare the present scene to the past scene by changing the transparency of the device camera image.

3.2   Detailed Design for On-Site Exhibition

Through some user tests, we determined that there are three requirements for realizing an on-site exhibition.

Registration Between a Device and the Real Place. The first requirement is to obtain the correct starting position and orientation of the device. It is difficult to place measurement devices or AR markers in a public location, as mentioned earlier. Some mobile AR systems use GPS-based positioning. However, GPS cannot provide sufficient accuracy, especially inside buildings or in urban districts where many blocking objects exist. Therefore, we specify the starting position based only on image feature points without the use of any other equipment, and achieve a high registration accuracy.

First, we take a photograph of the present scene in advance at the same location where a photograph of a past scene was taken. This photo is used as a reference image to recognize the target scene retrieved by the camera of the users device. Within the center rectangle region of the device frame, a translucent reference image is displayed along with the divided camera image covering the whole frame. The users can then look for the point where the reference image was taken by seeing a translucent image on their device display. The system extracts the feature points of both the reference and device camera image, and calculates the position and orientation of the device. We adopted SURF [15] for the feature points, which realizes a fast calculation even on a mobile device. We also use RANSAC [16] to remove incorrect matches. Finally, if the system determines that the camera image of the device is sufficiently similar to the reference image, it shows a panoramic image of the past scene aligned with the reference image in advance. There is a problem in that the visual performance is different between daytime and nighttime. To realize robust matching and registration, we prepare two different reference images for the daytime and nighttime, and switch them according to the present time. Our user test showed that the proposed system can achieve a robust recognition if users stand within a 1-m radius of the correct point where the reference photo was taken. In addition to automatic matching, we optionally provide a manually matching button for users to push when they judge that a correct registration has been achieved.

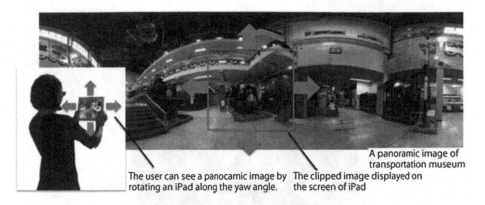

A panoramic image of transportation museum

The user can see a panocamic image by rotating an iPad along the yaw angle.   The clipped image displayed on the screen of iPad

Fig. 1. Interactive display of a panoramic image

Fig. 2. Screen capture of our system: The background image is a past image, and the central rectangle shows the camera view of the device.

Interactive Image Presentation Based on Actual Photographs. An interactive image presentation requires an operation that is sufficiently easy to understand even without the use of a docent. In our system, we mainly use panoramic images compounded from digitalized photographs through panoramic stitching, and users can appreciate a past scene by rotating their devices at the proper location (Fig. 1). We used Microsofts Image Composite Editor [12] to generate panoramic images based on material photographs belonging to our research group. To reproduce a past scene location, we place a spheroidal polygon on a virtual space and attach a panoramic image to it as a texture. The device calculates the position using its acceleration and gyro sensor, and displays the image clipped from the panoramic image according to the direction that the device is facing. However, a gyro sensor cannot retrieve the absolute angle, although it can retrieve the relative angle. In our system, the users first obtain the starting position based on image features, and the system then calculates the orientation of the device on the relative yaw angle from the direction of the reference image. Figure 2 shows a screen capture of our proposed system. The image covering the

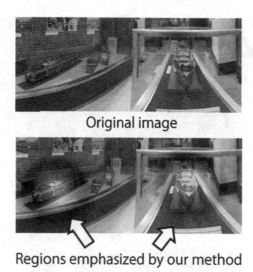

Fig. 3. Visual guidance using a brightness change filter

whole screen is a past scene image clipped from a panoramic image, and the central rectangle is the current camera view of the device. To view a wider area of the scene, the system enables the users to adjust the size of the displayed area using a slider placed on the right side of the screen. Moreover, users can change the transparency of the camera view using another slider on the left side (Figure 3).

Guiding User's Visual Line. All content provided has a point of attention, where we expect users to look at without fail. In a sustainable outside exhibition, however, it is difficult to provide a description using panels or a docent. For this research, we generated a method to easily notify the users of a specific area of an image [13], and the user's active experience is assured by displaying the image area according to the direction they are facing.

Applying our method in a laboratory environment, the users tended to keep an eye on a high-saliency area, and our method did not prevent them from discovering other parts of the image when compared to a method that points out symbols or words. By applying this method to the proposed system, we expect the users to look at and observe the point of attention in more detail. In our implementation, changing the intensity can be achieved very quickly even on a mobile device through a parallel computation using the programmable shader of the GPU when the image is rendered as a 3DCG.

4   Field Experiments

4.1   Experimental Settings and Procedures

To evaluate the educational effect of our system and verify whether it can induce the appropriate level of appreciation in an unattended environment, we

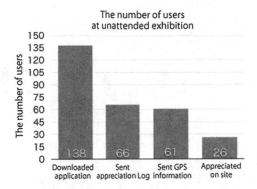

Fig. 4. The number of users who downloaded the application

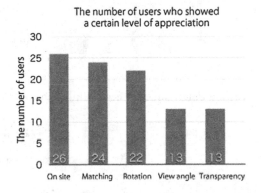

Fig. 5. The number of users who showed a certain level of appreciation

conducted two types of field experiments for the general public. One experiment is for an attended exhibition, in which users are guided by docents available at the site, and the other experiment is for an unattended exhibition, in which users can experience our proposed system using their own mobile device. We evaluated whether the proposed system functions effectively as an on-site exhibition method by measuring the level of appreciation and questionnaire results of the users. We also evaluated the effect of our method under an on-site environment.

For the exhibition location, we adopted mAAch Ecute Kanda Manseibashi and the JR Kanda Manseibashi Building, which are commercial facilities and an office building in Akihabara, Tokyo, respectively. Manseibashi Station existed at this location until 1943, as did a transportation museum until 2006. While this place is very valuable when considering the evolution of the railway development and changes in local culture in Tokyo, it is difficult to realize an exhibition that conveys such history because additional equipment cannot be installed here. We developed an exhibition at this location by applying seven panoramic images and one normal image. A plan view showing the arrangement of the content of the eight different images is displayed on the device screen to help the users discover the starting point of each content.

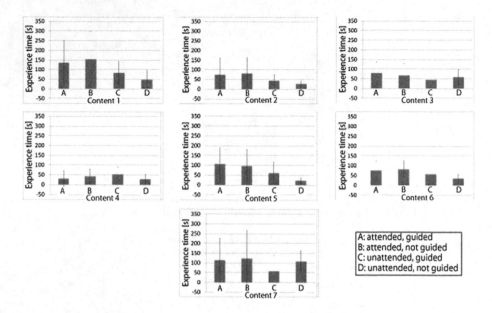

Fig. 6. Experience time for each exhibition content

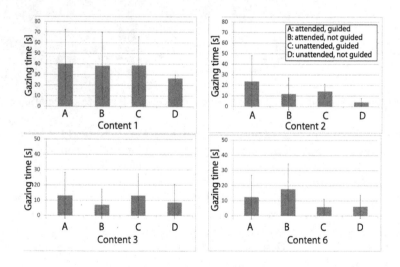

Fig. 7. The time gazing at certain spots

Attended Exhibition with Navigation Using Docents. We conducted an attended exhibition for six days from August 2013 to January 2014, in which docents and explainers were available on-site. The subjects were general participants recruited through an Internet announcement and on-site, and a total of about 100 subjects used our system during these six days. The exhibition was carried out using a tour format with one docent, or a student who received historical education from a docent, made available. We guided the subjects to move on to the next content after we determined that they were sufficiently satisfied with the current content. To use the proposed system, we lent an iPad to the subjects. We continuously measured and recorded the values of the device's gyro sensor as the user's level of appreciation. When the docents or explainers were unavailable, we judged whether the subjects sufficiently understood the objects shown in the exhibition by setting this level of appreciation as the target value for the unattended exhibition.

Unattended Exhibition Using User's Personal Mobile Device. To evaluate the effectiveness of our system in a real environment, we distributed our system through a free iPad and iPhone application, which was downloadable from the Internet. To allow the users to see how to use the system even when a docent was not present, we provided a simple tutorial on how to find the starting point and how to change the transparency and viewing angle. By measuring the level of appreciation of an unspecified number of users, we verified whether our system can motivate users to experience an exhibition in a public space, whether they can appreciate our system appropriately, and whether our system can sustain user interest regarding the content provided.

We registered our system as a free application in the App Store, which is an application distribution service managed by Apple, Inc., allowing the users to download it freely onto their own mobile device. At startup, the application displayed messages to the users promoting their cooperation during the experiment. If the users consented, a log of their level of appreciation was saved on their device and sent to our own personal server. We issued a press release on the Internet on January 17th, 2014, and collected the appreciation logs for the unattended exhibition sent by unspecified users until January 28th, 2014.

4.2 Evaluation Based on Level of User Appreciation

For the attended exhibition, all subjects were able to appreciate our system appropriately because docents and explainers were available to guide them how to use the system. For the unattended exhibition, however, some of the subjects were considered unable to achieve the desired level of appreciation. Therefore, we analyzed the subject's level of appreciation and evaluated to what extent they understood the format of the proposed system.

Figure 4 shows the number of users who downloaded the application. Within 12 days after its release, 138 users had downloaded and installed the application onto their own mobile device. Sixty-six of the users accepted their cooperation in the experiment and sent a log of their level of appreciation to our server. Sixty-one of the users allowed their location information to be sent based on GPS or WiFi. Therefore, most of the users had little resistance to using their location information. A total of 26 users actually visited the exhibition location and experienced the on-site exhibition, which is 42.6 % of the number of users who showed a level of appreciation toward the content provided and sent a log containing their location information.

For these 26 users, we analyzed their level of appreciation. Figure 5 shows the number of users who surpassed the intended level of appreciation. Out of 26 users, 24 succeeded to find the starting position of at least one of the provided contents and to match the present scene with the corresponding past image either automatically or manually. These 24 users were able to rotate their device by more than 30 degrees along the yaw angle, and showed a level of appreciation regarding a past panoramic image after it was superimposed onto the current scene. However, only 13 of the users were able to change the transparency and viewing angle of the past panoramic image. These results indicate that, although users could achieve a level of appreciation by rotating their device along the yaw angle through a simple tutorial, they had difficulty with operating the screen.

4.3   Quantitative Evaluation of Appreciation Level

Quantitative Evaluation of Experience Time. To evaluate our system in greater detail, we quantitatively analyzed the log of each user's level of appreciation. The experience time for each content is an important indicator related to the user's degree of interest.

Figure 6 shows the experience time for each exhibition content. We verified the experience time through a two-way factorial analysis of variance based on whether a docent navigated the user and the effect of the user's visual line. As a result, for six of the contents, there was no significant difference between the experience time for the attended and unattended exhibitions with a significance level of 5 %. However, there was a significant difference ($p = 0.026$) in one of the contents, i.e., the outside appearance, where the docents first explained the whole exhibition and introduced our system at the attended exhibition.

Therefore, it is natural that a significant difference exists between the experience time of the attended and unattended exhibitions. On the other hand, no significant difference in the other six contents indicates that an unattended exhibition can attract the user's interest as much as an attended exhibition.

Quantitative Evaluation of the Gazing Time at Certain Spots. To evaluate whether our method for guiding the user's visual line through a brightness change filter works in a real environment, we measured the amount of time the users gazed at a spot where a change in brightness was added. We extracted the valid experience logs, which show the locations where such an effect appeared at least once on the device screen. In three out of the seven contents, there were no valid experience logs. Therefore, we verified the gazing time for the other four contents using a two-way factorial analysis of variance based on the existence of a docent navigation and the inducing effect of the user's visual line (Fig. 7). The results show that, for one of the contents, there is a significant difference between the gazing time with and without a guidance effect ($p = 0.088$). The reason why only this content shows such a significant difference may be that users were more interested in the past content than the real scene because this content was farthest from the remains of Manseibashi Station and there is little similarity between the past and present scenes. One of the reasons why the effectiveness of the guidance decreased in the real environment compared to the laboratory environment may be because the visibility of the device screen decreased according to the sunlight conditions. A method for changing the brightness dynamically according to the lighting intensity or angular velocity can help resolve this problem.

4.4 Subjective Questionnaire Evaluation

For the attended exhibition, we asked the subjects to fill out a questionnaire regarding the exhibition. Many of the subjects answered that they became more interested in the exhibited contents and the digital exhibition itself. They also answered that they wanted to experience other contents through our system. For the unattended exhibition, we could not obtain questionnaire responses from the users directly. However, some SNS posts on the Internet regarding our system stated that our application was quite enjoyable because its operation is intuitive and easy to understand. These remarks suggest that the proposed on-site AR exhibition system is acceptable to users and that similar on-site exhibitions can be developed in various locations in the future.

5   Conclusion

In this research, as a method to hold exhibitions in public spaces outside a museum, we proposed an on-site AR exhibition system using a users own mobile device. As the exhibition objects, we used past panoramic images of Manseibashi Station and the Transportation Museum in Akihabara, Tokyo, which are historically important locations. We designed the proposed on-site AR exhibition system after analyzing the limitations of an on-site exhibition. We distributed this system as an iOS application through the Internet and held attended and unattended exhibitions as an experimental evaluation.

As a result of analyzing the level of appreciation of the users for both the attended and unattended exhibitions, no significant differences were shown between the experience times for most of the contents. This shows that our system can attract the user's interest even for an unattended exhibition. The evaluation results of our guidance of the users visual line shows a marginally significant difference between the gazing time with and without a brightness effect for one of the contents, revealing the need for a refinement of the guidance method for a real exhibition. In addition, the number of downloads of the application is continuously increasing, proving the sustainability of our exhibition system. In conclusion, we established a new outside exhibition form for a public space in an urban district, which is sustainable even without the use of a docent. Our system has allowed the introduction of commercial facilities that are conducting economic activities within society, and succeeded in motivating an unspecified number of people to appreciate an exhibition in a public space.

This suggests the applicability of the proposed system to other exhibitions in public spaces dealing with other subjects.

As future work, we aim to establish an interface applicable for an exhibition requiring more complicated levels of appreciation using 3D models restored from real moving sequences or images. In addition, we intend to develop a guidance method to induce the user's translational motion and attract the users interest to a particular spot. From the subjects who attended our exhibitions, we determined that they would like to be able to use photographs they took themselves. If users can view their own photographs and video sequences on an exhibition system and share their content with others, it will vitalize the on-site exhibition and thus the local community. To realize such a service, we are developing a method to easily match past images with a current scene. We intend to install such a method into our system and refine it to allow users to share their own content with others.

Acknowledgments. This work was partially supported by the MEXT, Grant-in-Aid for Scientific Research (A), 25249957. The authors would like to thank all the members of our project especially staff members of THE RAILWAY MUSEUM and JR Station Retailing Co., Ltd..

References

1. Narumi, T., Hayashi, O., Kasada, K., Yamazaki, M., Tanikawa, T., Hirose, M.: Digital diorama: AR exhibition system to convey background information for museums. In: Shumaker, R. (ed.) Virtual and Mixed Reality, HCII 2011, Part I. LNCS, vol. 6773, pp. 76–86. Springer, Heidelberg (2011)
2. Tanikawa, T., Narumi, T., Hirose, M.: Mixed reality digital museum project. In: Yamamoto, S. (ed.) HCI 2013, Part III. LNCS, vol. 8018, pp. 248–257. Springer, Heidelberg (2013)
3. Arakawa, T., Kasada, K., Narumi, T., Tanikawa, T., Hirose, M.: Reliving video experiences with mobile devices. In: 18th International Conference on, Virtual Systems and Multimedia (VSMM), 2012, pp. 581–584. IEEE (2012)
4. Nakasugi, H., Yamauchi, Y.: Past viewer: development of wearable learning system for history education. In: Proceedings of the International Conference on Computers in Education, 2002, pp. 1311–1312. IEEE (2002)
5. Nakano, J., Narumi, T., Tanikawa, T., Hirose, M.: Implementation of on-site virtual time machine for mobile devices. In: Virtual Reality (VR), 2015. IEEE (2015)
6. Snavely, N., Seitz, S.M., Szeliski, R.: Photo tourism: exploring photo collections in 3d. ACM Trans. Graph. (TOG) **25**(3), 835–846 (2006)
7. Klein, G., Murray, D.: Parallel tracking and mapping for small ar workspaces. In: 6th IEEE and ACM International Symposium on, Mixed and Augmented Reality, ISMAR 2007, pp. 225–234. IEEE (2007)
8. Vlahakis, V., Ioannidis, N., Karigiannis, J., Tsotros, M., Gounaris, M., Stricker, D., Gleue, T., Daehne, P., Almeida, L.: Archeoguide: an augmented reality guide for archaeological sites. IEEE Comput. Graph. Appl. **22**(5), 52–60 (2002)
9. Ikeuchi, K., Oishi, T., Kagesawa, M., Banno, A., Kawakami, R., Kakuta, T., Okamoto, Y., Lu, B.V.: Outdoor gallery and its photometric issues. In: Proceedings of the 9th ACM SIGGRAPH Conference on Virtual-Reality Continuum and its Applications in Industry, pp. 361–364. ACM (2010)

10. Uchiyama, S., Takemoto, K., Satoh, K., Yamamoto, H., Tamura, H.: Mr platform: a basic body on which mixed reality applications are built. In: Proceedings of the 1st International Symposium on Mixed and Augmented Reality, p. 246. IEEE Computer Society (2002)
11. Chen, S.E.: Quicktime vr: an image-based approach to virtual environment navigation. In: Proceedings of the 22nd Annual Conference on Computer Graphics and Interactive Techniques, pp. 29–38. ACM (1995)
12. Microsoft image composite editor. http://research.microsoft.com/en-us/um/redmond/groups/ivm/ICE/
13. Imura, J., Kasada, K., Narumi, T., Tanikawa, T., Hirose, M.: Paper reliving past scene experience system by inducing a video-camera operator's motion with overlaying a video-sequence onto real environment. ITE Trans. Media Technol. Appl. **2**(3), 225–235 (2014)
14. Kim, Y., Varshney, A.: Saliency-guided enhancement for volume visualization. Vis. Comput. Graphics, IEEE Trans. **12**(5), 925–932 (2006)
15. Bay, H., Ess, A., Tuytelaars, T., Van Gool, L.: Speeded-up robust features (surf). Comput. Vis. Image Underst. **110**(3), 346–359 (2008)
16. Fischler, M.A., Bolles, R.C.: Random sample consensus: a paradigm for model fitting with applications to image analysis and automated cartography. Commun. ACM **24**(6), 381–395 (1981)

Enhancing Facial Impression
for Video Conference

Sungyeon Park[1,2], Heeseung Choi[2], and Ig-Jae Kim[1,2(✉)]

[1] HCI Robotics, University of Science and Technology, Seoul
Republic of Korea
[2] Imaging Media Research Center, Korea Institute of Science and Technology,
Seoul, Republic of Korea
{sy.park,hschoi,kij}@imrc.kist.re.kr

Abstract. Most people have their preferred impression to be seen by others. Our face warping method can make this real. In this paper, we propose a new technique for automatic transformation of facial impression, for example, look more attractive or baby-face from the original. We build an impression score function, trained by scores from human raters, and the function is used to get displacement vectors for a given face. To preserve the facial identity as much as possible, we constrain the facial deformation range with facial classification. In case of real time application, such as video conference, there are frequent facial expressions variation and position changes. Face tracker is used to cope with this changing situation. Through our experiments, our proposed method can be one of the promising methods for future video conference system.

Keywords: Transformation of facial impression · Face warping · Face tracker · Machine learning · Deformation of face

1 Introduction

People have developed many kinds of advanced digital technologies that make us enrich all our lives. Among them, smartphone is one of the fascinating inventions. Owing to smartphone, it becomes no surprise that more people can talk to or see others who live in the distant whenever or wherever they are. Since nearly everyone has a smartphone capable of handling video chats, we can enjoy a video chat or teleconference easily. Consequently, we have more chances to talk to someone else face-to-face with digital devices.

When it comes to video conferencing, most people want to look well to others. People have their preferred impression to be seen by others regarding the situation en-countered. For instance, we might want to be seen as trustworthy in a case such as job interview and talking with older people. People want to be seen as an attractive person to someone who is in their mind.

The human face conveys important information regarding not only the person's identity but also impressions of various personal attributes from biological ones such as age and gender to social ones such as personality and attractiveness [12]. If the relationship between the physical parameters representing variations in the face's

N. Streitz and P. Markopoulos (Eds.): DAPI 2015, LNCS 9189, pp. 362–369, 2015.
DOI: 10.1007/978-3-319-20804-6_33

appearance and the impression of the corresponding images perceived by humans is formalized in a mathematical model, the possibility of a computer capable of dealing with perceptual or subjective information conveyed by faces could become a reality [13].

From this background, we propose a new method to transform facial impression automatically for video chat or teleconference while maintaining identity of original face in this work. Since we transform the impression in regard to the shape of original face, it is possible to maintain close similarity with original face.

In Sect. 2, our transformation facial impression system framework consisting of three stages is presented. In Sects. 3 and 4, we explain details about transformation system and tracking and warping method for video sequence. Finally, we summarize and conclude the chapter in Sects. 5 and 6, respectively.

Fig. 1. System flow chart

2 Overview

We showed overview of our proposed method in Fig. 1. Once we capture a person in the frontal view through a camera, we detect the face region and extract 66 landmark points with facial features, such as two eyebrows, two eyes, nose, lips, and boundary of face, from it automatically. In the first stage, we use the detected frontal face image and the landmark points as an input image to the second stage.

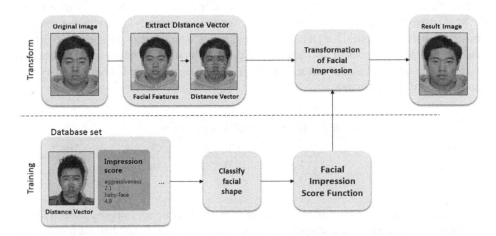

Fig. 2. Detail process for automatic transformation of facial impression

The key process in our system is an automatic transformation of facial impression (Fig. 2) based on our database which we trained. It is composed of frontal faces and their facial impression score that we gathered from groups of human raters. We built *facial impression score function*, modeled by a support vector regressor, with the classified data according to their facial shape. Finally, a deformed face is obtained by optimization of the function. We can transform facial impression as the user wants in this step, in the meanwhile our proposed algorithm can preserve the original face identity.

Facial features are detected in images and tracked across video sequences in the last step. According to the facial features detected through face tracker, original faces are substituted with the deformed face in real time. Our results indicate that the proposed method is capable of transforming facial impression and substituting the original face in real time.

3   Impression Transform Engine

3.1   Construction Database and Extract Facial Feature

The training set is consist of 846 frontal portraits of males with neutral expression. The impression (e.g. Attractiveness, baby-face and aggressiveness) degree of each face was rated by 10 human raters. The average rating of a face is its impression score (on a scale of 1 to 7). Since each rater has their own score range and deviation, we use the z-score (Eq. 1) for score normalization which is calculated using the arithmetic mean and standard deviation of the given data [1].

$$s'_k = \frac{s_k - \mu}{\sigma} \tag{1}$$

In our work, we use constrained local model (CLM) [11] and Chehra [10] face tracker to extract 66-landmark points (Fig. 3(a)). Since Chehra face tracker which is a good face alignment technique does not provide feature points for the boundary of a face, CLM is used to extract 17-landmark points for the boundary. The extracted feature points are used to construct a Delaunay triangulation which builds meshes (Fig. 3(b)). The triangulation consists of 166 edges, and the lengths of these edges are components of 166-dimensional distance vector (Fig. 3(c)). The distance vector is normalized by the square root of the face area.

Table 1. The number of data in each class

	Class 1	Class 2	Class 3	Class 4	Class 5
# of data	116	173	177	187	193

Face area is a sum of the all triangles from meshes. Training samples are classified as their facial shape in five classes by K-Means [8] classifier. Table 1 is the number of data in each class. Classified samples reduce computation and are used to build

Impression Score Function (Sect. 3.2). Constructing function through data which has similar facial shape with original face makes the result images preserve the original facial identity.

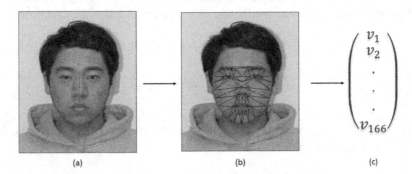

$$\begin{pmatrix} v_1 \\ v_2 \\ \cdot \\ \cdot \\ \cdot \\ v_{166} \end{pmatrix}$$

(a)   (b)   (c)

Fig. 3. (a) Facial feature points, (b) The mashes by Delaunay Triangulation, (c) The 166-D distance vector

3.2 Facial Impression Score Function

The image captured by user is original image as input. To seek suitable training sample class for original image, we should select training sample class which has the smallest Euclidean Distances between the center vector in each class and distance vector of original data. Impression Score Estimation function is built from training sample data consisted of selected distance vector and impression score by using Support Vector Regression (SVR) [4].

SVR is similar to Support Vector Machine (SVM) but used for data regression. SVR is an induction algorithm for fitting multidimensional data by using various kernels. Suppose we have training data $\{(x_1, y_1), \ldots, (x_l, y_l)\}$, where $x \in \mathbb{R}^d$ and $y \in \mathbb{R}$. In ε-SV regression [1], the goal is to find a function f(x) that has at most ε deviation from the actually obtained targets y_i for all the training data, and at the same time is as flat as possible. Describe the case of linear functions $f(x)$, taking the form

$$f(x) = <w, u> + b \tag{2}$$

where $<\cdot, \cdot>$ denotes the dot product. Flatness in the case of (Eq. 2) means that one seeks a small w. For small w, it is required to minimize the Euclidean norm i.e. $\| w \|^2$. This can be written as a convex optimization problem by requiring. We use a Radial Basis Function kernel, which is a popular kernel function used in various kernel method learning algorithms. Model selection was performed by a grid search over the width of the kernel σ, the slack parameter C and the tube width parameter ε. Leave-One-Out Cross Validation (LOOCV) method was used to determine adequate parameters. In the (1), u is 166-dimensional feature vectors and y is their corresponding impression score. Therefore, we can estimate impression score with above function.

3.3   Transformation of Facial Impression

Reduce Dimension and Constrain the Search Space with PCA. In this paper, we use Principal Component Analysis (PCA) to reduce a dimension of distance vector from 166 to 30. x is defined as the distance vector reduced. We regularize objective function (Eq. 3) to constrain the search space in valid human face. LP(X) (Eq. 4) define face space by multivariate Gaussian distribution. We set α to 0.3 following experimentation.

$$E(x) = -f(x) - \alpha(f(x) - LP(x)) \tag{3}$$

$$LP(x) = \sum_{i=1}^{d} \frac{(x - \bar{\mu})^2}{2 \Sigma_{jj}} + cons \tag{4}$$

In $LP(X)$, $\bar{\mu}$ is 30-D average vector of training sample data for selected class and Σ_{jj} is eigen-value obtained by PCA.

Modified Distance Vector. We use Powell's method [2] to seek modified distance vector. Powell's method is a proper optimization for problem where the optimal solution is close to the starting point. Since Modified distance vector should be near to original one to maintain close similarity with original, Powell's method is suitable one. Modified distance vector is obtained by minimizing objective function (Eq. 3) which is based on the impression score function. Original distance vector is staring point in optimization.

$$f(x') > f(x) \tag{5}$$

Modified distance vector should satisfy the condition (5). This means that modified data has higher score than original one.

Adjust Landmark Points as Modified Distance Vector. To transform the facial impression, landmark points should be placed to new landmark position according to the modified distance vector. New landmark points can be obtained by minimizing Eq. 6. This minimizing reduces the differences between the lengths of these edges and their corresponding modified distances. The Levenberg-Marquardt [5, 6] algorithm is used to perform this minimization.

$$D(q_1, \ldots, q_{166}) = \sum \alpha_{ij}(\| q_i - q_j \|^2 - d_{ij}^2)^2 \tag{6}$$

The variable q_i and q_j are target landmark point and d_{ij} is distance corresponded to q_i and q_j. We can obtain optimal landmark positions by considering global error.

Post-processing. To reduce distortion of deformed face with forehead and background, modified landmark points of face boundary is replaced original one. The modified landmark points $\{q_i\}$ should translate to the position of the original face. The reason is that it makes deformed face align in the background of the video. Post-processing can cause a decrease in target impression score, but it is necessary to realistic result image.

4   Face Tracking and Warping

We should replace original face image to deformed one in real time. For this, we detect face landmark points with Chehra Face Tracker and CLM in real time, and then add the moving amount to deformed landmark points to track the moving face.

We have the set of the original face landmark points $\{p_i\}$, which extracted on initial frame, and the set of the deformed one $\{q_i\}$ in initial image position. The set of difference $\{diff_i\}$ is acquired by subtracting from the set of original face landmark points $\{p_i\}$ to the set of moving original face one $\{p'_i\}$ (Eq. 7). The set of moving deformed face landmark points $\{q'_i\}$ is updated in every moment by sum of $\{q_i\}$ and $\{diff_i\}$ (Eq. 8).

$$diff_i = p_i - p'_i \tag{7}$$

$$q'_i = q_i + diff_i \tag{8}$$

According to the $\{p'_i\}$ and $\{q'_i\}$, we perform texture warping with the triangle mash which is a result of Delaunay triangulation. The texture images for warping are obtained from each frame to handle the problems of illumination and expression.

5   Experiment

We have implemented application for our system. The application automatically detects facial feature in video sequence image. The user looks camera straight with neutral expression and captures frontal image. Next, the application computes for transformation of the facial impression and displays the transformed image. The application track the face and the original face on the video is substituted with deformed faces in real time. Currently, our training sample images are only for Asian

(a)

(b)

Fig. 4. Transformation of facial impression example. (a) original image [14]. (b) deformed image (look much younger)

male. We have deformed face which is not included in training samples to enhance baby-face and transform Fig. 4(a) to (b) based on the training data. The difference between original face and deformed face are subtle on the eyes, nose and lips but this subtle changes have impact on the facial impression (Fig. 5).

Fig. 5. The results for transformation of facial impression video sequence images. Top two lines are original images and bottom two lines are deformed images to enhance baby-face. Asian male original and deformed face video sequence images [14].

6   Conclusion

In this paper, we propose a new system for automatic transformation of facial impression in real-time. Since we use trained dataset which is classified as their facial shape, the deformed face is close to original face. Since our database is composed of images of Asian male only, so we need to gather additional datasets, such as images for female and other races. In the future, we will gather more review scores for various kinds of impression for more wide use. And besides, we have to come up with a more sophisticated and objective method for evaluating impression than the current one based on human evaluators.

Acknowledgement. This work was supported by the KIST Institutional Program (Project No. 2E25660).

References

1. Jain, A., Nandakumar, K., Ross, A.: Score normalization in multimodal biometric systems. Pattern Recogn. **38**, 2270–2285 (2005)
2. Press, W.H., Flannery, B.P., Teukolasky, S.A., Vetterling, W.T.: Numerical Recipes: The Art of Scientific Computing, 2nd edn. Cambridge University Press, Cambridge (1992)
3. Eisenthal, Y., Dror, G., Ruppin, E.: Facial attractiveness: beauty and the machine. Neural Comput. **18**(1), 119–142 (2006)
4. Joachims, T.: Making Large-scale SVM Learning Practical. In: Schölkopf, B., Burges, C.J. C., Smola, A.J. (eds.) Advances in Kernel Methods: Support Vector Learning, pp. 169–184. MIT Press, Cambridge (1999)
5. Levenberg, K.: A method for the solution of certain problems in least squares. Quart. Appl. Math. **2**, 164–168 (1944)
6. Marquardt, D.: An algorithm for least-squares estimation of nonlinear parameters. SIAM J. Appl. Math. **11**(2), 431–441 (1963)
7. Leyvand, T., Cohen-Or, D., Dror, G., Lischinski, D.: Data-driven enhancement of facial attractiveness. ACM Trans. Graph. SIGGRAPH **27**(3), 38 (2008)
8. Wagstaff, K., Rogers, S.: Constrained K-means cluastering with background knowledge. In: Proceedings of the 18th International Conference on Machine Learning, pp. 577–584 (2001)
9. Milborrow, S., Nicolls, F.: Locating facial features with an extended active shape model. In: Forsyth, D., Torr, P., Zisserman, A. (eds.) ECCV 2008, Part IV. LNCS, vol. 5305, pp. 504–513. Springer, Heidelberg (2008)
10. Asthana, A., Zafeiriou, S., Cheng, S., Pantic, M.: Incremental face alignment in the wild. In: CVPR (2014)
11. Cristinacce, D., Cootes, T.F.: Feature detection and tracking with constrained local models. In: Proceeding of British Machine Vision Conference, vol. 3, pp. 929–938 (2006)
12. Bruce, V.: Recognizing Faces. Lawrence Erlbaum Associates, London (1988)
13. Hashimoto, S.: KANSEI as the third target of information processing and related topics in Japan. In: Proceeding of KANSEI – The Technology of Emotion, AIMI International Workshop, pp. 101–104, October 1997
14. https://www.youtube.com/watch?v=sPaRCtGu9zQ

Art and Coffee in the Museum

Nikolaos Partarakis[1(✉)], Emmanouil Zidianakis[1],
Margherita Antona[1], and Constantine Stephanidis[1,2]

[1] Foundation for Research and Technology – Hellas (FORTH),
Institute of Computer Science,
70013 Heraklion, Crete, Greece
{partarak, antona, cs}@ics.forth.gr
[2] Department of Computer Science, University of Crete, Rethimno, Greece

Abstract. Natural interaction refers to people interacting with technology as they are used to interact with the real world in everyday life, through gestures, expressions, movements, etc., and discovering the world by looking around and manipulating physical objects [16]. In the domain of cultural heritage research has been conducted in a number of directions including (a) Personalised Information in Museums, (b) Interactive Exhibits, (c) Interactive Games Installations in Museums, (d) Museum Mobile Applications, (e) Museums presence on the Web and (f) Museum Social Applications. Most museums target family groups and organize family-oriented events in their programs but how families choose to visit particular museums in response to their leisure needs has rarely been highlighted. This work exploits the possibility of extending the usage of AmI technology, and thus the user experience, within leisure spaces provided by museums such as cafeterias. The Museum Coffee Table is an augmented physical surface where physical objects can be used for accessing information about artists and their creations. At the same entertainment for children is facilitated through the integration of popular games on the surface. As a result, the entire family can seat around the table, drink coffee and complete their visit to the museum acquiring additional knowledge and playing games.

Keywords: Ambient intelligence · Tabletop interaction · Augmented reality · Cultural heritage · Interactive surfaces

1 Introduction

Currently, Cultural Heritage Institutions (CHIs) in Europe are experiencing growth and change, they are increasing in number, expanding in size, and attracting more diverse audiences every day with heritage tourism alone accounting for more than 5 % of European GDP. New demands and challenges are emerging in every aspect of the cultural heritage landscape, making innovations in information and communication technologies an increasingly integrated part of the related strategies. Novel approaches are emerging for understanding people's art and cultural experiences and for designing interactive technologies to support these experiences. In this context, new expectations of the public are emerging with regard to the fruition of cultural experiences, focusing

© Springer International Publishing Switzerland 2015
N. Streitz and P. Markopoulos (Eds.): DAPI 2015, LNCS 9189, pp. 370–381, 2015.
DOI: 10.1007/978-3-319-20804-6_34

on factors such as easiness and fun, cultural entertainment, personal identification, historical reminiscences and escapism [25]. This paper, taking into account the fact that most museums target family groups and organize family-oriented events, explores the possibility of extending the usage of AmI technology, and thus the user experience, within leisure spaces provided by museums such as cafeterias.

2 Background and Related Work

The evolution of ICT has raised the expectations regarding its usage in the CH sector. Family visitors with children account for a significant segment of CHIs audiences. Most CHIs target family groups and organize family-oriented events in their programs. Table 1 summarizes five major family motivations to visit museums, including: education (opportunities for informal learning or education benefits to children), entertainment (having fun), quality family time, the need of social outings and the need of children.

Table 1. Five major family motivations to visit museums

Researcher	Key motivational themes
Falk & Dierking (1992)	Social interaction, Education, Entertainment, Family history
McManus (1994)	Education, entertainment
Hooper- Greenhill (1994) & MORI (2001)	The need of the children
Baillie (1996)	Education, Entertainment, Quality family time
Moussouri (2003)	Education, Family life-cycle, Entertainment, Quality family time
Kelly et al. (2004)	Social interaction, Education, Purposes of day out, Quality family time, Enjoyment of children
Sterry (2004)	Need of social outing, Entertainment, Educational benefits to children, Intergenerational benefit

The perspectives of adults' prevail in deciding regarding museum experiences [17–24]. Apparently, parents can articulate what they perceive as the need of their children. However, the opinion of children should not been ignored in order to reflect the nature of a family's choice. Various studies have evaluated the relationship between the motivation that families have when visiting a museum and its impact on the their learning experience [17, 18, 22]. How families choose to visit particular museums in response to their leisure needs has rarely been highlighted. Baillie criticizes that most museum professionals tend to concentrate museum missions on collection, preservation and interpretation; as a result, how effective an exhibition is delivered to visitors in terms of learning becomes a key issue [20]. Last but not least, these motivational studies were mainly investigated through quantitative questionnaire surveys. The motivational factors were defined by the researchers. Motivations are treated as the triggers for the decisions to visit museums. All these researchers studied family choices of museum participation in an exclusive museum context without acknowledging general leisure contexts. Some researchers suggested that these motivational factors are intertwined and interrelated. However, only few attempts have been made at revealing a more holistic and detailed picture of reflecting the complex needs of families from museum products in leisure contexts.

The importance of family leisure needs as outlined by researcher has led museums to turn their interest to the introduction of ICT technology within their premises. Worldwide, there have been a number of museums that have installed, temporarily or permanently, interactive exhibits. The "Fire and the Mountain" exhibition comprised four hybrid exhibits aiming to promote awareness about the cultural heritage of the people living around the Como Lake [11]. ARoS, an art museum in Denmark, employed four interactive exhibits targeted in an exhibition of the Japanese artist Mariko Mori [12]. The Austrian Technical Museum in Vienna opened a digitally augmented exhibition on the history of modern media [13]. The Archaeological Museum of Thessaloniki hosts "Macedonia from Fragment to Pixels" [14], an inter- active exhibition of prototypical interactive systems with subjects drawn from ancient Macedonia. The Panoptes system allows the browsing of artefact collections, while Polyapton offers multi-touch, multiuser gaming experiences with archaeological arte- facts [10]. The ArtEFact Project [2, 4] has developed a generic platform for interactive storytelling in Mixed Reality that facilitates access to a knowledge base of objects of art and art history. One installation was placed in the Bargello Museum (Soprintendenza Speciale pei il Polo Museale Fiorentino).

In the same context, interactive surfaces are today more broadly facilitated in CHIs. The etx surface[1] is an art exploration system that uses an infrared camera system to track reflective-taped wooden paddles on a table surface. Located at the Indianapolis Museum of Art, etx uses the PercepTable [26] recognition and display system devel- oped at Indiana University's Visualization and Interactive Spaces Laboratory, which is part of the Pervasive Technology Laboratories. A permanent display (see http://www. asiasociety.org/about/buildingtour/) at the headquarters of the Asia Society and Museum in New York gives a visual way for visitors to explore six aspects of Asian culture, region by region. A small, round table supports six palm-sized stones, vari- ously labelled food/cuisine, news, art, country profiles, Asian Americans, and Asia for kids. The Churchill Lifeline is a permanent, central exhibit at the Churchill Museum and Cabinet War Rooms (visit http://www.churchillmuseum.iwm.org.uk) in London. Projected from above onto this 40-foot-long table are summaries of events in the statesperson's life, arranged in chronological order. A series of touch-strips (force-sensitive resistors) on both long sides of the table gives visitors greater detail about these events, via access to more than 4,000 relevant digital documents. The Dialog Table at the Walker Art Centre in Minneapolis, Minnesota, presents further insight into items in the centre's collection and serves to stimulate discussion among visitors. Part of the permanent exhibit, it is one of the few table-top displays using rear projection: images are projected via a system of mirrors inside a kiosk onto two horizontal, head-to-head displays [27]. Floating numbers is an associative presentation

---

[1] http://www.ima-art.org/xRoom.asp#etx

of information that's part of a temporary exhibit at the Jewish Museum Berlin. Floating numbers presented a dynamic river of digits that flow from one end to the other.

The work presented here expands the potential contexts where such technology is typically installed by promoting the usage of interactive displays within the leisure spaces of cultural heritage institutions (restaurants, coffee shops, etc.). To this end, the Museum Coffee Table expands the visiting experience for parents while providing entertainment for children targeting to general leisure markets and contexts within CHIs.

3 Museum Coffee Table

The Museum Coffee Table facilitates the beverage coaster metaphor to provide access to the life and works of famous artists. A number of augmented beverage coasters have been developed integrating tags to be recognised by the Microsoft SUR40 surface device. This augmented beverage coasters present on their front side (where the beverage is placed) a famous artist while the tag for object recognition is located on the back side (see Fig. 1 left). When a coaster is placed on the table surface, it is augmented by a digital menu of options. This menu offers access to the life and works of the selected Artist (see Fig. 1 right). Another set of augmented beverage coasters which are smaller in size and more playful in terms of appearance (circle, triangle, star, rectangle etc.) are also contained in the collection. These beverage coasters are meant to be used by children and are employed by the table to adapt and personalise its content to children. The adaptations currently supported include the limitation of menu options (simplified access to collections of paintings, memory and puzzle games are available for children) and the adaptation of information presented (only a simplified text description of the painting is presented to children). Using separate collections of augmented objects for interaction was a conscious decision aiming at getting implicit input from users in order to provide personalised content. Each coaster is not only linked to information about the artist but also to a specific age group.

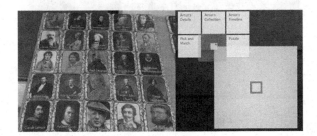

Fig. 1. Left: Collection of augmented beverage coasters, **Right:** Augmenting a coaster with a menu of information

Through the aforementioned artist's menu a variety of information about the pictured artist can be accessed such as demographic details (name, movement, art period etc.), the artist's collection of works and a timeline of the artist's life (that presents important events in conjunction with artistic accomplishments). The Artist's collection is a library bar that contains the works of the selected artist (see Fig. 2). It presents a list of thumbnails containing all the artistic accomplishment of an artist's lifetime. From this library users can select (drag on the surface) and manipulate paintings.

Fig. 2. The Artist's collection library bar

The Artist's timeline is designed to present important events of the artist's life in conjunction to artistic accomplishments (see Fig. 3). Users can manipulate through touch these timelines using basic gestures (touch from left to right to move the timeline forward and from right to left to move the timeline backwards). Selection of an event results in the display of extra information. At the same time duration of events is visualised by bar on top of each event.

Fig. 3. El Greco's timeline

A manipulated painting provides extra information using the embedded menu as shown in Fig. 4. Information includes details about the creation of the artefact, techniques used by the artist, the composition scheme followed etc. At the same time users can access a very large scale digital image of the painting where deep zooming can be employed to present the details of the original masterpiece (that are traditional lost by low resolution digital copies).

Games are considered an important add-on to the interactive table as long as they allow parents to get more information about art while their children get entertained through games. In this sense the Museum Coffee Table can be considered as a facility for the whole family and a valuable partner of their museum experiences. Currently two games are supported a cards based memory game and a puzzle game. The cards game is a simple memory game where children are prompted to locate the same pairs of cards within a collection of initially hidden cards (see Fig. 5 left). The game gets added value when integrated to the museum coffee table where the game cards are coupled with the selected coaster offering access to a vast number of alternative gaming possibilities. For example if the coaster represents Domenikos Theotokopoulos a game is randomly generated by his works. In the same manner the puzzle extracts information from the currently selected artist to produce a collection of puzzles using the artist's works (see Fig. 5 right).

Fig. 4. The painting's menu

Fig. 5. Left: memory game, Right: Puzzle game

"Museum Coffee Table" is currently deployed for demonstration purposes on a Samsung SUR40 at FORTH-ICS Ami facility [1] and is considered part of the work conducted in the field of Ambient Intelligence for Learning and Education [2]. Samsung SUR40 is the new generation of Microsoft® Surface® experience featuring PixelSense™ technology, which gives LCD panels the power to see without the use of cameras [3]. Figure 6 presents the educational facilities provided by "Museum Coffee Table" running on the aforementioned device while Fig. 7 presents the entertainment facilities. At the same time the usage of physical augmented objects for accessing these facilities is highlighted.

Fig. 6. Education facilities

Fig. 7. Entertainment facilities

4 Implementation

For implementing the Coffee Table a quite straight forward architecture was used that contains four distinct layers (Fig. 8).

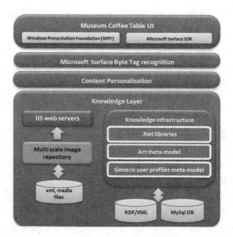

Fig. 8. Architecture

The upper most layer stands for the UI of the system building on two UI frameworks, the Microsoft Windows Workflow Foundation and the Microsoft Surface 2.0 UI library [5]. The Microsoft Byte Tag recognition layer provided by the device through the Microsoft Surface SDK offers access to information about beverage coasters to be in turn used by the Content Personalisation layer to form the appropriate queries to the Knowledge layer. The Knowledge layer contains the models to represent art and generic user profiles. These models have been defined in RDF [6] and were developed with the Protégé ontology editor [7], while SemWeb [8] was used for querying the ontology using the SPARQL syntax [9]. The Art Model is based on CIDOC-CRM, a domain standard for CH extended accordingly to support the purposes of this research work. Finally to support scaling of media content in extremely large resolution multi scale representations of paintings are stored in the appropriate format (converted through the usage of appropriate tools such as the Microsoft Deep Zoom composer) and served to the application through an IIS web server.

5 Evaluation

One of the most important considerations during an evaluation procedure is to prepare the environment in which the user testing will be performed, since the context of use can greatly affect a product's usability [28]. In the case of the Museum Coffee Table, the test has been performed within an in vitro setup of the coffee table in of the simulation spaces of FORTH-ICS's AmI research facility with the participation of twelve users. Five of them were children aged from eight to twelve years old. Adults were requested to fill in a pre-test questionnaire containing demographic information and information regarding their attitude towards CHIs in general and the usage of modern technology within CHIs. Subsequently, the users were requested to complete a number of interaction scenarios through the system and then fill in the post-test questionnaire. The second phase of the evaluation and the completion of the post-test questionnaires was conducted by all users including children. In the case of children, a separate questionnaire was used to assess playability while for adults the assessment concerned usability and educational value.

Interaction of users with the system was recorded for offline analysis by the evaluators. The scenario conducted by users in the context of the usability evaluation contained 5 tasks (adults). Additionally in the case of children three tasks were used. An example of one of the tasks is presented below:

The **pre-test questionnaire** has shown that $\sim$ 66 % of the users visit a museum once a year. At the same time their interest in paintings and modern art covers a percentage of $\sim$ 53 % but they do not follow some specific art style or trend. More importantly, $\sim$ 56 % of the users have visited a museum with some form of interactive exhibits. Regarding their satisfaction from museum visits, $\sim$ 89 % are not satisfied from the information gathered from museum while, $\sim$ 67 % feel that museums are boring. Additionally, $\sim$ 85 % of the participants stated that interactive technology within museums can improve their museum experience, especially when visiting with family.

In the case of adults the results gathered through the **post-test questionnaire** are used to calculate four factors (see Fig. 9). The OVERALL factor expresses the overall satisfaction of the users regarding the system. The SYUSE factor measures the satis-faction of users when using the system, while the INFOQUAL measures the information quality provided by the system. Finally, INTERQUAL is a factor that captures user satisfaction regarding the interface provided by the system. The OVERALL factor, shows that the users were generally satisfied (∼ 87 % of the users are within the range 5 to 7 while 30.56 % of the users provided a grade of 7 to all questions) by the overall usability of the system. However, there are 5 % of the users that state that were not satisfied. According to the SYUSE factor users were generally satisfied (∼ 85 % of the users are within the range 5 to 7 while 37, 04 % of the users provided a grade of 7 to all questions) by the overall satisfaction by using the system. However, there are ∼ 14 % of the users that state that they were little to medium satisfied. Regarding the quality of information (INFOQUAL), users were generally satisfied (∼ 88 % of the users are within the range 5 to 7 while ∼ 25 % of the users provided a grade of 7 to all questions). However, there are ∼ 43 % of the users that scored 6 which implies that are is a substantial amount of users that requires some form of improvement in the way that information is presented. To identify this aspect, a more detailed analysis of questionnaire data is reported below. The interaction quality (INTERQUAL) shows that the users were generally satisfied (∼ 83 % of the users are within the range 5 to 7 while ∼ 35 % of the users provided a grade of 7 to all questions). However, there are ∼ 25 % of the users that scored 5 and ∼ 24 % that score 6 which implies that are is a substantial amount of users that requires some form of improvement in the interaction.

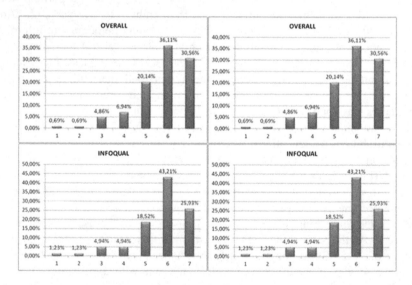

Fig. 9. Usability factors

A more in depth analysis of the questionnaire data was conducted in order to highlight potential areas of improvement. To do so the questions where categorised, analysed and presented graphically:

General User Satisfaction: Regarding the general user satisfaction $\sim$ 12 % of the users score a medium satisfaction while also $\sim$ 76 % score 6 while only $\sim$ 12 were fully satisfied. These results also empower the need for identifying areas of improvement.

Interaction Metaphors: In this section the questions relevant to the interaction metaphors employed by the system are analysed. The touch and byte tag recognition metaphors scored high grades in all questions but some of the supported gestures were not well appreciated by users. For example the dragging gesture required to remove an item from the list of artist's works and place it on the surface was not always understood by users. On the contrary most of the users were trying to tap or double tap the item. This resulted to a satisfaction rate of $\sim$ 50 % for gestures.

Augmented Objects for Interaction: As long as augmented objects are used for interaction users were in general very satisfied ($\sim$ 90 % in question 12 and 100 % in question 9 scored within the range 5 to 7). In both cases there is a percentage of $\sim$ 33 % that scored 5. An analysis of the feedback received by users pointed out that in some cases faced difficulties identifying the usage of augmented objects.

Information Representation and Extraction: Regarding the ways that information is represented and extracted users were in general very satisfied ($\sim$ 85 % scored from 5 to 7 in all questions). Nevertheless there is a percentage of $\sim$ 55 % that are not fully satisfied in the way that information is browsed in general. For example 33 % scored 5 in the way that information is browsed through the timeline (in some cases events overlapped with multimedia content).

General System Use: Finally in questions that affect general system use the results pin point that the system in general was very well received while living a percentage of $\sim$ 24 % scoring 5 and 6 pointing the need of further improvements.

In the case of children the results of the questionnaire were employed to assess the playability of the games and partially the usability of the provided interface. The results were analyzed together with the recording of the children interaction and informal interviews with children. The outcome of this process were compiled in the form of problems encountered together with suggestions for improvement. More specifically, some usability issues identified by children were:

- The coaster menu does not seem playful. Text labels should be replaced with icons or just include also icons for each of the available games
- The difficulty bar on the puzzle is not easily understood by children. Children use to judge the difficulty of puzzles based on the number of pieces
- In some cases especially in the case of the cards game input from children with small fingers was lost. Touch interface should be made more responsive for children
- In some cases especially when the original paintings have unconventional dimensions (the one dimension is proportionally many times larger than the other) puzzle pieces are not well formed and appear stretched. Dynamic rendering of puzzle pieces should be improved

Additionally there were comments regarding playability:

- In some cases regardless of the game children elbows on the surface were producing false input. Is it possible to make touch available only of the game surface?
- In the puzzle game pieces can get out of the puzzle surface. This seems confusing and should not be allowed
- On the cards game you cannot rearrange cards. It would be useful to have at least the option to rearrange matched pairs. Another suggestion was to hide matched pairs of cards.
- Some children also suggested that the cards should increase in size because the painting were not easily distinguished
- Some children (especially the older ones) requested that the table should also integrate games that have a more "arcade" character using the rational that they could easily get bored.

6   Discussion and Future Work

The work presented by this paper aimed at augmenting the user experience within museum leisure spaces focusing both on information and entertainment. Targeting family visitors of CHIs within leisure spaces the Coffee Table offers extra information about the CHI's exhibits to parents while providing an entertainment environment for children. At the same time the usage of a standard's compliant knowledge base provides extensibility and scalability. The Museum Coffee Table falls into the research line currently conducted within FORTH-ICS to use AmI technologies in CHIs contexts so as to enhance the museum experience at large. In this context, one of the most important goals for future work is to seek possibilities of practical exploiting the proposed functionality and concepts in vivo. To do so the improvement of the current instantiation is a prerequisite starting with the comments received from the initial user based evaluation.

Acknowledgements. This work is supported by the FORTH-ICS internal RTD Programme 'Ambient Intelligence and Smart Environments' [1, 15, 29].

References

1. FORTH-ICS AmI Programme. http://www.ics.forth.gr/index_main.php?l=e&c=4
2. Art Games. http://www.ics.forth.gr/ami/education/Art_Games.html
3. http://www.samsunglfd.com/product/feature.do?modelCd=SUR40
4. Iurgel, I.: From another point of view: Art-E-Fact. In: Göbel, S., Spierling, U., Hoffmann, A., Iurgel, I., Schneider, O., Dechau, J., Feix, A. (eds.) TIDSE 2004. LNCS, vol. 3105, pp. 26–35. Springer, Heidelberg (2004)
5. Microsoft® Surface® SDK and Runtime. http://www.microsoft.com/en-us/download/details.aspx?id=26716
6. RDF Vocabulary Description Language 1.0: RDF Schema, W3C Recommendation, 10 February 2004. http://www.w3.org/TR/rdf-schema/ (2004)

7. Protégé. http://protege.stanford.edu/
8. SemWeb.NET: http://razor.occams.info/code/semweb/
9. SPARQL Query Language for RDF. http://www.w3.org/TR/rdf-sparql-query/
10. Grammenos, D., Zabulis, X., Michel, D., Sarmis, T., Georgalis, G., Tzevanidis, K., Argyros, A., Stephanidis, C.: Design and development of four prototype interactive edutainment exhibits for museums. In: Stephanidis, C. (ed.) Universal Access in HCI, Part III, HCII 2011. LNCS, vol. 6767, pp. 173–182. Springer, Heidelberg (2011)
11. Conversational agent at the Heinz Nixdorf MuseumsForum. In: Proceedings of Re-Thinking Technology in Museums (2011). http://www.idc.ul.ie/techmuseums11/index.php?option=com_content&view=article&id=15&Itemid=7
12. Garzotto, F., Rizzo, F.: Interaction paradigms in technology-enhanced social spaces: a case study in museums. In: Proceedings of DPPI 2007, pp. 343–356 (2007)
13. Kortbek, K.J., Grønbæk, K.: Interactive spatial multimedia for communication of art in the physical museum space. In: Proceeding of MM 2008, pp. 609–618 (2008)
14. Hornecker, E., Stifter, M.: Learning from interactive museum installations about interaction design for public settings. In: Proceedings of OZCHI 2006, pp. 135–142 (2006)
15. Aarts, E., Encarnacao, J.L.: True Visions: The Emergence of Ambient Intelligence. Springer, Heidelberg (2008). ISBN 978-3-540-28972-2
16. Valli, A.: The design of natural interaction. Multimedia Tools Appl. 38(3), 295–305 (2008)
17. Falk, J.H., Dierking, L.D.: The Museum Experience. Whalesback Books, Washington D.C. (1992)
18. McManus, P.M.: Families in museums. In: Miles, R., Zavalac, L. (eds.) 16 Towards the Museum of the Future: New European Perspectives. Routledge, London and New York (1994)
19. Hooper-Greenhill, E.: Museums and Their Visitors. Routledge, London (1994)
20. Baillie, A.: Empowering the visitor: the family experience of museums, a pilot study of ten family group visits to the Queensland Museum. In: Museums Australia Annual Conference (1996)
21. MORI: Visitors to Museums and Galleries in the UK, Research Study Conducted for the Council for Museums Archives and Libraries (2001)
22. Moussouri, T.: Negotiated agendas: families in science and technology museums. Int. J. Technol. Manage. 25(5), 477–489 (2003)
23. Kelly, L., Savage, G., Griffin, J., Tonkin, S.: Knowledge Quest: Australian Families Visit Museums. Australian Museum and National Museum of Australia, Sydney (2004)
24. Sterry, P.: An insight into the dynamics of family group visitors to cultural tourism destinations: initiating the research agenda'. In: Smith, K.A., Schott, C. (eds.) Proceedings of the New Zealand Tourism and Hospitality Research Conference 2004, Wellington, 8–10 December, pp. 298–406 (2004)
25. Sheng, C.-W., Chen, M.-C.: A study of experience expectations of museum visitors. Tourism Manage. 33(1), 53–60 (2012)
26. McRobbie, M., et al.: Pervasive Technology Labs Program Report, August 2005
27. Walczak, M., McAllister, M., Segen, J.: Dialog table. In: Proceedings of the 5th Conference on Designing Interactive Systems: Processes, Practices, Methods, and Techniques. ACM (2004)
28. Karat, C., Campbell, R.L., Fiegel, T.: Comparison of empirical testing and walkthrough methods in user interface evaluation. In: Proceedings ACM CHI 1992 Conference, Monterey, CA, 3–7 May, pp. 397–404 (1992)
29. Nielsen, J.: Paper versus computer implementations as mock-up scenarios for heuristic evaluation. In: Proceedings of INTERACT 1990 3rd IFIP Conference on HCI, pp. 315 – 320 (1990)

Context-Based Document Management in Smart Living Environments

Julian von Wilmsdorf[1], Alexander Marinc[2], and Arjan Kuijper[1,2](✉)

[1] Technische Universität Darmstadt, Darmstadt, Germany
[2] Fraunhofer IGD, Darmstadt, Germany
arjan.kuijper@igd.fraunhofer.de

Abstract. Nowadays an increasingly wide variety of multimedia devices can be networked together in ever-growing smart environments. Although these networks, thanks to mobile technology and Wi-Fi, are almost ubiquitous by now, the players therein are still working largely distinct from one another. To simply play a file on the playback device A, which is originally housed on device B, is therefore a complicated task, despite the theoretical possibility provided by existing networking. Especially playing and viewing files on multimedia devices under various circumstances and limited reproduction capabilities is a non-trivial problem. Current solutions from industry still put little interoperable approaches in proprietary systems. Individual multimedia devices of the same manufacturer can be combined intelligently, but with respect to the usability the system scales poorly, the (also physical) distribution increases the difficulty of access to the functions and control is largely independent of the user's context. In this work, a solution is developed, which focuses in particular on the context-based playback of files: sending video, music, image and text files to output devices with different display options, as well as the distribution of these multimedia files between devices. Activities are centered on a mobile device for visualizing the spatial distribution of all devices, including the user's position and the intuitive movement of files of various types between them.

Keywords: Image processing and computer vision · Enhancement · Filtering

1 Introduction and Motivation

Smart living environments are increasingly becoming a part of the reality of modern new buildings. This includes not only different concepts of building automation but also increasing networking static and mobile clients in the catchment area. Current multimedia devices are getting more integrated into existing networks. A stereo system or a TV can be just as connected via TCP/IP to a home network as the computer, a tablet PC or mobile phone. In current architectures, the distribution of multimedia files is normally regulated by a corresponding media server, which manages files centrally and allows/manages

© Springer International Publishing Switzerland 2015
N. Streitz and P. Markopoulos (Eds.): DAPI 2015, LNCS 9189, pp. 382–394, 2015.
DOI: 10.1007/978-3-319-20804-6_35

access. This is in practice often possible through the use of a single operating system and specially tailored software. In modern apartments, this is hardly the case, as in most cases, installations from different manufacturers are found and interoperable solutions generally do not exist. The variety of existing devices makes it difficult for inexperienced users to use targeted selection of individual devices and functionalities. Finally multi-modal aspects are largely ignored in the management of multimedia files in available on the market applications. Thus, a stereo system cannot play a movie, but at least one can listen to the sound, if there is no TV available in the room of the user.

In order to meet identified problems an architecture for the distribution of multimedia files is suggested that simplifies the complexity of this process on the one hand, but also extends to multi-modal aspects. Core of the concept is a mobile device, which as a central point allows files to distribute to various other devices. With the integrated sensors and an external localization system it is possible to transmit a specific file through simple gestures with the mobile device to another one. Depending on the capabilities of the device, the file is now given in the format that is best suited. We present a prototypical implementation of this concept. Text files, as well as movies and music, can now be distributed via a graphical user interface to the various devices. If one moves for example a text to a stereo system, a text-to-speech application is used to read this over a loudspeaker. The basis is a client-server structure, which allows dynamically moving files. Testing the implementation shows not only the validation of the basic functionalities, but also the satisfaction of the system for the test users.

2 Background and Previous Work

Intelligent living environments form already for some time a large area of research and are becoming increasingly important. This section describes some partial solutions that work and highlighted the problems existing solutions. Mark Weiser's prediction of the development of modern distributed environments [20] is increasingly becoming a part of reality. Rather than to interact specifically with each device, there is a growing tendency to always and everywhere to get in touch with a distributed intelligence. Multimedia applications are a strong example.

2.1 Service Mobility

Moving multimedia files between devices within a network or even the network-wide transfer falls within the concept of service mobility. It is a type of mobility where, in contrast to physical mobility, rather than individual devices regardless of their current location are permanently online, but sessions are adjusted based on the user's spatial movement [11]. For example, a user leaves the living room while he was playing a movie, and goes into the kitchen, this means that the movie is playing on a monitor in the kitchen. The so-called session (later also called session) is in this scenario the summary of the playback information of the movie, so e.g. file name, title used, current movie position and selected audio language. In the context of service mobility, one must differentiate between a complete session transmission as well as the partial session transfer. The previous scenario includes a full session transfer: processing a file is stopped and continued on another multimedia device. A partial session transfer would, for example, be maintaining the sound output on a tablet PC on which currently a movie is playing, whereas the video stream is redirected to a larger display.

Although service mobility includes already playing files on multiple, networked multimedia devices, moving sessions between the players is only considered for target devices with the same reproduction procedures. A transfer of a pure text file from a display device to a device that limit its ability to audio output is ignored. Since all network participants need to have access to the same pool of files to reflect the appropriate time, the question for the file synchronization arises.

2.2 Network Topologies

Various network topologies and techniques are available to solve this problem. As in [2], a central data server can easily solve this problem, at least for local networks. But due to the strong advent of P2P systems, such as in [18] or [13], the dynamic distribution of files plays an increasingly important role and the use of the concept of this work is to be examined.

An existing architecture for file synchronization with mobile devices is given in [15]. Since the resources of mobile devices, such as bandwidth and computing power, restricted by mostly high energy consumption, are limited, also energy efficient peer-to-peer synchronization models as in [5] are worth to be mentioned.

2.3 Indoor Localization in Science

Indoor localization is also an important approach for interacting with smart environments and mostly based on the user of a residential environment. For interaction with a mobile device his position must be determined. Since the Global Positioning System is not available indoors, this task is a challenge in itself. Suitable approaches for determining the position in the living area are mainly those who use the existing infrastructure of existing networks. Several access points of a wireless network can be used for this purpose as described in [12].

This principle can also be applied on Bluetooth nodes [3]. The accuracy of position determination can be improved by the combination of different sensors. In [9] as sensors we used a wireless network, an altimeter, and image data: a promising approach, since at least one interface for wireless communication and a camera are now to be found in almost any mobile device.

Also sensor networks specially designed for indoor localization are a common variant. At Fraunhofer IGD in Darmstadt a solution is developed which uses a concatenation of capacitive sensors. These systems can take many different designs and are easily installed, for example in the form of a carpet that determines the position of a person [4,6–8,10].

3   An Approach for Context-Based Multimedia

This work will focus on the context-based document management. Since this is a very broad notion we narrow it: in relation to this work, we mean managing and playback of electronic documents. Managing includes activities such as creating, deleting, indexing, searching, viewing, sharing, and manipulating files. The focus of this paper is just on the distributing and viewing files on different devices.

3.1   Modern Multimedia Distribution

In a modern apartment, a plethora of technical multimedia devices are distributed over different rooms. The difficulty for the user is to gain a quick overview of all devices, their positions and playing options. Even for users who know all multimedia devices on the network well this gives rise to yet another problem. The rapid distribution and redistribution of documents between all devices is a difficult and very time-consuming task for most users in general.

As listed in [11], a variety of ways exist for moving a file in an intelligent environment. An architecture for which all devices are addressed in the event of a transfer, would make more sense for largely interaction-free applications, i.e. in cases in which the user causes a session transfer by change in position. In such a scenario, each device could decide for itself whether it is positioned close enough to the user to take over the session. In our case, a mobile device will take over this decision, since it is always near the user when he wants to initiate a file transfer.

Another design decision is to use the "Device Centric Approach" [11]. This means that the entire complexity to initiate the file transfer between multiple devices, can be found in the participating network nodes. This approach is used, since the network infrastructure must not be changed, as would be the case with an intelligent network. In an intelligent network, the network itself would be responsible for the transfer. This results in the difficult extensibility of such a network, which is with the "Device Centric Approach" no problem, as described in [11].

3.2   File Formats and Playback Context

Very relevant is the problem of different file formats. Nowadays there are lots of different formats in all areas of IT. Alone the range of different video containers, video formats and codecs is almost unlimited. The problem of the approach of several players with partially limited edition options is that not all combinations of players and file types are allowed and that not all multimedia devices are equally suitable for outputting different file types in an intelligent environment. It is possible to play text files to actually inappropriately playback devices with text-to-speech programs. Nevertheless, there are two combinations technically very difficult to implement:

1. Reproducing image files on pure audio devices is difficult to imagine. Conceivable are programs that filter out features from images, bring them in

connection with semantic concepts and then read these terms. This is similar to the human gift of "describing" images. However, this requires a high level of artificial intelligence.

2. To view a music file on a fully visual equipment is also problematic. Possible solutions are visualizations of the audio file. For example, the individual notes can be displayed in case of music. If the file contains language it could be tried to convert them to text and display the resulting text on the screen. Sounds could be filtered out and visualized through images.

As shown in [16], there are already approaches that describe the way towards the above mentioned solutions. The possibility should also be considered, that file types are automatically converted towards each other so that they can possibly been shown better on the target device. In [1] a framework is demonstrated that could make such a conversion possible. This work is limited to basic classes of files, such as audio, video, text and image formats. They are sufficient to demonstrate to play files in a seemingly inappropriate context, such as playing text files on a radio.

3.3   Solutions for Localization

The location determination of the mobile device, which will be used to manage the files, is a non-trivial problem. There are different approaches that can be divided into solutions with smartphone-integrated sensors and solutions with external sensors, as well as equipment and people localization. Each solution has its advantages and disadvantages, depending on the intended application area and place (buildings, unpopulated areas and in urban areas, large or small radius). In our case, especially solutions to limit the position of mobile devices are interesting. These are often technically easier and will be sufficient, since a mobile device is a core of the solution approach located at the relevant times at the user itself.

It is e.g. possible by using the camera of a smartphone to scan multiple, in advance placed QR codes. This works theoretically in any of those types of areas, but is in practice only feasible in small areas [3]. Alternatively, one can use the in most of today's smartphones integrated wireless network to measure the reception strength to several previously known Hotspots in order to calculate the position. The same principle is transferable to Bluetooth [3]. There are also implementations that compute a motion path profile using the acceleration and orientation sensors and are thus dependent on relatively few really reliable, location decisions [14].

Conceivable are, of course, combinations of all of these ideas. The most obvious determination of the device position through the Global Positioning System, is inappropriate in our application due to mainly two reasons. On the one hand, the position can not be determined accurately enough for the purposes of this work due to the low resolution of the GPS. On the other hand, GPS is in the main area of application of the program, inside buildings, often not available since for the localization a satellite network is used.

As described the exact location of mobile devices within a few decimeters is often associated with complex work and thus an subject of many works. Needed for our purposes is a user or the mobile device localization of about 20 to 30 cm so that the measurement errors can not "skip" major obstacles. In order to guarantee a continuous handling of the final application, the position measurements are to be performed in a time frame of few seconds.

3.4 File Synchronization

As many devices on the network need access to one and the same file, this raises another problem: The bandwidth of the network in which the equipment is located, or the transmission power of the devices themselves may be restricted. A complete file transfer can therefore take more time than is reasonable. However, large files like videos should be played instantly on all devices. Possible solutions would be the media streaming or pre-synchronization of files. Mobile systems have only limited computing and storage capacity. The storage of the entire media library should therefore take place somewhere else if possible, as document collections and multimedia libraries are usually very large. The problem of limited space on mobile devices, and in following described file synchronization is solved using a cloud services.

Before a document can be reproduced on a device, one must ensure that it is also available for all devices in the network. Here is a variety of implementation options to choose from. Conceivable peer to peer approaches or solutions have one or more central servers as the core. These can be further divided into applications where a file synchronization must occur before the document can be reproduced, and on-demand streaming solutions, such as described in [17]. In this work a cloud service for synchronizing files is used [19]. This is primarily due to its ease of use and the high scalability in use. In this way also enhancements to file management with multiple users at very little expense can be integrated.

3.5 System Architecture

The greatest complexity of the overall architecture is transferred to the central mobile device, since here the graphical user interface can be found. The event handling includes the processing of sensor data of the mobile device as well as the handling of user input, such as a touch screen. The world view, which is graphically displayed in the user interface, can now be replaced with the actual data of the event handling in terms of user position, device status of the individual network nodes and spatial orientation of the user.

4 FourD - a Prototypical Implementation

The user interface is the Android app "Drag and Drop Document Distribution". For this concept, the name derives FourD, an allusion to the alliteration of the program name. FourD consists not only of the visible servers, but also, possibly several, client devices. Each client represents a separate unit and offers a variety of contexts for files to be displayed or played. Depending on device capabilities should other services offered by the unit responsible for each client program.

4.1   The Server

FourD was developed for the Android version 2.3.3 or higher. Thus FourD can be performed in over 80 % of all Android devices. OpenGLES 2.0 is used for an appealing graphical processing: the 3D OpenGL interface for embedded systems, i.e. for embedded systems such as tablet PCs and smartphones. The server itself exists of several so-called activities. An activity is similar to the concept of window-known operating systems, adapted to smaller display devices. One limitation is that only one activity at the same time can be displayed. Since activities seek to track the facts of a real, natural action of people, it is useful to divide the explanation of the FourD server in its activities. Thus it becomes clear what the user can accomplish with what activity.

Starting Activity - User Interface. The class "Start Activity" is responsible for displaying the home environment. It forms a key part of FourD server. Here the user can recognize all devices which are available for playback of files and can distribute the documents according to them. The start activity consists only of a single control, namely a so-called "GLSurfaceView". This surface supports the output of three-dimensional data using an "open Grahpics Library" interface, short OpenGL. In this work, we used the most recent implementation of the OpenGL API for mobile devices. It falls under the name "OpenGL for Embedded Systems", Version 2.0 or "OpenGLES 2.0". By using this graphics library, the necessary spatial representation of all nodes in the network can be implemented with relatively simple means.

After the start, firstly the configuration file is loaded in which all existing network nodes are listed. This configuration file consists of several lines, each line contains a string in the format "ClientIP; port; model; X-coordinate; Y-coordinate;". The tuple ClientIP: Port is not only the address of each client on the network, but also serves to uniquely identify this. Although several output devices can be connected to a physical computer, these are managed by exactly one client per device. The distinction of multiple client programs on a computer is done via different port numbers. Thus, the FourD server can, for example, report on which connected monitor the just opened video file is to be display.

Also the device type is passed from the configuration file. Although the decision whether a file on the selected device can be processed is done actually the client, still the server must be told the device type to ensure the correct presentation to the user. This can be seen on the mobile device of the user at a glance which player it is and what file types are particularly well suited for it.

In addition to the actual devices and their abilities, the spatial location of each multimedia players must be specified. This is necessary so that the mobile device on the server of FourD is used, can calculate the relative position of the

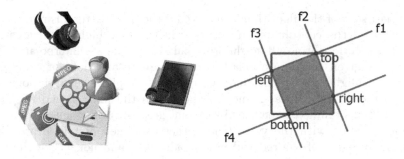

Fig. 1. Left: Starting activity. Right: Collision detection

individual playback devices to the user perspective. In this way, the user can at any time be made recognizable which output channels the device in front of him supports. At this point, an interface for changing the position of the user is also provided. An internal spatial localization has not been implemented but it could be integrated here.

The graphical interface elements (Fig. 1, left) are rendered by OpenGLES 2.0. Each element consists of at least a textured square, in turn consisting of two triangles. The files that were loaded on the management interface can be individually moved by a drag-and-drop gesture. The GUI of FourD also supports multi-touch gestures. Thus, it is possible with two fingers to "grab" a graphical representation to file and rotate, resize and move it. The decision whether a square is at a finger touching the display of the mobile device, is taken by the function "isPartOfTile (float x, float y)". If the given pair of coordinates (x, y) lies in the quadrant of the visible rectangle, the function returns the Boolean true. Since not the coordinates of all four corner points of a quadrangle are stored, but only the position of the center of gravity of the quadrangle as well as its rotation, and scale, the algorithm of isPartOfTile function must first calculate the position of the four corner points.

This is done by a unit matrix shifted according to the square, rotated and scaled and then multiplied by each point in the untouched original condition. For this, the matrix operations of the OpenGL API were used. Once the "real" coordinates are known, it is determined which point is most on the right, top, etc. In Fig. 1, right, these points are denoted with left/right/top/bottom.

Now the first evaluation takes place. If the supplied coordinates to the function are not within the blue marked area, the function is terminated immediately with the return value false. This evaluation may seem redundant in retrospect, but must be carried out to prevent a division by zero later.

If the coordinates are given within the blue rectangle, it is checked whether the point "left" is identical to the point "top" or "bottom". If this is the case, it means that the investigated square is exactly horizontally aligned. The blue square spanned by the vertices has the same edges as the actual quadrilateral. And since, as previously already checked the coordinates given are within the blue range, they are also within the actual square. In the case of the identity of the item "left" with "top" or "bottom" thus true is returned.

The last step of the algorithm is achieved if the quadrilateral is not perfectly horizontal and the coordinates are at least in the blue highlighted area. Now four linear functions from all neighboring pairs of points are interpolated. Thus in order the given coordinate pair lies in the square and not, for example, in the green highlighted area, the following rule must apply: The given point must be below the straight lines f1 and f2, and above the lines f3 and f4. Are all these conditions fulfilled, then the given point is in the orange marked area and the function ends with the value true. Otherwise, the point is located in an intermediate region of the red and blue quadrangle, and not within the tested quadrilateral.

Furthermore, each in the Start Activity displayed device can be selected. If a device is selected, then the activity "SessenInfoActivity" starts. Then it can be seen what the current status of the device is, or what the file being just played is.

4.2   Activity Open File - File Explorer

The activity "Open File Activity" is started from the "Start Activity", after it was informed that the user wants to manage a new file with FourD. It checks a predetermined directory for existing files and lists them. Filtering of the different file types and file formats is not done, since it depends on the corresponding client and its associated player, which formats can be processed and which not. If a file has been selected from the list, on the original calling Start Activity the event "onActivityResult" is called by the Android system. In case of selecting files, Start Activity is informed of a successful display of the Open File Activity using a result code and a string containing the file name and path of the file to be opened is passed.

In the case that the user after starting the Open File Activity does not want to add a new file to the management, there is a cancel button. Then start the Activity via an invalid result code is informed that no a valid string is available for further processing.

4.3   SessionInfoActivity - The Device Status

If the user touches one of the displayed multimedia devices, the SessionInfoActivity is started. This displays the current device status. Information about device type, distance of the multimedia device to the user, as well as the currently playing and displayed file (if available) can be shown. When the user wants to play or view the file on another multimedia device, he can delete the file from the device with this button. A click on OK closes the session Infoactivity without making any changes.

4.4   The Client

The client is the second major component of the solution presented here. His duties include playback of files and management of the available multimedia

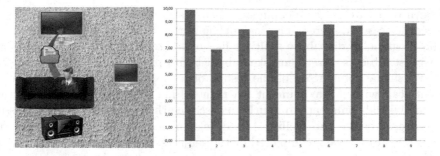

Fig. 2. Left: Testing scenarios, distributing several filetypes to several devices from the couch via a swipe. Right: Average points per question

device. Since the Android framework of the server-side application is programmed exclusively with the programming language Java, an implementation of the client is also done with Java.

The client is configured before starting to use a fixed scenario. This is done via a configuration file that is passed to the client as a startup parameter. If no configuration file is specified, the client uses the default "config.txt" as the file name.

In this work, two screens and a stereo system can be used. This means that three instances of the client program must be started because each client uses a device. To illustrate the functionality of FourD better only one of the two screens has own speakers. The second screen is therefore not in a position to independently reproduce audio streams.

If the client has device data of the available playback units, it opens a port and waits for the server sending the playback information. In this implementation, no parallel connections of multiple servers are supported. Altough this is quite possible, additional effects such as concurrent processes and race conditions must be considered.

Once a server has connected to the client, the server has several request options. Each available device in the network is controlled by a FourD client, and each FourD client precisely controls a single device. So as each client represents a device easily a network environment can be provided with a variety of devices to simulate. A stereo system is represented by a client that can only generate audio outputs, a network-compatible projector is analogous to a client only displaying output. Of course, a client, such as a real device can have a plurality of output channels, such as a television. This is simulated by a client with both audio and video output. Furthermore, this model is realistic in terms of the IP addresses. All clients can run on different computers on the network and so naturally getdifferent IP addresses, just as it would involve multiple, autonomous devices.

5   Results

This section analyzes whether FourD is an improvement over other methods for the control of various multimedia devices. To achieve this the user interface has been tested by several people ($n = 11$). The system consisted of two video-enabled devices and stereo. The task of the user was, after a short introduction to the program, to distribute multiple files of different types to the players.

All test subjects were then asked about their opinion on the experiment. To ensure a simple comparison of the results of each question this was done with a point scale with a maximum of ten points. Finally, the subjects could write down individual comments to FourD to describe other strengths and weaknesses of the user interface and facilitate its development. After several test tasks on the FourD interface were completed by the subjects, they evaluated the following questions:

1. How often do you use mobile devices with touch screen control?
2. How much experience do you have with applications to mobile devices that behave similar to a remote control?
3. How did you like the user interface?
4. Was the operation intuitive?
5. Did you find the information displayed clearly presented?
6. Do you think that the tasks were easy to do?
7. How accurate was the multi-touch operation Move/Rotate/Scale of Files?
8. Would you prefer FourD compared to other device controllers (e.g. remote controls)?
9. How clear was the audio output of text files?

Figure 2, right, illustrates the responses of all test subjects. The points awarded by the participants were arithmetically averaged.

Remarkable is that all the users claim to have very high experience with devices based on touch screens. A more representative survey would be one that also includes people with less experience. On the other hand, the judgment of a larger number of experienced testers is significant because the subjects can compare the application with others. Nowadays, most people have such experience, and the application is targeted towards such users. The user comments strengthen the solid impression of the user interface. The following are some unchanged excerpts to the questions: which has appealed the test persons particularly or where did they see flaws in the execution.

What did you like most about FourD?: "The intuitive handling of different types of files"; "The touch surface and the reaction rate, nearly as fast as remotes"; "Intuitive operation, no problems, very reliable. Cute visualization. The program is very useful, I want to have it!"; "Quick service, all units visible at a glance"; "No buttons with functions that I do not use anyway. Since FourD is running on the smartphone, it is always within reach".

What you did not like about FourD?: "Partial execution error"; "Display of the phone a bit too small. In landscape mode, accidentally file removed"; "There was no help service during operation"; "Drag and drop could be useful, not just 'shooting'. Double-click is relatively slowly recognized. One may make three clicks and then select a file directly". "Device disappeared. The "Mii" in both sexes variations or completely unisex".

As seen from the user comments, the surface may indeed be further improved, particularly with regard to the presentation on small screens, but the user interface is widely accepted. We therefore succeeded in creating a natural user interaction with various distributed devices in the home environment.

6   Conclusions

Context-based document management in intelligent environments is a very complex problem. Our concept with a mobile device as a controller and the consideration of the abilities of different players, and developed software solution for context-based distributing and displaying various types of files is a good step towards a comprehensive document management for smart living environments. It is successfully evaluated and provides scope for extensions and improvements. The integration of an appropriate method for determining the position of the user or the mobile device needs to be further elaborated with. Also, using FourD more research toward "ubiquitous multimedia" can be operated, i.e. how media distribution networks behave with multiple active users.

References

1. Bajcsy, P., Kooper, R., Marini, L., McHenry, K., Ondrejcek, M.: A framework for understanding file format conversions. In: Proceedings of the 2010 Roadmap for Digital Preservation Interoperability Framework Workshop, US-DPIF 2010, pp. 10:1–10:7. ACM (2010)
2. Baugher, M., French, S., Stephens, A., Horn, I.V.: A multimedia client to the ibm lan server. In: ACM Multimedia, pp. 105–112. ACM Press (1993)
3. Bittins, B., Sieck, J.: Multisensor and collaborative localization for diverse environments. In: EMS, pp. 406–411. IEEE (2011)
4. Braun, A., Neumann, S., Schmidt, S., Wichert, R., Kuijper, A.: Towards interactive car interiors: the active armrest. In: Proceedings of the 8th Nordic Conference on Human-Computer Interaction, pp. 911–914 (2014)
5. Chandrasekar, A., Chandrasekar, K., Ramasatagopan, H., Rafica, R.A.: Smc: an energy conserving p2p file sharing model for mobile devices. In: MobiDE, pp. 66–73. ACM (2012)
6. Grosse-Puppendahl, T., Herber, S., Wimmer, R., Englert, F., Beck, S., von Wilmsdorff, J., Wichert, R., Kuijper, A.: Capacitive near-field communication for ubiquitous interaction and perception. In: ACM UbiComp 2014, pp. 231–242 (2014)
7. Grosse-Puppendahl, T.A., Berghoefer, Y., Braun, A., Wimmer, R., Kuijper, A.: Opencapsense: A rapid prototyping toolkit for pervasive interaction using capacitive sensing. In: 2013 IEEE PerCom, pp. 152–159 (2013)
8. Grosse-Puppendahl, T.A., Braun, A., Kamieth, F., Kuijper, A.: Swiss-cheese extended: an object recognition method for ubiquitous interfaces based on capacitive proximity sensing. In: 2013 ACM SIGCHI Conference on Human Factors in Computing Systems, CHI 2013, pp. 1401–1410 (2013)
9. Lemieux, N., Lutfiyya, H.: Whlocator: Hybrid indoor positioning system. In: International Conference on Pervasive Services, pp. 55–64. ACM (2009)

10. Majewski, M., Braun, A., Marinc, A., Kuijper, A.: Providing visual support for selecting reactive elements in intelligent environments. Trans. Comput. Sci. **18**, 248–263 (2013)
11. Mate, S., Chandra, U., Curcio, I.D.D.: Movable-multimedia: session mobility in ubiquitous computing ecosystem. In: Proceedings of the 5th International Conference on Mobile and Ubiquitous Multimedia, MUM 2006, p. 8 (2006)
12. Milioris, D., Kriara, L., Papakonstantinou, A., Tzagkarakis, G., Tsakalides, P., Papadopouli, M.: Empirical evaluation of signal-strength fingerprint positioning in wireless lans. In: MSWiM, pp. 5–13. ACM (2010)
13. Mokhtarian, K., Hefeeda, M.: Analysis of peer-assisted video-on-demand systems with scalable video streams. In: MMSys, pp. 133–144. ACM (2010)
14. Ookura, H., Yamamoto, H., Yamazaki, K.: Development and evaluation of walking path estimation system using sensors of android device and vector map matching. In: ICOIN, pp. 25–29. IEEE (2012)
15. Ribeiro, J., Barreto, J., Ferreira, P.: Multirep: Asynchronous multi-device consistency. In: Third International Workshop on Middleware for Pervasive Mobile and Embedded Computing, pp. 7:1–7:6. ACM, New York (2011)
16. Salamin, P., Thalmann, D., Vexo, F.: Context aware, multimodal, and semantic rendering engine. In: VRCAI, pp. 11–16. ACM (2009)
17. Sharman, R., Ramanna, S.S., Ramesh, R., Gopal, R.D.: Cache architecture for on-demand streaming on the web. TWEB **1**(3) (2007)
18. Vu, L., Gupta, I., Nahrstedt, K., Liang, J.: Understanding overlay characteristics of a large-scale peer-to-peer iptv system. ACM Trans. Multimedia Comput. Commun. Appl. **6**(4), 31:1–31:24 (2010)
19. Wang, H., Shea, R., Wang, F., Liu, J.: On the impact of virtualization on dropbox-like cloud file storage/synchronization services. In: IWQoS, pp. 1–9. IEEE (2012)
20. Weiser, M.: The computer for the 21st century. In: Baecker, R.M., Grudin, J., Buxton, W.A.S., Greenberg, S. (eds.) Human-computer Interaction, pp. 933–940. Morgan Kaufmann Publishers Inc., San Francisco (1995)

Smart Devices, Objects and Materials

The Capacitive Chair

Andreas Braun[1]([⊠]), Sebastian Frank[2], and Reiner Wichert[1]

[1] Fraunhofer Institute for Computer Graphics Research IGD,
Darmstadt, Germany
{andreas.braun,reiner.wichert}@igd.fraunhofer.de
[2] Hochschule Rhein-Main, Wiesbaden, Germany
SebastianFrank87@gmx.de

Abstract. Modern office work often consists of spending long hours in a sitting position. This can cause a number of health-related issues, including chronic back pain. Ergonomic sitting requires suitably adjusted chairs and switching through a variety of different sitting positions throughout the day. Smart furniture can support this positive behavior, by recognizing poses and activities and giving suitable feedback to the occupant. In this work we present the Capacitive Chair. A number of capacitive proximity sensors are integrated into a regular office chair and can sense various physiological parameters, ranging from pose to activity levels or breathing rate recognition. We discuss a suitable sensor layouts and processing methods that enable detecting activity levels, posture and breathing rate. The system is evaluated in two user studies that test the activity recognition throughout a work week and the recognition rate of different poses.

Keywords: Capacitive proximity sensor · Posture recognition · Smart furniture

1 Introduction

The modern office worker spends a considerable amount of time sitting on a chair in front of a screen. The popularity of this style of work has led to the growth of related health issues in recent decades. Most notably lower back pain is a major risk factor that causes considerable economic impact in many western countries [1]. Supporting the office worker by providing more ergonomic seating, as well as encouraging physical exercise in the office can alleviate some of this impact [2]. In this work we present the Capacitive Chair. This office chair is equipped with eight capacitive proximity sensors that are able to detect body posture, respiratory rate and work activities. In order to detect a high number of poses, the electrodes have to be applied on the chair in a suitable layout. To demonstrate potential adaptations to common chair features we use a variety of different electrode materials and shapes, including one conductive thread electrode integrated into the mesh of a back rest. This thread electrode reacts to both presence and geometric deformation, which makes it suitable to detect subtle movements, such as respiration.

We envision three different use cases that can be supported by the Capacitive Chair. The first is the tracking of working situations, based on the current level of movement. We can determine if the chair is occupied and how active a person has been moving on

© Springer International Publishing Switzerland 2015
N. Streitz and P. Markopoulos (Eds.): DAPI 2015, LNCS 9189, pp. 397–407, 2015.
DOI: 10.1007/978-3-319-20804-6_36

it. The second use case is a posture recognition that recognizes different common poses on a chair. The last use case is breathing rate recognition, based on analyzing the chest movement. We have performed two different studies. The first tracked the working activity of a single user throughout a week. The results are activity graphs that show active phases, inactive phases and periods of not being at the chair. In a second evaluation we were testing the posture recognition of the chair in a short study with 10 participants. This work is extended from internal technical reports and project reports. Excerpts and intermediate results can be found in [3, 4].

2 Related Works

In the previous years there have been various attempts to attach different sensors to pieces of furniture, in order to provide additional functionality or provide contextual information for other systems in the environment.

The Health Chair by Griffiths et al. uses pressure sensors in the backrest to detect the respiratory rate from chest movement and EKG electrodes on the armrests to measure the heart rate [5]. Based on a pre-study with several hundred users focusing on common sitting postures, they have optimized their data processing for detecting physiological signals of users in those postures. They conducted a study with 18 users that were taking different poses on an equipped chair. The Health Chair was able to detect the heart rate in 32 % of the cases and respiratory rate in 52 % of the time.

The Smart Bed is a system created by our group that integrates capacitive proximity sensors into a bed [6]. A first algorithm detects the posture of one or two persons on the bed and the estimated stress distribution on the spine, using a combination of pressure and presence. This data is acquired by attaching flexible electrodes to a slatted frame. In an extended work a movement-based algorithm was added that evaluates the current sleep phase [7]. Based on the variance of sensor signals over time the extent of user movement can be estimated. This is correlated to the current sleep phase. This method was adapted for detecting the work activity levels of the Capacitive Chair. It will be briefly discussed in the following sections.

Another similar prototype is the Smart Couch [8]. This system by Grosse-Puppendahl et al. uses capacitive proximity sensors integrated into a regular couch to recognize different postures of one or two occupants based on a machine learning classifier. A similar approach is used for the posture recognition in this paper. We extend on this work by providing an integrated layout for capacitive proximity sensors in a chair and a classification method that is focused on the requirements of one person on one chair.

3 Layout for Capacitive Sensors in an Office Chair

The layout of capacitive proximity sensor systems should be driven by the requirements of the chosen applications. In our case there are three measured properties - posture, activity and breathing rate. The requirements for the first two are similar. Posture can be determined by the position of body parts relative to the sensors, while activity is calculated based on the change in position of body parts relative to the sensors. Therefore, a high number of sensors should be reserved for placement close to the body parts performing most of the movement - the limbs. As the office chair has no parts around the lower legs or feet the leg movement is instead indicated by a sensor in front of the seat area that detects presence of the upper legs. The chair has two armrests that can be equipped to estimate arm positions and activity. In order to detect postures that are similar but vary on orientation of the user the weight distribution of the body should be identified - whether it is more on the left or right side. For this purpose two electrodes are added in the back area of the seat. This is suitable as most of the body weight is put in this area and variations can be easily identified.

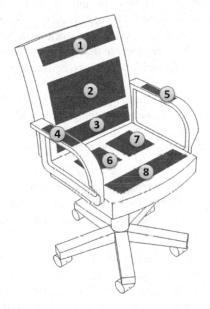

Fig. 1. Electrode layout of the capacitive chair

To detect how far an occupant is leaning to the front several electrodes should be attached in the back rest. Here, the third requirement comes into play. The detection of the respiratory rate is based on the movement of the chest. As it is beneficial if electrodes are approximately the size of the object to be detected, the electrodes are not evenly spaced - instead we are using a larger electrode close to the chest. This leads to the final electrode layout shown in Fig. 1. (1) electrode on the upper part of the backrest (covered by faux leather), (2) electrode in the central part of the backrest (using conductive thread), (3) electrode in the lower part of the backrest (covered by faux leather), (4) electrode below the right armrest (5), electrode below the left armrest, (6) electrode for the left hip area below the left part of the seat, (7) electrode for the right hip area below the right part of the seat, and (8) electrode for detecting both legs below the front part of the seat.

4 Data Processing

In this section we describe three different data processing methods that allows us to detect activity levels, recognize the posture and acquire a breathing rate from a single sensor.

4.1 Activity Level Detection

Detecting a general activity level during work is a useful measure for long term data analysis and in an aggregated form allows an organizational oversight of how workers behave during a regular work day. Thus it may inform changes in organization of work if undesired activity levels are detected. The individual user is getting a feedback on his activity. This may prompt a more active style of work with less sitting and increased activity on and off the chair. It is foreseeable that this could be combined with different gamification approaches, e.g. to facilitate activity competition between workers of a group.

The chosen method is similar to an approach we previously used for sleep detection. The variations in subsequent sensor readings are used to determine an activity level. We will at this point just give a shortened description of this process with a thorough description being found in Djakow et al. [7]. The following three steps are performed:

1. Acquire a time-series of sensor readings and their variations
2. Detect movement if aggregate or individual variation exceeds a certain threshold
3. Analyze the frequency of movements over time and associate them to a certain activity level

For the Capacitive Chair we are considering three activity levels. The first is "not at chair", whereas no occupancy is recorded on the chair. This usually occurs during lunch break or certain meetings. The second level is "active work", such as writing and typing. The third level is "inactive work" that does not involve movement, such as reading screen content. The tasks of writing and typing are indicated by considerable movement of the hands and arms. Thus, we can use the electrode layout to our advantage and prefer readings from the sensors attached to the arm rests. We tested two approaches - the first explicitly favored variation from armrest sensors, while the second implicitly uses the sensors with most significant variation. The first method is preferable if we only want to detect writing and typing, as it will ignore movements of other body parts. The second method considers activity whenever any sensor has high variations. We observed that typing and writing often lead to selection of armrest sensors. However, since we wanted to capture more styles of active movement of the chair the second method is used in this work.

4.2   Posture Recognition

Support vector machines (SVM) are a supervised learning method that is primarily used for linear classification of n-dimensional features [10]. They are clustering data by calculating a hyperplane from training data that maximizes the distance from the closest features. A fast learning method is using sequential minimal optimization and was proposed by Platt [11]. The algorithm requires normalized values. A dynamic normalization algorithm constantly analyzes the sensor data for minimum and maximum values and accordingly calculates the normalized value. There is a variety of different software frameworks for machine learning that support training and recall of SVMs, thus there is no need for reimplementing these methods. As there is an implicit weighting of features according to significance, there is no need to preprocess or weigh the sensor data. The training data is collected from a set of persons that have a significant variance in body shapes in both height and girth. SVMs support an arbitrary number of different groups for classification. However, the number of significant poses on a chair is limited. The Global Posture Study by office furniture manufacturer Steelcase Inc. analyzes the most common poses with a focus on information consumption from modern technical devices, such as smart phones or tablets [9]. The different postures are shown in Fig. 2. A capacitive office chair should be able to distinguish most of these poses if training data has been collected from a sufficiently large number of suitable candidates. Additionally, using sensors clearly positioned on a certain side of the chair, e.g. the armrest, it is possible to associate directional varieties of the asymmetric postures.

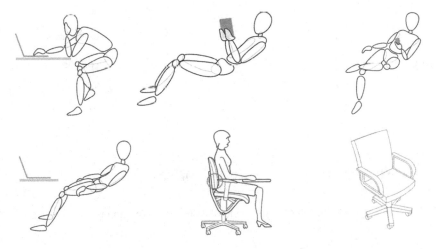

Fig. 2. Selected set of postures from global posture study and own gestures. From top left to bottom right: The strunch, the draw, the smart lean, the take it in, upright, no person (first four taken from [9])

The processed values of all sensors are compared to previously trained sitting positions of a user. The position with the lowest deviation is considered the current posture.

4.3 Detection of Breathing Rate

The volume changes of the chest while breathing have been a topic of research for a long time [12]. If the body of a person is not moving and can be considered at a static distance from a capacitive proximity sensor, the chest movement should translate into a periodically changing sensor value. The breathing rate detection is operating on a single electrode that is placed close to the chest. The basic concept is shown in Fig. 2. The surface of the electrode is large and close to the surface. Therefore, it is able to pick up the chest movement. Two different methods of data processing are used and fused to get the final breathing rate. Using a fast Fourier transformation the signal is transformed into the frequency space. We are looking for significant signal portions in frequency areas that can be associated to breathing, between 0.1 Hz and 3 Hz. The above Fig. 3 shows an example of the sensor data curve generated by the conductive thread sensor behind the back of a person. The chest movement is clearly visible as sinusoidal oscillation of the sensor value. If there is a sufficiently stable baseline, the zero-crossings can be calculated. However, as this can't be guaranteed in all cases an adaptive baseline should be used that is reconfigured according to changing states of the sitting person.

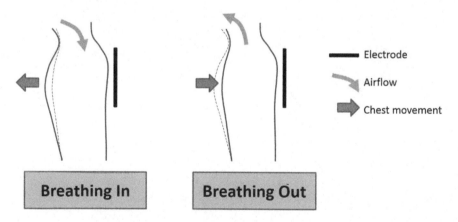

Fig. 3. Chest movement when breathing in and out

5 Capacitive Chair Prototype

As our basis we are using a regular office chair that was acquired from a local furniture store for approximately €40. Its backrest has a mesh texture in the middle and two non-movable armrests on each side. The electrode locations are chosen according to the layout present in Sect. 3. It is outlined in Fig. 4. Electrodes 1 and 3 are created from flexible copper foil suspended and held in place by duct tape that is attached to the aluminum frame of the backrest. Electrode 2 is created by weaving conductive thread through the mesh and fixing it on two sides using conductive copper tape. This structure is shown in Fig. 5. Electrodes 4 and 5 are also based on copper foil, yet fixed below the hard plastic of the armrests. In order to avoid signal attenuation from the aluminum pipe in the armrest, they are cut to be wider and cover the whole lower structure. Electrodes 6, 7 and 8 are made from single layer PCB boards that are glued to the bottom of the seat area.

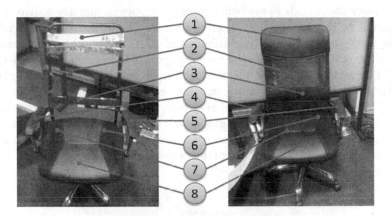

Fig. 4. Capacitive chair electrode positions on actual prototype

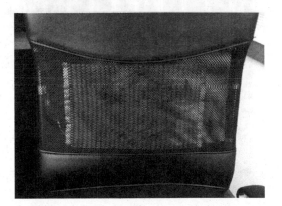

Fig. 5. Capacitive electrode based on conductive thread woven through the mesh of the chair

The different electrodes of the Capacitive Chair are connected to a single Open-CapSense board that supports eight channels [13]. This board additionally supports various pre-processing steps. In this case we use a floating average filter to attenuate high-frequency noise. OpenCapSense provides non-normalized integer values that are sent to a connected PC through a USB cable. Any further processing is done on this PC. Normalization is used before all further steps. The Activity Level detection and Posture

Recognition use these normalized value for their processing, while the Breathing Rate recognition performs a FFT with a sliding window of 20 s and a 200 ms overlap. This provides sufficient information in the required range between 0.1 Hz and 3 Hz. The most significant amplitude in this interval is considered the user's breathing rate.

6   User Studies

We have performed two different studies. The first tracked the working activity of a single user throughout a week. The results are activity graphs that show active phases, inactive phases and periods of not being at the chair. An example day activity graph is shown in Fig. 6. The test user was asked to annotate specific activities throughout the day. The graph shows the hourly distribution of the three phase. Notable are a very inactive phase at the beginning of the workday (green), in this case caused by reading emails. At the middle of the work day the lunch break is visible as "not at chair" period (grey). However, the distinction between active and inactive work often is not closely correlated to noted activities. In general even fairly active work periods only resulted in a low percentage of active work. The method has to be either tuned to individually set different activity levels on a per-person basis or consider other data sources, such as sensors attached in different places of the work environment or monitoring tools installed on the work computer.

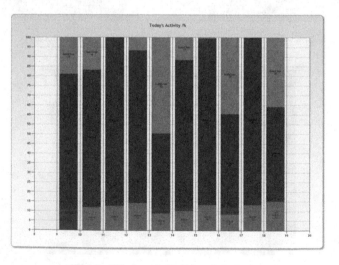

Fig. 6. Work activity throughout a day

The aggregated values enable self-monitoring of levels of activity throughout the week. This can be used as feedback to employ a more active lifestyle or in an aggregated fashion by management to facilitate a more active style of work, e.g. by using micro break programs.

In a second evaluation we were testing the posture recognition of the chair in a short study with 10 participants. Our system was tuned to distinguish three poses from the global posture study and a non-pose: sitting upright, the strunch, take it in, and close to chair. The latter is defined by providing some signal due to presence without actually sitting on the chair.

Before the study a set of training samples was collected by two of the developers and used to train the system. The data collected from the study participants was not used in the training process, in order to test a pre-trained system.

The persons were given a short introduction, in which the different postures were displayed. After that the participants were asked to perform the postures in order. When testing "close-to-chair" the subjects were asked to rattle at the chair, stand close, move it around and thus disturb the potential sensor readings. Each class was tested for 10 s, collecting 200 samples. Overall the results were very convincing. Of the 40 different measurements series only two were not achieving 100 % accuracy. The upright and "close to chair" positions were classified correctly for all candidates. A single candidate had an 86 % rating on the strunch posture. A different candidate had a 55 % rating on the "take it in" position. The average of correctly classified postures is 98.5 %.

The following Table 1 shows the percentage of correct samples for each posture of all participants.

Table 1. Results of posture recognition test in percent

	S1	S2	S3	S4	S5	S6	S7	S8	S9	S10	Avg
Upright	100	100	100	100	100	100	100	100	100	100	100
The strunch	100	100	100	100	86	100	100	100	100	100	98,6
Take it in	100	100	100	100	100	100	100	100	55	100	95,5
Close to chair	100	100	100	100	100	100	100	100	100	100	100

7 Conclusion and Future Work

On the previous pages we have presented the Capacitive Chair - a regular office chair equipped with eight capacitive proximity sensors that is able to detect presence, posture, activity level and breathing rate of its occupants. The sensor system is invisibly integrated into the chair and uses variations of electric fields to determine the physiological data over a distance. We have shown that a combination of different electrode materials and shapes that are attached to a single evaluation board for capacitive proximity sensors provide sufficient information about presence and proximity of occupants to gather physiological data. The system was installed in a prototype and evaluated during a long term study for activity level monitoring at work, as well as a test on the precision of the posture recognition method with ten subjects. The activity levels correlate with the noted activities, however active and inactive work are difficult to distinguish using the chair alone. The posture recognition achieved a very high overall classification rate of 98.6 %. However, the set of postures is limited to only four. A test with more postures might require modifications to our method or adding a higher number of sensors.

As future work we are planning to improve the range of recognized postures by collecting a more comprehensive set of training data from various subjects. Another approach is to use the proximity data, in order to allow a more fine-grained posture recognition, e.g. to enable tracking of office chair exercises. This can create various applications in the domain of applied ergonomics. We are working on expanding our breathing rate recognition to also detect the heart rate of occupants. However, as the movement of the heart muscle within the chest is weak compared to the chest movement while breathing this may require higher precision sensors and higher data acquisition frequencies. Notably, the breathing rate recognition wasn't evaluated in this work, which is planned in the immediate future.

There are a few factors related to the hardware that can be improved. A major point to improve is the restriction to a single chair. It took approximately 12 h to equip a single chair with our sensing system. Ideally, the electrodes and sensors should be able to be installed as a kit that can be easily attached to various different types of chairs. Also, the system has a comparatively high energy consumption of about 200 mA. Therefore, it is currently wired and should be modified for reasonable battery powered application.

Acknowledgments. We would like to thank all volunteers that participated in our studies and provided valuable feedback for future iterations. This work was partially funded by EIT ICT Labs SSP14267 and HWB13031.

References

1. Maniadakis, N., Gray, A.: The economic burden of back pain in the UK. Pain **84**, 95–103 (2000)
2. Robertson, M., Amick III, B.C., DeRango, K., Rooney, T., Bazzani, L., Harrist, R., Moore, A.: The effects of an office ergonomics training and chair intervention on worker knowledge, behavior and musculoskeletal risk. Appl. Ergon. **40**, 124–135 (2009)
3. Braun, A.: Application and validation of capacitive proximity sensing systems in smart environments. Dissertation, TU Darmstadt (2014). http://tuprints.ulb.tu-darmstadt.de/4175/
4. Braun, A., Wichert, R., Kuijper, A., Fellner, D.W.: Capacitive proximity sensing in smart environments. J. Ambient Intell. Smart Environ. (2015, in press)
5. Griffiths, E., Saponas, T.S., Brush, A.J.B.: Health chair: implicitly sensing heart and respiratory rate. UbiComp Adjunct., pp. 661–671 (2014)
6. Braun, A., Heggen, H.: Context recognition using capacitive sensor arrays in beds. In: Proceedings AAL-Kongress (2012)
7. Djakow, M., Braun, A., Marinc, A.: MoviBed - sleep analysis using capacitive sensors. In: Proceedings UAHCI, pp. 171–181 (2014)
8. Grosse-Puppendahl, T., Marinc, A., Braun, A.: Classification of user postures with capacitive proximity sensors in AAL-environments. In: Proceedings AmI International, pp. 314–323 (2011)
9. Steelcase Inc.: Global posture study. http://www.steelcase.com/en/products/category/seating/task/gesture/pages/global-posture-study.aspx. Accessed 30 Jan 2015
10. Hearst, M.A., Dumais, S.T., Osman, E., Platt, J., Scholkopf, B.: Support vector machines. IEEE Intell. Syst. Appl. **13**, 18–28 (1998)

11. Platt, J.C.: Fast training of support vector machines using sequential minimal optimization. Advances in Kernel Methods - Support Vector Learning, pp. 185–208. MIT Press, Cambridge (1999)
12. Wade, O.L.: Movements of the thoracic cage and diaphragm in respiration. J. Physiol. **124**, 193–212 (1954)
13. Grosse-Puppendahl, T., Berghoefer, Y., Braun, A., Wimmer, R., Kuijper, A.: OpenCapSense: a rapid prototyping toolkit for pervasive interaction using capacitive sensing. In: Proceedings PerCom, pp. 152–159 (2013)

Aspects Concerning the Calibration Procedure for a Dual Camera Smartphone Based ADAS

Mihai Duguleana$^{(\boxtimes)}$, Florin Girbacia, Cristian Postelnicu,
Andreea Beraru, and Gheoghe Mogan

Department of Automotive and Transport Engineering, University Transilvania
of Brasov, Brașov, Romania
{mihai.duguleana, garbacia, cristian-cezar.postelnicu,
aberaru, mogan}@unitbv.ro

Abstract. We present the architecture of an Advanced Driver Assistance System (ADAS) based on common dual camera smartphones, emphasizing on the calibration procedure which is active during the initialization phase (prior to the actual driving). NAVIEYES project attempts to make use of the video information received from both the front and the rear cameras of the phone in order to infer and alert drivers upon potential dangerous situations. This study focuses on the information received from the front camera. 10 different mobile devices were tested, in order to choose the most powerful and ergonomic platform. A calibration experiment is carried by 22 subjects, and the first version of the application is tested using a driving simulator. The system is deployed on a real car, and several warning paradigms such as audio, video and mixed alerts are also analyzed. We present the HCI questionnaire, analyze the data and propose further developments.

Keywords: Personal navigation assistant · Smartphone · Dual camera · Driver assistant · ADAS

1 Introduction

Traffic accidents have always been a weak point of road transportation. A 2010 report from the World Health Organization (WHO) shows that more than 1.2 million traffic accidents occur each year [1]. In hope of diminishing the effects of this phenomenon, the United Nations General Assembly adopted resolution which proclaims the period 2011–2020 as the Decade of Action for Road Safety. Today we find ourselves at the middle of this period, and although several safety systems have been deployed on the latest car models, things are not improving radically. As an active component of the initiative, WHO has released in 2013 the Global status report on road safety [2]. Making the vehicles safer is an important objective resulted from this report, not only from a social and psychological point of view, but also from economical point of view, as the cost of traffic incidents (whether they are fatal or non-fatal) has been estimated to average 1.5 % of the gross national product in EU partner countries, totaling a global cost of approximately \$500 B per year [3]. WHO identified distracted driving and fatigue among the most common causes of accidents.

© Springer International Publishing Switzerland 2015
N. Streitz and P. Markopoulos (Eds.): DAPI 2015, LNCS 9189, pp. 408–417, 2015.
DOI: 10.1007/978-3-319-20804-6_37

The project NAVIEYES [4] started in 2014 and aims to research new means of preventing at least a small part of potential dangerous driving situations. NAVIEYES proposes to improve classic Advanced Driver Assistance Systems (ADASs) by using computer vision capabilities to track driver's eyes and head, along with the traffic environment. The ADAS developed within NAVIEYES can be deployed on smart-phones with dual cameras. The application will alert the driver for front obstacles (static or dynamic), change of direction (lane change), specific traffic signs or whether his drowsiness level is high. The core of the system is based on 3 concurrent modules: an estimator of eye gaze, head orientation and drowsiness level, a detector of road obstacles, lanes and traffic signs and an API necessary to integrate the first 2 modules. The outcome solution will work with any car kit that allows visibility for both smartphone cameras, as seen in Fig. 1.

Fig. 1. Positioning the smart phone (yellow area), with the rear camera facing outside the car (blue area) and the front camera facing the car interior (red area) (Colour figure online).

2 Related Work

Concerning the information received from the front camera (the car interior and the driver), computer vision is at the moment used within actual ADASs for 2 not nec-essarily disjunctive purposes: evaluating the drowsiness level (the fatigue level) and analyzing the behavior of the driver. While the first plane of development focuses on studying eye movements, specifically eye blinks, the later includes the analysis of body postures, possibly face detection and recognition, head orientation, prediction of future actions and the assessment of driver's cognitive load among several others.

2.1 Drowsiness

Drowsiness appears due to several reasons, including long periods of driving, stress, diseases (such as sleep disorders, medication side effects), or even radio music. As some of the driver's actions are a direct result of the high levels of fatigue, and additionally, as several activities are hard to categorize and include in structural patterns, most scientists which research driver information focus on calculating just the most common parameter from the first area: PERCLOS (PERCentage of eye CLOSure) [5]. Calculating PERCLOS based on video processing algorithms usually takes the following route:

- First, face detection will be computed. Ideally, face detection will make use of a fusion of methods such as Haar classifiers, filters, Viola-Jones, landmark model matching and others.
- After retrieving the image segment which contains driver's face, the eyes are usually classified and followed through consecutive frames, using other techniques such as neural networks (NNs), template matching, Haar classifiers, Dynamic Time Window, or particle swarm optimization. The biggest problem of this approach is the high sensitivity to even the slightest light variations.
- The number of blink occurrences is accounted over a period of time and compared with specific threshold.

Besides PERCLOS, another visual clue analyzed by researchers is yawning. Several studies inferred that yawning is triggered by low vigilance levels, during progressive drowsiness. However, the main issue when analyzing yawning is the weak quantification possibility. There is still a public debate on what exactly triggers yawns [6], and some studies also argue the precision of correlation between facial muscles and drowsiness (60 %) with respect to the correlation between blinking and drowsiness (>80 %) [7]. It has been proved that people may have high yawning levels without even experiencing drowsiness, and the other way around – sleep can occur without yawning. Another drowsiness cue is head movement. It has been shown that head movement distance and velocity has a strong correlation to somnolence [8]. Taken together, eye blinking, yawning and head movements provide critical data necessary to determine the drowsiness level of the subject.

2.2 Driver Behavior

The behavior of the driver can prove to be useful to ADASs. The focus of most studies is on inferring the eye gaze (if possible, the gaze intersection point) and the head orientation, or better said, driver's region of interest (ROI) and within this region, driver's point of interest (POI). Another important region is the focus of expansion (FOE). Since almost 2 decades ago, it has been concluded that at their simplest, drivers' fixation patterns on straight roads can be described as concentrating on a point near to the FOE (i.e. the horizontal line, where objects appear stationary). Researchers assumed that the reliance on the FOE is trivial, as it provides precise directional information to the driver and is the location near to which future traffic hazards are most likely to be first visible. Other researchers refer to the fixations on the tangent point (TP) - the inner lane marking (the boundary between the asphalted road and the adjacent green) bearing the highest curvature in the 2D retinal image, or in other terms, the innermost point of this boundary (see Fig. 2a). Other fixation strategy slightly different from TP relies on the retinal flow theory. As the driver moves through the environment, the objects projected on his retina change with the movement, creating a "retinal flow" in a manner fairly similar with the optical flow computer vision algorithm. This flow depends on several parameters like the heading direction, car speed, the depth structure of the environment and whether objects themselves are static or dynamic. Basically, drivers fixate a spot on their future path (i.e. the middle of the lane) and track it for some time as they approach it. When the point comes too near to the car front, drivers will look for a new point to track. Depending on the curvature of the flow lines, drivers make steering decisions, as straight retinal flow lines emerge if the driver steers correctly (see Fig. 2b).

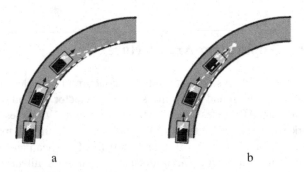

       a   b

Fig. 2. (a) TP theory; (b) retinal flow theory

Processing a video stream from a single camera provides approximate results. Luckily, most assistance systems do not require detailed eye gaze direction, but only the coarse gaze direction, in order to reduce false stressful alarms. Coarse gaze direction can be computed based on the head orientation vector. Humans have a limited FOV, thus in order to gaze on some scene element, they will move their head to a comfortable position before orienting their eyes. If the coarse gaze direction extends to an angle higher than ±35 degrees, the driver will most likely rotate his head and from this point on, coarse gaze direction may be calculated by tracking the orientation of the head [9]. Several methods are used for head tracking. Most of the make use of information such as eye position and facial features. The active appearance model (AAM) was used to find facial features in various situations. Other methods are based on shape features, such as the cylindrical face model technique. The methods based on texture features work by finding driver's face (partial face) in the video stream and analyzing the intensity pattern of the facial image in order to estimate the head orientation. Among texture-based methods one can count the Principal Component Analysis (PCA), Kernel Principal Component Analysis (KPCA) and the Linear Discriminant Analysis (LDA). Furthermore, some scientists used Local Gradient Orientation (LGO) and Support Vector Regression (SVR) to estimate the driver's continuous yaw and pitch, while others analyzed the asymmetry of the facial image by using a Fourier transform to estimate the driver's continuous yaw.

2.3   Integrated Research

Both research areas (drowsiness and driver behavior) are integrated in just a few studies. Furthermore, only a few analyze the possibility of using a dual camera mobile phones as a sensorial system. Most of the work relies on using special laboratory equipment (head mounted eye trackers, infrared light cameras and so on). In [10], authors propose a similar system, with several drawbacks: the system is designed specifically for a test car and doesn't take into consideration the general case, in which a calibration procedure is required. This subject is precisely treated by this paper. In [11], researchers use only on the front camera to compute where the driver is looking, and produce a finite set: the road, top, left and right mirrors, street signs, car board or phone.

3   NAVIEYES Application Architecture

The core of the NAVIEYES system is based on 3 concurrent modules: an estimator of the eye gaze, head orientation and drowsiness level, a detector of road obstacles, lanes and traffic signs and an API necessary to integrate the first 2 modules. The outcome solution will work with any car kit that allows visibility for both smartphone cameras.

The first module handles the recording and analysis of the head and eye movement and provides important clues vital for understanding driver's intentions, for taking appropriate accident countermeasures. The output of this module is the gaze vector, the head orientation vector and PERCLOS. The first module is based on the video stream received from the front camera and requires a calibration procedure before actually retrieving data (see Fig. 3).

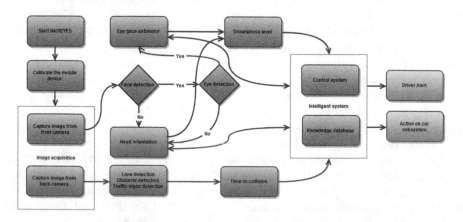

Fig. 3. NAVIEYES application architecture

The second module analyses the exterior traffic environment, and produces 3 outputs: front collision warning (FCW), traffic sign detection (TSD) and lane departure warning (LDW). The second module receives the video stream from the rear camera. This assumes that the rear camera is correctly facing the car exterior environment.

The third module integrates the first 2 modules. The output from the first module is used to determine if the driver is actually paying attention to potential dangerous situations (front collision or lane switching). Although traffic signs are not considered in this category, based on the computed vectors (eye gaze and head orientation), the system can also infer if the driver actually sees the traffic sign.

4 Calibration Procedure

The calibration system starts as soon as the user enters a vehicle and opens the application. The calibration phase ensures that both the front and the rear cameras are positioned correctly (they are both able to receive the desired video streams). This assumes setting a correct position for the car kit and a video calibration of the device, by following these steps (see Fig. 4):

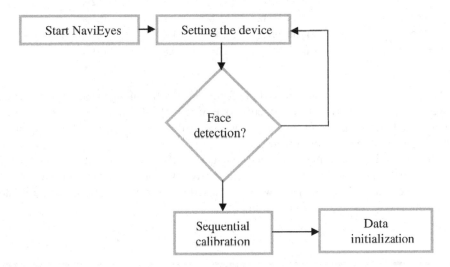

Fig. 4. Calibration procedure

- The device is mounted into the car kit.
- The app tries to detect the face of the user.
- If the face is detected, the user is guided into a calibration sequence which quantifies what a look to left or right really means. The user is asked to maintain its head fixed, and to look at the maximum left and right. If not, the app asks the user to reposition the device, based also on the gyroscope sensor.
- If the calibration is a success (the eye gaze is established), previous session data is initialized (PERCLOS average, GPS position, total driving distance and others).

Before running the HCI experiment trials, 10 mobile phones were taken into account, based on their hardware specifications, their switching delay (the simultaneous use of both cameras is impossible by design of CameraService for Android, and a similar problem exists on IOS) and on their face detection rate (using the basic OpenCv haar classifier). The following data resulted from our primary tests (Table 1):

Table 1. Smartphones tested for Navieyes deployment

Model	Processor	Memory	Switching delay	Face detection overhead
Samsung Galaxy S3	1400 MHz	1 Gb	1.2 s	0.3 s
Samsung Galaxy S4 mini	1700 MHz	1.5 Gb	1 s	0.2 s
Samsung Galaxy S4	1900 MHz	2 Gb	0.9 s	0.2 s
Samsung Galaxy S5	2500 MHz	2 Gb	0.9 s	0.2 s
HTC One Mini 2	1200 MHz	1 Gb	1.3 s	0.2 s
HTC One M8	2300 MHz	2 Gb	1.1 s	0.2 s
LG G3	2500 MHz	2 Gb	1.1 s	0.2 s
iPhone 4S	1000 MHz	512 Mb	1 s	0.1 s
iPhone 5S	1300 MHz	1 Gb	1 s	0.1 s
iPhone 6	1400 MHz	1 Gb	0.8 s	0.1 s

We've concluded that all Android platforms are mostly taking around 1 s to switch between cameras, and their face detection overhead is 0.2–0.3 s, while iPhones switch cameras and detect faces faster. Thus, we've settled for using the Android based Samsung S3 within our experiments.

The calibration procedure was tested in a real vehicle, on 22 subjects (18 students, 3 Ph.D. students and 1 person from the administrative staff of our university). The car kit was already mounted, the subjects were just asked to insert the smartphone into it and to run the NaviEyes application (see Fig. 5).

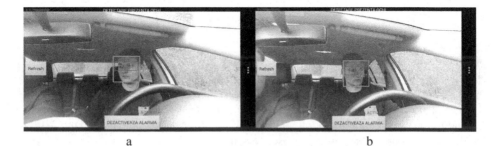

a   b

Fig. 5. Calibration procedure. Driver looks right (a) and left (b)

5 Virtual Experiment Setup

The same subjects were asked to use the ECA Faros Simulator and drive within an urban scenario with medium traffic for 3 min, on a designated route, while using the first version of the application. Each participant was involved in 3 trials, each using a different alert: sound alert coming from the phone, light alert coming from the phone and sound alert coming from the stereo speakers of the VR simulator. Subjects were asked to perform various activities within each trial, in no particular order: send a text message, look behind, and close their eyes for 3 s. The application was set to trigger the alarm after receiving 0.6 s of continuous invalid readings (no face detection, Fig. 6).

Fig. 6. Experiment setup: VR simulator and Samsung Galaxy S3 running Navieyes app

6 HCI Questionnaire

The HCI questionnaire proposed in this study was developed to acquire data on subjects' interaction with the application. Most questions from the quiz could be answered on a scale of 1 to 10, and were divided into 3 sections:

- The biographic section was designed to gather data related to the technological background of the participant. We tried to cluster subjects by their age and sex, their driving and computer skills and their experience with smartphones by using questions such as "How often do you drive?", "How often do you use smartphones?", "How familiarized are you with mobile apps?".

- The <u>calibration section</u> treats only aspects concerning the calibration procedure, with questions such as "How easy going was to set up the system?" or "How good do you find the detection rate?". We also addressed an open question: "How would you improve the calibration procedure?".
- The <u>usability section</u> treats the issues participants encounter during the VR experiment. In order to measure the usability of the application while driving on the car simulator, this section includes questions such as "How stressful is the alarm system no. 1 (phone sound alarm)?" or "How good is the 0.6 s timeframe?". The overall usability of the system is assessed with the question "How useful do you find the Navieyes application?" (Table 2).

Table 2. HCI questionnaire

Section	Question	Answer
Biographic section	Age?	20 years – 11
		21 years – 7
		25 years – 2
		26 years – 1
		37 years – 1
	Sex?	M – 17 F – 5
	How often do you drive?	6.95 (0 – never, 10 – all the time)
	How often do you use smartphones?	9.04 (0 – never, 10 – every day)
	How familiarized are you with mobile apps?	8.22 (0 – never heard, 10 – always using)
Calibration section	How easy going was to set up the system?	7.90 (0 – easy, 10 – hard)
	How good do you find the detection rate?	7.81 (0 – bad, 10 – good)
	How would you improve the calibration procedure?	–
Usability section	How stressful is the alarm system no. 1 (phone sound alarm)?	6.59 (0 – stressful, 10 – not stressful)
	How stressful is the alarm system no. 2 (phone light alarm)?	7.40 (0 – stressful, 10 – not stressful)
	How stressful is the alarm system no. 3 (environment sound alarm)?	7.5 (0 – stressful, 10 – not stressful)
	How do you find the 0.6 s timeframe?	6.18 (0 – too long/short, 10 – perfect)
	How useful do you find the Navieyes application?	8.72 (0 – useless, 10 – useful)

The open question received advices on improving the detection rate, the sound alarm jingle or the application user interface.

7   Conclusions and Further Development

The centralized results from the HCI questionnaire conclude that Navieyes app will improve driver's road safety. According to question 13, the usability of the initial version of the application is rated at 8.72 on a 1-to-10 scale. Most study participants are rather young and have extensive experience with smartphones and mobile apps, according to the first section of the questionnaire. Due to the fact that only about half of them own a personal car, they however don't have too much driving experience according to question 3 (6.95). The calibration procedure was rated with 7.9 out of 10, and the most accepted form of alarm was the environment sound alarm.

As future development, we plan to further expand the application by integrating the data received from the rear camera, which will in term lower the stress emitted by the application alarm (as it will produce far less notifications).

Acknowledgements. This paper is supported by the Romanian Government, specifically MEN – UEFISCDI authority under the program PNII "Partnerships in priority areas", under the project number 240/2014 - NAVIEYES, supporting the collaboration between the company Route 66 and University Transilvania of Braşov.

References

1. World Health Organization. Data and statistics of the World Health Organization. http://www.who.int/research/en/. Accessed 20 Feb 2015
2. World Health Organization. Global status report on road safety 2013. http://www.who.int/research/en/. Accessed 20 Feb 2015
3. Pedan, M., et al.: World Report on Road Traffic Injury Prevention. WHO Press, Geneva (2004)
4. NaviEyes site. http://navieyes.unitbv.ro. Accessed 20 Feb 2015
5. Dinges, D., Grace, R.: Perclos: a valid psychophysiological measure of alertness as assessed by psychomotor vigilance. Technical report, FHWA-MCRT-98-006, Federal Highway Administration, US Department of Transportation (1998)
6. Guggisberg, A.G., Mathis, J., Schnider, A., Hess, C.W.: Why do we yawn? The importance of evidence for specific yawn-induced effects. Neurosci. Bio-behav. Rev. **35**(5), 1302–1304 (2011)
7. Vural, E., Cetin, M., Ercil, A., Littlewort, G., Bartlett, M., Movellan, J.R.: Drowsy driver detection through facial movement analysis. In: Lew, M., Sebe, N., Huang, T.S., Bakker, E.M. (eds.) HCI 2007. LNCS, vol. 4796, pp. 6–18. Springer, Heidelberg (2007)
8. Van Den Berg, J.: Sleepiness and head movements. Ind. Health **44**(4), 564–576 (2006)
9. Cai, H., Lin, Y.: An integrated head pose and eye gaze tracking approach to non-intrusive visual attention measurement for wide FOV simulators. Virtual Real. **16**(1), 25–32 (2012)
10. You, C.W., et al.: Carsafe app: alerting drowsy and distracted drivers using dual cameras on smartphones. In: Proceeding of the 11th Annual International Conference on Mobile Systems, Applications, and Services, pp. 13–26, ACM, June 2013
11. Chuang, M.C., Bala, R., Bernal, E.A., Paul, P., Burry, A.: Estimating gaze direction of vehicle drivers using a smartphone camera. In: 2014 IEEE Conference on Computer Vision and Pattern Recognition Workshops (CVPRW), pp. 165–170, IEEE, June 2014

Task Specific Paper Controller that Can Be Created by Users for a Specific Computer Operation

Daisuke Komoriya[✉], Buntarou Shizuki, and Jiro Tanaka

University of Tsukuba, Tsukuba, Japan
{komoriya,shizuki,jiro}@iplab.cs.tsukuba.ac.jp

Abstract. We describe Paper Controller, a paper based controller that allows users to design and create their own task specific controllers with touch-sensing capability for controlling a desktop computer. Casual users of computers can design and create a task specific Paper Controller by printing and/or drawing buttons freely with conductive ink and by drawing annotations including text and figures with regular ink. We implemented a prototype system for the Paper Controller. The system consists of the Paper Controller, a Clipboard for the Paper Controller, and a parameterization software running on a computer. We conducted an experiment to examine whether users can create a Paper Controller. The results show that the users can create and use their own Paper Controllers.

Keywords: Paper controller · Prototyping · Conductive ink · Capacitive sensing

1 Introduction

While buttons on the controllers of consumer electronics, including desktop computers, are necessary to execute all the available functions of the electronics, the controllers suffer from a lack of usability in some cases; for example, there are too many buttons on the controller, making it difficult for certain users to perform the user's specific daily tasks.

One supporting example is shown in Fig. 2. This task specific controller is designed for casual users of consumer electronics, such as for a grandmother to control her television. Moreover, although this photograph might seem comical, examining this controller suggests two designs principles:

– A limited number of buttons is necessary for a task specific controller.
– Annotation improves the usability of a task specific controller.

© Springer International Publishing Switzerland 2015
N. Streitz and P. Markopoulos (Eds.): DAPI 2015, LNCS 9189, pp. 418–428, 2015.
DOI: 10.1007/978-3-319-20804-6_38

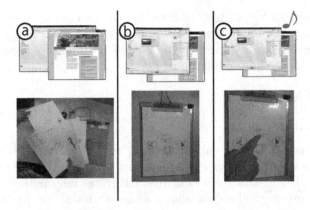

Fig. 1. How to use a Paper Controller. (a) The user selects a Paper Controller that suits the specific task that she wants to perform among her own Paper Controllers. (b) She then clips the Paper Controller on a Clipboard for Paper Controllers. (c) Now, she can use the Paper Controller by touching the buttons on it.

A possible solution to the above problem would be a controller designed to be suitable for a specific user to perform the user's specific task; if one can design and create such a controller easily, the problem will be solved.

In this paper, we present a novel approach to solve the above problem, which involves these two design principles. This approach uses paper with touch-sensing capability, which we call *Paper Controller*. Casual users of computers can design and create a task specific Paper Controller by printing and/or drawing buttons freely with conductive ink and drawing annotations including text and figures with regular ink. It is low cost and easy to duplicate and distribute because a Paper Controller consists of a sheet of paper and conductive ink. Additionally, a

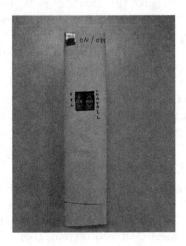

Fig. 2. Most basic television remote controller for casual users of consumer electronics.

Paper Controller can be printed out if the user has its data. Moreover, the user can easily store many Paper Controllers with a clipboard or in a folder. As the first step to explore the feasibility of the Paper Controller, we focused on Paper Controllers for controlling a desktop computer.

2 Related Work

2.1 Enhanced Paper

Similar to our research that enhanced paper to create interactive controllers, some researches enhanced paper to create user interfaces. Koike et al. [1] proposed EnhancedDesk, which is a desk that integrates information on a sheet of paper and a computer. The desk allows a user to touch the paper to interact with it by computer vision. A paper control panel [2] is a camera based paper controller. It allows the user to operate a computer by touching shapes drawn on normal paper. In contrast to these researches that enhanced paper to allow interaction with paper through cameras, we use touch sensors instead of cameras, which allows for little setup with occlusion-free touch interactions.

Some researches enhanced paper by using conductive ink and electronic components put on the paper. Qi et al. [3] enhanced paper by using traditional pop-up mechanisms and paper-based electronics. Lo et al. [4] proposed electronic circuits that allow sketching and shrinking. Untoolkit [5] combined micro controllers with a craft drawing circuit on paper with conductive ink. Saul et al. [6] proposed interactive paper devices that users can create and build their own designs. In contrast to the above research, we use conductive ink to make touch-sensitive paper. Moreover, in our research, we do not use electronic components on the paper. Therefore, a Paper Controller is flat, thin, and easy to duplicate and distribute.

Conductive ink has been focused on and used in some researches as a material for building interactive paper-like functional objects. Karagozler et al. [7] proposed a technology for harvesting energy from users' interactions with paper-like materials. PrintScreen [8] is a technology for digital fabrication of customized flexible displays. Both are composed of various materials including conductive ink. Jacoby et al. [9] proposed interactive paper for storytelling. When a user touches a part of a paper, the system detects it and plays the story. Olberding et al. [10] proposed a cuttable multi-touch sensor. Both use conductive ink for building touch sensors on paper. Similarly, we use conductive ink to allow users to design touch-sensitive paper.

2.2 GUI as Freehand Drawings

Similar to our research, some researches used freehand drawings to design GUIs. For example, Coyette et al. [11] proposed a converter that converts freehand drawings into XML code. This allows users to create GUIs by drawing figures. UISKEI [12] is a sketch based GUI prototyping tool for designers. It converts sketches into GUI components such as buttons, checkboxes, and textboxes. In contrast, our research uses freehand drawings to create touch interfaces.

2.3 Customizable Controller

Various methods to fabricate customizable controllers have been proposed. Villar et al. [13] proposed a malleable structure on which users can freely arrange controls, such as buttons, sliders, dials, and joysticks, and assign functionality to each control. Holman et al. [14] used conductive tape to customize everyday objects into touch-sensitive controllers. Corsten et al. [15] changed everyday objects into controllers by using cameras. Reference [16–18] allow users to design a physical controller by assigning an operation such as a shortcut key to a physical controller. Klemmer et al. [19] proposed an everyday object input interface that uses a RGB camera and RFID. In contrast, our research uses touch sensors drawn/printed by using conductive ink on a sheet of paper to fabricate customizable controllers, whose sizes and shapes can be designed freely, providing users with a large degree of freedom in designing.

3 Paper Controller

The Paper Controller is a paper-based controller. Each Paper Controller is designed to be suitable for a specific user to perform the user's specific task on a desktop computer.

3.1 Using

To use a Paper Controller, the user selects a Paper Controller that is suitable to the specific task that he or she wants to perform among many of their own Paper Controllers, and clips it on a Clipboard made for Paper Controllers that is a specialized clipboard for our system. Then, the system detects the clipped Paper Controller by reading the ID printed on it and makes the windows necessary for the task active. Now, the user can use the Paper Controller by touching the buttons on it. Every time a button is touched, the system sends the assigned commands to the windows. The user can easily perform another task by simply changing the Paper Controller on the clipboard.

Figure 1 shows an example use case. Here, the user is going to play songs from their favorite musician. Assume that the user is currently performing another task (Fig. 1a). When the user clips the Paper Controller assigned to playing songs, the system detects the clipped Paper Controller and makes the media player active. After that, the system opens the assigned playlist (Fig. 1b). When the user touches the play button on the Paper Controller, the media player plays the songs from the play list (Fig. 1c).

3.2 Designing and Creating

To allow a user to design and create a Paper Controller, we provide the parameterization software that will be used on a desktop computer. After the user prints and/or draws buttons freely by using conductive ink on a Paper Controller, the user can easily assign an operation (e.g., opening a specific file, opening a specific play list, or jumping to a web site with a specific URL) to each button on the Paper Controller by using the GUI of this parameterization software.

4   Implementation

Our prototype system consists of the Paper Controllers, a Clipboard for the Paper Controller, and the parameterization software running on a computer.

4.1   Paper Controller

A Paper Controller has buttons and pins printed by using conductive ink (we use AgIC silver nano-particle ink [20] in our current implementation). Figure 3 shows both sides of a Paper Controller. The user draws freehand drawings including figures and text on the front side by using regular ink. The buttons drawn on the back side correspond to the figures on the front side. There are two kinds of pins printed on the back side. One kind is pins for the ID (the four pins in the top left in Fig. 3 right). The ID is binary encoded by using the pins (the short-circuited pins mean 0s; the other mean 1s; the ID is 010 in Fig. 3 right). The others kind is pins for buttons (the five pins in the top right in Fig. 3 right). Each button is connected to a pin.

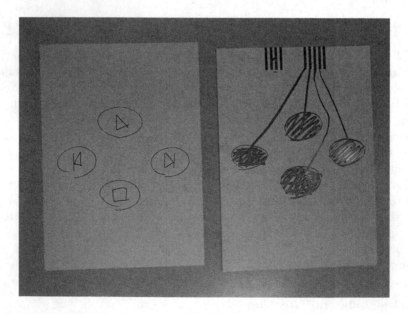

Fig. 3. Both sides of a Paper Controller (left: front side; right: back side).

4.2   Clipboard for Paper Controllers

The clip of the Clipboard for the Paper Controller also has pins that are connected to the pins on the back of a Paper Controller (Fig. 4). All the pins of the clip are connected to a micro controller (Arduino) to read the ID and detect button touches. The clipboard sends an event to the computer when a Paper Controller is changed or a touch is detected. When a Paper Controller is changed, the clipboard sends the "change Paper Controller" event along with the Paper Controller ID. We use capacitive touch sensing [21] to detect the touches. When the micro controller detects a touch, it sends a touch event to the computer with the Paper Controller ID and the button ID.

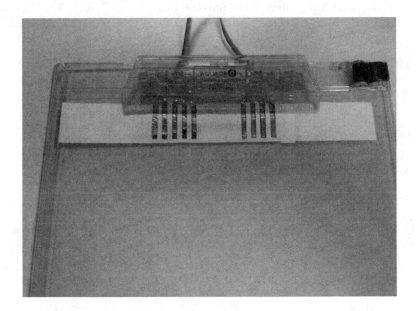

Fig. 4. The clip of the Clipboard for the Paper Controller.

4.3   Parameterization Software

We implemented parameterization software to assign a button of a Paper Controller to a window and its commands (we use shortcut keys in our current implementation). This parameterization software is built on the .NET Framework 4.0. When the parameterization software receives a touch event from the clipboard, it sends the assigned shortcut keys to the assigned window.

5   Experiment

We conducted an experiment to examine whether and how users can create a Paper Controller.

5.1   Participants

Four Participants (3 males and 1 female) ranging in age from 22 to 23 took part in this experiment as volunteers. All of them are majoring in Computer Science. Three of them were graduate school students; one was an undergraduate.

5.2   Apparatus

We used a personal computer (Lenovo ThinkPad X201i; Intel Core i3 processor and 4 GB of RAM) running the parameterization software, sheets of paper (Mitsubishi Paper Mills NB-WF-3GF100) on which we printed pins to connect to the clipboard (Fig. 5), and a conductive ink pen (AgIC Circuit Marker) which is a pen containing AgIC silver nano-particle ink.

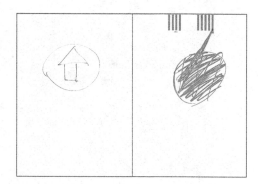

Fig. 5. Paper Controller with pins already printed to connect with the clipboard.

Fig. 6. Paper Controller designed as an example (left: front side; right: back side).

5.3   Procedure

We explained the concept of the Paper Controller and handed them a Paper Controller that we had already designed as an example (Fig. 6). After that, the participants used the Paper Controller for approximately 5 min to play Flappy Bird[1], a one-button game running inside a web browser, to familiarize themselves with the concept of the Paper Controllers. We used Internet Explorer 11 as the web browser. Then, we explained how to create a Paper Controller. First, draw figures on the front side. Second, draw buttons and lines from each button to a pin to connect them with the conductive ink pen. Third, clip the Paper Controller to the clipboard. We note that, in this experiment, the shortcut key was already assigned by us by using the parameterization software. After that, the participants created their own Paper Controllers. During the experiment, we answered questions from the participants. After that, we asked them to complete the questionnaires. Each participant took about 15 min to complete this experiment.

---

[1] http://www.freeflappybird.org/.

5.4   Results

Figure 7 shows the Paper Controllers that were created by the participants. All figures were drawn on the upper half of the sheet. This may be caused by the pins being placed at the top of the Paper Controller.

P1 drew a character that represented a bird and a triangle as the button for flapping up. The task in this experiment is a game. In this game, users tap a button shaped like a bird to make the character flap upward. Therefore, P1 drew a triangle to flap up. P2 drew five circles that represent the places of the fingers. In P4's experiment, the line that connects the pin to the button was too thin at first, therefore the touch sensor did not work. We asked him to draw a thicker one. After that, the touch sensor worked.

5.5   Comments

We collected the following comments from the questionnaires:

It is difficult to draw a circuit on the back side to make it match the button on the front. (P1)
Since the paper we used in this experiment was thick, the participants could not see through to the front side when the paper was placed on the table. We observed that some of the participants held the Paper Controller up to look through to the front side.

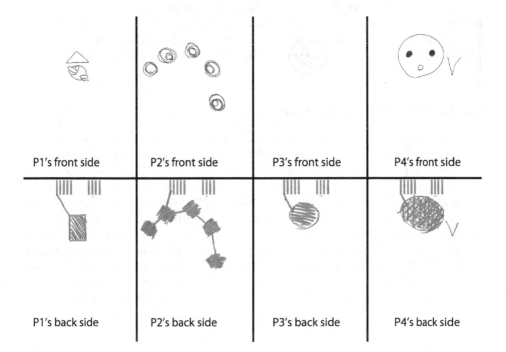

Fig. 7. Participants' Paper Controllers. The back side is mirrored to improve visibility.

It is good that I can draw something that I like. (P1, P2, and P3)
> Paper Controllers created by participants affirmed this comment as the four Paper Controllers had quite different designs from each other in spite of the fact that all of them had the same functionality.

A user doesn't need to remember shortcut keys. (P3)
> Since shortcut keys are assigned to buttons, only the user of the parameterization software needs to know the shortcut keys.

6 Discussion and Future Work

6.1 Experiment

As the first step to explore the feasibility of the Paper Controller, we conducted an experiment where we asked participants whose major is Computer Science, i.e., having satisfactory knowledge of computers, to create a Paper Controller after we show an example. Therefore, to further examine the feasibility of the Paper Controller, we plan to conduct experiments where we ask participants not majoring in Computer Science to freely design their own Paper Controllers.

6.2 Authoring Editor

As we described above, P4 had a problem where the line was too thin during the experiment. To solve this problem, we plan to implement a authoring editor for the Paper Controller that helps users lay buttons out more easily. Ideally, the user would scan the front side of a Paper Controller. After that, the editor would create the circuits. After that, the circuits can be printed out by using printer with conductive ink.

6.3 Realizing Other Touch Gestures

In our prototype, we used conductive ink to create capacitive touch sensors. This makes it possible for users to draw touchable buttons and to use printers to print them. However, we consider that conductive ink provides us with many chances to design and implement various touch gestures and GUIs, thus improving the functionality and usability of the Paper Controller. For one approach, we will consider providing not only simple touch but also other touch gestures, such as tap and flick; this can be realized by printing specialized patterns of conductive ink [22]. For another approach, we also plan to implement sliders and knobs by also printing specialized patterns. Moreover, we plan to reduce the number of connectors by using the technique described in [23] and to investigate other touch sensing techniques such as TempTouch [24] to enrich touch gestures.

6.4 Target

In this paper, the Paper Controller was used for controlling a window based GUI as the first step to explore the feasibility of the Paper Controller because window based GUIs are popular and complicated. As the next step, we plan to improve the system of the Paper Controller to apply it to consumer electronics including TV, air conditioners, and microwaves, therefore we plan to add an IR remote control function to the clipboard.

7 Conclusion

We presented Paper Controller, a paper based controller that allows users to design and create their own task specific controllers with touch-sensing capability for controlling a desktop computer. We conducted an experiment to examine whether and how users can create a Paper Controller. The result shows that users can create and use their own Paper Controllers.

References

1. Hideki, K., Yoichi, S., Yoshinori, K.: Integrating paper and digital information on EnhancedDesk: a method for realtime finger tracking on an augmented desk system. ACM Trans. Comput.-Hum. Interact. 8(4), 307–322 (2001)
2. Kaneko, M., Tanaka, J.: Paper control panel: making paper-based touch interface. Proc. Interact. 2014, 562–567 (2014). (In Japanese)
3. Qi, J., Buechley, L.: Electronic popables: exploring paper-based computing through an interactive pop-up book. In: Proceedings of TEI 2010, pp. 121–128 (2010)
4. Lo, J., Paulos, E.: ShrinkyCircuits : sketching, shrinking, and formgiving for electronic circuits. In: Proceedings of UIST 2014, pp. 291–299 (2014)
5. Mellis, D.A., Jacoby, S., Buechley, L., Perner-Wilson, H., Qi, J.: Microcontrollers as material: crafting circuits with paper, conductive ink, electronic components, and an "untoolkit". In: Proceedings of TEI 2013, pp. 83–90 (2013)
6. Saul, G., Xu, C., Gross, M.D.: Interactive paper devices: end-user design and fabrication. In: Proceedings of TEI 2010, pp. 205–212 (2010)
7. Karagozler, M.E., Poupyrev, I., Fedder, G.K., Suzuki, Y.: Paper generators: harvesting energy from touching, rubbing and sliding. In: Proceedings of UIST 2013, pp. 23–30 (2013)
8. Olberding, S., Wessely, M., Steimle, J.: PrintScreen: fabricating highly customizable thin-film touch-displays. In: Proceedings of UIST 2014, pp. 281–290 (2014)
9. Jacoby, S., Buechley, L.: Drawing the electric: storytelling with conductive ink. In: Proceedings of IDC 2013, pp. 265–268 (2013)
10. Olberding, S., Gong, N.-W., Tiab, J., Paradiso, J.A., Steimle, J.: A cuttable multi-touch sensor. In Proceedings of UIST 2013, pp. 245–254 (2013)
11. Coyette, A., Faulkner, S., Kolp, M., Limbourg, Q., Vanderdonckt, J.: SketchiXML: towards a multi-agent design tool for sketching user interfaces based on USIXML. In: Proceedings of TAMODIA 2004, pp. 75–82 (2004)
12. Segura, V.C.V.B., Barbosa, S.D.J., Simões, F.P.: UISKEI: a sketch-based prototyping tool for defining and evaluating user interface behavior. In: Proceedings of AVI 2012, pp. 18–25 (2012)

13. Villar, N., Gellersen, H.: A malleable control structure for softwired user interfaces. In: Proceedings of TEI 2007, pp. 49–56 (2007)
14. Holman, D., Vertegaal, R.: TactileTape: low-cost touch sensing on curved surfaces. In: Proceedings of UIST 2011 Adjunct, pp. 17–18 (2011)
15. Corsten, C., Avellino, I., Möllers, M., Borchers, J.: Instant user interfaces: repurposing everyday objects as input devices. In: Proceedings of ITS 2013, pp. 71–80 (2013)
16. Hudson, S.E., Mankoff, J.: Rapid construction of functioning physical interfaces from cardboard, thumbtacks, tin foil and masking tape. In: Proceedings of UIST 2006, pp. 289–298 (2006)
17. Greenberg, S., Boyle, M.: Customizable physical interfaces for interacting with conventional applications. In: Proceedings of UIST 2002, pp. 31–40 (2002)
18. Spiessl, W., Villar, N., Gellersen, H., Schmidt, A.: VoodooFlash: authoring across physical and digital form. In: Proceedings of TEI 2007, pp. 97–100 (2007)
19. Klemmer, S.R., Li, J., Lin, J., Landay, J.A.: Papier-Mâché: toolkit support for tangible input. In: Proceedings of CHI 2004, pp. 399–406 (2004)
20. Kawahara, Y., Hodges, S., Cook, B.S., Zhang, C., Abowd, G.D.: Instant inkjet circuits: lab-based inkjet printing to support rapid prototyping of ubicomp devices. In: Proceedings of UbiComp 2013, pp. 363–372 (2013)
21. Arduino Playground - CapacitiveSensor. http://playground.arduino.cc/main/capacitivesensor. Last accessed: February 2015
22. Manabe, H., Inamura, H.: Single capacitive touch sensor that detects multi-touch gestures. In: Proceedings of ISWC 2014, pp. 137–138 (2014)
23. Wimmer, R., Baudisch, P.: Modular and deformable touch-sensitive surfaces based on time domain reflectometry. In: Proceedings of UIST 2011, pp. 517–526 (2011)
24. Peiris, R.L., Nakatsu, R.: TempTouch: a novel touch sensor using temperature controllers for surface based textile displays. In: Proceedings of ITS 2013, pp. 105–114 (2013)

Re-appropriating Old Furniture via IoT, in an Artistic Context: The Case of "DolceVita"

Irene Mavrommati[1(✉)] and Konstantinos Grivas[1,2,3]

[1] School of Applied Arts, Hellenic Open University, Patras, Greece
[2] Griik Architects and Designers, Patras, Greece
[3] Department of Architecture, University of Patras, Patras, Greece
mavrommati@eap.gr, kostas@griik.gr

Abstract. An old 1950's buffet was re-appropriated with QR tagging and internet resources, in the context of a design exhibition. This paper describes its concept and IoT realization for a monthly deployment in the AntiDesign2014 venue.

Keywords: IoT · WPF · QR code recognition · Dropbox · Vintage furniture · Design

1 The Case: IoT Re-appropriation of Obsolete Furniture

The project "Dolce-Vita" consists of the re-appropriation of a 1950's buffet and the modification of objects inside it, using IoT technology and internet resources, in order to augment its function and transform it into an interactive art installation and a mediating device. This paper provides a detailed description of the concept development and the process of implementation of this project.

The old cabinet had become functionally and stylistically obsolete. It originally belonged to the designers' grandparents and its style was very prominent in the working and middle class households in Greece during the 1950s and early 1960s, but currently this old cabinet had no commercial value and it was not in a very good condition. Yet it had emotional significance for its present owners (designers) for it carried childhood memories, and this was the main reason why the designers decided to give this cabinet a renewed life transforming it into the central piece for the "Dolce Vita" installation. The occasion presented itself in the context of the AntiDesign2014 venue, a month-long exhibition themed: *Proposals for a zero budget era,* at Athens "Technopolis" art and Culture Park. The venue specifically addressed design in times of financial crisis. The design team decided to augment and re-appropriate the old piece of furniture for AntiDesign2014, challenged not only by creatively using recycled objects, but also by observing the perception of well-being during the past decades (as documented in decorative items, lifestyle consumer products, photographic and film material). The resulting overall design, through the use of rituals and iconography, aimed to provoke contemplation related to urban Greek lifestyle and the perception of affluence and comfort.

N. Streitz and P. Markopoulos (Eds.): DAPI 2015, LNCS 9189, pp. 429–436, 2015.
DOI: 10.1007/978-3-319-20804-6_39

The installation aimed to invite participants into a conceptual roaming/wandering/stroll through the post-war era of optimism making use of the modified cabinet and the artefacts inside which influence a triptych projection. Both the cabinet itself and the theme of the adhesive tapestry that lines the interior shelves are symbols of the working class aspirations for social rise, affluence, and entering into the glorified realm of bourgeois life; tasting the delights of "good life" of the 1960s–1970s. The pictorial content of the digital photographic triptychs refers to that age of hope in contrast to the current financial crisis and pessimism.

The buffet itself resonated with collective memories to many visitors/users. The projection, although comprising of randomly selected images found in the internet, is constructed by the respective software so as to maintain a very strong aesthetic coherence as a triptych (see Fig. 1). The experience of interaction with *Dolce Vita* oscillates between a set of direct sensory stimuli provided by the old buffet and the plates inside it, and a series of visual and conceptual stimuli effected by the dynamics of the changing projections. The interaction with the *Dolce Vita* buffet refers simultaneously to the experience of the kid that digs into her grandmother's buffet, to the ritual of serving treats to guests (a typical Greek custom for visitors), but also to the contemporary practice of web searching/browsing with often unexpected results.

Fig. 1. The buffet, its content, and the triptych projection on the wall behind it

QR codes were used as an IoT mediator subtype [1] via which a *"device mediates the interactions between Physical Entities and Digital Proxies"*. The plates from inside the buffet when placed on top, act as a means to select the theme of the triptych projection, which relates each time to the icon on the selected plate. As a result, the buffet obtains a new function: beyond the storage and display of physical objects (dishes, glasses etc.) it allows the storage, seeking and display of digital archive material (for archive interactive art strategy see [2]), and reflection upon the produced associations. An analogous process of reuse and re-signification could be expanded in other obsolete elements of home furniture – bearing similarity with the approach in [3].

2   Design and Interaction

The *Dolce Vita* installation consists of two main visible parts: the augmented buffet and its contents, and a digital projection on the wall behind the buffet. There are design relations and functional links between both the physical and the projected parts of the installation at various levels. Users choose among the thematically coded plates, found inside the buffet, and place them on the tray which is atop the buffet in order to alter the theme of the triptych images projected on the wall behind the buffet. The installation is complemented by simple electronic equipment, several web-accessed photographic collections/archives and a dedicated programme that compiles and manages the projections.

The tripartite structure of the buffet is reflected to the triptych form of the projection, which is following the same visual proportions as the doors and internal divisions of the cabinet. The iconic 1960's imagery of the inside adhesive tapestry resonates on the crockery found inside the cabinet. The plates are artefacts that one would normally expect to find inside a 1950's–1960's urban home cabinet, blending naturally to the style and period of the buffet. Images selected from the adhesive tapestry are imprinted on the plates that have a matching QR code sticker beneath them. The 17 specially decorated plates inside the buffet, when served on top of the tray, alter the theme of the triptych images (drinks, food, horses, gambling, travels, home décor, etc.), relating directly to the icon of each plate (Figs. 2 and 3).

The buffet is internally lit inviting one to search inside. The custom-made wooden tray on top of the buffet hides a small webcam that reads the QR codes beneath the plates. The tray provides enough space on both sides so one can place and try various plates at the same time. The hidden lights inside the tray enable the reading of the QR codes (beneath each plate) by the webcam, and a luminous transparent circle in the middle serves as visual aid for the targeted placing of the plates.

The associative triptych projection triggers virtual wanderings. For example, the fruit-plate-icon generates still-nature fruit-bowls in (signifiers of affluence) but also Carmen-Miranda playful fruit-hat images. Likewise, the "boat-in-a-bottle" plate generates a triptych with recreational sailing around islands, juxtaposed with miniature sailing boats entrapped into decorative bottles. Photographs selected attempted to relate to and comment on the greek crisis situation or urban lifestyle; thus they included typical decorative items to be encountered in such cabinets. The images compiling the galleries where the projection retrieves its material from are a result of internet image

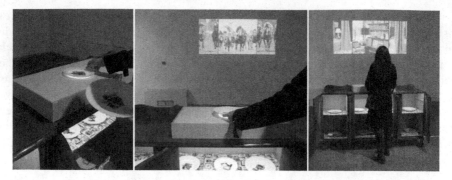

Fig. 2. Visitors may take a plate from the cabinet and place it on top (on the luminous circle) thus initiating a coherent triptych visual, relating to the dish image. The QR tags at the back of each plate, detected via the webcam and a PC, trigger the projection of related content.

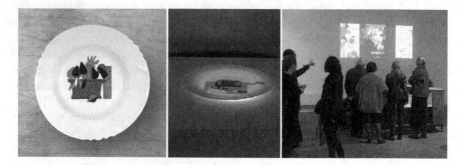

Fig. 3. Each plate is printed with a distinct image extracted from the patterns of the inside tapestry of the buffet; when placed on the top surface (webcam reader) each printed dish represents a theme for images projected behind the cabinet.

search and are used via a Dropbox folder, nevertheless any digitized or archive material can equally well be used as resources.

3   Implementation

As mentioned before, the installation consists of the cabinet (buffet 2.00 × 0.60 × 1.00 m), specially modified plates inside it (17 plates), a simple device (wooden tray with hidden webcam) for recognizing the plates placed on top of the buffet, and a triptych digital projection on the wall behind the buffet (3–4 m distance). A laptop and a digital projector were also used. During the installation these were placed simply in an inconspicuous position on the floor behind the buffet with no effort to hide or disguise them.

The buffet was left untreated and unrepaired. The internal shelves had a plastic adhesive decorative cover with specific images shown in Fig. 5. It was necessary to remove some newer adhesive tapestries that covered the initial tapestry and clean its surface. LED light strips were attached and hidden beneath the top surface of the buffet in order to light up the interior of the buffet. A small web-cam was attached beneath the centre of the top surface of the buffet facing upwards, and a very small hole (~ 5 mm diameter) was drilled on that surface so that the web-cam can "view" the QR codes of the plates when placed on the tray. The buffet had a drawer in its right compartment which was temporarily removed.

The wooden tray ($74 \times 37 \times 10$ cm) on top of the buffet is made out of 5 mm untreated plywood, and the transparent circular hole in its top surface is 15 cm in diameter and covered with 5 mm clear Perspex. Simple LED light strips are attached inside the wooden tray.

The 17 themed plates are cheap, plain white, glass plates purchased from a local hardware hypermarket. They are 6 fruit plates, 6 dinner plates and 5 soup plates. They were chosen so that they match in style with the plates originally found inside the buffet. Each plate was decorated with an icon selected from the adhesive tapestry of the buffet (Figs. 3 and 5). Those icons were laser printed on decal paper and applied to the top surface of the plates. A small square adhesive with a unique QR code was applied beneath the base of each plate.

Technologies used in this installation were: WPF and QR code recognition. *Triptych* (Triptych.codeplex.com) is the software developed for this occasion and made available as open source, for interactive visual art experiments on the theme of triptych displays. The team used a WPF based Windows desktop application, which shows a tripartite 1:2:1-sized display using images from a local file folder that are organized in thematic subfolders (including a "Startup" subfolder). By pointing a respective QR code to a webcam, an image subfolder is picked (QR code contains a URL with subfolder's name). The left and right panes on the Triptych have their leftmost and rightmost halves cropped out of the display respectively (Figs. 1 and 2). Those panes are both using right-to-left (RTL) display option, so that they show the respective image horizontally flipped. Since they're both assigned to show the same image this results in them showing the left and right halves respectively of the horizontally flipped image. A timer (background thread) picks another image as source for the middle and the left/right panes of the triptych, from a random-ordered list of the images in the currently chosen subfolder. The middle and the left/right images are picked from the same list with a different frequency (time delay), so that different combinations of images (Triptychs) can be achieved in a visually coherent manner, as time passes. Periodically, the same image may be picked for both the middle and the left/right panes on the triptych, unfolding a mirroring, kaleidoscope-like panorama, since the vertical borders between the triptych panes are practically mirroring axes. This effect was inspired from the left and right doors of the tripartite cabinet with 1:2:1 part ratios, that open to respective directions, splitting a view in half and flipping its parts outwards to the left and right sides (Fig. 4). The software run on a recycled screenless laptop, salvaged from trash and hidden under the cabinet.

Using the Cloud: The images folder and the application can be on Dropbox or other Cloud Storage solution that is synchronized to a local folder so that they are easily updated from a remote location. This also facilitates offline updates, even when the installation computer is shut down, so that it catches up with any updates when the

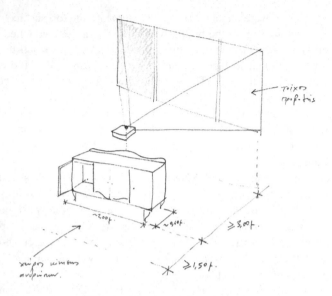

Fig. 4. Sketch of the installation

Fig. 5. Detail of the adhesive tapestry inside the cabinet

system and local cloud storage synchronization agent is restarted. One can have the QR codes contain custom short URLs generated out of shared web links provided by a cloud storage that hosts the image subfolders. For example, Dropbox allows to right-click a subfolder under its local synchronization folder and select to copy a sharing URL to the system clipboard to paste elsewhere and share. Such short URLs can be constructed using services like TinyUrl.com, but also using link tracking ones like Bit.ly. Thus web analytics (statistical info) can be obtained for user visits to the URLs hosted by the respective QR codes (e.g. using a smartphone's camera via a QR reader app). Such URLs apart from being used as tokens to point to a local image subfolder, can serve as online web galleries displaying the same images of those folders (e.g. Dropbox sharing URLs point to photo galleries on the web for those cloud-shared folders that contain only images).

4 Reception and Use Observations

The DolceVita installation was exposed to the public and used during the course of a month by more than 600 people. Many, primarily female, visitors expressed emotional contemplation, since the exhibit evoked to many childhood memories.

The luminous, open design and the available RFID dishes inside caused many visitors to interact, by 'serving' the dishes and causing a related thematic triptych display, exposed a technology fascination and curiosity that was in turn triggered by the interaction. Visitors searched for the seams and the details of the construction elements. Many visitors subsequently reflected on the hybrid nature of the design item and its implications to other obsolete pieces of furniture.

Relatively few of the visitors contemplated on the specific projected images which pointed at the perception of crisis through the filter of urban lifestyle.

Only a handful visited the folder's url to see the resulting triptychs that were generated from the physical handling of the exhibit.

Many acclaimed artists designers and architects visited and discussed aspects of the installation. On the aesthetic and artistic aspects it seemed that there were no such remarks received, indicating that the exhibit was successful in providing an artistic experience perceived as a unified whole, (in spite of its inherent complexity).

5 Conclusions

This paper presented a process re-appropriating furniture in combination with virtual resources (internet searched photographs, QR codes, cloud shared resources), and re-combining them for artistic and aesthetic contemplation. For the latter, in terms of aesthetics, it is worth to mention the challenge of generation of a coherent visual triptych, when this is composed from preexisting web-searched images – and not a priori made with triptych-views in mind. This challenge was successfully handled by the design of dedicated software that was subsequently released as open source.

A process of augmentation and reuse similar to the one described here can be attempted in other obsolete furniture or decorative objects that can be easily re-appropriated via widely available IoT resources. It is a process affordable and quick to implement, laying the challenge in people's artistic creativity and design imagination.

Acknowledgements. The DolceVita design team includes George Birbilis, computer engineer and application developer, and Natasa Kyriakidi, *griik architects,* as well as the authors; this paper reflects on the results this team's collaboration, all people involved being a great pleasure to work with. DolceVita Installation was publicly used in *Anti-Design 2014*, Technopolis, Athens, curated by E. Krouska, P. Zervopoulou, 15/1-15/2/2014.

References

1. Serbanati, A., Medaglia, C.M., Ceipidor, U.B.: Building blocks of the internet of things state of the art and beyond. In: Turcu, C. (ed.) Deploying RFID-Challenges Solutions and Open Issues. InTech, Rijeka (2011)
2. Kluszczynski, R.W.: Strategies of interactive art. J. Aesthet. Cult. **2**, 1–27 (2010)
3. van den Hoven, E.: A future-proof past: designing for remembering experiences. Mem. Stud. **7**(3), 373–387 (2014)

Novel Method for Notification from Interactive Smart Cover

Young Hoon Oh and Da Young Ju[⊠]

School of Integrated Technology, Yonsei Institute of Convergence Technology,
Yonsei University, Incheon, Republic of Korea
{50hoon, dyju}@yonsei.ac.kr

Abstract. Traditional interaction method on mobile device often causes notification stress. Several research projects based on the software approach were attempted but it is not always perfect solution. In this design work, we propose a new interaction method with Interactive Smart Cover. This mobile device accessory adds a new notification channel as well as protects device. We extend its potential to future devices such as smartwatch. Future applicability of the accessory and its limitation will be discussed as well.

Keywords: Notification · Interactive · Accessory · Appcessory · Cover

1 Introduction

Current mobile device supports varieties of functions. People can use it to manage finance, view documents or design creative contents. However, its primary use is limited to lightweight activities [9, 29] such as checking E-mail, communicating on Facebook, or playing games. All these start from checking notifications. For instance, when you receive new E-mail from your friend, you would receive push message for the reply. This means that our mobile device is always ready for communicating with people, other software, or even with other devices.

Although the push notification system has contributed to the formation of application ecosystem, method of checking notifications is not heavily changed. People still head down to read texts displayed on the screen or prick up ears to hear ring tone. This lasting interaction method might stress out users while communicating with social network. Yoon et al. investigated [8] the causes of notification stress from mobile messenger and revealed that current method of notification does not properly express the importance and kind. In this regard, we have looked back on the notification system and devised the way to complement users.

We think device accessory will play greater role in the future. Surveys [1, 2] and potential growth of device accessory [10, 11] also backs up our vision. Academic community also recognized the infinite potential of mobile accessory and defined Appcessory, [5] a smart accessory that can be integrated with mobile applications. Appcessory is now widely distributed in commercial market and some research projects using accessory type device were presented [3, 4, 6, 7] as well.

© Springer International Publishing Switzerland 2015
N. Streitz and P. Markopoulos (Eds.): DAPI 2015, LNCS 9189, pp. 437–448, 2015.
DOI: 10.1007/978-3-319-20804-6_40

Therefore, we revisit research on the interruption of notification system and improvement on that issue. We also briefly report on the current use of mobile accessory. Next, we propose our new notification method with simple magnetic cover, Interactive Smart Cover, the cover that we were inspired by the Apple Smart Cover [30]. The specific design and concept of the cover is proposed, and we extend its potential to flexible device like smartwatch. Functional integration on mobile device and limitation of the proposed item will be discussed as well.

2 Related Work

Although notifications provide valuable information, it often interrupts people in real life and even stresses people. Herein, we will focus on the notification system, its stress and interruption while using mobile devices. The disruptiveness of notification and proposed solution by other researchers will be presented as well.

2.1 Notification, Stress, and Interruption

People receive a lot of push messages every day but we do not know how frequently they get notifications and what the leading cause of stress is. In this regard, Pielot et al. reported the quantitative analysis on real-world notifications through logging user actions [15]. The objective data revealed that participant received about 65 notifications every day and messenger applications took the biggest portion. Czerwinski et al. and Iqbal et al. reported on the effects of Instant Messenger on the desktop environment [25, 26]. They showed two findings; one is that the relevance between notification and task is related to productivity [26] and the other is that the disruptiveness of notifications varies according to the phase of task [25].

In mobile environment, Fischer et al. [24] also found the result that timing of notification is important. It is known that opportune moment of notification is end of the task. Yoon et al. pointed out the problem of intrusive notification and surveyed the notification stress of mobile messenger [8]. They elicited from participants that tons of messages in multi-user chat room cause huge stress to users. From the in-depth interview, several interviewees said they felt like they had heard auditory hallucinations of notifications. On this issue, Fallman et al. put emphasis on the necessity of context aware notification [23] and discussed which modality could be important.

Several research projects attempted to mediate notification stress. To reduce the disruptiveness of notification, Horvitz et al. physically deferred the frequency of E-mail notification [14]. Iqbal et al. devised the concept of scheduling notification and developed the system [26], Oasis, which is able to defer notifications until interruptible moments. Scheduling notification was pretty effective [26] in that it yields faster reaction time compared to immediate notification. Another improved notification design within specific mobile application is done by Böhmer et al. [12]. Researchers pointed out the limitation of previous phone call user interface and developed the improved visual design of dialer application [12], which enables users to get out of full screen notification and helps them to prepare for incoming call. Perhaps disabling notification for a while could be helpful to users. This extreme idea has also been discussed from Iqbal et al., who conducted an experiment [27] which compares E-mail client access rate in two conditions; with notifications and without notifications. Ironically, some of the participants said [27] they are willing to turn on notification and accept the potential disruption because they want to monitor whether new information arrived. This clearly indicates that mitigating stress with traditional interaction method is not always perfect solution for everybody.

Interaction method itself is obviously important factor of notification system. There are some unique research projects based on the technological advance. MorePhone [28] is the representative case of notification method using shape-changing flexible display. The actuated smartphone is able to describe both urgency and type of notification. This seems a bit different approach from previous projects because most have adopted software approach [12, 14, 25, 26]. On the other hand, Vibkinesis [6] is obviously unusual research project. Yamanaka et al. proposed a smartphone-attachable case [6] that can control its angle and directions of movement. The proposed hardware enables the smartphone to move and notice the alarm by tapping user's hand. The external accessory rotates with vibration motors, and the specific rotation angle can be used to notify the number of new E-mail.

In summary, majority of prior works have focused on reducing the stress within its device – software application, optimizing algorithm, or device integrated sensors. But there is little research which tried to mitigate notification stress in the perspective of accessory devices. From the following section, we revisit the current mobile accessories and propose futuristic notification method using them.

2.2 Revisiting the Mobile Accessory

In this section, we briefly look around the mobile accessory and interaction with it. It includes the following categories; Protective accessory, music receivers (Headphone and earphone), or chargers. Given the distribution of accessory [31], we will narrow down the subject to protective accessories.

Protective accessory is the most representative category among mobile accessories [31]. It can be categorized according to the protecting area. Cover-type accessory generally refers to the item which covers only the one side of the device (Reversely if the cover only protects backside of device, it is named back cover in the market.). On the other hand, case-type accessory protects rear and side of the device. Case cover accessory which protects all the face exists as well.

To improve interaction of using device, we have to know how people use their accessories on their devices. Following is the typical way people use protective cover to check notifications (Except for backside cover):

1. Device receives a push message.
2. Device notifies.
3. User recognizes, opens the cover.
4. Reads information.

From these steps, we found that manually opening the cover to read message might be cumbersome to whole accessory users. This comes from the contradiction that people want both safety and instant access. The contradiction gave rise to a number of unique commercial items that not only cover devices but also provide instant access. Samsung S View Flip Cover is an example [32] which displays summarized information through rectangular hole on the cover. The Flip Cover helps users not to open the cover for checking notification. However, the cover still has the limitation that users must open it by hand whenever they want to look detail information. The small size of notification area and its top-sided location is also regarded as weak point.

3   Interactive Smart Cover

Assuming most people use their own protective cover on their device, the key problem while using cover-type accessory is that visual feedback is blocked. When people receive a new message, text tone sounds but users cannot catch the information before they open the cover. In this respect, we introduce the futuristic notification method with Interactive Smart Cover, which does not require us to manually check the notifications.

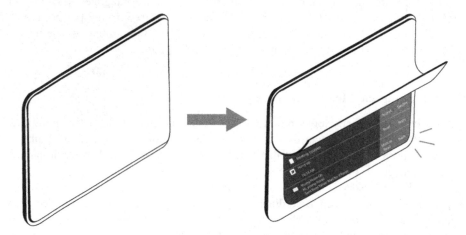

Fig. 1. (a) Before receiving notification (Left), (b) Example of notification list and buttons (Right).

The proposed item differs from existing Smart Cover by Apple [30] because our cover has interactive feature. This means that the cover automatically opens/closes itself and alerts new notifications. When the cover is automatically opened, it shows the list of notifications and extended buttons for users to take action. Figure 1 illustrates what happens when users receive users receive a new mail.

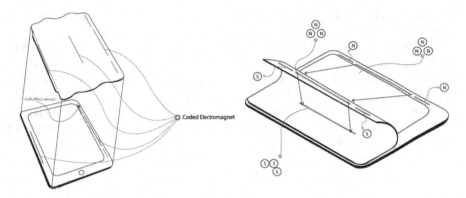

Fig. 2. (a) Arrangement of electromagnets (Left), (b) Disclosure of screen using repulsive force (Right).

3.1 Method

Interactive Smart Cover is operated by arrays of coded electromagnet which is placed both on the cover and device (Please note the Fig. 2(a)). Coded magnets or programmable magnets refer to the magnetic structures which can be programmed dynamically by using multiple correlated patterns of magnets. For example, when current is applied to the electromagnetic elements they will produce the magnetic field. Thus, we have designed the magnets on device to exert repulsive forces to the magnets on the cover. This results in the disclosure of screen as shown in Fig. 2(b).

Figure 2(a) describes the blueprint of the proposed accessory. All red lines on Fig. 2 describe the sets of coded electromagnets. There are four separate sets of magnets on the device – Two sets of long magnets and two sets of short magnets. Interactive Smart Cover has three long magnets and two short magnets. One of the long size magnets on device is for clamping the Interactive Smart cover and another one is limited to exert repulsive force only if the device receives message. Both have same magnetic polarity such as north polar (Also noted in Fig. 2(b)). Two short-sized magnets is also North pole and they are used to cover touchscreen same as previous Apple Smart Cover. Among five separate magnets of the cover, all are South pole except for the long-sized one which is used to make repulsive force. Therefore, two separate long-sized magnets are used to uncover touchscreen as shown in Fig. 1(b).

3.2 Benefit

Here are some following benefits of the *Interactive Smart* Cover. Uncoordinated notification has been important issue [8, 15]. One of the leading causes might be repetitive visual/auditory notification which occurs all at once. *Interactive Smart Cover* not only provides physical convenience but also gives peace of mind from the rush. The proposed cover does not repeat opening and closing every time device receives notification but it is gradually opened according to the number of push messages. This means that the more messages it receives the more area it exposes (Compare Fig. 1(b) and Fig. 3(a)).

Unlike previous cover products, the proposed cover does not intrusively distract users. Imagine a situation that an office worker's phone sounds 'Marimba' during an important meeting. If it happens, you may feel embarrassed. This interruption comes from the fact that sound is originally "designed to attract maximum attention" [13]. The proposed item, however, is able to silently notice when the device is within the range of one's vision. It could reduce the notification stress from sound and even save some time to prepare for the interruption [12].

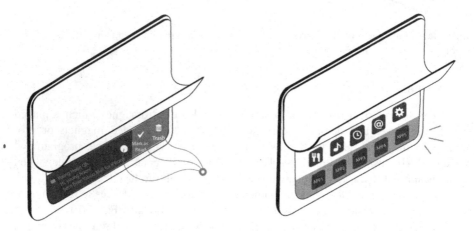

Fig. 3. (a) Uncovered screen with Interactive Smart Cover (Left), (b) Uncovered home screen with previous cover (Right).

There has been no option for people using non-interactive smart cover [30] to check notification instantly since existing products display the last screen when cover is opened (Assume device is unlocked). However, when Interactive Smart Cover exposes the touchscreen, the mobile device displays notification first (See Fig. 3(a)). The touchless notification enables users to use their mobile devices as if they are not using accessories. If user manually uncovers the device himself/herself, it shows the home screen or last app screen as previous products (Also in Fig. 3(b)). Therefore, the cover improves adaptability as well as usability.

From the perspective of Appcessory, Interactive Smart Cover adds a new personalized notification channel. It can be configured to response only when the device receives important notification. For instance, if users receive phone call from starred contact which is personally set on the phone, the phone would be uncovered and incoming call screen will be displayed. It makes sense because the cover does not block visual feedback and it does not make sound even the device is mute mode. Third party applications might provide detail preference such as combining notification channel – sound notification and cover movement for important phone call, vibration and cover movement for important new E-mail. This will help people who are worried about missing important notification [8] or who want to minimize daily interruptions [14]. With further integration with mobile application, proposed cover will be able to provide context-aware notification in the future.

4 Interactive Smart Cover on Watch-Type Device

Interaction with wearable computing devices has attracted HCI Community's attention. Large amount of previous works have focused on the supporting input modality [33] but little work is gone into integrating notification system on smartwatch with accessories. Since steady growth of smartwatch is reported [20], accessory design supporting its own nature would be required. In this section we propose the notification method of Interactive Smart Cover for watch-type devices and account for the reason why its interaction design is suitable for them and other future devices.

Fig. 4. Example of Interactive Smart Cover's notification for watch-type device – closed (Left), opened (Right).

The question on how to deal with the integration of accessory and device has heavily led us to devise various designs. Figure 4 is an example of application for flexible device (or current non-flexible device). The flexible watch is on the wrist and the cover is uncovered to show notifications. However, the watch might lose its natural feature if the cover is closed all the time. In this regard Interactive Smart Cover not only protects the flexible device but also improve the noticeability of watch device with its interactive feature.

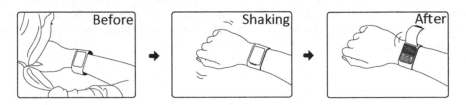

Fig. 5. Example of using watch-type device with flexible cover (Before > Shaking > after)

Although small screen of watch-type device causes discomfort for users to check notification, current smartwatch users actively check notification/information from the mobile devices [16]. In accordance with the activity trend, we have added one more way to check notifications; shaking devices. Figure 5 shows another method to check notifications. It presents three simple steps. When people shake their own device, it senses the direction of motion. For example, if the flexible watch is shaken twice to the right, the OS forces the coded magnet to be opened. Users can trigger opening of the cover with motion sensor, which is widely packed in the watch device. This enables users to check notifications as if they are not using accessories. Of course, they can close it by shaking or by hand.

The proposed interaction for watch-type is applicable to most mobile devices. Past research on the utility of motion sensing [17, 18] supports that shaking accessory can be adapted to users naturally. Chernbumroong et al. had experiment on detecting five daily activities with single wrist-worn sensor [22] and Partidge et al. developed the TiltType technique [19], a text entry complementing system which is designed for small mobile devices such as current watch-type devices. Motion sensor is already distributed in the commercial market. For instance, Moto 360 which was the most popular in 2014 [21] has accelerometer sensor and gyro sensor (Fig. 6).

Fig. 6. Rear side of typical watch-type device

The original nature of smartwatch also supports the necessity of our interaction technique. Assuming most users need protective accessories for watches, front screen is vulnerable to be damaged in practice. On the other hand, the rear surface of the watch has lower chance of getting damaged. This means that cover-type accessory is suitable for watches. In addition, given that the most-used feature of smartwatch is checking notification [16], frequent notification might be stressful to watch users. Regarding this inconvenience, Interactive Smart Cover would be used as helpful customized notification channel.

5 Discussion

Noticeability varies depending on the context. In public spaces people usually set their phone to mute mode. This means that sound notification is not available at specific location. In case of time modality, "Do Not Disturb" or "Quiet time" feature in mobile OS blocks auditory notification during scheduled time [8]. In this regard, Interactive Smart Cover has obvious advantage that it does not explicitly make noise. Since we only proposed the interaction method and design of the cover from this paper, comparison of actual noticeability should be explored from the further research.

The proposed cover has some limitations as well. As we have previously mentioned, the cover's movement is visible only within the user's vision. This means that if s/he is distant from devices, the cover loses immediate notification. In this case, maintaining uncovering of the cover, it is able to notify arrival of new message just like the dying message [6]. Dark place might be problematic as well, but light from touchscreen and illumination sensor would be helpful to deal with the situation. We can find another weak point from the proposed interaction method (See Fig. 5). In respect of wearable device, whole user activities should be concerned. For instance, if table tennis player wears watch-type device with Interactive Smart Cover, their stroke could trigger the disclosure of the cover. To cope with extreme situations, further integration with mobile device is required. If motion sensor packed in the smartphone detects the exercising state, the phone would inhibit the trigger of paired device for a while. In addition to the case of small devices, strength of magnetic force should be tested for the feasibility.

For our future work, we will develop the hardware and compare the noticeability with traditional notifications. Significance of the cover would be the following. Based on the development of Interactive Smart Cover, we plan to apply some specific functions to the mobile device. Since our cover could expose private information publicly, we also devised how to avoid unwanted cases. One possible option is detecting user with front camera on tablet PC. If face of user is not detected, display would be turned off earlier. Other detail algorithm and steps will be addressed in the future work.

6 Conclusion

In this paper we review current notification system and several improvements on its problem. We also suggest new notification method using mobile device accessory which has been little focused. The design of Interactive Smart Cover is presented and it extends its potential to provide customized notification channel. We also propose a new interaction method for wrist-worn device. Further development and noticeability will be discussed in the future work.

Acknowledgements. I would like to address special thanks to So Yon Jeong for her insightful comments and very useful materials.

This research was supported by the MSIP (Ministry of Science, ICT and Future Planning), Korea, under the "IT Consilience Creative Program" (NIPA-2014-H0201-14-1002) supervised by the NIPA(National IT Industry Promotion Agency).

References

1. One-in-four Smartphone Owners Don't User a Case to Protect Their Phone According to NPD (2013). https://www.npd.com/wps/portal/npd/us/news/press-releases/one-in-four-smartphone-owners-dont-use-a-case-to-protect-their-phone-according-to-npd/
2. REVEALED: Here's Who Uses iPhone Cases And Why. http://www.businessinsider.sg/iphone-case-survey-2014-7/
3. Bianchi, A., Ian, O.: Designing tangible magnetic appcessories. In: Proceedings of the 7th International Conference on Tangible, pp. 255–258. ACM Press, New York (2013)
4. Weiss, M.G., Nathan, A., Kropp, J.B., Lockhart, W.J.: WagTag: a dog collar accessory for monitoring canine activity levels. In: Proceedings of the 2013 ACM Conference on Pervasive and Ubiquitous Computing Adjunct Publication, pp. 405–414. ACM Press, New York (2013)
5. Holtman, K.: Appcessory Economics: Enabling loosely coupled hardware/software innovation. Technical Note, arXiv preprint (2012)
6. Yamanaka, S., Miyashita, H.: Vibkinesis: notification by direct tap and 'dying message' using vibronic movement controllable smartphones. In: Proceedings of the 27th Annual ACM Symposium on User Interface Software and Technology, pp. 535–540. ACM Press, New York (2014)
7. Lee, J.-u., Lim, J.-M., Shin, H., Kyung, K.-U.: SHIFT: interactive smartphone bumper case. In: Isokoski, P., Springare, J. (eds.) EuroHaptics 2012, Part II. LNCS, vol. 7283, pp. 91–96. Springer, Heidelberg (2012)
8. Yoon, S., Lee, S.S., Lee, J.M., Lee, K.: Understanding notification stress of smartphone messenger app. In: CHI 2014 Extended Abstracts on Human Factors in Computing Systems, pp. 1735–1740. ACM Press, New York (2014)
9. Müller, H., Jennifer, G., John, W.: Understanding tablet use: a multi-method exploration. In: Proceedings of the 14th International Conference on Human-Computer Interaction with Mobile Devices and Services, pp. 1–10. ACM Press, New York (2012)
10. Aftermarket Mobile Accessory Revenues to Reach $62 Billion by 2017 as Market Value Moves to Smart Accessories. https://www.abiresearch.com/press/aftermarket-mobile-accessory-revenues-to-reach-62-
11. Smartphone Accessory Revenues Valued at $20 Billion in 2012. https://www.abiresearch.com/press/smartphone-accessory-revenues-valued-at-20-billion
12. Böhmer, M., Lander, C., Gering, S., Brumpy, D.P., Krüger, A.: Interrupted by a phone call: exploring designs for lowering the impact of call notifications for smartphone users. In: Proceedings of the 32nd Annual ACM Conference on Human Factors in Computing Systems, pp. 3045–3054. ACM Press, New York (2014)
13. Hansson, R., Peter, L., Johan, R.: Subtle and public notification cues for mobile devices. In: Streitz, N., Stephanidis, C. (eds.) Ubicomp 2001: Ubiquitous Computing. LNCS, vol. 2201, pp. 240–246. Springer, Heidelberg (2001)
14. Horvitz, E., Johnson, A., Muru, S.: Balancing awareness and interruption: Investigation of notification deferral policies. In: Ardissono, L., Brna, P., Mitrovic, A. (eds.) UM 2005. LNCS, vol. 3538, pp. 433–437. Springer, Heidelberg (2005)

15. Pielot, M., Karen, C., de Oliveira, R.: An in-situ study of mobile phone notifications. In: Proceedings of the 16th International Conference on Human-Computer Interaction with Mobile Devices and Services. pp. 233–242. ACM Press, New York (2014)

16. We Surveyed People About Smartphone Ownership and Their Answers Reveal Just How Loyal People Are to Apple and Android. http://www.businessinsider.com/smartphone-survey-platform-loyalty-2014-11

17. Hinckley, K., Pierce, J., Sinclair, M., Horvitz, E.: Sensing techniques for mobile interaction. In: Proceedings of the 13th Annual ACM Symposium on User Interface Software and Technology. pp. 91–100. ACM Press, New York (2000)

18. Oakley, I., O'Modhrain, S.: Tilt to scroll: evaluating a motion based vibrotactile mobile interface. In: Eurohaptics Conference, 2005 and Symposium on Haptic Interfaces for Virtual Environment and Teleoperator Systems, 2005. World Haptics 2005. First Joint, pp. 40–49. IEEE Press, New York (2005)

19. Partridge, K., Chatterjee, S., Sazawal, V., Borriello, G., Want, R.: TiltType: accelerometer-supported text entry for very small devices. In: Proceedings of the 15th Annual ACM Symposium on User Interface Software and Technology, pp. 201–204. ACM Press, New York (2002)

20. Smartwatch Market is Expected to Reach $32.9 Billion by 2020. http://www.prnewswire.com/news-releases/smartwatch-market-is-expected-to-reach-329-billion-by-2020—allied-market-research-287902311.html

21. Over 720,000 Android Wear devices shipped in 2014. http://www.canalys.com/newsroom/over-720000-android-wear-devices-shipped-2014

22. Chernbumroong, S., Atkins, A.S., Yu, H.: Activity classification using a single wrist-worn accelerometer. In: 2011 5th International Conference on Software, Knowledge Information, Industrial Management and Applications (SKIMA), pp. 1–6. IEEE Press, New York (2011)

23. Fallman, D., Yttergren, B.: Meeting in quiet: choosing suitable notification modalities for mobile phones. In: Proceedings of the 2005 Conference on Designing for User eXperience, pp. 55. AIGA Press, New York (2005)

24. Fischer, J.E., Greenhalgh, C., Benford, S.: Investigating episodes of mobile phone activity as indicators of opportune moments to deliver notifications. In: Proceedings of the 13th International Conference on Human Computer Interaction with Mobile Devices and Services. pp. 181–190. ACM Press, New York (2011)

25. Czerwinski, M., Cutrell, E., Horvitz, E.: Instant messaging: effects of relevance and timing. In: People and Computers XIV: Proceedings of HCI 2000. pp. 71–76. Springer, Sutherland (2000)

26. Iqbal, S.T., Brian, B.P.: Effects of intelligent notification management on users and their tasks. In: Proceedings of the SIGCHI Conference on Human Factors in Computing Systems. pp. 93–102. ACM Press, New York (2008)

27. Iqbal, S.T., Horvitz, E.: Notifications and awareness: a field study of alert usage and preferences. In: Proceedings of the 2010 ACM Conference on Computer Supported Cooperative Work, pp. 27–30. ACM Press, New York (2010)

28. Gomes, A., Nesbitt, A., Vertegaal, R.: MorePhone: a study of actuated shape deformations for flexible thin-film smartphone notifications. In: Proceedings of the SIGCHI Conference on Human Factors in Computing Systems. pp. 583–592. ACM Press, New York (2013)

29. Sahami Shirazi, A., Henze, N., Dingler, T., Pielot, M., Weber, D., Schmidt, A.: Large-scale assessment of mobile notifications. In: Proceedings of the 32nd Annual ACM Conference on Human Factors in Computing Systems. pp. 3055–3064. ACM Press, New York (2014)

30. Apple – iPad – Accessories. http://www.apple.com/ipad/accessories/

31. The NPD Group: Mobile Phone Cases Lead 32 Percent Increase in Mobile Phone Accessories Sales. https://www.npd.com/wps/portal/npd/us/news/press-releases/pr_120821/
32. Galaxy S® 5 S-View® Flip Cover, Black. http://www.samsung.com/us/mobile/cell-phones-accessories/EF-CG900BBESTA
33. Huang, D.Y., Tsai, M.C., Tung, Y.C., Tsai, M.L., Yeh, Y.T., Chan, L., Hung, Y., Chen, M.Y.: TouchSense: expanding touchscreen input vocabulary using different areas of users' finger pads. In: Proceedings of the 32nd Annual ACM Conference on Human Factors in Computing Systems, pp. 189–192. ACM Press, New York (2014)

Combining Generative Art and Physiological Information for New Situation of Garden Restaurant

Tung-Chen Tsai[(✉)] and Chao-Ming Wang

National Yunlin University of Science and Technology, Douliu, Taiwan
{M10234003,wangcm}@yuntech.edu.tw

Abstract. Restaurant consumers often spend most of their time queuing outside garden restaurants during mealtimes, waiting for a table. If restaurant owners and customers can effectively utilize these idle times, both of them will inevitably benefit. This study developed an interactive device that can be used to divert customers' attention during waiting times and enable them to enjoy the fun of using this device, thereby helping restaurant owners promote their garden restaurants and local postcards.

A literature review on human–computer interaction, wearable devices, and generative art was conducted to propose the design principle of the interactive device. Subsequently, prototyping, user manual, and recommendations for users were developed, and the effectiveness of the prototype was assessed.

This study developed an interactive device with which users can use during their waiting or idling time. The prototype of this interactive device involves combining the concept of generative art and a pulse sensor. Participants can use the garden restaurant's postcard as an interactive media, which can then be converted into images through image processing. According to rules and motion of a graphics, the prototype can provide unique visual feedback. In addition, the proposed prototype entails a wearable pulse sensor that enhances the graphic rules and motions, enabling users to see their own heartbeat information. Moreover, a novel interactive thinking for wearable devices was proposed.

The contributions of this study included (1) completing the prototyping of a pulse sensor based on the concept of generative arts, and (2) developing a novel wearable interactive device that can be used in garden restaurants.

Keywords: Generative art · Human-computer interaction · Pulse sensor · Interactive technology

1 Introduction

As information technology advances, digital media has become an integral part of people's daily life, in which each information product is developed through a series of design thinking process. During this design process, interactive design is a crucial topic for designing an interactive device that satisfies user needs. The article will design the

© Springer International Publishing Switzerland 2015
N. Streitz and P. Markopoulos (Eds.): DAPI 2015, LNCS 9189, pp. 449–460, 2015.
DOI: 10.1007/978-3-319-20804-6_41

interactive device for garden restaurant, and arrange the customer at a waiting for idle time can interact with the device.

Restaurant customers often spend most of their time either queuing outside garden restaurants waiting for a table or waiting for their food after placing their orders. Moreover, some restaurants require customers to collect table numbers as a mean of acquiring a table (Fig. 1). If restaurant owners and customers can effectively utilize these idle times, both of them will inevitably benefit. Therefore, this study developed an interactive device for a garden restaurant, where customers can play and interact with it while waiting for a table or their meals, thereby effectively utilizing their idle times.

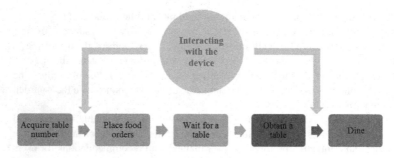

Fig. 1. Dining procedure

Generative art is crucial for the development of new media art. Generative art is a unique type of art that combines technology with the concept of aesthetics, enabling computers to autonomously create artworks through a set of rules. Therefore, it is also referred to as an automatic art-creation system. In this study, the concept of generative art was integrated with the interactive system, thus allowing users to appreciate the beauty of generative art and enjoy the fun of interacting with the system.

We developed an interactive device by using a landscape postcard of a garden restaurant as the basis. When getting a table number, the restaurant offers customers landscape postcard and inform that the postcard can interact with the device. Hopes to promote local cultures and landscape through interaction, thereby raising the popularity of the restaurant. Heartbeat sensing is smart watches are equipped with the function. If a wearable device can provide various types of information such as users' physiological information, or interact with peripheral devices, such device will be interesting application. In this study a wearable device that provides users' heart rate information and immediately transmits information to the device. The objectives of this study were as follows:

(1) To Design a Generative Art-Based Interactive Device Integrated with a Pulse Sensor. By combining a postcard, image processing, and wearable technology, a prototype of an interactive device was proposed to provide customers with a device that enables them to enjoy the fun of an interactive experience. In addition, a novel concept related to the application of wearable devices was proposed.

(2) To Promote Local Attractions Through the Device and Enhance the Restaurant's Popularity. Sceneries near the garden restaurant can be promoted through the postcard–device interaction, leaving a deep impression in users of the landscape presented on the postcard and thus to elevate restaurant popularity.

2 Related Work

In this study the interactive device involved image processing, pulse sensor and algorithm. The device can transmit heartbeat signals through a wearable device to a computer, and an automated function for graphical visualization. Therefore, we reviewed literature on human–computer interaction, wearable devices, and generative art.

2.1 Human Computer Interaction

Kantowitz and Sorkin (1983) proposed human factors view of the human operator in a work environment, stating that in human–computer interactions, the brain receives information that stimulates the human body to control the keyboard. Subsequently, the computer provides feedback on the screen, the information on which is transmitted back to the brain through the human eye. The brain continually receives information, which forms the basis for the human to make a decision. The concept of human factors has gradually evolved, forming the concept of human–computer interaction.

An interactive system considers the nature of a design, using user as the basis for system design and determining whether the entire human–computer interaction satisfied people's needs (Benyon, 2010). The device applied computer vision as the human–computer interface. Computer vision is the capability of a machine to visualize and make judgments like how the human eyes do. The machine acquires images through a video camera, converting the captured objects into image information, which is then subjected to image processing. Image characteristics are obtained by analyzing the pixel distributions, brightness, and color of the processed image. Subsequently, the machine uses the processed information to make a decision and execute an action (Learned-Miller, 2007). In the design of the device comprising a wearable device and computer vision two input interface, to clarify the structure of Human-computer interaction is very important part.

2.2 Wearable Technology

"Wearable computing" is a study of physical devices that comprise microprocessor and sensor. Wearable computing involves converting detected physiological information into usable data. Wearable devices such as smart glasses, watches, clothing, and shoes can be attached to the human body (Mann, 1996). In recent years, smart watches have been widely used in people's daily lives, and smart watches of various brands are equipped with a pulse sensor. Therefore, the application of smart watches will be one of the focus of future technology developments. This paper adopted a wearable device to detect users heartbeat in real-time. And input heartbeat information into the device, which then processes it through image processing and provides it as feedback to users. Through real-time interaction with field or device feature, the formation of a novel type of wearable device interaction.

2.3 Generative Art

This study employed wearable computing as a means of interacting with the wearable device. Wearable computing entails providing raw physiological data to the device. To achieve real-time visualization, we reviewed literature on generative art. Galanter (2003) defined generative art as follows:

Generative art refers to any art practice where the artist uses a system, such as a set of natural language rules, a computer program, a machine, or other procedural invention, which is set into motion with some degree of autonomy contributing to or resulting in a completed work of art.

In other words, using language programming or mechanical procedures to formulate rules and constraints enables a system to autonomously generate results that feature the following characteristics: chance, unpredictability, surprise, and indeterminacy (Monro, 2008). This design of visual feedback develop to definitions and rules for the graphics, and the two parts of the practice, hoping that through computational design, allowing users to experience a unique presentation.

2.4 Case Study

In this chapter provides a review of case studies on interactive installations and digital display. These cases are based on interactive experience, allowing users to attain pleasure and fun for of an interactive experience. We analyzed and compared human-computer interface, display and feedback for each case. Hoping to generalize the case of design methods, and learn design method from case. To develop design principles of prototype.

(1) Wooden Mirror (Rozin, 1999). "Wooden mirror" is an interactive art, designed by Rozin and exhibited in 1999. This work is a mechanical mirror that combining computer vision and a various materials. Device via camera to capture each pixels of grayscale image and each wooden chips corresponding part in image; by motor drive to achieve each wooden chips.

(2) Living Shapes Interactive Wall (Philips, 2012). Philips Electronics develop interactive intelligent mirror with OLED (Organic Light-Emitting) in 2012. Device uses infrared cameras to sense the body shape and display on the OLED wall. Each OLED with a unique display brightness, and achieve device illumination. "Living shapes interactive wall" is a set of interactive devices and stylish lighting device.

(3) Sketch Aquarium (teamLab, 2013). "Sketch Aquarium" is a digital interactive installation which combining with e-learning experience for children. User can get a draft of ocean creature, and allows users to freely draw. And then put the ocean creature in the scanner, people will see the creature come life on the wall. This work using artificial intelligence and simple human-computer interface to lead children learn graffiti.

(4) Visualizing Perlin Noise (Hingorani, 2014).**"Visualizing Perlin Noise"** is designed by Hingorani and displayed in 2014's MAT 200C: Pattern Formation. This work is an interactive device of visualized Perlin noise, the device presents life cycle and motion trail of a particle by utilizing Kinect to identify the hand gesture and project the images in an interactive experience space. Besides the strong visual effect, users also can fell Generative art its feature of randomness, unpredictability, surprise and uncertainty.

(5) Time Traveler - The 120th Anniversary Exhibition on Chen Cheng-po (Bright Ideas Design, 2014). "Time traveler" is multi-screen projection interactive installation to recode painting of artist Chen Cheng-po each period. Through multi-screen projection will be converted into the artist's creative period the year and complete record of Chen's life course. This interactive installation using gesture recognition as human-computer interface, let user can waving right hand or left hand to browse painting.

2.5 Summary

This chapter presents a review of case studies on interactive interfaces and feedback in Table 1. The standing type of interactive installation typically used computer vision as the interactive interface. Specifically, the Sketch Aquarium is an interactive installation where participants can sketch pictures and interact with it through a device. The designer of the Sketch Aquarium considered using intuitive simply interactive interfaces that allow users to assimilate into a scenario. Regarding feedback design, the former two designs involve using a physical structure to achieve digital display, whereas the latter three designs entail using projection to digitally display. This study selected computer vision as the human-computer interface, and used a wearable device to simulate the pulse sensor functions of smart watches, thereby providing a novel thinking approach that enables users to experience the interactive functions of smart watches.

3 Design Method

3.1 Design Concept

Prototype systems are expected to effectively utilize the waiting time to divert the focus of users through fun of an interactive experience, and to promote postcards and restaurants popularity. Customers can interact with the device through the postcard by inserting the card into the device, which will then perform image processing, and display the images of postcard onto the screen as feedback for users. In addition, the pulse sensor function of the wearable device transmits users' heartbeat information to the device, and the motion and speed of the graphics change according to users' physiological information to generate unique feedback to users (Fig. 2).

Table 1. Case studies summary

Title	User interface	Display	Feedback
Wooden mirror (1999)	Detection of approaching objects.	Dynamic structure	Each wooden piece corresponding part in image.
Living shapes interactive wall (2012)	Infrared cameras for skeleton detection	OLED	Each OLED corresponding part in depth image.
Sketch aquarium (2013)	By scanning the sketch, interact indirect with computer	Multi-screen projection	Simulation of fish swarm behavior.
Visualizing Perlin noise (2014)	Infrared cameras for skeleton detection	Screen projection	Flow field visualization
Time traveler (2014)	Hand gesture recognition	Multi-screen projection	Display of artist painting each period.

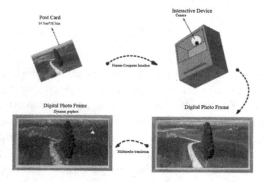

Fig. 2. Storyboard

In this study, the research method involved first conducting a background and literature review, compiling case studies relevant to interactive installation. Various human-computer interface, display, and feedback approaches were summarized to determine the design principles of various cases, which were then used as the basis for developing the system prototype in Table 2. The human-computer interface method of the prototype involved using computer vision to capture the image information on the postcard and displaying the image according to the concept of generative art. Moreover, the parameters produced when the graph changed according to the information generated from the pulse sensor were also one of the features of this work.

3.2 Visual Feedback Design

The prototype displayed digital contents through Processing. Users can view a display that is achieved through design computation and is distinct from conventional image display methods. This section presents the definition and rules for a unit square planar,

Table 2. Disign principles

Interface	Display	Feedback
Computer vision: insert postcard into device./Wearable device: detecting heartbeat.	45-inch screen display.	Dynamic image composite digital postcard image. And corresponding to the change of heart rate parameters of the graphics.

and how an image can be sketched using the motion of a graphics. The graphics definitions included the x-coordinates, y-coordinates, size, rotational angle, and quantity of squares, and the rules for a square planar comprised the x-axis and y-axis motion, and the colors of display (Tables 3 and 4). According to displacement rules, the system automatically generates unique feedback for users to experience (Fig. 3).

Table 3. Definition of graph

Definition	Content
X-coordinate	The default value of graphics x-coordinate is 0.
Y-coordinate	The default value of graphics y-coordinate is random that stage height.
Size	The default value of graphics size default value is random $5 \sim 20$.
Rotation angle	In the center of the graphics as a benchmark towards 2π clockwise rotate.
Quantity	Set of multiple units square that has definitions and rules.

Table 4. Rule of graph

Rule	Content
X-axis motion	Graphics x-axis motion from 0 to scene width, and each graph shift value of random $0.5 \sim 2$.
Y-axis motion	Graphics y-coordinate as a reference point from the upper or lower movement, and using noise that variable shift offset limited to between -100 and $+100$, let the graph move smoother.
Color	Graphics color captures images each pixel as a graph coloring.

3.3 Production of the Pulse Sensor

According to the Human factors View of the human operator in a work environment, we produced the framework diagram for the prototype (Fig. 4). Regarding the framework for a human–computer interaction, users insert the postcard into a device, subsequently activating the device. Device can use the camera to take pictures. When the computer captures an image, it stores the image to the database; processes the image; computes the graphics; and defines the rules of the graph. Then computed image is then displayed on the screen for users. The wearable device is a simulation of the smart watch; it wirelessly transmits the received heartbeat information to the computer, which converts the physical information into graphics so that the rules correspond to the information, thereby forming an environment where human–computer interactions take place.

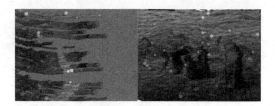

Fig. 3. Visual feedback

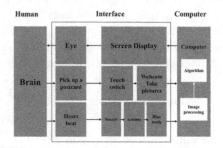

Fig. 4. Human-computer interaction framework (Source: Kantowitz and Sorkin 1983) (This article redraws).

The sensor for the system prototype was developed by integrating the computer vision technology and using the wearable device. The computer vision captures the image information of the postcard, and the wearable device is used to correspond users' heart rate information to the rules of the graphic, thus leading users into the scenario.

(1) Integrating Computer Vision Technology. Prototype was used computer vision as the input for capturing images. It captures images, stores them, and algorithm according to processing procedures (Fig. 5), which involve three parts: device activation, image process, and data processing.

Regarding device activation, Arduino was used as the interface for hardware and computer communication. Once users insert a postcard into the device, the device will be activated. For image processing, the camera automatically focuses on the image of the postcard and then captures it. The images are stored in the database and subjected to image processing. The device system extracts the processed image for graphics computation and then displays it on the screen for users to view.

(2) Using Wearable Device. A pulse sensor was used as the wearable device. The sensor captures heartbeat information expressed in terms of inter beat interval (IBI) and beats per minute (BPM). According to the developer of Oregon Scientific, the heart rate of an adult resting is approximately 60–80 bpm, and the heart rate of an adult working is approximately 140–180 bpm and a maximum of 190 bpm. Because a pulse sensor generates errors when in use, we adopted a heart rate of 50–200 bpm as the change parameter for the rule of graphics. Fixed graphics were used, and the heartbeat (in BPM and IBI) parameters were quantified and added to the base values (Table 5). The Arduino then wirelessly transmits the detected heartbeat information via Bluetooth to the computer (Fig. 6).

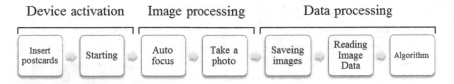

Device activation   Image processing   Data processing

| Insert postcards | → | Starting | Auto focus | → | Take a photo | Saveing images | → | Reading Image Data | Algorithm |

Fig. 5. Processing procedures

4 Research and Analysis

The prototype comprised three portions: visual feedback, wearable device, and tangible user interface. This section describes the steps and interfaces of the interaction process and details the process through users interact with the interface (Fig. 7 and Table 6).

Table 5. Heartbeat correspondence table

Heartbeat data	Definition or rule	Content
IBI, Inter beat interval	Size	Set of various parameter between −10 to +10, and added to graph size.
BMP, Beats per minute	Graph motion of x-coordinate or graph motion y-coordinate.	Set of various parameter between −1 to +1, and added to the x-coordinate. Set of various parameter between −100 to +100, and added to the y-coordinate.

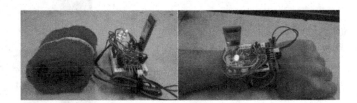

Fig. 6. Prototype of wearable device

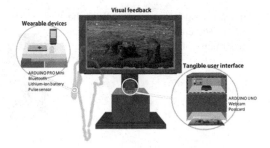

Fig. 7. A schematic diagram

Table 6. Interactive process

Step	Interface	Content	Photographs
1	Wearable device	Users wear a wearable device with a pulse sensor, which corresponded to heartbeat sensing display heartbeat.	
2	Tangible user interface	After wearing wearable device, user can select a postcard, and insert in the device.	
3	Tangible user interface	System process image capturing and image processing.	
4	Visual feedback	The screen will display the postcard images. According to heartbeat to display graph size, motion and speed.	
5	Visual feedback	After a period time, graph will fill the entire screen, and allow users to see the image of the original postcard.	

5 Conclusions and Future Directions

(1) Conclusions. The contributions of this study included (1) completing the prototyping of a pulse sensor based on the concept of generative arts, and (2) developing a novel wearable interactive device that can be used in garden restaurants. The results can be provided as reference to future researchers.

(2) Future Directions. In this study, we applied the garden restaurant's postcard and implemented the prototype. During the implementation process, the following three revisions to the prototype can be made in future:

(a) *Highlighting the application of heartbeat information derived from the wearable device.*

   1. The heartbeat information did not effectively correspond to the result of the graph computation in the system prototype. Therefore, users could not know the changes in their heartbeat from the interactive device. The design for the graphics computation generated an exceedingly small parameter error and failed to identify the changes in the pulses. Thus, revisions should be made to these aspects of the system prototype.

(b) *Enriching the visualization approach.*

   2. Users who used the interactive device mentioned that they were attracted to the content of the visual feedback during their first use. This prompted them to play with the device for the second time, but the experience was not as fun as the first time. This indicates that the visual feedback provided accorded with users' expectation. Thus, future in-depth studies can be conducted according to the graphics computation, and try to create various graphics algorithm..

(c) *Assessing system display and effectiveness.*

   3. Regarding the on-site exhibition and system evaluation, we intend to exhibit the system in the garden restaurant and conduct on-site observations and questionnaire survey to assess the effectiveness of the system and public participation. From this process, concrete recommendations for system modification can be obtained.

References

Benyon, D.: Designing Interactive Systems: A Comprehensive Guide to HCI and Interaction Design. Addison-Wesley, Boston (2010)

BrightIdeasDesign: Time Traveler - the 120th Anniversary Exhibition on Chen Cheng-po. (2014). http://chenchengpo.brightideas.com.tw/, Retrieved 7 June 2015

Galanter, P.:What is generative art? complexity theory as a context for art theory. Paper presented at the GA2003–6th Generative Art Conference (2003)

Greenberg, I.: Processing: Creative Coding and Computational Art. Apress, New York (2007)

Huang, G.B., Ramesh, M., Berg, T., Learned-Miller, E.: Labeled faces in the wild: a database for studying face recognition in unconstrained environments. Technical Report 07–49, vol. 1(2), p. 3. University of Massachusetts, Amherst (2007)

Hingorani, M.: Visualizing Perlin Noise. (2014). https://www.youtube.com/watch?v=Go2nXtn-dEl0, Retrieved 3 May 2015

Jennifer, P., Yvonne, R., Helen, S.: Interaction Design: Beyond Human-Computer Interaction. Wiley, New York (2002)

Lazzeroni, C., Bohnacker, H., Groß, B., Laub, J.: Generative Design: Visualize, Program, and Create with Processing. Princeton Architectural, New Jersey (2012)

MacKenzie, I.S.: Human-Computer Interaction: an Empirical Research Perspective. Newnes, Oxford (2012)

Mann, S.: Smart clothing: the shift to wearable computing. Commun. ACM **39**(8), 23–24 (1996). doi:10.1145/232014.232021

Monro, G.: The Concept of Emergence in Generative Art. University of Sydney, Sydney (2008)

Pearson, M.: Generative Art: A Practical Guide Using Processing. Manning, New York (2011)

Philips: Living shapes interactive wall. (2012). http://www.lumiblade-experience.com/livingshapes, Retrieved 7 June 2015

Reeves, W.T.: Particle systems & mdash;a technique for modeling a class of fuzzy objects. SIGGRAPH Comput. Graph. **17**(3), 359–375 (1983). doi:10.1145/964967.801167

Rozin, D.: Wooden Mirror. (1999). http://www.smoothware.com/danny/woodenmirror.html, Retrieved 7 June 2015

Shiffman, D.: The Nature of Code: [Simulating Natural Systems with Processing]. Selbstverl (2012)

teamLab: Sketch Aquarium. (2013). http://www.teamlab.net/tw/all/products/aquarium.html, Retrieved 3 May 2015

Design of Co-evolving Textiles Applied to Smart Products

Rachel Zuanon$^{(\boxtimes)}$ and Geraldo Coelho Lima Júnior

Sense Design Lab, PhD and Master's Design Program, Anhembi Morumbi
University, São Paulo, Brazil
rzuanon@anhembi.br1, rachel.z@zuannon.com.br1,
glimadesign58@gmail.com2

Abstract. Among the main barriers to the production of smart textiles on an industrial scale, there are the difficulty of integration of electronic and textile raw materials; the maintenance of textiles, especially with regard to their washing; and the poor durability of smart capabilities associated with the textile structure. Moreover, most breakthroughs in the development of smart textiles occur in a limited way and targeted to meet the specific features of the project or wearable product. This article proposes the hypothesis of co-evolving smart textile as a contribution to overcome these problems. Memorization and customization features are viable due to nanotechnology and assigned to the textile basis. These characteristics aim to contribute to the progress in the design and production process of smart textiles in large scale, aimed at daily use, and able to co-evolve with the user's body and the surrounding environment.

Keywords: Textile design · Smart textile · Co-evolving smart textile · Smart products

1 Introduction

Textiles and, therefore, the clothes made from them are in an interface between the body and the surrounding environment. Its characteristics are varied and able to stimulate and promote different kinds of perception to the user. Nevertheless, fundamentally, textiles are made up of fibers. These fibers can be differentiated between natural and chemical, the latter comprising the synthetic and artificial materials. However, the performance and appearance of the final textile are linked to how these fibers are wove, as well as the way the stitching yarn is manufactured. In contrast, "the finishing and treatments can be applied to a textile at any stage of their production, in the form of fiber, stitching yarn, textile or final clothing" [1]. In this context, there were considered the basic principles of textile design related to scale, texture, color, patterned, repeat, positioning and weight, as these parameters are articulated in functional designs for use in the contemporary context. In summary, the structural qualities of the raw material of each textile, the finishing processes and processing confirm the construction of sensory relations among body-textile-environment.

Advances in the creation of textiles follow two paths: those arising from technological advances in the area, and those derived from ethical and environmental concerns, and in the intersection point of these two paths, the textiles of the future will be

© Springer International Publishing Switzerland 2015
N. Streitz and P. Markopoulos (Eds.): DAPI 2015, LNCS 9189, pp. 461–470, 2015.
DOI: 10.1007/978-3-319-20804-6_42

produced [1]. In addition, there are experimental textiles that do not arise from the influence of existing textiles, but from references obtained in different areas, such as the architecture, arts, contemporary culture, such as the nature itself. In an emerging era of biotechnology, nature is not only being copied by biological imitation (biomimetics), nor just being exploited in the development of bioactive materials, but mostly collaborating with the emergence of other "natural" versions through textile engineering.

With the development of electronic textiles (e-textiles), these possibilities are enhanced with fibers, stitching yarns, ribbons and textiles that can conduct electricity [2]. These textiles can feel when and how they are being touched, acting as sensors, switches, transistors, cables, antennas, displays; and react to stimuli and the user's body conditions and environment [3, 4] derived from mechanical, thermal, chemical, electrical and magnetic sources, among others. In this field, textile techniques can create conductive textile and clothes with the application of carbon, stainless steel, silver and, even, gold [2]. Moreover, interactivity provided by the association of smart materials to the fibers or stitching yarns constitute circuits and communication networks in which information such as heat, light, pressure, magnetic forces, electricity, heartbeats and other neurophysiological data of the user may be transferred and promote changes on shape, color, sound or size of this textile.

With the nanotextiles, this potential is intensified, once the nanotechnology operates at the molecular level, allowing the creation of smart textiles capable to structural reconfigurations. Thus, a textile acquires unique properties such as, for example, chemicals that can be administered as a drug or a cosmetic.

The smart textile presents different expressions according to its ability to feel and react. Such expressions constitute the current categories: passive smart textile; active smart textile and very smart textile. The passive condition attributed to the textile indicates its ability to feel only environmental stimuli without, however, expressing any reaction to them. However, the active condition ensures the expression of reactions to stimuli interpreted by the textile, whereas a higher degree of intelligence provides the textile to feel, react and adapt to the conditions identified [5].

The technological systems consisting of sensors, actuators and control units are related to different levels of intelligence, that are assigned to each of these categories. The sensors are responsible for the detection of stimuli sent by the environment or by the user's body, and transform it into a kind of intelligible signal. Several different types of sensors operate in this sense: temperature, humidity, pressure, tension, chemical sensors, biosensors, nanosensors, among others, and their presence is identified as essential in the three categories of textile intelligence.

In passive smart textile, the sensors are sovereign and essential. In active smart textile, they work in cooperation with actuators and are responsible for generating transformations in response to the interpretation of the signals delivered by the sensors. The example of the chromatic materials that change their optical properties in response to temperature, light, chemical, mechanical stress stimuli, among others; hydrogel swells and releases chemicals in response to changes in pH, electric field or temperature; shape memory materials, which move in response to temperature changes; and electroluminescent materials that send light in response to voltage application. In very smart textiles, sensors operate in interface with the control units, which act as a brain, with cognition, reasoning and action capabilities [5] to interpret and generate real-time answers to the data sent by different sensors.

Despite significant breakthroughs in the development of smart textiles, there are still several challenges to overcome for its extensive application in clothing products, which are the following: the difficulty of integration of electronic and textile raw materials, caused by the differences between their manufacturing processes that results in the textile flexibility as opposed to the solidity of most electronic components [6]; the maintenance-related problem, especially the clothing washing, due to differences between the physical properties of the T = textile and embedded electronics; and the poor durability of smart capabilities, aggregated to the textile structure in the processing stage, after repeated washings.

Several research projects [7–15] are focused on overcoming these challenges. However, all design developments in this regard reinforce the textile development restricted to meet only the specific features of the desired product. That is, the wearable product features end up defining the characteristics of the textile, restricting its application to the development of only one product. This condition represents an impact restrictor to diversified production of smart textile products, from the single textile structure.

Driven by identification of this gap, this article aims the design of textile with features and physico-chemical and technological qualities capable of providing interactive and uninterrupted flow between textile material, user and environment, in order to promote continuous adaptability of these systems. This textile behavior, called by the authors of this article as co-evolving smart textile, is set up in the hypothesis aimed to contribute to the transposition of the main obstacles that limit the extensive use of smart textiles in the production of varied everyday clothes considering their daily and continuous use.

Therefore, the design of co-evolving smart textiles is intended to provide memorization of the interaction process among body-textile-environment from co-evolving nanosensors present in the textile structure. In addition to the memory capacity, co-evolving nanosensors are also able to monitor biological data provided by the user body, comfortable and safe, by excluding the need to display electrodes to the skin; responding to different stimuli coming from the surrounding environment; and promoting the reuse through repeated washings, without losing their functionalities. These characteristics aim to contribute to advances in smart and co-evolving textile products design with the user's body and the surrounding environment, since its configuration enables customization. That is, with the application of co-evolving nanosensors, the development of smart textile is not restricted to the product use specifications. Instead, the smart textile structure becomes customizable in order to allow different design purposes.

2 Literature Review

Given the hypothesis defined by this article, this section will be restricted to the research approach performed in the active smart textile and very smart textile and represent relevant references to the approach proposed here.

The development of active smart textiles involving the application of sensors and actuators in the cooperative operation is part of the study of photosensitive materials, optical fibers, conductive polymers, thermosensitive materials, shape memory materials, smart coatings/membranes, responsive chemical polymers, responsive mechanical materials, microcapsules, micro and nano materials [5].

In this sense, Hardaker et al. [12] present a study on fibers and textile coatings with optical, magnetic and electric properties for commercial and military applications. According to these researchers, there are significant research efforts directed to the development of new materials with coloring properties through the visible spectrum, including the electromagnetic spectrum of infrared and ultraviolet regions. This fibers system of responsive color, also known as chameleon, also aims a range of applications not restricted to textile, such as in the fields of optical communication and electronics.

Karaguzel et al. [11] investigate screen printing of the transmission lines in a variety of non-textile substrates, using different conductive inks focused on long-lasting application in e-textiles. In this scope, the researchers developed a porous textile coating for the printed lines, aiming the conductivity function durability.

It is noteworthy the studies involving the development of textiles and its application in wearables. Among them, the projects Wealthy (Fig. 1), My Heart, Lifeshirt by Biometrics (Fig. 2), Nike IPod Sport Sistem by Biomedia are studied by several authors [16–19]. These projects have, as a guiding concept, the health care and, accordingly, aim to the monitoring of vital signs, using textile bases in which there are sensors, able to enhance the implementation of outpatient monitoring systems for health, safety, security and well-being of the individual. Such researches aim to examine the characteristics of textiles and the responses for the control of heart rate and oxygen rate, and other neurophysiological parameters. Lifeshirt project provides, besides these data, the position of the user [17].

Regarding the development of very smart textile, there are two research lines: the first is related to the transmission, processing and monitoring of signals, in which are inserted neural networks and control systems as well as cognition theories and systems; the second research line investigates processes and integrated products in electronic and photonic wearable, adaptive and responsive structures, biomimetic, bioprocessors, and materials with the release of chemicals/drugs [5].

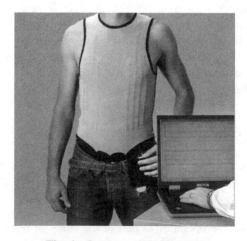

Fig. 1. Smartex – Wealthy [28]

Fig. 2. Lifeshirt [29]

In the first research line, Holland et al. [15] discuss the development of electrically conductive textile, which acts as a sensor for detection and localization of body fluids (for example, blood), wounds (for instance, cuts, wounds caused by bullets) and, potentially, vital signs.

In the second research line, Linz et al. [8] conducted a study on the use of non-invasive sensors integrated into the textile for monitoring human health in electromyography tests. The main purpose is the sensor fusion to the textile structure so as to avoid contact of the sensors with the patient's body.

Carpus et al. [9] present as a result of their research a knit textile with integrated resistive sensor for monitoring fetal heart rate in intrauterine development period.

Other studies [16] refer to the use of textiles to measure the sugar level in the user's body by monitoring the sweat. In this case, the authors indicate the possibility of verification of pathological disorders through the sensors system integrated to the textile, which identify the subject's body hydration and re-mineralization in order to prevent bodily reactions such as irritability, headache, vomiting, in addition to identifying the body temperature and heart rate.

Other research projects [20] move forward to the area of e-textiles, capable of electrical conduction from the stitching yarns developed with conductive characteristics, such as the Textro-Yarns®, elastic, highly conductive composite yarns with constant and high conductivity over a wide range of elongation. However, these studies did not show the physical properties of electronic textiles made with these stitching yarns, with respect to handling possibilities, intrinsic to everyday use, perspiration and washing (Fig. 3).

As of this scenario, it is possible to identify the subordination of smart textiles development related to the functional characteristics of wearable products in most developing wearable projects and textile products on the market. It is possible to note

Fig. 3. Textro-Yarns® [30]

the configuration of a production process that, different from that employed in other textiles in clothing industry, focus on the textile development with properties targeted to specifically meet the wearable product design needs, such as the Wealthy.

Therefore, the success of such textiles is related to the implementation of these specific properties that will result in the exclusive manufacturing of the clothing smartly designed. Despite the recognition of the significant progress already achieved in this area, the question is, in this article, about the development of smart textile able to meet different design needs in clothing and, therefore, wider productive range. Moreover, consequently, perspectives opening for the development of wearable products whose projects originate from implementation potential and viability provided by the textile.

3   Co-evolving Smart Textile Concept

Feeling is a vital necessity for the survival of every human being. Different stimuli are capable of promoting the ways to perceive and feel the surrounding reality, and among them, there is the act of dressing. The body fells the contact with the textile, and shall also respond to these tactile stimuli, combining actions to the textile movements that folds, pleats, stretchs, warms and refreshes. "Although touching is not itself an emotion, its sensory elements induce neuronal, glandular, muscular and mental changes that, combined, are called emotion" [21]. The use of each type of textile and fiber can provide the user with different sensations with respect to the touch, the textile in contact with the body.

As an extension of the epidermis, the skin overlying the skin [22], the textile acts as an interface, through which the individual interacts with the surrounding environment and stimulates its sensory device in different ways, in a dialogical relationship with numerous references capable of association and recognition by this body. In this mediation, co-evolving smart textile appears as a possibility to simultaneously promote and expand the scope of sensations to the human body and, thus, provide the differentiated management of body-environment communication.

In biology, the concept of co-evolution comprises the reciprocal selective interaction between two major groups of organisms in a close ecological relationship [23]. Moreover, in a broader perspective of the concept, "the co-evolution of biological and physico-chemical systems created the conditions for the development of human beings, which introduced a new type of interaction: human interaction" [24].

Using the concept of co-evolution for textile applications means strengthening a systemic vision, as considered by Bertalanffy [25, 26], in which all the behavior is more complex than the sum of the behaviors of the parts, so that events appear to involve more than only the individual decisions and actions.

It is possible to state, therefore, the intelligence of an open system assigned to the textile remains in continuous exchange of matter with the environment. Open systems exchange information with the part of reality external to them. This reality denominates the system environment. It is possible to say that the environment of a system is a group of all things that are not part of the composition of such system, but act over it or suffer some action from it [27]. In this continuous exchange with the environment, the open system cannot only maintain, but even evolve to a higher degree of complexity.

This exchange of information is also extended to the user's body and sets up intersystem interactions contexts, in which the boundaries are dynamic, as permeable membranes able to change and take on new forms from exchanges carried out in this relationship [26]. In this process, the adaptability of the textile structure to continuous interaction with the user's body and the environment is stored and, at the same time, externalized as outputs in the textile surface. Such outputs denote not only the textile adaptability process to stimuli coming from the user's body and the environment, but also express the textile intelligence in ongoing management of uninterrupted information flows that build this triad.

Thus, it is important to emphasize smart co-evolving textile is inherent to the textile itself as an intrinsic feature to its structure and, therefore, far from that intelligence coming from electronic devices coupled to the textile surface or woven by the textile frame.

This development proves to be feasible due to the use of nanotechnology, which, by operating at the molecular level, enables the creation of smart textiles, made of fibers and sensors in nanoscale, capable of structural rearrangements. Such structural rearrangements result from a process of "individual molecular manufacturing", which consists precisely in the construction of textile material, molecule by molecule, and enable the features presented by the co-evolving smart textiles, memorization of the interactive processes among body-textile-environment, and customization of responses to different stimuli coming from the user's body and the surrounding environment. These molecular arrangements are responsible for monitoring biological data provided by the user's body, comfortable and safe, due to the absence of electrodes attached to the skin; and the reuse condition by providing successive washings without losing their functionalities (Fig. 4).

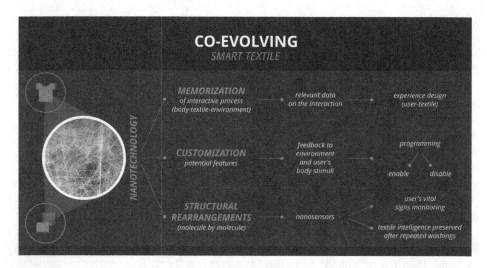

Fig. 4. Co-evolving smart textile features

Memorization is directly related to the potential of collecting relevant data to the experience design of wearable textile product. Thus, it becomes possible to identify positive and negative aspects that affect the body-textile-environment interaction, and can be reinforced or canceled respectively, in a continuous refinement process. While the possibility of customization, by providing the configuration of the textile structure, with respect to the feedback given to the user as a result of the interactive process among body-textile-environment, it enables different design purposes from the same textile matrix. Both properties give the smart textile an active behavior, consisting of dynamic features, and continuously adaptable to the user's body and the environment in which it is inserted. These features enhance smart textile design on a large scale, since it expands the scope of possible applications from a single textile basis.

4   Conclusion

The way the body is covered or uncovered over time and textile quality for each of these moments are reflected in technological and industrial developments.

Despite significant efforts made in the development of smart textiles, there are barriers, such as the difficulty of integration of electronic and textile raw materials; successive washings; and poor durability of smart capabilities, that still need to be overcome to enable its extensive application in clothing products. In addition to this context, there is fact that the vast majority of advances made in this area and available in the market are the result of a process guided by the specific features as a result of a wearable product or project.

Identifying this scenario as a constraint to the production process of smart textiles in large scale and focused on everyday use, this article proposes the concept of co-evolving smart textile. Among its features, the ability to store the interactive processes among body-textile-environment and to offer a customizable textile matrix, both feasible due to the use of nanotechnology, constitute significant contributions to overcoming the problems above-mentioned.

Future developments of this research aim at evaluating the evolution of this concept from the results obtained in practical experiments in the development of a co-evolving smart textile.

References

1. Udale, J.: Fundamentos de design de moda: tecidos e moda. tradução: Edson Furmankiewicz. Porto Alegre: Bookman (2009)
2. Lee, S.: Fashioning the Future: Tomorrow's Wardrobe. Thames & Hudson, London (2005)
3. Baurley, S.: Interactive and experiential design in smart textile products and applications. In: Tao, X. (ed.) Personal and Ubiquitous Computing, vol. 8(3–4), pp. 274–281. (2009)
4. Davis, F., Roseway, A., Carroll, E., Czerwinski, M.: Actuating mood: design of the textile mirror. In: Proceedings of the 7th International Conference on Tangible Embedded and Embodied Interaction, pp. 99–106. ACM, New York (2004)
5. Tao, X.: Smart Technology for Textiles and Clothing – Introduction and Overview. Woodhead Publishing Editions and The Textile Institute, Cambridge (2001)
6. Cho, G., Lee, S., Cho, J.: Review and reappraisal of smart clothing. Int. J. Hum. Comput. Interact. 25(6), 582–617 (2013)
7. Alomainy, A., Hao, Y., Davenport, D.M.: Parametric study of wearable antennas with varying distances from the body and different on-body positions. In: 2007 IET Seminar on Antennas and Propagation for Body-Centric Wireless Communication. http://yadda.icm.edu.pl/yadda/element/bwmeta1.element.ieee-000004231228
8. Linz, T., Gourmelon, L., Langereis, G.: Contactless EMG sensors embroidered onto textile. In: 4th International Workshop on Wearable and Implantable Body Sensor Networks (BSN 2007) (2007)
9. IFMBE Proceedings, vol. 13, pp 29–34. Springer, Heidelberg (2007) http://link.springer.com/chapter/10.1007%2F978-3-540-70994-7_5
10. Carpus, E., Dorogan, A., Visileanu, E., Ignat, M., Onosc, G., Nanu, D., Carpus, I., Buzdugan, M., Radu, M.: Accomplishing of convergent systems for mobile personalized information monitoring. In: Vincenzini, P., Paradiso, R. (eds.) Advances in Science and Technology, vol. 60, pp. 95–100. (2009)
11. Jiménez, L., Rocha, A.M., Aranberri, I., Covas, J.A., Catarino, A.P.: Electrically conductive monofilaments for smart textiles. In: Vincenzini, P., Paradiso, R. (eds.) Advances in Science and Technology, vol. 60, pp. 58–63. (2009)
12. Karaguzel, B., Merritt, C.R., Wilson, J.M., Nagle, H.T., Grant, E., Pourdeyhimi, B.: Flexible, durable printed electrical circuits. J. Text. Inst. 100(1), 1–9 (2009)
13. Hardaker, S.S., Gregory, R.V.: Progress toward dynamic color-responsive "chameleon" fiber systems. MRS Bull. 28, 564–567 (2003)
14. Hertleer, C., Langenhove, L.V., Rogier, H.: Printed textile antennas for off-body communication. In: Vincenzini, P., Paradiso, R. (eds.) Advances in Science and Technology, vol. 60, pp. 64–68. (2009)
15. Vanfleteren, J., Gonzalez, M., Bossuyt, F., Hsu, Y.Y., Vervust, T., Wolf, I., Jablonski, M.: Printed circuit board technology inspired stretchable circuits. MRS Bull. 37(03), 254–260 (2012). Rao, G.R. (ed.)

16. Holland, S.A., Mahan, C.A., Kuhn, M.J., Rowe, N.C.: Utilizing metalized fabrics for liquid and rip detection and localization. In: Brian M.C., Eric S.M. (eds.) Smart Biomedical and Physiological Sensor Technology X, Baltimore (29 April 2013)
17. Morris, D., Coyle, S., Wu, Y., Lau, K.T., Wallace, G., Diamond, D.: Bio-sensing textile based patch integrated optical system for sweat monitoring. Sensors and Actuators B: Chemical **139**(1), 1–258 (2008). In: EUROPT(R)ODE IX Proceedings of the 9th European Conference on Optical Chemical Sensors and Biosensors, Dublin (30 March–2 April) (20 May 2009)
18. Axisa, F., Schmitt, P.M., Gehin, C., Delhomme, G., Mcadams, E., Dittmar, A.: Flexible technologies and smart clothing for citizen medicine, home healthcare, and disease prevention. Inf. Technol. Biomed. **9**(3), 325–336 (2005). IEEE Press
19. Paradiso, R.: Wearable health care system for vital signs monitoring. In: 4th International IEEE EMBS Special Topic Conference on Information Technology Applications in Biomedicine 2003 (2003)
20. Caldani, L., Pacelli, M., Gamboni, P.G., Luprano, J., Paradiso, R.: Real-time monitoring trough wearable systems. In: 5th pHealth Workshop on Wearable Micro and Nano Systems for Personalised Health, Valencia (2008)
21. Suh, M.: E-Textiles for Wearability: Review on Electrical and Mechanical Properties. In Textile World., Atlanta (2010)
22. Montagu, A.: Tocar: o significado humano da pele. Summus, São Paulo (1988)
23. Saltzman, A.: El cuerpo diseñado. Paidos, Buenos Aires (2004)
24. Odum, E.: Fundamentos de ecologia. Fundação Calouste Gulbenkian, Lisboa (1988)
25. Moraes, E.: A construção do conhecimento integrado diante do desafio ambiental: uma estratégia educacional. In: Noal, F.O., et al. (Orgs.). Tendências da educação ambiental brasileira. Santa Cruz do Sul: EDUNISC, pp. 35–54 (1998)
26. Bertalanffy, L.: Robots, hombres y mentes. Ediciones Guadarrama, La psicologia en el mundo modern. Madri (1971)
27. Bertalanffy, L.: Teoria geral dos sistemas. Vozes, Petrópolis (1973)
28. Albuquerque, J.: Singularidade e território na teoria geral dos sistemas. Território das Artes, São Paulo (2006)
29. Smartex – Wealthy. http://trender.ru/archives/898
30. Lifeshirt. http://www.virtualworldlets.net/Shop/ProductsDisplay/ VRInterface.php?ID = 49
31. Textro-Yarns®. http://www.textronicsinc.com/products/textro-yarns

Location, Motion and Activity Recognition

User Location Modeling Based on Heterogeneous Data Sources

Patrick Gottschaemmer[1], Tobias Grosse-Puppendahl[1(✉)], and Arjan Kuijper[1,2]

[1] Fraunhofer IGD, Fraunhoferstr. 5, 64283 Darmstadt, Germany
{patrick.gottschaemmer,tobias.grosse-puppendahl}@igd.fraunhofer.de
[2] Technische Universität Darmstadt, Hochschulstr. 10, 64289 Darmstadt, Germany
arjan.kuijper@gris.tu-darmstadt.de

Abstract. Over the past decade, interest in home automation systems constantly grew. This yields especially for daily life - considering the connection of intelligent everyday devices through the Internet of Things. To allow automatic actions on these devices, user localization systems have become a major input modality for smart home systems. The location of a user (or rather a subject) can be determined by different localization techniques, such as sensitive floor systems, discrete activity sensors like light switches or RSSI-based WLAN/Bluetooth beacons (e.g. smartphones). These heterogeneous data sources provide various means of user location certainty, the ability to identify a user or the ability to recognize multiple subjects in the same location. In order to achieve a higher grade of accuracy, multiple data sources can be combined by location fusioning algorithms. However, to allow the integration of such algorithms on a hardware independent basis, a commmon user location model is needed, which can represent all important aspects of these localization techniques. This paper investigates the concepts of existing user localization systems and develops a new model to represent the location of subjects based on already existing location models. An implementation is provided based on Eclipse SmartHome, an open-source building automation framework.

Keywords: Location modeling · User location · Location fusion

1 Introduction

In recent years, the terms *smarthome* and *home automation* have received a lot of attention when it comes to the question, how we will deal with our daily lives in the future, especially at our homes. However, a Smart Home is not just a bunch of connected devices, like light bulbs controlled by a smartphone app. One of the key focuses lies in the *automation* aspect. Users do not want to control everything in their homes manually, specific things should "just happen when needed". For instance, the lights in a room should be switched on when someone enters it and the heating should be turned off if everyone leaves the house in order to save energy. There are two main issues to enable such automatic features:

© Springer International Publishing Switzerland 2015
N. Streitz and P. Markopoulos (Eds.): DAPI 2015, LNCS 9189, pp. 473–484, 2015.
DOI: 10.1007/978-3-319-20804-6_43

The system needs to know *where* a user is and *when* these actions should happen. The first issue, knowing where a user is, requires two things: On the one hand, the Smart Home system needs to know the user interesting locations, like *Bedroom* or *Couch in living room*. So a location model of the user's home (or even more: of the whole environment) is needed. On the other hand, a (physical) device is needed which can detect where the user is located (at a specific time). The second issue, knowing when something should happen, does not mean *when* in a temporal manner - more in a conditional way, determined by automation rules. Rules like: "When a user enters his house, the air conditioning should be turned on." And in the best case, both aspects (the location model and the automation rules) should be configurable by the user himself. Otherwise, it would neither be *smart* nor an *automation*.

By now, there are dozens of implementations of smarthome systems, most of them are proprietary, like *RWE Smart Home*[1], *Phillips HUE*[2] or *EnOcean*[3]. However, proprietary systems share a common lack of interoperability (in most cases, there are exceptions like *Qivicon*[4]). These systems are not compatible to each other, meaning a device of system A cannot work together with a device of system B. In addition, the market of smarthome products for end users is very fragmented at the present. And it does not look as if there will be any change in this respect in the short term. Since there is no single system, protocol or standard which could possibly fulfill all potential (future) requirements, it is very difficult for end-users to choose the right system fitting their needs.

This is where open-source systems like *Eclipse SmartHome*[5] come into place. The Eclipse SmartHome project aims to offer a flexible framework, which allows the integration of different systems and protocols into a single platform solution, providing an uniform way of user interaction and access to higher level services. Like said before, a user location model is needed, which represents the current (and past) location(s) of a user, in and outside of buildings. These user locations can be determined based on multiple heterogeneous data sources, like capacitive localization systems, discrete activity sensors (e.g. Light Switches), or GPS devices. A user location model needs to offer the ability to collect the data of these heterogeneous sources and combine them to a correct user location, using a fusion based technique. Additionally, user locations could either be continuous (e.g. an absolute geographic coordinate) or discrete (e.g. *Living Room*) and needs to be able to be put in relation to each other. The user should be able to ask questions like: "Is the user in *Living Room* close to the user at a specific GPS coordinate?".

In this paper, a user location model will be investigated and implemented, fulfilling the mentioned requirements. The model will allow the usage of multiple heterogeneous data sources, integrated in the Eclipse SmartHome Framework.

---

[1] http://www.rwe-smarthome.de/web/cms/en/448330/smarthome/.

[2] http://meethue.com/en-us/this-is-hue.

[3] http://www.enocean.com/en/building-automation/.

[4] https://www.qivicon.com/.

[5] https://www.eclipse.org/smarthome/.

2   Related Work

2.1   Location Provider

Localization systems for users (but also items, pets, etc.) use Location Providers which can be grouped and separated by three different criteria:

- Is the location provider assignable to an identified user?
- Is the location provided discrete (like a room) or continuous (e.g. a Cartesian coordinate)?
- Is the location provided absolute or in relation to a fixed point (a parent node in a tree)?

In the following, we present a few exemplary systems to outline these properties in detail.

Sensitive Floor Systems and Intelligent Furniture: Sensitive floor systems, as described in [1,5] and [18], are often based on proximity or pressure sensors, which are placed under the actual floor. In the case of SensFloor [15], a whole underlay mat beneath the actual floor is needed, which transmits the sensor events wireless to a receiver in the room. Sensitive (resp. capacitive) floor systems are often not assignable to an identified user, as they simply recognize a physical weight on their sensors, which could be any person (or item). They provide the locations of recognized objects via Cartesian coordinates, thus are continuous Location Providers. However, these Cartesian coordinates are not absolute, they are related to a fixed point. From a mathematical point of view, Cartesian coordinates are always related to a fixed point - the origin of the Cartesian coordinate system. Interactions with furniture may also be of interest, however, this data will be more or less discrete. For example, a couch or a bed may measure the number of occupants and the type of activity [6].

Global Navigation Satellite System Receivers: The integration of GPS devices (or in general: GNSS devices) in modern smartphones raised user localization in distributed systems to the next level. When a smartphone is connected to the Internet (or local network), the GPS status can be requested by a smarthome environment system and the provided location can be assigned to a user. The GPS receiver in the smartphone not even has to be turned on all the time, as polling can be used based on a fixed period or other events. Nevertheless, GPS in smartphones costs a lot of energy and drains the battery very fast, even at low update rates. Reference [10] introduces an approach which needs 3 orders of magnitude less power to obtain a location fix. This is achieved by only using 5*2 ms chunks of GPS raw data (a conventional GPS fix needs 30 s) which are uploaded to the internet (40 kB). A cloud service derives the location fix by using publicly informations like GNSS satellite ephemeris and an Earth elevations. Unfortunately, the accuracy of these fixes is only ¡35 m. Another drawback of GPS is the fact, that it only works outside of buildings, as you need a line of sight to the satellites. However, [12] introduces a technique which tries to solve this issue by using a steerable directional antenna, the cloud based computing approach of [12] and the acquisition of results from different directions over time. A location fix is achieved in 20 of 31 tested spots with a median error of less than 10m. But the localization errors vary from less than 2 m to more than 70 m. A GPS-based Location Provider is assignable to a specific user in the system, considered smartphones as GPS-based Location Providers are not shared between users. Yet it should be kept in mind that a smartphone is maybe not always at his users, e.g. if it is misplaced. Since GPS-based devices are providing coordinates, they are continuous Location Providers. Even more, the provided continuous locations are absolute, as a geographic coordinate has no relation to a fixed point in a location model. Technically speaking, there is no parent location. Of course, all geographic coordinate have a *real* fixed point, like the center of the earth in WGS84. It could be considered that a geographic location has possible sub-locations, which are geographic locations with a higher accuracy inside this location.

RF-Based Location Estimation Systems: Radio Frequency Location Providers are trying to estimate the location of a user carrying a radio frequency sensor device (like a Bluetooth beacon or a WLAN chip in a smartphone). A radio signal offers (aside from the actual data packets) additional informations which can be useful for a location estimation. With one (or several) base stations, whose locations are known to the sensor, the location of the sensor itself can be computed with various methods. These methods are based for example on time-measurement (TOA/TDOA) [14], signal strength (RSSI) [9] or direction of arrival (DOA) [17]. The RSSI and DOA based methods are especially interesting for WLAN networks, which could be deployed in a smarthome environment. The error distances of DOA and signal strength based approaches for WLAN APs are compared in [7]. RF-based Location Providers can be assigned to an identified user in the system, carrying a radio frequency sensor device. For WLAN and Bluetooth, this could be the user's smartphone. The locations provided by these systems can be continuous, as they provide a coordinate with a given accuracy. However, if the accuracy is too low, a discrete location could be used instead.

Electronic Switches: One of the main benefits of using heterogenous data sources in location models is the possibility to integrate already existent systems and use them for other purposes than they had been primarily defined for. Home automation systems, like KNX[6] or Z-Wave[7], offer the possibility to receive events which happened on connected devices. If a user operates a KNX light switch and the KNX IP router is connected to our location model system, this event can be used to locate user activity and estimate a user location. Of course, locations provided by these events are not assignable to a user in the system, but the

---

[6] http://www.knx.org/knx-en/.
[7] http://www.z-wave.com/.

information can be used for further user location processing. The location of such a light switch event can be either discrete (the room in which the light switch is located) or even continuous (if the coordinates of the pressed light switch are modeled). Both are in relation to a parent location.

Other Technologies: In addition to the systems listed above, there are other possible technologies which could be used as location providers. They are depicted in Table 1.

Table 1. Summary of location providers

Location provider	Assignability	Type	Parent relation
Sensitive floor systems	No	Continuous	Yes
GNSS receivers	Yes	Continuous	No
Rf-based providers	Yes	Continuous or discrete	Yes
Electronic switches	No	Discrete	Yes
Motion sensors	No	Discrete	Yes
Observation cameras	Yes	Continuous	Yes
Gesture recognition devices	No	Continuous	Yes
RFID	Yes	Discrete	Yes
Access terminals	Yes	Discrete	Yes
Power consumption	No	Discrete	Yes
Network pings	Yes	Discrete	Yes

2.2 User Location Models

We can differentiate between three types of location models: Symbolic location models, geometric coordinate-based location models, and hybrid location models, which combine the geometric and symbolic approach. These approaches and their properties will be discussed in the following.

Symbolic Models: Symbolic location models, as described in [13,16], only use discrete locations, classified by names. Symbolic Location models can be implemented based on sets, graphs or a combination of them. Symbolic models can be easily configured by the user, representing the structure of a smart home environment with adjacent and parent symbolic locations. Moreover, *things* can be represented, e.g. a *Couch in the living room*. A pure symbolic location model does not support continuous locations. Providers like GPS devices or sensitive floor systems forfeit their benefits of supplying coordinates and are thus reduced to discrete Location Providers. A symbolic location model could satisfy all requirements of a smarthome environment, if ALL thinkable discrete locations of interest would be modeled by the user. The continuous Location Provider would then need to know, which coordinate maps to which location and thus provide the proper discrete location. Nevertheless, question like "Is user John in a 5 m range of user Jane" could not be answered (at least not without additional informations about the discrete locations, like distance to each other).

Geometric Coordinate Based Models: Geometric coordinate based models, as introduced in [11], only support continuous locations based on coordinates. These locations are great for tasks like automatic gathering POIs for users or learn routes between them for trajectories. However, they miss the ability of representing the structure of a building. Furthermore, when working only with continuous locations, each discrete Location Provider would need to be configured with a coordinate and a radius to provide a continuous location. This would be a very cumbersome work for the user and makes state queries much more complex.

Hybrid Location Models: Hybrid location models try to combine the benefits of symbolic and coordinate based locations, allowing to use the advantages of both types of Location Providers (discrete and continuous). The hybrid model described in [8] is based on a computable location identifier, which integrates both types of location, symbolic hierarchical and coordinates. To compare two locations (and calculate the distance between them via coordinate translation), a sub-location must define its coordinates within its super-location for a coordinate translation. Thus, both information snippets needs to be available to represent a valid user location, preventing the usage of only discrete based Location Providers. This is very cumbersome and complex for simple private smarthome solutions. Furthermore, the authors used PostgreSQL[8] with a user-defined datatype as database. There is no possibility to change the persistence layer. Reference [3] introduces a jsrLocation[9] compliant API implementation with an underlying hybrid location model for location-aware client services. The service API is technology-independent and allows the integration of multiple heterogeneous positioning technologies (Location Providers). In addition, the concept for a position-fusion-based location estimator is presented, which combines measurements coming from different sensors. This fusion-based estimator is also responsible for automatic selecting and switching between the positioning technologies (Bluetooth RSSI, GPS, WLAN) to minimize the use of resources. This is achieved by holding a schema which positioning technology is responsible for each possible area to locate. While the hybrid model and service API in [3] is great for the usage of positioning in single embedded systems (like smartphones) with limited power resources and only one user, it yet lacks in the following points:

---

[8] http://www.postgresql.org/.

[9] https://www.jcp.org/en/jsr/detail?id=179.

3   Proposed Location Model

3.1   Requirements

In order to investigate the requirements on our proposed location model, we asked a number of users to formulate goals which they would like to achieve in their smarthome. User stories are simple sentences in the everyday language of an end user which capture what a user needs or wants to do with a system. We use the following format for user stories as suggested by Mark Cohn in [2]: A subset of our collected user stories is listed in the following:

- As a user, I want to turn down the heating when nobody is home in order to save energy.
- As a user, I want to switch off the lights in rooms I am not using in order to save energy.
- In order to increase my comfort as a user, I want that the light switches on in a room I am heading to.
- As a house owner, I want to know which users are currently in my house.
- As a user, I want that the music follows myself to rooms I am using in order to increase my comfort.
- As a user, I want to trigger a nice light mood when I am lying on the couch.
- As a user, I want to automatically activate the burglar alarm when nobody is home in order to increase home security.
- As a user, I want to activate the outdoor light, when I come home at night to increase my comfort.
- As a family member, I want to be notified if (and which) a family member comes home (e.g. kid from school).
- As a user, I want to be notified if my pet leaves a section (e.g. ground floor) of my house to prevent it from escaping.

As mentioned in our related work, there are a lot of different technologies for user localization (resp. user presence detection). Based on these technologies and the user stories above, we can derive the following functional requirements to a user location model in a smarthome system:

1. Symbolic and geometric locations should be modeled
2. Multiple heterogenous data sources (Location Providers) should be used
3. Assignable and non-assignable Location Providers (and thus, locations) should be considered
4. The ability to include location fusioning algorithms, which can be easily interchangeable
5. The location fusioning algorithms should be included positioning technology independent
6. Event based localization updates ("Push a switch")
7. Eventuality of a domain specific language (DSL) for rule based queries of users ("When user *John* enters location *LivingRoom*, then...").

3.2 Concept

The Eclipse SmartHome framework offers an open-source solution of these concepts and services for smarthome systems. It provides a widely extensible API for new components purely based on the OSGi specifications[10]. This means that Eclipse SmartHome can be used on any device which is capable of running an OSGi runtime (like Apache Karaf[11]). A Raspberry Pi[12] or BeagleBone[13] is all that is needed as special hardware for running Eclipse SmartHome.

The underlying structure of the proposed hybrid location model is an undirected graph within a composite pattern (see [4], P. 163–173), allowing the definition of symbolic neighbor locations within and between the composites, represented as edges between the nodes. To be more specific, the graph is a tree as locations can have sub locations (*child nodes*). In this implementation, symbolic and coordinate based locations are represented through the classes *DiscreteLocation* resp. *ContinuousLocation*. The model and API class diagram is notated in Fig. 1.

In order to understand how the Eclipse SmartHome Framework can be extended with new functionality, an overview of the Thing and Item concept in Eclipse SmartHome will be given. There are two types of important entities in Eclipse SmartHome: *Things & Items*. While Things represent real physical devices devices or services, Items are the virtual or technical representation and configuration of them in the system. For example, the smartphone of a user would be a "Location Provider Thing", while it's ip address and presentation in a user interface are Items. Things can be bound to Items by *Channels* in order to receive updates of them and handle these. The Eclipse SmartHome Framework can be extended with two mechanisms: The subclassing of Items and the implementation of ThingHandlers. ThingHandlers are added to the system by providing OSGi services (see [19]). Things cannot be subclassed. However, their channels (and thus, Items) have *States* of certain types (like String, DateTime, etc.). These can be subclassed to represent new types of states. All things are registered in the *ThingRegistry*, which can be used to keep track of removed or new added things during runtime.

The important API interfaces for operations and updates on the location graph are `LocationProvider`, `LocationListener` and `LocationMerger`. The class `Location` and its subclasses will be used for both: The static location model (the structure of the user's environment) and updates (called events) on this location model provided by `LocationProviders`.

A `LocationProvider` is responsible for the localization of objects in the system. Clients can call `provideLocations(...)` in order to receive location models outside of location update events. If a client wants to be informed about every location update the provider detects, he can register an instance of the interface `LocationListener` through calling the method `register(...)`.

---

[10] http://www.osgi.org/Specifications/HomePage.
[11] http://karaf.apache.org/.
[12] http://www.raspberrypi.org/.
[13] http://beagleboard.org/.

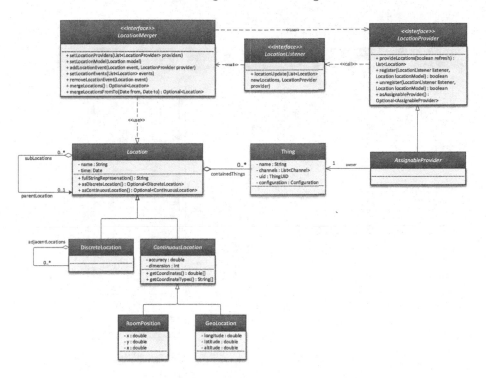

Fig. 1. UML class diagram for the Location Model and API

For this, he needs to pass a valid location model for which he wants to receive updates. If a `LocationProvider` is of subtype `AssignableProvider`, the method `asAssignableProvider()` will return itself as the subclassed instance of `AssignableProvider`, using the Java type `Optional<?>`[14]. If the provider is not an instance of `AssignableProvider`, `Optional.empty()` will be returned.

A LocationMerger is responsible for the fusion of a series of location events. Usually, it is called by a `LocationListener` which wants to merge its updated location events through calling the method `mergeLocations()`. In the beginning, the `LocationMerger` needs to be passed in the location model and all `LocationProviders` with `setLocationModel(...)` and `setLocationProviders(...)`. Before calling `mergeLocations()`, the interested client has to add every location event to the `LocationMerger` with `addLocationEvent(...)`. In addition, he can call `mergeLocationsFromTo(...)` in order to only merge locations in a specific time interval. `LocationMergers` are consumed and used through OSGi services.

The sequence diagram in Fig. 2 illustrates a possible sequence of events in the system. A user first enter his WLAN area with his assigned smartphone and presses the switch for the kitchen light afterwards. To reduce the complexity of the diagram, not all system procedure calls are explicitly notated, these events

---

[14] http://docs.oracle.com/javase/8/docs/api/java/util/Optional.html.

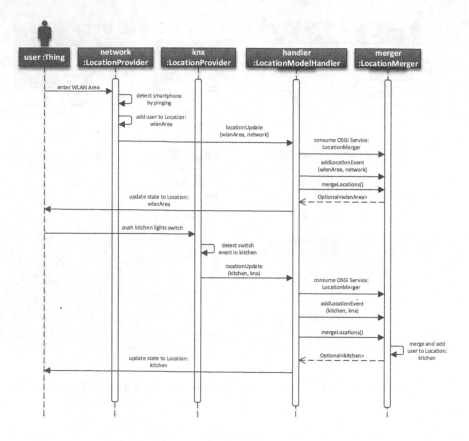

Fig. 2. Sequence diagram of event processing

are abstracted in red color. The merge algorithm in this case assumes that only a single user environment is specified. Thus it can compute that the user which entered his WLAN area is the same which pressed the switch for the kitchen light.

4   Conclusion and Outlook

In this paper, the current concepts of user localization models in smarthome environments were investigated. Related work on (hybrid) location models was introduced and their correspondence to heterogeneous data sources in home automation system were stated. Based on related work and our design requirements, we introduced a concept and implementation of a suitable location model. The location model uses both symbolic and geometric coordinates. This allows to abstract from the concrete location providers after a location event was detected and published in the system. The new location model was provided with an extensible API for new Location Providers, listeners and location fusioning algorithms. It is purely implemented on an OSGi basis and within the Eclipse SmartHome framework. This allows an easy integration of new hardware bindings.

It could be furthermore observed that the new location model is capable of dealing with multiple heterogeneous data sources and allows the usage of technology independent location fusioning algorithms. This enables the computation of better locations for users, dependent on the environment conditions. However, the introduced location fusioning algorithm is rather simple and not widely usable. For future work, there are two possible problem areas: First, location fusioning algorithms which work technology (in)dependent needs to be further investigated. Location fusioning algorithms will always be a main issue when it comes to locate subjects based on heterogeneous data sources. Additionally, it should be researched which and how many technology dependent information snippets a location fusioning algorithm could need from the system. Currently, there is no possibility to retrieve such information from the Location Providers through their interface for the location fusioning algorithm in the presented API.

References

1. Braun, A., Heggen, H., Wichert, R.: CapFloor – a flexible capacitive indoor localization system. In: Chessa, S., Knauth, S. (eds.) EvAAL 2011. CCIS, vol. 309, pp. 26 35. Springer, Heidelberg (2012). http://dx.doi.org/10.1007/978-3-642-33533-4_3
2. Cohn, M.: User Stories Applied: For Agile Software Development. Addison Wesley Longman Publishing Co., Inc, Redwood City, CA (2004)
3. Ficco, M., Russo, S.: A hybrid positioning system for technology-independent location-aware computing. Softw. Pract. Exper **39**(13), 1095–1125 (2009). http://dx.doi.org/10.1002/spe.v39:13
4. Gamma, E., Helm, R., Johnson, R., Vlissides, J.: Design Patterns: Elements of Reusable Object-oriented Software. Addison-Wesley Longman Publishing Co., Inc, Boston, MA (1995)
5. Grosse-Puppendahl, T., Berghoefer, Y., Braun, A., Wimmer, R., Kuijper, A.: Opencapsense: a rapid prototyping toolkit for pervasive interaction using capacitive sensing. In: PerCom 2013, pp. 152–159 (2013)
6. Große-Puppendahl, T.A., Marinc, A., Braun, A.: Classification of user postures with capacitive proximity sensors in AAL-Environments. In: Keyson, D.V., Maher, M.L., Streitz, N., Cheok, A., Augusto, J.C., Wichert, R., Englebienne, G., Aghajan, H., Kröse, B.J.A. (eds.) AmI 2011. LNCS, vol. 7040, pp. 314–323. Springer, Heidelberg (2011)
7. Hafiizh, A., Obote, S., Kagoshima, K.: Doa-rssi multiple subcarrier indoor location estimation in mimo-ofdm wlan aps structure
8. Jiang, C., Steenkiste, P.: A hybrid location model with a computable location identifier for ubiquitous computing. In: Borriello, G., Holmquist, L.E. (eds.) UbiComp 2002. LNCS, vol. 2498, p. 246. Springer, Heidelberg (2002). http://dl.acm.org/citation.cfm?id=647988.741480
9. Lim, H., Kung, L.C., Hou, J.C., Luo, H.: Zero-configuration indoor localization over ieee 802.11 wireless infrastructure. Wirel. Netw. **16**(2), 405–420 (2010). http://dx.doi.org/10.1007/s11276-008-0140-3

10. Liu, J., Priyantha, B., Hart, T., Ramos, H.S., Loureiro, A.A.F., Wang, Q.: Energy efficient gps sensing with cloud offloading. In: Proceedings of the 10th ACM Conference on Embedded Network Sensor Systems, SenSys 2012, pp. 85–98. ACM, New York, NY, USA (2012). http://doi.acm.org/10.1145/2426656.2426666
11. Marmasse, N.: A user-centered location model. Pers. Ubiquit. Comput. **6**(5–6), 318–321 (2002). http://dx.doi.org/10.1007/s007790200035
12. Nirjon, S., Liu, J., DeJean, G., Priyantha, B., Jin, Y., Hart, T.: Coin-gps: indoor localization from direct gps receiving. In: Proceedings of the 12th Annual International Conference on Mobile Systems, Applications, and Services, MobiSys 2014, pp. 301–314. ACM, New York, NY, USA (2014). http://doi.acm.org/10.1145/2594368.2594378
13. Satoh, I.: Location-aware communications in smart environments. Information Systems Frontiers **11**(5), 501–512 (2009). http://dx.doi.org/10.1007/s10796-008-9120-5
14. Shin, D.H., Sung, T.K.: Comparisons of error characteristics between toa and tdoa positioning. IEEE Trans. Aerosp. Electron. Syst. **38**(1), 307–311 (2002). http://dx.doi.org/10.1109/7.993253
15. Sousa, M., Techmer, A., Steinhage, A., Lauterbach, C., Lukowicz, P.: Human tracking and identification using a sensitive floor and wearable accelerometers. In: PerCom 2013, vol. 18, p. 22 (2013)
16. Stirbu, V., Selonen, P., Palin, A.: The location graph: towards a symbolic location architecture for the web. In: Proceedings of the 3rd International Workshop on Location and the Web, LocWeb 2010, pp. 10:1–10:8. ACM, New York, NY, USA (2010). http://doi.acm.org/10.1145/1899662.1899672
17. Terada, J., Takahashi, H., Sato, Y., Mutoh, S.: A novel location-estimation method using direction-of-arrival estimation. In: 2005 IEEE 62nd Vehicular Technology Conference, VTC-2005-Fall, vol. 1, pp. 424–428, September 2005
18. Valtonen, M., Maentausta, J., Vanhala, J.: Tiletrack: Capacitive human tracking using floor tiles. In: Proceedings of the 2009 IEEE International Conference on Pervasive Computing and Communications, PERCOM 2009, pp. 1–10. IEEE Computer Society, Washington, DC, USA (2009). http://dx.doi.org/10.1109/PERCOM.2009.4912749
19. Vogel, L.: Osgi services - tutorial (2013). http://www.vogella.com/tutorials/OSGiServices/article.html

Monitoring Wildlife in Contaminated Environments via the Carrier Pigeon-Like Sensing System

Hiroki Kobayashi$^{(\boxtimes)}$, Hiromi Kudo, and Kaoru Sezaki

Center of Spatial Information Science, The University of Tokyo,
Kashiwa, Chiba 277-8568, Japan
{kobayashi,kudo3,sezaki}@csis.u-tokyo.ac.jp

Abstract. This paper presents a Carrier Pigeon-like Sensing System (CPSS), a future–present archetype that will enable the observation of inaccessible and contaminated environments, such as the area surrounding the Fukushima Daiichi nuclear power plant. Our system employs wildlife-borne sensing devices with Animal- Touch'n Go (ATG) and animal-to-animal Internet sharing capabilities; such devices expand the size of monitoring areas where electricity and information infrastructures are limited or nonexistent. Through our approach, monitoring information can be collected from remote areas safely and cost-effectively. Based on the human–computer–biosphere interaction (HCBI) concept, CPSS is presented in this paper, with an overview of the concept, methods employed, and current work in progress. We provide a clear scope for CPSS in the context of natural ecosystems. Furthermore, we implement a documentation framework that describes how complex interactions between living organisms within such natural ecosystems are connected with HCI.

1 Introduction

The Chernobyl nuclear disaster report of the International Atomic Energy Agency [1] states that it is academically and socially important to conduct ecological studies regarding the levels and effects of radiation exposure on the wild animal populations over several generations. Immediately following the Fukushima Daiichi nuclear power plant disaster, remnants of which are shown in Fig. 1, Ishida (a research collaborator at the University of Tokyo) started conducting regular ecological studies of wild animals in the northern Abukuma Mountains near the Fukushima Daiichi nuclear power plant, where high levels of radiation were detected. Ishida aims to place automatic recording devices at over 500 locations, and has been collecting and analyzing vocalizations of target wild animals. The long-term and wide-range monitoring is required to understand the effects of the nuclear accident because he has not yet little evidence of the direct effects of radioactivity on wildlife at Fukushima [2].

Ecological studies of wild animals involve recording and analyzing spatial information associated with animal species (e.g., vocalizations, locations, food sources, and environmental conditions, such as weather information) using ubiquitous and wearable technologies. In studying wild animals in environments close to urban areas,

© Springer International Publishing Switzerland 2015
N. Streitz and P. Markopoulos (Eds.): DAPI 2015, LNCS 9189, pp. 485–495, 2015.
DOI: 10.1007/978-3-319-20804-6_44

a ubiquitous system can provide the means for achieving an effective study [3]. In studying wild animals in their habitats, however, electric power sources and information network infrastructures are often limited, because the provision of such resources is expensive in the wild (e.g., near the ground surface of the forest) and tend to be in areas with limited number of users. As an example, mobile phones are out of range in approximately 70% of Japan; note that this is not a population coverage ratio [4].

Fig. 1. Wildlife near the Fukushima Daiichi nuclear power plant [5]

In this paper, we present our vision of CPSS (based on human–computer–biosphere interaction (HCBI), illustrated in Fig. 2) by offering a conceptual overview, currently developed interfaces, related work, and a discussion. Not only do we propose a solution to the sustainability problem, we also implement a documentation framework describing how complex interactions of living organisms within such natural ecosystems can be connected via human–computer interaction (HCI). Using a multidisciplinary approach, we propose a view of CPSS-based design and interfaces to support our future society.

2   Background

Human communities employ a wide variety of technologies that interact with nature. One of the most ancient forms of information communication technology involves the use of carrier pigeons: homing pigeons that can carry messages and find their way home over extremely long distances. In the United States, the 1800 km pigeon race, wherein specially trained racing pigeons are released and return to their houses over carefully measured distances, is the longest pigeon race in the world [6]. In the field of computer network engineering, on April 1, 1990, Waitzman announced a proposal to carry Internet Protocol (IP) traffic by birds such as homing pigeons (RFC 1149) [7]. Even though this was an April Fool's joke, several experiments proved that the method was effective [8, 9].

April Fool's jokes aside, wild animals adapt to their habitat and environment. They maintain their biological diversity by internetworking with a wide variety of other animals on the basis of a cloud-like food chain. Their actions comprise individual actions (ranging from a few kilometers to a few tens of kilometers) and group actions (ranging from a few tens of kilometers to a few hundred kilometers). Through individual actions, animals sense spatial information necessary for survival in their own territory, whereas through group actions, they periodically share obtained information, optimizing for the entire group, and therefore achieving evolution and the prosperity of the species.

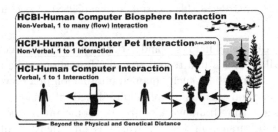

Fig. 2. Human–computer–biosphere interaction (HCBI) concept [10], an extension of human–computer interaction (HCI) [11] and human–computer–pet interaction (HCPI) concepts [3].

In this study, we integrate these wild animal actions with an advanced HCI technology to solve the problem with existing systems described in backgounrd section. Specifically, in this study, we aim to achieve our goal by developing a system in which wild animals carry a wearable sensor that records spatial information in their territory through individual actions and then shares the information obtained through group actions, all with reduced power requirements, eventually uploading the shared information to the Internet.

Our prototype CPSS concept, illustrated in Fig. 3, expands our research results to date and obtains spatial information using wild animals with the specific goal of supporting ecological studies. We have already conducted preliminary research and obtained results in regards to recording sensor data and sharing information using wild animals as well as guiding wild animals [10, 12–14].

As described above, researchers have started to address and study wearable systems for wild animals. In the United States, the "Crittercam" project [15] is proceeding under the leadership of multiple academic institutions. In Japan, Takahashi's research group at Fukushima University has played a key role in measuring radiation exposure by mounting collar-shaped sensor equipment on wild Japanese macaques [16]; however, in both these projects, it has been necessary to recapture monitored subjects, which limits the geographical area of the study. To our knowledge, our proposed system is the first innovative sensing framework in the world. CPSS will produce results for wearable systems for animals that goes significantly beyond existing research.

3 CPSS Conceptual Overview

Fig. 3. Carrier Pigeon-like Sensing System (CPSS) concept image

As noted above and illustrated in Figs. 3 and 4, our proposed system comprises wearable sensors worn by wild animals that record spatial information in the animals' territory through individual actions, share such obtained information in a power-saving manner through group actions, and eventually upload the shared information to the Internet. In short, our system is a sensing framework optimized for the environment that is based on the HCBI concept illustrated in Fig. 2, which is an extension of both HCI [11] and human–computer–pet interaction (HCPI) [3]. In the field of computer-supported cooperative work (CSCW), such computer-interaction paradigms support specific activities. For example, we exchange our ideas, thoughts, theories, and messages by encoding them into transferable words, communicating these words through space via computer systems, and then decoding them; however, in our daily lives, we implicitly exchange and share a great deal of additional nonverbal information, such as the presence and mood of others, to maintain our social relationships [17].

Considering implicit (background) information opens up new possibilities for interactions through nonlinguistic wearable forms and nonverbal remote communications between different species. Wearable computing devices enable us to extend our spatial interactions and develop human-to-human communication beyond physical distance [18].

HCPI as illustrated in Fig. 2, is a novel physical interaction paradigm that proposes a symbiosis between humans and pets via computers and the Internet as a new form of media. As an example, Botanicalls was developed to provide a new interaction method between plants and people to develop better and longer-lasting relationships that go beyond physical and genetic distances [19]. From this paradigm, computer systems become a medium through which a telepresence can be expressed among different species in the biosphere through nonlinguistic means that are perceived and understood by individuals, thus violating the rules of linguistic science.

Regardless of how advanced the aforementioned technologies are, these are spatial interactions. We expect some feedback from others before we issue a command to end an interaction; however, there are many temporal interactions in our daily lives. The sounds of singing birds, buzzing insects, swaying leaves, and trickling water implicitly imprint the presence of space in our minds. When we are not in a forest, recalling the memory of a forest takes us back to the same place. The crucial factor here is not the means of conveyance (i.e., words or language) but the intangible "something" that hovers around us, an atmosphere we cannot exactly identify but lasts beyond generations [20]. This interaction follows the theory of natural selection proposed by Charles Darwin. The theory of evolution, which has become a fundamental cornerstone science, was introduced to readers in Darwin's book on the origin of species that he wrote after visiting the Galápagos Islands [21].

We propose that, much like elements of natural selection, the concept of HCBI can be extended to spatial interactions from countable objects, such as animals and plants in space, to their temporal environment, which is an uncountable, complex, nonlinguistic, "something" beyond generations.

In the HCBI framework, the sounds of a forest or other such natural environments are all information cues that help us understand natural selection. Thus, through HCBI, we can experience the wonderment of the global ecological system with all living beings and their relationships, including their interactions with the elements of the biosphere. With HCBI, we begin to interact with inaccessible ecological natural systems beyond space and time.

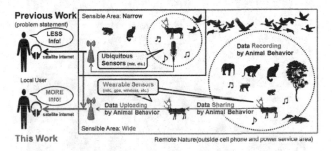

Fig. 4. Comparing previous methods with our proposed prototype

4 Research Prototypes

4.1 Ubiquitous Real-Time Systems

As introduced above, in ecological studies, it is desirable to develop a technology that most effectively supports the study with minimal resources. More specifically, we aim to establish a long-term continuously operating ubiquitous system that delivers, in real time, environmental information, such as sound. Researchers worldwide are conducting ecological studies by recording and analyzing the spatial information of wild animal vocalizations [22]. Furthermore, ecological studies of the environment close to urban areas are being conducted using cells phones [3]; however, it is difficult to confirm the behavior of wild animals using cell phones.

To record vocalizations of wild animals whose behaviors are difficult to predict, it is necessary to continuously operate a monitoring system. As it is difficult to conduct system maintenance due to severe environmental conditions of wild animal habitats (e.g., out of infrastructure service areas, and high-temperature and high-humidity environments), system redundancy becomes crucial. In a previous study, we have researched and developed a proprietary system that delivers and records environmental sounds in real-time [10]. This system has been almost continuously operational on Iriomote Island in Okinawa since 1996, using equipment such as that shown in Fig. 5. To date, the basic research on Iriomote Island has been expanded to include 18 domestic and international sites, including Los Angeles and the San Francisco Bay area in the United States, Sanshiro Pond at the Hongo Campus of the University of Tokyo in Japan, Kyoto Shokokuji Mizuharu in Suikinkutsu, Mumbai City in India, Antarctica Syowa Station (under construction), Morotsuka Village in Miyazaki, and Fukushima University in Japan. We have worked with project collaborators and have introduced our system to the University of Tokyo Chichibu Forest; Otsuchi in Iwate; Shinshu University; the University of Tokyo Fuji Forest; the University of Tokyo Hokkaido Forest (under construction); the University of Tokyo International Coastal Research Center; and on an uninhabited island in Iwate (also under construction). We have also been conducting research on ubiquitous interfaces for ecology studies of wild animals since April 1997. Illustrated in Fig. 5.

Fig. 5. Ubiquitous systems for real-time delivery of environmental sounds, and its long-term and continuous operation.

4.2   Uploading Individual Actions Data from Wild Animals

Fig. 6. A system that allows data obtained through individual actions to be uploaded from wild animals [13, 23].

As described above, the applicability of ubiquitous systems is limited in ecological studies. In computer science, individuals and wild animals carrying wearable sensors to monitor behaviors and surrounding environments have been reported in early sensor network research [24]; however, it is not feasible to collect data from sensors on wild animals on a regular basis because of their unpredictability. To collect sensor data, wild animals need to come in contact with a sink node (in a ubiquitous system) connected to an external network such as the Internet; however, the chance of this occurring spontaneously is not high. Thus, it becomes important to guide wild animals. We proposed a method to guide wild animals based on Uexküll's Umwelt theory [25] and verified its effectiveness with the NTT Docomo CSR research funding in 2007 [13]. In our study, Iriomote cats were equipped with wearable sensors and collected spatial information in their territory for two years. They were then remotely controlled and guided to a predetermined location to upload the data, as shown in the left-hand side image of Fig. 6. We verified the long-term operation of the system and repeated the experiments using wild deer in 2013, as shown in the right-hand side image of Fig. 6. Through these activities, we have established the ability to create a system in which wild animals carry wearable sensors, record spatial information in their territory through their individual actions, and upload this shared information to the Internet (Animal- Touch'n Go).

4.3   Sharing Group Actions Data with Limited Power Resources

From the above, the use of wearable sensors to monitor behaviors and surrounding environments is useful for collecting individual actions data; however, it is not feasible to recharge such devices on a regular basis when they are used for wild animals. As noted above, to collect sensor data, wild animals need to encounter a sink node connected to an external network such as the Internet. Since the chances of this occurring are not high, it becomes important to reduce the power consumption and increase the lifetime of the sensor nodes. For a wireless sensor node, the power consumed by an acceleration sensor during operation is 100 times greater than that consumed by a sensor during communication [26].

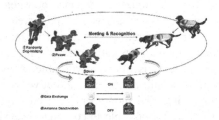

Fig. 7. A system wherein wild animals record data through individual actions and share such data, with limited power requirements, through group actions [14].

We know from ethology that when land mammals with natural habitats near the ground surface of a forest encounter other land mammals, they exhibit behaviors that are different from those that they exhibit when they are alone [27]. When land mammals encounter other land mammals, it is likely that they are within communication range of the sensor node they carry. Thus, it is possible to significantly reduce power consumption and increase the lifetime of sensor nodes by activating communication among sensor nodes only upon detecting land mammals encountering other land mammals. Until this condition occurs, the sensor could and should be in the sleep mode.

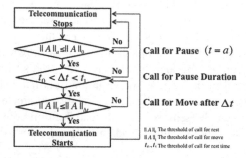

Fig. 8. Algorithm for data sharing between animals [14]

Based on our research conducted on Iriomote cats, we designed an algorithm (shown in Fig. 8), verified its effectiveness using multiple mammals (four dogs), and implemented a system that can detect encounters among multiple mammals with 70% accuracy, illustrated in Fig. 7 [14]. In that study, we successfully established a system in which wild animals were equipped with wearable sensors that recorded spatial information in the animals' territory through individual actions and shared the acquired information, with reduced power requirements, through group actions.

5   Discussion

As humans expand their sphere of influence, the clash between the benefits to human society and the conservation of ecosystems has become increasingly serious. We have seen spikes in the number of endangered species and crop damage caused by harmful wildlife species [13]. When humans physically interact with surrounding ecosystems, the destruction of such ecosystems is often unavoidable. Although physically separating humans and ecosystems would be the most effective means to conserving such ecosystems, natural heritage sites and monuments are closely tied to tourism, agriculture, and forestry. Thus, it is not possible to completely separate these entities.

In our previous study, we proposed HCBI [10], a concept wherein humans and ecosystems interact via computers to avoid major conflicts between one another. More specifically, we integrated computers and art, proposing an interaction model for cooperation between real spaces at remote locations and ordinary everyday spaces; this is accomplished through information spaces that consider various physical, economic, and ethical constraints. With active support from users, we plan to provide our research results to society.

The Japanese government and research institutions have funded research in technological support of ecological studies of wild animals involving wearable monitoring systems. Funding for research related to the conservation of ecosystems has primarily been from the Ministry of the Environment and science-oriented institutions. In addition, the Ministry of Agriculture, Forestry and Fisheries, and other agriculture-oriented institutions have funded research on countermeasures against harmful wildlife species. There is no single research framework at any educational or research institutions in Japan that fosters research with an information science focus in such areas because computer science research generally requires information and power supply infrastructures.

At the time of writing, it has been 28 years since the Chernobyl nuclear disaster. In that time, wildlife has returned and appears to be thriving in the surrounding forests [28]. Although a staggering 20-million wild animals were killed in the immediate aftermath of the disaster [29], it is believed that a very small number of wild animals survived and adapted to the changed environment. These animals evolved and prospered in high-radiation areas; however, it took a long time to establish research organizations to conduct ecological studies, and the evolutionary process of the surviving animals remains unknown.

Insights into the survival and evolution of radiation-exposed wild animals may result in insights into agriculture and forestry, animal husbandry, and medical care; however, long-term ecological studies of wild animals and their radiation exposure levels are required [1]. Regarding the recovery efforts after the Fukushima nuclear power plant disaster, the importance of ecological studies being conducted from the very beginning of a disaster has been pointed out [30]. As described above, Ishida, who has conducted ecological studies since immediately after the disaster, has stated that it would be extremely difficult to continue conducting ecological studies on an ongoing basis [2]; however, HCI can address these issues, and we claim with confidence that our proposed project will successfully address these issues.

6   Conclusion

Investigations into natural environments consider living creatures and their surrounding environments; such investigations are important for reviewing the value of biological diversity from various perspectives. It is currently possible to obtain ecological information regarding wild animals in remote areas using various ubiquitous systems; however, information and electrical power supply infrastructures are essential to the success of these systems, and thus, they are limited to areas serviced by such infrastructure.

To address this limitation, researchers have started applying wearable sensors to wild animals. To collect the data recorded by these wearable sensors, it is usually necessary to recapture the monitored subjects; thus, wearable sensors are limited. To solve such problems with existing systems, we proposed the Carrier Pigeon-like Sensing System (CPSS), a system in which wild animals carry a wearable sensor that records spatial information in their territory through individual actions, shares the information obtained through group actions (with reduced power requirements), and eventually uploads the shared information to the Internet.

More specifically, in this paper, we (a) integrated results established through preliminary research into a system for specific wild animals, (b) evaluated the effectiveness of our implemented system through ecological studies conducted by system users, and (c) constructed a framework to support ecological studies around the Fukushima Daiichi nuclear power plant through collaboration with international institutions within the domain of HCI.

Acknowledgments. This study was supported by JSPS KAKENHI Grant 26700015, MIC SCOPE Grant 142103015, the Okawa Foundation for Information and Telecommunications Research Grant, the Telecommunications Advancement Foundation Research Grant, Tepco Memorial Foundation Support for International Technological Interaction, the Moritani Scholarship Foundation Research Grant, Hatakeyma Culture Foundation Research Grant, the Mitsubishi Foundation Science and Technology Research Grant, and the Ogasawara Foundation for the Promotion of Science & Engineering Research Grant.

References

1. Chernobyl Forum Expert Group 'Environment'. and International Atomic Energy Agency., Environmental consequences of the Chernobyl accident and their remediation : twenty years of experience; report of the Chernobyl Forum Expert Group 'Environment'. Radiological assessment reports series, p. 166. International Atomic Energy Agency, Vienna (2006)
2. Ishida, K.: Contamination of wild animals: effects on wildlife in high radioactivity areas of the agricultural and forest landscape. In: Nakanishi, T.M., Tanoi, K. (eds.) Agricultural Implications of the Fukushima Nuclear Accident, pp. 119–129. Springer, Japan (2013)
3. Lee, P., et al.: A mobile pet wearable computer and mixed reality system for human poultry interaction through the internet. Pers. Ubiquit. Comput. **10**(5), 301–317 (2006)
4. Statistics Bureau M.o.I.A.a.C., Japan. Islands, length of coastline and area of national land. Chapter 1 Land and Climate, Japan Statistical Yearbook (2014)
5. mosamosa1010. fukushima 1F LIVE 20110602c. [movie] 1 Jun 2011–4 Sep 2014. https://www.youtube.com/watch?v=cIzanzeUejw]
6. Walcott, C.: Pigeon homing: observations, experiments and confusions. J. Exp. Biol. **199**(1), 21–27 (1996)
7. Waitzman, D.: Standard for the transmission of IP datagrams on avian carriers, RFC Editor (1990)
8. Govender, P.: Pigeon transfers data faster than South Africa's Telkom (2009). http://www.reuters.com/article/2009/09/09/us-safrica-pigeon-idUSTRE5885PM20090909. Accessed 2014
9. Ozimek, J.F. BT feathers ruffled over pigeon-based file transfer caper (2010). http://www.theregister.co.uk/2010/09/17/bt_bird/. Accessed 2014
10. Kobayashi, H., Ueoka, R., Hirose, M.: Human computer biosphere interaction: towards a sustainable society. In: CHI 2009 Extended Abstracts on Human Factors in Computing Systems, pp. 2509–2518. ACM, Boston, MA, USA (2009)
11. Hewett, T.T., Baecker, R.,Card, S., Carey,T., Gasen, J.,Mantei, M.,Perlman, G.,Strong, G., Verplank, W.: Definition of Human Computer Interaction (1992). http://old.sigchi.org/cdg/cdg2.html

12. Kobayashi, H., et al.: Wild Theremin: electronic music instrument for remote wildlife observation. Trans. Hum. Interface Soc. **12**(1), 15–22 (2010)

13. Kobayashi, H.: Basic Research in Human-Computer-Biosphere Interaction. In: Department of Advanced Interdisciplinary Studies, Division of Engineering. The University of Tokyo, Tokyo, Japan (2010)

14. Nakagawa, K., Kobayashi, H., Sezaki, K.: Carrier pigeon-like sensing system: animal-computer interface design for opportunistic data exchange interaction for a wildlife monitoring application. In: Proceedings of the 5th Augmented Human International Conference, pp. 1–2. ACM, Kobe, Japan (2014)

15. Gad, S.D.: Crittercam - a new tool in animal-borne imaging. Curr. Sci. **95**(2), 153–154 (2008)

16. Satherley, J.: Japanese to fit 1,000 monkeys with Geiger counters to test radiation levels in Fukushima (2011)

17. Itoh, Y., Miyajima, A., Watanabe, T.: 'TSUNAGARI' communication: fostering a feeling of connection between family members. In: CHI 2002 Extended Abstracts on Human Factors in Computing Systems, pp. 810–811. ACM, Minneapolis, Minnesota, USA. (2002)

18. Stead, L., et al.: The emotional wardrobe. Pers. Ubiquit. Comput. **8**(3–4), 282–290 (2004)

19. Bray, R., et al.: Botanicalls. (2009). http://www.botanicalls.com/

20. Suzuki, D.T.: Zen and Japanese culture. Rev. and enl. Bollingen series, 2nd edn. Pantheon Books, New York (1959). xxiii, p. 478

21. Darwin, C.: On the Origin of Species by Means of Natural Selection, or The Preservation of Favoured Races in the Struggle for Life, p. 432. D Appleton and company, New York (1860)

22. Krause, B.L.: Bioacoustics: habitat ambience in ecological balance. Whole Earth Rev. **57**, 14–18 (1987)

23. Muramatsu, K., et al.: The realization of new virtual forestexperience environment through PDA. In: MobileHCI 2014 Extended Abstracts on Human-Computer Interaction with Mobile Devices and Services. ACM (2014)

24. Juang, P., et al.: Energy-efficient computing for wildlife tracking: design tradeoffs and early experiences with ZebraNet. In: Proceedings of the 10th International Conference on Architectural Support for Programming Languages and Operating Systems, pp. 96–107. ACM, San Jose, California (2002)

25. Vonuexkull, T.: Uexkull, Jakob, Von a 'stroll through the worlds of animals and men' + preface and introduction. Semiotica **89**(4), 277 (1992)

26. Shimizu, K., Iwai, M., Sezaki, K.: Social link analysis using wireless beaconing and accelerometer. In: 2013 27th International Conference on Advanced Information Networking and Applications Workshops (WAINA) (2013)

27. Smith, R.H.: Ecology - individuals, populations and communities - Begon, M, Harper, Jl, Townsend, Cr. Nature **319**(6056), 809–809 (1986)

28. Mycio, M.: Wormwood Forest: A Natural History of Chernobyl. The National Academies Press, Washington, D.C. (2005)

29. Mycio, M.: Wormwood forest : a natural history of Chernobyl. Joseph Henry Press, Washington, D.C. (2005). xii, p. 259, p. 4 of plates

30. group, n.p.: Japan earthquake and nuclear crisis. http://www.nature.com/news/specials/japanquake/index.html

Crowd Monitoring

Critical Situations Prevention Using Smartphones and Group Detection

Joseph El Mallah, Francesco Carrino$^{(\boxtimes)}$, Omar Abou Khaled,
and Elena Mugellini

University of Applied Sciences and Arts Western Switzerland,
Delémont, Switzerland
{francesco.carrino,omar.abouKhaled,elena.mugellini}@hes-so.ch
joseph.elmallah@master.hes-so.ch

Abstract. Festivals and big scale events are becoming more and more popular, they can attract thousands of spectators. Ensuring the safety of the crowd has become a top priority to many organisers after the multitude of dramatic accidents that resulted in losses in human lives. Monitoring the crowd via smartphones is a relatively new technique that emerged recently with the capabilities of mobile phones to transmit their GPS location data. We present a novel approach, based on the local crowd pressure, combined with the detection of groups in a crowd, to detect critical situations and propose evacuation plans that does not separate groups of people that are together. Groups were detected using DBSCAN clustering algorithm with 80 % accuracy. Location acquisition was tested during the Campus Fever event, and 87 % of the collected data had an accuracy lower than 10 m while 29 % of the total data had 5 m of accuracy. During 2 h of monitoring, activity of the application, reduced the battery of 20 %.

1 Introduction

The number of festivals and special events that take place each year is in a constant growth. More than 670 events take place each year in Britain. The top 200 of them generating more than £450 million to the economy [16]. This is one of the reasons why this industry has flourished so much during these 25 past years [12]. The number of attendees at top world vents can reach more than a million people. Such a big number of attendees can cause serious troubles if not managed correctly. Various techniques of estimation are used to plan pedestrian flows and capacities [10]. Despite all the preparations, crowds should be monitored during the event to detect abnormal situations and act on solving them. Many events ended in a tragic way due to people being crushed to death, like the *Love Parade* held in Duisberg, Germany in 2010 were 21 attendees where killed and more than 500 injured [11]. Vision-based monitoring techniques, like CCTVs, are the most used worldwide to monitor events [18]. They provide a reliable video stream of the event in real-time. Vision-based monitoring requires good lighting condition

© Springer International Publishing Switzerland 2015
N. Streitz and P. Markopoulos (Eds.): DAPI 2015, LNCS 9189, pp. 496–505, 2015.
DOI: 10.1007/978-3-319-20804-6_45

and clear weather conditions, which is not the case in many nocturnal events. With the arising of smartphones, capturing the location of participants became possible [23]. The collected data is used for real-time analysis like crowd density and pressure computation [13]. These results combined with group recognition features, enable us to detect the possibility of a disaster, and propose evacuation solutions to groups. Many researches handled the monitoring of crowd via location aware smartphones. Real tests were made during the Lord Mayors Show 2011 in London [22] and Züri Fäscht 2013 [5]. Defining groups detection algorithms were made by McPhail et al. [16] and implemented using vision based techniques [8] or wearable sensors [23].

In this paper, we are going to propose a method to prevent critical situations during mass gatherings by monitoring the crowd via their smartphones, an implementation of the local crowd pressure algorithm, a comparison between potential algorithms for group recognition inside a crowd, and test results taken from the Campus Fever [1] event alongside with simulated data. The goal is to prove that the smartphone monitoring technique can assist events organisers to enhance the safety level.

2   Related Work

This section examines the related work. Section 2.1 presents the crowd characteristics that can determine the criticality of a situation. Section 2.2 discuss the different techniques used to monitor the crowds during events. Section 2.3 discuss multiple techniques of group detection.

2.1   Crowd Dynamics

Personal space preferences and interaction with others are essentials to understand pedestrian requirements. Normally people try to avoid contact between each other, but contact could be tolerated when there is an overcrowded place. Fruin [7] modeled the human as an ellipse defined by the body depth and shoulder breadth measurements. Therefore the personal space required by a person can be represented by an ellipse. The required personal space to keep people from touching each others should be less than 2.17 person/m^2. Also Fruin showed that the normal walking speed vary from 0.76 and 1.76 m/s with an average of 1.37 m/s. Still [20] in his work made a point that Fruin measurements were made in a street environment and may vary if used in an event environment. In addition, the population body dimensions vary a significantly between different countries and ethnic groups [19].

When density rises inside a crowd there is less room to move and therefore less speed. At high densities movement doesn't stop completely. Movement is involuntary and individuals are carried on by the crowd general flow. Density alone can not reflect the dangerousness of the situation. Higher densities can be reached with a stationary crowd than a moving crowd [6]. Therefore Helbing introduced the crowd pressure [10], which depends on the local density (1) and the local speed (2).

$$\rho(\boldsymbol{r}, t) = \frac{1}{\pi R^2} \sum_i \exp[-\frac{||\boldsymbol{r}_i(t) - \boldsymbol{r}||^2}{R^2}] \qquad (1)$$

$$v(\boldsymbol{r}, t) = \frac{\sum_i v_i \exp[-\frac{||\boldsymbol{r}_i(t) - \boldsymbol{r}||^2}{R^2}]}{\sum_i \exp[-\frac{||\boldsymbol{r}_i(t) - \boldsymbol{r}||^2}{R^2}]} \qquad (2)$$

where v_i represent the speed of the pedestrian i at the location $\boldsymbol{r}_i$ and time t. R represent the kernel radius.

Local measures are used over global ones, because human behaviours differs from liquid behaviour. Instead of filling the available area we can find over-crowded areas and empty ones on the same surface. Stop-and-go waves in a crowd is a manifestation of a potential critical situation. It becomes lethal when it translates to crowd turbulences resulting in a very packed crowd where individuals are moved involuntarily by the crowd [13].

2.2 Crowd Monitoring

Crowd monitoring techniques can be divided into two categories: vision-based techniques and mobile phone techniques. The first one relies on video streams captured by surveillance cameras, while the second one collects location data from the attendees devices.

Vision-Based Techniques: are well used in event monitoring, because they provide a reliable and constant flow of video. The basic technique is to have a TV monitor per video stream coming from a camera installed in a strategic place. Other elaborated techniques consist of analysing the video stream by monitoring algorithms that can assist security agents. Vision-based monitoring has several advantages: it is an independent technique that does not rely on the collaboration of the crowd, it is a real-time technique providing instant feedback. Despite its numerous advantages vision-based techniques present many limitations. Lighting is essential to have a clear vision of the crowd, poor lighting condition makes this technique useless. Cameras can be obstructed by obstacles in their field of vision, resulting in a part of the crowd being hidden. Gong et al. [9] demonstrated in his paper that currently deployed vision-based system suffers from poor scalability due to deployment complexity and the necessity of manual judgment of critical situations. Managing multiple video streams at the same time is a difficult task that needs many training and abilities of a person. Other techniques propose to fuse the different video streams with computer vision algorithms to offer an auto-matic monitoring of the crowd. Despite the progresses of computer vision and pattern recognition techniques, this remains a challenging way to automatically monitor crowds accurately.

Mobile Phone Techniques: Finding alternative technologies to monitor crowds during events has oriented research to profit from the sensors embedded in smartphones who became very popular among people. To track the crowd conditions and detect critical situations, gathering the location of attendees of a mass gathering is required. Different approaches to capture smartphones location can be divided into two classes: in-network and on-device. While the in-network uses the CDRs (Call data records) to track a user's position, the on-device technique uses the GPS sensors to do that. In-network estimate the position of a user by locating the cell tower who logged the phone call or message, the accuracy is approximately 300 m and CDRs only occur when an activity is taken, like making a call or sending an SMS [4]. On-device methods rely on GPS and Wi-Fi/GSM-fingerprinting [15] can get an accuracy up to 5 m for the GPS and around 20 m for the Wi-Fi. One clear advantage of on-device methods over in-network is the capability of recording data on a periodic basis. Another method is the usage of Bluetooth beacons distributed in the events environment [21] to track users positions. This method gives a good approximation, but is limited to the availability of a beacon in the surroundings of users and a need to deploy many beacons to cover all the events area. An attempt to deploy the monitoring via smartphone technique took place at the Lord Mayors Show 2011 in London. During this event location information was gathered from pedestrians smartphone devices. Wirz et al. [22] suggested being able to calculate the density of the crowd even if a limited number of attendees shared their location, because the walking speed is affected directly by the density. 828 pedestrians participated which enabled them to verify their theory an average calibration error of 0.36 m^{-2}. A second attempt was made during the Züri Fäscht 2013 [5]. 28,000 people contributed and a total of 25M locations updates were submitted.

In summary, using a mobile device with a GPS localisation approach gives us much more accurate location estimation compared to in-network approaches. On-device methods does not suffer from occlusion, limitation in bad lighting, coverage of large spaces, or scalability. On the other hand, on-device techniques face a big challenge: in contrary to in-network based approach the location is collected from the users device directly. To access location information users have to allow its use. Also a dedicated piece of software should be running on the attendee's phone. The short battery life that most of the smartphones suffer from, and the need for an active internet connection can limit the usage of this technique.

2.3   Group Detection Inside a Crowd

Being able to identify groups of people in the crowd is very helpful to correctly propose evacuation plans to people according to their proximities to exits. People tend to attend events in small groups rather than coming alone. Johnson [14] argues that most crowds consist of small groups rather than isolated individuals. An unpublished study by McPhail concluded that 89 percent of all people present during an event came with the company of at least another person, 52 percent with at least 2 others, 32 percent with at least 3 others, and 94 percent of those who came to the event with someone left with the same people they came with. McPhail's [16] algorithm considers two or more people as a group, if they walk within a distance of 2 m from each others, have the same direction within 3 degrees of difference and have the same speed within 0.15 m/s of difference.

Other techniques consist of using a clustering algorithm in order to cluster the people of the crowd into separated groups. The dimensions used as input vectors for the clustering algorithms are the longitude, latitude, velocity and heading. These dimensions can be easily acquired via the attendee smartphone. Ge et al. [8] used a bottom-up hierarchical clustering approach that starts with individuals as separate clusters and gradually builds larger groups by merging two clusters with the strongest intergroup closeness. The DBSCAN is a density-based algorithm, that is fast, robust against outliers and does not require the number of groups as an input. DeLiClu and OPTICS clustering algorithms will be tested along with DBSCAN in Sect. 5 in order to determine the best fitted algorithm in our case.

3   Data Collection

To collect data from attendees via their smartphones, a custom application had to be installed and launched during the event. We developed the application SmartCrowd [3] that is capable of recording location data and sending them to a centralised server. Privacy protection was taken into consideration by assigning for each user a unique identifier (UUID) that is not traceable back. The application first explains in a short tutorial how the app helps enhance the user's safety and then asks for his permission to capture GPS data. Secondly, a connection with the server is established and location monitoring can begin. The application runs in the background enabling the user to continue doing his normal activities. At each submit, the collected data during two consecutive submits are sent through an HTTP POST request, in response the server refreshes the next submit time based on the user's location. Controlling dynamically the submit time helped us maintain a high submit time in potential critical places (stage area, food stands), and enables us to save the user's battery by maximising the submit time when he is far from the critical places. The submitted data contains: latitude, longitude, altitude, accuracy, speed, heading, battery percentage and a timestamp. To incite attendees to download the app, a reward was unlocked if the user left the app running for 2 h during the event peak time.

We deployed the application during the Campus Fever 2014 event. 36 attendees participated and submitted a total of 144060 location update, from 19h00 until 21h00. Where 29 % had 5 m of accuracy and 87 % had between 5–10 m of accuracy. Only 18 users completed the challenge and won a prize. After investigating, many attendees could not complete the challenge because their battery was low and their phone switched off. The maximum submit time was fixed to 4 submits/minutes. Figure 1 shows the average battery percentage of the participating devices. We can conclude that from 19 h until 21 h, the monitoring activity of the application, plus the user's normal activity reduced the battery of 20 %.

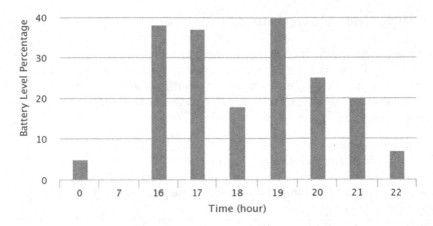

Fig. 1. Average battery percentage statistics during the CampusFever event.

4   Crowd Pressure Computation

Since the collected data during the CampusFever was not enough to test the crowd pressure computation algorithm, we altered the JuPedSim [2] simulator to generate GPS like coordinate instead of local scene unites. As discussed in Sect. 2.1 the developed algorithm relies on the computation of the local crowd pressure. The algorithm was first tested on 500,000 simulated agents and finished the computations after 5 min. To keep the time execution near the second so it can be used in real-time:

- We took into consideration only the agents present in a 2 m radius circle around a point of interest, due to the exponential factor in the Eqs. (1) and (2).
- We divided the event into clusters of 1 m^2 to accelerate the location search performed by the algorithm.
- Instead of computing the local pressure on each agent, we only computed it for the center of each 1 m^2 division.

Table 1 shows the test results made on a MacbookPro with a 2.5 GHz Intel Core i5 processor. The error introduced in the final local crowd pressure value by trimming off all the agents outside the 2 m circle was 0.08 in average.

Table 1. Execution time of crowd pressure computing algorithm with different stress tests.

Test settings	Execution time (s)
300 × 300 m size - 500,000 agents	0.51
500 × 500 m size - 1,000,000 agents	1.18

5   Clustering Algorithms Comparison

Despite of the accuracy, the collected amount of data during the event, was not enough to provide statistical evidence relevant to group detection. The majority of users was not moving due to weather conditions and the small size of the events. In order to address the lack of exploitable real data, we simulated 7 different scenarios:

- Group intersection.
- Group passing near a stationary group.
- A person leaving a group, a person joining a group.
- Resilience to outliers. Outliers are people walking alone, therefor they don't belong to any group.
- Big event with multiple groups.

The data needs to be normalised before clustering it. We compared DBSCAN, DeLiClu and OPTICS because they can cluster data without knowing in advance the number of clusters. The clustering results of a simulated dataset containing 600 people distributed into 40 groups, are showen in Table 2 and Fig. 2. DBSCAN proved to be better than DeLiClu and OPTICS in terms of accuracy and execution time. OPTICS long time is explained by the fact that the algorithm is an amelioration of DBSCAN that does not need the specification of a maximum distance (epsilon) but adds some overhead. The DeLiClu have a long execution time (nearly 400 ms) and this is due to the indexing phase that takes nearly 25 % of the total time. DBSCAN enable us to set a maximal distance between two entries (epsilon). Because of the low variation of density between groups, OPTICS and DeLiClu try to group together distant point by considering their density as low. With it's fixed minimal distance (epsilon) DBSCAN can detect approximately the exact number of simulated clusters. In other words, setting epsilon can limit the density and therefor avoid the problem that OPTICS and DeLiClu face. Other comparisons where made between DBSCAN and other algorithms like DBCLASD, CLARANS [24], DENCLUE [17] which are all density based clustering techniques. In these comparisons DBSCAN also showed a high percentage of precision relatively to its low consumption of time.

6   Evacuation of Groups in Case of Emergency

Groups can be formed by family members or friends. Splitting a group by transmitting different direction information to each member will result in failure. Proposing a unified solution to a group have a better probability to be executed, since a group tends to stay together, if one member of the group reads the notification he can communicate it to the others. In addition the majority of groups has one person who leads them. This person, known to have the highest level of communication [25], is always in the centre of the group, and other members try to follow him. Groups have also an internal auto organisation, members take

Table 2. Results of DBASCAN, DeLiClu and OPTICS clustering algorithms.

Algorithm	Accuracy	Duration(s)	Number of groups
DBSCAN	80.2%	11 ms	38
DeLiClu	73%	395 ms	27
OPTICS	71%	55 ms	27

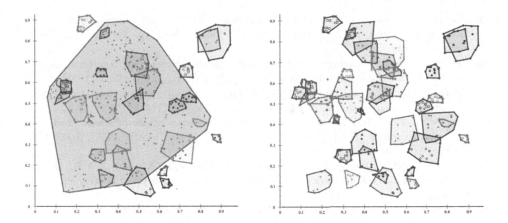

Fig. 2. Example of group detection results for OPTICS and DBSCAN respectively.

care of each others. Based on these observations, we can conclude that communicating an information to a group will be better perceived.

When a critical situation is detected, an algorithm finds the nearest exit for each group to evacuate and then sends it on the members smartphones.

7 Conclusion

In this paper, we presented a technique to collect location updates from smartphones and compute the crowd pressure in real-time. Once a critical situation is detected, a evacuation plan is set and sent to the attendees on their smartphones. The evacuation plan takes into consideration the groups formed by the attendees to avoid splitting them. We presented results of the CampusFever data collection and concluded that the major downside of smartphone monitoring is the short battery life. 29% of the collected data had an accuracy of 5 m while 87% had an accuracy between 5–10 m. We also showed that by reducing the radius of the considered people around a point of interest to 2 m, we can speed up the local crowd pressure computation. We demonstrated that a clustering algorithm, like DBSCAN, can be used to detect groups inside a crowd with an accuracy of 80% over a simulated dataset. Finally we put in place a shortest path algorithm to select the nearest exit for a group in case of emergency and transmit this information to the group through their smartphones.

References

1. Campusfever website. http://www.campusfever.ch
2. Jupedsim official webpage. http://www.jupedsim.org
3. Smartcrowd website. http://smartcrowd.tic.eia-fr.ch
4. Becker, R.A., Cceres, R., Hanson, K., Loh, J.M., Urbanek, S., Varshavsky, A., Volinsky, C.: A tale of one city: using cellular network data for urban planning (2011)
5. Blanke, U., Tröster, G., Franke, T., Lukowicz, P.: Capturing crowd dynamics at large scale events using participatory GPS-localization, pp. 21–24, April 2014. www.ulfblanke.de
6. Fruin, J.: Crowd disasters-a systems evaluation of causes and countermeasures. Inc. in US National Bureau of Standards, pub. NBSIR, pp. 81–3261 (1981)
7. Fruin, J.: Pedestrian Planning and Design. Metropolitan Association of Urban Designers and Environmental Planners, New York (1971)
8. Ge, W., Collins, R.T., Ruback, R.B.: Vision-based analysis of small groups in pedestrian crowds. IEEE Trans. Pattern Anal. Mach. Intell. **34**(5), 1003–1016 (2012)
9. Gong, S., Loy, C., Xiang, T.: Security and surveillance. In: Moeslund, T.B., Hilton, A., Krger, V., Sigal, L. (eds.) Visual Analysis of Humans, pp. 455–472. Springer, London (2011)
10. Helbing, D., Johansson, A., Al-Abideen, H.Z.: The dynamics of crowd disasters: an empirical study, January 2007
11. Helbing, D., Mukerji, P.: Crowd disasters as systemic failures: analysis of the Love Parade disaster. EPJ Data Sci. **1**(1), 7 (2012)
12. Janeczko, B., Mules, T., Ritchie, B.: Estimating the economic impacts of festivals and events: a research guide (2002)
13. Johansson, A., Helbing, D., Al-Abideen, H.Z., Al-Bosta, S.: From crowd dynamics to crowd safety: a video-based analysis, October 2008
14. Johnson, N.R.: Panic at the who concert stampede: an empirical assessment. Soc. Probl. **34**(4), 362–373 (1987)
15. Kim, D.H., Kim, Y., Estrin, D., Srivastava, M.B.: Sensloc: sensing everyday places and paths using less energy. In: Proceedings of the 8th ACM Conference on Embedded Networked Sensor Systems, SenSys 2010, pp. 43–56. ACM, New York, NY, USA (2010)
16. McPHAIL, C., Wohlstein, R.T.: Using film to analyze pedestrian behavior. Sociol. Methods Res. **10**(3), 347–375 (1982)
17. Nagpal, P.B., Mann, P.A.: Comparative study of density based clustering algorithms. Int. J. Comput. Appl. **27**(11), 44–47 (2011)
18. Norris, C., Mccahill, M., Wood, D.: Editorial. The Growth of CCTV : a global perspective on the international diffusion of video surveillance in publicly accessible space, vol. 2, pp. 110–135
19. Pheasants, S.: Bodyspace, September 1988
20. Still, G.: Crowd dynamics. Ph.D. thesis (2000)
21. Versichele, M., Neutens, T., Delafontaine, M., Van de Weghe, N.: The use of bluetooth for analysing spatiotemporal dynamics of human movement at mass events: a case study of the ghent festivities. Appl. Geogr. **32**(2), 208–220 (2012)
22. Wirz, M., Franke, T., Roggen, D.: Probing crowd density through smartphones in city-scale mass gatherings. EPJ Data Sci. **2**(1), 5 (2013)

23. Wirz, M., Roggen, D., Troster, G.: Decentralized detection of group formations from wearable acceleration sensors. In: 2009 International Conference on Computational Science and Engineering, pp. 952–959 (2009)
24. Xu, X., Ester, M., Kriegel, H.P., Sander, J.: A distribution-based clustering algorithm for mining in large spatial databases. In: Proceedings of the 14th International Conference on Data Engineering, pp. 324–331, February 1998
25. Zhang, Y., Pettre, J., Qin, X., Donikian, S., Peng, Q.: A local behavior model for small pedestrian groups. In: 2011 12th International Conference on Computer-Aided Design and Computer Graphics, pp. 275–281, September 2011

Indirect Monitoring of Cared Person by Onomatopoeic Text of Environmental Sound and User's Physical State

Yusuke Naka[✉], Naoto Yoshida, and Tomoko Yonezawa

Kansai University, Takatsuki, Japan
{k361326,k463362,yone}@kansai-u.ac.jp

Abstract. In this paper, we propose a nonverbal, descriptive method for creating daily life logs, in text format, on behalf of people who require monitoring and/or assistance in taking care of themselves. The users environmental situations are converted into and recorded as onomatopoeic texts in order to preserve their privacy. The users ambient context is detected by the accelerometer, gyro sensor, and microphone in her/his smart device. We propose a soft monitoring system that utilizes nonverbal expressions of both onomatopoeic text logs and symbolic sound expressions that is named Soundgram. We have investigated impressions regarding the monitoring of the elderly and the proposed system via a questionnaire distributed to two groups of potential users, the elderly and middle-aged people, which captures the viewpoint of both the recipient and the caregiver.

1 Introduction

In daily life, elderly people often face various dangerous situations, such as falling, which are caused by a decline in physical strength, muscular strength, and concentration. Even if they live with their families, it is difficult for other family members to remain with the elderly person all day. Present observing systems became to be able to transmit the living conditions of elderly people to their caregivers in detail through various media, such as video. These systems prevent or predict larger problems from small accidents, and they can also notify caregivers when an elderly person is in danger. However, such observing systems may sacrifice elderly peoples privacy in the interest of ensuring they are safely cared for, in some cases. This problem can create a mental burden for elderly people who are under the observation of such systems and cause them to hesitate to use such systems long term. In addition, caregivers have a physical burden because of the cost of the observation and because they need to continually verify the status of the person for whom they are caring all day, every day. Thus, currently available observing methods present various problems for both people who require care and caregivers.

Against such problems, we have proposed a push-type observing system that automatically captures information regarding physical movement, contexts,

N. Streitz and P. Markopoulos (Eds.): DAPI 2015, LNCS 9189, pp. 506–517, 2015.
DOI: 10.1007/978-3-319-20804-6_46

state, and environmental sounds near the person requiring monitoring and/or care as a text-based log that sends selective notifications only in situations when the system detects a high risk of danger. Text-based, onomatopoeic information expresses various things in daily life. It is expected that a caregiver can use this method to simply and intuitively confirm the state of an elderly person without interfering with the latters privacy. In this study, we defined onomatopoeic expression as an onomatopoeic text that represents (1) a sound or the voice of something or someone and (2) a mimetic word that imitates and represents a physical state.

When a caregiver reads such text logs after they have been gathered for a certain period of time, it takes time to read them all. Therefore, we propose the adoption of onomatopoeic texts and Soundgrams in order to communicate the physical movement states and sounds in the environment that surrounds elderly people. The text expressions are easy to read and it takes less time than watching a video log. The Soundgrams provides caregivers with an intuitive, rough understanding and overview of the text logs by creating an active stimulus while the listener passively receives the information without needing to go through special training. A Soundgram is an expressive series of sound files of fixed length that concretely expresses various things. It is expected that Soundgram expressions can also be used as an emergency notice when combined with information about the contents.

2   Related Works

There have been various studies on methods for automatic recognition of physical dangers and predictable movements, such as falls [1–4]. One study developed an algorithm of automatic fall detection based on threshold values using the bi-axial gyroscope sensor that is built into most commonly available cell phones [1]. The results of the experiment showed recognition to be effective only when the users physical movement changed. Moreover, there is a possibility of detection errors when using a threshold-based system for a bi-axial gyro sensor. From the viewpoint of the risk of detection error in emergencies, the elderly people may lose their confidence in the system and, therefore, they will not use it for a long period of time. Furthermore, their proposed method focuses only on detection and does not consider the importance of communication and expression for both emergency and daily life signals. In contrast, our proposed system recognizes the physical state of elderly people by using a tri-axial acceleration sensor and a tri-axial gyroscope sensor with cyclical information, combined with environmental sounds for rough sound recognition in daily life events. Moreover, our system transmits information not as high-level information, such as a physical action and actual environmental sounds, but as an expression that is a combination of onomatopoeic text and Soundgram. Text-based logs seem to be an appropriate method of checking, at a glance, upon people who require care when the caregiver is busy, the text logs. For checking up on people while doing something else at the same time, Soundgram expression is considered to be appropriate. Text format files are able to preserve data for a long time because the data increase corresponds to the length of the period, especially if we use media with high storage capacity.

In addition, the text onomatopoeia reduces the quality and quantity of the information enough that our proposed method may prevent an excessive intrusion into the privacy of the elderly person who is receiving care. For this reason, we believe that the burden of the caregiver, which is rooted in the need to constantly observe his/her elderly ward, can be reduced by using our system. The push-type notification is limited only to emergencies, and the results of the daily observation are passively uploaded as a text log.

There have been many studies on safety and privacy while observing elderly people [5–8]. Generally, safety is the most pressing issue of such systems, which seek to physically protect elderly people. On the other hand, many studies aimed at protecting the privacy of elderly people consider the psychological problems inherent to using observation systems. Yonezawa et al. have proposed a daily observation system of elderly peoples status that utilizes environmental sounds [8]. The system adopted multiple microphones and simplified spectrogram data to recognize environmental sounds and the sounds location to provide privacy-protected observation. In this research, the environmental sounds are classified by a Support Vector Machine (SVM) with features from a simplified spectrogram. However, there is a problem with recognition accuracy. For this reason, we propose to adopt a spectrum envelope of environmental sounds.

3   System Implementation

3.1   System Concept

We focus on a pull-type observation system with a partial push-type notification. Our concept is based on the automatic detection and conversion of the sonic and bodily events of elderly peoples daily lives into text logs (Fig. 1). We then focused on onomatopoeic texts and a method of expressing them using Soundgrams. The text logs with nonverbal onomatopoeia can intuitively and plainly show abstract information to be able to help the caregiver understand what is happening with the elderly person. The Soundgram, a series of expressive sound files of short and fixed length, is also used to provide caregivers with an auditory representation of the digest that uses a virtual agent as though it was speaking the text logs.

3.2   System Overview

This system realizes an observational method that provides pull-type information by automatically collecting events of (1) physical movement and (2) environmental sound in the daily lives of elderly people (see Fig. 2). The accumulated information is able to be read at a glance in the form of text logs We adopt the onomatopoeic text of the users contexts in order to (a) protect their privacy, (b) provide caregivers with a rough understanding, (c) reduce the amount of the

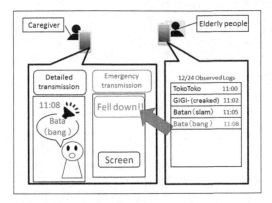

Fig. 1. Soft-Observed System of the elderly

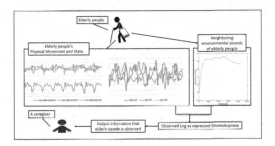

Fig. 2. The communication that improved an understanding degree of the situation

data, and (d) reduce the psychological burden upon elderly people by minimizing feelings of discomfort. In this paper, we propose an observational system that recognizes and automatically classifies the users physical movements and neighboring environmental sounds in order to convert them into onomatopoeia. From the preliminary survey, the classification uses a SVM (support vector machine) by learning features of both physical movements and environmental sounds. SVM is suitable for a classification with high-dimensional features and can operate at high speed, especially in real-time processing.

3.3 Recognition of User's Body Motion

Our system for data acquisition and recognition is premised on the use of the internal sensors in the individuals smart devices. The values of three-dimensional accelerometers and three-dimensional gyro sensors (in total, six axes) are used to detect user events. Sampling frequency of the sensor values is 100 Hz, and window size of the data process is 128 samples. Means, variances, and cyclical features are used as features of bodily motion. Regarding cyclical features, FFT (Fast Fourier Transformation) is used for low frequencies (from 0.78 to 4.69 Hz). In order to classify the users various situations, the system first learns the features using

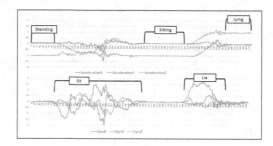

Fig. 3. Classification of body movements using a tri-axial acceleration sensor and tri-axial gyroscope sensor

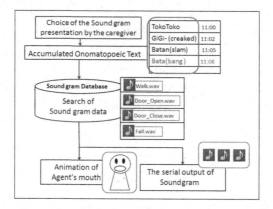

Fig. 4. Generation process of the Soundgram

SVM (Fig. 3). From the preliminary test [9], it was conjectured that the system can recognize and classify, with approximately 85 % to 90 % accuracy, sitting, running, lying, walking, and standing. Next, for short-term motions, such as standing up or lying down, we adopted the mean and variances as features of the window by dividing it into four regions. The preliminary test showed about 75 % accuracy in classifying stand up, sit down, lie down, and sit up.

3.4   Recognition of Environmental Sound

In order to automatically classify environmental sound into typical consonants for onomatopoeias (p, t, k, b, d, g, s, z/j), we focused on a spectrum envelope. As features of machine learning using SVM, the 128 cepstrum coefficients from 5.38 to 172 Hz are calculated by FFT and iFFT with 8192 samples of the window size at a sampling frequency of 44,100 Hz. As a result of our preliminary test, an accuracy rate of more than 85 % was confirmed. The length and envelope of the environmental sound determines the existence of the following marks at the ending of the word: long vowel, promote sound, and nasal sound. The long vowel mark is attached when the sound length is more than 150 ms. The promote sound mark is attached when the sound length is less than 75 ms. The nasal sound mark is attached when the release time is less than 750 ms. These rules were defined by a preliminary subjective test.

3.5 Design of Virtual Agent with Soundgram

Corresponding to the need of the detailed information of the cared person for the caregiver, our proposed system makes sound of the Soundgram, that is the auditory expression more concrete than onomatopoeic texts (Fig. 4). In the set of Soundgram, audio files assigned to onomatopoeic texts and word texts beforehand is searched based on the log texts of the elderlys daily-life information. The audio files are expressed serially as a script of an agent with a digest of the log texts.

In particular, when people communicate from different backgrounds, such as different languages, it is not possible for them to directly communicate with each other. In order to mediate human-human communication, an expressive agent, such as a robot or virtual agent, is used as a facilitator [10]. The nonverbal and verbal expression of the anthropomorphic agent helps provide intuitive understanding of the contents. In this research, we aim to express the daily life events of people who require daily observation and/or assistance with their activities of daily living by using Soundgram expressions as a script of a virtual agent that talks to the caregiver. Soundgrams are serially played back in correspondence with onomatopoeic texts. The serial sound flow expresses the flow of the users daily life without creating confusion by mixing the sounds Soundgrams are expected to be a common means of expression for various people that provides presentational sound without learning prerequisites.

4 Questionnaire About Needs for Watching for Elderly and the Middle-Aged People

We performed a survey about the need of observation from the standpoint of both the cared people and caregivers by a questionnaire sheet for elderly people and middle aged people. In order to verify the possibility of the proposed method, the questionnaire sheet asked the positive/negative feedbacks for various situations of the observation of elderly people in different places and different methods with showing our proposed method as Fig. 1. The elderly participant answered to the questions from the viewpoint of the cared situation, and the middle aged people answered to the question from the viewpoint of the situation of caregiver.

4.1 Questionnaire About Watching for Elderly and the Middle-Aged People

Respondents: Nine participants aged from 70 to 90 years old as elderly (two males, seven females), and ten participants aged from 44 to 62 years old as middle-aged people (three males, seven females).

Table 1. Questionnaire count for the elderly

Item	Answer(number of the respondents of the elderly)
1	Smartphone(2)cell-phone other than a smartphone(4)none(3)
2	Living together(6)Living near(3)Living in the distance(0)
3	1-2 people(3)3-6 people(6)More than 7 people(0)
4	Under one hour(1)From one hour to three hours(3)From three hours to five hours(5)More than five hours(0)
5	Necessary(3)Unnecessary(6)
6	Necessary(6)Unnecessary(3)
7	Necessary(3)Unnecessary(6)
8	Necessary(2)Unnecessary(7)
9	Necessary(3)Unnecessary(6)
10	Necessary(4)Unnecessary(5)
11	Under going out(4)Bedroom(1)Stairs(0)
12	Movie(0)Sound(3)Wearable Device(3)Household appliance(1)Unnecessary(1)Snuggle up(1)
13	Bath(3)restroom(4)Room of oneself(1)Hobby(0)
14	Privacy (high)It is observed in the future, but is ashamed now (high)
15	Foot(4)Waist(4)Back(1)Reflex nerve(1)Knee(1) Eyesight(0)Muscular strength(0)Joint(0)
16	Necessary(7)Unnecessary(2)

Survey Item: Item: We asked the participants to answer for each question with selective choices as following 12 items. The middle-aged participants answered to the questions by assuming the standpoint of the elderly people.

1: Kind of the cell-phone [smartphone/cellphone (non-smartphone type)/none]
2: The living families [Living together/Living near/Living in the distance or no family]
3: Number of family member living together [1-2 people/3-6 people/More than 7 people]
4: Going out time per day [Under one hour/From one hour to three hours/From three hours to five hours/More than five hours]
5: Observation in the restroom [Necessary/Unnecessary]
6: Observation in stairs [Necessary/Unnecessary]
7: Observation in the kitchen [Necessary/Unnecessary]
8: Observation in the entrance [Necessary/Unnecessary]
9: Observation in the living [Necessary/Unnecessary]
10: Observation in the bath [Necessary/Unnecessary]
11: Other places/situation to be observed [free description]
12: Method of observation [Movie/Sound/Wearable Device/Household appliance]

Table 2. Questionnaire count as the situation of the elderly for the middle-aged people

Item	Answer(number of the respondents of the middle-aged people)
1	Smartphone(7)cell-phone other than a smartphone(3)none(0)
2	Living together(6/10)Living near(3/0)Living in the distance(0/0)
3	1-2 people(1)3-6 people(9)More than 7 people(0)
4	Under one hour(4)From one hour to three hours(3)From three hours to five hours(3)More than five hours(0)
5	Necessary(8)Unnecessary(2)
6	Necessary(9)Unnecessary(1)
7	Necessary(8)Unnecessary(2)
8	Necessary(7)Unnecessary(3)
9	Necessary(5)Unnecessary(5)
10	Necessary(10)Unnecessary(0)
11	Under going out(2)Bedroom(2)Stairs(1)
12	Movie(1)Sound(1)Wearable device(8)Household appliance(2)Unnecessary(0)Snuggle up(0)
13	Bath(5)restroom(5)Room of oneself(1)Hobby(1)
14	Privacy (high)It is observed in the future, but is ashamed now (high)
15	Foot(4)Waist(4)Back(0)Reflex nerve(0)Knee(2) Eyesight(3)Muscular strength(1)Joint(2)
16	Necessary(10)Unnecessary(0)

13: Other places/situation not to be observed [free description]
14: Reason for the previous question [free description]
15: Bodily problems if you have [free description]
16: Necessity of the proposed system[Necessary/Unnecessary]

Results: Tables 1 and 2 shows the summary of the questionnaire for both elderly people and middle-aged people. Less than a half of the elderly people who participated in this survey answered that they need the daily-life observation in this stage. On the other hand, more than a half of the middle-aged people answered that they feel the necessity of the observation to their parents. Thus there was a difference of the feelings for necessity of the observation between two generations. In the case where the cared people believe that observation is unnecessary, it is possible that the system would become hard to be accepted. Therefore, it is important to provide the observing method of cared people without consciousness of the observed state.

Next, we show the results of the questionnaire by different places in daily life. In the question 6, it is confirmed that more than a half of the elderly people feel the necessity of the observation in the stairs while the other places showed low scores. There were extra opinions for the necessary observation in outings. In contrast, a half of middle-aged people consider that the observation in various places in the house is necessary. In particular, all of the middle-aged participants replied necessary to the question 10, that is the observation in the bath. For privacy protected observation in the private places in the house such as bath and toilet, it is important to protect the cared peoples privacy as well as possible.

Table 3. Questionnaire count as the situation of the caregiver for the middle-aged people

Item	Answer (the number of the respondents)
1	Necessary(9)Unnecessary(1)
2	Necessary(9)Unnecessary(1)
3	Necessary(9)Unnecessary(1)
4	Necessary(7)Unnecessary(3)
5	Necessary(7)Unnecessary(3)
6	Necessary(10)Unnecessary(0)
7	Under going out(2)Bedroom(2)During a meal(1)
8	Meeting(3)Movie(0)Sound(4)Wearable Device(2)Household appliance(1)
9	Bath(4)Restroom(3)
10	PrivacyApology

In the question of the observing method, the elderly people preferred sound logs or wearable devices, and most of the middle-aged people preferred wearable devices. It is conjectured that people in the generation accustomed to wear the smartphone devices can become familiar to the observation using such devices. Most of the elderly people and all of the middle-aged people replied that our proposed method of the observation is necessary. From the result, the embarrassed or hesitated feeling of the observation may decrease by the proposed method.

4.2 Questionnaire About Watching as a Viewpoint of the Caregivers for the Middle-Aged People

Respondents: Ten participants aged from 44 to 62 years old as middle-aged people (three males, seven females).
Survey Item: We asked the participants to answer for each question with selective choices as following 10 items. The middle-aged participants answered to the questions by assuming the standpoint of the caregiver.

1: Observation in the restroom [Necessary/Unnecessary]
2: Observation in stairs [Necessary/Unnecessary]
3: Observation in the kitchen [Necessary/Unnecessary]
4: Observation in the entrance [Necessary/Unnecessary]
5: Observation in the living [Necessary/Unnecessary]
6: Observation in the bath [Necessary/Unnecessary]

7: Other places/situation to be observed [free description]
8: Method of observing [Meeting/Sound/Household appliance/Signal of the cell-phone]
9: Other places/situation not to observe [free description]
10: Reason for the previous question [free description]

Results: Table 3 shows the summary of the questionnaire for middle-aged people. Almost all of the middle-aged people who participated in this survey answered that they need daily-life observation from the viewpoint of caregivers. In particular, all responders answered that the observation in the bath is necessary. Furthermore, some of the participants had indicated that it is necessary for observation during the going out or in the bedroom in the house. However, it was found that a lot of people do not like to observe in the bath or a restroom because of privacy. In comparison to this result and the survey for the elderly people, it seemed that the middle-aged people felt the necessary of observation from the viewpoint of the caregiver, while they cared the privacy from the viewpoint of the cared people. From the results, it is conjectured that the system should cover differences of both consciousness for the observation between the standpoint of caregiver and cared people. In addition, there were a lot of comments that the preferred observation method should in real-time media such as sounds.

5 Discussion

We investigate the effectiveness and possibility of our proposed method of the soft observation from the results of the questionnaire. There were several differences of the consideration for the observation necessity between the elderly people and the middle-aged people. The middle-aged people who do not face the problems from living alone responded that they are going to need observation of themselves in the future. In contrast, the elderly participants responded that they do not need to observation at the present stage.

The result of the elderly people was considered to be relieved because they live with their family or live close to their family. From the situation, they do not feel anxiety about the emergency although most of family members are busy for some other works to do in their lives. Some of the elderly participants told that they would need the observation in the future while they do not need the observed life at this moment. The need for help or observation causes the acceptable attitude to the all-time observation. Even when they adopt the observing system, it is also important to consider the psychological acceptance.

Now we discuss the place and the situation for observation. There were many answers with strong needs for the observation and strong resistance to the observation at the same time in the private places such as a bath and a restroom. The bathing time is one of the most frequent scene of the elderlys accidents such as falls or attacks. The washroom is also one of the most frequent place of attacks by the sudden change of blood pressure. These results are considered as the recognition of both the private places and increased risks. Accordingly, it is important to observe the cared people to prevent the elderlys uncomfortable feeling from the privacy problems In order to consider the privacy, it would be effective to limit the pull-type observation in the private place, the push-type notification only in the case of the emergency should be allowed. In addition, it is necessary to examine the feeling of privacy by detective method of physical movements and environmental sounds of the elderly people.

There were the results of the questionnaire of the observation needs in the stairs and outings while there were several participants who have various troubles and physical anxiety of their legs and backs, we suppose that observation is necessary especially for the activities using their legs. Accordingly, the system should make log text using various onomatopoeias related to the action of the users large motion. The detailed recognition of the physical state of the elderly people would help the caregivers to predict the dangerous situation. Mobile systems for the observation during outing [11] are also important for the fall detection [12]. In addition, the device of the system should not become load to the elderly people.

There were many answers that the real time media such as sound were preferred for observation. It is supposed that push-type and real time media were considered to become appropriate as an emergent notification. From some comments with the strong endorsements of the face-to-face observation, the most important thing in the observation is to be ready for various situations of the cared people. From the viewpoint of the human observer in daily life, the presence of the human caregiver gives a relieved feeling. The proposed Soundgram can provide such real-time information by push-type sound media while the privacy is protected. In addition, intuitive understandability, one of the important characteristic of anthropomorphic agents, can be adopted to the virtual source of Soundgram expressions as its utterance.

6   Conclusion

In this paper, we proposed an observational system that converts physical movements and environmental sounds in the daily lives of elderly people into a text format with onomatopoeic expressions. The automatic reading system for the text logs uses Soundgram, a series of expressive sound files of short and fixed length. In addition, we investigated the need of the observation and the adaptation of this system for elderly and middle-aged people from the standpoint of both people who require care and caregivers. As a result, it was confirmed that it is necessary for elderly people to be observed without feeling uncomfortable and to have a way of reporting emergencies without invading their privacy. As future work, we plan to improve the observation method and its correspondence to typical scenes in a persons daily life in order to fulfill the needs of caregivers and the elderly. We are also going to verify the effectiveness of our proposed system.

Acknowledgement. This research was supported in part by KAKENHI 24300047 and KAKENHI 25700021.

References

1. Bourke, A.K., Lyons, G.M.: A threshold-based fall-detection algorithm using a bi-axial gyroscope sensor. Med. Eng. Phys. **30**(1), 84–90 (2008)
2. Boehner, A.: A smartphone application for a portable fall detection system. In: Proceedings of the National Conference on Undergraduate Research (NCUR) 2013, pp. 213–219 (2013)
3. Lutrek, M., Kalua, B.: Fall detection and activity recognition with machine learning. Informatica **33**, 205–212 (2009)
4. Doukas, C., Maglogiannis, I.: Advanced patient or elder fall detection based on movement and sound data, pervasive computing technologies for healthcare, 2008. In: Second International Conference on PervasiveHealth 2008, pp 103–107 (2008)
5. Melander-Wikman, A.: Safety vs. privacy: elderly persons experiences of a mobile safety alarm. Health Soc. Care Community **16**(4), 337–346 (2008)
6. Lin, C.-C., Lin, P.-Y., Po-Kuan, L., Hsieh, G.-Y., Lee, W.-L., Lee, R.-G.: A healthcare integration system for disease assessment and safety monitoring of dementia patients. IEEE Trans. Inf. Technol. Biomed. **12**(5), 579–586 (2008)
7. Sharkey, A., Sharkey, N.: Granny and the robots: ethical issues in robot care for the elderly. Ethics Inf. Technol. **14**(1), 27–40 (2012)
8. Yonezawa, T., Okamoto, N., Yamazoe, H. Abe, S., Hattori, F., Hagita, N.: Privacy protected life-context-aware alert by simplified sound spectrogram from microphone sensor. In: Proceedings of the ACM the 6th Workshop of CASEMANS, pp. 4 9 (2011)
9. Naka, Y., Ino, Y., Yoshida, N., Yonezawa, T.: Embedded text communication with onomatopoeia of user's bodily motion and environmental sounds. Hum. Interface Soc. J., **17**(2) (2015, in press)
10. Fujiwara, K., Nishinaka, J., Yoshida, N., Yonezawa, T.: Shedule managing agent among group members with caring expressions. In: Proceedings of the SCIS-ISIS 2014, pp. 1564–1567 (2014)
11. Yonezawa, T., Yamazoe, H.: Wearable partner agent with anthropomorphic physical contact with awareness of clothing and posture. In: Proceedings of the ISWC 2013, pp. 77–80 (2013)
12. Bourke, A.K., Obrien, J.V., Lyons, G.M.: Evaluation of a threshold-based tri-axial accelerometer fall detection algorithm. Gait Posture **26**(2), 194–199 (2007)

Estimating Positions of Students in a Classroom from Camera Images Captured by the Lecturer's PC

Junki Nishikawa[1], Koh Kakusho[1(✉)], Masaaki Iiyama[2],
Satoshi Nishiguchi[3], and Masayuki Murakami[4]

[1] School of Science and Technology, Kwansei Gakuin University,
Sanda, Japan
{jun-nishikawa,kakusho}@kwansei.ac.jp
[2] Academic Center for Computing and Media Studies,
Kyoto University, Kyoto, Japan
iiyama@mm.media.kyoto-u.ac.jp
[3] Faculty of Information Science and Technology,
Osaka Institute of Technology, Hirakata, Japan
satoshi.nishiguchi@oit.ac.jp
[4] Research Center for Multimedia Education,
Kyoto University of Foreign Studies, Kyoto, Japan
masayuki@murakami-lab.org

Abstract. We propose to estimate the position of each student in a classroom by observing the classroom with a camera attached on the notebook or tablet PC of the lecturer. The position of each student in the classroom is useful to keep observing his/her learning behavior as well as taking attendance, continuously during the lecture. Although there are many previous works on estimating positions of humans from camera images in the field of computer vision, the arrangement of humans in a classroom is quite different from usual scenes. Since students in a classroom sit on closely-spaced seats, they appear with many overlaps among their regions in camera images. To cope with this difficulty, we keep observing students to capture their faces once they appear, and recover the positions in the classroom with the geometric constraint that requires those positions to be distributed on the same plane parallel to the floor.

Keywords: Classroom · Position estimation · Student positions · Continuous observation

1 Introduction

In the field of higher education, it becomes quite usual to record videos of lectures [1–3]. Those videos are used for various purposes including self-learning by students, reviewing the recorded lectures for faculty development, and so on. In addition to simply recording videos of lectures, it is also proposed to recognize various situations of the lecturer or the students during each lecture by observing it with cameras or sensors installed in the classroom. Those recognized situations are assumed to be

© Springer International Publishing Switzerland 2015
N. Streitz and P. Markopoulos (Eds.): DAPI 2015, LNCS 9189, pp. 518–526, 2015.
DOI: 10.1007/978-3-319-20804-6_47

employed as indices to find remarkable scenes from the recorded video for viewing the video or analyzing the procedures of the lecture efficiently [4–7].

In this article, we propose to estimate the position of each student sitting in a classroom during a lecture by observing the classroom with a camera, as one of the situations of the lecture. Positions of the students sitting in the classroom are useful for analyzing their learning behavior, grasping their attendance and so on during the lecture. Information about the leaning behavior or attendance of students can be used for guiding their learning activities by considering their type of participation in the class. For observing the classroom, we employ the camera attached on the notebook or tablet PC of the lecturer, because recent lectures are usually given by the lecturers with their own PCs, which are often equipped with cameras.

In the field of computer vision, there are many previous works on estimating positions of humans from camera images [8, 9]. However, the arrangement of humans in a classroom is quite different from usual scenes discussed in those previous works. Since students in a classroom sit on closely-spaced seats, many occlusions often occur among those students in their image if it is captured by the camera on the lecture's PC. However, each student keeps sitting on the same seat, and the camera on the lecture's PC can keep observing the students from their fronts throughout the whole time of the lecture. Thus, even if some students happen to be occluded by other students in their camera image at a moment of the lecture, they should appear in the image at another moment. Moreover, although all the students may not be able to be observed by the camera at the same single moment, they could be observed if the lecturer sometimes moves the PC during the lecture to change the camera angle.

Our method first recovers the 3D position of each student appearing in the camera image at each moment of the lecture from his/her face. Then the position and the orientation of the floor of the classroom in relation to the camera at each moment is estimated based on the distribution of the recovered 3D positions of the students by introducing the geometric constraint that the students sit on the seats arranged on the plane parallel to the floor. The seat location of each student is obtained by estimating the seat arrangement on the floor based on the geometric constraint that the 2D positions of the students on the floor are arranged in a grid pattern. In the remainder of this article, we will describe our method above in Sect. 2 and experimental results in Sect. 3, before giving conclusions in Sect. 4.

2   Estimating Seat Locations of Students

2.1   Recovering 3D Facial Positions

Our method first estimates the 3D positions of the students in relation to the camera from the appearance of their faces in the camera image (see Fig. 1). We detect faces in the image before extracting the eyes as well as estimating the 3D orientation for each detected face by facial image processing. For the k-th face detected in the image, let s_k^C denote the 3D position of the midpoint between the eyes in the camera-centered coordinate system with the origin at the optical center, the z axis along with the optical axis and the x, y axes parallel to the image plane. When the 2D positions of the left eye and the right eye extracted for the k-th face in the image are represented by l_k^I and r_k^I respectively, s_k^C can be obtained from the following equations:

$$l_k^I = \lambda A \left(R_k l_k^F + s_k^C \right) \tag{1}$$

$$r_k^I = \lambda A \left(R_k r_k^F + s_k^C \right) \tag{2}$$

where l_k^F and r_k^F denote the actual 3D positions of the left eye and the right eye of the k-th face in its face-centered coordinate system with the origin at the midpoint between the eyes and the x, y, z axes rightward, upward and forward of the face. The coordinates of these 3D positions are given as $l_k^F = (-d, 0, 0)^T$ and $r_k^F = (d, 0, 0)^T$, where d denotes the intraocular distance. Matrix A, which consists of the inner camera parameters, represents the process of optical projection together with scaling parameter λ. Matrix R_i denotes the pose of the face in the camera-centered coordinate system, and is given by the 3D orientation of the face obtained by the facial image processing described above.

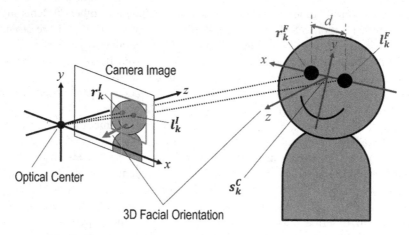

Fig. 1. Recovery of the 3D facial position relative to the camera

2.2 Estimating 2D Positions on the Floor

In order to further obtain the 2D position of the student with the k-th face on the floor of the classroom from s_k^C, we need to know the position and the orientation of the floor in the camera-centered coordinate system. However, these position and orientation are unknown, because the camera is attached on the PC of the lecturer and the PC is moved so that all the students are captured by the camera. Since the students sit on the seats arranged on the floor, the 3D positions of their faces should be distributed on the same 3D plane parallel to the floor, if we neglect the difference in their sitting heights. Thus, we estimate the position and the orientation of this plane P instead of the floor by fitting a 3D plane with s_k^C for all the faces in the image.

Let us represent a 3D plane in the camera-centered coordinate system as follows:

$$\pi(x; \alpha, \beta, \gamma, \delta) = \alpha x + \beta y + \gamma z + \delta = 0 \tag{3}$$

where $x = (x, y, z)^T$. The normal vector of the plane is represented by $n = (\alpha, \beta, \gamma)^T$ and the position of the plane among all the planes with the same normal vector n is specified by δ. In order for s_k^C for all the faces detected in the image to be on this plane, the following constraint needs to be satisfied:

$$E_P(\alpha, \beta, \gamma, \delta) \equiv \sum_{k=1}^{N} \pi\left(s_k^C; \alpha, \beta, \gamma, \delta\right) = 0 \tag{4}$$

where N is the number of the faces detected in the image. The values of α, β, γ and δ satisfying Eq. (4) are obtained by minimizing E_P with these variables.

The 2D position of the student with the k-th face on the floor is denoted by s_k^P. Since the floor and the plane P are parallel to each other and both perpendicular to n, we represent s_k^P by the plane-centered coordinate system with the x, y axes orthogonal to each other and both perpendicular to n. The unit vectors of these x, y axes are denoted by p_x and p_y respectively. We set $p_x = (1, 0, 0)^T$ so that it coincides with the x axis of the camera-centered coordinate system and $p_y = \hat{n} \times p_x$, where $\hat{n} = n/\|n\|$. In this plane-centered coordinate system, s_k^P is given as follows:

$$s_k^P = \begin{pmatrix} p_x^T \\ p_y^T \end{pmatrix} s_k^C \tag{5}$$

2.3   Obtaining Seat Location of Each Student

In order to know the seat location (the row and column of the seat) of each student in a grid arrangement of the seats in the classroom, we further need to obtain the position and the orientation of the grid arrangement on the floor. Let $s_k^S = (i_k, j_k)^T$ denote the seat location of the student with the k-th face in the image, where i_k and j_k are the numbers of the column and the row of the seat counted from the seat at a corner of the grid seat arrangement, and the seat at the corner is represented as $(0, 0)^T$. When we represent the 2D position of this corner and the orientation of the grid seat arrangement by o^P and R^P respectively, the following equation should be satisfied for s_k^P and s_k^S for all the faces in the image:

$$\sigma\left(s_1^S, .., s_N^S; o^P, R^P\right) \equiv \sum_{k=1}^{N} \left\| R^P \begin{pmatrix} w i_k \\ h j_k \end{pmatrix} + o^P - s_k^P \right\|^2 = 0 \tag{6}$$

where w and h are constant values for the intervals between adjacent columns and adjacent rows of the grid seat arrangement. Moreover, the following constraint should also be satisfied because different students do not sit on the same seat:

$$\delta\left(s_1^S, .., s_N^S\right) \equiv \sum_{\substack{k,\, l\, =\, 1 \\ k\, \neq\, l}}^{N} \left\| s_k^S - s_l^S \right\|^2 > 0 \tag{7}$$

For finding seat locations of all the students with the faces in the image, we minimize the following function for $s_1^S, .., s_N^S$ together with o^P and R^P:

$$E_S\left(s_1^S, .., s_N^S; o^P, R^P\right) \equiv \sigma\left(s_1^S, .., s_N^S; o^P, R^P\right) - \delta\left(s_1^S, .., s_N^S\right) \tag{8}$$

2.4   Merging Results in Different Frames

In order to obtain the seat locations for all the students whose faces can be captured by the camera at any moment during the lecture, we need to merge the seat locations obtained for the images of all the frames. Since o^P could be different for the images of different frames, we need to shift the seat locations obtained for the faces detected in the images of different frames before overlapping them.

Among all the pair of faces detected respectively in the t-th frame and the $(t + 1)$-th frame, we first find the pairs recognized as the same face by face recognition using facial image processing. Then we overlap the seat locations obtained for those frames by shifting the seat locations obtained for the $(t + 1)$-th frame so that the same seat location is assigned to the pair of the faces that are given the best similarity by the face recognition. In this overlapping, other pairs of faces recognized as the same face may be given different seat location. Currently, we simply give higher priority to the seat location obtained in the latter frame, although we may need to employ more sophisticated conflict resolution strategy in near future.

3   Experimental Results

We evaluated our method described above using the camera images of the students in a seminar supervised by one of the authors in his university. We employed OKAO Vision of OMRON Corporation for facial image processing include face detection, eye extraction, facial orientation estimation and face recognition, OpenCV for the other image processing, and the Powell method [10] for minimizing functions E_P and E_S. The value of d is set as 63 mm based on the data of the standard human face.

Figure 2 are sample image frames of the camera at the moments when it observes the central area, the right side and the left side of the classroom. These images are captured by the same camera oriented in different directions from around the left corner in the front side of the classroom. The numbered squares in red and blue in each image are the faces detected in that frame and the other frames. Figure 3(a)–(c) are the results of estimating the seat locations of the students whose faces are extracted in Fig. 2. Figure 3(d) is the overall seat locations obtained by merging (a)–(c). This result is obtained by consecutively overlapping the partial seat locations of (c) after overlapping

(a) Facial regions extracted from an image of the central area of the classroom

(b) Facial regions extracted from an image of the right side of the classroom

(c) Facial regions extracted from an image of the left side of the classroom

Fig. 2. Sample results for extracting facial regions (represented by the numbered squares)

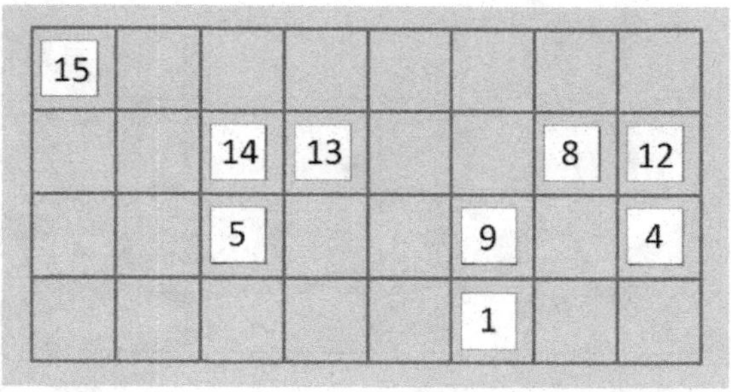

(a) Partial seat locations estimated for the facial regions in Fig.2 (a)

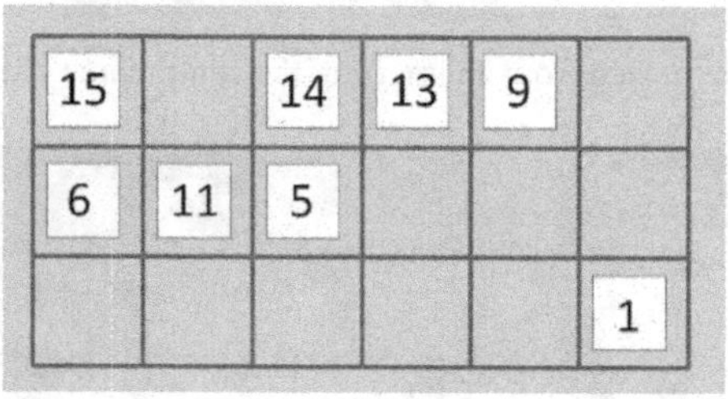

(b) Partial seat locations estimated for the facial regions in Fig.2 (b)

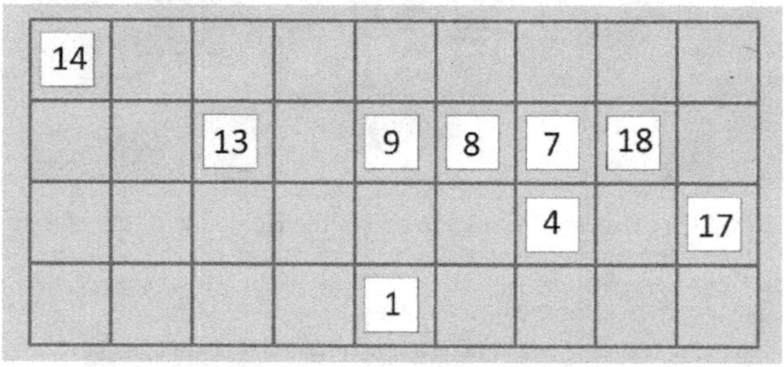

(c) Partial seat locations estimated for the facial regions in Fig.2 (c)

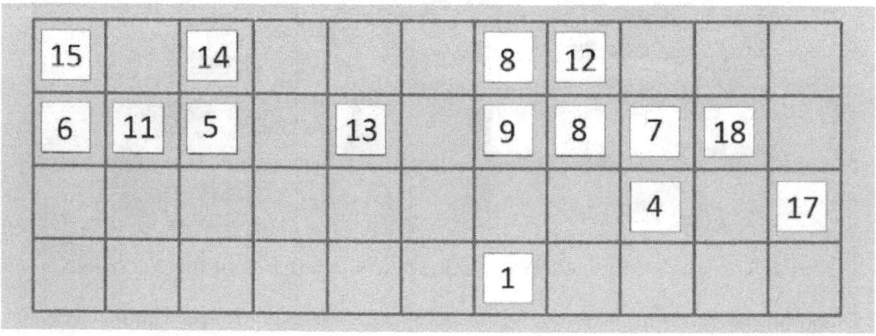

(d) Total seat locations after overlapping (a), (b) and (c), consecutively

Fig. 3. Resultant seat locations estimated for the facial regions in Fig. 2

the seat locations of (b) to (a). This result roughly reflects the actual positional relations among the seat locations of the students, although the rows and the columns for the seat locations of several students include errors within a single row and a column. These errors are mainly caused by the error in the process of recovering the 3D position of each students in the camera-centered coordinate system from their face detected in each image frame. As described in Sect. 2.1, this process employs the 3D orientation of the face together with the 2D positions of the eyes, which are obtained by facial image processing. However, the result of this facial image processing often includes some errors especially for small facial regions. We need to consider additional constraints to cope with this error in one of our future steps.

4   Conclusions

We proposed a method to estimate the position of each student in a classroom from the images of a camera observing the classroom, assuming that the camera is attached on the PC used for the lecture by the lecturer. First, the 3D position of each student in the camera-centered coordinate system is recovered from his/her face detected in the image using the 3D orientation of the face and the 2D positions of the eyes extracted from the detected face by facial image processing together with the knowledge of the intraocular distance of the standard human face as the clues for the recovery. Then the position and the orientation of the floor in the camera-centered coordinate system are estimated by fitting a plane to the recovered 3D positions of all the detected faces, because all the students are sitting on the seats on the same floor of the classroom. The 2D position of each student on the floor is obtained by projecting the recovered 3D position onto the estimated plane. Finally, the position and the orientation of the grid arrangement of the seats on the floor are estimated from the obtained 2D positions of all the students detected in the image. The seat location of each student is obtained by specifying the row and the column of the seat in the grid seat arrangement with the estimated position and orientation for his/her 2D position on the floor. Overall seat locations of all the students in the classroom are obtained by overlapping the local seat locations in the results for different image frames after finding the correspondence between the faces detected in those different frames based on face recognition.

We evaluated our method by the experiment using video images of a seminar. We confirmed from the result that our method can estimate rough positional relations among the seat locations of the students in the classroom, as far as their faces can be detected. However, the estimated seat locations include some errors in their rows and the columns in the grid arrangement of the seats, although the amount of errors is just within a single row and a column. Since these errors are caused by the error of facial image processing for estimating the 3D orientation of the detected face and the 2D position of the eyes by facial image processing, it is possible to assume that the faces detected in the image are oriented toward the camera. It is also useful to introduce additional geometric constraints to cope with this error. Possible constraints are the invariance of the seat location of the students and continuity of the position and orientation of the camera. These are the possible future steps of this work.

References

1. Minoh, M., Nishiguchi, S.: Environmental Media – In the Case of Lecture Archiving System –. In: Palade, V., Howlett, R.J., Jain, L. (eds.) KES 2003. LNCS, vol. 2774. Springer, Heidelberg (2003)
2. https://www.coursera.org/
3. https://www.edx.org/
4. Shimada, A., Suganuma, A., Taniguchi, R.: Automatic camera control system for a distant lecture based on estimation of teacher's behavior. In: IASTED International Conference on Computers and Advanced Technology in Education, pp. 106–111 (2004)
5. Onishi, M., Fukunaga, K.: Shooting the lecture scene using computer-controlled cameras based on situation understanding and evaluation of video images. In: International Conference on Pattern Recognition (ICPR), pp. 781–784 (2004)
6. Nishiguchi, S., Kameda, Y., Kakusho, K., Minoh, M.: Automatic video recording of lecture considering variety of motion and equability of scale for observing students. J. Adv. Comput. Intell. Intell. Inf. 8(2), 180–188 (2004)
7. Wulff, B., Rolf, R.: OpenTrack – Automated Camera Control for Lecture Recording. In: IEEE International Symposium on Multimedia (ISM), pp. 549–552 (2011)
8. Turaga, P.T., Chellappa, R., Subrahmanian, V.S., Udrea, O.: Machine recognition of human activities: a survey. IEEE Trans. Circ. Syst. Video Technol. 18(11), 1473–1488 (2008)
9. Aggarwal, J.K., Ryoo, M.S.: Human activity analysis: a review. ACM Comput. Surv. 43(3), 16 (2011)
10. Press, W.H., Teukolsky, S.A., Vetterling, W.T., Flannery, B.P.: Numerical Recipes, 3rd edn. Cambridge University Press, New York (2007)

Activity Context Integration in Mobile Computing Environments

Yoosoo Oh[(⊠)]

School of Computer and Communication Engineering, Daegu University,
Gyeongsan 712-714, Republic of Korea
yoosoo.oh@daegu.ac.kr

Abstract. In this paper, we propose an approach of activity context integration as a means of evaluating semantic information, by integrating situational information from heterogeneous sensors in a smartphone. The proposed activity context integration is a method to provide a foundation for interacting with situation-aware mobile computing systems. Moreover, we develop a context-aware embedded middleware that generates high-level integrated contexts through the fusion of internal • external sensors in a smartphone. The proposed system extracts semantic information such as the user's activities.

Keywords: Activity recognition · Context integration · Embedded middleware

1 Introduction

In mobile computing environments, there are growths on applications, which provide appropriate services to users by utilizing sensing data (physiological signal, profiles, and physical phenomena). Besides the existing manual service delivery, recent mobile applications provide a personalized service and selective information to users. In particular, a smartphone embeds various sensors such as acceleration, gyroscope, GPS, microphone, proximity, illuminance, NFC. Since a user always has a smartphone, the smartphone is a useful device that recognizes the user's location as well as the moving speed, direction and basic behavior.

In order to provide personalized services to mobile users, it is necessary to interpret the users' activities. Various types of sensors, which are embedded in smartphones, are an important factor as the input information to identify the user's activities. Activity recognition provides personalized services to a user by fusing and reasoning information gathered from the sensors. A context-aware technique, which makes a decision for current situation with a user's activity, can provide appropriate services to the user. The context-aware technique describes meaningful contexts about given situation and then integrates the contexts. Especially, an embedded middleware, which recognizes a user's activity in mobile computing environments, has high industrial impact as a mobile app, connected cars, smart home, simulation, education, and games.

This research was supported by Basic Science Research Program through the National Re-search Foundation of Korea(NRF) funded by the Ministry of Education(NRF-2014R1A1A2056194)

© Springer International Publishing Switzerland 2015
N. Streitz and P. Markopoulos (Eds.): DAPI 2015, LNCS 9189, pp. 527–535, 2015.
DOI: 10.1007/978-3-319-20804-6_48

As spreading the concept of ubiquitous computing, activity recognition research is being actively investigated in many interdisciplinary fields [1]. In human-computer interaction field, technologies for an intelligent system have been studied. The technologies include indirect information (for example, user's gender, age, location, etc.) as well as a direct input of a user [2]. Especially, applications using context information in mobile computing environments have been received lots of attention. The developed context-aware services exploit the information obtained from various sensors in mobile devices. For example, there are a mobile tour guide services which recommend appropriate paths to users according to users' location and orientation information, and a mobile augmented reality service which augments appropriate contents on objects of interest by using acceleration, orientation, and other sensor information.

It is difficult to clearly identify a user's activity or intentions, because the existing activity recognition research for mobile application systems integrates a wide variety of sensing information in a single way. Also, the existing decision-making technologies have been developed for the special purpose in a given domain such as smart home, smart office, and smart building. Furthermore, there is no consideration for a generalized algorithm to infer the high level decision by collecting a large number of data (context) obtained from various sensors [3–14]. And to conclude, it is not enough for the decision-making approach to fuse the different types of contexts obtained from different sensors in order to extract the semantics exactly. Thus, we need to design a middleware that adaptively integrates various contexts and makes user's activities according to each user's environment.

In order to deduce the high-level semantic information from internal • external sensors in a smartphone, an embedded middleware should classify inputted data according to each characteristic and integrate them. For the operation of the embedded middleware, the generalized architecture of a context-aware embedded middleware should be developed in mobile computing environments. Therefore, we propose a context-aware embedded middleware that infers a user's activity according to a given context by adopting a user-centric context integration technique. The proposed middleware recognizes the user's activity by integrating the sensing information from internal and external sensors of the smartphone in real time.

2   Activity Recognition and Context Awareness

In this paper, we define a systematic approach, which is listed by key technologies and effectively links with them to develop context fusion, activity detection, and reasoning. By utilizing recently released smartphones, we design and implement an algorithm that recognizes, fuses, and reasons about activity contexts obtained from mobile and environmental sensors in a mobile computing environment. In addition, we make a lightweight version of context fusion, activity detection, and reasoning module to effectively use limited resources in a mobile computing environment.

Context fusion, activity detection, and reasoning are key properties of the context integration process. Context fusion is processed by specific fusion methods, activity detection takes contexts as well as user activities into account and reasoning is done by rule-based or statistical reasoning methods. The activity context integration comprises the process of the analysis, fusion, and reasoning. Our ultimate goal is to design and develop an approach of context fusion, activity detection, and reasoning to interact with situation-aware mobile computing systems. The proposed middleware consists of activity context integration and context reasoning. Activity context integration entails classifying and integrating inputted contexts according to each user in smart environments.

Many of the existing research activities have been mainly addressed context- and activity-awareness in their desktop environments [5–9]. In order to obtain high-level semantic information in real-time on mobile devices, however, a context-aware middleware, which collects and integrates various contexts is required. In particular, it is important to develop architecture for activity context integration that enables a decision to be made based on context data from large numbers of heterogeneous sensors (e.g., mobile & environmental sensors). In addition, to produce meaningful information in a smartphone, activity context integration should be done according to the characteristics of the activity context. Therefore, in this paper we propose a context-aware embedded middleware that generates high-level integrated contexts through the fusion of internal • external sensors in a smartphone. The proposed system extracts semantic information such as the user's attention, orientation, activities, the object of interest and the surrounding environment by fusing and reasoning about various contexts obtained from heterogeneous sensors in a mobile computing environment. As available sensors in a mobile computing environment, there are internal sensors (e.g., accelerometer, gyroscope, ambient light sensor, digital compass, internal GPS, and internal Wi-Fi) and external sensors (e.g., input device, external light sensor, temperature sensor, and noise sensor). The proposed middleware generates a reliable integrated context through sensor fusion in smartphones by filtering unnecessary context information. In addition, the proposed middleware creates a robust integrated context according to the characteristics of information obtained from internal or external sensors of the smartphone.

3 Activity Context Integration

3.1 Activity Recognition Approach

The proposed middleware is operated as shown in Fig. 1. First, the proposed middleware extracts features like sinusoidal peak from raw data from smartphone internal sensors and external sensors by using signal processing and feature extraction. Next it operates an application by creating appropriate activities after activity context integration based on the 5W1H contexts.

Table 1 describes the analysis of possible algorithms for context fusion and reasoning. A user activity, which can be obtained by applying the algorithm, is related to the basic daily behavior. The user activity comprises a primary activity for a simple action, and a secondary activity which can be determined by reinforcing the primary activity and surroundings information. For example, the primary activity is walking, running, sitting, hiking, jogging, and stair climbing up/down, and the second activity is to cook, to eat, to move hand, watching TV, and talk to. The following Fig. 2 represents a structure of the context-aware embedded middleware. The proposed middleware classifies the 5W1H (Who, What, Where, When, Why, and How) context of various sensors according to each user. The middleware recognizes user activities by applying

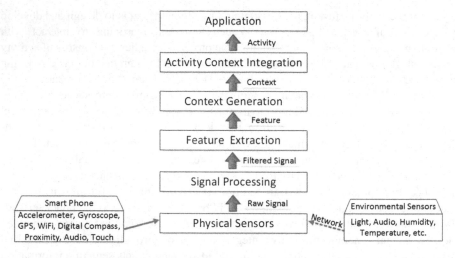

Fig. 1. Process of activity context integration

reasoning algorithms for the characteristics of six elements of the 5W1H context. The process of activity recognition makes a proper decision by utilizing learned information in knowledge base.

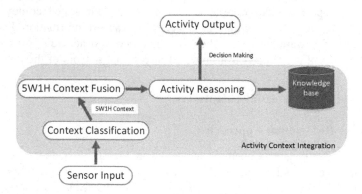

Fig. 2. Structure of the context-aware embedded middleware

3.2 Activity Recognition Implementation

The proposed middleware supports a recognition algorithm that integrates a user's location, interaction, and internal/external sensors in a smartphone. For the temporal consistency, we applied the HMM (Hidden Markov Model) in the activity recognition process. The activity recognition process based on HMM is as a following 4 steps. At an initial step, our hypothesis is that a user is using a smartphone. Figure 3 illustrates the process of usages of various sensors inside the smartphone. Our middleware operates to validate the user's activity by utilizing the above sensors, as shown in Fig. 1.

Table 1. Analysis of reasoning algorithms

Item	Algorithm	Description
Feature selection/extraction	Principal Component Analysis (PCA)	• to reduce dimensionality • to discard some of the original features • to map the original features into a lower dimensional subspace
	Independent Component Analysis (ICA)	
Stochastic static classifiers	Naive Bayes	
	Decision tree	
	k-nearest neighbor (k-NN)	
	Support Vector Machine (SVM)	
Temporal classifiers	Hidden Markov Model (HMM)	• a temporal probabilistic model • to model user interactions • to recognize multi-user activities • the inference of hidden states(activity labels) given the observations • stochastic process using temporal information • infer stable states from a sequential and noisy observation stream (e.g., eye-gaze without noise)
	Dynamic Bayesian Network (DBN)	
	Conditional Random Field (CRF)	
	Coupled Hidden Markov Model (CHMM)	
Sequence of activities	Quantitative temporal Bayesian networks	• recognition of hierarchical events where each level has a different temporal granularity (e.g., activity recognition using eye-gaze movements)
	Propagation networks	
	Aggregate dynamic Bayesian models	
	Abstract Hidden Markov Model (AHMM)	

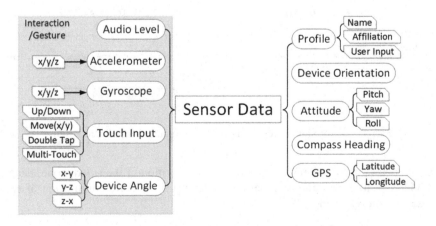

Fig. 3. Used sensory data in a smartphone

- Initial Step: Since an audio sensor for measuring the ambient noise is difficult to process the input values, we apply a FFT (Fast Fourier Transform) to convert the magnitude in dB level (as shown in Fig. 4). We correct an acceleration sensor, a gyroscope sensor, and device motion (smartphone's motion) by applying a Lowpass filter because the sensors are sensitive to changes of their input values. Figure 4 shows the result of experiments by explicitly changing values of the x-axis (y-axis and z-axis are fixed).

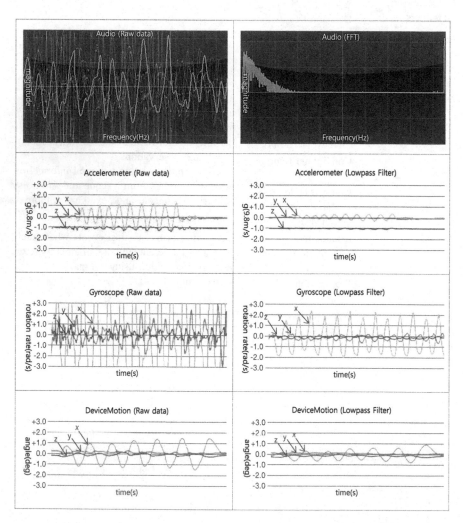

Fig. 4. Sensor signal processing (left: raw input, right: filtered output)

- Step 1: Next, we compensate the posture and position of the smartphone using the device orientation, digital compass, user input for the correct utilization of sensor data. (as shown in Fig. 5)

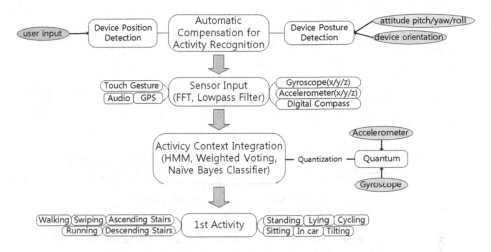

Fig. 5. Implemented activity context integration method

- Step 2: As shown in Fig. 5, we develop the quantization procedure for switching a continuous value to a discrete value in order to solve a frequent change of the gyroscope and acceleration data, and apply them to the HMM. The acceleration sensor has an advantage to recognize the user's action with minimizing the loss of data, because it can detect the change and vibration or impact of the speed per unit time. In particular, if we utilize a gyroscope with an accelerometer we can easily determine the user's activity by using six-axis information. If the shock caused by the user's motion is transmitted to the smartphone, we can extract a specific pattern of the acceleration and gyroscope data. We then make the inference of 1st activity (standing, sitting, walking, and running) by using the state transition of the HMM. Figure 6 represents the state transition diagram of the HMM. An initial state of the state transition diagram begins with the Standing state, which is the most frequent activity in probability distribution.

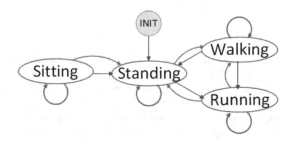

Fig. 6. State transition diagram

- Step 3: In next step, we reason out the 2nd activity by using the user's location information, user input information, and the 1st activity inference result. The reasoning method is to apply both rule based reasoning and Naïve Bayes classifier, as shown in Fig. 7.

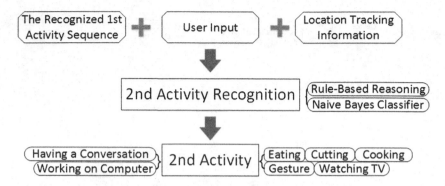

Fig. 7. The secondary activity recognition process

- Step 4: Finally, we develop an embedded middleware application that recognizes the user's activity in mobile computing environments.

4   Conclusion

In this paper we proposed an approach of activity context integration as a means of evaluating semantic information, by integrating situational information from heterogeneous sensors in a smartphone. The proposed activity context integration is a method to provide a foundation for interacting with situation-aware mobile computing systems. The proposed approach evaluates, assesses, adopts and extends multiple fusion methods to find solution for robust activity context integration. It incorporates real-time fusion of contexts, which are obtained from multiple sensors, and facilitates real-time maintenance by information fusion for online dynamic changes of sensors in mobile computing environments.

References

1. Mitchell, K.: A survey of context-awareness. Internal Technical report, Lancaster University, Computing Department (2002)
2. Schmidt, A., Laerhoven, K.V.: How to build smart appliances. IEEE Pers. Commun. Spec. Issue Pervasive Comput. **8**(4), 66–71 (2001)
3. Guanling, C., Ming, L., David, K.: Design and implementation of a large-scale context fusion network. In: Proceedings of the First Annual International Conference on Mobile and Ubiquitous Systems: Networking and Services MobiQuitous 2004, Boston, Massachusetts, pp. 246–255 (August, 2004)
4. Thomas, B., Michael, K., Claudia, L.-P., Michael, S.: CoCo: dynamic composition of context information. In: Proceedings of the First Annual International Conference on Mobile and Ubiquitous Systems: Networking and Services MobiQuitous 2004, Boston, Massachusetts, pp. 335–343 (August, 2004)

5. Karen, H., Jadwiga, I.: A software engineering framework for context-aware pervasive computing. In: Proceedings of the Second IEEE international Conference on Pervasive Computing and Communications Percom 2004, Orlando, Florida, pp. 77–86 (March, 2004)
6. Norman, C., Apratim, P., Luke, W., Danny, Y.: iQueue: a pervasive data composition framework. In: Proceedings of Third International Conference on Mobile Data Management, Singapore, pp. 146–153 (January, 2002)
7. Norman, C., Hui, L., Paul, C., John, D., Apratim, P.: Composing pervasive data using iQL. In: Proceedings of Fourth IEEE Workshop on Mobile Computing Systems and Applications, Callicoon, New York, pp. 94–104 (June, 2002)
8. Huadong, W.: Sensor data fusion for context-aware computing using Dempster-Shafer theory. Carnegie Mellon University Doctoral thesis, UMI Order Number: AAI3126933 (2004)
9. Daniel, S., Anind, D., Gregory, A.: The context toolkit: aiding the development of context-aware applications. In: Proceedings of the ACM Conference on Human Factors and Computing Systems (CHI 1999), Pittsburgh, USA, pp. 434–441 (May, 1999)
10. Jan, B., Karin, C.: Towards integrated design of context-sensitive interactive systems. In: Proceedings of the 3rd IEEE International Conference on Pervasive Computing and Communications Workshops (PerCom Workshops 2005), Hawaii, USA, pp. 30–34 (March, 2005)
11. Oh, Y., Han, J., Woo, W.: A context management architecture for large-scale smart environments. IEEE Commun. Mag. **48**, 118–126 (2010)
12. Siljee, J., Vintges, S., Nijhuis, J.: A context architecture for service-centric systems. In: Strang, T., Linnhoff-Popien, C. (eds.) LoCA 2005. LNCS, vol. 3479, pp. 16–25. Springer, Heidelberg (2005)
13. Gregory, B., Vinny, C.: A framework for developing mobile, context-aware applications. In: Proceedings of the Second IEEE International Conference on Pervasive Computing and Communications (PerCom 2004), Orlando, Florida, pp. 361–365 (March, 2004)
14. Bardram, J.E.: The Java Context Awareness Framework (JCAF)–a service infrastructure and programming framework for context-aware applications. In: Gellersen, H.-W., Want, R., Schmidt, A. (eds.) PERVASIVE 2005. LNCS, vol. 3468, pp. 98–115. Springer, Heidelberg (2005)

BearWatcher: Animal Motion Estimation Application for Tourism and Welfare

Keni Ren[1]([⊠]), Jani Hourunranta[2], Joni Tolonen[2], and Johannes Karlsson[1]

[1] Embedded Systems Laboratory, Umeå University, 90187, Umeå, Sweden
{keni.ren,johannes.karlsson}@umu.se
[2] Centria Reseach and Development, Vierimaantie 7, 84100 Ylivieska, Finland
{jani.hourunranta,joni.tolonen}@centria.fi

Abstract. This paper purposes an application based on video supervision systems in the zoo for human animal computer interaction. BearWatcher system covers the entire process from collecting animal's visual data, analyzing their movement and behavior, and presenting them to user interface for tourism and animal welfare. With the interaction between the users and animal movement information, the system gives the tourist more digital, more available, more involved experience. In the meanwhile, zoo keepers get reliable, accurate, cost-effective way to take care of animals.

Keywords: Animal sensor networks · Computer vision · Motion tracking · Interaction

1 Introduction

The video supervision system represents a new paradigm for reliable surrounding information collection. The applications widely covered from agriculture [1, 2] to monitoring wild animal movement and distribution [3, 4]. Nowadays, the video supervision systems are widely deployed in modern zoos. These supervision systems provide animal's raw video streams for attracting online visitors. In this paper, we introduce a system which can estimate animal's movement and evaluate their behavior for digital zoo visitors and local zoo keepers. In BearWatcher system, zoo's visitors can get more meaningful message with the animals' activity and set up friend-to-friend connection between each other. Meanwhile, we explore the possibility of analyzing animal's behavior and their surroundings to significantly assist zoology.

The BearWatcher concept is based on the Animal Sensor Networks project [5] that uses wireless sensor networks to capture information about the animals and their surroundings. The project is part of the Botnia-Atlantica cross-border cooperation program including Sweden, Finland, and Norway.

The BearWatcher application is implemented for zoology and tourism in Lycksele Zoo in Sweden and Predator Center in Kuusamo, Finland. The Predator Center, which is located in north east of Finland near the town of Kuusamo, is best known for all their bears. Tourism, arranging photo shoots of the animals for

© Springer International Publishing Switzerland 2015
N. Streitz and P. Markopoulos (Eds.): DAPI 2015, LNCS 9189, pp. 536–546, 2015.
DOI: 10.1007/978-3-319-20804-6_49

TV programs and animal photographers are its main attractions. The Lycksele Zoo in Sweden, which is one of the biggest attractions in northern Sweden, has been test bed of Animal Sensor Networks and Digital Djurpark projects [6]. The BearWatcher system has been running successfully in bear area of Lycksele Zoo for 1 year.

2 System Architecture

Figure 1 shows the overview of the system architecture. Thanks to the employment of sensor networks, rich content information about the animals and their surroundings, such as video, picture, sound, and temperature are captured. Computer vision system manages, analyses and extracts information from sensors. To present the semantic information, BearWatcher website and smartphone applications are designed. The feedback conveys to animals through the welfare.

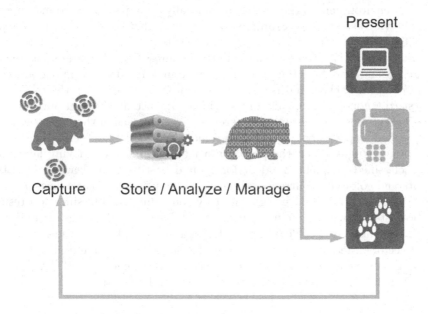

Fig. 1. Overview of the system architecture

2.1 Sensor Networks Setup

The deployment in the Lycksele Zoo consists of 18 video transmitting nodes distributed over the whole zoo. The sensors connect themselves in a wireless ad-hoc network. In the bear area, we set up temperature sensor, three pan-tilt-zoom cameras for outdoor, and two cameras including one IR camera for bear den where bear hibernates and gives birth to cubs during winter. Various data as video, picture, sound, and temperature provide rich content information about the animals and their surroundings.

2.2   Computer Vision System

In the computer vision system, the major efforts are focused on providing the effective information of interest from the sensor's raw data. In this case, capturing the bear's activity is essential to understand bear's behavior. To achieve this task, four steps are carried out:

- Background/foreground estimation: Separate the foreground from the background.
- Motion detection: Detect the motion of the animals.
- Motion score: Evaluate the motion. The motion data combining time and position information are prepared for estimating animal's behavior.
- Store and manage activity data: Generate daily/weekly/monthly activity report, and automatically publish images with high activity.

In the real environment of the zoo, there is usually a complex background appearing in the video stream, for example a background that contains shadows, moving objects, or illumination changing. In the bear den, the light condition is poor, and ventilation systems cause noisy pictures. To solve these challenges, the background and foreground estimation from a real-time video steam containing complex background is designed based on Bayes decision theory [7].

First, the non-change pixels in the video sequence are filtered out by using simple background and temporal differences. The changes in the video sequence are separated as pixels belonging to stationary and moving objects according to inter-frame changes. Then the pixels associated with still or moving labels are further classified as background or foreground based on the learned statistics of colors and color co-occurrences respectively by using the Bayes decision rule. Then foreground objects are segmented by combining the classification results from both stationary and moving parts. At last, background models are updated. Both gradual and Once-off learning strategies are utilized to learn the statistics of feature vectors. Meanwhile, a reference background image is maintained to make the background difference accurate and adaptive to the background changing [8]. Figure 2 shows the result of background/foreground estimation.

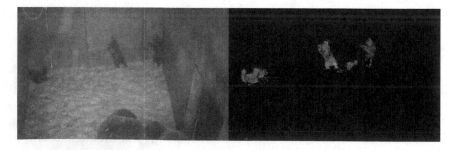

Fig. 2. Result of background/foreground estimation

The purpose of using motion detection is to find the video which contains animal activity. Motion detection works by comparing the intensity of pixels between new video sequence image and reference image. The connected component analysis uses the foreground pixels result to detect the close moving object. The motion score is calculated as the size of moving object to the scene. To reduce the noise, the moving object should be continuous moving for 10 frames.

By setting the threshold of the motion score, the system will record the bear's high activity data, and plot them into statistical graphics in web application. In the meantime, the pictures with large movement will be saved and pushed to the web application. Figure 3 shows bears' activity for the whole day in the bear den.

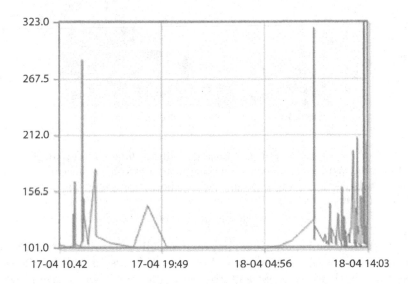

Fig. 3. 28 h bear activity in the bear den

In traditional zoo management way, when bears hibernate, they will sleep in their cave for the whole winter without disturbance, which means the zoo keepers will not know when the bear gives birth to cubs, neither how many kids she has until the next spring. By analyzing the long-term activity data, bear's behavior can be predicted. During winter 2013/2014, BearWatcher recorded the activity data during bear hibernation and giving birth to cubs. Figure 4 shows bear activity changes during this period. From the 1 month activity data we can see the week before labor, bear mother started to move double amount than normal hebetation days during sleep. The activity kept increasing. Bear started to wake up and walked inside the cave more and more. While the motion scores of the labor day (marked as red) is 5 times more than the score from normal hibernation days. With BearWatcher monitoring the animal's movement, zoo keeper can get reliable, accurate help to predict and understand animal's behavior.

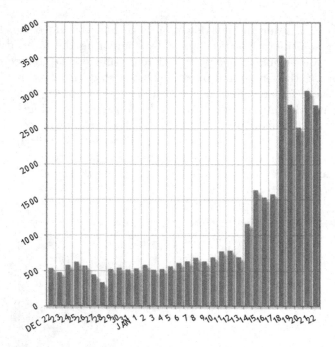

Fig. 4. 30 days bear's activity in the bear den during hibernation and giving birth period. Labor day's data is marked as red. Bear mother started to move double amount than normal hebetation days from 4 days before labor, on the labor day is 5 times more than normal (Color figure online).

Motion estimation is performed for automatically capturing the bear's activity from all cameras. Activity data will be recorded. System will automatically push pictures with large movement to web application, which means visitors can receive the zoo's fun moments, instead of sleepy animals. In the meantime, bear's activity data will be stored and managed as activity daily/weekly/monthly report and presented to zoo keepers.

2.3   Interaction Design for BearWatcher

In traditional zoos, information flow from animal to visitors is passive. Based on the sensor networks setup and computer vision system analyzed bears' activity data, BearWatcher is designed that give the users a more interactive visiting experience. Three components are concerned by BearWatcher to enhance the interactive experience: Information Component, Web Application Component, Interactor Component. These components take charge of their own function, give different outputs. In the meantime, they relate to each other, use each other's output as input, update and communicate with each other. Figure 5 shows the relationship of three components:

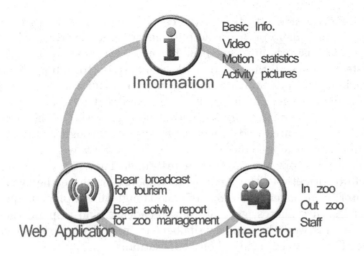

Fig. 5. 3 interactive components in BearWatcher

- Information Component contains basic information which shows the knowledge and events of the zoo: maps, directions, animal's fact, etc. Sensor networks capture live stream and their surrounding features. Activity report and bear's photos with high activity are pushed by computer vision system. The design of this component focuses on meaningful context used to present to the Interactor Component. The information will be automatically updated, and always in the background making Interactors, if only subconsciously, aware of the state of on-going processes.
- Interactor Component refers all the people, both visitors and zoo keepers, involved as active users of the information. They make interaction through the Web Application Component with both animals and other people; we give them a new name, Interactors [9].
- Web Application Component concerns how to present the Information Component to the Interactor Component. BearWatcher developed two web applications: bear broadcast for tourism and bear activity report for zoo management. They both use website and smartphone application as interface.

Bear Broadcast for Tourism. In the traditional zoo visiting experience, information flow is passive. Visitors walk around the zoo, look at animals, and in some zoos they can pet animals. Every so often, animals are sleeping in the cave, or hiding in the bush. By estimating activity and motion of the animals in the digital zoo, BearWatcher enhances the visiting experience with information containing richer content. The purpose of this application is to provide visitor, as Interactor, more opportunities to get direct way following the animals and get to know animals a little better in personal way.

In the BearWatcher website, visitors can select different live streams of the bears; browse the gallery of bear's activity images. Moreover, to help the bears involving in the visitor's life, social media such as Twitter is used. Computer Vision System pushes all the photos with high activity to web application. The photos combine the position information and time information can generate the meaningful message. For instance, high activity at feeding place around 5 p.m. indicates bears are eating. A Twitter message says "Dinner time!" with a photo will be generated and broadcast by system through phone application and Twitter. The message communicates as the same way as friend to friend in real life, the visitors are engaged in real-time. They can comment directly on the website or retweet the message to response or share the event. As the administrator in management, zoo staff can manage all the photos, upload some extra behind scenes photos, generate new broadcast, and respond the visitor's comments. In this way, the two-way dialogue is created. Figure 6 is the activity function for Bear watcher smartphone application.

Fig. 6. Activity function for BearWatcher smartphone application

With the help of bear broadcast application, the zoos can keep connection with their visitors even after their attendees leave. A broadcast with a series of bear's activity posts, can surface their story to engage their global audiences. One of the usage scenarios was when the Lycksele zoo got the news of baby bears will be born at the zoo in the winter. Bear Mama's expecting cubs photo started the story, followed with she was walking around the cave which means babies were on their way, to the first look of the small cubs gathered together without clear number of the babies, until finally clear photos of three cubs.

In this way, the relationship between the visitors and bears is more interactive. System gives the visitors of the zoo a more digital, more available, more attractive experience.

Bear Activity Report for Zoo Management. In most traditional zoos, zoo keepers need to write welfare diary about the animal's behavior such as feeding, sleeping and abnormal behaviors for every animal that he, or she, takes care of everyday. The content of the welfare diary is based on the observations and staff's experience. Bear activity report application for zoo management aiming for helping with zoo keepers develop a more efficient, more accurate and easier way to take care of animals.

In this application, interaction design focuses on how to present the information organized, and easy to handle by the Interactor, which means something that is easy and appealing to use by non-technical users. BearWatcher present all the information to zoo's staff by using the same web application system just with log-in function. After log-in as zoo keeper account, the administration organized into three catalogues: Activity report, Tweet and Control Room. In Activity Report page, by selecting different cameras, detail of daily/weekly/monthly individual animal's activity line chart is shown; zoo keepers can directly export the graph to their welfare diary. In Tweet page, an easy to use Tweet function is designed for generate quick Twitter message. Bear's photos during the whole day with high activity are list on the right side of the page, user can select the fun picture from them, drag and drop to the Tweet box, send it with short description. User can edit Twitter Messages that generated automatically by computer vision system. Control Room page lists recent posts, latest 24 h activity chart, recent comments from visitors, and recent activity photos. Figure 7 shows the control page for the zoo staff. Figure 8 is the twitter update page.

3   Discussion

BearWatcher is a system sensing animal's movement, analyzing their activity, and present them to website and smartphone application. The purpose of the system is using computer vision and media technology to improve interactive experience of the zoo and help animal's welfare. From a marketing aspect, modern zoo representatives increase in value of having contact with their visitors [10]. This shows that modern zoos combining local zoo physical environment, live streaming digital world, animal welfare information, and social media interaction can create tourist attractions. In the meantime, using digital world's record to analyze and help physical animal's welfare can generate more accurate and cost-effective method to take care of the animals.

The whole system is created to enhance user experience. The system is designed to meet the user experience hierarchy of needs: functional, reliable, usable, convenient, pleasurable and meaningful [11]. The sensor networks and

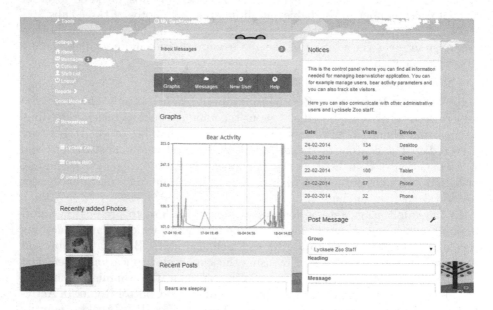

Fig. 7. Control page for the zoo staff.

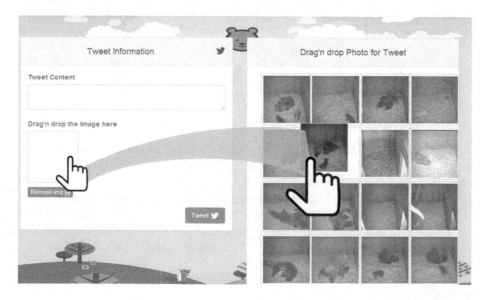

Fig. 8. Twitter update page using easy drag and drop function

computer vision system provide the basic functional and reliable result, which have been running successfully in bear area of Lycksele Zoo for 1 year. The challenge of the system in the future work focuses on truly creating a convenient and meaningful product. In the further work, the system needs more participants for the user experience evaluations.

4 Conclusion

In this paper, we introduce an application based on animal motion estimation in the zoo. BearWatcher is a system sensing animal's movement, analyzing their activity, and presenting them to website and smartphone applications. With the interactive experience design, the system bridges the gap between digital zoo and their visitors. The system gives the zoo visitors more active, more involved experience. Meanwhile it provides more accurate and cost-effective welfare conveys to animals.

References

1. Wark, T., Corke, P., Sikka, P., Klingbeil, L., Guo, Y., Crossman, C., Valencia, P., Swain, D., Bishop-Hurley, G.: Transforming agriculture through pervasive wireless sensor networks. In: IEEE Pervasive Computing, vol. 6, no. 2, pp. 50 57, April 2007
2. Handcock, R.N., Swain, D.L., Bishop-Hurley, G.J., Patison, K.P., Wark, T., Valencia, P., Corke, P., ONeill, C.J.: Monitoring animal behaviour and environmental interactions using wireless sensor networks, GPS collars and satellite remote sensing. Sensors 9(5), 3586–3603 (2009)
3. Kays, R., Kranstauber, B., Jansen, P., Carbone, C., Rowcliffe, M., Fountain, T., Tilak, S.: Camera traps as sensor networks for monitoring animal communities. In: IEEE 34th Conference on Local Computer Networks, LCN 2009, pp. 811–818, 20–23, Oct 2009
4. Juang, P., Oki, H., Wang, Y., Martonosi, M., Peh, L.S., Rubenstein, D.: Energy-efficient computing for wildlife tracking: design tradeoffs and early experiences with ZebraNet. SIGPLAN Not. 37(10), 96–107 (2002)
5. Mohamad, Y., Mustafa, I.H., Eilertsen, S.: Animal sensor networks: animal welfare under arctic conditions. In: Seventh International Conference on Sensor Technologies and Applications, Barcelona, Spain, pp. 231–235, August 2013
6. Karlsson, J.: Wireless video sensor network and its applications in Digital Zoo 1652–6295, 13 (2010)
7. Li, L., Huang, W., Gu, I.Y.H., Tian, Q.: Foreground object detection from videos containing complex background. In: The Eleventh ACM International Conference on Multimedia (MULTIMEDIA 2003), pp. 2–10. ACM, New York (2003)
8. Karlsson, J., Ren, K., Li, H.: Tracking and identification of animals for a digital zoo. In: 2010 IEEE/ACM International Conference on Green Computing and Communications International Conference on Cyber, Physical and Social Computing, pp. 510–515. IEEE Computer Society (2010)

9. Karlsson, J., Wark, T., Ren, K., Fahlquist, K., Li, H.: Applications for wireless visual sensor networks. In: Visual Information Processing in Wireless Sensor Networks: Technology, Trends and Applications, IGI Global, Chap. 15, p. 325–339 (2012)
10. Fahlquist, K.: Creating New Experience for Zoo Visitors by Using Media Techniques. Licentiate thesis, Ume: Department of Applied Physics and Electronics, Ume University, 78 p. (2014)
11. Anderson, S.P.: Seductive Interaction Design: Creating Playful, Fun, and Effective user Experiences. Pearson Education, Harlow (2011)

Children Tracking System in Indoor and Outdoor Places

Mounira Taileb[✉], Wejdan Wajdi, Hind Hamdi, Galia Al-Garni,
Sarah Al-Shehri, and Manal Al-Marwani

Faculty of Computing and Information Technology, Information Technology
Department, King Abdulaziz University, P.O Box 42808, Jeddah 21551,
Saudi Arabia
mtaileb@kau.edu.sa

Abstract. The issue of loss or kidnapping children has become unfortunately a widespread phenomenon in many countries. To address this issue, this paper presents a children tracking system. It consists of a small device carried by the child and a mobile application that enables the user to track his child movements by tracking that device. That will be done by using GPS and Bluetooth 4.0 technology to track children in indoor and outdoor locations. For indoor, the application searches for the child by detecting the beacon device using Bluetooth 4.0. And for the outdoor locations, the application uses the GPS/GPRS chip.

Keywords: GPS/GPRS · Bluetooth 4.0 · Beacon

1 Introduction

The issue of missing children in the markets, malls and public places has become a real concern and a major threat to children and their families. Statistics about missing children are shocking. Approximately 100,000 children in Germany, 41,000 children in Canada, and 20,000 children in Spain and Australia are reported missing each year. Also 800,000 children go missing each year in the United States [1]. In India, a child goes missing every eight minutes, 40 % of those children have not been found [2]. Unfortunately, there is a lack of information about the missing children in Saudi Arabia and in the Gulf countries in general, but according to the articles published about this issue, many families have suffered from losing a child and some of them have lost a child for a short duration because he walks away his family and doesn't know his family name, his home address or his neighborhood which delay their return to their families.

To address this issue, this paper presents a children tracking system. It consists of a small device carried by the child and a mobile application that enables the user to track his child movements by tracking that device. That will be done by using GPS and Bluetooth 4.0 technology for tracking the child in indoor and outdoor locations.

© Springer International Publishing Switzerland 2015
N. Streitz and P. Markopoulos (Eds.): DAPI 2015, LNCS 9189, pp. 547–553, 2015.
DOI: 10.1007/978-3-319-20804-6_50

For indoor, the application searches for the child by detecting the beacon device using Bluetooth 4.0. And for the outdoor locations, the application uses the GPS/GPRS chip.

The rest of the paper is organized as follows. In Sect. 2, a brief overview of related work is given, followed by the description of the proposed system in Sect. 3. In Sect. 4, results of the usability testing and system testing are discussed. Finally, the Sect. 5 concludes the paper.

2 Related Work

Many systems have been proposed to track and locate children; in some of them researchers use the Global Positioning System (GPS) to locate a child in outdoor places [3–7]. However, GPS and even cell phones are not useful in indoor places. The accuracy of cell phone positioning technology is not sufficient and GPS systems cannot penetrate building and other obstacles. Other systems use alternative technologies for indoor places, such as Bluetooth [8, 9] and RFID [10]. There are many commercial devices used by parents to track and locate their children such as Amber Alert GPS [11], Pocket finder [12], Spark Nano GPS Tracker [13] and iTrail [14].

The proposed and commercialized systems consist of tracking the child's cell phone or tracking the chip carried by the child to locate him. However they are insufficient because they don't support commonly the indoor and outdoor tracking. Furthermore, the size of the tracking device for others systems is not suitable for the child. Also these systems are expensive and not all of them support the Arabic language.

3 System Methodology and Design

The proposed children tracking system consists of developing a mobile application that enables users to track their children movements in indoor and outdoor locations. The child holds a small device and the applications tracks that device. That will be done by using GPS and Bluetooth 4.0 technology for tracking the child in indoor and outdoor locations.

For indoor, the application searches for the child by detecting the beacon device using Bluetooth 4.0. Beacons are small wireless devices that transmit small amount of data to other beacons or smart phones by using Bluetooth 4.0 technology. They consume a little amount of energy, can transmit up to 2.4 GHz Bluetooth signals and serve up to 300 feet space. If the child is found, the distance between the child device and the parent's phone will be displayed on the phone screen. And if the location of the child was not found in the range of Bluetooth 4.0, the application searches the child using GPS/GSM chip. GPS/GSM chip sends an SMS message to the parent's phone containing child location on Google map, and that what we are using for the outdoor locations. Internet connection is not required for all of the services. The architecture of the proposed system is illustrated in Fig. 1.

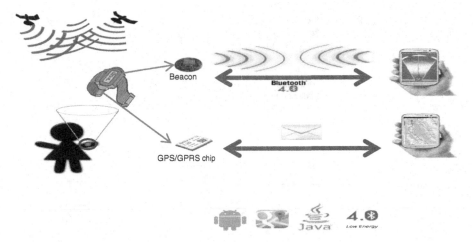

Fig. 1. System architecture

Step 1: Search for the child by detecting the beacon device using Bluetooth 4.0. If the child is found, the distance between the device carried by the child and the parent's phone will be displayed.

Step 2: If the location of the child was not found in the range of Bluetooth 4.0, the application searches for the child using the GPS/GSM chip, the chip sends an SMS to the parent's phone containing the child location on Google map.

3.1   Flow Chart Diagram

The flow chart diagram, presented in Fig. 2, shows the logical representation of the find function in child tracking system. It starts by searching for a selected device using Bluetooth. After selecting the device, the search starts using Bluetooth first, if the device is found within the Bluetooth range, the location is displayed. Otherwise, if the device is not found, it means that it is out of the Bluetooth range, so the GPS is used in the search process.

3.2   Graphical User Interfaces

When the user runs the application, he can search for his child or one of his children by clicking on the child's profile in the list, as shown in Fig. 3. After clicking on a child's profile, the child's indoor location will be displayed, as illustrated in Fig. 4(a). If the child is out of the range, the user has to click on GPS button, and another GUI is displayed with the child's location on Google map, as shown in Fig. 4(b).

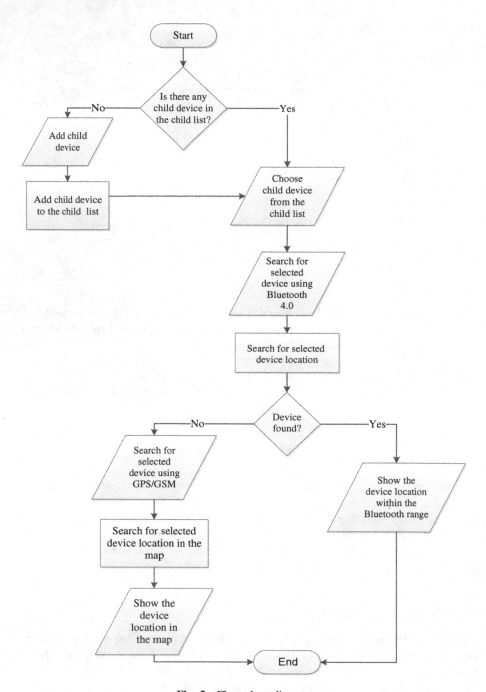

Fig. 2. Flow chart diagram

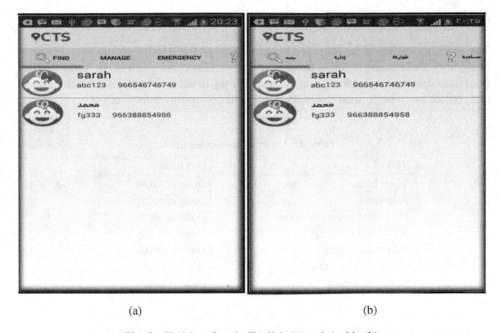

(a)   (b)

Fig. 3. Find interface in English (a) and Arabic (b)

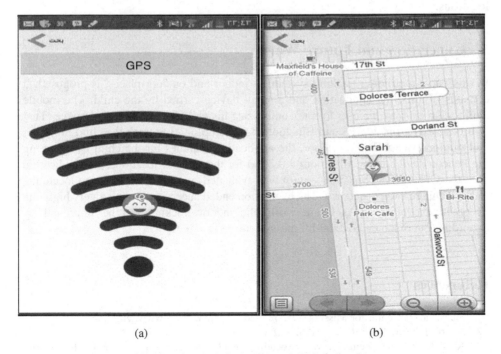

(a)   (b)

Fig. 4. Bluetooth finder (a) and GPS finder (b)

4 System Testing

The usability testing of the proposed system was performed by 10 people with different ages; both genders and different level of education. Tasks are given in the Table 1. The goal is to determine whether the application is easy to use and her GUIs are friendly or not. All of users performed the tasks easily and give positive feedbacks.

Table 1. Usability testing results

Task	Comment
View help.	Done correctly
Add child.	Done correctly
Find child using Bluetooth 4.0.	Done correctly
Find child using GPS.	Done correctly
Edit child profile.	Done correctly
Delete child profile.	Done correctly
View emergency information.	Done correctly

On the other hand, the system testing has shown that the proposed tracking system is capable to locate the children, carrying the device, in the indoor and outdoor locations.

5 Conclusion and Future Work

In this paper a children tracking system, in indoor and outdoor places, is proposed. It consists of a mobile application and a small device carried by the child. The mobile application enables the user to track and locate his child by locating that device. That will be done by using GPS and Bluetooth 4.0 technologies to track the child in indoor and outdoor locations. For indoor, the application searches for the child by detecting the beacon device using Bluetooth 4.0. And for the outdoor locations, the application uses the GPS/GPRS chip. The system was evaluated by testing its ability to locate the tracked children with accuracy. The evaluation ended successfully with a very high rate of positive outcomes. As future work, the indoor tracking can be improved by extending the distance covered by the system.

References

1. International Centre for Missing & Exploited Children. http://www.icmec.org
2. National Crime Records Bureau. http://ncrb.gov.in
3. Al-Suwaidi, G.B., Zemerly, M.J.: Locating friends and family using mobile phones with global positioning system (GPS). In: IEEE/ACS International Conference on Computer Systems and Applications (2009)

4. Almomani, I.M., Alkhalil, N.Y., Ahmad, E.M., Jodeh, R.M.: Ubiquitous GPS vehicle tracking and management system. In: IEEE Jordan Conference on Applied Electrical Engineering and Computing Technologies (AEECT), pp. 1–6 (2011)
5. Chandra, A., Jain, S., Qadeer, M.A.: GPS Locator: An application for location tracking and sharing using GPS for Java enabled handhelds. In: International Conference on Computational Intelligence and Communication Networks (CICN), pp. 406–410 (2011)
6. Anderson, R.E., et al.: Building a transportation information system using only GPS and basic SMS infrastructure. In: International Conference on Information and Communication Technologies and Development (ICTD). IEEE (2009)
7. Al-Mazloum, A., Omer, E., Abdullah, M.F.A.: GPS and SMS-based child tracking system using smart phone. Int. J. Electr. Comput. Electron. Commun. Eng. **7**(2), 171–174 (2013)
8. Opoku, S.K.: An indoor tracking system based on bluetooth technology. Cyber J. Multi. J. Sci. Technol. J. Sel. Area. Telecommun. (JSAT) **2**(12), 1–8 (2011)
9. Morii, K., Taketa, K., Mori, Y., Kojima, H., Kohno, E., Inoue, S., Ohta, T., Kakuda, Y.: A new generation children tracking system using bluetooth MANET composed of android mobile terminals. In: 9th International Conference on Ubiquitous Intelligence & Computing and 9th International Conference on Autonomic & Trusted Computing (UIC/ATC), pp. 405–407 (2012)
10. Al-Ali, A.R., Aloul, F.A., Aji, N.R., Al-Zarouni, A.A., Fakhro, N.H.: Mobile RFID tracking system. In: 3rd International Conference on Information and Communication Technologies: From Theory to Applications ICTTA, pp. 1–4 (2008)
11. Amber Alert GPS. http://www.amberalertgps.com
12. Pocket Finder. http://www.pocketfinder.com
13. Spark GPS. http://sparkgps.com
14. iTrail. http://itrailgpstracker.com

Smart Cities and Communities

Spending Precious Travel Time More Wisely: A Service Model that Provides Instant Travel Assistance Using Input from Locals

Kenro Aihara[1,2]($\boxtimes$), Susumu Kono[2], and Shizuhiro Sugino[3]

[1] National Institute of Informatics, Tokyo, Japan
kenro.aihara@nii.ac.jp
[2] SOKENDAI (The Graduate University for Advanced Studies),
2-1-2 Hitotsubashi, Chiyoda-ku, Tokyo 101-8430, Japan
su-kono@nii.ac.jp
[3] SPC Co., Ltd., 7-3-5 Minato-cho, Matsuyama, Ehime 790-8586, Japan
sugino@ma.kk-spc.co.jp

Abstract. We propose a new service model that incorporates input from locals to provide instant travel assistance.

No matter how well travelers plan, circumstances at their destination invariably force them to modify their plans, especially towards the end of a tour. However, it is difficult for travelers to get useful information or support.

Accordingly, we propose a service model whereby on-site travelers can instantly access planning suggestions from locals. Travelers send a personalized plan request with conditions such as desired end point (destination and time), preferences (e.g. dining, historical spots, etc.), and group information. The service delivers this to participating locals, who create appropriate plans and register them with the service.

We conducted a preliminary survey of the model in March, 2014 in Matsuyama, Japan. Despite an insufficient volume of data the questionnaire results support our approach. Locals provided useful information that was perceived as more credible than online search results.

Keywords: Context-aware computing · Location-based service · Cyber-physical systems · Behavior log

1 Introduction

No matter how well travelers have planned prior to departure, they must invariably modify their travel plans after arrival at their destination. For example, they may find themselves more tired than expected and hence decide to cancel planned visits to certain spots. Plan change is a reality that travelers must confront, especially towards the end of their tour.

Cyber-physical systems (CPS) seek to provide users with optimal control of the world they correspond with by modeling physical space in cyber space,

© Springer International Publishing Switzerland 2015
N. Streitz and P. Markopoulos (Eds.): DAPI 2015, LNCS 9189, pp. 557–567, 2015.
DOI: 10.1007/978-3-319-20804-6_51

coupled with the use of related databases. More than big data systems, social CPS is the operating system of urban society. It provides a user environment that supports the agency of people in decision-making. Social CPS is increasingly necessary for building sustainable, safe, and secure urban societies. The prerequisite basic technologies are maturing rapidly. Remaining efforts include opening data silos maintained by both the private sector and government, and analyzing massive, complex data that cannot be fully described with a single monolithic model. Tantalizing research and development challenges exist in relation to Social CPS.

This paper proposes a new service model for instant travel assistance that uses input from locals. We consider the model an example of Social CPS that aims to develop a framework to collect traveler needs based on sensor data that reflects microscopic personal-scale events, in a similar manner to crowd-sourcing, and organizes locals to collect knowledge and recommendations that can support travelers.

2   Background

Travelers may have to modify their initial plans en-route, and various factors can require this. Weather is one of the biggest influences. Travelers can also find that their interests change during a long journey. Even if circumspect travelers can prepare alternative options to deal with such uncertainty, it is difficult to develop alternatives for all eventualities prior to their travel. Plan change thus is one certainty that travelers confront, especially towards the end of their itineraries.

We assume that a problem exists in that it is difficult for travelers to get useful information or effective support to help them modify their plans. This problem may cause not only the loss of opportunities for travelers to experience local interesting places and things, but also the loss of opportunities for local businesses to sell products and services.

2.1   Travel Assistance

Many travel assistance services have been proposed, using several approaches. One approach is online travel guides, such as Lonely Planet and AAA TourBook guides. Another approach is to supplement travel guides with user comments and reviews, in the manner of TripAdvisor. Social networking sites like Twitter and Facebook are a natural source of destination information. Web searches like Google must be frequently used. We suppose that, for various reasons, such existing services are insufficient to support travelers, especially on-site. One reason is limited time. In contrast to the situation when preparing for travel, once on-site travelers have limited time to research and plan. Another reason is limited tools. Once at their destinations travelers can only use their own smartphones for navigation. Hence they need to efficiently find things of interest using only their smartphones and while working under time restrictions. The problem thus is one of content accessibility. We also suppose that another essential problem involves insufficient local content. Generally, we often confront a lack of listed candidates when running searches for local restaurants. This is a problem of sparseness of content. Additionally, both social networking site content and "recommended" content on commercialized media may have low credibility. We must consider not only how to efficiently provide credible information to users, but also how to incrementally produce useful local content.

2.2 Mobile Applications

Numerous network services for mobile users with location data have been created, and some, such as foursquare[1], are becoming popular. Location information is usually given in the form of geographical coordinates, i.e. latitude and longitude, a location identifier such as a facility ID entered into geographical information services (GIS), or a postal address. Google has launched Google Places[2], which gathers place information from participating networkers and delivers it via Google's website and application programmable interface (API). Google thus tries to obtain information on activities in the real world, information it lacks despite being the omniscient giant of the cyber world. Google already uses its own physical resources to capture real world information. For example, it gathers landscape images for the Google Street View service[3] using its own fleet of specially adapted cars. However, capturing and digitizing facts and activities in the real world is generally very expensive beyond a superficial level, such as capturing photo images associated with geographical information. Although Google Places may be a reasonable solution to gathering information in the real world, these is no guarantee it can become an effective and reliable source reflecting the real world.

Existing social information services, such as Facebook and Twitter, are expanding to attach location data to user content.

2.3 Social CPS

To capture situations and help solve problems in the real world, research on CPS has recently become increasingly important. CPS is a promising new class of systems that deeply embed cyber capabilities in the physical world, either on humans, infrastructure or platforms, to transform interactions with the physical world [5,10]. CPS facilitates the use of information available from the physical environment. Advances in the cyber world, such as communications, networking, sensing, computing, storage, and control, as well as in the physical world, such as materials and hardware, are rapidly converging to realize a class of highly collaborative computational systems that rely on sensors and actuators to monitor and effect change. In this technology-rich scenario, real-world components interact with cyberspace via sensing, computing and communication elements.

---

[1] http://foursquare.com/.
[2] http://www.google.com/places/.
[3] http://www.google.com/streetview/.

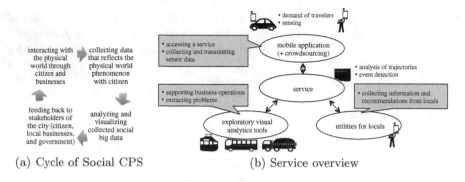

(a) Cycle of Social CPS   (b) Service overview

Fig. 1. Social CPS

Social CPS focuses human aspects in the parallel world because humans are not only subjects that exploit such systems but also objects that are observed and affected by the systems. Information flows from the physical to the cyber world, and vice-versa, adapting the converged world to human behavior and social dynamics. Indeed humans occupy the center of this converged world since information on their operating context is the key to the adaptation of CPS applications and services. The concept of social CPS is shown in Fig. 1(a).

2.4 Crowdsourcing for Civil Problems

The term "crowdsourcing" was coined by Jeff Howe in 2006 [7] to describe the act of taking a task traditionally performed by a designated agent and outsourcing it via an open call to a large but undefined group of people [8]. Crowdsourcing can involve peer-production, but is also often undertaken by solitary individuals [6].

The concept of smart cities can be viewed as a recognition of the growing importance of digital technologies to competitiveness and sustainability [11]. The smart city agenda, which sets ICTs strategic urban development goals such as improving the life quality of citizens and creating sustainable growth, has recently gained considerable momentum. In smart cities, collaborative digital environments facilitate the development of innovative applications, starting from local human capital, rather than believing digitalization can transform and improve cities.

Tools such as smartphones provide the opportunity to facilitate co-creation between citizens and the authorities. Such tools have potential to organize and stimulate communication between citizens and the authorities, and allow citizens to participate in the public domain [4,12]. One example is FixMyStreet[4], which enables citizens to report broken streetlights and potholes [9].

Incidentally, to capture situations involving a town, such as local events or the feelings of locals and visitors, the author believes that it is not enough to collect tweets and behavior logs of locations, simply because the number of geotagged

---

[4] https://www.fixmystreet.com/.

tweets is limited. In a previous work by the author [1,3], only 1 % of LBS users posted microblogs while strolling in town. Therefore, for microscopic analysis of town situations in small resolution of time and space, more information sources that reflect pedestrian behaviors and emotions are needed [2]. Unconstrained crowdsourcing approaches will not succeed automatically and social standards like trust, openness, and consideration of mutual interests must be guaranteed to make citizen engagement in the public domain challenging.

3   Methodology

In the case where a traveler's initial plans change on-site, we assume that it is difficult for travelers to get useful information or effective support to modify their plans. To solve this problem, we propose a new service model for the provision of instant travel assistance. The service targets on-site travelers and aims to help travelers make instant plans by providing them with plan proposals by locals.

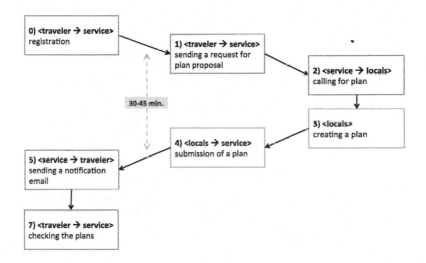

Fig. 2. Service process flow

3.1   Service Scenario

Travelers can send a plan request that incorporates various important conditions, such as an end point (destination and time), preferences (including those regarding cuisine, historical spots, etc.), and group information. They do this by completing the web form (Fig. 2. (1)), (Fig. 3(a)).

When the service receives the request (Fig. 2. (2)), it is delivered to cooperating locals (Fig. 2. (3)).

According to the request, locals make their own plans and register these with the service by the deadline (Fig. 2. (4)). If a plan includes a destination not registered in the service database, that destination will be added at this time.

On the arrival of the deadline, a plan proposal is composed using plans collected from locals and an email that includes a URL pointer to the plan proposal is sent to the requester (Fig. 2. (5)).

The requester can get the plan proposal, including plans proposed by Locals, by clicking the URL pointer in the email (Figs. 2. (6), 3(b)).

(a) Plan request form   (b) Example plan

Fig. 3. Snapshot images of the service

3.2   Features

This service model contains the following features:

- Sending the request is simple and quick.
- Plans are not only ready-made but also made-to-order by locals who know the area well.
- Previously created plans and content are registered in the service DB and can be reused; the volume of local content thus gradually grows.

Figure 4 shows examples of plans created by locals. Each plan (Fig. 4(a)) includes the planner's profile with a photo image, some general comments, and finally the details of the plan. In contrast to plans by locals, web search plans are simple; that is, they merely comprise the result of a web search related to the request.

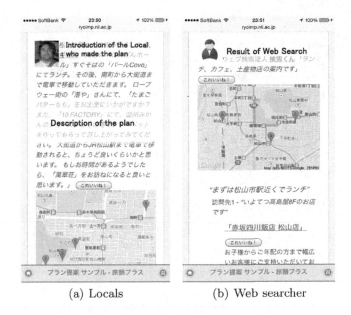

(a) Locals   (b) Web searcher

Fig. 4. Snapshot images of the service

3.3 User Functions

Typical Plans. Users can browse typical plans prepared by locals.

Spot List. Users can look up a list of already registered spots. They can also sort those spots according to distance from their current location.

When they select one spot on the list, spot information is shown. Figure 5 illustrates examples of spot information. Spot information consists of short descriptions of the spot, a map and business hours, as well as a "Like" button that users can use to express interest.

3.4 Sensing Functions

User Data. The service collects the following user attributes:

– gender
– generation
– zip code

The service collects users' demographic attributes on their first access.

Location. The service is accessed via web browser. When users post their plan request and search nearby spots, the browser sends the service their current location.

Fig. 5. Examples of Spot Information

4   Survey

4.1   Overview

We conducted a preliminary survey of the proposed model at the beginning of March, 2014 in Matsuyama, Japan. We asked 26 actual travelers who carried their own Android smartphones to participate in the survey. The travelers were asked to use our proposed service at least once; that is, they were asked to request a plan proposal. Doing this required participants to install our smartphone application, "Ryoimp"[5], to allow collection their behavior logs in background mode.

Participants also had to compete an online survey after completing their travel.

4.2   Results

Sixteen participants completed the software installation and registration. Unfortunately, only seven participants sent plan proposal requests while eight answered the online survey.

Online Survey. We requested monitors to answer questionnaires on the following:

1. about plans provided by locals
   (a) expertise, consideration of preferences, and usefulness

---

[5] https://play.google.com/store/apps/details?id=jp.ryoin.

    (b) comparative acceptance of plans created by locals and plans obtained from web search

    (c) whether the spots in provided plans were visited

2. acceptance of agent reservation service

3. services used during travel

    (a) useful internet services

    (b) useful information sources.

Expertise, Consideration of Preferences, and Usefulness. Two in five agreed that the plans provided by the service displayed expertise and consideration of requesters' expressed preferences. Three acknowledged that the service was useful. None of the monitors who responded to the online survey gave negative ratings.

Comparison of Acceptance Between Plans Provided by Locals and Web Search Results. When examining the credibility questionnaire results, we found plans provided by locals to be more credible than those resulting from a web search (Table 1).

Table 1. Credibility: "Is the plan by {locals | web search} credible for you?"

	Locals	Web search
Good	0	0
Better	4	1
Neutral	1	4
Worse	0	0
Bad	0	0

Four out of five participants who completed the survey and used the service at least once answered "real locals with viewable profiles providing customized plans is credible". We suppose that these results support our assumption, namely that plans provided by locals with viewable profiles can be accepted as credible and preferable.

Actual Traveler Behavior. Table 2 shows the behavior of travelers who used the application, received customized plans and provided behavior logs. Unfortunately only a few participants provided such feedback, but four out of six recommended spots were accepted by these participants. We regard responses of "satisfied" and "want to visit" as indicating acceptance.

Figure 6 illustrates an example of traveler trajectory.

Table 2. Recommended spots and traveler behavior

Motivation	Visited	Not visited	
	Visited/satisfied?	Reason	Not visited/want to visit?
Recommended	1/1	No time	1/1
		Not interested	1/0
		Unsure spot	1/0
Self directed	2/2		

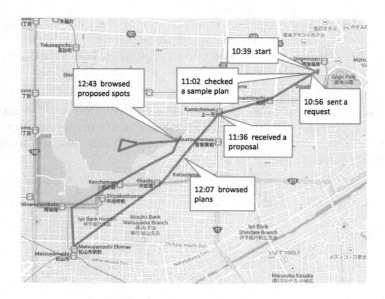

Fig. 6. Examples of a traveler's log

5   Conclusions

This paper proposes a new service model whereby travelers receive instant travel assistance from locals. Although we have not collected enough data, the questionnaire results support our approach. For example, participants found information from locals extremely useful, and regarded plans provided by locals as more credible than content obtained through a simple web search.

The authors are continuing to develop this service model, and experiments are being planned to evaluate its effectiveness.

Acknowledgments. This work was partly supported by JSPS KAKENHI Grant-in-Aid for Scientific Research (C) Grant Number 24611035 and Strategic Information and Communications R&D Promotion Programme (SCOPE) Number 122309007 from the Ministry of Internal Affairs and Communications of Japan.

References

1. Aihara, K.: Do strollers in town needs recommendation?: on preferences of recommender in location-based services. In: Streitz, N., Stephanidis, C. (eds.) DAPI 2013. LNCS, vol. 8028, pp. 275–283. Springer, Heidelberg (2013)
2. Aihara, K.: Collecting behavior logs with emotions in town. In: Streitz, N., Markopoulos, P. (eds.) DAPI 2014. LNCS, vol. 8530, pp. 231–240. Springer, Heidelberg (2014)
3. Aihara, K., Koshiba, H., Takeda, H.: Behavioral cost-based recommendation model for wanderers in town. In: Jacko, J.A. (ed.) Human-Computer Interaction, Part III, HCII 2011. LNCS, vol. 6763, pp. 271–279. Springer, Heidelberg (2011)
4. Amichai-Hamburger, Y.: Potential and promise of online volunteering. Comput. Hum. Behav. **24**(2), 544–562 (2008)
5. Conti, M., Das, S.K., Bisdikian, C., Kumar, M., Ni, L.M., Passarella, A., Roussos, G., Tröster, G., Tsudik, G., Zambonelli, F.: Looking ahead in pervasive computing: Challenges and opportunities in the era of cyber-physical convergence. Pervasive Mob. Comput. **8**(1), 2–21 (2012)
6. Howe, J.: Crowdsourcing: A definition. Crowdsourcing: Tracking the Rise of the Amateur (2006)
7. Howe, J.: The rise of crowdsourcing. Wired Mag. **14**(6), 1–4 (2006)
8. Howe, J.: Crowdsourcing: How the Power of the Crowd is Driving the Future of Business. Random House, New York (2008)
9. King, S.F., Brown, P.: Fix my street or else: Using the internet to voice local public service concerns. In: Proceedings of the 1st International Conference on Theory and Practice of Electronic Governance, pp. 72–80 (2007)
10. Poovendran, R.: Cyber-physical systems: Close encounters between two parallel worlds. Proc. IEEE **98**(8), 1363–1366 (2010)
11. Schuurman, D., Baccarne, B., De Marez, L., Mechant, P.: Smart ideas for smart cities: investigating crowdsourcing for generating and selecting ideas for ict innovation in a city context. J. Theor. Appl. Electron. Commer. Res. **7**(3), 49–62 (2012)
12. Stembert, N., Mulder, I.J.: Love your city! an interactive platform empowering citizens to turn the public domain into a participatory domain. In: International Conference Using ICT, Social Media and Mobile Technologies to Foster Self-Organisation in Urban and Neighbourhood Governance (2013)

Interpreting Food-Venue Visits: Spatial and Social Contexts of Mobile Consumption in Urban Spaces

Shin'ichi Konomi[1]([✉]), Kenta Shoji[2], and Tomoyo Sasao[2]

[1] Center for Spatial Information Science, The University of Tokyo, 5-1-5, Kashiwanoha, Kashiwa, Chiba 277-8568, Japan
konomi@csis.u-tokyo.ac.jp
[2] Graduate School of Frontier Sciences, The University of Tokyo, 5-1-5, Kashiwanoha, Kashiwa, Chiba 277-8563, Japan

Abstract. The increasing amount of mobility data introduces an opportunity to develop novel urban applications that are integrated with everyday practices. Although simple events (e.g., visits to places) can be inferred from mobility traces, events have very different meanings in different contexts. To contribute to the body of work that aims to uncover effective methods to integrate ubiquitous computing technologies in urban spaces and context, we discuss interpretation of ubiquitous events in urban computing: food-venue visits. Based on a survey and a small supplemental study, we identify the spatial and social contexts that influence the meanings of food-venue visits. We also suggest a possibility of novel technological support for eating out.

Keywords: Eating out · Food · Consumption · Urban context

1 Introduction

There is an increasing amount of mobility data captured and accumulated by using GPS, WiFi access points, cell-towers, video cameras, laser range scanners, embedded sensors, foursquare check-ins, etc. It is of interest to many people to identify visits to places based on mobility data because a visit to a venue can signify some meaning, and be useful for providing context-aware services. Also, collective patterns of visits can be visualized to interpret the state of the city. However, it is not always easy to interpret venue-visit data as their meaning depends on contexts. This makes it difficult to fully exploit the data in urban applications.

Food consumption is a pervasive activity in urban spaces, and it would be extremely useful for service provides and consumers to understand (or automatically infer) its patterns, meanings and contexts. For example, such understanding can be used to build effective recommender systems for food venues. Therefore, we have studied the spatial and social contexts that influence the meanings of food-venue visits in Japan.

© Springer International Publishing Switzerland 2015
N. Streitz and P. Markopoulos (Eds.): DAPI 2015, LNCS 9189, pp. 568–577, 2015.
DOI: 10.1007/978-3-319-20804-6_52

Japan, as a site for investigating food-venue visits, can be characterized by many different types of food venues clustered in urban spaces, as well as the large amount of information about food venues available in print, broadcast, outdoor and digital media. Urban sociology researchers selected the country as a non-Western context for comparative studies of consumption, with Western countries (e.g., [4]). More than 66 % of the country's population live in cities, and Tokyo, in particular, has a very large number of food venues as shown in Fig. 1 [22].

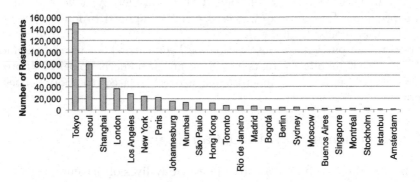

Fig. 1. Number of restaurants in cities

Based on a survey and a small supplemental study, we identify and discuss spatial and social contexts of food venue visits. The discussions also suggest a possibility of some technological support for eating out.

2   Related Works

2.1   Mobile Tourist Guides and Recommenders

Many mobile applications have been developed to support consumption-centric activities such as tours [8]. The earliest examples include Cyberguide [1], and GUIDE [3] for city visitors. More recently, a mobile recommender system has been proposed to infer user preferences to recommend nearby points of interest (POIs) [2]. Paay et al. discuss a design approach for context-aware urban guides by combining rapid ethnography, architectural analysis, design sketching, and paper prototyping, without a particular focus on urban consumption or eating out [13].

Although there are many commercial applications that suggest food venues to mobile users [6,7,14,18,23,24], there is relative scarcity of research systems that focus on food venues. An interesting example is the experimental system by Lee et al., which recommends restaurants based on users' location, demographic data and environmental information such as weather and temperature [12]. However, this system does not consider social contexts.

2.2 Mobility and Context

Context awareness is a popular feature of many mobile applications. To support urban activities effectively, we need to rethink mobility and context, going beyond a clean model of geometric spaces. In contrast to common approaches to context-aware urban applications that focus on cities as generic settings for *"mobile users,"* Williams and Dourish discuss an approach that views cities as products of social practices [21].

Interpreting urban mobility data, including food venue visits, is closely related to an alternative view of context that consider dynamic and interactional aspects [5]. This notion of context could be applied to food venue visits to examine their contexts in depth.

Ethnographic participant observation has been carried out to analyze microscopic aspects of mobile contexts based on an ethnomethodological approach [17]. We focus on a more macroscopic aspects related to food venues in particular.

3 Food Consumption in Urban Spaces

Consumption plays an important role in everyday lives of urbanites [4]. One of the pervasive consumption activities in urban spaces is eating out.

The practice of eating out has been studied in depth by sociologists [20]. Some of their findings can be useful for interpreting food venue visits. First, different food venues attract different types of people. For example, social class and gender as well as life styles can influence the choice of food venues. Second, people have different attitudes towards eating out. For example, some people are interested in learning and enjoy trying out new food. Other people like to stick to the food that they know they like. Third, there are different reasons to eat out, besides the necessity to fill one's stomach. People may do it to socialize, celebrate, relax, or trying out something new; or because of social obligation.

Moreover, the act of eating out can be understood in terms of its symbolic significance, or *sign value*, as well. Having a cup of coffee at a trendy cafe could be a form of expression through food consumption, and the coffee may not necessarily taste good.

4 Venue Visits in Context: A Survey

We have conducted a survey to understand patterns and contexts of food-venue visits in Japan using a crowdsourcing service called Lancers [10].

4.1 Method

Crowdsourcing such as Mechanical Turnk [9] has been used for running user studies. Lancers [10] is the largest crowdsourcing service in Japan (and in Japanese), which has 279 thousand registered users as of March 2014. Unlike Mechanical

Turk, almost all ($> 99\%$) workers on Lancers live in Japan [11]. It supports microtasking as well as other forms of crowdsourcing, and more than 70 % of the workers live outside Tokyo [11].

We developed survey questions that asked about food-venue visits. After testing and revising survey questions, we obtained a permission from our institutional review board. A microtask request was then posted on Lancers, which is linked to a corresponding online survey form on SurveyMonkey [16]. Filling out the survey form takes approximately 5 min with the payment of 50 Japanese Yen (i.e., about 50 US Cents). Workers had to be adults ($\geq$ 20 years old) and answer the survey no more than once.

Figure 2 shows the overview of the survey questions[1].

1. Age, gender, and occupation.
2. How many times a week do you eat out on average?
3. When you eat out with other people, do you think you have discretion over the choice of the venue? Provide answers for different group sizes: 2, 3-4, 5-10, and more than 10.
4. During the last 7 days, did you compromise when eating out? (e.g., went to an undesirable venue just to be sociable; went to a nearby venue because the lunch break was short; went to a different venue because the preferred venue was crowded.) If your answer is yes, how many times did you compromise and what are the reasons for compromising.
5. Do you have a favorite venue? How many times do you use the favorite venue? Do you want to tell your acquaintances and friends having a similar taste as you about the favorite venue? Do you want to know about venues whose food taste and ambience are similar to the favorite venue?
6. Do you want to use a service or a system that automatically recommends venues based on the records of usage and activity?
7. Do you use information from words-of-mouth communication websites when using a venue that you have never used before? If your answer is yes, how much do you use words-of-mouth communication websites? If your answer is no, provide the reason for not using.

Fig. 2. Overview of survey questions

4.2   Findings

After filtering out invalid responses, we analyzed responses from 193 people, 130 (67 %) of which are female and 63 (33 %) male. Figure 3 shows distributions of respondents by age groups, occupations and the numbers of times to eat out in a week. Similarly to what has been reported about the demographics of Mechanical Turk [15], there are more female respondents than male respondents, and the largest age group is 30–39 years old.

---

[1] The original survey questions are in Japanese, and they were translated into English by the authors.

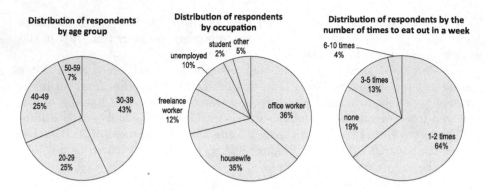

Fig. 3. Distributions of respondents by age group, occupation and eat-out frequency

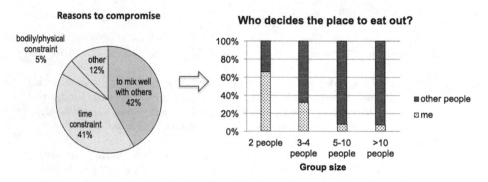

Fig. 4. Patterns of compromise in selecting place to eat out

32 % of the respondents compromised in the last 7 days, by going to food venues that they did not think were the best. Visiting a food venue many times does not necessarily mean that one likes the venue.

We asked the people who compromised why they did so. Figure 4 shows the summary of the responses. Apparently, time constraints are a major reason for compromising. What seems interesting is that as many people said that the reason was to *mix well with others*[2]. Respondents' comments point to concrete situations in which they selected suboptimal food venues, as they said *"That was the only food venue nearby," "The venue was busy, so I dropped in a vacant venue,"* and *"I made myself agreeable to my peer in terms of taste."*

As this suggests the importance of social contexts in eating out, we examine the impact of group size on discretion. Among the people who said that they compromise to mix well with others, 66 % said that they decide the venue by themselves when eating out in a group of two people, but only 7 % when eating out in a group of more than 10 people.

---

[2] The responses are originally in Japanese as well. They were translated into English by the authors.

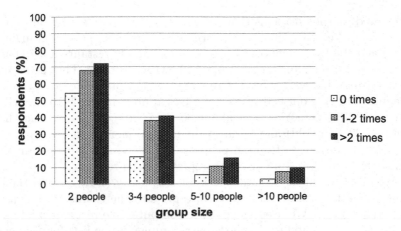

Fig. 5. Ratio of people who decide the place to eat by themselves, by group size and weekly eat-out frequency

As this seems to simply reinforce a common sense understanding that the more people one eat out with, the more likely to compromise, there is a less trivial pattern related to the frequency of eating out. As shown in Fig. 5, respondents who eat-out frequently are more likely to decide the place to eat by themselves. Moreover, this impact of eat-out frequency on discretion is statistically significant for a certain group size only.

There is a statistically significant association between eat-out frequency and discretion for the group size of 3–4 people ($\chi(2) = 6.661, p = 0.036$). However, when the group size is 2 ($\chi(2) = 3.001, p = 0.223$), 5–10 ($\chi(2) = 1.935, p = 0.380$), or more than 10 ($\chi(2) = 1.367, p = 0.505$), the association is weak and *not* statistically significant. The impact of eat-out frequency is the strongest.

5   Chain Restaurants and Time of Day

In a preliminary study that supplements the survey, we looked into the impact of two additional contexts: time of day and chain restaurants in different food categories.

5.1   Method

We examine it by creating recommendation lists of food venues based on time of day and food chains, and collecting feedback about the lists from a small number of citizens in person.

We crowdsourced the data collection to build a database from which recommendation lists are derived by using user-based collaborative filtering. The microtask request we posted on Lancers asked people to provide the names of at most seven favorite food venues in Shibuya along with the frequency to visit them, followed by the questions that asked the frequency of eating out in different time of day (i.e., early morning, morning, around noon, evening, night, and midnight) and the frequency of using 9 chains of family restaurants, 7 chains of hamburger restaurants, and 4 chains of beef bowl restaurants. They serve similar food with comparable prices, yet, interestingly, people prefer a certain chain over other chains. Carrying out this microtask takes approximately 5–10 min with the payment of 80 Japanese Yen (i.e., about 80 US Cents). Again, workers had to be adults ($\geq$ 20 years old) and perform the task no more than once.

We collected responses from 36 people on Lancers, and 3 people in person, and built two databases, one of which represents the relationship between the people and the time of day to eat out most frequently (DB_{tod}), and the other represents the relationship between the people and the chains they visit most frequently (DB_{chain}). We used the data to compute nine recommendation lists for the 3 people, p_1, p_2 and p_3. Of the three recommendation lists for each person, one is based on DB_{tod}, another based on DB_{chain}, and another based on an equally weighted sum of the interpersonal similarities (i.e., Pearson correlation coefficients) based on DB_{tod} and DB_{chain}.

5.2   Preliminary Results

p_1 liked the recommendation list based on DB_{chain} the best because it prioritizes venues that are not chain restaurants. In contrast, p_2 liked the recommendation list based on DB_{tod} the best because it recommends a venue in a shopping mall that p_2 frequently visits.

This anecdotal finding complements the survey in that it suggests (1) time of day is a relevant context for interpreting and using venue-visit logs, (2) chain restaurants are also a relevant context and they can connect people in different areas or cities, which could be potentially useful for recommending venues in unfamiliar environments, and (3) these two contexts needs to be interpreted and prioritized in different ways for different people and/or contexts. These three points are more relevant for venue visits in urban spaces than page visits on the web or an e-commerce site.

6   Discussion

Our findings suggest the importance of group size, visit frequency, distance, crowding, time of day, and other contextual factors in understanding food venue visits. We now discuss them in more depth based on relevant conceptual frameworks, and suggests some technological interventions for eating out, which is a pervasive consumption activity in urban spaces.

The sheer amount of food venues in cities facilitate people to eat out without the physical and social constraints of traditional "eating home with family members." Although people often associate eating out with reduced spatial and social constraints, people's decision making about food venues is under constant tension and *satisficing* solutions need to be sought by considering social, temporal, and spatial constraints. One often has to conform to peer-group norms in groups of different sizes and social distances. Indeed, *"there are many graduations of experience between freely willing and feeling inescapably obliged to participate in any given social practice"* [20, p. 66]. Moreover, not only physical distances, accessibility, travel costs, available alternatives and financial circumstances but also life styles and symbolic aspects of food venues make the decision making process a dynamic and multi-faceted one in the context of everyday practices.

It can be useful to make a distinction between consumption for necessity and luxury. When eating out of necessity, it is often under many circumstantial pressures such as the available time and money, nutritional requirements, and proximity to daily or planned trajectories through time and space. This distinction seems to be reflected in the design of physical food venues such as eat-in convenience stores, food court in shopping malls, and *"Eki Naka"* (in-station) fast-food restaurants although such distinction is not as apparent in the design of conventional urban applications such as location-based services.

When purchasing a book on an e-commerce site, it does not matter very much whether one buys it in the morning or in the evening. However, meanings of a visit to a restaurant in the morning and in the evening can be very different because people who eat out in the morning can have different daily life patterns than the ones who eat out in the evening, and the restaurant may provide different food and services for breakfast, lunch, and dinner. Time of day is a context which is particularly relevant to mobile, ubiquitous consumption, and it could have some impact on the quality of recommendation lists.

Another factor that differentiates eating out from online consumption is that eating out is an embodied, situated activity in which different kinds of consumption are combined as people consume visual, auditory, olfactory and gustatory information as well as physical food. This suggests potential use of various sensors and locative media for the support of food venue visits.

In many cases, food venue visits cannot be simply defined as the conduct of market exchange. For example, the association between eat-out frequency and discretionary venue choices can be analyzed based on a more holistic view that consumption is embedded in practices. What the discussion on consumption and theory of practice suggests is the importance of participation and learning to be competent in consuming food and services appropriately [19]. In some cases, the level of participation and competence could be reflected in the frequency of eating out as well as the influence on decision making in a social eat-out setting. More generally, different degrees of involvement in practices can generate behavioral variation, and patterns of food venue visits can be interpreted and used based on relevant practices.

Based on a traditional view on consumption, food venue visits can be interpreted as the act of satisfying hunger, or expressing personal tastes in relation to their *sign values*. However, a view based on practices interprets food venue visits in terms of competence, participation, and cultural conventions. We believe that the latter view is also important in ubicomp applications for food consumption as much as in physical environments for eating out.

Finally, information about preferred chain restaurants could have some impact on the quality of recommendation lists as well. Chain restaurants are an interesting class of food venues because many of them are distributed across the nation at somewhat regular intervals, thereby enabling association of food venue visits in different areas. This suggest that other types of *spatially connective structures*, besides the spreading patterns of networked chain stores, could potentially be relevant as well.

7   Conclusion

In this paper, we discussed spatial and social contexts of food venue visits in urban spaces based on a survey and a supplemental study. We identified several important contexts and discussed how they might come into play in different settings based on an existing conceptual framework about consumption and practices.

The discussions related to chain restaurants and time of day are based on preliminary results and rather speculative. Therefore, we avoided making strong conclusions on these issues. That said, our findings from the survey and overall discussions suggest directions towards novel design strategies for urban applications, and open up opportunities for further research in ubiquitous computing for urban consumption.

Acknowledgments. This research was supported by the Environmental Information project under the Green Network of Excellence (GRENE) program of MEXT, Japan.

References

1. Abowd, G.D., Atkeson, C.G., Hong, J., Long, S., Kooper, R., Pinkerton, M.: Cyberguide: A mobile context-aware tour guide. Wireless Netw. **3**, 421–433 (1997)
2. Biancalana, C., Gasparetti, F., Micarelli, A., Sansonetti, G.: An approach to social recommendation for context-aware mobile services. ACM Trans. Intell. Syst. Technol. **4**(1), 1–31 (2013)
3. Cheverst, K., Davies, N., Mitchell, K., Friday, A., Efstratiou, C.: Developing a context-aware electronic tourist guide: some issues and experiences. In: Proceedings of the CHI 2000, pp. 17–24 (2000)
4. Clammer, J.: Contemporary Urban Japan. Blackwell Publishers, Oxford (1997)
5. Dourish, P.: What we talk about when we talk about context. Pers. Ubiquit. Comput. **8**(1), 19–30 (2004)
6. Foodspotting. http://www.foodspotting.com/
7. GURUNAVI. http://www.gnavi.co.jp/en/
8. Kenteris, M., Gavalas, D., Economou, D.: Electronic mobile guides: a survey. Pers. Ubiquit. Comput. **15**(1), 97–111 (2010)
9. Kittur, A., Chi, E.H., Suh, B.: Crowdsourcing user studies with Mechanical Turk. In: Proceedings of the CHI 2008, pp. 453–456. ACM Press, New York (2008)

10. Lancers. http://www.lancers.jp
11. Lancers (2012). http://www.lancers.co.jp/news/pr/482
12. Lee, B.-H., Kim, H.-N., Jung, J.-G., Jo, G.-S.: Location-based service with context data for a restaurant recommendation. In: Bressan, S., Küng, J., Wagner, R. (eds.) DEXA 2006. LNCS, vol. 4080, pp. 430–438. Springer, Heidelberg (2006)
13. Paay, J., Kjeldskov, J., Howard, S., Dave, B.: Out on the town: a socio-physical approach to the design of a context-aware urban guide. ACM Trans. Comput.-Human Interact. **16**(2), 1–34 (2009)
14. Retty. http://www.retty.me/
15. Ross, J., Irani, L., Silberman, M.: Who are the crowdworkers?: shifting demographics in mechanical turk. In: Proceedings of the CHI 2010 Extended Abstracts, pp. 2863–2872 (2010)
16. SurveyMonkey. http://www.surveymonkey.com
17. Tamminen, S., Oulasvirta, A., Toiskallio, K., Kankainen, A.: Understanding mobile contexts. Pers. Ubiquit. Comput. **8**(2), 135–143 (2004)
18. Urbanspoon. http://www.urbanspoon.com/
19. Warde, A.: Consumption and theories of practice. J. Consum. Cult. **5**(2), 131–153 (2005)
20. Warde, A., Martens, L.: Eating Out: Social Differentiation, Consumption and Pleasure. Cambridge University Press, Cambridge (2000)
21. Williams, A., Dourish, P.: Imagining the city: The cultural dimensions of urban computing. Computer **39**, 38–43 (2006)
22. World Cities Culture Forum: World cities culture report 2014 (2014)
23. Yelp. http://www.yelp.com/
24. Zagat. http://www.zagat.com/

Co-design Practice in a Smart City Context Through the Gamification Approach: A Survey About the Most Suitable Applications

Antonio Opromolla[1,2(✉)], Valentina Volpi[1,2], Andrea Ingrosso[1], and Carlo Maria Medaglia[1]

[1] Link Campus University, Via Nomentana 335,
00162 Rome, Italy
{a.opromolla, v.volpi, a.ingrosso,
c.medaglia}@unilink.it
[2] ISIA Roma Design, Piazza della Maddalena 53,
00196 Rome, Italy

Abstract. In a "smart" city context, citizens' participation allows to create public services and products meeting the real people's needs. In this regard, the co-design process is a useful practice for encouraging city users to co-create new effective solutions. However, it is fundamental to renovate methodologies and tools for citizens' engagement. In this paper, we argue that the gamification approach could increase the willingness of city users in getting involved in Public Administration (PA) decision-making processes and in co-design practices. Assuming that, we present the main findings of a survey conducted to investigate city users' behaviours and needs on gamification and co-design issues. These findings will be useful to identify the most suitable applications combining these two practices.

Keywords: Co-design · Gamification · Game design · Survey · Smart city · Decision-making processes · Citizen engagement and participation

1 Introduction

The academic literature has widely discussed the "smart city" phenomenon, focusing on various factors (e.g.: technology, governance, economy, etc.), mainly depending on different disciplinary areas. According to Chourabi et al. [1], the quality of life of people and communities is one of the essential components of a city that aims to be defined "smart".

In this field, citizens' participation is an important factor, since it allows to create public services and products meeting the real people's needs. In order to do that, it is fundamental to use specific tools and methodologies aiming to engage city users in city issues. The *co-design* process, i.e. a design approach in which the different stakeholders of a city (e.g.: citizens, institutions, enterprises, associations, etc.) work together in order to ideate new services and products [2], is useful to encourage city users to co-create new solutions [3].

© Springer International Publishing Switzerland 2015
N. Streitz and P. Markopoulos (Eds.): DAPI 2015, LNCS 9189, pp. 578–589, 2015.
DOI: 10.1007/978-3-319-20804-6_53

Therefore, renovating approaches, methodologies and tools for the citizens' engagement could increase their participation in decision-making processes. In this regard, the hypothesis we support in this work is that the *gamification* approach, which consists in "the use of game elements in non-game context" [4], could increase the willingness of the city users in getting involved in these processes.

Indeed, according to McGonigal [5], games can really be used in order to improve the world and to solve real problems in a real environment. From this points of view, the gamification approach aims to encourage an active behaviour by motivating people to achieve specific purposes (mainly in activities that could be boring or uninspiring) through specific game mechanics (e.g.: point, levels, badges, etc.).

Although the gamification approach was applied mainly in marketing and education fields, the urban context is becoming an increasingly important sector of implementation. In details, the purpose of the gamification approach applied to the city context is making people aware of the issues affecting the territory in which they live. In this regard, as we pointed out in a previous study [6], the current academic contributions underestimated the application of this approach to engage citizens and co-design new solutions.

So, with this work we intend to proceed with the research toward that unexplored direction by observing how gamification can be combined with co-design. In the next section we report the basic game design elements we considered as the more suitable in the implementation of new co-design solutions. In the third section we report the methodology followed for the design of a survey aiming to investigate city users' behaviours and needs on gamification and co-design issues. In the fourth section we focus on the main findings of this survey. Finally, in the fifth section the conclusions and the future work.

2 Defining the Basic Design Elements to Use for Combining Co-design and Gamification

In order to identify how the gamification approach can be integrated in co-design practice to increase city users' participation in decision-making processes, it was necessary to define the "boundaries" within which the possible solutions should move.

For this purpose, we investigated in depth the main characteristics of "co-design" and "gamification", by identifying, for both of them, the related practices, tools, purposes, involved stakeholders, fields of application, etc., and by pointing out the connections between the single characteristics. On the basis of these connections, we identified some basic required features that we consider as the more suitable in combining co-design and gamification. In detail, they are summarized in the following game design elements.

1. *Multiplayer mode*: the "gamified" applications should involve several people, playing simultaneously or not. Indeed, the presence of more than one person is fundamental both in a co-design practice, where new solutions arise from the consideration of more than one perspective, and in a gamification approach, where "the other" is a central element.

2. *Roles*: in the "gamified" solutions any player should "play a role". Indeed, on the one hand, co-design practice considers the joined work of different stakeholders, with different characteristics; on the other hand, the "role" is an important element of specific typologies of games.
3. *Cooperative gameplay*: the solutions should involve players working together to reach a common goal. The "gameplay" identify the modes through which players interact with a game [7] and the relations with the others. In the solutions combining co-design and gamification players should have the same importance, as well as the different perspectives of the participants of a co-design session are on the same level of relevance.
4. *Dynamic game balancing*: during the co-design session the single player should receive benefits, awards, and acknowledgments. Since the single player may not be strongly motivated in realizing new "co-designed" products and services, the use of game mechanics (e.g.: points, badges, awards, etc.) is a key requirement for increasing participation. Indeed, during a co-design session, or during consecutive co-design sessions (that could be considered as different levels of a game), the user arises his/her abilities and he/she should be rewarded as a consequence.
5. *Socializer players*: the solutions should be firstly addressed to the players that Bartle define "socializer" [8], i.e. those who within the game are interested in people, rather than only in the game. Indeed, the interaction among participants of a co-design session is more important than the single perspective, as well as "socializer" focuses on human relations.
6. *Emergent gameplay*: in the solutions the actions and the creativity of the players should influence the game process and its result. Indeed, their ideas, needs, and thoughts should be the most important game tools.
7. *Story-based game*: the solutions should be based on an open and a "not defined a priori" process, because it should be built by the interaction among participants.
8. *Results*: the solutions should aim to achieve a clear goal, which consists in the creation of a new product or service. So, it is important not only the "game" side (e.g.: declaring a winner), but also obtaining useful elements for the real implementation of the identified outputs.
9. *Clear rules*, allowing to really reach a result.
10. *Real or virtual mentor*, who should follow the process without direct it, as well as during a co-design practice designers drive users and in some "gamified" solutions a "master" presents and maintains game settings.

On the basis of these elements, we identified five typologies of games that present the basic required features to proper combine co-design and gamification. They are: *role-playing games (RPG)*, *serious games*, *board games*, *videogames*, *urban games*. Although the aim of the "gamification" approach is to offer a gameful experience and not to create a real game, the list in the Table 1 was useful to observe (as a speculative reference) existing game solutions and game elements that appear to be really close to the scope of the solutions combining co-design and gamification.

Table 1. Five typologies of games that present the basic required features to proper combine co-design and gamification.

Games	Characteristics of the games
RPGs	Unpredictability of the results; clear rules; story-based; collective consciousness shared among players; central role of the mentor; different players with different roles; social interaction; creativity as a central element.
	Examples of RPGs: *massively multiplayer online role-playing games (MMORPG), role-playing video game, live action role-playing game (LARP), game committee.*
Serious games	"Serious" purposes; adaptability to different devices; clear goals; improvement of player conditions; different typologies of players as users.
Board games	Different game tools (e.g.: game table, tokens, bricks, etc.); social interactions; possibility to realize a story; clear rules; focus on the player abilities; high flexibility.
	Example of board games: *cooperative board games.*
Videogames	Different typologies of videogames; possibility to employ different devices, platforms, and controllers; high interactivity; focus on the game environment; clear rules; possibility to create a story.
	Examples of videogames: *role-playing video game, city building games, government simulation games.*
Urban games	Real city as game environment; possibility to use different mobile technologies (e.g.: GPS, NFC, mobile social network, etc.); usually organized as a team game.

3   A Survey on Gamification and Co-design Issues: The Followed Methodology

Identifying the basic game design elements useful to combine co-design and gamification led us to the identification of the "boundaries" within which the possible solutions should move. The next step was to investigate, within these "boundaries", people's behaviours and needs on both gamification and co-design issues. So, we create a survey to collect the related data.

We decided to administer the questionnaire to Italian people potentially willing in being involved in Public Administration (PA) decision-making processes and/or more interested in games. To identify the characteristics of this target, we considered as variables age, gender, and education level. On the one hand, according to the ISTAT (Italian National Institute of Statistics) [9], the age groups more willing to an active participation in public and/or social issues are 25–34, 35–44, and 45–54 years old, with an education level equal or higher than a high school diploma, and without a significant difference between males and females. On the other hand, according to the Osservatorio gioco online [10], the more active Italian gamers belong to the age group 25–34 and 35–44 (followed by 18–24 and 45–54 age groups) and they are mostly males. However, some studies (e.g. that of ISFE [11]) show that women players are on the rise also in the Italian context.

So, the respondents of our survey had the following characteristics: age range between 25 and 54 years old; education level equal or higher than a high school diploma; uniform distribution between males and females.

A *structured survey questionnaire* composed of the following 5 sections was administrated to them:

1. *Personal details.* Investigation on: age, gender, educational level and job.
2. *Participation in decision-making processes.* Investigation on: consideration of co-design practice, perceived advantages and disadvantages of this practice, willingness in being involved in decision-making processes, evaluation of the co-design experiences already carried out. In order to get the respondents familiar with the participation in decision-making processes issue, we showed them videos and images explaining the main concepts and procedures of the co-design practice.
3. *Game experience.* Investigation on: frequency of play, types of games conducted more frequently.
4. *Gamification approach.* Investigation on: consideration of the gamification approach, willingness in using applications and services based on the gamification approach, evaluation of the "gamified" experiences already carried out. Also in this section, we showed the respondents videos and images, in order to get them familiar with the gamification concepts and procedures.
5. *Gamification in urban area.* Investigation on: consideration of the solutions involving citizens, businesses, associations, etc. in PA decision-making processes through the gamification approach and user needs about the most suitable co-design activities, organization modes, fields of application, game mechanics and tools, etc. in the solutions combining co-design and gamification.

The questionnaire was composed of multiple choice questions with only one answer allowed or with more than one answer allowed, open questions and 5-point Likert scale questions. The latter were used in order to identify the agreement/disagreement level with different design alternatives regarding specific elements. The survey questionnaire was administered online to a sample of 200 respondents.

4   The Main Findings from the Survey

In this section, we show the main findings from the survey, according to the 5 sections investigated: personal details, participation in decision-making processes, game experience, gamification approach, and gamification in urban area.

4.1   Respondents' Personal Details

The respondents have an average age of 34 years. The most part of them has a master degree (38 %). People with a PhD (24,5 %), a bachelor degree (19 %) and a high school diploma (18,5 %) follow. They are equally distributed in males (51 %) and females (49 %).

4.2 Participation in Decision-Making Processes

83,5 % of the respondents consider positive or totally positive the possibility of involving citizens, businesses, organizations, etc. in the PA decision-making processes, 13,5 % consider this possibility neither positive nor negative, and 3 % negative or totally negative.

The three main perceived advantages of co-design practice are: "increasing the sense of belonging to a community" (65 % of the respondents), "creating products and services really useful" (61 %), and "making people aware of the issues related to the territory in which they live" (59 %).

On the contrary, the three main perceived disadvantages of this practice are: "the lack of interest on the part of the PA" (59 %), "the difficulties in meeting all the people needs" (46 %), and "the difficulty in finding people willing to get involved in co-design practice" (45 %).

71,5 % of the respondents are willing or absolutely willing to be involved in decision-making processes aiming to develop products/services in a given area. However, only 24 % of the respondents took part in these processes in the past. The main purpose of the co-design sessions in which they have been involved, were: the urban regeneration of public places (squares, urban gardens, shared spaces, train station, etc.), buildings, neighbourhoods; the (re)design of digital services; the design of public services in environment, mobility, and touristic fields. 52,1 % of the respondents that took part in these processes describe this experience positive or totally positive, defining it "effective", "activating", "involving", "connecting citizens", "meeting people needs", and "low-cost". On the other hand, 27,1 % of the respondents that took part in these processes describe their experience negative or totally negative, defining it "ineffective", "without a real involvement", "complicated", "confused", "unstructured", "excessively driven", and "without a real participation". Finally, 20,8 % of the respondents who already took part in these processes consider this experience neither positive nor negative.

4.3 Game Experience

56 % of the respondents consider themselves fans of games. The three main types of game conducted are: board games (49 %), mind games (41 %), and card games (41 %). 24 % of the respondents declare to play daily, 41 % at least once a week, 19,5 % at least once a month, 11 % at least once every six months, 3,5 % at least once a year, 0,5 % less than once a year, and 0,5 % never.

4.4 Gamification Approach

78 % of the respondents consider positive or totally positive the use of the game mechanics with the aim to engage people in different fields of application, 18 % consider this possibility neither positive nor negative, and 4 % negative or totally negative.

73,5 % are willing or absolutely willing to use applications and services based on a gamification approach. However, only 28 % of the respondents used them in the past. The main fields of application of the solutions they used were: marketing (loyalty features), learning (primarily foreign languages), work (team building, skills development, and evaluation of work activities purposes), well-being (e.g.: sport, diet, etc.), and organization of daily activities. In the city environment the main aims of the employed applications were: traffic control, public works construction, and conflict resolution (between two neighbourhoods).

Among the respondents who used these applications or services, 8,9 % consider this experience negative or totally negative. They define it "ineffective", "disadvantageous", "unwieldy", "complicated", "not exciting", "trivial", "repetitive", and "boring". 62,5 % of the respondents who used these applications or services consider their experience with these systems positive or totally positive, by defining it "captivating", "pleasant", "engaging", "leading to collaborate", "motivating", "enjoyable", "improving", "mild-expanding", "outside the box", "learning", "activating", "effective", and "fascinating". Finally, 28,6 % of the respondents who used these applications or services consider their experience neither positive nor negative.

4.5 Gamification in Urban Area

76,5 % of the respondents consider positive or totally positive the application of gamification approach with the aim of involving citizens, businesses, associations, etc. in PA decision-making processes. See Fig. 1.

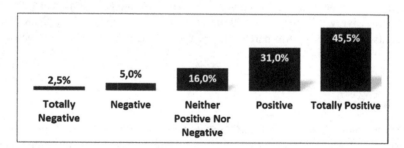

Fig. 1. Online structured questionnaire. Question: "In the range of 1 to 5, how do you consider a game involving citizens, businesses, associations in PA decision-making processes? (1: totally negative; 5: totally positive)". Total: 200 respondents.

70,5 % of respondents declare that the gamification approach could increase their involvement in PA decision-making processes. See Fig. 2.

The respondents who would increase their involvement in these processes through the gamification approach are:

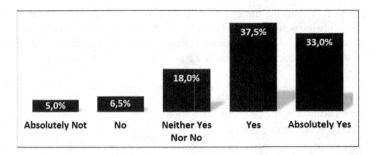

Fig. 2. Online structured questionnaire. Question: "In theory, such a game could increase your participation in PA decision-making processes? (1: absolutely not; 5: absolutely yes)". Total: 200 respondents.

1. considering the age, 72,2 % of the respondents belonging to the 25–34 years age range, 70,8 % of the respondents belonging to the 35–44 years age range, and 64 % of the respondents belonging to the 45–54 years age range;
2. considering the gender, they are 72,4 % of the females and 68,6 % of the males;
3. considering the education qualification level, they are 65,7 % of the respondents with a high school diploma, 63,2 % of the respondents with a bachelor degree, 77,6 % of the respondents with a master degree, and 67,3 % of the respondents with a PhD;
4. 76,2 % of the respondents willing to be involved in PA decision-making processes and 50 % of the respondents not willing (or absolutely not willing) to be involved in PA decision-making processes;
5. 64,6 % of the respondents already involved in PA decision-making processes and 71,5 % of the respondents not involved, neither in the past, in these processes;
6. 77,7 % of the game fans and 61,4 % of the respondents who do not consider themselves fans of games;
7. 79,6 % of the respondents willing to use services and applications based on the gamification approach and 21,4 % of the respondents not willing to use them;
8. 69,6 % of the respondents who used services and applications based on the gamification approach and 68,6 % of the respondents who did not use them.

The following data identify the respondents' agreement/disagreement level, in the range of 1 to 5 (1: strongly disagree; 5: strongly agree), with different options related to 5 elements regarding the combination between co-design and gamification. These 5 elements are: the more suitable activities, application areas, people categories, game tools, and game mechanics.

In each of the following table the findings about each of the 5 investigated elements are summarized. In details, each table illustrates the results about the different options provided for one of the 5 different investigated elements, showing the average (from 1 to 5) value calculated on a total of 200 answers.

As presented in Table 2, the respondents believe that solutions combining co-design and gamification could mainly facilitate the identification of the problems in a specific area. Indeed, almost 78 % of the respondents are agree or strongly agree to use these solutions with this aim. (Please note that the activities listed in Table 2 are the main phases of a co-design session).

Table 2. Evaluation through 5-points Likert scale. Question: "Which of the following activities could be facilitated by a game? For each of the activities, express your agreement/disagreement level in a range of 1 (strongly disagree) to 5 (strongly agree)". Total: 200 respondents.

Activities	Average
Identification of people needs	3,89
Identification of the problems in a specific area	4,15
Collaboration with other people	3,69
Design of new products and services	3,85
Development of new products and services	3,76

Considering the gender, females are more interested in the "design phase" than males. Moreover, the age range 45–54 years old is more inclined towards the "development of new products and services".

Table 3 shows the city application areas in which respondents would like the solutions to be implemented. Environment and mobility are the favourite ones: almost 76 % of the respondents are agree or strongly agree to use these solutions in the environment area and the 75 % in the mobility area. The listed city application areas are those identified by Giffinger et al. [12].

Table 3. Evaluation through 5-points Likert scale. Question: "Which of the following application areas could be affected by a game? For each of the application areas, express your agreement/disagreement level in a range of 1 (strongly disagree) to 5 (strongly agree)". Total: 200 respondents.

Application Areas	Average
Mobility	4,02
Environment	4,11
Governance	3,62
Living	3,84
People	3,84
Economy	3,59

Considering the age range, the respondents belonging to the age group 45–54 years old prefer "Governance" as main city application area; on the contrary, the respondents with a high school diploma expressed interest for "Economy" and "Living" areas.

The respondents consider also that young adults are the most suitable category for the solutions combining co-design and gamification (see Table 4). Almost 90 % of the respondents are agree or strongly agree with this category.

Table 5 shows the tools considered as the most suitable for the solutions combining co-design and gamification. Digital tools in the mobility environment (mobile applications, smartphone, etc.) are the preferred ones.

Table 4. Evaluation through 5-points Likert scale. Question: "in your opinion, which of the following categories would be the most suitable for solutions combining co-design and gamification? For each of the categories, express your agreement/disagreement level in a range of 1 (strongly disagree) to 5 (strongly agree)". Total: 200 respondents.

Categories	Average
Children	3,16
Teens	3,78
Young adults	4,33
Adults	3,80
Elderly	2,68

Table 5. Evaluation through 5-points Likert scale. Question: "in your opinion, which of the following tools are the most suitable for solutions combining co-design and gamification? For each of the tools, express your agreement/disagreement level in a range of 1 (strongly disagree) to 5 (strongly agree)". Total: 200 respondents.

Tools	Average
PC (Personal Computer)	3,61
Playing cards	2,57
Videogames	2,97
Internet	4,06
Mobile applications	4,15
Pen and paper	2,89
Dice	2,10
Toy models (e.g. of the city furniture)	2,98
Smart objects	3,81
Smartphone	4,17
Augmented reality	3,34
Tablet	3,95
Virtual reality	3,17
3D graphics	3,10
Console	2,59
Totem/Interactive screens	3,34
NFC (Near Field Communication)	2,76
GPS (Global Positioning System)	3,37
Board game	2,77
Tokens	2,64
Game table	2,57
Bricks	2,93
Social networks	3,90

In details, males prefer videogames and consoles. Females instead prefer social networks, totem, toy models, and bricks. Moreover, by increasing with age, the preference for videogames and no-digital tools (playing cards, pen and paper, toy models, board game, tokens) rises, while the preference for digital tools (mobile, PC, totem, smart objects) decreases. Finally, respondents with a more high education qualification level prefer augmented and virtual reality and 3D graphics, to the detriment of PC, toy models, tokens, game table.

The respondents also indicated additional tools they would like to use. Among them: everyday and wearable objects (e.g.: bracelets, watches, odometer, fidelity cards, etc.) that could interact with the physical environment; urban furniture; open data (i.e., the data released by the PAs); photos.

The preference for tools usually used in mobility is confirmed by the fact that the respondents (especially the younger) would like to use these solutions all around the city rather than in a dedicated place.

Moreover, the respondents prefer solutions organized in "micro-goals" rather than in "one final goal".

About that, the respondents have preference for solutions that allow them to play (and co-design) while performing other activities at the same time (e.g.: a walk, visit a place, etc.), rather than to play during a dedicated co-design session.

Finally, Table 6 shows the game mechanics considered the most suitable ones for the solutions combining co-design and gamification.

Table 6. Evaluation through 5-points Likert scale. Question: "in your opinion, which of the following games mechanics are the most suitable for solutions combining co-design and gamification? For each of the tools, express your agreement/disagreement level in a range of 1 (strongly disagree) to 5 (strongly agree)". Total: 200 respondents.

Tools	Average
Points and leader boards	3,57
Badges	2,97
Prizes and rewards	3,82
Challenges	3,55

5 Conclusion and Future Work

In this paper we assumed that the gamification approach could be integrated in co-design practice to increase city users' participation in decision-making processes. On the basis of this hypothesis, we showed the main findings from a survey conducted in the Italian context aiming to investigate city users' behaviours and needs on gamification and co-design issues.

In general, the respondents are strongly willing to be involved in a co-design practice through a "gamified" solution. One of the main results emerged from the survey is the interest of the respondents in mobility and environment city issues (e.g.:

accessibility, sustainability and innovation of transport systems, pollution, environmental protection, etc.) and in mobile digital game tools (e.g.: smartphone, mobile applications, smart object, etc.). Moreover, the respondents prefer to play (and co-design) while performing other activities at the same time, rather than to play during a dedicated co-design session, as well as all around the city rather than in a dedicated place. Finally, the respondents declare that such a game could be implemented in order to identify the specific problems of a given area.

So, in the future, we will use the findings of this survey in order to design at least three "gamified" solutions meeting the behaviours and needs of the identified target. In details, we intend to realize these solutions not only for the people who declared to be willing to use these solutions, but also for people not willing. Indeed, the aim is to identify how the applications that combine gamification and co-design could be useful in involving also this category.

Finally, we are identifying a specific urban area in the Italian territory, with the aim to realize and test in this area the designed solutions.

References

1. Chourabi, H., Taewoo, N., Walker, S., Gil-Garcia, J.R., Mellouli, S., Nahon, K., Pardo, D. A., Scholl, H.J.: Understanding smart cities: an integrative framework. In: 45th Hawaii International Conference on System Science, pp. 2289–2297. IEEE Computer Society, Washington (2012)
2. Sanders, E.B.-N., Stappers, P.J.: Co-Creation and the new landscapes of design. Co-design Int. J co-creation Des. arts **4**(1), 5–18 (2008)
3. Smart cities: Co-Design in Smart Cities. A Guide for Municipalities from Smart Cities (2011)
4. Deterding, S., Sicart, M., Nacke, L., O'Hara, K., Dixon, D.: Gamification. using game design elements in non-gaming contexts. In: CHI 2011 Extended Abstracts on Human Factors in Computing Systems, pp. 2425–2428. ACM, New York (2011)
5. McGonigal, J.: Reality is broken: Why Games Make us Better and How They Can Change the World. Penguin Books, USA (2010)
6. Opromolla, A., Ingrosso, A., Volpi, V., Medaglia, C.M., Palatucci, M., Pazzola, M.: Gamification in a smart city context. An analysis and a proposal for its application in co-design processes. In: Games and Learning Alliance Conference (2014)
7. Lindley, C.A.: Narrative, game play, and alternative time structures for virtual environments. In: Göbel, S., Spierling, U., Hoffmann, A., Iurgel, I., Schneider, O., Dechau, J., Feix, A. (eds.) TIDSE 2004. LNCS, vol. 3105, pp. 183–194. Springer, Heidelberg (2004)
8. Bartle, R.: Hearts, clubs, diamonds, spades: players who suit MUDs'. J. MUD Res. **1**(1), (1996)
9. ISTAT (Italian National Institute of Statistics): La Partecipazione Politica in Italia. Report, ISTAT (2014)
10. Osservatorio Gioco Online: Il Gioco Online in Italia: tra Maturità e Innovazione. Report, Politecnico di Milano (2014)
11. ISFE (Interactive Software Federation of Europe): Videogames in Europe: Consumer study-Italy. Report, ISFE (2012)
12. Giffinger, R., Pichler-Milanovic, N.: Smart Cities, Ranking of European Medium-Sized Cities. Report, Centre of Regional Science Vienna (2007)

Activity Recipe: Spreading Cooperative Outdoor Activities for Local Communities Using Contexual Reminders

Tomoyo Sasao[1(✉)], Shin'ichi Konomi[2], and Keisuke Kuribayashi[1]

[1] Department of Socio-Cultural Environmental Studies,
The University of Tokyo, Kashiwa, Chiba 277-8563, Japan
{sasaotomoyo,kuri}@csis.u-tokyo.ac.jp
[2] Center for Spatial Information Science, The University of Tokyo,
Kashiwa, Chiba 277-8568, Japan
konomi@csis.u-tokyo.ac.jp

Abstract. Recently, many civic engagement platforms have appeared on the web and for mobile devices to collect public comments and local information. However, it is difficult to cope with diminishing civic engagement due to the loss of diverse outdoor activities in towns using existing civic engagement platforms. In this paper we present Activity Recipe, a framework for supporting citizens to create and share activities in public spaces and thereby promoting their cooperative outdoor activities. We discuss the methods to 'spread' effective activities for local communities and cultivate citizens' awareness for these activities based on Activity Recipe.

Keywords: Activity recipe · Mobile phones · Civic engagement · Community development · Sharing citizen's activity

1 Introduction

Recently, social connections between friends are increasing through online services such as Facebook and Twitter. On the contrary, interactions between neighbors are becoming weaker and the diversity of citizen's outdoor activities seems to be diminishing in many cities as many urban planning experts pointed out including Jan Gehl [1] and Jane Jacobs [2]. Consequently, many urban design projects are based on the understanding that just building civic facilities is not enough, and it is important to build civic engagement for increasing citizen's motivation and power to challenge problems of their surroundings.

Following that movement, many web platforms such as OpenIDEO [3] and Neighborland [4] pursue a collaborative/corporative working space that match and introduce mates who have similar social aims, and encourage a user participate in creating social problems' solutions with the mates. These open access approaches are succeeding to create opportunities to directly collect grass-roots opinions and ideas more easily. Moreover, nowadays, mobile devices become earning a new position as civic engagement platforms, which support citizen's outdoor activities for local community

© Springer International Publishing Switzerland 2015
N. Streitz and P. Markopoulos (Eds.): DAPI 2015, LNCS 9189, pp. 590–601, 2015.
DOI: 10.1007/978-3-319-20804-6_54

such as Pirika, volunteered trash-picking platform [5], and FixMyStreet, problem reporting in neighborhood [6]. These mobile platforms for civic engagement are excel in supporting simple actions within few minutes in field as in citizen science (e.g., [7]), volunteered geographic information (VGI) projects (e.g., OpenStreetMap [8]), and participatory sensing projects (e.g., [9]). However, little work has been done to support other many complex activities existing in the field flexibly. In other words, many towns suffer from losing diversity of citizen's outdoor activities but they are beyond saving.

In this paper we focus on recipes as a civic engagement framework to encourage citizen's outdoor activities as well as easy/simple tasks. A typical recipe has succeeded as a worldwide tool that can be sharing long/complex cooking processes and DIY (Do it Yourself) instructions. Almost everyone can produce something by following recipe instructions and can write original recipes by themselves. We present Activity Recipe, a contextual reminder framework extended a recipe structure that citizens can create and share activities in public spaces, and thereby seeding and fostering activities that positively impact local communities.

First, we discussed key issues in existing outdoor activities with three scenarios and elicited our research questions, how to 'spread' effective activities for local community and cultivate citizens' awareness for these activities based on Activity Recipe. Second, we introduced the powers of online recipes, which have a potential of promoting their outdoor activities. Based on these discussions, finally, we presented Activity Recipe framework including several modules, which provide opportunities to access recipes and encourage citizens to readily try activities with the recipes.

2   Issues in Outdoor Activities

In this section, we present three scenarios for showing the problems in existing outdoor activities. These scenarios are based on actual experiences of people.

2.1   Problem Scenarios

Use of the Newly Developed Public Square. *Miki* has been running a restaurant for thirty years in front of a train station. Recently, the area around the station had been redeveloped and new public squares, wide sidewalks, and benches were installed gradually. However many people do not use them frequently. *Miki* thinks if people receive ideas how to use and enjoy these facilities, people living/coming her town will make full use of the new public space better.

Use of Vacant Lands and Forestry. Recently, as vacant lands including house lot, parking, rice field and forests, given up manage by the landowners grow in number, crime risks become higher and towns spoil the sight. *Ryoko* is an urban designer who tackles this problem. She thinks it is important to give opportunities to experience of playing in vacant lands and teach various skills to enjoy outdoor life with neighbors. She rent several vacant lands and conducts citizen workshops recreating arid vacant places to common garden, farm, and park with the neighbors in several cities. *Ryoko* want to expand her programs in more many cities, however, it is difficult to do just by herself. She has published a magazine to promote her programs but she felt it was not enough to make citizens to start acting.

Anticrime Patrol. *Yasutaka* is a businessman and he has lived with his family in this city for 5 years. His office is also in this city so he can go back home in early evening everyday. In the past few months, he worries about his family and neighborhood because he often hears small crime news in the city. He decides to join a local anticrime patrol group in his town every week because he wants to do something for the problem. In the patrol group, most members are retired elderlies or people who come back home in early evening, such as like *Yasutaka*. This is one day of his anticrime patrol; Today's patrol started at 6 pm. *Yasutaka* and other 3 members gathered in a park, then they walked around and check any suspiciousness on one hour in the south part of the town. They greeted passerby and gave them to anticrime goods such as a light reflection band. Recently, *Yasutaka* became realizing that the number of patrol participants are decreasing and in this month, there are even two times that they could not find enough participants for the patrol. *Yasutaka* feels anxiety about this activity's future.

2.2   Research Questions

From these three scenarios, key problems in outdoor activities can be summarized as follows: the first and second scenarios show that many places cannot afford fertile outdoor activities by themselves and the difficulty of penetrating new activities in a target place. The former one implies the luck of ideas of how to use the place well. The later one implies the luck of spreading power of good activities for local communities. While, third scenario shows the difficulty of working with neighbors together. If these activities disappear, citizens will lose their quality of life, however it becomes difficult to participate in and continue such social activities by citizens nowadays.

Consequently, the key research questions we address are: (1) how to spread effective activities for local community and (2) how to cultivate citizens' awareness for these activities based on Activity Recipe.

3   Recipes for Activity

In this section, we summarize our survey about online recipes focusing on their formats and the environment for sharing their repositories, in order to uncover applicable recipe essentials in supporting outdoor activities.

3.1   Recipe Formats

For discussing typical recipe formats effects, we pickup three kinds of recipe formats from representative online recipe sharing services, hRecipe [10], Cookpad [11], and Instructables [12] (see Table 1).

hRecipe is one of the widely used cooking recipe formats on the web because the format is used for a crawling service by Google search. If people upload their recipes

Table 1. Recipe formats of hRecipe, Cookpad, and Instructables

Recipe format contents	Title	Author	Images	Instructions	Licenses	Published date	Tag / Keywords	Categories	Ingredient, Field	Duration	Introduction	Summary	Tips, Caution points	Background	Social Network
I. Necessary information	N	N	N	N	N	N	N								
II. Information for Searching	S	S	S		S		S	S	S	S					S
III. Information for Performing	P	P	P	P	P				P	P	P	P	P	P	P
hRecipe	✔	✔	✔	✔	✔	✔	✔	✔	✔	✔		✔			
Cookpad	✔	✔	✔	✔	✔	✔	✔		✔		✔		✔	✔	✔
Instructables	✔	✔	✔	✔	✔	✔	✔	✔			✔				✔

written in this format on blogs, Google automatically create a summary (Rich Snippets) from their cooking recipes; therefore we expect that this format contain common attributes for many recipes. For users searching proper ones from a large number of recipes, the format prepares various tags to generate several categories helpful in many situations such as nutrition automatically, and also use duration and ingredients data for generate categories to be helped exploring a recipe.

Cookpad is one of popular sharing recipe site in Japan, which stock 1,920,000 cooking recipes and has 50,420,000 unique visitors in one month (in December, 2014). This recipe format seems to include some contrivances to increase cooking motivation such as introduction, tips, and background of a recipe. This information becomes important when choosing one recipe in many similar choices after searching recipes. In addition, comments and ratings of recipes using social network services are also strong information to influence whether to try or not.

Instructables is an online sharing recipe service for not only cooking but also anything including Food, Living, Outside, Tech, Play and Workshop. Although we may think we need to prepare proper instructions in proper ways for each type, Instructables provides just one recipe format for all types and it seems to be enough. Especially in the format contents, 'introduction' covers various kinds of information, which is not provided own form, such as ingredients, duration, tips and backgrounds. However the diverseness of coverage and the facility of searching are tradeoff relation, this service inspires us that outdoor activities will be able to be described and shared by using recipe formats.

From them, we propose essentials for extending recipe formats to outdoor activities. A recipe format for an outdoor activity needs to include not only *necessary information*, but also, *information for searching*, and *information for performing*. For information for searching, we can consider a possibility of automatically narrowing down recipes with current location and other surrounding context from mobile sensors as well as generating useful categories. While for information for performing, we can consider showing recipe contents directly when affording the recipe activity, because the impression from these information inside of the recipe are big factors to decide whether to try it or not.

3.2   Recipe Sharing Environment

Nowadays, online repositories for recipes or something similar to a recipe can be found in many fields other than cooking. To understand the potentials of recipe sharing environments, we surveyed interfaces and functions of following online repositories in several fields: cooking (Cookpad), anything (Instructables), 3D modeling (Thingiverse [13]), programming (wonderfl [14]), furniture (Architecture for Dogs [15]), and personal smart task (IFTTT [16]). From this survey, we can summarize key roles and corresponding components of sharing recipe environment as follows:

Search. Most of repositories provide a search box for narrowing down recipes. This component is used by people who have already decided what he creates with rough details, such as what ingredients they use, or what event they prepare for. They can meet by chance and practice a better process, which is someone's knowhow. Additionally, this component is useful especially when a repository holds large number of recipes.

Explore. Many repositories provide several components for exploring recipes such as various unique categories, keywords/tags. Furthermore, a top-page of sharing recipe sites arranges popularity ranking and featuring contents (e.g., 5 min cooking, for diet, seasonal ingredient in Cookpad). These components is used by people who want to create something but do not decide to create what and make opportunities of finding good recipes.

Perform. Some repositories promote links between a recipe and performing environments. First, a video component for the recipe instruction is one of easy and popular methods to link performing and can help to perform step by step (e.g., [11, 12]). As a second example, some repositories provide sub-repositories of tools (e.g., outsourced 3D print [17]) and materials (e.g., furniture blueprints, dress pattern, and 3D drawing data). These components support troublesome preparing phases for performing and encourage people to quick start. As a third example, some repositories include execution environments, which are directly connected with recipes and contribute to the ease of making recipes. For example, in wonderfl [14], sharing ActionScript codes can be done in a preview screen on the web, which provides the functions to perform and refine the codes easily.

Create. Unless people attempt to serve carefully selected high quality contents, they can use the recipe design components provided by repositories for anyone. Because they have good user interfaces and provide samples of recipes, most recipes can be created easily. In addition, some provide special user support including a staff calling to advise a draft phase of recipes. Without such services, people still have a lot of chances to learn how to write recipes better because they are familiar with recipes by reading and performing. In some repositories, people can create branch recipes based on other one's recipe [14]. This way can cut a workload for writing recipes and improve recipe qualities cooperating with each other.

Furthermore, we found an essential but overlooked characteristic in online repositories, 'encounter'. Most of online repositories just premise active access (i.e., 'pull'), and *searching, exploring, performing, and creating recipes* are ushered by user's active action. In other words, we cannot obtain recipes in the repositories without our active actions. While, we may know intuitively that 'encountering' recipes are valuable experiences for us. Indeed, we encounter recipes frequently in our lives. For example, about cooking, recipes appear on TV cooking show in lunchtime, on a package of food, and in a supermarket vegetable corner. They sometimes plant an idea, "let's try to do it" in people's mind. We consider that encountering recipes is a necessary idea for spreading outdoor activities in neighborhood.

For supporting this idea in outdoor activities, location-based contextual reminder technologies can be focused on. These technologies will create a chance to encounter recipes in proper place and proper timing. Then, the possibility that people try to perform the activity will become higher. We have developed Community Reminder, a smartphone-based contextual reminder system for local communities, which include notification co-design platform and local information notification repository [18]. It can encourage citizens to do small tasks that will benefit their neighborhoods. We finished testing the prototype in 1-month field study and revealed that this system worked well in serving opportunity to 'encounter' local issues with small works or local relevant knowledge. In addition, the encounter experiences put high concerns in neighborhood into participant's mind long time [19]. From these results, we expect to embed an Activity Recipe as a contextual notification, in Community Reminder frame for spreading outdoor activities in local community.

4 Activity Recipe Environment

In this section, we present the Activity Recipe Environment model and the four key modules strongly tying recipes to citizen's activities based on the strengths and weaknesses of recipes discussed in Sect. 3. To illustrate how the Activity Recipe environment can support citizens, we also show an activity scenario that describes the case when people use this system. This scenario is based on one of the problem scenarios in Sect. 2.

4.1 Activity Recipe Environment Model and Four Supporting Modules

As shown in Fig. 1, we designed the Activity Recipe environment model based on an online recipe repository. We learned that a recipe could encourage people to perform not only cooking but also other types of activities enhancing a connection between people and creative artifacts (e.g., programming, DIY). From this finding, we believe that outdoor activities should be also described with a proper format and collected in an online repository. Then, the Activity Recipe environment provides various methods of repository access to increase a chance to encounter recipes. It can be accessed while searching, exploring, performing, and creating recipes and from several platforms including the web and mobile devices. In this model, searching and exploring recipes supposes a user-driven access (i.e., 'pull'). In contrast, system-driven access (i.e., 'push') is necessary for performing and creating recipes on mobile devices so that recipes embedded in the real world can be discovered and elicit people's actions in a natural way. This environment model uses extended context reminder engine to support a system driven access by notifying recipes to citizens with appropriate formats and timing.

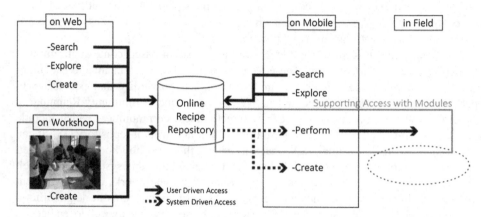

Fig. 1. Activity Recipe environment model. Online Recipe Repository can be accessed various purposes and platforms. Four modules support system driven access on mobile (see the red rectangle) (Color figure online).

Furthermore, we focus on the mobile platform in Activity Recipe environment because it has a potential to connect recipes and citizens' activities tightly in their life. We propose four modules that support system driven access on smartphones based on different approaches to involve citizens widely in outdoor activities and enhance their awareness of their surroundings, which can produce various activities. (1) *Trial recipe module* and (2) *Neighbor Sourcing module* provides triggers for enhancing people's motivations to try recipes and (3) *Notification control module* provides a scheme for controlling suitable timing of a recipe encounter in outdoor spaces. (4) *Activity Sprinkler module* focuses on passers-by near the people who are performing a recipe to change the mind of the passers-by.

4.2   Trial Recipe Module

A Recipe is One Thing and Doing is Another. An ordinary recipe is separated from action, so unless we try, we won't know whether the activity is interesting or not, or provides good effects or not for our city. As instructables, many workshops provide people experiences of trying recipes in a real space such as "instructables restaurant".

We also should remark the hurdle when designing ways of access to activity recipes and prepare a mechanism of decreasing the starting hurdle.

Trial recipe module focuses on user-friendly recipe format. It generates a short trial guidance, which work as a stepping stone to perform a recipe's activity easily by converting a regular recipe automatically. A role of trial recipe is to encourage people to perform a short version of activity described in a regular recipe and afford great understanding of a recipe content. The following shows four conditions on trial recipe that is able to lower the starting hurdle:

- Allowing to comple the process within x minutes
- Including a start point and an end point in the process
- Providing a opportunity that information of regular recipes is clear
- Providing a opportunity to try the process empty-handed

The method of trial recipe creation is described in Fig. 2. First, an Activity Recipe creator fills out a target activity title, introduction, performing conditions, duration, and all steps to perform a target activity with a feature tag showing appropriate place in digital format of a regular recipe (Fig. 2a). Changing from current format to map-based format, the creator can plot all steps at each appropriate location (Fig. 2b). Then the recipe is completed as regular one. Additionally, he can collect and setup photos and location data used for the recipe in the field so Activity Recipe can be created quickly.

To set up a trial recipe, the recipe creator needs to segment partial steps in the regular recipe and set proper duration, which will be shorter than regular one (Fig. 2a). After the setup, this module can notify the trial recipe as well as regular one automatically in proper place and at proper timing referring conditions described in these recipes (Fig. 2c). The trial recipe interface is very simple; it displays the activity title, the short introduction and just one instruction of the steps. The recipe notification changes the display of the activity process step by step along with a user's move. Moreover, it equips two buttons, one is "next step", and the other is "view a regular recipe".

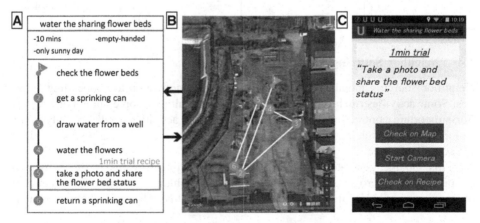

Fig. 2. A regular recipe converts into a trial recipe notification automatically

4.3   Notification Control Module

Notification control module supports timely access to the activity recipe repository because it is important to calculate appropriate timing from user circumstances as well as appropriate situation described in a recipe and also difficult to setup timely notifications to a recipe under complex context by laypeople.

Some researches revealed that a notification is less annoying when pausing manipulation of smartphones [20] and when shifting to another action mode (e.g., start walking when sitting) [21]. Fischer et al. discuss that notifying content is important more than notifying timing [22].

In our notification control, first, this module narrows the list of activity recipes down referring the proper conditions described in each recipe (e.g., weather, hour), then narrow down the list again with current user's circumstances (e.g., weather, hour, location) and situation (e.g., busy, free, walking, stay in same place) earned from sensors in user smartphone. Consequently, this module notifies a proper trial or a regular recipe in a timely manner. We confirmed two rules of notification control for different targets (see Table 2). One target is people walking periphery of recipe points because they have high potential of dropping in a recipe spot on the way. Trial recipes are easier to perform in the spare time than regular one. The other one is people staying within walking distance of recipe points. They also have potential of dropping in a recipe spot but they need some motivations or purposes to go there in particular. This rule finds people's spare time from smartphone use, and triggers and notifies regular recipes.

Table 2. Two rules of notification control for different targets

Target	Aim	Recipe Type	Conditions
People walking periphery of recipe points	encourage to drop in and make the attempt	trial recipe	enter within a 50-meter radius of the city on foot
People staying within walking distance of recipe points	encourage to visit and make the attempt	regular recipe	still or walk within a 800-meter radius of the city (walkable distance) more than 1 hour, and when unlocking a smartphone display

4.4   Neighbor Sourcing Module

Neighbor Sourcing module focuses on participative motivation to cooperating activities. Some activities can be continued/concluded by multiple people but not one person. For supporting continuous working, a recipe of such activities needs not only notification control module but also additional set of functions to tell some urgency and ask for some assistance.

This module generates another type of notification, a status board visualizing cooperative work progress (e.g., counting individual achievements) and notifies them in order of priority to rise in neighbor's awareness of status of tasks for their community existing their surrounding. This interface has referring recipe button, so that someone interested in the status immediately join and try the activity using the trial recipe.

4.5   Activity Sprinkler Module

Activity sprinkler module focuses on rise in awareness of someone performing recipe activities for increasing neighbors' motivation of participating various activities in their surroundings. This module supports several physical outputs (e.g., shining key holder, smart street lamp) visualizing "doing the activity now" and it can draw attentions of passers-by. It can be expected that increasing participants of the activity can increase the opportunity attracting people's notice.

4.6   Scenario in Case Using Activity Recipe – Activate Anticrime Patrol

Yasutaka worried about sustainability of the voluntary anticrime patrol activity in his town because of decreasing the group members. He had known Activity Recipe because his friend living different city told him that his friend's town uses it for sightseeing. Accordingly, he conceived of eliciting cooperation from citizens such as people who take a dog walk and who come back home in evening by Activity Recipe environment. *Yasutaka* described his 1 h patrol activity process, significance, and several proper conditions into a regular format of Activity Recipe. He wrote 10 checkpoints and the tips about anticrime in each step based on his anticrime patrol experiences and plotted these steps in the map view of his town (e.g., This parking is a poor visibility so you need to check to the bottom.) He also wrote "17:00–19:00" as proper time to do it and "walking with a dog, coming back home" as a better situation in the condition blank. Then the regular recipe is completed. Additionally, he decided to design a trial recipe because he wants to give many busy people an opportunity to experience small actions for anticrime contribution. He cut and divided the regular recipe's 10 steps into 4 parts, grouping some steps if they are close, then each part of work could be finished in 5–10 min. Just from this operation, *trial recipe module* in the Activity Recipe environment generated 4 trial recipe notifications from Yasutaka's anticrime patrol recipe. Moreover, to encourage the participation in this activity, he created anticrime key holders for dogs with LED lighted during taking the recipe action using *activity sprinkler module*. The key holder includes an NFC tag inside, and people can receive the patrol recipe just approaching their smartphones to it when getting out of a house and thereby start blinking and start guiding the recipe on their smartphones. He distributed the key holders to his friends and passers-by with dogs.

Yoshie is an office worker and she is interested in anticrime activities. However she usually came home at 8 pm, so it is difficult to participate in anticrime patrol in her town. It is a reason she installed the smartphone app, Activity Recipe in her phone. Today, she was able to leave her office earlier than usual and receive one notification at 18:30 at the bus stop near her home. Because her current place is close to one of the recipe points, *the notification control module* sent a trial recipe notification to her. The notification was an anticrime patrol recipe telling that you could do it in just 10 min.

Yoshie decided to try it because she usually thinks that she wants to contribute some activities for her town. When she pushed start button in the trial recipe, the trial recipe start navigating a first checkpoint that is a parking side of a supermarket. Arriving the point, the recipe asked to check whether this parking is safe and take a photo. She did these steps then the recipe displayed "Thank you for your cooperation! This recipe was completed." She felt small satisfaction.

Toru is a student and today he was on duty for walking with a dog. Walking around his town with his dog, suddenly his smartphone received a notification. He checked it right away and then the notification told the urgent place to treat an anticrime patrol. At that time, *a neighbor sourcing module* works because Toru was coming near the recipe point where is less traffic street and not treated well recently. He understood the urgent message from attached information of the regular recipe for the patrol and decided to go the street to check safety. When he pushed start button on the notification, a recipe was appeared and started to navigate the first step spot of the recipe. At last, he completed all steps of the recipe easily and this minor street was taken care by him.

Reiko was drinking tea and talking with her friend in a café. When she checked her phone, a notification arrived on her phone. The notification told her introduction of anticrime patrol in her town. At that time, *a notification control module* works and sent a regular recipe to her because Reiko was staying long time in the café, which was not 800 m far from one recipe spot. Her friend and she didn't know well about the anticrime patrol group, and they were interested in the activity. So they decided to perform a trial recipe on the way their home.

Recently, *Takashi* often saw dogs wearing neck bands with blinking key holders. One day, by word of mouth, he knew that the blinking dogs are related with anticrime patrol in his town then he wanted to try it and started the activity getting the key holder from official anticrime patrol group.

After designing and sharing the anticrime patrol recipe, *Yasutaka* was surprised and now he knows that many people participate in his designed trial recipe of anticrime patrol. This trial activity is different from an official patrol way but it also contribute to anticrime.

5   Conclusion and Future Works

We have proposed Activity Recipe environment, a civic engagement platform to encourage outdoor activities using the recipe framework. We focused on recipes' potential, and our survey made clear that proper formats and sharing environments are needed to encourage people to "try to do it." To integrate the recipes' potential with outdoor activities, we decided to prepare a flexible access model of online recipe repository including mobile-based contextual notification and four modules to facilitate performing recipes.

We verified our approach using several scenarios in this paper, however, we are yet to verify its effects and feasibility in real towns. In addition, we will explore other triggers to encourage outdoor activities in cities besides context notification on mobile devices. We believe that outdoor activity information included in recipes can seed and foster activities to positively impact local communities and make cities better places.

References

1. Gehl, J.: Life Between Buildings: Using Public Space. Island Press, Washington, DC (2011)
2. Jacobs, J.: The Death and Life of Great American Cities. Random House LLC, New York (1961)
3. OpenIDEO. https://openideo.com
4. Neighborland. https://neighborland.com
5. Pirika. https://www.pirika.org
6. FixMyStreet. http://www.fixmystreet.jp/
7. Kim, S., Mankoff, J., Paulos, E.: Sensr: evaluating a flexible framework for authoring mobile data-collection tools for citizen science. In: Proceedings of CSCW, pp. 1453–1462 (2013)
8. OpenStreetMap. http://www.openstreetmap.org/
9. Willett, W., Aoki, P., Kumar, N., Subramanian, S., Woodruff, A.: Common sense community: scaffolding mobile sensing and analysis for novice users. In: Pervasive Computing, pp. 301–318 (2010)
10. hRecipe. http://microformats.org/wiki/hrecipe
11. Cookpad. http://cookpad.com
12. Instructables. http://www.instructables.com
13. Thingiverse. http://www.thingiverse.com/
14. wonderfl. http://wonderfl.net/
15. Architecture for Dogs. http://architecturefordogs.com/
16. Ur, B., McManus, E., Ho, P.Y., M., Littman, M.L.: Practical trigger-action programming in the smart home. In: Proceedings of the SIGCHI Conference on Human Factors in Computing Systems (CHI 2014), NY, USA, pp. 803–812. ACM, New York (2014)
17. Ponoko. http://www.ponoko.com
18. Sasao, T., Konomi, S.: U.App: an urban application design environment based on citizen workshops. In: Streitz, N., Markopoulos, P. (eds.) DAPI 2014. LNCS, vol. 8530, pp. 605–616. Springer, Heidelberg (2014)
19. Sasao, T.: Support environment for co-designing micro tasks in Suburban communities. In: CHI 2015 Doctoral Consortium, Seoul, Republic of Korea (2015)
20. Fischer, J.E., Greenhalgh, C., Benford, S.: Investigating episodes of mobile phone activity as indicators of opportune moments to deliver notifications. In: Proceedings of MobileHCI 2011, pp. 181–190 (2011)
21. Ho, J., Intille, S.S.: Using context-aware computing to reduce the perceived burden of interruptions from mobile devices. In: Proceedings of CHI 2005, pp. 909–918 (2005)
22. Fischer, J.E., Yee, N., Bellotti, V., Good, N., Benford, S., Greenhalgh, C.: Effects of content and time of delivery on receptivity to mobile interruptions. In: Proceedings of MobileHCI 2010, pp. 103–112 (2010)

Personalized Energy Reduction Cyber-physical System (PERCS): A Gamified End-User Platform for Energy Efficiency and Demand Response

Nicole D. Sintov[1,2(✉)], Michael D. Orosz[1], and P. Wesley Schultz[3]

[1] Viterbi School of Engineering, Information Sciences Institute,
University of Southern California, Los Angeles, CA, USA
{nisintov,mdorosz}@isi.edu
[2] Department of Psychology and Environmental Studies Program,
University of Southern California, Los Angeles, CA, USA
[3] Department of Psychology, California State University at San Marcos,
San Marcos, CA, USA
wschultz@csusm.edu

Abstract. The mission of the Personalized Energy Reduction Cyber-physical System (PERCS) is to create new possibilities for improving building operating efficiency, enhancing grid reliability, avoiding costly power interruptions, and mitigating greenhouse gas emissions. PERCS proposes to achieve these outcomes by engaging building occupants as partners in a user-centered smart service platform. Using a non-intrusive load monitoring approach, PERCS uses a single sensing point in each home to capture smart electric meter data in real time. The household energy signal is disaggregated into individual load signatures of common appliances (e.g., air conditioners), yielding near real-time appliance-level energy information. Users interact with PERCS via a mobile phone platform that provides household- and appliance-level energy feedback, tailored recommendations, and a competitive game tied to energy use and behavioral changes. PERCS challenges traditional energy management approaches by directly engaging occupant as key elements in a technological system.

Keywords: Games · Gamification · Psychology · Energy efficiency · Human factors · Cyber-physical systems

1 Introduction

Smart grid systems are rapidly being deployed across the world. They provide opportunities for improving the reliability, efficiency, and adaptability of the electric grid. Among an array of hardware and software upgrades, smart grid systems include high-resolution meters to measure electricity use. For example, advanced metering infrastructure (AMI) technology involves meters that collect near real-time usage data ("smart meters"). However, the meters alone do not generate electricity savings.

Changing end-user behavior is key to an optimally functioning smart grid system. A variety of technologies and programs already exist to involve end-users in power

© Springer International Publishing Switzerland 2015
N. Streitz and P. Markopoulos (Eds.): DAPI 2015, LNCS 9189, pp. 602–613, 2015.
DOI: 10.1007/978-3-319-20804-6_55

systems, but consumers are often not central considerations in technology design. Technologies that consider end-users as key players in power systems are urgently needed.

Leveraging behavioral science can improve our understanding of how to partner with consumers in the smart grid to develop these technologies, and ultimately lead to more efficient uses of energy. A wealth of research supports the effectiveness of various tools in changing end-user energy behaviors. For instance, the provision of real-time energy feedback to customers has proven to be a reliable strategy for achieving conservation. Energy savings tend to be higher for more granular feedback, which has been greatly facilitated by smart meters. However, granularity in terms of specific behaviors remains on the frontier of the field: no systematic study to date has had the ability to provide real-time, personalized behavioral recommendations to reduce energy use—they have been limited to providing household-level data, leaving end users to contemplate which behavioral changes might result in large savings. Separately, recent advances in non-intrusive load monitoring (NILM) research are enabling the provision of appliance-level feedback, though training NILM algorithms has proven challenging and applications have not been widely tested. Involving end-users in the training process offers one potential for addressing NILM research challenges.

To this end, the Personalized Energy Reduction Cyber-physical System (PERCS) aims to promote energy efficiency and peak load curtailment by engaging building occupants as partners in a user-centered smart service platform. PERCS uses a single sensing point–a Wi-Fi-enabled service gateway-installed in end-user homes–to capture smart meter data in real time. Machine-learning algorithms disaggregate the household energy signal into individual load signatures of common appliances (e.g., air conditioners), yielding near real-time appliance-level energy information, and creating a smart home area network without the requirement of purchasing smart appliances. This level of customization marks a substantial innovation from the status quo of whole-house feedback. It eliminates the need for consumers to generate a mental list of what is using energy in their home, which can be overwhelming and inhibit action. Building additional opportunities for utility-customer engagement, users interact with PERCS via a mobile phone platform that provides household- and appliance-level energy feedback and timely, tailored recommendations. The user experience is tied to a competitive game that leverages social influence. The system also solicits feedback directly from end-users to improve disaggregation results. Finally, PERCS joins anomaly detection approaches with NILM to enable appliance fault detection.

In the remainder of this paper, we describe shifting priorities in energy systems, and describe how PERCS is designed to achieve future energy efficiency and demand response (DR) goals. We also discuss how this system has been informed by and makes contributions to the fields of computer science and behavioral science.

2 Literature Review

2.1 Shifting Priorities in Energy Systems

Despite the growing availability of renewable energy resources, current demand for electricity, particularly at peak times of day, contributes substantially to greenhouse gas

(GHG) emissions, which are associated with rising global temperatures [1] and negative public health outcomes, including increased mortality rates [2]. The residential and commercial sector is a major consumer of electrical energy and contributor to electric power-related GHG emissions: from 1990–2012, the residential and commercial sector accounted for the largest portion (35 %) of electric power-related GHG emissions of any sector [3]. In addition to environmental and health impacts, even relatively brief lapses in electric power reliability, which often occur when an over-stressed grid cannot meet peak demand, have significant economic consequences. Annual losses from power interruptions range from 150 billion Euros among European Union businesses [4] to $80 billion in the U.S. [5]. Accordingly, electric utilities allocate considerable resources to avoiding such interruptions and historically, have invested in additional peak generating capacity (e.g., "peaker plants"), which generally relies on traditional, higher-polluting generation sources (e.g., coal; [6]). Although these strategies can help accommodate increasing demand, the associated economic and environmental costs are substantial. As an alternative, growing efforts are being made to manage demand by curtailing peak loads [6]. Advances in "smart grid" technologies have facilitated this approach by improving demand predictions (e.g., [7]). However, solving the problem of *how* to reduce demand merits further attention.

The U.S. Federal Energy Regulatory Commission (FERC) calls for DR programs that encourage electric customers to make behavioral changes to curtail energy use [8]. Such programs can be effective in promoting overall energy conservation, with home energy savings as high as 21 % [9]. With regards to peak demand and load-shifting programs, however, the literature is relatively sparse. Despite the prevalence of these programs, many have not been evaluated or published, and among those that have, methodological limitations suggest areas for improvement (e.g., [10]).

Achieving the load reduction objectives of the coming decades will require higher levels of customer engagement. The California Energy Commission (CEC) found that the state's DR programs have not met load reduction goals [11]. With DR program participation rates estimated at less than 10 %, and actual compliance rates likely lower [8], the CEC recommends focusing on customer engagement to move closer to DR targets [11]. Toward this end, utility-consumer connectivity must be enhanced. Programs must shift from a one-way, utility-to-consumer approach to a more interactive relationship. Research suggests that "gamified" programs may be better equipped to attract users and sustain program engagement [12] and energy savings, over time. With recent advances in human interface platforms, smart building infrastructures, and real-time mobile technology, now is the time to focus on the rapidly developing area of technology-enabled behavior change.

Building occupants need actionable energy feedback (i.e., information about their building's energy use) in order to make informed energy management decisions. Feedback has been found to be most effective when it is tailored, accompanied by specific recommendations for reductions, and delivered digitally at the appliance-level in an interactive manner [13, 14]. However, monitoring individual loads (e.g., at the appliance level) is cost prohibitive [15, 16]. Instead, a solution that gathers highly granular information while minimizing instrumentation is needed. PERCS offers these features using a single sensing point, making it cost-effective and scalable.

2.2 Computer Science Foundations

Energy disaggregation describes a set of statistical approaches to identify individual loads (e.g., appliances) within a whole-building energy signal. Two primary methods have been applied to electric energy disaggregation: (1) distributed direct sensing, which involves monitoring individual appliance loads; and (2) single-point sensing, also known as non-intrusive load monitoring (NILM), which uses statistical algorithms to determine the state and energy use of individual appliances based on measurements collected (e.g., voltage, current, frequency, harmonics, real and reactive power) via a single sensing point on the incoming building power feed. Because load metering requires more instrumentation and tends to be expensive, limiting its scalability, much work has focused on NILM.

NILM approaches emerged in the 1980s [17]. As power data are collected, statistical approaches identify "events", which represent state changes, and cluster them into groups, which represent individual appliances. Correctly classifying appliances with similar signatures presents a challenge. One recent advance for improving classification accuracy is to increase sampling rates, which addresses noise in the signal, thereby improving multi-event discrimination and detection of state changes [15, 16]. To this end, studies suggest leveraging data streams from installed AMI meters [15, 16], in part because such solutions can be cost-effective and scalable, given that electric utilities have deployed millions of smart meters globally that provide whole-home power measurements in intervals of seconds to minutes. Other studies have achieved improvements in classification accuracy by considering non-power data, such as time of day and temperature (e.g., [18]). It is noteworthy that approaches for advancing algorithm performance have relied on pattern detection using non-human inputs.

A major limitation of this work is minimizing the human factors element, a missed opportunity that has resulted in the limited training of algorithms [16, 19, 20]. The few studies that have considered user input and behavioral data have found a direct relationship between behavior and device usage [21] and have increased classification accuracy [22]. These findings suggest that incorporating direct user input into the NILM process can improve NILM results, and point to new research directions.

Also relevant to NILM is the issue of appliance performance degradation over time. NILM can deliver an additional service by identifying, tracking, and addressing suboptimal appliance performance (i.e., appliance fault detection). To this end, anomaly detection, which has been extensively studied among the signal intelligence (SIGINT) community [23], offers a viable model. For example, Hidden Markov Models have proven successful in detecting changes in observed behaviors [24]. However, little, if any, of this research has been applied to the NILM context, in which there is opportunity to improve equipment operating efficiency. For instance, in a typical household, anomalies can result from innocuous changes in end-user behavior (e.g., change in frequency of opening/closing refrigerator door) or due to appliance performance problems (e.g., fan bearing failure, etc.). A primary innovation of the current study is to extend NILM research by leveraging SIGINT approaches.

Finally, little work has leveraged NILM to investigate real-world potential for energy savings. The few studies that have done so have been on limited scales (e.g.,

[16], [19]) with the exception of Chakravarty's study [25], which showed promising results of 14 % energy savings following provision of disaggregated energy feedback via web and mobile interfaces among a sample of California households. Limitations in the methodology of this latter study underscore the need for additional research.

PERCS extends NILM research in three fundamentally novel ways, by: (1) engaging users as partners, directly building user feedback into training the models; (2) integrating SIGINT anomaly detection approaches with NILM to enable appliance fault detection; and (3) mapping the output of the NILM process to actionable insights for end-users, offering a cost-effective smart service.

2.3   Behavioral Science Foundations

Previous behavioral science studies on residential electricity consumption have estimated that households could realistically use 5–10 % less energy without adversely impacting occupant comfort or well-being [26]. Newer technologies allow users to achieve comparable output with less energy input, and upgrading appliances or using appliances more efficiently offers an excellent opportunity to achieve reductions [3, 27]. In addition, people tend to underestimate the amount of energy required for household activities, especially those that involve major household appliances [28].

Smart meter infrastructure can be leveraged to motivate residents to increase energy efficiency through feedback. Historically, residents received only aggregated feedback on a monthly or quarterly basis, making it difficult to connect their behaviors with consumption. Behavioral research has shown that feedback can play an important role in reducing energy consumption, with high-resolution feedback associated with greater savings [13]. For instance, a recent meta-analysis of 57 residential energy feedback studies found that disaggregated, real-time feedback was associated the highest mean reduction of energy use at 12 % [9]. The same meta-analysis found a mean peak load reduction of 13 % among 11 studies that targeted load curtailment. Although these findings are promising, many of the studies included in the meta-analysis did not undergo rigorous peer-review, as is true for the bulk of DR projects.

More importantly, energy feedback by itself may not be sufficient to motivate change [29]. For feedback to generate a behavioral response, the individual must also have a goal, and creating a specific plan for achieving an energy reduction goal has been associated with greater savings [30]. In addition, research on financial framing and incentives suggest that these tools are generally not effective at motivating reductions in electricity consumption, and in some cases they result in increased consumption [31]. Among the feedback-frames tested to date, social comparison to peers has emerged as a promising strategy for motivating electricity conservation [32, 33].

Finally, in line with the Theory of Planned Behavior [34], studies suggest that energy technology acceptance is partially explained by perceived control over the technology [35]. Direct control DR programs may achieve reliable reductions, but participation rates are estimated at 10 % [8]. Evidence suggests that consumers may be deterred from these programs due to privacy and autonomy concerns. Among the most well-documented customer concerns regarding smart grid technologies are perceptions that utilities can (1) directly control a variety of home equipment without consumer permissions or opt-out; and (2) infer specific behaviors in which occupants are engaging [36]. In a similar vein, many consumers prefer choosing their own methods for curtailing consumption to direct control technologies [35]. To gain greater acceptance, smart grid technologies should provide some level of consumer choice.

PERCS provides residents with near real-time feedback about their household and appliance electricity consumption, along with specific recommendations for reductions. This allows consumers to link discrete actions with electricity data, and to decide whether they will change their behavior. The feedback is delivered in a gamified context that allows for social comparison and for a non-pecuniary reward system, a strategy that can potentially motivate users to reduce their consumption [32].

3 PERCS

The mission of PERCS is to create new possibilities for improving building operating efficiency, enhancing grid reliability, avoiding costly power interruptions, and mitigating GHG emissions. PERCS proposes to achieve these outcomes by engaging building occupants as partners in a user-centered smart service platform that motivates behavioral changes. See Fig. 1 for a systems diagram.

3.1 Objectives

Our research objectives are to (1) improve energy disaggregation classification by incorporating non-power features, most notably direct user input, into algorithm training; (2) integrate anomaly detection approaches with NILM to enable appliance fault detection along with a user alert system; (3) test the energy efficiency and peak load curtailment potentials of deploying a gamified, user-centered NILM platform at scale, with energy reduction goals of 15 % per DR event and 15 % for overall energy efficiency; and (4) evaluate the effectiveness of appliance-level feedback and behavior-contingent social rewards on electricity use among residential end-users.

3.2 Technical Approach

PERCS uses a single sensing point – a Wi-Fi-enabled service gateway installed in a residence – to capture smart electric meter data at high resolution, and push the data through a server where it is processed. The processed data are then presented to users as novel information about their home energy use via a mobile phone application (app), providing actionable, appliance-level information without the requirement of purchasing individual smart appliances or smart plugs. The NILM process identifies "events" in the power feed that indicate a state change of an appliance, typically signifying a change of power. Machine learning algorithms then attribute non-power features to that event, such as delta-power, time of day, and outdoor temperature, which enable discrimination between similar load characteristics. Using these features, a clustering algorithm groups these events into groups of similar events. Event-groups that co-occur are then grouped into an "appliance-pattern", which is linked to specific appliances based on additional non-power characteristics of state changes (i.e., only runs when outdoor temperature is above 80 F). PERCS aims to refine appliance classifications through soliciting feedback from users as part of the training process, described below. Additionally, the system identifies patterns of suboptimal appliance functioning and alerts users when it would be advantageous to replace or service inefficient or failing appliances. PERCS features the following:

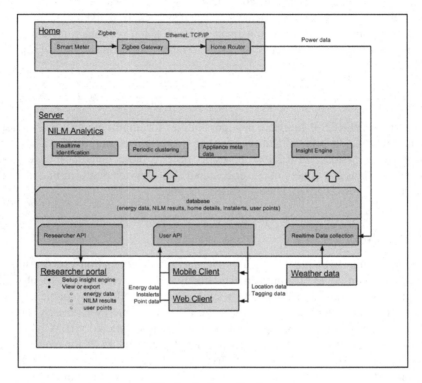

Fig. 1. Systems diagram

Leveraging User Input to Improve Classification. PERCS builds user feedback directly into the NILM workflow through a process called "tagging". PERCS prompts users to identify an appliance that changed state in real time by sending notifications to users' mobile phones. This data improves differentiation between similar appliances (e.g., stove and grill) as well as identification of appliances with multiple signals. To encourage responses to tagging prompts, users earn points for responding as part of the competitive mobile platform game, described in detail below.

Real-Time Algorithm Training. Running the entire NILM process continuously can be computationally intensive. In PERCS, we add a unique parallel process that streamlines the process, enabling it to run as new data are received. This real-time identification process uses characteristic appliance data to identify state changes, updating classification as appropriate as new data are received.

Smart Appliance Insights for Users. Perhaps the most transformational of the PERCS innovations is the insight engine, which uses NILM results to provide a valuable service to end-users by triggering user notifications. The trigger comprises a decision tree with specific conditional triggers, such as time of day, total power demand and consumption, specific appliance power and run time, appliance efficiency, and other metrics. From the insight engine, PERCS sends "Action of the Week" notifications to users every week, each of which is a request to engage in one specific behavior tailored to each user's household based on identified appliances (e.g., "Keep your A/C off every day this week from 1–4 pm"). These notifications serve as behavioral "triggers", which have been identified as a key component of behavior change [12]. This level of customization marks a significant innovation from the status quo of whole-house feedback. It eliminates the need for consumers to generate a mental list of what is using energy in their home, which can be overwhelming and ultimately inhibit action. By eliminating this step, PERCS provides a valuable service that enables consumers to focus on executing a single, straightforward action to save energy.

Enhancing User Engagement. To produce and sustain an engaging user experience, PERCS includes a game as part of the mobile platform under which users earn points for complying with "Action of the Week" requests. Each "Action of the Week" is presented to users via a push notification sent to their mobile phones, and includes the following information: concise description of specific action to be taken, number of points that can be earned for compliance, and dates and times of requested compliance. Any given "Action" is active for a 1-week period, and users can earn points for complying each day during that particular week. To maintain user engagement over time, the platform offers opportunities to earn bonus points, which will be awarded on intermittent schedules of reinforcement (e.g., points awarded for logging in, participating in tagging process). Users compete against one another for the highest rank among the PERCS community via a public leaderboard that displays each participating household's selected username, point total, and rank, introducing social norms as motivation to reduce usage. Point totals and leaderboard ranks are updated daily to encourage frequent participation. To enable households who join the game relatively later than others to "catch up" to households that joined earlier, leaderboard ranks are adjusted daily to account for level of participation. For DR events, users receive special push notifications one day ahead and one hour ahead of the scheduled event, with a request to engage in a specific behavior to save energy.

Protecting User Data Privacy. To protect users' data privacy, energy data, disaggregation results, and other anonymous data are linked to an Anonymous User ID. All identifiable data (e.g., address) are stored separately, linked by an Identifiable User ID. Only the study team has access to both IDs to enable mapping between datasets. Select pieces of secure code in the application programming interface have access to the proper private keys required to link the Anonymous and Identifiable User IDs.

Anomaly Detection. PERCS expands on the disaggregation process by adding anomaly detection to the platform in order to identify failing or inefficient appliances. We leverage research from the U.S. Department of Energy-funded Building Level Energy Management System (BLEMS; [37]) and the U.S. Office of Naval Research

(ONR)-funded Geospatial Analysis of Motion-Based Intelligence and Tracking (GAMBIT) projects [38]. In BLEMS, artificial neural networks and Bayesian Belief Networks (BBNs) were trained to recognize office building occupancy patterns and to detect anomalies. This information was used to calculate HVAC set points to simultaneously optimize energy efficiency and meet occupant comfort preferences. In GAMBIT, BBNs were trained to recognize movement data (signals) and detect normal and abnormal movement behaviors. PERCS incorporates these approaches to identify, track, and address appliance degradation, using findings to trigger user alerts regarding appliance functioning along with recommendations to service or replace failing appliances at the optimal time.

Smart Building Services. We view energy efficiency, peak load reduction, user satisfaction, and equipment performance as services – each often competing with the other. A smart service platform that is designed to add capabilities over time, PERCS currently offers the following: (1) detect and differentiate energy usage anomalies from appliance performance degradation, including identifying the economic and environmental "cross-over" point at which it is advantageous to replace an appliance; (2) tailored to each participating household, suggest specific behaviors to improve energy efficiency and reduce peak demand; (3) provide an engaging experience to occupants using relatable information and social incentives.

If successful, future extensions of PERCS would enable remote appliance control, integrate with DR forecasting to improve peak demand management, and/or offer redemption of points earned as part of the game (e.g., gift cards, utility bill rebates).

4 Conclusions

PERCS introduces new possibilities for improving building operating efficiency, enhancing grid reliability, avoiding costly power interruptions, and mitigating GHG emissions. Using minimal instrumentation, we provide a cost-effective and scalable solution for intelligent sensing. Additionally, PERCS offers a new model for engaging utility customers, which may prove to be valuable for meeting DR and energy efficiency goals. The platform allows end-users to monitor their behavior, receive personalized feedback, and motivates behavior change via competition. If successful, PERCS could be expanded to promote behavior change for other applications.

Using an interdisciplinary approach that combines social psychology, machine learning, energy informatics, and network computing, PERCS challenges traditional energy management approaches by directly engaging end-users as key elements in a technological system, and provides a solution to the problem of *how* to achieve reductions in peak demand. PERCS advances behavioral science and computer science research by creatively mapping the output of the NILM process to actionable insights via a relatable user platform; it improves the NILM training process without burdening, but rather by engaging, end-users. Coupled with DR forecasting, PERCS holds promise for reshaping the energy landscape.

Acknowledgments. The authors thank J. Cole Hershkowitz, and Nicholas Roome for their helpful input on previous drafts of this paper.

References

1. United States Environmental Protection Agency: Causes of climate change (2014). http://www.epa.gov/climatechange/science/causes.html#greenhouseeffect/. Accessed 3 Feb 2015
2. Smith, K.R., Jerrett, M., Anderson, H.R., Burnett, R.T., Stone, V., Derwent, R., Thurston, G.: Public health benefits of strategies to reduce greenhouse-gas emissions: health implications of short-lived greenhouse pollutants. Lancet **374**(9707), 2091–2103 (2009)
3. United States Environmental Protection Agency: Sources of greenhouse gas emissions (2014). http://www.epa.gov/climatechange/ghgemissions/sources/electricity.html/. Accessed 3 Feb 2015
4. Targosz, R., Manson, J.: Pan European LPQI power quality survey. In: Proceedings of the 19th International Conference on Electricity Distribution, Paper 0263 (2007). http://www.cired.net
5. LaCommare, K.H., Eto, J.H.: Understanding the cost of power interruptions to U.S. electricity consumers. Lawrence Berkeley National Laboratory, Berkeley (2004). http://emp.lbl.gov/publications/understanding-cost-power-interruptions-us-electricity-consumers. Accessed 21 Mar 2014
6. California Independent Systems Operator: Demand response and energy efficiency roadmap: maximizing preferred resources. California Independent Systems Operator, Folsom (2013). http://www.caiso.com/Documents/DR-EERoadmap.pdf. Accessed 4 Apr 2014
7. Zhou, Q., Natarajan, S., Simmhan, Y., Prasanna, V.: Semantic information modeling for emerging applications in smart grid. In: Proceedings of the 9th Annual International Conference on Information Technology: New Generations, pp. 775–782. IEEE, Las Vegas (2012). http://ieeexplore.ieee.org/xpl/articleDetails.jsp?arnumber=6209085
8. United States Federal Energy Regulatory Commission: A national assessment of demand response potential (2009). http://www.ferc.gov/legal/staff-reports/06-09-demand-response.pdf. Accessed 18 Mar 2014
9. Ehrhardt-Martinez, K., Donnelly K., Laitner, J.: Advanced metering initiatives and residential feedback programs: a meta-review for household electricity-saving opportunities. American Council for an Energy-Efficient Economy, Washington, D.C. (2010). http://www.aceee.org/research-report/e105
10. Wang, K., Swisher, J., Stewart, S.: Comprehensive home energy management systems for demand response: are they worth the cost? In: Proceedings of the 2005 International Energy Program Evaluation Conference: Reducing Uncertainty Through Evaluation, pp. 165–176. International Energy Program Evaluation Conference, New York (2005). http://www.iepec.org/index.htm. Accessed 4 Apr 2014
11. Anderson, G., Bailey, S., Franco, G., Fugate, N., Grau, J., Hestsers, M., Hungerford, D., Jaske, M., Kavalec, C., Kondoleon, D., Korosec, S., Gallardo, C.L., Giyenko, E., Gravely, M., Loyer, J., McKinney, J., Milliron, M., Neff, B., O'Neill, E., O'Neill-Mariscal, G., Olon, T., Patterson, J., Rhyne, I., Spiegel, L., Stom, D., Vidaver, D., Walter, J., Wilhelm, S.: Integrated Energy Policy Report: 2013. California Energy Commission, Sacramento (2014)
12. Fogg, B.J.: Persuasive Technology: Using Computers to Change What We Think and Do. Morgan Koffman Publishers, San Francisco (2002)
13. Abrahamse, W., Steg, L., Vlek, C., Rothengatter, T.: A review of intervention studies aimed at household energy conservation. J. Environ. Psychol. **25**, 273–290 (2005)
14. Vine, D., Buys, L., Morris, P.: The effectiveness of energy feedback for conservation and peak demand: A literature review. Open J. Energ. Effi. **2**, 7–15 (2013)
15. Armel, K.C., Gupta, A., Shrimali, G., Albert, A.: Is disaggregation the holy grail of energy efficiency? the case of electricity. Energy Policy **52**, 213–234 (2013)

16. Berges, M., Goldman, E., Matthews, S.H., Soibelman, L.: Enhancing electricity audits in residential buildings with nonintrusive load monitoring. J. Ind. Ecol. **14**(5), 844–858 (2010)
17. Hart, G.W.: Nonintrusive appliance load monitoring. Proc. IEEE **80**(12), 1870–1891 (1992). http://ieeexplore.ieee.org/xpl/login.jsp?tp=&arnumber=192069&url=http%3A%2F% 2Fieeexplore.ieee.org%2Fxpls%2Fabs_all.jsp%3Farnumber%3D192069
18. Kim, H., Marwah, M., Arlitt, M., Lyon, G., Jan, J.: Unsupervised disaggregation of low frequency power measurements. In: Proceedings of the 11th SIAM International Conference on Data Mining. SIAM, Mesa (2011)
19. Berges, M., Goldman, E., Matthews, H.S., Soibelman, L., Anderson, K.: User-centered non-intrusive electricity load monitoring for residential buildings. J. Comput. Civil Eng. **25**, 471–480 (2011)
20. Zoha, A., Gluhak, A., Imran, M.A., Rajasegarar, S.: Non-intrusive load monitoring approaches for disaggregated energy sensing: a survey. Sensors **12**, 16839–16866 (2012)
21. Lee, S.C., Lin, G.Y., Jih, W.R., Hsu, J.Y.J.: Appliance recognition and unattended appliance detection for energy conservation. In: Proceedings of the Workshops at the Twenty-Fourth AAAI Conference on Artificial Intelligence, pp. 37–44. Association for the Advancement of Artificial Intelligence, Atlanta (2010). http://www.aaai.org/ocs/index.php/WS/AAAIW10/ paper/viewFile/2012/2445
22. Kolter, J.Z., Jaakkola, T.: Approximate inference in additive factorial HMMs. In: Proceedings of the 15th International Conference on Artificial Intelligence and Statistics. Artificial Intelligence and Statistics, La Palma (2012). http://www.cs.cmu.edu/~zkolter/ pubs/kolter-aistats12.pdf
23. Seibert, M., Rhodes, B.J., Bomberger, N.A., Beane, P.O., Sroka, J., Kogel, W., Stauffer, C., Kirschner, L., Chalom, E., Bosse, M., Tillson, R.: See coast port surveillance. In: Proceedings of the 2006 Conference on SPIE: Photonics for Port and Harbor Security II, 62040B (2006). doi:10.1117/12.666980, http://dx.doi.org/10.1117/12.666980
24. Joshi, S.S., Phoha, V.V.: Investigating hidden markov models capabilities in anomaly detection. In: Proceedings of the 43rd ACM Southeast Conference, pp. 98–103. ACM, Kennesaw (2005). http://neuro.bstu.by/ai/To-dom/My_research/failed%201%20subitem/ For-research/D-mining/Anomaly-D/KDD-cup-99/Joshi-Phoha%2520ACMSE%252005.pdf
25. Chakravarty, P.: The power of data. In: Proceedings of the 6th Annual Conference on Behavior, Energy, and Climate Change. American Council for an Energy-Efficient Economy, Sacramento (2013). http://beccconference.org/wpcontent/uploads/2013/12/ Chakravarty_TheHolyGrail_EnergyDisaggregation_Bidgely_2013-11.pdf
26. Dietz, T., Gardner, G., Gilligan, J., Stern, P., Vandenbergh, M.: Household actions can provide a behavioral wedge to rapidly reduce U.S. carbon emissions. Proc. Natl. Acad. Sci. **106**, 18452–18456 (2009)
27. Gardner, G., Stern, P.C.: The short list: the most effective actions U.S. households can take to curb climate change. Environ. Mag. 1–10 (2009). Electronic (2012)
28. Attari, S.Z., DeKay, M.L., Davidson, C.I., de Bruin, W.B.: Public perceptions of energy consumption and savings. Proc. Natl. Acad. Sci. **107**, 16054–16059 (2010)
29. Schultz, P.W.: Making energy conservation the norm. In: Ehrhardt-Martinez, K., Laitner, J. (eds.) People-Centered Initiatives for Increasing Energy Savings. American Council for an Energy-Efficient Economy, Washington, DC (2010)
30. Sintov, N.D., Angulo, A., Vezich, S., Goldstein, N.J.: New directions in goal setting: the effects of action planning on electricity conservation. Presented at the 7th Annual Behavior, Energy, and Climate Change Meeting. American Council for an Energy-Efficient Economy, Sacramento (2013)
31. Asensio, O.I., Delmas, M.A.: Nonprice incentives and energy conservation. Proc. Natl. Acad. Sci. **112**(6), E510–E515 (2015)

32. Abrahamse, W., Steg, L.: Social influence approaches to encourage resource conservation: a meta-analysis. Glob. Environ. Change **23**(6), 1773–1785 (2013)
33. Schultz, W.P., Nolan, J.N., Cialdini, R.B., Goldstein, N.J., Griskevicius, V.: The constructive, destructive, and reconstructive power of social norms. Psychol. Sci. **18**, 429–434 (2007)
34. Ajzen, I.: The theory of planned behavior. Organ. Behav. Hum. Decis. Process. **50**, 179–211 (1991)
35. Leijten, F.R.M., Bolderdijk, J.W., Keizer, K., Gorira, M., van der Werff, E., Steg, L.: Factors that influence consumers' acceptance of future energy systems: the effects of adjustment type, production level, and price. Energ. Effi. **7**, 973–985 (2014)
36. Hess, D.J.: Smart meters and public acceptance: comparative analysis and governance implications. Health Risk Soc. **16**(3), 243–258 (2014)
37. Jazizadeh, F., Ghahramani, A., Becerik-Gerber, B., Kichkaylo, T., Orosz, M.: A human-building interaction framework for personalized thermal comfort driven systems in office buildings. J. Comput. Civil Eng. **28**(1), 2–16 (2014)
38. Ramakrishna, A., Chang, Y.-H., Maheswaran, R.: An interactive web based spatio-temporal visualization system. In: Bebis, G., Boyle, R., Parvin, B., Koracin, D., Li, B., Porikli, F., Zordan, V., Klosowski, J., Coquillart, S., Luo, X., Chen, M., Gotz, D. (eds.) ISVC 2013, Part II. LNCS, vol. 8034, pp. 673–680. Springer, Heidelberg (2013)

Tou Hsiang Kun – A Platform for Elderly and Neighborhood to Help Each Other

Yi-Sin Wu[1], Teng-Wen Chang[1(✉)], Ying-Ru He[1], Yi Wang[1,2],
Wei-Hung Chen[1], and You-Cheng Zhang[1]

[1] National Yunlin University of Science and Technology, Douliu, Taiwan
{m10234017, tengwen, m10130014, m10131030, m10131022}
@yuntech.edu.tw,
[2] Huazhong University of Science and Technology, Wuhan, China
m201273022@hust.edu.cn

Abstract. Tou Hsiang Kun, with the meaning of "assistance" in Minnan dialect, is a platform developed by people who help each other in communities. Society or geographical features cause the isolation in Xizhou, but it aids residents to strengthen the network of neighborhood. Hence, the relationship of mutual help is built by helping the elderly with chronic diseases or with the need for articles of daily use. Five services provided are shopping, government information, diet, repair and medical. Interactive TV and Pad are used for prototypes as well as cloud service are designed. Except for accepting assistance, elderly people who live alone can serve others at the same time.

Keywords: Elderly · Solitary Elders · iTv · TV · Platform · User-centered design

1 Introduction – Use Tou Hsiang Kun to Help the Community

This study aimed to discuss the lifestyle of elderly who lived alone in Xizhou community, Yunlin County, trying to get a better understanding on their needs through their lives. Research on lifestyle attempted to find its mutual aspect between individuals and groups. Further, the study tried to explain and expect the actions the group may take later on after getting some ideas on the particular group [1]. Because of the lack of care over a long period of time, elderly who lived alone tended to be degenerated, both mentally and physically. Therefore, the aim of the study was not only to provide the elderly who live by themselves a healthier and better life, but further to enhance their quality of life.

Five orientations included "confidence-learning," "family-conservative," "leisure-directed," "society-directed" and "society-caring" could be induced by the research concerning the lifestyle of elderly [2]. Moreover, because of isolating by societies or geographical features, the elderly developed mutual care when being ill or encountering difficulties, creating powerful networks of family and neighborhood among regional residents [3]. To sum up, Social Mutual Aid, consisting of mutual identification and interdependence, was one of the basic concepts and behaviors on human society.

© Springer International Publishing Switzerland 2015
N. Streitz and P. Markopoulos (Eds.): DAPI 2015, LNCS 9189, pp. 614–624, 2015.
DOI: 10.1007/978-3-319-20804-6_56

Community-based services provided elderly for medical and welfare needs. Communities had a variety of services; however, elderly who were desperate for those services were not able to employ them. As a veteran of social work, several reasons claimed by researchers were as follows. (1) Elderly with low level of education or acquired disability were not able to apply for services through written words. (2) Elderly didn't have much information about community services because they were unable to move freely and tended to stay at home for a long time; in addition, people who live with them were physically handicapped, or they were disadvantaged elders as well. (3) Elderly were not willing to receive social welfare services because of their temperament and negative images. (4) Elderly had no idea about social services and were not willing to accept it owning to mental retardation. (5) With the reason "don't wash your dirty linen in public," the elderly can't apply the services because they were not getting along well with family members or people who live with them. (6) Elderly were unable to take advantage of services because transportation in their domicile was inconvenient.

In addition to the reasons mentioned above that unable the elderly to obtain welfare, according to contextual approach, it found out that in Xizhou community, the rate of elderly who lived alone is higher, because farming is mostly the main industry there, resulting in high emigration of young people. Besides, the remoteness blocked the networks between Xizhou community and its community-based services. By collecting the lifestyle of the elderly who lived by themselves and contextual analysis, the neighborhood in Xizhou community tended to be "society-directed" and "society-caring." Tou Hsiang Kun, with the meaning of "assistance" in Minnan dialect, was developed to help the elderly who lived alone in Xizhou community, and to enhance community-based services and networks.

2 Literature Review

This study was conducted by setting up a platform for the elderly, and principles proposed by researchers were consulted as a basis of designing Tou Hsiang Kun. Therefore, known mistakes could be avoided in advance, the rate of making mistakes could be declined, and thus the feasibility of the platform could be increased. Several ideas were in common between the real platform and Tou Hsiang Kun. (1) The elderly used specific remote control to manipulate the TV screen when employing the platform. (2) By using the platform could shorten the distance between elderly people and the society. (3) The support of social activities was a key to enhance aged people's quality of life, especially those who lived alone. In that case, how to provide a TV screen that suited the elderly lived individually? This study proposed some principles based on eCAALYX Project. (1) Use concordant design and meaningful icons for the elderly so that they could distinguish them more easily. (2) Show the service functions on the interface. (3) Use simple words.

2.1   The VITAL Platform for Elderly

In order to understand the potential needs from aged people's lives, the VITAL project, a European Community 6th Framework financed project, was employed in the case of the elderly in Spain [5], and its techniques were used to develop platforms and applications. Researchers believed that the support of social activities was a key; therefore, they considered the needs that elderly people may want, for example, being fond of chatting or having social contact with friends and relatives to strengthen the connection between families and the society. In addition, researchers also considered that how to enhance senior citizens' quality of life through far-end services provided by the platform.

The remote control provided by VITAL was used to master the table of contents shown on TV screen, and a variety of social activities could be chosen. (Figure 1 Information service page and communication interface when using webcam) For example, many kinds of games were provided for encouraging elderly people to interact with other users. Besides, the system provided audio books, which could read the content of the books aloud. In addition, far-end education courses such as cooking and homemaking were provided as well. Among those functions, the "Information service and personal newspaper" is similar to the "Government information service" provided by Tou Hsiang Kun, helping the elderly be able to get information promptly. However, testers indicated that they still preferred to p-newspapers, the overall type-setting and typeface of "information service and personal newspaper" in VITAL were subject to correction, and its function was more suitable for the young.

Fig. 1. Information service page and communication interface when using webcam

2.2   The ECAALYX Project

Previous studies showed no best suggestions on websites and TV interface specially designed for the elderly. Therefore, with persistent design, tests and the results of development, the eCAALYX project proposed some principles concerning the design of TV interface for elderly people [4]. eCAALYX (Enhanced Complete Ambient Assisted Living Experiment) is a project of European Union, with the aim to provide an overall solution for patients. Its technique was to set up the set top box at home, and the elderly could lighten their burdens by using TV to monitor their health conditions and to receive useful information about their conditions through Healthy Channel.

At the first stage of usability evaluation, with persistent design and usability evaluation, researchers got the procedures and steps needed to be revised and fitted icons by using low vision simulation model with Wizard of Oz [6]. Then researchers used the original one to carry the second stage of the test out, and discovered that the results were similar to the first test. However, in addition to the similarity, the second stage of the test not only appointed tasks more completely, but proceeded the size of the typeface and put appropriate words in each line.

After combining the usability evaluations, researchers proposed some suggestions concerning the design for the elderly, which could regard as a basis of future study. Researchers also indicated that the list would increase if there are other ways of input such as voice and gestures. Thirteen suggestions so far are as follows. (1) Minimize the number of steps it takes to reach a given screen. (2) Use consistency to facilitate recognition. (3) Make error recovery as painless as possible. (4) Reduce the information presented so users can focus on a single concept at a time. (5) Indicate current location clearly. (6) Show the current selection clearly. (7) Use meaningful icons and labels. (8) Concentrate on information at the center of the screen. (9) Use scrolling with caution. (10) Use a high contrast color. (11) Use large, sans serif and left-aligned text. (12) Use simple languages. (13) Give users time to read.

3   Combined Analysis on Elderly People Live Individually in Xizhou Community

Owing to the high rate of solitary elders in Xizhou, there were many inconveniences in their lives. For example, elderly people who lived alone had difficulties obtaining government information and receiving welfare funds or food provided by the government, because Xizhou belonged to rural area, except for watching TV series, residents seldom used tech-products such as computers or smart phones. In addition, aged people lived individually were suffering from chronic diseases, and they needed long-term medical care and medicines. However, physical degeneration was unable them to move freely, which may bring some persecutions. Many problems in solitary elders' lives still remained unsolved, but some of them were regarded as mental problems, which should be improved through social interaction. For example, care. Therefore, two factors included fundamental element and lifestyle that elderly people lived individually in Xizhou community would be addressed in this study.

3.1   Fundamental Element for Solitary Elders

Two elderly people who lived alone were analyzed by interviews. For example, "How do you get along with your family members?" "How many children do you have?" "How often do you and your family get together?" "Do you close with the community?" "Do you have any experience on participating in activities in the community?" and "Whether or not you are cared by both family members and the community?" From those questions, researchers found some similarities between two participants. By considering three aspects "Family members-Care-Social groups," they also discovered the "Questions-Influences-Actual demands" of solitary elders, and finally concluded that the potential demands the elderly want were (1) hearing (2) vision (3) communication (4) action and (5) care. (Figure 2 Fundamental Element).

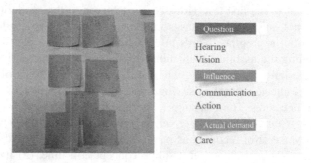

Fig. 2. 「Question- Influence- Actual demand」 The potential demand for elderly

3.2   Lifestyle of Solitary Elders

From the items and behaviors two participants owned, researchers came up with some aspects like food, accommodation, transportation, purchase, recreation and government organization as conception, in order to understand the motivations and goals behind elderly people's behaviors, and to find appropriate methods to help them. To take "accommodation" as an example, senior citizens lived in three-section compound or bungalow; they may do chores such as paying fees or cleaning the house. When senior citizens who lived alone had the need concerning gas or repair, they had to contact with gas store or general contractors. But how did they carry out those actions and where did they execute the behaviors? (Figure 3) Results from the interview were induced as follows.

Food-How to Eat Healthier? For economic reasons, elderly people lived individually only eat lunch in a day, other meals are replaced by brewing up tea. However, it is necessary to replenish nutritious food appropriately since the physical condition of aged people is gradually degenerate.

Accommodation-How to Find an Assistant? It is dangerous for the elderly when items need to be repaired, since children are not allowed to accompany them. And it is difficult to find someone to give them a hand.

Transportation-How to Obtain Things and Medicines in Need? Both the participants in the interview had the experiences of going out, and the aim of being out was to get medical care or medicines for chronic diseases.

Purchase-How to Obtain more Information or Knowledge from Markets? For economic reasons, nonscheduled activities held in large outlets such as specific goods are on sale can lower the burden of aged people.

Recreation-How to Shorten the Distance Between the Elderly and the Society? Reading, watching TV and chatting with neighbors are common recreations for the elderly who live by themselves. If the elderly haven't contacted with their children for a long time, the rate of being lack of care could be higher.

Government Organization-How to Obtain the Latest Information from the Government? The participants of the interview indicated that they were not informed of the information concerning receiving free food supply. Though the government has tried its best to take care of people with low income, it's a pity that elderly people can't get supplies and information in time.

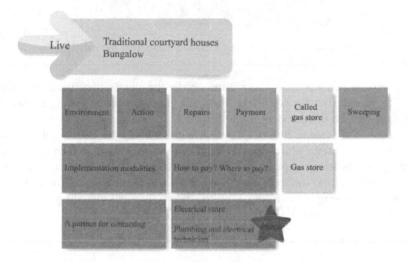

Fig. 3. An example of accommodation, consisting of several considerations such as environment, actions, behaviors, locations, and people the elderly may contact with.

3.3 The Idea of Tou Hsiang Kun

After discussion, researchers believed that transportation was not the priority problem, since the elderly seldom go out after physically degenerated. To aged people who live alone, interacting with residents is their recreation. Therefore, the demand of recreation was combined to other items. While solving the problems of food, accommodation, purchase and government organization, the aim should let the elderly able to interact with the society. Based on the definition of fundamental elements, the platform should flexibly adjust to aged people's vision and hearing; and it should function as communication, action and care while the service is provided. (Figure 4 fundamental elements and lifestyle of the elderly).

4   The Platform of Tou Hsiang Kun

From the interview, researchers found that in Xizhou community, interpersonal cooperation does exist. Therefore, building the platform there will have a great effect on helping residents. People in the community could use the demand-service matching

Fig. 4. Fundamental elements and lifestyle of the elderly

function, which can not only help them obtain the goods they need, but provide services to the elderly who need help. Thus, the opportunities of getting assistance for aged people will be increased.

To operate the system, first of all, ask relatives to help the elderly set up personal information, and then the elderly put their demands in the system, which will search for the appropriate assistant and provide services to them. The helper could be another senior or residents from different ages. (Figure 5 Basic procedures of Tou Hsiang Kun) Therefore, while using Tou Hsiang Kun, the elderly live individually will be a helper and the cared at the same time.

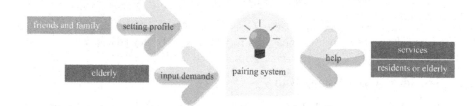

Fig. 5. Basic procedures of Tou Hsiang Kun. Personal information will be asked to fill in for the first time of use. Then, all the elderly need to do is to put their demands in the system, through matching to find a helper (another elderly person or resident in the community).

4.1   Matching Service/Information Service

The system will start matching as soon as demands are inputted. If the user is able to purchase the goods on his/her own, the system will show the information of the item nearby, and the elderly can decide to buy it or not. If the user needs a helper, then the system will find someone who is suitable for him/her. After successfully matched, the helper can decide to call the elderly or not after the demand shown on his/her cell phone. (Figure 6 Service of Tou Hsiang Kun) Both parties will discuss about the goods need to be purchased, the number of the specific product and delivery location by phone. The helper delivers the goods and the elder person pays for the product

Fig. 6. After inputting their demands, matching service or information service will be shown on the interface. Then the system helps to find a helper, and communication through phones between both parties will be developed.

simultaneously, and the interpersonal interaction between the elderly and the society works.

4.2 Prototype Design-Personal/in-Shop Device

The system is divided into cared-end and service-end, and six services are provided for the elderly, including (1) service (2) purchase (3) medical care (4) diet (5) household maintenance and (6) government information. Household TV is commonly used and widely accepted by elderly people; therefore, the instrument chose household TV as a platform of conveying messages, and handheld device is employed as a combination of telephone and remote control, which also provides photographic function, so that the user can take a photo of the goods and input it into the system. (Figure 7 Operating procedures of Tou Hsiang Kun, taking purchase as an example).

The service-end is divided into personal and in-shop. Personal mobile device (also called smart phones) receives demands released by the elderly through APP, if it can provide the service; users can hold conversations by a simple click. In-shop device is

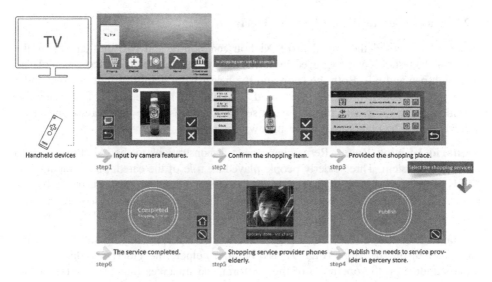

Fig. 7. Operating procedures of Tou Hsiang Kun, taking purchase as an example

installed in the tablet, which is put on the checkout counter. When residents finish purchasing and come to the checkout counter, they can see the goods that need to be purchased. If they are willing to help, just click "I can help" bottom, then the elderly in need can be helped in time.

5   Test on Tou Hsiang Kun

Backed to the manipulation of users from the system and through the interview and generalization, researchers aimed to see if the interface and operation performance of Tou Hsiang Kun are suitable for elderly people's actual conditions and lifestyle; besides, how is the acceptance of household TV, which is used as a media for the elderly? Two stages of evaluation would be tested, and the results would be regarded as a basis of revising the procedures and system in the future.

5.1   Stage 1-Experts' Evaluation

First stage of evaluation was made by experts before the system tested by the elderly in Xizhou community. They indicated that choosing TVs as the media is suitable for the elderly. However, TVs are different from cell phones and tablets, so the manipulation of the system should fit with household TV, and the interface of TV should adjust to future operation as well. Besides, researchers could provide the design of interface that more suit TVs while switching the items or pages. To sum up, the design of interface of Tou Hsiang Kun should fit household TV, with which can correspond manipulation naturally. And the designing of handheld device derived from the remote control should be improved to fit operation of the interface.

5.2   Stage 2-Actual Usage by the Elderly

Researchers invited the president of Xizhou community and two participants as the users of the test. TV was replaced by touch screen, and handheld device was replaced by touch pen and wii. Both the shop and the helper were equipped with a tablet and a smart phone, and a notebook was used to deal with the feedback. Two scenarios included living-room and in-shop were set up in the test. The procedures and video records would be elaborated in the following session.

Scenario 1-Living Room. Researchers made demonstrations to the elderly on how to operate the system. Three elderly people played the role of the cared, photographing the goods in the scenario and inputted them to the system, completing three tasks on buying tissues, designating buying goods, and dispensing medicines. Through the test, researchers could find mistakes and check if any procedures need to be improved. (Figure 8).

Scenario 2-In-shop. The elderly played the role as a helper, buying salt through the tablet set up in the store (Fig. 9). By being a helper, the elderly could get more understanding on the operation of the platform, and mistakes found in the test would have great help in future development.

Fig. 8. Demonstrations on the operation and instruments used in the test, including the screen, touch pen, and remote control.

Fig. 9. Demonstrations on how to help the elderly buying goods through the platform in in-shop scenario.

6   Conclusion

After the test, all three participants indicated that they were willing to use the system. They suggested that it is convenient to obtain goods and dispense medicines through Tou Hsiang Kun when people are unable to move freely or go out. However, the prototype design of Tou Hsiang Kun still needs improvements. Based on the first and second stages of evaluation and suggestions, corrections on the device are as follows.

(1) **Use Daily Goods to Design the Interface Icons.** Icons on the interface are easy to understand, but few are expressed unclearly; therefore, the choice of icons should close to the elderly people's lifestyle and fit with their cognition and experiences, designing easily distinguished icons for the elderly.

(2) **The Design Should Fit in with TV Interface While Switching Items or Pages.** Experts suggested that household TV fits elderly people's lifestyle. However, it is different from cell phones and tablets, so the interface of TV and the appearance of the interface should adjust to future operation. Besides, while switching items or pages, the design of interface should be more suitable for TV.

(3) **Improvement on Handheld Device Which Derived from Remote Control of TV.** Tou Hsiang Kun used household TV as the handheld device, but it should be designed based on the operation on the interface.

(4) **Create more Realistic Scenarios on the test.** Interface and hardware should closer to real operations, so that the elderly could get more experiences and feedbacks. During the test, wireless control was replaced by touch pen, but the effectiveness was low because the user was not familiar with the timing and power while clicking.

Therefore, it is necessary to adjust handheld device from household TV to wireless sensor or rocker, increasing the distance and space without touching the screen, and enhancing the operation experience.

References

1. Chiang, P.-C.: A Study on the Correlationship Between Life Styles and Degrees of Acceptance on City Spa. Department of Land Management, p. 98. Feng Chia University (2002)
2. Kuo, Y.-C., Kao, S.-K.: A study on the effect between lifestyle and learning needs of older adults in elder college of Kaohsiung City. Rev. Agric. Extension Sci. 20, 57–80 (2003)
3. Zhu, P.-L.: The Elderly Care and Social Work. Chinese University Press, Hong Kong (2001)
4. Nunes, F., Kerwin, M., Silva, P.A.: Design recommendations for TV user interfaces for older adults: findings from the eCAALYX project. In: Proceedings of the 14th International ACM SIGACCESS Conference on Computers and Accessibility, pp. 41–48. ACM, Boulder (2012)
5. Díaz, U., Etxaniz, A., Urdaneta, E., Epelde, G., Valencia, X.: A TV platform to improve older people's quality of life: lessons learned from the evaluation of the VITAL project with Spanish elderly users. In: Proceedings of the 4th International Conference on PErvasive Technologies Related to Assistive Environments, pp. 1–6. ACM, Heraklion (2011)
6. Kelley, J.F.: An iterative design methodology for user-friendly natural language office information applications. ACM Trans. Inf. Syst. 2, 26–41 (1984)

Consumer Concerns About Smart Meters

Rani Yesudas[⊠] and Roger Clarke

College of Engineering and Computer Science,
The Australian National University, Canberra, Australia
{rani.yesudas,roger.clarke}@anu.edu.au

Abstract. Modernisation of the grid is inevitable as aging and outdated traditional power infrastructure is subject to challenges of cost, climate change,
distributed power generation, and unstable demand patterns. Engineers identified smart meters as a vital element for modernisation and hastily implemented
and deployed them without fully considering their implications. There has been
significant consumer concern, and rollouts in various countries have been
delayed and even stopped entirely. The resistance from consumers makes it
evident that their requirements were inadequately addressed. A major reason for
this is that the requirements elicitation process was seriously deficient. This
article first analyses the functionalities of a smart metering system from a
consumer perspective and discusses the risks to consumer assets that are perceived to, and in some cases do, arise from the introduction of smart meters. It
then proposes that proponents of smart meter schemes need to improve their risk
assessment and requirements elicitation processes, in order to better understand
user realities, needs and concerns and ensure that their designs address them
effectively.

Keywords: Consumer perspective · Risk · Smart meters · Consumer concerns · Consumer segments

1 Introduction

Smart metering emerged from a need to effectively manage the electricity requirements
of increasingly large populations making more extensive and intensive use of electrical
devices. Though the initial interests were focused on accurately measuring power
usage, they have progressed to contributing to reductions in production cost and carbon
emissions.

Traditional accumulation meters display the cumulative amount of electricity used,
in order to enable manual reading on a periodic, typically quarterly basis. Smart meters,
on the other hand, record the time of use during short intervals and can be read
remotely by the utility. Smart metering technologies offer various possibilities for
electricity system stakeholders. For electricity utilities and electricity system operators,
they provide tools to address peak demand. With smart meters that enable time-of-use
(TOU) tariff, it is expected that peak electricity consumption could be reduced;
deferring and even avoiding the need to construct new power plants [1, 2].

From the viewpoint of the utility, the introduction of smart meters was intended to
encourage consumers to manage their power usage by showing them how much they

© Springer International Publishing Switzerland 2015
N. Streitz and P. Markopoulos (Eds.): DAPI 2015, LNCS 9189, pp. 625–635, 2015.
DOI: 10.1007/978-3-319-20804-6_57

are consuming and how much more they will have to pay for using electricity during peak periods. That was claimed to offer consumers the chance to change their energy usage patterns. It has also reinforced messages communicated to them by other means, drawing attention to the scope to use renewable sources of energy by installing solar panels [1, 2]. But are consumers sufficiently well-educated and motivated to manage their power usage? And, even if they are, is the proposal practicable?

After smart meter rollouts started in various countries across the globe, consumer concerns arose. In many places, rollouts have been delayed and even stopped, including in some where the scheme had initially been mandated [3]. It appears that industry will face years of battling to convince consumers of the benefits of smart meters. Resolving the impasse is not just a question of technology but of end-user requirements, behaviour and choices.

Most residential consumers have neither time nor inclination to check when critical peak pricing periods have been declared by their supplier, let alone continually follow energy pricing in real time. Consumers have other priorities besides their electricity bill and will prefer to spend only a little time to tweak their appliances' settings.

Promoters of smart grids talk about the potential for a home automation network where all appliances could be operated remotely via the smart meter [4]. On the other hand, current smart metering systems only support remote switching of the entire or partial load. The technologies have not yet advanced to the stage where selective appliances on the consumer side can be turned on and off without manual intervention. Even if smart metering systems reach the stage where such features are supported, residences will remain a long way from full automation. Major appliances like air conditioning systems will need to be retrofitted or replaced to be able to communicate with the smart meter. This modification will be expensive and for most households this will happen very slowly and mostly when systems reach the end of their normal life [1, 2].

Where utilities have imposed functionalities that address their own business needs but are not beneficial to consumers, furious responses have been triggered. It is crucial to that scheme sponsors ensure that consumers are on board and that the power grid transformation is tailored to meet their needs and their willingness to pay.

This paper commences by reviewing the context within which smart meter schemes have been conceived and implemented. It then examines the consumer concerns that have arisen, distinguishing between real and perceived risks. It is proposed that significant enhancements are needed to the risk assessment and requirements elicitation processes used in smart meter projects.

2 Background

The conventional grid assumes central generation of power, and dispersed consumption. The efficiency of the traditional grid is low, because the excess from centrally generated power can't be re-used or stored. Bottlenecks occur in the transmission system and this interferes with the reliability, efficiency, and delivery of electricity. Almost 8 % of output is lost along the transmission lines, while 20 % of the generation capacity exists to meet the peak demand only [5, 6]. To meet increases in demand, it is necessary to build new power plants, transmission and distribution infrastructures.

Modernisation of the grid is essential to address the drawbacks in the traditional system. The key requirements identified for Smart Grid are [7, 8]:

- Accurately measure usage and identify leaks and thefts.
- Identify the demand profile and provide measures to smooth the curves and thereby reduce the overall production cost.
- Enable detection of power failure in real time and speed up the recovery service.
- Provide quicker response to events and alerts

The solution that engineers identified for modernising the grid was to collect detailed consumption data from network end-points by means of Advanced Metering Infrastructure (AMI), and transmit that data frequently to the utility. The replacement of traditional meters with smart meters was considered as a major building block towards the implementation of the Smart Grid. With automated readings, engineers expected that utility operations would become more accurate and more responsive to changing conditions in the power reticulation network.

Over time, the detailed data collected from smart metering systems was seen as enabling the utility industry to introduce TOU billing. Designers assumed that the majority of the users would then be encouraged to switch their usage to off-peak hours to take advantage of the cheaper rates, thereby reducing the demand during peak period. But in a great many, and perhaps most, scenarios, peak hour usage is not easily avoidable by consumers. This is a sensitive social issue in some countries, and utilities and related government entities are being forced to continue with flat tariff rates even after smart meter roll-out. That defeats a principal justification for smart meters.

Meanwhile, additional challenges have confronted the electricity generation and supply industries. There is great pressure for central generation to switch progressively towards lower-carbon-emission alternatives. There has been an explosion in small-scale electricity generation, widely dispersed, and attached to the distribution network. There are at this stage only limited options for control of dispersed generation and hence of managing the risks of voltage fluctuations outside the range dictated by operational Standards. Electric car projects are promising to change demand profiles, but to some extent also supply and storage patterns.

These challenges compound the difficulties for an industry that has been strongly focused on a means of better managing demand, but by means of schemes that are being delayed and even still-born.

3 Consumer Concerns

An analysis of consumer concerns has distinguished a number of issues with the adoption of smart meters. Table 1 provides a summary.

Among the most significant obstacles are inadequate financial incentives, health concerns, security issues and violation of privacy [9–11]. The remainder of this section expands on some of the key issues. There have been reports of increased electricity bills associated with the use of smart meters. The complaints include an uninhabited home being billed more than double previous amounts following the installation of a smart meter. Utilities respond that the bills are accurate and that increases may be due to the precision of measurements which was not available with traditional meters, or leakage or theft of power [12].

Table 1. Consumer concerns over smart meter functionalities

	Smart Meter Functionality	Consumer Concerns	Consumer Assets Affected
1	Storage of fine grained consumption data.	Will provide insights into a household's living patterns to the extent that it could reveal the appliances used and activities conducted by the household.	Confidentiality, Security, Safety, Privacy
2	Two way communication and automated meter reading using various technologies.	Data susceptible to interception during transmission leading to modification or destruction of information.	Integrity, Availability of data and power, Privacy, Security
		Exposures to radio frequency waves causing electro hypersensitive (EHS).	Health, Safety
3	TOU tariff to reduce peak demand.	Unable to avoid the peak period due to various reasons.	Comfort, Convenience, Financial
4	Remote switching (disable and enable) of supply.	Possibility of getting disconnected by error or deliberate attempts by anti-social elements.	Safety, Security, Control
5	Enable energy export and calculation of net usage.	Currently smart meter does not check before injecting the energy into the system and that could destabilise the system.	Availability of power, Safety

There have also been complaints that smart meters are causing health problems. The terms idiopathic environmental intolerance attributed to electromagnetic fields (IEI-EMF) and electromagnetic hypersensitivity (EHS) have been coined to refer to a range of complaints that arise from, or are at least perceived to arise from, among other devices, smart meters and/or associated data transmission devices. Utilities respond that the meters comply with industry standards, and that radiation from smart meters is much lower than that from mobile phones [12, 13].

The concerns over security and privacy arise from collection and transmission of fine-granularity consumer data from AMI modules. Some reports suggest that Smart Meters are capable of revealing a considerable amount of sensitive data about people and their lifestyle and that it would let the observer know about the occupancy and contents of premises [14]. Current installations lack strong cyber security features, and hence data is susceptible to interception during transmission, which creates the possibilities of modification and destruction of information [15, 16]. There are also fears that malicious hackers may be able to intrude into the grid and cause harm to individuals' equipment, or blackout an area, or perhaps even undermine critical infrastructure.

There are also safety concerns. It has been reported that power surges have caused some smart meters to overheat and start a fire. Poor quality components and improper assembly of meters has been noted as the reason for overheating [17, 18].Utilities respond that smart meters are subject to rigorous safety standards and that the fires are caused by faulty switchboards and unsafe wiring that had hitherto remained undetected. In some cases investigations conducted by a safety regulator have determined that criminal damage was the cause of the fire [18].

There are also concerns about some consumers being unable to avoid peak demand, resulting in huge electricity bills. Utilities expect consumers to utilise smart meter facilities, and adjust their consumption behaviours and patterns accordingly. On the other hand, consumers such as pensioners and others who stay at home most of the time can't survive without heating/cooling systems and without operating other essential appliances during the peak period. People belonging to low income groups cannot afford to have expensive solar panels installed as an alternative. People requiring disability or medical assistance, e.g. for life support systems, also cannot adjust their demand in response to price changes.

4 Perceived vs Actual Risk

When a system embodies risk to the vital assets of the stakeholder, there will be resistance to it. That is clearly evident in the case of smart meters. From the perspective of a consumer, there are significant risks to assets that they value, and there is little evidence of significant gains. To a consumer, it will appear that the utility is forcibly introducing a system that is beneficial to the utility's business but not to the consumer.

But are all described concerns actual risks or are the problems perceived rather than real? Different actors participating in the same system may have a different perception of risk and they react according to those perceptions. The following insights into perceived risk by Bruce Schneider and Daniel Gilbert [19] are useful in analysing the consumer concerns about smart meters.

1. "People overreact to intentional actions and under-react to accidents, abstract events, and natural phenomena" [19].

   – The majority of computer and Internet users are not cautious when using public terminals or do not change the password regularly, thereby exposing personal data. But the same users are worried that personal data will be exposed by smart meters. Most smart meter systems have basic encryption and firewall protection. There are numerous ways in which antisocial elements can cause harm to the public. Even without smart meters, houses are being robbed and occasionally terrorists are planning attacks. What would be the motivation to use the smart meter for future attacks? Are they easier than existing methods?

2. "People underestimate risks they willingly take and overestimate risks in situations they can't control" [19].

   – Electronic devices emit radiation. RF emissions are produced by many wireless devices already found in the home, not just by smart meters. Research suggests that smart meter emissions are lower than those of wireless routers used for internet connectivity, and even less than wireless baby monitors. But unlike those devices, smart meters transmit in short bursts during only a fraction of the day.

3. "People under-react to changes that occur slowly and over time" [19].

   – Residential electricity prices have increased over 90 % in many countries over the past five years and consumers have been paying high flat-rate bills. With TOU tariff the consumer is showing resistance to paying high prices during peak periods. If flat rates continue, it is likely that consumers as a whole will pay more under flat-rate arrangements than they would if a TOU tariff were introduced and production costs were able to be reduced.

4. The way in which risks are communicated can affect user perceptions.

   – Closely associated with consumer protests about health hazards breaches have been media reports to the effect that smart meters cause such problems.
   – Similarly, the smart meter has been described as a spy in the home [20]. This was based on a report that found that detailed smart meter data at one-minute intervals could provide insights into a household's living patterns to the extent that it could reveal the appliances used and activities conducted by the household [14]. This accurately reflects the intentions of the visionaries and even of some design engineers. But it does not describe contemporary capabilities. Most smart meter data is generated on intervals far less frequent than one minute, and inferences are accordingly much harder to draw. Even if and when smart meter data becomes very fine-grained, detailed knowledge of the appliances present in the home and the habits of the consumer might also be required in order to infer living patterns [20].

The above examples showcase some exaggerations that are communicated through social media. If erroneous information sources find ready access to the mass media without effective remedies, then large social impacts, even for minor events, becomes possible [21]. A number of consumer concerns do, however, reflect actual risks that need to be addressed.

1. Fires and explosions arising from the introduction of smart meters is an actual risk. It is unacceptable to reduce cost of production by using poor quality components, inadequate assembly or short-changed quality control. In addition, a utility cannot blame existing conditions for causing a fire. When a traditional meter is replaced as part of a utility-sponsored scheme, it is the sponsor's responsibility to ensure that the existing wiring and conditions are safe for smart meter operations.
2. Software quality must be assured. The meter firmware that calculates the power usage needs to be demonstrated to be accurate and free from bugs. Erroneous billing due to firmware and system defects is unacceptable.

3. Discrimination against some categories of consumer is an issue that needs to be addressed, not ignored. This applies to individuals who depend on electrical devices for life-support, safety or maintenance of critical quality-of-life services; and to low-income and low-educational-level households.
4. Data Disclosure appears to be a design fault in many schemes. Data with potential sensitivity is passed from smart meters up through other organisations, without controls in place to minimise its distribution and to maximise its aggregation.
5. Data Interception is a genuine risk in many scheme designs.
6. Remote switching of devices, although not at this stage delivered functionality, is more than a gleam in the eyes of utilities and ambitious designers.
7. Instability of Supply is a genuine risk where distributed generation is closely coupled to medium- and low-voltage transmission lines.

For smart meters' potential benefits to be realised, a thorough risk assessment is necessary, to ensure that the drawbacks are understood and their impacts minimized on all stakeholders. Ultimately it will be the consumer who will have to bear the cost of running such a system and if the system's safety and security aren't guaranteed, consumer preparedness to accept the scheme will inevitably be harmed.

An important insight arising from the analysis conducted in this section is that not only is it essential that real risks be addressed, but it is also necessary that potential misperceptions be recognised in advance, fears allayed, and the ground prepared to counter misinformation when it appears within communities, in social media and in mass media venues. We have earlier devised a risk analysis framework specifically for Smart Grid with a perspective based approach [22]. Using our framework, risk analysis can be easily conducted from the perspective of a consumer.

5 Consumer Requirements Elicitation

The previous section has established the need for risk assessment to be conducted from the consumer perspective. It is common to perform a risk assessment late in a project, and all too often it is performed only once deployment is already under way. However, in most cases, retro-fit costs are far greater than designed-in costs and hence it is highly beneficial if the necessary features are incorporated within the design at the earliest possible stage, rather than deferred until after deployment.

To ensure early discovery of features that are needed to ensure consumer acceptance, a suitable framework needs to be selected for the specification of requirements and the subsequent design and deployment activities. The project's objectives and scope need to reflect consumer needs, rather than only those of the sponsor and the other organisations that exercise institutional and market power within the domain. For this to be achieved, it is crucial that the framework selected place great stress on the very early phase of requirements elicitation.

Consumers need to be identified as stakeholders. Means need to be devised to not merely gain their feedback on requirements specifications, prototypes and design documents, but also to meet with them, or suitable proxies for them, at the very outset of the project, and develop an understanding of their perspectives. Great care must be taken not to rely unduly on intermediaries, because many of them are too far removed from consumers themselves to provide designers with appropriate understanding [23].

The authors, as the next phase of the project, are developing the selection criteria for a suitable requirements engineering framework for smart grid and smart meter projects.

6   Consumer Segmentation

The previous section identified the need for consumers to be identified as stakeholders. Earlier sections established that consumers behave according to their perceptions of risks rather than to actual risks. The perception of risk is dependent on consumer expectations, preferences, and ability to tolerate the risk. Different consumers have different expectations for the same situation. For instance, if an event creates a loss, there is a possibility that one consumer is able to tolerate it whereas another is not. A further relevant factor is the opportunities that the consumer has available to them when they are contemplating taking a risk [16, 24]. Figure 1 is a representation of response of different consumer groups using an adaptation of CORAS.

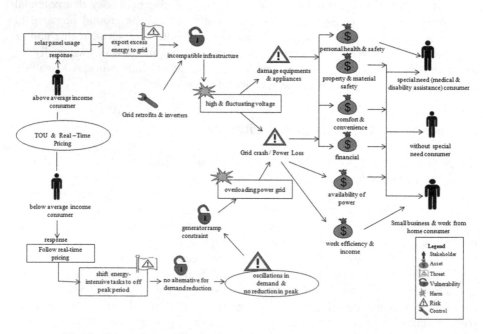

Fig. 1. Issues that could arise from renewable resources and TOU tariffs

Despite the many sources of difference among consumers, there is a tendency by designers to lump all customers together into a single entity. All users are considered to want the same things [25].

In order to avoid public reactions against smart meter schemes, sponsors must take stakeholder analysis beyond this limited conception of an army of undifferentiated consumers. Stakeholder segmentation offers details that the traditional "one lump" views cannot. Representatives for each stakeholder segment need to be identified, and included in requirements elicitation activities. In order to avoid a coarse-grained stakeholder analysis, intensive focus groups and other structured brainstorming activities are required [26].

In the specific context of smart meter schemes, some relevant consumer segments that have different requirements are as follows:

- People requiring medical and disability assistance.
- Pensioners and concession card holders.
- Households with low incomes, a single income, or a single parent.
- Wealthy people with additional security requirements for person and property.
- Households living in particular types of premises, including free standing houses, and units, flats and apartments.
- Households that include the owner of the property – variously as head-of-family and as landlord – tenants/renters/lessees, and boarders/sub-lessees.

The possibility exists that the agendas of different stakeholder segments may give rise to incompatible and inconsistent requirements. In such circumstances, stakeholder segments need to be ranked, in order to resolve requirements conflicts and make appropriate decisions.

7 Conclusions

Smart meters have great potential, but harbour risks for various stakeholders, particularly for consumers. The perception by end-user that they are subject to significant cost, safety, security and privacy risks has proven to be a significant impediment to progress.

In this article we have discussed consumer concerns about smart meters, and have identified how consumers perceive risk. The analysis identified the need for recognition of consumers as stakeholders, and a much more careful approach to requirements elicitation from consumers, including consumer segmentation. We contend that these measures are essential pre-conditions for successful smart meter projects.

The context is rapidly changing, however, and parallel developments also need to be factored into smart meter projects. Of particular significance is distributed power generation through domestic solar panel installations, and the sale of surplus power into the grid. Legacy architecture was designed for electrical flows from central power stations to appliances. In areas with a high concentration of solar cells, voltage levels may become unstable. This can have negative consequences for consumers' equipment, but it can also trigger shutdowns in order to take load off the grid [27]. Some of the measures suggested are battery storage and retrofits to present infrastructure, but those will be costly.

A further concern is that real-time pricing could overload the power grid. If enough consumer power usage does become highly responsive to real-time price changes, it is quite feasible that rapid swings in demand could represent a serious threat to the reliability of supply. The careful analysis of consumer requirements advocated in this paper is relevant not only to smart meter projects but also to many other aspects of grid modernisation.

References

1. DOE, The Smart Grid: An Introduction. US Department of Energy (2008)
2. Kemp, J.: Are consumers ready for smart meters? Climate - Smart Energy (2013)
3. UKERC, Future Research Requirements for Smart Metering Workshop, in UKERC/ MR/HQ/2011/006. The UK Energy Research Centre (2011)
4. Yesudas, R., Clarke, R.: Identifying consumer requirements as an antidote to resistance to smart meters. In: Innovative Smart Grid Technologies Conference Europe (ISGT-Europe). IEEE PES (2014)
5. Farhangi, H.: The path of the smart grid. IEEE Power Energ. Mag. 8(1), 18–28 (2010)
6. Amin, S.M., Wollenberg, B.F.: Toward a smart grid: power delivery for the 21st century. IEEE Power Energy Mag. 3(5), 34–41 (2005)
7. Zheng, J.X., Gao, D.W., Lin, L.: Smart meters in smart grid: an overview. In: 2013 IEEE Green Technologies Conference, pp. 57–64 (2013)
8. Fang, X., et al.: Smart grid - the new and improved power grid: a survey. IEEE Commun. Surv. Tutorials 14(4), 944–980 (2012)
9. Khurana, H., et al.: Smart-grid security issues. IEEE Secur. Priv. 8(1), 81–85 (2010)
10. Amin, S.M.: Smart grid security, privacy, and resilient architectures: opportunities and challenges. In: 2012 IEEE Power and Energy Society General Meeting (2012)
11. Yan, Y., et al.: A survey on cyber security for smart grid communications. IEEE Commun. Surv. Tutorials 14(4), 998–1010 (2012)
12. Betz, J.: Smart meters under fire as electric bills soar. In: Convention for the Protection of Human Rights and Fundamental Freedoms as amended by Protocol No. 11 (2010)
13. Baliatsas, C., et al.: Idiopathic environmental intolerance attributed to electromagnetic fields (IEI-EMF): a systematic review of identifying criteria. BMC Public Health 12(1), 643 (2012)
14. Quinn, E.L., Privacy and the new energy infrastructure. 2009, SSRN eLibrary. p. 25
15. Angermeier, D., et al.: A secure architecture for smart meter systems. In: Xiang, Y., Lopez, J., Kuo, C.C., Zhou, W. (eds.) Cyberspace Safety and Security, pp. 108–122 (2012)
16. Baumeister, T.: Literature Review on Smart Grid Cyber Security. Department of Information and Computer Sciences, University of Hawaii: Honolulu, Hawaii (2010)
17. EMFSN, Smart meter fires and explosions. In: EMF Safety Network (2012)
18. ESV Safety of Advanced Metering Infrastructure in Victoria (2012)
19. Schneier, B.: Perceived risk vs. actual risk. Schneier on Security (2006)
20. Roberts, S., Redgrove, Z.: The Smart Metering Programme: A Consumer Review – A Report to Which?. The Centre for Sustainable Energy, Bristol (2011)
21. Kasperson, R.E., et al.: The social amplification of risk - a conceptual-framework. Risk Anal. 8, 177–187 (1988)
22. Yesudas, R., Clarke, R.: A framework for risk analysis in smart grid. In: Luiijf, E., Hartel, P. (eds.) CRITIS 2013. LNCS, vol. 8328, pp. 84–95. Springer, Heidelberg (2013)
23. Wiegers, K.E.: Software Requirements, 2nd edn. Microsoft Press (2003). 2 Sub edition

24. Asnar, Y., Zannone, N.: Perceived risk assessment. In: Proceedings of the 4th ACM Workshop on Quality of Protection. ACM (2008)
25. Davis, K.W.: Why utilities should care about customer segmentation (2013)
26. Laplante, P.A.: Stakeholder Analysis for Smart Grid Systems. Penn State (2010)
27. Roozbehani, M., Dahleh, M.A., Mitter, S.K.: Volatility of power grids under real-time pricing. IEEE Trans. Power Syst. **27**(4), 1926–1940 (2012)

Humor in Ambient Intelligence

Laughter as the Best Medicine: Exploring Humour-Mediated Health Applications

Claire Dormann[1,2(✉)]

[1] University of Ottawa, 55 Laurier East, Ottawa,
ON K1N 6N5, Canada
[2] Institute of Dementia, University of Salford, Salford, UK
cdormann@gmail.com

Abstract. Despite the physiological and psychological benefits of humour on health, many health applications for aging hold very little humour. We investigate the potential of humour in health for aging, reviewing studies from humour therapy. To show the potential of humour in this domain, we look at the functions of humour and discuss their application to the design of virtual agents. Then, we propose new conceptual designs based on the therapeutic use of humour: agents as comic relief, agent as comic partners, and agents as virtual clowns. We aim to initiate a new research agenda in this domain and stimulate further investigations in the use of humour-mediated technology.

Keywords: Humour · Virtual health agent · Therapeutic agent · Aging · Seniors

1 Introduction

In most industrialized nations, the population is aging and living longer. An important trend in the development of healthcare to support aging relates to well being and quality of life. Healthcare applications are designed to maintain and supplement declining physical and cognitive abilities. Hence, technology assists seniors in performing their daily activities and maintaining a healthy life style. Examples are medication adherence, medical appointment, diet, and exercise. In a therapeutic context, exergames, virtual agents, and social robots have been developed to stimulate activity, rehabilitation, and social interaction. Quality of life, in the form of active social participation and emotional well-being, is also a fundamental component of aging successfully.

Despite an increasing number of older adults going online and playing digital games there is still a gap in seniors' acceptance of digital technology, especially for older groups or users with impairments. To minimize barriers in using technology, virtual agents, avatars, or embodied conversational agents provide notable benefits. Agents provide interfaces for seniors that are less confusing and more natural than traditional interfaces [1]. They also build on a strength that most older users retain: conversation. They communicate through different modalities, including non-verbal behaviour, which can be tremendously advantageous when designing for older user groups. Studies on the acceptance of robots and agents by seniors show that an agent who displays social signals is better able to gain users' trust and interest [2]. As Bickmore et al. [1] highlight

© Springer International Publishing Switzerland 2015
N. Streitz and P. Markopoulos (Eds.): DAPI 2015, LNCS 9189, pp. 639–650, 2015.
DOI: 10.1007/978-3-319-20804-6_58

in their study, agents help to support long-term socio-emotional relationships. Advantages often associated with agents relate to naturalness, trustworthiness, and believability [3].

In recent years, the idea that humour and laughter have positive health benefits has become increasingly popular. Humour is widely accepted for its positive physiological and psychological effects in a variety of situations. Humour is recognized as an essential communication skill and coping device for patients, their families, and their healthcare providers [4]. Moreover, humour is at the heart of many health campaigns that try to change behaviour, such as 2014 UK Stoptober campaign for stopping smoking. In this campaign, well-known comedians pledged their support and jokes to help motivate people and get them through the 28 days needed to stop [5]. Humour enhances persuasion, augments positive emotions, and creates a link with the audience.

Despite this, many health applications for healthy aging contain very little humour. Thus, we propose to investigate the role of humour in this context: how it mediates technology to benefit and support aging seniors. In the first part of the paper, we review the functions and benefits of humour on health, focusing on humour in the context of aging. In the second part of the paper, we consider the application of humour to virtual health agents. We first discuss how humour enhances the design of health agents then we propose new conceptual designs based on the therapeutic use of humour. We aim to initiate a new research agenda in this domain to stimulate further investigations in the application of humour for healthy aging and well-being.

2   Humour, Health, and the Aging Process

Humour has positive physiological (e.g., amelioration of pain and discomfort) and psychological effects (e.g., mental wellness) [6]. Stevens [7] carried out a review of the literature on humour and laughter and found positive physiological changes on the immune system, heart disease, and cardiac rehabilitation. Nuttman-Shwatz et al. [8] examining studies in humour for healthcare, observed that humour was shown to facilitate relationships and communication. Moreover, they found that humour was deemed to improve coping and well-being as well as help to release tension. In a review dedicated to older adults, Berk [9] established that humour reduced stress, anxiety, tension, and depression, by order of importance. Quite a few studies also indicated that humour improved self-esteem. As Martin [6] suggested, some caution is needed, as there were some methodological limitations with these studies, such as the numbers of respondents or inadequate control groups.

The impact of humour on the lives of older adults is manifold. Adults do enjoy and maintain a sense of humour into the later years of life. Proyer et al. [10] suggest that a sense of humour is stable across age groups. In their study, elderly participants gave higher rating for mood in association with humour but laughed less, and less easily, than younger participants did. Damianakis and Marziali [11] found that affiliative as well as authentic humour were key components of the use of humour by older adults. Affiliative humour was used to strengthen interpersonal relationships and sharing with others. Marziali et al. [12] surveyed older adults in their use of humour as a coping device. The authors suggest that humour is a self-efficacious strategy for coping with life adversity used to ward off stress caused by challenges surrounding the aging process. Despite their circumstances, patients in palliative and end-of-life care were still able to laugh and experience joy [13].

As can be understood, some precautions are needed when using humour as a tool to improve health. A study by Mak and Carpenter [14] comparing older adults with students observed that older adults performed worst on comprehension of humour tests, as cognitive abilities decline with age. However, research by Liptak et al. [15] suggests that older adults with cognitive impairment do not lose the ability to appreciate humour, but rather that initiating humour and responding appropriately can be more difficult. Greengross [16] showed that aging is a sensitive process and thus, understandably, seniors dislike jokes mocking age-related vulnerabilities and stereotypes related to aging. When using humour in this context, we must keep in mind factors related to aging that can diminish humour efficiency.

Humour has also been used as a specific intervention to improve the well-being of older adults. The oldest and simplest method consists of watching comedies. Then programs were elaborated to include a number of humorous activities, which demanded a more active and participative role from the senior. The most common intervention in this group is the work of Clown Doctors or Elder Clowns. Besides the interventions, the elderly are surrounded by further humorous stimulus, for example, through the provision of a humour cart. The most participative interventions are based on stand-up comedy performed as skits or as a long-term activity, culminating in stand-up performances.

Not all initiatives are evaluated but assessed interventions are presented here. In the Clemson Project, seniors watched comedies over the period of the study. In their evaluation of this project, McGuire et al. [17] concluded that affect appeared to be an area where humour can be an effective agent for change. Mathieu [18] implemented a humour program to increase life satisfaction among older adults. She found that program participants were thinking more positively and were more accepting of their life circumstances. Seniors also appeared to feel more comfortable socializing and less lonely.

In their small study of Elder Clowns, Thomson [19] observed that after a few clown visits, seniors with severe dementia showed an overall increase in positive behaviours and a decrease in negative behaviours during the sessions. Similarly, the largest and most systematic study, conducted in Australia, with Elder Clowns showed that levels of agitation in residents decreased but they did not show any significant improvement with depression [20]. Some positive results on quality of life were also found in the preliminary results.

In two small studies of stand-up comedy conducted with adults suffering from mild dementia, benefits of the programs included enhanced socialization and communication as well as improved mood and happiness [7, 21]. As importantly, these interventions show that people with dementia still have a sense of humour, can participate in improvisational comedy, and demonstrated better skills for it than anticipated.

3   The Work of Elder Clowns

Clown Doctors or medical clowning has become quite pervasive, now reaching geriatric hospital wards and residential care. Although the number of formal studies of Elder Clowns is not high, their practice is well documented. Thus looking at Elder

Clowns should give us a better understanding of the role of humour in this context and provide some insights for the design of health agents.

Elder Clowns aims to create a playful and joyful atmosphere for patients and provide comic relief from the usual hospital atmosphere [22]. Indeed, there is a sharp contrast between the playful, magical, comical world of the clowns and the sterile, formal medical care space. Clowns give emotional support and establish a strong empathic relationship with patients; they acknowledge the human being as a living adult, and not as a patient or long-term resident in need of care. They allow elders to express positive emotions through laughter, but also give them the freedom to express negative feelings without fear of repercussion. Clown interventions reframe time and space through their work. Through humour, clowns activate pleasant memories by making links to the past and the present. Important strategies include evoking patients' memories with them, telling humorous stories from the past, as well as commenting news from the present. Clowns break routine and passivity by reaching out to the elderly. They solicit reactions, communication, and participation to achieve positive changes. Elder Clowns can improve cognitive functioning, through small memory games and jokes. They empower seniors to participate in the action through play, magic, and games. Finally, they aim to stimulate and enhance relationships and communication with different members involved in care: medical staff, family members, and the residents/patients themselves.

Elder Clowns elaborate a light comic persona, usually wearing a small token of their profession: a red nose, make-up, a lab coat and a stethoscope. Elder Clowns often worked in pairs, performing short routines, varying in length from a few minutes to ten minutes. Routines are tailored to individual patients, depending on their physical, emotional, and mental condition. Clowns will often incorporate visitors into their routines, and sometimes offer group sessions. Most of their practice involves the same elements, including a range of techniques from juggling, and magic to small games and singing (with patients) [22, 23].

Warren and Spitzer [23] looking at clown production in hospital settings, defined their practice around verbal, physical, or musical jests. Clowns use a range of verbal humour from the most sophisticated, such as puns and riddles, to the simplest, such as playing with sounds, songs, and music. Verbal humour is complemented through facial expression, body posture, gesture, and movement. Physical comedy is also a very important tool in the clown routine, from pratfalls, imitations, pantomime, and playing with objects and props. The role of non-verbal humour can be especially significant in these institutional settings, especially with patients with diminished cognitive abilities, when verbal communication becomes difficult.

Unfortunately, the work of Elder Clowns is still quite limited, both in terms of coverage, where programs have been setup, but also within hospitals and residences in terms of number of individuals they can visit, or the time they can spend with each patient (or group). Within context of children hospitals, the use of virtual clowning is emerging, for example, to support a child receiving palliative care at home [24]. The red nose report [25] (2014) also mentioned an online clown doctor service for children provided by a hospital in the Czech Republic. It is anticipated that such services will grow and reach geriatric hospital wards and residential care.

4 Humour-Mediated Technology: Health Agents

Now we focus on virtual agents as the platform upon which to investigate the role humour can play in health applications for well-being and healthy aging. As we have discussed, agents have important characteristics that make them suitable to this context. An important element is their ability to support socio-emotional interaction, an important function of humour in healthcare. Thus, we first review the functions of humour and then discuss how humour can be used to strengthen the design of health agents. Next, based on our review of humour for aging, we propose new developments in this domain as therapeutic humour agents.

5 Humour and Health Agents

Looking at the three main classical theories of humour superiority, relief, and incongruity theories gives us some indication of how to use humour in the design of agents. Superiority theory is the oldest, humour theory, and relates to mockery and ridicule: we laugh at the misfortunes of others, their faults, and their deviance. Humour can be used to criticize behaviour gently, but overly aggressive humour and mocking patients is obviously not done in a health context. Nonetheless, superiority theory suggests more generally the social functions of humour. Humour helps to sustain social relationships and interaction. Humour and laughter also support social emotions such as friendship, sympathy, and solidarity, as well as intimacy or empathy. This is a well-know aspect of agent design. For example, humour combined with praise and small talk can smooth social relationships and enhance intimacy [26]. Moreover, a humorous agent was better liked than a non-humorous agent. The importance of caring and intimacy is widely known in healthcare to improve patient satisfaction and also to ameliorate treatment adherence and outcome [4].

We want to highlight most particularly relief theory, an aspect of humour that has not been discussed in depth with virtual agents. Relief theory is linked to the release of tension, nervous energy, or suppressed emotion. Comic relief is a well-know function of humour use in games to relieve stress and frustration and to lighten the mood [27]. A laughing and humorous virtual agent could lead to greater positive feelings through mimicry and emotional contagion. Beyond the use of humour to support communication and social relationships, humour in virtual agents could have a calming effect and make people happier.

Last, we should not underestimate the value of humour as comic fun. Humour has a value and is an end in itself. People play with ideas and words, exchange riddles and comic anecdotes, and perform practical jokes to provoke mirth and create a highly pleasurable experience. Humour is a device specifically used to elicit joy and happiness. Incongruity theories explain jokes, where an idea is situated within two contrasting frames of reference resulting in an unexpected ending. We can also build on the surprising value of humour to make people laugh.

Thus, we believe that health agents can benefit from the addition of humour, especially coach, advisor, or persuasive agents that try to motivate change. Agents through humour can improve compliance to treatments, as they enhance the patient's mood. By providing support, empathy, or sympathy, a humorous agent can facilitate procedural daily routines. As a coach, the agent enhances engagement by producing a fun experience, providing both relief from boredom and motivation through mirth. As with computer games, humour can change the pace, breaking the monotonies of routine exercises to provide an element of reward through laughter. Anyone who has been in a fitness class realizes the importance of humour and praise to create an upbeat mood and to motivate users through drills and practices. Playful and dynamic applications that generate mirth contribute to a willingness for use, leading to a reduction in apathy among users/patients. A humorous health agent is thus more likely to motivate a user to continue interacting, thus increasing exposure to the behaviour change components embedded in the application.

6   Therapeutic Humour Agents

Following the role that humour plays in the aging process, and the utilization of therapeutic humour with seniors, we are developing new conceptual designs. From our scenarios and preliminary sketches, we are proposing three types of therapeutic agents: agents as comic relief, agents as comic partners, and agents as virtual clowns. Basic elements of our designs are presented here to illustrate the application of humour in this context and to advance the use of humour-mediated technology.

To accommodate multimodal humour and forms of non-verbal communication, we advocate using full-embodied conversational agents rather than talking heads. Furthermore, speech output would enable richer expressions of humour and laughter, while speech input would facilitate user interaction, especially with frailer seniors. Speech input is thus highly recommended for virtual clowns.

An important function of humour with these agents is to break boredom and loneliness, to improve mood and diminish anxiety and stress. The therapeutic agents all share fundamental components: the agents should support a high level of social interaction and should be built to harness the socio-emotional functions of humour. Even so, the uses of humour with the different agents move in a continuum, from active listening to participative engagement, where the senior is a full partner in the humour production.

As we have seen with the simpler forms of humour therapy, or with clown doctors and their humour carts, comic relief can be provided to seniors by surrounding them with as many humorous objects as possible (e.g., watching videos, cartoons, providing a joke calendar, etc.). Thus for residential care, the hospital environment, or even home care, we can design a personal agent application, or agent, as *Comic Relief*, on computer or interactive television, to provide humour on demand.

Nowadays, the Internet is filled with cartoons, jokes, funny cat videos, and podcasts posted by professional humorists. Seniors write blogs and provide many jokes and humorous anecdotes on aging. The comic relief agent would drive a resource-based application tailored to the cognitive abilities and situations of seniors. To sustain social presence and build an intimate relationship with the senior, the agent would first engage in small talk, tell jokes, and create a positive atmosphere. Then the agent would give seniors a few options, such as a choice of three comedies, podcasts, or programs.

Depending on their abilities, needs, and situations, seniors could be given access directly to the full resource or to programs with specific humour sequences. Humour sequences would be put together with the help of therapists to cheer but also to engage seniors and patients with various humorous stimuli. To conclude, the agent would ask for feedback and provide closure to the session. The aim here is to provide comic relief, making seniors laugh but also stimulating regular use of the agent.

An important element in the success of humour therapy is seniors' participation. They should interact with the humour stimuli, engage with the humorist, and perform. Thus, the second virtual agent that we are elaborating would act as a *comic partner*. Nakatsu and Tosa [28] have developed an AI comedy system, based on the art of Mazai or comic dialogue generation. In their system, the agent and user engage in comic banter. *Comedy Night* (2012), an indie game for the Xbox, is a virtual comedy club, where players can join in as stand-up comedians performing comic routines.

We are elaborating this agent application for more able seniors. The setting can be a comedy club or day care centre. The application would start with some performances by two characters (stand-up comedians), to stimulate laughter and create a positive climate. An agent would then engage a senior through a small skit, and comic banter. The agent would first coach the user, providing guidance or prompts. Then, as the seniors become accustomed to the agent and the comic performance, a variety of scenarios would be given to the user. The agent could continue to coach the user, providing feedback and praise after each skit. To make the application more engaging, seniors could be given different comic partners (such as famous comedians). Then again, users would be rewarded with more comic performances. This agent aims to engage seniors in comic fun, to stimulate their cognitive abilities and to strengthen their sense of humour to use in daily interactions.

For less able seniors, a slightly altered design might be more suitable. As shown by Stevens [7], skits should be based on situations that seniors can relate to and engage in. The agents would be designed to take the appearance and persona of the characters in the skits, with visual clues given as prompts. An important consideration for the agent, especially in this case, is not the quality of the humour exchange but ensuring that users cannot fail, feel intimidated, or feel anxious while using the agent. Besides guidance, the agent should be able to repair breaks in the conversation (e.g., prolonged silence or poor feedback) through dialogue lines but also through non-verbal expression, physical humour, or animation.

The last concepts relate to *agents as virtual clowns,* based on the work of Elder Clowns. Virtual Clowns would be used by and for seniors in hospital and long-term-care residence, most particularly with those who have reduced physical and mental ability or severe illness. The purpose of the virtual clown would not be to replace Elder Clowns, but to complement or supplement their visits. In some cases, volunteer caregivers and family members might have to mediate the virtual clown utilization, as they participate during Elder Clown visits.

To work best, the agent should have some knowledge of the patient, medical as well personal, thus some data entry or integration with a medical database would be necessary. The design of these agents should follow Elder Clown routines: small comic performances, dialogues, jokes, and participative actions such as games, singing, music, etc. A number of design issues should be resolved relating to the agent and the expression of humour in its multi-modalities. Questions around agent representation are not new in agent research, but have a slightly different emphasis here. Due to the medical context and patient condition, we believe that the design of the agent should align with the Elder Clown persona. Such design might enhance social presence and emotional identification.

7   Design of Therapeutic Humour Agents

There are several issues to consider for the design of virtual humorous agents and therapeutic agents; clown agents are not really at the forefront of agent research! Although models of laughing agents exist, and new research has emerged in the generation of laughter sounds, their range is still too limited for our purpose. Comic characters and performers giggle, chuckles, chortle, snicker, guffaw, roar, or hoot with laughter. The laughter and tears of a clown are highly prototypical in their exaggeration.

We have highlighted the importance of non-verbal humour in these therapeutic agents, through the body and physical humour, especially for users with cognitive or emotional impairment. Full-embodied agents communicate through postures, gestures, and body movements but lack the vocabulary for full comical expressiveness.

As Bergson [29] stated, humour and laughter are created by people's characteristics, including shape and appearance as well as behaviour (e.g., gestures and movements). The study of *Mr. Bean, Monty Python,* and old film comedies shows how the exaggeration of body posture and gesture as well as acceleration of movement can create a comic effect. Designing a comical agent after Mr. Bean or a clown would demand very different models of animations, body postures, and movements than the more naturalistic representations generally use in virtual agent design. Physical comedians transcend language barriers, communicating emotions, thoughts, and ideas without using words. Harpo in the Marx Brothers comedies never said a word but communicated by means of honks, whistles, and pantomime. Thawonmas et al. [30] system, where an agent mimics one controlled by a user, a classic of pantomime, was a step in the right direction.

The playful spirit of humour is also demonstrated through the enjoyment of language for its own sake the witty play on words and jokes that make us laugh. Besides humour engines such as JAPE (Joke Analysis and Production Engine), or the HA-HAcronym, among others, various conversational agents have been equipped to support some form of verbal humour [31]. All the same, the production of sound, voices and Foley effects, has not been discussed much with the production of verbal humour. Stylized voices and speech patterns can add to or produce the comic effect in many ways: rhythm, alliteration, foreign languages, specific accents, or distortion. Using the wrong type of voice with a character or imitating the voice of a well-known actor can be hilarious. We should also consider Foley effects or sound made by humans (e.g., footsteps, manipulation of tools) as a source of humour. Foley effects might not be used as much with agents as they are in animation, but they can still be utilized, for example, to characterize some emotional states (e.g., anger by the sound of blowing steam or love by the sound of a beating heart).

We have discussed some issues related the design of humour for therapeutic agents, looking more specifically at issues related to non-verbal humour. We also need to develop humour models for comic agents and comic performances. The studies of comedy devices and memes, as well as film comedies, clown doctors, and stand-up comedies should give us some preliminary ideas.

8 Discussion

We have focused on virtual agents to illustrate some new conceptual designs for humour-mediated technology to support well-being and healthy aging. As we are still early in the design process, we review issues that would sustain the development of the therapeutic humour agents. To discuss these issues, we follow an iterative design process, from user research, to design and evaluation.

We need to better understand preferences of humour within the older population as there are not many studies on what makes seniors laugh. We can expect socio-demographic differences with the use of humour. First, we might want to look in more depth at aging, as cognitive abilities decline and lifestyle changes drastically over the years, age differences could mitigate preferences or responses to humour. Gender differences in humour do exist, but would they be more pronounced with age? Should we consider designing a female-centric agent for use with the older user groups? Then again, what would be the impact of ethnicity or religion? More studies are also needed with special user groups, such as dementia patients.

We have discussed issues related to the design of comic agents and the development of new humour models. We should also more fully acknowledge the multi-sensory dimensions of humour: visual, music, smell, and touch. Humour can be expressed though music. Indeed, a music score can become the source of the comic effect by manipulating and distorting normal music conventions: any rules can be broken [32]. A popular form of comedy in music is parody, and unexpected juxtaposition of musical genres: remix culture is full of hilarious mash-ups. Within the visual medium, visual puns and jokes occupy the same place as word games. Specific visual humour devices are caricature (graphics) and visual gags (film). The multi-sensory dimensions of humour will more fully enter into the design of humour programs or routines. We are using the humour games of Elder clowns or the Improv Comedy games (1985) as inspiration. These programs should be informed and reviewed by therapists, caregivers, and professional humorists, including clown doctors, as well as seniors.

Another important question for the design of therapeutic humour applications relates to the number of agents (single agent vs. multi-agent characters) thus the number of users that the application can accommodate. Using a single agent as a virtual clown could be less confusing and could enhance intimacy. Nevertheless, for frailer or more dependent adults, caregivers or family members could mediate the use of a therapeutic agent. Elder Clowns often work in pairs, thus the virtual clown could be a given a sidekick (the caregiver as the laughter boss). The potential of comic duos are well-know from films to games [33]. Comic duos act as foils for each other, possessing complementary personalities and types of humour. It also allows for greater socio-emotional interaction between the characters. The agent as a comic partner has been conceptualized for a single user. In the future, however, it could be interesting to allow multi-users for a group of elders to stimulate social interaction and comic fun.

The technological implementation of the therapeutic agent is beyond the scope of this paper. However, to conclude we want to outline two issues. Building on the latest research on computational humour, in which agents can recognize the user's humour and detect laughter to respond accordingly, would greatly enhance the design of therapeutic agents. Personalization of the agent and customization of the intervention in the function of the user profile could also augment the efficiency and enjoyment of the humour therapy.

The last set of issues relates to the assessment of the therapeutic agents, from usability to socio-emotional issues such as likability and trust. We also need to evaluate more particularly the design of humour, and the overall impact of the agents on, for example, life satisfaction, well-being, or anxiety. Note that in some instances, these evaluations can be more complex than anticipated. The work of Elder Clowns highlights the difficulties in assessing older adults with impairments or severe illnesses. These patients are not always very responsive so standard psychometric tools will not work well with them. Alternative procedures and tools will have to be considered.

9 Conclusion

We have focused on virtual agents as the platforms of choice to illustrate some new conceptual designs for humour-mediated technology to sustain well-being and healthy aging. To do so, we first investigated the potential of humour in health for aging, reviewing studies from humour therapy and looking more particularly at the work of Elder Clowns. The benefits of humour in this domain include reducing stress or negative behaviour, and providing joy and enhancing mood. Then, we discussed the use of humour for health agents, focusing on two humour functions: comic relief and comic fun. Next, we proposed three types of therapeutic humour agents: agents as comic relief, agents as comic partners, and agents as virtual clowns. We also highlighted more specifically problems related to humour design. Designing therapeutic humour agents might demand a shift in the design paradigm of agents to accommodate new models of comic representation. Last, to initiate a new research agenda in this domain and to further the design of therapeutic agents, we discussed a number of issues connected to user research, humour design and evaluation. Even so, we expect other issues to emerge as we refine the design of the therapeutic agents.

We hope to stimulate new research in computational humour, health agents, and more generally in persuasive health technology. A day without laughter is a day wasted. Humour is so much a part of human society that we should capitalize on it to develop new applications for virtual agents, health games, or intergenerational games. Moreover, we believe that there are still many possibilities remaining to be explored for humour-mediated technology.

References

1. Bickmore, T.W., Caruso, L., Clough-Gorr, K., Heeren, T.: 'It's just Like you Talk to a Friend' relational agents for older adults. Interact. Comput. **17**(6), 711–735 (2005)
2. Sakai, Y., Nonaka, Y., Yasuda, K., Nakano, Y.I.: Listener agent for elderly people with dementia. In: Seventh Annual ACM/IEEE International Conference on Human-Robot Interaction, pp. 199–200. ACM, New York (2012)
3. Ortiz, A., del Puy Carretero, M., Oyarzun, D., Yanguas, J.J., Buiza, C., Gonzalez, M., Etxeberria, I.: Elderly users in ambient intelligence: does an avatar improve the interaction? In: Stephanidis, C., Pieper, M. (eds.) ERCIM Ws UI4ALL 2006. LNCS, vol. 4397, pp. 99–114. Springer, Heidelberg (2007)
4. Scholl, J.C.: The use of humor to promote patient centered care. J. Appl. Commun. Res. **35**(2), 156–176 (2007)
5. UK Stopober. http://www.nhs.uk/smokefree/stoptober
6. Martin, R.A.: Humor, laughter, and physical health: methodological issues and research findings. Psychol. Bull. **127**(4), 504–519 (2001)
7. Stevens, J.: Stand up for dementia: performance, Improvisation and Stand up Comedy as therapy for people with dementia; a qualitative study. Dementia **11**(1), 61–73 (2012)
8. Nuttman-Shwartz, O., Scheyer, R., Tzioni, H.: Medical clowning: even adults deserve a dream. Soc. Work Health Care **49**(6), 581–598 (2010)
9. Berk, R.: The active ingredients in humor: psychophysiological benefits and risks for older adults. Educ. Gerontol. **27**(3–4), 323–339 (2001)
10. Proyer, R., Ruch, W., Müller, L.: Sense of humor among the elderly. Zeitschrift Für Gerontologie Und Geriatrie **43**(1), 19–24 (2010)
11. Damianakis, T., Marziali, E.: Community-dwelling older adults' contextual experiencing of humour. Ageing Soc. **31**(1), 110–124 (2011)
12. Marziali, E., McDonald, L., Donahue, P.: The role of coping humor in the physical and mental health of older adults. Aging Ment. Health **12**(6), 713–718 (2008)
13. Adamale, A.K., Ludwick, R.: Humor in hospice care: who, where, and how much? Am. J. Hosp. Palliat. Med. **22**(4), 287–290 (2010)
14. Mak, W., Carpenter, M.: Humor comprehension in older adults. J. Int. Neuropsychol. Soc. **13**(4), 606–614 (2007)
15. Liptak, A., Tate, J., Flatt, J., Oakley, M., Lingler, J.: Humor and laughter in persons with cognitive impairment and their caregivers. J. Holist. Nurs. **32**(1), 25–34 (2014)
16. Greengross, G.: Humor and aging - a mini-review. Gerontology **59**(5), 448–453 (2013)
17. McGuire, F.A., Boyd, R.K., James, A.: Therapeutic Humor with the Elderly. The Haworth Press Inc., New York (1992)
18. Mathieu, S.I.: Happiness and humor group promotes life satisfaction for senior center participants. Activities Adapt. Aging **32**(2), 134–148 (2008)
19. Thomson, R.: Evaluation of the use of a clown therapy group with dementia sufferers. NHS Borders Psychological Services, 3–4 (2005)
20. Low, L.F., Brodaty, H., Goodenough, B., Spitzer, P., Bell, J.P., Fleming, R., Chenoweth, L.: The Sydney Multisite Intervention of LaughterBosses and ElderClowns (SMILE) study: cluster randomised trial of humour therapy in nursing homes. BMJ Open (2013). http://bmjopen.bmj.com/
21. Hafford-Letchfield, T.: Funny things happen at the grange: introducing comedy activities in day services to older people with dementia-innovative practice. Dementia **12**(6), 840–852 (2013)

22. Raviv, A.: The clown's carnival in the hospital: a semiotic analysis of the medical clown's performance. Soc. Semiot. **24**(5), 599–607 (2014)
23. Warren, B., Spitzer, P.: Smiles are Everywhere: Integrating Clown-Play into Healthcare Practice. Routledge, London (2013)
24. Armfield, N.R., Bradford, N., White, M.M., Spitzer, P., Smith, A.C.: Humour sans frontieres: the feasibility of providing clown care at a distance. TeleMedecine e-Health **17**(4), 316–318 (2011)
25. Seeliger, G., Culen, M.: Red Noses Clowndoctors International. Annual Report (2011). http:// www.rednoses.eu/fileadmin/rni/medien/bilder/About_us/Jahresbericht/Jahresbericht_RNI_ 2011_E_FINAL_Web.pdf
26. Campbell, R.H., Grimshaw, M.N., Green, G.M.: Relational agents: a critical review. Open Virtual Real. J. **1**, 1–7 (2009)
27. Dormann, C., Biddle, R.: A Review of humor for computer games: play, laugh and more. Simul. Gaming **40**(6), 802–824 (2009)
28. Tosa, N., Nakatsu, R.: Interactive comedy: laughter as the next intelligence system. In: International Symposium on Micromechatronics and Human Science, pp. 135–138. IEEE Press, New York (2002)
29. Bergson, H.: Le Rire - Essai sur la Signification du Comique. In: Oeuvres, pp. 382–485. Press Universitaire de France, Paris (1970)
30. Thawonmas, R., Hassaku, H., Tanaka, K.: Mimicry: another approach for interactive comedy. In: Conference on Simulation and AI in Computer Games, pp. 135–138 (2003)
31. Mihalcea, R., Strapparava, C.: Technologies that make you smile: adding humor to text-based applications. IEEE Intell. Syst. **21**(5), 33–39 (2006)
32. Mera, M.: Is funny music funny? contexts and case studies of film music humor. J. Pop. Music Stud. **14**(2), 91–113 (2002)
33. Dormann, C., Boutet, M.: Incongruous avatars and hilarious sidekicks: design patterns for comical game characters. In: Digital Games Research Association (2013)

An AI for Humorously Reframing Interaction Narratives with Human Users

Christian F. Hempelmann[1,2(✉)] and Max Petrenko[1,2]

[1] Ontological Semantic Technology Laboratory, Texas A&M University–Commerce, 2600 South Neal Street, Commerce, TX 75428, USA
[2] NTENT, Research and Development, 1808 Aston Avenue, Suite 170, Carlsbad, CA 92008, USA
c.hempelmann@tamuc.edu, mpetrenko@ntent.com

Abstract. This paper presents a hybrid approach to computational humor generation. The approach consists (a) of a probabilistic, LSA-based method to identify text instances in HCI environments, specifically computer games, where humor can be inserted, and (b) a knowledge-based method to generate the actual humorous text by minimally varying the input to create an appropriate incongruity. We discuss two examples in detail and provide suggestions for the actual implementation.

Keywords: Computational humor · Video games · Human-computer interaction · LSA · Spreading activation

1 Introduction

Humor is a quality of symbolic interaction, i.e., a semiotic phenomenon. More specifically, it is a connotative semiotics, that is, a symbolic system of a signifier and a signified that itself has a meaning, namely to be funny [1]. As such, non-symbolic humor is not possible. What is possible, is non-verbal humor that operates in other semiotic domains than language. But even non verbal humor will always be a quality of symbolic communication, e.g. gestures, narrative reframing, as in pranks, humorous music, or visual humor in cartoons. Finally, humorous narratives can be enacted rather than told as in cut scenes and the largely scripted interaction between players and non-player characters. Conversely, any non-verbal humorous act can be described in language, because as the most arbitrary semiotic system, language is universally available to express what can be denoted in any other semiotic system.

Therefore, if we're interested in true humor generation, not just template filling or selection from a list of prefabricated humorous items, for HCI to move into non-verbal humor [2] could mean to attempt entering these somewhat non-prototypical types of humor [3] For body and facial gestures, the computer program would need to become embodied in an avatar or robot, neither of which is primarily an issue of humor or knowledge-based systems, which is what the present paper intends to elaborate. For visual cartoon humor, there is practically no spontaneous generation even by humans [4, fn. 3], so spontaneous computational cartooning would be a unique artificial expression of intelligence.

N. Streitz and P. Markopoulos (Eds.): DAPI 2015, LNCS 9189, pp. 651–658, 2015.
DOI: 10.1007/978-3-319-20804-6_59

Rather, much in line with Ritchie [5, 6], the paper presents additional evidence towards the methodological and computational benefits of approaching the subjects of humor recognition and humor generation in the context of HCI from the perspective of knowledge-based systems. Unlike the above-mentioned contributions, though, the paper attempts to mitigate the hard methodological dichotomy between knowledge-based and probabilistic approaches to humor analysis by adopting the position that the two could complement each other by distributing their scopes to areas most appropriate to each.

2   Humor in Human-Computer Interaction

The literature that describes the behavioral functional prerequisites for a humor-aware interactive computer system converges on three core properties:

(a) the ability to detect acceptable triggering conditions, i.e., a specific combination of circumstances at a given point in an interaction that, upon appropriate modification, would yield a humorous effect by casting the wide net of a probabilistic approach;
(b) the ability to select and apply the most appropriate modification (given the properties derived in (a)) that would yield a humorous effect most successfully by doing pin-point changes with a sophisticated knowledge-based approach; and optionally
(c) the ability to solicit feedback from the user that has been exposed to the output of (b).

A vast amount of research has been produced that discusses the methodological and practical intricacies of all three properties. Under the reconciliatory position stated above, it would appear that approaches focused on attaining (a) from the machine-learning perspective report measurable results, whereas approaches focused on attaining (b) from the knowledge-based perspective present an apparatus which imparts the depth and robustness for any application that aspires to meet the very high scalability requirements in computational humor.

More specifically, [7] present a machine-learning classifier of "that's what she said" cues, but also offer a methodology that could be applied to any type of humor, provided the features are defined appropriately. Similar models are of the same methodological type [8]. On the other hand, research on knowledge-based systems offers extensive discussion of the prerequisites and strategies of generating humorous narratives, puns, jokes in interactive contexts [9–11].

3   Reframing in Hybrid Approach to Humor Generation

As an implementation of the hybrid approach, we're proposing the spontaneous humorous reframing [11, 12] of in-game narratives in computer games. Humor in computer games can have the same range of functions that humor has in general [13, 14]. Therefore its use in computer games, both primarily humorous ones and interspersed in generally serious games, is as advantageous as its general use. The approach is in spirit similar to [7], but instead of a machine-learning approach, we use a probabilistic simulation of semantics [15], but different in two crucial respects. First, our approach includes knowledge-based methods. Second, it is generalized and should be triggered at a substantially higher rate.

The knowledge base has as one purpose to let the system determine when a statement in the user input is compatible with two scripts [16], but almost completely disambiguated to one of its readings through co-text and/or context. Moderate generation abilities will then generate a reframing statement that a non-player character (NPC) in a game utters.

By way of illustrating the benefits of approaching the issue of humor analysis from the knowledge-based perspective, the paper will discuss how reframing could be performed by an interactive computer system in computer games. Here, "reframing" is tentatively defined as a communicative act of rendering an alternative reading of a previously produced utterance by structurally imposing novel properties on the utterance. By "structurally" we mean augmenting the original utterance with a phrase or sentence (normally with a repetitive syntactic structure), which imposes the novel interpretation on the original utterance by imparting novel properties to it. In humor, a standard example of reframing is a type of "what she said" jokes, where the sexual reading is imposed on an utterance. While the (undoubtedly challenging) problem of recognizing utterances amenable to a potential double entendre was addressed in [7], the problem of modeling and implementing a computational system capable of reframing has not received any attention in computational linguistics and humor research.

It should be noted that the mechanism of reframing is not strictly confined to "what she said jokes." an arguably semantically and syntactically rigid phenomenon. Reframing appears to be common across various domains of discourse including bona-fide interaction. The common feature all such cases share is that the constructed frame either exposes a default premise (in bona-fide cases) or declares a novel property for the utterance, thus imposing a novel interpretation (in non-bona-fide cases) [17].

3.1 Detecting Humor Occasions Broadly and Making Use of Them Precisely

From the humor analysis perspective, and recasting the general behavioral functional prerequisites described above, a knowledge-based system generating reframing would have to follow a two-step procedure:

(1) find an utterance deemed semantically sufficient to support an appropriate script opposition;
(2) embed the statement in another statement of a specific and likely pre-defined structure (e.g. comment, quote, etc.) that "grafts" an explicit property from the opposing script onto the original utterance.

LSA-Based Setup Detection. The Semantic Script Theory of Humor (SSTH, [17]) proposes humor necessarily requires script opposition, wherein two overlapping scripts conflict. These scripts are triggered by the text (or whatever symbolic system the humor is communicated by). In the most simplified scenario a text can be parsed in terms of one script, or reading, but at some point, often implicitly, another script is the only possible interpretation of the text, often revealing that parts of the previous text were compatible with this second reading as well. For this scenario to play out, part of the text must be compatible with both scripts, which, again, are in a relation of opposition.

For the present approach, we are adopting an operationalization of this opposition in relation to a use case explored in [18]: Suppose you are a writer for a news-based comedy show like Jon Stewart's Daily Show [19], Larry Wilmore's Nightly Show [20], or Stephen Colbert's former The Colbert Report [21]. In addition to working on major daily news items, much of the preliminary work of the writer's rooms for these shows involves scanning the current day's news for potential material to write humor about for the show of that night.

Our approach takes printed news items as input, segments it into sentences and determines for every non-stop word, the semantic distance between them in terms of their LSA-cosine. If the cosine is above an established threshold, the sentence is flagged as a potential setup for a humorous punch. The assumption is that there is a more common sense/$script_b$ to $word_1$ that is potentially opposed to the sense/$script_a$ triggered by $word_2$. LSA picked the more frequent sense/$script_b$ of $word_1$ because it reflects word-co-occurrence and is insensitive to semantic contexts, which would have disambiguated to sense/$script_a$ for $word_1$, beyond co-occurrence. The approach then serves this sentence as a setup to the writers' room, whose members can focus on generating a punchline instead of scouring news sources for potential setups in addition to writing the punchline.

Our approach is intended to consider LSA-cosines generated against two corpora: (a) a news corpus, which means priming the system against an LSA-emulation of humor semantics as the expected output text, but for the emulation of news semantics as the expected input text, and (b) a corpus of jokes, which means priming the system for an LSA-emulation of humor semantics as the expected output text, but against the emulation of news semantics as the expected input text. As far as we know, this testing of choice of LSA training corpora contrasting input vs. output genre is a novel research issue with interesting implications to be solved empirically. Our hypothesis is that the a news corpus will be the more relevant training set, because it will not feature the two trigger words as frequently near each other as humorous corpus would, thus yielding high LSA-cosines indicating large semantic difference. In other words, a humor-only corpus for training would already contain the punchline thus put the input words in frequent proximity, thus making LSA blind to semantic contrasts, which are necessarily frequent in humorous texts, while they are to be avoided in bona-fide news text. But because this is a hybrid approach, we can be prepared to find our hypothesis falsified by the empirical data to be derived and to adjust accordingly.

As a simplified example, consider a news item with the headline "court strikes a blow to religious freedom" [22]. Stop-word removal leaves the approach with the following input words:

- court
- strike
- blow

- religious
- freedom.

Our assumption is that, especially as trained on a news corpus, the word pair *blow-religious* will yield a high LSA-cosine, i.e., indicate that in terms of most frequent usage the dominant senses of these words in a news context don't co-occur significantly. Let us assume the *blow* has the most news-frequent literal sense of STRIKE (note that "strike a blow" is an idiomatic and semantically redundant way to trigger a single event), in contrast to the literal sense EXPEL-AIR, which is related to the metaphorical sense ORAL-SEX.

Our assumption is that not having been trained to consider the ORAL-SEX sense because it is infrequent in the training corpus of news texts, the *blow-religious* pair will receive a cosine above the empirically established threshold. This will make the input sentence a candidate output for the writers' newsroom, whose staff can now proceed to human-generate a punchline, e.g., "not much blowing allowed in religion otherwise." Lame as it is, this relieves that writers of the most time-consuming part of their job, that of scanning news items.

In an AI system, we need to not only have the setup identification automated, but also the punch line generation. As discussed we leave the former here to LSA as a probabilistic machine-learning system for the presumed sakes of high speed and broad output. Another reason is the brittleness of knowledge-based systems from the false confidence that their algorithms lead to and that lead to false positives (see [6, 23]), which tend to get compounded in knowledge-bases systems.

Spreading-Activation Network-Based Humor Permutation. In the previous subsection we referred to sources that discussed the following example of inadvertent computational humor. This example was selected by a knowledge-based NLP system as the most likely meaning of an input sentence, given the system's set of resources. The system missed the correct meaning by a few semantic constraints, so that a human interpretation of the output could detect funny opposition as compared to the intended interpretation. In other words, the computer generated no humor at all, but a human can see that the intended meaning of the following sentence and its automatically processed meaning by an Ontological Semantic Technology system [24] are in humorous contrast: *Meggett has been acquitted on sex-related charges*; (a) "a football player called Meggett was not sentenced for a crime that involved an illegal sexual act that he was accused of" and (b) "a football player called Meggett was not sentenced for a crime that he was accused of, and this non-sentencing took place while he was located on top of an explosive device that is used for sex".

The funniness of this contrast lies in the fact that the incongruity that the text interpretation by the NLP system carries in contrast to the human-intended and – processed interpretation lies in a small mis-disambiguation of *charges*. The context-disambiguated interpretation is ACCUSATION, but the NLP system failed because it had insufficient semantic connections between this concept and the other legal concepts triggered by *acquitted*. Instead it went for another sense of *charges* as EXPLOSIVE-DEVICE, not being aware that its constraint satisfactions are insufficient to exclude such devices from being instruments in a SEX-ACT. As computational linguists involved in the testing of the knowledge-based systems we have engineered over the years, we share the experience with our colleagues that our systems often get close to the correct interpretation of natural language input (are contextually appropriate), but not close enough (reflect ontological incongruity), reflecting the main claim for the essence of humor [17] as phrased in [25].

Appropriate incongruity points to our main mechanism for the second part of our approach: minimal violation of the constraints of the knowledge base as an operationalization of a local incongruity that is not (a) violating the knowledge stored in the comprehensive knowledge base or (b) not even violating the knowledge base information because it is too sparse. We will not discuss the lucky case (b) any further as it requires an additional interpretation layer by the human user as in the *Meggett* example above. In other words, in the (b) scenario the system does not know that it's wrong and can't report that it's wrong; its' just caught in its mistake at a metalevel. But we will explore case (a) further.

Based on this observation, for this part of our currently proposed system, providing the punchline to a probabilistically chosen potential setup by reframing the setup based on a spreading-activation network (for a relevant psycholinguistic approach to meaning activation in verbal humor, see [26]).

Based on specific examples, the full paper will address various strategies of performing (1), based on the existing research (including [7]) and discuss the knowledge-based strategies of modeling, supporting and implementing (2) in computer games.

Assuming a statement in dialogue by a player character that uses the same or similar input as the headline in [22], that is use of the highly ambiguous word *blow* and another word with predominantly religious senses, let's consider how a spreading activation network could provide the knowledge base that (a) processes the relation between these senses, (b) "knows" that a strategic tweak could lead to humorous reframing, and (c) can actually produce this tweak.

In the proprietary system we are consulting, the following semantic connections are activated between senses of *blow* and *religion*, two words flagged as semantically different enough to provide a potential script opposition, while known to be occurring in the same sentence in the LSA-based step 1. $Blow_1$ as EXPEL-AIR is not connecting to any subcollection of RELIGION through any relation, but known to have an animate AGENT. $Blow_2$ as in STRIKE is very remotely connecting to a subcollection of RELIGION as an event sense connected to RELIGIOUS-STRUGGLE, both sharing an animate AGENT. $Blow_3$ as in ORAL-SEX is slightly more actively connected to RELIGIOUS-STRUGGLE as an event known to also have an animate AGENT and HUMAN-THEME. Thus, the system has three choices, starting from spreading activation and then considering constraint satisfaction. It's constraints point it to one of the metaphorical senses of *blow*, namely the third sense as satisfying more constraints than the other, while violating the CHRISTIAN-RELIGION vs. SEX disjointment violation of the knowledge base as the main humorous tweak. The final IOU of our approach remains the tweak that in response to the input produces the punchline output. This will be our main area of research, in parallel to the LSA approach in [18] for this presentation.

4 Summary and Outlook

We have discussed reframing a probabilistically identified potential setup for a punchline based on a knowledge-based system. Several questions remain open, not least the proof in eating this pudding. But in the course of our discussion we have highlighted many relevant, and some new, issues in computational humor in a novel fashion: hybrid approaches and distribution of labor in such approaches, choice of training corpora for probabilistic approaches where input and output fall into different genres, and spreading activation networks as used beyond spreading activation. We have also outlined solutions to most of these issues and provided the sketch of an application type in which they can be tested.

References

1. Attardo, S.: Semiotics and pragmatics of humor communication. Special issue of BABEL Aspectos de Filoloxia Inglesa e Alemana. Aspectos Lingüísticos y Literarios do Humor, pp. 25–66 (2002)
2. Nijholt, A.: Towards humor modelling and facilitation in smart environment. In: Ahram, T., Karwowski, W., Marek, T. (eds.) Proceedings of the 5th International Conference on Applied Human Factors and Ergonomics AHFE 2014, Kraków, Poland, 19–23 July 2014, pp. 2997–3006 (2014)
3. Wendt, C.S., Berghe, G.: Nonverbal humor as a new dimension of HRI. In: Proceedings of the 18th IEEE International Symposium on Robot and Human Interactive Communication, Toyama, Japan, September 27–October 2 2009, pp. 183–188 (2009)
4. Hempelmann, C.F., Samson, A.C.: Cartoons: drawn jokes? In: Raskin, V. (ed.) The Primer of Humor Research, pp. 613–644. Mouton de Gruyter, Berlin, New York (2008)
5. Ritchie, G.: Can computers create humor? AI Mag. **30**–3, 71–81 (2009)
6. Raskin, V., Hempelmann, C.F., Taylor, J.M.: How to understand and assess a theory: the evolution of the SSTH into the GTVH and now into the OSTH. J. Literary Theor. **3**–2, 285–312 (2010)
7. Kiddon, C., Brun, Y.: That's what she said: double entendre identification. In: Proceedings of the 49th Annual Meeting of the Association for Computational Linguistics, pp. 89–94 (2011)
8. Mihalcea, R., Strapparava, C., Pulman, S.: Computational models for incongruity detection in humour. In: Gelbukh, A. (ed.) CICLing 2010. LNCS, vol. 6008, pp. 364–374. Springer, Heidelberg (2010)
9. Binsted, K., Ritchie, G.: Computational rules for generating punning riddles. Humor **10**(1), 25–76 (1997)
10. Stock, O., Strapparava, C.: HAHAcronym: Humorous Agents for Humorous Acronyms. Humor, **16**(3), 297–314 (2003)
11. Mason, Z.J.: CorMet: a computational, corpus-based conventional metaphor extraction system. Comput. Linguist. **30**(1), 23–44 (2004)
12. Goffman, E.: Frame Analysis: An Essay on the Organization of Experience. Harper and Row, London (1974)
13. Gregson, J.: Reframing. In: Attardo, S. (ed.) Encyclopedia of Humor Studies, pp. 630–632. Sage, London (2014)

14. Dormann, C., Barr, P., Biddle, R.: Humour theory and videogames: laughter in the slaughter. In: Sandbox 2006 Proceedings of the 2006 ACM SIGGRAPH symposium on Videogames, pp. 95–98 (2006)
15. Dormann, C., Biddle, R.: A review of humor for computer games: play, laugh and more. Simul. Gaming **40–6**, 802–824 (2009)
16. Deerwester, S., Dumais, S.T., Furnas, G.W., Landauer, T.K.: Indexing by latent semantic analysis. J. Am. Soc. Inf. Sci. **41**(6), 391–407 (1990)
17. Raskin, V.: Semantic Mechanisms of Humor. Reidel, Dordrecht (1985)
18. Hempelmann, C.F., Morris, T.: Using LSA to automatically identifying the setup for daily news satire shows. Paper Presentation at the 2015 International Society for Humor Studies Conference, Oakland, CA, July 2015 (2015)
19. http://thedailyshow.cc.com/
20. http://www.cc.com/shows/the-nightly-show
21. http://thecolbertreport.cc.com/
22. http://www.publiceye.org/ifas/fw/9004/court.html
23. Hempelmann, C.F.: Computational approximations of human humor processing. Invited Lecture at the International Summer School and Symposium on Humour and Laughter, Magdeburg, Germany, July 2013 (2013)
24. Nirenburg, S., Raskin, V.: Ontological Semantics. MIT Press, CambridgeMA (2004)
25. Oring, E.: Appropriate Incongruity Redux. In: Oring, E. (ed.) Engaging Humor, pp. 1–12. University of Illinois Press, Urbana und Chicago (2003)
26. Vaid, J., Hull, R., Heredia, R., Gerkens, D., Martinez, F.: Getting a joke: the time course of meaning activation in verbal humor. J. Pragmat. **35**, 1431–1449 (2003)

Humor Techniques: From Real World and Game Environments to Smart Environments

Anton Nijholt[⊠]

Faculty EEMCS, Human Media Interaction, University of Twente,
PO Box 217, Enschede, The Netherlands
anijholt@cs.utwente.nl

Abstract. In this paper we explore how future smart environments can be given a sense of humor. Humor requires smartness. Entering witty remarks in a conversation requires understanding of the conversation, the conversational partner, the context and the history of the conversation. We can try to model interaction smartness and how to use it in creating not only witty remarks, but also to create humorous events. Smart sensors and actuators, embedded in our environments and our wearables allow us to make changes to a digitally enhanced physical environment. Witty remarks in language can have their counterpart in witty events in digital environments, including social media environments with their own communication characteristics. Sequential and parallel juxtapositions of incongruous and contrasting events invade our communication and, in addition, can be expected to emerge or to be created in digitally enhanced physical environments too, accidentally and intentionally.

Keywords: Incongruity humor · Computational humor · Intended humor · Accidental humor · Sense of humor · Ambient intelligence · Internet of things

1 Introduction

Humor is universal, but different cultures have different kinds of humor. Humor has different functions. When we look at existing humor theories the incongruity theory focuses on the cognitive effort to understand humor, the superiority theory is about how we experience humor, and the relief theory is about the function of humor [1]. Relief theory, introduced by Sigmund Freud [2], tells us that jokes help us to release tension and allows us to suppress emotional censors, hence, allowing us to include taboos in a conversation. Minsky [3] talked about the suppression of cognitive sensors and in later years also the suppression of social censors were mentioned, for example by Junco [4], in his observations on cartoon humor.

Almost all humor researchers focus on verbal humor and jokes. Language is not the only tool that can be used to create humor. In our daily life we often encounter situations that make us laugh and that we consider to be humorous. It certainly may be the case that also in these situations protest against social censors plays a role, however, in our research we just assume that people, for whatever reason, like to get amused by

© Springer International Publishing Switzerland 2015
N. Streitz and P. Markopoulos (Eds.): DAPI 2015, LNCS 9189, pp. 659–670, 2015.
DOI: 10.1007/978-3-319-20804-6_60

humor. When looking at digital technology, can it help in providing conditions that lead or are expected to lead to humorous situations? Think of 'practical jokes' that are performed in the physical world and that make use of 'building blocks' provided by the environment. But there can also be lots of humorous situations emerging because of wrong expectations, unusual behavior, or failure to deal with a situation. This design of humor is exploited in comedy writing, whether it is on stage, on television, or in movies, for example the silent movies of the beginning of the twentieth century. Our traditional natural, physical environments, and the people that inhabit them, can of course not be controlled in a way that compares with the way a movie or stage director can control a physical environment, its inhabitants (the actors) and events that are designed to happen there. Our hypothesis is that this will change. Users will have more control of their environment. Obviously, they already have devices that allow them to control aspects of their house and garden. Or devices that assist them in controlling their health or intended changes of behavior, such as doing more sports. They can maintain and control their social life by being active on social media. But, when we continue to increase the numbers of sensors and actuators in our daily environments we can expect to be able to use them for humor creation just as we can use words, speech, and prosody for verbal humor generation.

The aim of this paper is to support this hypothesis by surveying the possible ways humor can appear in smart environments. The focus is on nonverbal humor, that is, humorous behavior and humorous events. Unfortunately, most of the humor research is on verbal humor, so, we need to spend time on surveying what has been said about nonverbal humor in the past and we need to discuss whether observations from earlier research, not taking into account digital technology, can be used for our purposes. But we can also look at nonverbal humor in situations where the user (audience member) can just watch and enjoy what is presented to him of her: a stand-up comedian, a silent movie, a sitcom, a comedy on stage? What kind of humorous events are constructed there? Can we design similar humorous events in smart environments? One step closer to smart environments are game environments, in particular videogames. Here the user (gamer) has an active role. She can interact with the game environment and her behavior and decisions will have impact on her experience of the humor that has been designed in the game. In particular when we adhere to the view that our society will become more gamified, we probably can learn from the way humor has been integrated in game design. There are also examples where videogames have been given an implementation in the physical world, where digitally augmented and controlled human players represent the avatars in a particular videogame.

The organization of this paper is as follows. In Sect. 2 we have a preliminary discussion on the various forms of digital humor that can appear in smart environments. In particular we distinguish between accidental and intended humor, and possibilities to increase accidental humor. Section 3 has observations on verbal and nonverbal humor with the aim to inspire thoughts about introducing humor in smart environments. Unfortunately we have to leave out many useful observations that are available in the literature on comedy writing, sight gags in movies and explanations of humor in sitcoms. In Sect. 4 we discuss videogames and humor. Section 5 summarizes our observations from the point of view of smart environments and provides some concluding remarks.

2 Humor in Smart Environments: Senses of Humor?

In smart environments we can use our smart devices and the environment, whether it is the environment that physically surrounds us or our social media network that virtually surrounds us, can assist us in our needs and activities, whether they are work, health, recreational, mood, or socially related. There is not always need to use devices, the environment can monitor and interpret our behavior and can decide to be pro-active, take the initiative, and suggest, persuade or force the user to perform certain actions. Obviously, there can be more friendly and humorous interaction between environment and user too. That is, we can have human-human-like interactions with the environment and with its digital devices (wearables, tangibles, virtual pets) and other inhabitants (social robots, virtual and holographic humans, digitally augmented humans). Devices and inhabitants should allow humorous interactions, taking into account and using the context and the history of interaction [5]. Some related research is already performed. For example, interpreting various forms of laughter and generating various forms of laughter are research topics that aim at providing virtual humans with non-verbal speech characteristics [6]. Other research aims at providing social robots with the ability to recognize or generate humorous remarks or jokes in a conversation [7]. Clearly, this research requires knowledge of what is happening nowadays in computational linguistic research on dialogue modelling and dialogue management.

Humor in smart environments can occur in interaction with social robots, digital pets, virtual humans, interactive products, and whatever the smart environment has to offer. When humor is introduced in such interactions it is meant to be intended humor. But not all humor that we experience is intended. We can make innocent remarks that turn out to be humorous. The shortness of newspaper headings introduces ambiguities that allow humorous interpretations. We often laugh about the errors we make. Digital technology is not always that perfect either. We can sometimes laugh about failures of digital technology, or about people that are confronted with new digital technology and are unsuccessful in using it. It is also possible to explore imperfections of digital technology in digital environments to create humorous situations. Hence, when discussing humor in smart environments we need to look at both intended and unintended humor. Unintended humor can appear when technology fails, when technology is not understood and someone tries unsuccessfully to interact with this technology. Technology failures or possible misunderstandings arising from new technology can also be exploited to generate intended humor. For example, gamers exploit imperfections in game engines in order to create, record and edit humorous events using in-built or external editors [8].

Accidental humor and ways to increase occurrences of accidental humor in smart environments is an interesting approach to humor in smart environments. We will return to this view later. But in addition to increasing the possibility of accidental humor, for example by creating incongruous situations in smart environments, we would like to investigate intended humor, humor that is created and controlled, either by the environment or by an inhabitant (human, social robot, virtual pet, furniture, walls, et cetera) of the environment.

In smart environments sensors and actuators can be controlled and can be configured in order to facilitate humor generation. This can be done by those that own or maintain our smart environments. Depending on how much control is left for the environment's inhabitants, it can be done by its human inhabitants using available interfaces, including wearables, to control, configure and play with the environment and prepare it for a digital practical joke. In this way we can distinguish a 'weak' sense of humor and a 'strong' sense of humor. In the 'weak' sense the human or digital practical joker sets up unexpected and surprising events, but not yet necessarily humorous. Suggestions for such events can be given by the environment to the human joker or partly performed by the environment itself. In the 'strong' sense it is assumed that the environment has a sense of humor that allows it to autonomously generate humorous incongruities in the digital and/or digitally enhanced physical environment. Clearly, there is a continuum from the weak variant to the strong variant where there is a decreasing involvement of a human joker and an increasing involvement of the smart and playful environment that takes care of humorous event generation. This continuum allows the introduction of degrees of sense of humor.

Unfortunately, sense of humor – involving both creation and appreciation of humor – is hard to quantify [9], let alone, hard to model. That is, controlling humor settings for robots as is suggested in the 2014/15 *Interstellar* movie is still some years away. Nevertheless we can think of environments that more or less are receptive to humor appreciation and generation. Being able to control the humor level of smart environments is an important issue, but as well important is to have some consistency in the kind of humor that is generated. We can think of environments or their non-human inhabitants and devices as having some kind of personality and their humor should meet their artificial personality characteristics.

Humor styles associated with personality characteristics have been identified [10]. There is the affiliate style (meant to enhance the relationship with others), the self-enhancing style (related to an optimistic view on circumstances and life in general), the aggressive style (potentially detrimental towards others), and the self-defeating style (potentially detrimental towards the self). When designing smart environments with a sense of humor it is useful to know when what kind of style is useful, keeping into mind that some consistency in humor creation and appreciation is required.

Another issue that can be addressed is the quality of humor that is created by a smart environment or its users. Can we and do we want to distinguish between bad quality and good-quality humor? The aesthetics of humor has been discussed by John Morreall [11]. Criticism on his views appeared in [12]. At this moment there is hardly a way to embed such notions (sense of humor, styles of humor, and quality of humor) in the design of humorous smart environments. But, obviously, when designing future smart environments, these notions should be kept in mind and should appear in the design, even if it is in a rudimentary form.

3   Verbal and Nonverbal Interaction Humor

In texts, for example in verbal jokes, incongruity humor is introduced by a stereo-type set-up of a situation that, although it is ambiguous, its ambiguity is only recognized when the next text lines or a punch line introduces additional, non-stereotypical dis-ambiguating information to the listener or reader of a joke. The listener or reader understands that he or she has been fooled. There is a cognitive shift involved; one interpretation has to be exchanged with a second interpretation. And, moreover, this second interpretation often requires an unusual view of the world, a view that is not in accordance with what we assume to be appropriate, morally acceptable, logical, or physically possible. This incongruity humor research follows the interests of language researchers interested in non-literal language use, in irony, in sarcasm, and humorous utterances, whether they are part of conversations, texts, or part of joke telling. That is, traditional humor researchers focus on language and expect their linguistic techniques, sometimes supplemented with artificial intelligence techniques, to provide answers to questions why a particular text, a joke, or a particular conversational act, can be considered to be humorous.

3.1 Humor in Conversations

We use humor in conversations. For example, we can do it to humor our partner, to deal with disappointment, to catch attention or to smooth down a heated discussion. During parties and other informal gatherings we sometimes enter a situation where there is an accumulation of witty remarks. There is humor, but not by telling jokes. It is spontaneous and its ingredients are taken from the situation.

Often we see the possibility to make a humorous remark by given an incongruous (illogical, inappropriate, absurd, …) turn to a discussion or make a remark that is based on an intentional wrong and absurd interpretation of a preceding remark. In order to do so we need a relation between our witty remark and the context in which this remark is made. With context we mean the conversation so far, knowledge about the conversational partners, or events happening during the conversation, for example, watching a sports game or ordering drinks. Knowledge of this context makes it possible to make implicit or explicit reference to it and at the same time distorting it.

Obviously, in smart environments we can expect to have conversations and interactions with the environment and its artificial inhabitants such as virtual humans, social robots or pets. Unlike the usual approaches to textual humor, focusing on analysis, this requires humor generation, that is, as outlined above, humorous use of the knowledge about the dialogue so far and the context in which it takes place. Two examples for the case of virtual agents are:

- Elmo is a chatterbot-like agent [13] that lives in a virtual world where it can assist human users that have questions about this world. The chatterbot is integrated with JAPE, a pun generating system [14]. Using keywords (or WordNet synonyms) from a user's input, Elmo searches the JAPE database and can add a punning riddle to an answer.
- More sophisticated linguistic techniques (syntactic analysis of the user's input, applying reference resolution techniques, using ConceptNet) are used in [15] in an attempt to generate humor by purposely using a wrong antecedent of an anaphor, preferably an antecedent that opposes properties of the real antecedent.

There are some modest attempts to investigate the use of humor by social robots. For example, doing Wizard-of-Oz experiments in order to look at the effect of a robot's nonverbal behavior on humor appreciation. A robot butler with funny interaction behavior was introduced in [16]. Using principles from verbal humor and getting inspiration from movies about robots (WALL-E) and butlers ('Dinner for One'), they looked at funny ways for the robot butler to deliver objects and hand them over.

Virtual humans or social robots interacting with their human partners have to update their view of the world (new knowledge follows from the interaction) and due to their interactions they may want or are commanded to make changes in their virtual and physical world. Virtual humans and social robots are integrated with their environments, we can ask a virtual human to turn off the light when we leave a room and we can ask a domestic robot to provide information about his activities to an environment monitored by a virtual human. Virtual humans and social robots can make changes to their environments. When they have a sense of humor, they can provide a human partner with suggestions about a next configuration of their worlds that allows him or her to introduce a humorous event. And, as mentioned when we introduced the humor continuum in Sect. 2, there can be a cooperative decision with a human partner, but also an autonomous decision by a smart environment (and its digital inhabitants) to make a humorous event happen.

3.2 Humorous Events

In the discussion above we focused on the humor intelligence of virtual humans and social robots and how it can play a role in face-to-face interaction. A broader view is needed. There are also many situations in real live that amuse us, make us smile or make us laugh. There is no way yet that we can formalize such situations and have algorithms that decide when and how we find pleasure and enjoy a particular event. However, this does not mean that we cannot have incongruities introduced by smart technology into our lives. Such incongruities will not necessarily lead to humorous situations. Incongruities can be confusing or even threatening, but here we assume that when we are aware of potential incongruities we can understand and manipulate them to introduce humorous situations. So we can ask how we can control an environment and its virtual and human inhabitants, making use of sensors and actuators embedded in these inhabitants (e.g. using wearables or implants) and in other devices and objects in the environment, to generate humorous events. What kind of digital banana peel can we introduce in a smart environment?

Incongruity humor theories seem to be the most promising approach to the 'digital banana peel' problem. This approach may assume a view on a particular situation that has to be replaced by a different and surprising new view because of newly obtained information about that situation. Surprising, because it is in contrast with our initial interpretation of the situation. This is comparable to when someone tells us a joke or when we read a text that is ambiguous and later we realize that although at that moment our interpretation best fitted a stereotypical interpretation, the situation's description also allowed a less stereotypical and very much contrasting interpretation. However, in non-text humor, whether it is in cartoons, movies, stage performances or real life, different interpretations of a particular situation do not necessarily follow from a succession of events. It is as in a cartoon, where we see drawing and text at the same time, although there can be differences in 'scanning behavior' of a cartoon. In a similar way we use our senses to interpret an event in real life and become aware of incongruities. Unlike cartoons, we don't think that a snapshot of a humorous real-life event will turn out to be humorous. The dynamics of the event have to be taken into account. And, unless the single-modal incongruities that can appear in language, in the physical world we can have cross-modal incongruities, where our senses reach a conclusion, based on partly incomplete and partly conflicting information, that later has to be revised based on newly received information. We have been 'tricked'.

As the authors of [16] mention, there is no theory of funny behavior. They are right, but indeed, as they argue, there are principles from verbal humor that we can turn to and there is a wealth of funny behavior and funny events in movies and comedy that have been analyzed. There exist also many interesting observations on humor in daily life and there are some typologies for humor as it can appear in 'real' life. Clearly, 'real' life nowadays is different from 'real' life as we know it from twenty-five years ago when neither Internet, World Wide Web or mobile devices were integrated in our daily life. Existing typologies are however from the pre-Internet period and mostly focus on verbal humor or, when sight gags in movies are discussed, from the pre-'talkies' period. Noel Carroll [17] in his taxonomy of sight gags gives many examples of juxtaposition of incongruous elements in such movies. They include 'switch images', where an event is presented to the audience under one interpretation, but where subsequent information, for example obtained with a different camera view, makes clear that the situation was underdetermined and should have been given a different interpretation. They also include 'the mutual interference or interpenetration of two (or more) series of events (or scenarios), an incongruity also introduced by the French philosopher and Noble price winner Henri Bergson in his essay on laughter [18]. Bergson looked at humor in (French) comedy, but by doing so he had many observations on humor in real life situations with explanations that emphasized a 'mechanical' interpretation of events and human behavior in order to be considered humorous. Also accidental humor, following from thoughtlessness and not being able to deal with unexpected situations, is included in this 'mechanical' viewpoint (see also Nijholt [19]).

If we turn to humor researchers then, in Berger [20] we can find four basic categories of humor techniques: Language (the humor is verbal), Logic (the humor is ideational), Identity (the humor is existential), and Action (the humor is physical or nonverbal). The latter category only contains the techniques 'Chase', 'Slapstick', 'Speed', and 'Time', while the other categories all have more than ten techniques. But although illustrations of techniques usually address jokes, there are some techniques from other categories (for example, mimicry and impersonation) that can be used beyond language. This typology has been adapted in [21] for audiovisual media with the aim to use it to analyze humor in TV commercials. To answer the question what it is that generates humor in media they studied hundreds of commercials and seven humor technique categories were distinguished: (1) slapstick, (2) clownesque humor, (3) surprise, (4) misunderstanding, (5) irony, (6) satire and (7) parody.

Another useful typology has been introduced by Morreal [22]. We summarize his views, with a bias towards our interest in nonverbal humor that can be generated in smart environments as follows:

- Deficiency in an object or person. This is about physical deformity, ignorance or stupidity, moral shortcomings, or actions that fail. Hence, it is about inferiority, weakness and absentmindedness.
- One thing/situation seeming to be another. This is about mimicry/imitation, imposter, pretense, and mistaken identity, but also about giving different and opposing interpretations of events.
- Coincidence in things/situations. Everywhere we expect uniqueness unexpected repetition can have a humorous effect.
- Incongruous juxtaposition. The incongruous effect is obtained by having physical, social, and psychological opposites appear together in a situation.
- Presence of objects, people, behavior, opinions in appropriate situations. This includes situations where sequences of events inappropriately intersect.

With our aim to introduce humor in smart environments, whether it is done by a human, the environment itself or by a joint effort of human and environment, tools to realize these techniques using sensors and actuators need to be made available for a human joker, a controller of the environment or for the smart environment itself.

4   From Videogames to Smart Environments

Interestingly, there now are videogames that have been given an implementation in the digitally enhanced real world. That is, sensors and actuators make it possible to have playful and game-like experiences in smart environments. It is worthwhile to investigate videogames and how gamers use the virtual environments that are offered by the game companies. Unlike the passive listening and seeing experience when someone tells us a joke, when we watch a sitcom or a humorous TV commercial, when we watch a stage performance, or when we watch a movie, videogames are about interaction. In principle, a user's interactions are anticipated, including the many ways a user can fail to perform a certain interaction. Game designers, maybe not the designers of shooting games, have introduced humor in games, for example in adventure games, games where users have to exploit the environment and have to make decisions about how to continue, and while doing so get humorous commentary and sometimes are confronted with humorous actions of the non-playing characters (NPCs) or humorous behavior of the environment. In some games players are challenged, sometimes implicitly, to reach a goal as fast as possible. Other games can be played more leisurely and allow relaxed social interaction. In massively multiplayer online role-playing games (MMORPGs) we have teams of players that discuss strategies and try to humiliate and destroy opponents, preferring creative and humorous ways to do so.

Game designers do not systematically use humor techniques to design humor in a game, that is, in games we can recognize such techniques, but they have been introduced by a designer using his sense of humor and his intuition when and where to use it. In [23] a first attempt is made to offer game designers 'design patterns' that can help them to design comical game characters and events. Because at this moment there is not sufficient artificial intelligence that allows situation-aware autonomous behavior of NPCs, it is almost impossible to give them an active role in attempts to create spontaneous humor in games. Rather than canned or scripted humor and just as in the case of the human-robot interaction humor we discussed in Sect. 3, we would like to see situational humor.

Although it is not spontaneous, in good games 'canned' humor is as much integrated as it is the case with the sounds and music that accompany the game. Situational humor can be introduced in MMORPGs by human players without NPCs or game environment being aware of this humor and without a game designer intentionally having facilitated this kind of humor. We enter a grey area between canned humor and situational humor when the game designer introduces 'laws' in a physical engine that do not match with what we are used to in our daily life environments. Maybe we can walk through walls, see through walls, become invisible, or have eyes in the back of our head. Having unusual game physics, weird shortcuts, non-Euclidean geometries, intriguing perspective play and other surprising game elements (e.g., the use of panels and the portal mechanics in the *Portal* game) will certainly help to enter or introduce humorous situations during game play. Without verbal commentary such humorous situations can be recognized and we can consider this as intentional attempts of a game designer to introduce non-scripted humorous situations in a game. In order to make smart environments humorous we can make use of these videogame 'techniques'. They add to the techniques that were mentioned in the previous section. No systematic exploration of such techniques has been done so far.

There are more ways in which humor from videogame environments can be translated to humor in smart environments. In games we can encounter hackers, cheaters and gamers whose play is not (game) goal-oriented but rather to the exploitation of a game to see where things can go wrong and where you can be cleverer than the designers of the game. The general idea is that a game designer cannot anticipate every action a gamer can take and therefore cannot always choose an appropriate response for each of these actions. A gamer can choose to make unlikely decisions or to follow unlikely continuations of a conversation with a NPC. *Mass Effect 1* (2007) is an SF action game. It has a conversation wheel that allows choices in the conversation with NPCs. It is not really meant to introduce humor in the conversation, but dialogue choices, including 'charm' and 'intimidate' options allow the creation of verbal exchanges and decisions that can lead to intended bad endings, strange relationships and humorous situations. Creative play with a game's engine has led to the Machinima genre of gameplay videos, compilations of physical humor [8].

5 Conclusions: Humor in Smart Environments

Game environments are driven by a game engine. We can expect that future smart and interactive environments will be controlled by environment engines. It will depend on the goals of the environments or sub-environments how much control a user has when actively or passively interacting with the environment. Digital technology as it is available in sensors and actuators in our environments and as wearables on or in our bodies can extend existing humor techniques or introduce new techniques just as the game mechanics in a videogame can challenge us with situations we cannot encounter in a non-digitally enhanced physical world.

We can have canned humor in smart environments, without or hardly having a relation with the aims of the user, but scripted humor can also appear in a more integrated way, similar to what we see in game environments. Conversational interaction with physical robots, virtual agents and tangibles can also be sources of humor. Earlier we mentioned possibly funny behavior of robot butlers. Goal-oriented behavior of a human inhabitant can be accompanied with humorous comments that depend on the progress that is made, in this way getting closer to situational humor.

Just as in games we will have hacking, cheating, and exploitation behavior in smart environments. In particular exploitation behavior, not using the environment in the way it is supposed to be used, but searching for actions and creating events that have not been anticipated by the designers and that are humorous or potentially humorous. This provides the exploiter also with knowledge about the environment that can be used to make others the butt of a practical digital joke. Accidental humor can also follow from straightforward bugs in the environment or from clumsy use because of unfamiliarity with new technology. And, as mentioned in [24], due to our digital multitasking behavior, we will often be confronted with juxtapositions of information chunks that can be unexpected and potentially humorous.

Having (partial) control of an environment provides a user with the possibility to make changes to the environment and have the environment (and its objects and devices) act in a humorous way, to this particular user or to his or her audience, sometimes requiring a human or digital 'victim'. As mentioned in Sect. 2, we can consider a 'weak' and a 'strong' sense of humor, and a continuum from weak to strong with an increasing role of the environment and its objects and devices in creating humorous events. In this continuum we can make use of the typologies of humorous nonverbal behavior or humorous physical events that we mentioned in Sect. 3 and the humor emerging properties of game environments as discussed in Sect. 4.

Does every smart environment need a sense of humor? People use humor everywhere, even to cope with unbearable situations [25]. But clearly, when implementing a sense of humor in smart environments we can first look at rather 'innocent' domestic, public space and urban applications where our behavior is not always only goal-oriented, where we are more open to humor and where we can also engage in entertainment applications. In recent years we see, for example in research reported in the ACE (Advances in Computer Entertainment) or CHI (Computer-Human Interaction) conferences humorous aspects added to sitting in a bath, brushing your teeth, looking in a mirror, turn off an alarm clock, or let your microwave do its work by performing physical exercises. Playful and humorous interaction helps to persuade users to perform certain tasks. User-controlled smart sensors and actuators allow a user to manipulate the environment in order to create humorous events or humorous applications. Humor intelligence added to a smart environment allows the environment to recognize and introduce humorous events [26, 27].

However, it can be expected that in addition to government regulations that require monitoring our digital behavior, companies that provide us with domestic and safety applications, that take care of our energy, water and information needs and that provide us with smart environments will probably restrict our freedom to make changes to our smart environments. There is of course a chance that the sense of humor smart environments will have will be decided by others than its users [28].

References

1. Raskin, V.: The Primer of Humor Research. Mouton de Gruyter, Berlin (2008)
2. Freud, S.: Jokes and their relation to the unconscious. Translated by J. Strachey. W.W. Norton, New York (1960). (Original work published 1905)
3. Minsky, M.: Jokes and their relation to the cognitive unconscious. In: Vaina, L., Hintikka, J. (eds.) Cognitive Constraints on Communication, pp. 175–200. Reidel, Boston (1981)
4. Junco, M.A.: Designing the incorrect. Design and graphic humor. Des. Discourse **3**(2), 1–16 (2008)
5. Nijholt, A.: Conversational agents and the construction of humorous acts. In: Nishida, T. (ed.) Conversational Informatics: An Engineering Approach, pp. 21–47. Wiley, Chicester (2007)
6. Niewiadomski, R., Hofmann, J., Urbain, J., Platt, T., Wagner, J., Piot, B.: Laugh-aware virtual agent and its impact on user amusement. In: Ito, T., Jonker, C., Gini, M., Shehory, O. (eds.) 12th International Conference on Autonomous Agents and Multiagent Systems, pp. 619–626. ACM, New York (2013)
7. Becker-Asano, C., Kanda, T., Ishi, C., Ishiguro, H.: How about laughter? Perceived naturalness of two laughing humanoid robots. In: Cohn, J., Nijholt, A., Pantic, M. (eds.) 3rd International Conference on Affective Computing and Intelligent Interaction, pp. 49–51. IEEE Press, New York (2009)
8. Švelch, J.: Comedy of contingency: making physical humor in video game spaces. Int. J. Commun. **8**, 2530–2552 (2014)
9. Köhler, G., Ruch, W.: Sources of variance in current sense of humor inventories: how much substance, how much method variance? Humor Int. J. Humor Res. **9**(3–4), 363–397 (1996)
10. Martin, R., Puhlik-Doris, P., Larsen, G., Gray, J., Weir, K.: Individual differences in uses of humor and their relation to psychological well-being: development of the humor styles questionnaire. J. Res. Pers. **37**(1), 48–75 (2003)
11. Morreall, J.: Comic Relief: A Comprehensive Philosophy of Humor. Wiley-Blackwell, Oxford (2009)
12. Gordon, M.: What makes humor aesthetic? Int. J. Hum. Soc. Sci. **2**(1), 62–70 (2012)
13. Loehr, D.: An attempt at natural humor from a natural language robot. In: Hulstijn, J., Nijholt, A. (eds.) International Workshop on Computational Humor: Automatic Interpretation and Generation of Humor, pp. 161–171. University of Twente, Enschede (1996)
14. Binsted, K., Ritchie, G.: Computational rules for generating punning riddles. Humor Int. J. Humor Res. **10**(1), 25–76 (1997)
15. Tinholt, H.W., Nijholt, A.: Computational humour: utilizing cross-reference ambiguity for conversational jokes. In: Masulli, F., Mitra, S., Pasi, G. (eds.) WILF 2007. LNCS (LNAI), vol. 4578, pp. 477–483. Springer, Heidelberg (2007)
16. Wendt, C.S., Berg, G.: Nonverbal humor as a new dimension of HRI. In: 18th IEEE International Symposium on Robot and Human Interactive Communication, pp. 183–188. IEEE Press, New York (2009)
17. Carroll, N.: Theorizing the Moving Image. Cambridge Studies in Film. Cambridge University Press, Cambridge (1996)
18. Bergson, H.: Laughter: an essay on the meaning of the comic. Translated from Le Rire. Essai sur la signification du comique, 1900. Gutenberg project (2003)
19. Nijholt, A.: Incongruity humor in language and beyond: from bergson to digitally enhanced worlds. In: Fourteenth International Symposium on Comunicación Social: retos y perspectivas (Invited), vol. II, pp. 594–599. Ediciones Centro de Lingüística Aplicada, Santiago de Cuba (2015)

20. Berger, A.A.: An Anatomy of Humor. Transaction Publishers, New Brunswick (1993). (First edition in 1976)
21. Buijzen, M., Valkenburg, P.: Developing a typology of humor in audiovisual media. Media Psychol. **6**(2), 147–167 (2004)
22. Morreal, J.: Taking Laughter Seriously. State University of New York Press, New York (1983)
23. Dormann, C., Boutet, M.: Incongruous Avatars and hilarious sidekicks: design patterns for comical game characters. In: DiGRA 2013 Conference on Defragging Game Studies, pp. 1–16. DiGRA, Atlanta (2013)
24. Silber, M.J.: Digital humor theory. M.Sc. thesis, School of Art and Design, Pratt Institute, New York (2013)
25. Herzog, R.: Dead Funny. Humor in Hitler's Germany. Melville House, Brooklyn (2012)
26. French, J.H.: The identification of slapstick comedy using automatic affective video indexing techniques. In: 50th Annual Southeast Regional Conference (ACM-SE 2012), pp. 353–354. ACM, New York (2012)
27. Rekimoto, J., Tsujita, H.: Inconvenient interactions: an alternative interaction design approach to enrich our daily activities. In: International Working Conference on Advanced Visual Interfaces (AVI 2014), pp. 225–228. ACM, New York (2014)
28. Morozow, E.: Dafür sollte uns der Humor zu schade sein. Frankfurter Allgemeine Zeitung, 17 September 2014. http://www.faz.net/aktuell/feuilleton/silicon-demokratie/kolumne-silicon-demokratie-dafuer-sollte-uns-der-humor-zu-schade-sein-13130046.html

On Algorithmic Discovery and Computational Implementation of the Opposing Scripts Forming a Joke

Victor Raskin[(✉)]

Linguistics and CERIAS, Purdue University, West Lafayette, IN, USA
vraskin@purdue.edu

Abstract. The paper deals with the notion of 'script'. Scripts have been essential for the dominant formal theories of verbal humor since their inception in the late 1970s, and the formal theories gave rise to meaningful computational humor a decade or so later. Recent developments in computational semantics and computational humor have required a tighter definition of 'script' as a computational entity.

Keywords: Humor · Formal humor theory · Computational humor · Script

1 Introduction

The paper deals with the notion of 'script' and its readiness for computation, mostly in computational humor but also beyond. Computational humor does, of course, require the same computation as other meaning-based natural language processing applications (MB-NLP). Scripts formed the basis of the first full-fledged theory of humor, my Script-Based Semantic Theory of humor (SSTH: [1, 2]). They were kept on, without much elaboration, in Attardo's and my General Theory of Verbal Humor (GTVH: [3]). And it was not until the state of the art in computational semantics caught up with what the formal theory of humor needed for computation that the need to tighten up and to formalize, algorithmize, and compute actually arose, which led to the Ontological Semantic Theory of Humor (OSTH: [4]). In this section, we will introduce the notion of script first, as it was used in SSTH, which will be the very next item to be introduced, followed by GTVH and, finally, OSTH. We will then review computational humor, both how it should be done and why, and how it should not. The following sections will deal with the essence of the paper, i.e., how to algorithmize and compute scripts.

1.1 Scripts in Humor Theories

By the late 1970s, the notions of 'frame' and 'script' had been introduced at least in computer science [5, 6]. Neither had a formal definition, and its understanding depended on the reader's common sense: you know that a room has walls, a floor, a ceiling, always a door, often windows—so all of that is part of the frame for room. And

© Springer International Publishing Switzerland 2015
N. Streitz and P. Markopoulos (Eds.): DAPI 2015, LNCS 9189, pp. 671–679, 2015.
DOI: 10.1007/978-3-319-20804-6_61

the script of going to a restaurant includes these things that happen there: you are seated, offered the menus, etc. I did not feel compelled or enabled to go any further than that, so I referred to the script of DOCTOR and LOVER to explain how a most ordinary joke (1) worked:

(1) "Is the *doctor* at home?" the *patient* asked in his *bronchial* **whisper**. "No," the *doctor's* **young and pretty wife whispered** in reply. **"Come right in."**

The SSTH Main Hypothesis was that, to be a verbal joke, the text had to be compatible, in full or in part, with two opposing scripts. In the text above, the material that is compatible with the doctor script is italicized and the material compatible with the lover script boldfaced. The reader/hearer is strongly prompted towards the first script and pretty much ignores the material from the second script until he/she is stumped by the last-sentence punchline, which defeats, without any explanation like, *He will be back soon*, the patient's goal to get help. (Peter Derks' 1991 demo of the first MRI of his brain processing a joke actually demonstrated a total momentary collapse of all activity when the first script collapses and quickly recovers to handle the second script.) Then, the reader/hearer of (1) also quickly notices the second-script material and, given the premises and prejudices of the 1930s rural America, "gets" the joke.

This is the essence of SSTH, and one must understand the theoretical innocence of humor research at the time of its inception to figure out why the theory immediately gained the prominence it did. The theory did establish itself conditionally: it was supposed to work with a fully-fledged formal procedure of semantic representation. The whole pathos of the effort was that we can establish the joke potential of a text in the process of purely linguistic semantic processing. Only the semanticists, at least some of them, could appreciate the fact that such a processing was not then available, and there were no other semanticists among humor researchers.

Another reason for the immediate acceptance of the theory was that the field of humor research had been familiar with a purely household notion of theory, as in *I have a theory why Nicole left Jason*. Household wisdom rarely encompasses the philosophy of science, and the latter hardly ever discusses the properties of theories that are not of physics. The fact that theories must have purviews, premises, bodies, etc., that they must be falsifiable, justified, and evaluated, that they should have no unlisted exceptions [7] was a mystery to humor researchers then and have remained a mystery to many since—see, for instance, the "theory" of benign violations [8], which is a typical Nicole/Jason partial observation about undefined entities. Much more seriously, see [9], which is essentially the same, except for coming from a major humor scholar who does know all there is to know about humor but not about real theories. So, the reason for SSTH's easily achieved prominence was that it was a real theory even though it was not fully described as such until several decades later.

The next phase of the linguistic theory of humor was the General Theory of Verbal Humor (GTVH: [3]), which came up with 6 Knowledge Resources (KRs), three of which were introduced to make a linguistic theory interdisciplinary: Situation (action theory), Target (sociology), Narrative Strategy (narratology)—see also [11]. Two KRs, Script Opposition and Language, encapsulated SSTH, virtually unchanged. And the last KR, Logical Mechanisms, the only one, whose status in the sequence-of-funnels hierarchy was not confirmed in a famous massive psychological experiment [10], remains mysterious.

The linguistic component of GTVH continued to affirm that linguistic semantics could account for the joke potential of a text except for script opposition, treated in both theories rather dismissively: [2] came up with a couple of very short lists of script oppositions, such as sex vs. no sex, life vs. death, money vs. no money, that covered a huge majority of all jokes; [12] made a somewhat more careful attempt to inventory script oppositions. Unlike its two predecessors, OSTH, which emerged a couple of decades later, could rely on a mature system of linguistic semantic representation and computation, and as such, it fully incorporated script opposition into the Ontological Semantic Technology [13–16]: in other words, OSTH, not yet fully deployed but following pretty much the same main hypothesis of script opposition, is supposed to be a working theory, and the way it is supposed to work constitutes the idea of real computational humor.

1.2 Computational Humor

Computational humor encompasses approaches and systems that enable the computer to detect and/or generate verbal humor. Real computational humor is based on computer understanding rather than on the mechanical use of word lists early on and machine learning later. The term 'real' is not meant evaluatively but only to signify that this is how humans use humor—with understanding. And the major consequence of computability of anything is the conclusion that humans have come up with a rigorous formal theory of the computed phenomenon, a full-fledged theory of the kind described in the previous section, that was good enough to be encoded in machine language and to enable the computer to detect nad/or generate humor. A theory like that probides revealing insights into humor, on the one hand, and becomes a component of true, big-issue artificial intelligence (AI).

2 Scripts

After Schanck cavalry assault on the restaurant script, compromised mostly by his denial of any role to syntax and insistence on reducing all actions to 11 primitives, there has been surprisingly little work on computing scripts. But then, of course, there has been very little work on computational semantics at all, in an era, almost completely monopolized by meaning-free machine learning (ML), whose algorithms self-perpetuated and metamorphosed into a powerful industry. Since around 2005, however, voices from inside the ML have arisen that berate its low precision [24], and consumers have been unhappy with ML-based NLP applications, especially the more ambitious and sophisticated applications like e-discovery in litigation. Some ML leaders have actually led the charge towards semanticalizing the industry at least somewhat, by adding elements of meaning and/or ontology [25, 26]. Scripts are likely to re-emerge soon as well, and they are already raising their messy heads in our own Ontological Semantic Technology.

2.1   Scripts in Ontological Semantic Technology?

Don't let us beat about the bush: there have been no scripts in Ontological Semantic Technology (OST) so far, as there were none in Ontological Semantics [27] *per se*, of which OST has been a much improved and more (and better) implemented revision—see Fig. 1.

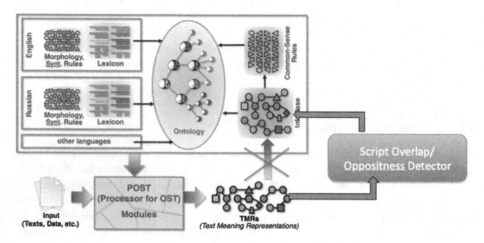

Fig. 1.   OST architecture for OSTH

Let us ignore the OSTH part in the bottom left corner for the moment and focus on what OST is and what it does. The oval language-independent ontology in the center is indeed the main basis of the approach. It is an initially manually crafted hierarchy of concepts organized on the subsumption IS-A basis but linked with several hundred other properties. It is an engineering ontology [28], built mostly semi-automatically, with the help of a well-evolved and tested acquisition tool [14], without any philosophical claim that it reflects how the world is or the psychobiological claim that our brain contains the same ontology. Its only justification is that it works—in meaning representation and communication, especially in practical applications.

The main function of the ontology is to provide conceptual support for the lexical items in a language-specific lexicon: English and Russian are listed on the left as just examples of languages, as confirmed by the lower "other languages" block; they do happen to have been languages OST has been implemented on, joined by Spanish, Korean, Arabic, and Hebrew. Thus, the English word *drive*, in one of its verb senses, may be anchored in the concept GO whose INSTRUMENT is restricted to a concept like AUTOMOBILE or VEHICLE. And so will the corresponding sense of the Russian word *vesti*.

Also in the large Resource block, are the language-specific lexicons, where every sense of every lexical item—word, acronym, phrasal—is defined in terms of the anchoring concept and restricted properties, as shown above. Also there, there is the language-specific ecological, morphological, and syntactic information [27]. InfoBase is where all the successfully processed sentences go to make up the language/knowledge experience of the system. And the common-sense rules, collected in processing.

The actual processing happens below the block: a text comes in, an OST software processes it in a variety of ways, and what comes out is a text-meaning representation (TMR), an ontological presentation of the meaning of the sentence. OST has used two different types of TMR calculation, pattern matching and graphic distances. The former one will present the English sentence Mary drove to Boston from New York yesterday, roughly, as in Fig. 2.

go
agent	Mary
instrument	automobile
direction-from	New York
direction-to	Boston
time	yesterday

Fig. 2.   Simplified OST TMR

The other software produces a graph TMR on the basis of the shortest distance between concepts in which the correct senses of the words in the sentence are anchored, and those graphs are much better visible to the computer than to human readers.

The successfully processed TMRs go to InfoStore. When the TMR fails the human engineer initiates the blame-assignment procedure, and that often diagnoses a common-sense failure, in which case a common-sense rule may be added to the Resource block. The rule may state, for instance, that one gets dressed before leaving home, and the rule, thus, supports an inference that people are dressed outside of their homes. The common-Common-Sense Rules block is, thus, the only place in OST where a whole sentence may—and does—typically appear. This is probably where scripts belong because they are also of that nature: if not common-sense rules, they are also part of our knowledge of the world.

2.2   Scripts as Language Entities

It was rather amazing to realize in the 1970s, when frames and scripts [5, 6] were introduced that it had not happened much earlier because human users definitely manipulate them all the time. As Schank could rely on his readers' knowledge of the script for attending a mid-toupscale restaurant, people fully dispose of a large number of ordinary scripts as well as developing scripts for shared experience, personally or professionally. Many scripts are culture-specific: thus the US morning routine differs from the continental European morning routine in a number of ways perhaps but most notably in the huge distinction between an American and continental breakfast. Couples develop sex routines. Colleagues establish meeting routines. There are fended bender routines, shopping routines, bill-paying routines, and so and so forth.

The most obvious way of handling a script is to present it as a set of sentences, each describing an individual attempt that is part of a script. This is what I must have felt intuitively when I invented a semi-formal presentation for the doctor and lover scripts when analyzing (1) in [1, 2]: a doctor was an adult human, who spent a considerable time at a medical school in the past and now sees patients, diagnoses them, and prescribes medication. A lover was an adult person, who has had sex at least once to a person of the (then) opposite sex, to whom he or she was not married. A bit more formally, something like the sequence of events in Figs. 3 and 4 must take place to establish X as a doctor and Y as a lover.

Figure 5 shows an abortive attempt to incorporate scripts into pre-OST Ontological Semantics [29] that OST has not yet picked up and incorporated. The if/then, and, and or logical operators had not, however, been actually incorporated into the system, even though [27] semi-tacitly allowed for them.

The scripts were developed for use in an application that would crawl the web and inform the officers of a company about the state of financial health of their partner companies, both suppliers and buyers. To my knowledge, such an application has not yet been implemented, and an expensive horde of human analysts provides an imperfect service. Obviously, an Ontological Semantic implementation would process the phrases and sentences into TMRs and develop a TMR-manipulating calculus for using scripts for inferencing and, more broadly, for reasoning.

2.3   Script Operations

Developing a TMR-manipulating calculus technically is a trivial algorithmic and programming task. Yet, inferencing and reasoning in NL, rather than in first-order logic as description logic does [30], is not simple, and the difficult part, as far as scripts are concerned, is script operations. What are they?

Obviously, it is a question whose significance goes far beyond computational humor but, almost equally obviously, for people in computational humor, this field can help to establish some helpful prompts for any form of HCI. One obvious exploitation of scripts in humor is the ability to mention scripts and to pretend to establish scripts, as in Jokes (2–3), respectively.

(2) It was such a hurried morning for me that I almost burned the trufle lasagna for the kids.

(3) Two Russian peasants chat over the fence between their outhouses early in the morning. "Ouch," one of them says, "The sun is almost up, and my cow has not been milked yet." "Nor has my woman been fucked yet," adds the other.

Similarly, in the financial world, a casual remark that a company applied for an unusual loan will bring up the much-feared specter of bankruptcy. But, then again, this may turn out to be the wrong conclusion. In spite of this and other difficulties with script operations, the initial problem is script acquisition. In [27], the complex event of teach is analyzed at length, setting up various sub-events. My co-author insisted on avoiding the notion of script there, and the legitimate part of his reservation was the finer grain size of that script. I had panicked when my over-enthusiastic Ph.D. students on the soft side started talking about the scripts of life or of poetry—that was much too

X is a doctor if and only if:
1. X went to an accredited medical school and graduated from it.
2. X passed an extended internship
3. X was licensed as a physician
4. X has opened or joined a medical practice or a hospital
5. X treats patients on a regular basis by examining or listening to them, diagnosing their condition and sending them to tests or specialists and/or prescribing them medication

Fig. 3.   "Script" for doctor

Y is a lover if and only if:
1. Y is a teenager or older
2. There is a Z of the opposite sex who is a teenager or older
3. Y and Z are not married to each other
4. Y and Z have had sex at least once

Fig. 4.   "Script" for lover.

APPROACH-BANKRUPTCY

If Or company has cash problems
company can't meet payroll
company misses loan payment
company seeks loan
Then company maynear bankruptcy

DECLARE-BANKRUPTCY

If company declares bankruptcy
And company files for Chapter 11
Or court appointsreceiver for company
Then And company officers lose control
company operates under receiver
Orcompany stops operating
company liquidates assets
creditors get partial payment

Fig. 5.   Two bankruptcy scripts

course. The fact that just about any event can be analyzed into sub-events arouses the fear of infinite regress. Not only does the joke punch line, largely not counterparted in non-humorous text, help to focus on the main script opposition in a joke [31] but it also establishes the appropriate grain size of the scripts.

References

1. Raskin, V.: Semantic mechanisms of humor. In: Chiarello, C., et al. (eds.) Proceedings of the Fifth Annual Meeting, Berkeley Linguistics Society. University of California, Berkeley (1979)
2. Raskin, V.: Semantic mechanisms of humor. D. Reidel, Dordrecht, Boston, Lancaster (1985)
3. Attardo, S., Raskin, V.: Script theory revis(it)ed: joke similarity and joke representation model. Humor Int. J. Humor Res. **4**, 293–348 (1991). doi:10.1515/humr.1991.4.3-4.293
4. Raskin, V., Hempelman, C., Taylor, J.: How to understand and assess a theory: the evolution of the SSTH into the GTVH and now into the OSTH. J. Literary Theor. **3**, 285–312 (2009)
5. Minsky, M.: A framework for representing knowledge. In: Winston, P.H. (ed.) The Psychology of Computer Vision, pp. 211–277. McGrow Hill, New York (1975)
6. Schank, R., Abelson, H.: Scripts, Plans, Goals and Understanding. Erlbaum, Hillsdale (1977)
7. Raskin, V.: A little metatheory: thoughts on what a theory of computational humor should look like. In: AAAI Symposium on the Artificial Intelligence of Humor, Arlington, VA (2012)
8. McGraw, P., Warren, C.: Benign violations: making immoral behavior funny. Psychol. Sci. **21**, 1141–1149 (2010)
9. Oring, E.: Parsing the joke: the general theory of verbal humor and appropriate incongruity. Humor Int. J. Verbal Humor **24**(2), 203–222 (2011)
10. Ruch, W., Attardo, S., Raskin, V.: Towards an empirical verification of the general theory of verbal humor. Humor Int. J. Humor Res. **6**(2), 123–136 (1993)
11. Taylor, J., Raskin, V.: Towards the Cognitive Informatics of Natural Language: The Case of Computational Humor. Int. J. Cogn. Inform. Nat. Intell. **7**, 3 (2013)
12. Raskin, V.: Linguistic heuristics of humor: a script-based semantic approach. In: Apte, M. (ed.) Language and Humor, Int. J. Sociol. Lang. (Special Issue) **65**(3), 11–26 (1987)
13. Raskin, V., Hempelmann, C., Taylor, J.: Guessing vs. knowing: the two approaches to semantics in natural language processing. In: Annual International Conference Dialogue (2010)
14. Taylor, J., Hempelmann, C., Raskin, V.: On an automatic acquisition toolbox for ontologies and lexicons in ontological semantics. In: International Conference in Artificial Intelligence: ICAI 2010 (2010)
15. Hempelman, C., Taylor, J., Raskin, V.: Application-guided ontological engineering. In: International Conference in Artificial Intelligence: ICAI 2010 (2010)
16. Taylor, J., Raskin, V., Hempelmann, C.: From disambiguation failures to common-sense knowledge acquisition: one day in the life of an ontological semantic system. In: Web Intelligence Conference (2011)
17. Raskin, V., Attardo, S.: Non-literalness and non-bona-fide in language: approaches to formal and computational treatments of language. Cogn. Pragamtics **2**, 1 (1994)
18. Binstead, K., Ritchie, G.: An implemented model of punning riddles. In: 12th National Conference on Artificial Intelligence (1994)
19. Stock, O.: Password swordfish: verbal humor in the interface. In: Hulstijn, J., Nijholt, A. (eds.) Proceedings of the International Workshop on Computational Humor, TWLT 12. University of Twente, Enschede (1996)
20. Wilks, Y.: Artificial companions. In: Bengio, S., Bourlard, H. (eds.) MLMI 2004. LNCS, vol. 3361, pp. 36–45. Springer, Heidelberg (2005)
21. Rosenthall, S., McKeown, K.: Sentiment detection of subjective phrases in social media. http://www.aclweb.org/anthology/S/S13/S13-2079.pdf

22. Mihalcea, R., Strapparava, C.: Computational laughing: automatic recognition of humorous one-liners. In: Cognitive Science Conference, pp. 1533–1538 (2005)
23. Mihalcea, R., Strapparava, C.: Learning to laugh (automatically): computational model for human recognition. Comput. Intell. **22**(2), 126–142 (2006)
24. Schiffman, B., McKeown, K.: Context and learning in novelty detection. In: HLT/EMNLP (2005)
25. Moldovan, D., Badulescu, A., Tatu, M., Antohe, D., Girju, R.: Models for the semantic classification of noun phrases. In: HLT/NAACL Workshop on Computational Lexical Semantics, pp. 60–67 (2005)
26. Mitchell, T., Cohen, W., Hruschka, E., Talukdar, P., Betteridge, J., Carlson, A., Dalvi, B., Gardner, M., Kisiel, B., Krishnamurthy, J., Lao, N., Mazaitis, K., Mohamed, T., Nakashole, N., Platanios, E., Ritter, A., Samadi, M., Settles, B., Wang, R., Wijaya, D., Gupta, A., Chen, X., Saparov, A., Greaves, M., Welling, J.: Never ending learning. In: Conference on Artificial Intelligence, AAAI 2015 (2015)
27. Nirenburg, S., Raskin, V.: Ontological Semantics. MIT Press, Cambridge (2004)
28. Gruber, T.: Toward principles for the design of ontologies used for knowledge sharing. In: Guarino, N., Poli, R. (eds.) The Role of Formal Ontology in the Information Technology, Int. J. Hum. Comput. Stud. (Special Issue) **43**(5–6), 907–928 (1995)
29. Raskin, V., Nirenburg, S., Hempelmann, C., Nirenburg, I., Triezenberg, K.: The genesis of a script for bankruptcy in ontological semantics. In: Hirst, G., Nirenburg, S. (eds.) Proceedings of the Text Meaning Workshop, HLT/NAACL 2003: Human Language Technology and North American Chapter of the Association of Computational Linguistics Conference. ACL, Edmonton (2003)
30. Baader, F., Calvanese, D., McGuiness, D., Nardi, D., Patel Schneider, P. (eds.): The Description Logic Handbook, pp. 47–100. Cambridge University Press, Cambridge (2003)
31. Taylor, J.: Different knowledge, same joke: response-based computational detection of humor. In: Streitz N., Markopoulos, P. (eds.) DAPI 2015. LNCS, vol. 9189, pp. xx–yy. Springer, Heidelberg (2015)

Different Knowledge, Same Joke: Response-Based Computational Detection of Humor

Julia M. Taylor[✉]

Computer and Information Technology Department, Purdue University,
401 N. Grant Street, West Lafayette, IN 47907, USA
jtaylor1@purdue.edu

Abstract. The paper explores the very basis of linguistic theories of humor with a view of applying them to computational humor. Computation requires tighter definitions. The paper analyzes joke-carrying texts based on the existing script-based methods. It compares jokes that have the same setup but different punchlines by examining the background knowledge that should be available to detect humor. It then moves into jokes where the same joke text elicits different responses from the reader, and conjectures that the responses are based on the readers' world knowledge and preferences. Such responses make it possible not only to analyze humor, but also to understand more about the people that produce the responses.

Keywords: Humor · Computational detection of humor · Semantics · Knowledge-based humor detection

1 Introduction

Since 1985, a text has been assumed to be joke-carrying [1] if it was compatible, fully or in part, with two scripts that overlap and oppose. The assumption is that any two scripts that a reader sees in a text would do the job, especially if communication is based on short canned-type jokes, which is what the theory was interested in. The (main) script oppositeness detection gets more difficult if the jokes are not canned, but a joke-carrying text is actually a spontaneous response to existing situation, or, as a simpler case, there must be response to the canned joke other than a non-verbal acknowledgment of the funny stimulus.

The reason why such detection is difficult is that each participant has their own fuzzy (in a technical sense of the word) view of the described situation, fill in the blanks according to their own understanding and experiences and may shift a conversation (whether the shift is picked up by others or not) to a different subscript or a set of scripts. In other words, it is these individual experiences that contribute to what part of the story a participant focuses on and it is likely that the oppositeness will be based on that focus, if one is to create one. While we are typically not blind to other possible scripts, or at least capable of recognizing them once they are recoverable from a stated utterance or sentence, their prediction is much more difficult as the result is based on

© Springer International Publishing Switzerland 2015
N. Streitz and P. Markopoulos (Eds.): DAPI 2015, LNCS 9189, pp. 680–688, 2015.
DOI: 10.1007/978-3-319-20804-6_62

something that may not be expressed (verbally or by another other means of communication).

With the development of computational humor, it becomes – at least theoretically – possible to detect more than one pair of scripts in a particular joke-carrying text. Moreover, it – again, at least theoretically – becomes possible to recognize scripts that may not be just visible to humans (due to lack of priming, for example), but may be visible to a machine as well (and, in the worst case scenario, only to machine but not to a human). Once a situation arises, where a person does not recognize a joke, but a computer does, due to its sensors or some (incorrectly?) weighted knowledge, a scientist may want to answer a question: is it possible to reduce such occurrences to match human expectations (or result appreciated by a human)? The next logical step, which we are not attempting to address here is, at which point we are willing to grant a computer a right to have an opinion over the jokeness value of a text. To put it into a less controversial and philosophical question, what constitutes an error in computational detection/generation of humor? Is it something that a (generic) human doesn't agree to, or is it a lack of (acceptable) explanation on the part of the computer why something is or isn't funny, based on known theories?

There is no argument that people have different senses or humor, and appreciate or do not appreciate different jokes. There is no argument that one person may think that something is a joke while another does not. There is also no argument that we allow such disagreements for humans. Luckily, computational humor is not at a state where a computer can address a question of why something is or isn't funny reliably (see [2] for initial attempts), but nevertheless such questions may be worth thinking about (at least relative to how do we report error rates). Should we allow a unique sense of humor for a computer? (For discussion on sense of humor see [3, 4])

Now that the controversial questions have been asked, we will leave them aside for the rest of the paper and proceed with examples where the same situation may lead to different response (different script oppositeness) and what can a system do about that.

2   Humor Theories

As mentioned in the Introduction, Script-based Semantic Theory of Humor (SSTH) [1] states that a text is joke-carrying if it contains two scripts that (partially) overlap and oppose. While the book was explaining only canned jokes, the theory can be applied to any type of joke (canned or not), and its extension—General Theory of Verbal Humor [5]—has been used in longer humorous texts [6, 7].

An extension of SSTH, the General Theory of Verbal Humor states that two jokes can be compared using six knowledge resources, namely, Script Overlap/oppositeness (SO), (pseudo-) Logical Mechanism (LM), Situation (SI), Target (TA), Narrative Strategy (NS), and Language (LA). The more knowledge resources they have in common, the more similar two jokes are. Moreover, the five knowledge resources form a strict hierarchy, SO– > [LM]– > SI– > TA– > NS-LA, and if two jokes vary only in one resource, the higher it is in the hierarchy, the more different the jokes are. For example, jokes that differ only in SI are more different than those jokes that differ only in NS. However, two jokes that differ only in SI are more similar than two jokes that differ in NS & LA together. The hierarchy was empirically verified [8] and confirmed, with the possible exception of LM.

It follows then from this hierarchy that two jokes that have different SOs should be rather different. The difference may vary depending on different scripts are. This should hold for cases ranging between:

- The jokes have identical setup, but differ only in punchline that leads to different SOs[1].
- The jokes that have setups that may vary in emphasis, but similar enough that the punchlines may be swapped.
- The joke have identical setup and punchline, but differ in the perception of either major scripts or subscripts.

The next sections provide examples on the both ends of the spectrum.

2.1   Identical Setup, Different Punchline

It is possible, although not entirely probable, to have a set of canned jokes that have the same setup, but different punchlines. As an example, consider the following pair, that works much better as a spoken joke rather than a written one:

$$\text{What's black and while and re(a)d all over?}$$
$$\text{- A newspaper} \tag{1}$$

This is an old joke that works due to the wordplay (homophone) between the color red and the past time of the verb read. The setup can be thought to ask what object consists of 3 colors, namely, that of black, white, and red. The punchline takes it to a different area, namely an object that has color white and black and has a property of being read (as in process information by reading) either from cover to cover or in its entirety.

Depending on whether the scripts are seen as semantic scripts in nature, and whether there exist overlap and semantic oppositeness, the text may be classified as a joke/pun or just a wordplay (see [9] for the differentiation between the two). The overlap of the two scripts – one being the reading of the newspaper, and the second one finding the object that has three colors – is the existence of some physical object that is white and black and has other characteristics. The oppositeness here is merely that of a homophone, and thus it serves as a good play on words in games for children.

The second part of the pair has identical setup to (1), but a totally different punchline, as demonstrated in (2), being one of many versions collected from the internet:

$$\text{What's black and white and red all over?}$$
$$\text{-An embarrassed zebra.} \tag{2}$$

---

[1] We are not considering cases where a different punchline varies only in LA, TA, etc., but does not activate different script pair.

The first script of the two is identical to that of the script of joke pair on (1): finding an object that contains three colors: black, white, and red. The second script takes an advantage of the word *red*, but in a milder form than (1) did: here the meaning of *red* changes slightly to denote not the prototypical color red, but the presumed human redness of a blushing face. The second script takes this human-like transformation and transposes it to an animal, thus making it possible for an animal to change color of skin in signifying embarrassment. Since it is widely known that zebras and black and white, and one turn reddish/pinkish when embarrassed, an embarrassed zebra could have some colors on the reddish/pinkish side if such transformation was possible for zebras. The overlap, again, is the physical object that could have some colors (at least white and black). The oppositeness here is not the fact that some objects turn red when they are embarrassed or not, but the fact that zebras in this joke are embarrassed, where the world knowledge, limited as may be, tells us that it is impossible. A humor informed reader may notice that this joke is a meta joke, and the script oppositeness is of a meta-level, namely, that between the zebra joke and the underlying newspaper joke.

Notice that the in (1) the punchline takes us from an object that is being either repeatedly or carefully studied, while in (2) we are concerned with the animal that possesses a human characteristic of embarrassment, which can hardly be attributed to an animal. The change of interpretation between the two jokes depends entirely on punchline.

While it is not theoretically possible to predict the word that the punchline will play on (that will serve as a trigger to SOs) and attempt to calculate every single possible interpretation, given a perfect world knowledge, it is possible to imagine what happens if the human specifies a second verse. It is also possible that a computer cannot tie the second verse to the first one due to the lack of world knowledge: it is rather difficult to get from red to blushing to embarrassment. It is possible then, for a computer to ask questions that would narrow down the interpretations of the second line and restrict the calculation of SOs. For example, in a response to *an embarrassed zebra*, a computer may ask a question about how such a zebra would look like (pointing back to the physical characteristics identified by the first line of the joke).

It should be stated that not all jokes are that complicated in nature. Another example of an internet provided response to a newspaper/zebra joke is demonstrated in (3);

$$\begin{aligned} &\text{—What's black and while and red all over?} \\ &\qquad \text{—A blushing zebra} \end{aligned} \qquad (3)$$

Notice that in this version the only connection that one needs to make to find SOs (and thus determine if this is a joke or not) is that from red to blushing, but removes the connection from blushing to embarrassment, thus significantly simplifying the problem at hand.

SOs Difference. The difference between (2) and (3) lie somewhere on the axis between totally different punchlines and identical punchlines that rely on the interpretation or emphasis that is seen by a user, but is not stated anywhere.

The difference between SOs pairs in (2) and (3) is minimal: while there is slight variation as to how to explain why the zebra is blushing – by embracement or not – the end result is the same. Thus, if we are looking at SO from the position of goal or a path to goal (as briefly suggested by [2]), we will arrive with approximately the same result for both blushing without a reason and blushing due to embarrassment. Thus, (2) and (3) are practically identical jokes – which follows a human's intuition as well.

The difference between (1) and (2) is much more pronounced: there is no intersection in meaning between the two second lines, or between how the pairs of scripts can be brought together. Thus, while the first scrip of the pairs is the same, the second scripts brings enough chaos into the jokes that the overall pair overlap is practically non-existent: we would have to compare an event of reading a particular printed material to an animal exhibiting human traits of being embarrassed.

2.2 Identical Setup, Identical Punchline, Different Knowledge of the World

On the other spectrum is the jokes that told exactly the same way, but get a totally different response from different people. As an example, consider the joke found on open Facebook political humor page:

Fig. 1 One of the jokes on the Facebook political humor page

The joke, if rephrase into a text form, could be analyzed as follows: a deadly Ebola virus was brought to America from one of African counties. This virus threatens lives of people who come in contact with those that already have Ebola and exhibit its symptoms. Over 500 years before, when Europeans came to America, they brought sickness, epidemic, and deaths to many Native Americans who were not immune to many European sicknesses. However, we now celebrate Columbus Day – observed as a second Monday in October – a legal holiday commemorating the discovery of the New World by Christopher Columbus in 1492.

The script overlap is the people from a different continent brought disease to people that live in America. The script oppositeness is the time of when the disease was brought, as well as the perception of the salience of the importance of the phenomenon: very salient in 2014, as perceived by 2014; and not at all salience 500 years ago as perceived in 2014.

The joke follows by hundreds of responses to the joke, indicating how it was perceived and which script played the most important role in this joke. It should be mentioned straight away that the responses to the joke do not indicate that the joke was entirely understood or appreciated, and some responses suggest just the opposite:

$$\text{Thousands of people have recently died. Not to be too big a sick in the mud but this is tasteless and not funny enough to make the crudeness worth it.} \quad (4)$$

The response indicates that the author of (4) perceived that was a joke, thus, supposedly, finding both scripts, while acknowledging only one of them: namely, that people die during virus outbreak/epidemics.

The acknowledgement of this script was one of the two major themes. Interestingly, however, such responses carried a second topic: who is responsible for the outbreak in America, and, at the same time exonerate the president. Examples of the responses are demonstrated in (5) and (6).

$$\text{Ebola} = \text{Enjoy Barack Obama's legacy America} \quad (5)$$

$$\text{And this is the Presidents fault how?? He is not God by any stretch of the imagination. This disease was not apparent when the guy got here.} [\ldots] \quad (6)$$

The second major theme was the European settlements on the Native American's territory as a consequence of the discovery of the new continent. Again, the topic of the response was an inference to the two major scripts directly accessed in a joke, namely, a conquest of the land and resettlement/eviction of the native population. As an example of such a response, see Fig. 2.

Fig. 2 One of the responses to the joke in Fig. 1

Again, the responses here identify which part of the background knowledge is salient to the reader and whether they are prepared to tolerate jokes of that nature. It is these responses that are helpful for identification of particular preferences in humor styles for an individual rather than a simple score [10].

Note all responses were negative, however, and some, such as (7) tried to joke back. The scripts at play are exactly the same, and the author is not explicitly using any inference to the secondary material, as the negative responses did. Instead, the focus is shifting from the recently salient Ebola and the deaths attributed to it, to the virus/epidemics that American Indians suffered from centuries ago. The playful shift, however, is acknowledged by the author through the second sentence, which also serves as a signal to the audience that the focus shift is intentional, not a result of a misunderstanding.

> Yeah just like the white settlers brought measles and chicken pox to American Indians. That's what you were thinking about right? RIGHT?   (7)

The response to perceived jokes, obviously, does not have to be negative. As described in [11], the same detection of what part of script or subscript was perceived by interlocutor is possible within friendly communication, especially when banter continues after initial joke, as shown in (8).

> [Friend 1:]So, I'm one of the last dinosaurs who just opened the
> LinkedIn profile. Not sure if I knew what I was doing but I think it's
> up and running. I am pretty sure I selected a terrific profile picture
> and connected with strangers that apparently were in my Gmail
> account It's great to be connected :)))[...]   (8)
> [Friend 2:] [...] u are kind of late in the game. Wanna buy a
> blackberry? [...]
> [Friend 1:] I dumped all my cash for Apple, I may spare some
> change for BB, a few cents now should be enough :)

While the conversation clearly rotates around BlackBerry, the intention of the friend 2 to produce a joke about BB being popular long time ago was misunderstood. Instead, Friend 1 caught on the fact that BB is no longer valuable, but not because is it nobody buys it anymore, but because their stock is very low. While one is likely to cause another, there are some parts of the (sub)script that were not activated by Friend 1, as intended by Friend 2. While not shown in this example, Friend 2 perceived the reasoning of low share argument and the banter continued. In other words, the intended joke was replaced by a different interpretation of the same explicitly stated material.

3   What About Embodied Humor?

We will assume for this section that a computational system that we are dealing with is not simply a read-write terminal, but that it has other senses: it can see (and has some ability to differentiate things), it can touch (and has some sensors to that effect), it can move (whether it is on wheels, legs or anything else), and it can hear (and process sounds at the same level of accuracy as it processes text). It would probably be very helpful if it could react in some way to the provided stimulus, based on existing research [12–16]. We will also assume that it can integrate the knowledge that it receives from all of its input channels and map it to its ontological representation, similarly to how it has been doing for text input. In essence, this computational system is a robot with some enhanced functionalities.

Such a system will have to sort a lot of knowledge out, including contradictory information. It will also have to address whether contradictory information is humorous or not. Let us consider a simple example: suppose, there is a bowl of raspberries on a table. Suppose, that our robot can differentiate colors and can differentiate objects such as table or bowl. Thus, he sees that the object in the bowl is reddish. Also, suppose, that he hears a comment from a person that the raspberries in the bowl are not ripe.

Now, suppose the robot can communicate in multiple natural languages. We will consider an example in Russian because of the convenient ambiguity words that mean things that can be easily perceived by a robot. Our robot hears the following sentence: *малина в вазе оказалось зеленой*. Our robot now has a problem: a word *зеленая* can mean 'unripe' (usually used in this sense with fruits or vegetables) or 'green.' This is where we either have a slight oppositeness or a potential misunderstanding: the robot can see that the color of the raspberries is close enough to red, even if it doesn't know the exact name of the color.

Now, suppose, a person who made the statement does not have in mind an interpretation of *зеленая* being the color (unless a person is a linguist, of course). Suppose, our robot responds, something like, *it looks rather red to me*. Technically, we have a joke-carrying conversation here, not unlike conversations that happen in many sitcoms. Will it be perceived as a joke by a person who is having such conversation with a robot?

Interestingly enough, the same phrase is translated by Google (11/14/2014, query "translate: малина в вазе оказалось зеленой") as *raspberry in a vase turned green*. This can be turned into a joke by a human (especially the one with linguistic knowledge), who should turn green from such translation.

What we have looked is a very simple case of when one agent (human or computational) has some knowledge or interpretation that the other one lacks (or doesn't see at first) and comments on the situation that is potentially humorous. It is up to the second participant to accept this situation as humorous, as suggested by the first, or to reject it. Provided that such situation is accepted, a further remark may be needed to acknowledge the acceptance.

References

1. Raskin, V.: Semantic Mechanisms of Humor. D. Reidel, Dordrecht, Boston, Lancaster (1985)
2. Taylor, J.M.: Towards informal computer human communication: detecting humor in restricted domain. Unpublished Ph.D. thesis. University of Cincinnati (2008)
3. Ruch, W.: The sense of humour: a new look at an old concept. In: Ruch, W. (ed.) The Sense of Humour: Explorations of a Personality Characteristic. Mouton de Gruyter, Berlin (1998)
4. Ruch, W. (ed.): Measurement of the sense of humor. Humor Int. J. Humor Res. 9(1/2), 273–302 (1996)
5. Attardo, S., Raskin, V.: Script theory revis(it)ed: joke similarity and joke representation model. Humor Int. J. Humor Res. 4(3–4), 83 (1991)
6. Ermida, I.: How to do humor with words: the linguistics of humor narratives. In: Raskin, V., Ruch, W. (eds.) Humor Research Series, vol. 9. Mouton de Gruyter, Berlin (2008)
7. Attardo, S.: Humorous texts: a semantic and pragamatic analysis. In: Raskin, V., Ruch, W. (eds.) Humor Research Series, vol. 6. Mouton de Gruyter, Berlin (2001)
8. Ruch, W., Attardo, S.: Raskin, V: Towards an empirical verification of the general theory of verbal humor. Humor Int. J. Humor Res. 6(2), 20 (1993)
9. Hempelmann, C.F.: Paronomasic puns: target recoverability towards automatic generation. Unpublished Ph.D. thesis. Purdue University (2003)
10. Hempelmann, C.F., Taylor, J.M, Raskin,V.: Tightening up joke structure: not by length alone. In: Cognitive Science Conference. Japan (2012)
11. Taylor, J.M.: Ontological semantic theory of humor in a context of humorous discourse. In: Chlopicki, W., Brzozowska, D. (eds.) Humorous Discourse. UK: Cambridge Scholarly Publishers, Cambridge (in press)
12. Nijholt, A.: Conversational agents and the construction of humorous acts. In: Nishida, T. (ed.) Conversational Informatics: An Engineering Approach. Wiley, Chicester (2007)
13. Sjöbergh, J., Araki, K.: Robots make things funnier. In: Hattori, H., Kawamura, T., Idé, T., Yokoo, M., Murakami, Y. (eds.) JSAI 2008. LNCS, vol. 5447, pp. 306–313. Springer, Heidelberg (2009)
14. Tinholt, H.W., Nijholt, A.: Computational humour: utilizing cross-reference ambiguity for conversational jokes. In: Masulli, F., Mitra, S., Pasi, G. (eds.) WILF 2007. LNCS (LNAI), vol. 4578, pp. 477–483. Springer, Heidelberg (2007)
15. Veale, T.: The ABCs of XYZs: creativity and conservativity in humorous epithets. In: Manjaly, J., Indurkhya, B. (eds.) Cognition, Experience, and Creativity. Orient Blackswan, New Delhi (2014)
16. Veale, T., Valitutti, A.: A world with or without you. In: Proceedings of AAAI-2014 Fall Symposium Series on Modeling Changing Perspectives: Re-conceptualizing Sensorimotor Experiences. Arlington, VA (2014)

Twitter: The Best of Bot Worlds
for Automated Wit

Tony Veale[✉], Alessandro Valitutti, and Guofu Li

School of Computer Science and Informatics, University College Dublin,
Belfield, Dublin 4, Ireland
{Tony.Veale,Alessandro.Valitutti,Guofu.Li}@UCD.ie

Abstract. Language affords a great many opportunities for the intelligent reuse
of linguistic content. Rather than always putting our own thoughts into our own
words, we often convey feelings through the words of others, by citing, quoting,
mimicking, borrowing, varying or ironically echoing what others have already
said. Social networking platforms such as Twitter elevate linguistic reuse into an
integral norm of digital interaction. On such platforms, *who* you follow and
what you re-tweet can say as much about you as the clothes you wear or the art
you hang on your walls. But not everyone that is worth following is human, and
not everything that is worth re-tweeting was first coined by a real person. More
and more of the witty and thought-provoking content on Twitter is generated by
bots, artificial systems that write their own material and vie for our attention just
as humans do. Real people knowingly follow artificial bots for reasons that are
subtle and diverse, but a significant reason is surely Twitter itself. This paper
explores Twitter as a smart environment for automated wit, and describes the
mechanics of a wittily inventive new Twitterbot named *@MetaphorMagnet*.

Keywords: Twitter · Twitterbot · Metaphor · Reuse · Irony · Social networks ·
Wit

1 We Can (Re)Tweet It for You Wholesale

The limitations on text length imposed by micro-blogging services such as Twitter do
nothing to dampen our ardour for creative language. Indeed, such limitations further
incentivize the use of creative devices such as metaphor, analogy and irony, as forms
such as these allow us to interact in ways that are witty, memorable and concise. As a
principally textual medium, Twitter supports all of the same compression strategies as
written language, but also adds some that are uniquely its own. Hashtags, for instance,
allow their originators to crystalize an emerging topic or movement into a single term,
thus allowing followers to hop onto an ever-accelerating bandwagon by appending the
hashtag *du jour* – such as *#CancelColbert* or *#GamerGate* – to their tweets. Twitter
also encourages its users to reuse, re-purpose and disseminate the tweets of others via a
simple re-tweeting mechanism. Re-tweeting is an action that creates added value for the
originator of a tweet *and* those that pass it along: for the former, it allows their texts to
reach a wider audience, and of latter it makes content intermediaries who – as
self-appointed social sensors – interactively filter what is worthy of greater attention.

© Springer International Publishing Switzerland 2015
N. Streitz and P. Markopoulos (Eds.): DAPI 2015, LNCS 9189, pp. 689–699, 2015.
DOI: 10.1007/978-3-319-20804-6_63

More and more, however, the texts that are so anointed by successive re-tweeting are not the texts of human writers but of artificial content-producers called *Twitterbots*.

A *Twitterbot* is an autonomous software system (a *bot*) that generates and tweets messages of its own design and composition. Ironically, many of these Twitterbots are popular precisely because their followers know them to be automated bots, and value the sense of the uncanny (what Freud called the *Unheimlich*) that they engender via their tweets, especially on those rare occasions when their tweets communicate an apparent insight that seems witty, profound or just enigmatic. Indeed, when humans interfere in the operation of a Twitterbot – to manually filter its outputs to improve its quality, or to manually (and fraudulently) write its tweets for themselves – users feel cheated and quickly *un*follow the bot. For users value the unusual perspective offered by non-human bots and are willing to tolerate large amounts of noise if a bot can occasionally generate a re-tweetable gem, even if these bots ultimately lack creative intent and cannot themselves tell the good from the bad from the unintelligible.

Twitterbots are an evolving technology and it is useful to distinguish the earliest or simplest exemplars from their more sophisticated and theory-guided successors. *First-generation* Twitterbots make little use of the rich techniques that linguistic theory has to offer, and rely instead on a combination of superficial language resources – such as word lists, rhyming dictionaries, thesauri – and recombinant aleatoric methods such as the *exquisite corpse* and *cut-up* techniques popularized by the early surrealists and by the beat poets William Burroughs and Brion Gysin [12, 13]. Popular Twitterbots such as @*Pentametron* achieve a great deal with superficial resources; @*Pentametron* re-tweets pairings of random tweets that each have ten syllables (for an iambic pentameter reading) and that each end with a rhyming syllable (as in *Pathetic people are everywhere/Your web-site sucks, @RyanAir*). First-generation Twitterbots do not generate messages from the semantic-level up; rather, they manipulate texts at the word-level, and thus lack any sense of the meaning of a tweet, or any rationale for why one tweet might be better – more provocative, more apt, more re-*tweetable* – than another. A bot such as @*MetaphorMinute*, which generates a random metaphor every two minutes (due to usage limitations imposed by the Twitter API) generates a great many outputs that are unintelligible for every one that a user might conceivably (with much effort) interpret as meaningful. In contrast, *next-generation* bots, such as the @*MetaphorMagnet* Twitterbot described here, use a panoply of linguistic and semantic techniques to craft their messages from the ground up. These theory-guided bots generate texts with specific rhetorical forms and semantics, to pithily reflect a bot's own semantic model of the world and to exploit its own inferential capabilities. Next-generation Twitterbots can thus generate observations, witticisms and metaphors that they themselves understand and recognize as interesting, surprising or ironic.

The simplest 1st-generation bots offer the clearest insights into why people actually follow mechanical content generators on Twitter. Consider @*everycolorbot*, which simply generates a random six-digit hex-code every hour. As each code denotes a different color from the RGB color space, @*everycolorbot* attaches a swatch of the corresponding color to each tweet. The bot's followers, which number in the tens of thousands, favorite and re-tweet its outputs not because they prefer certain RGB codes over others but because they bring their own visual appreciation to bear on each color. Thus, they favorite or retweet a color because of what that color says about their own aesthetics. Or consider @*everyword*, a bot which simply tweets the next word on its alphabetized inventory of English words every 30 min. (@*everyword* has since exhausted its word list, generating much media speculation as it neared the end of the Z's.) The bot, which attracted 100 thousand followers at its peak, tweeted words, not meanings, yet followers brought their own context and their own meanings to bear on those tweets that occasionally (and quite accidently) resonated with their times. For instance, the word "*woman*" – first tweeted on May 14, 2014 – was retweeted 243 times and favorited 228 times not because followers found the word new or unusual, but because the tweet coincided with the firing of the New York Times' first female executive editor, in a decision that drew the ire of many for its apparent sexism. First-generation bots do not offer their own meanings or insights, but give us opportunities to see, impose and share meanings of our own. Timely bot tweets are conversational hooks, allowing us to show that we are in on the joke and part of the conversation.

Though metaphors can often be witty, and witticisms are often based on figurative conceits, one does not imply the other. Nonetheless, though @*MetaphorMagnet* is principally a generator of metaphors, analogies and similes, its figurative outputs exhibit many of the same characteristics and are shaped by many of the same constraints as witty observations. For instance, Twitter's 140 character limitation on tweets leads @*MetaphorMagnet* to carefully ration its words, to favor brevity over verbosity and suggestiveness over detailed exposition. To attract the attention of new followers and encourage re-tweets from existing followers, the bot also aims to be provocative through its controlled use of semantic and pragmatic incongruity, realized at the textual level via semantic opposition (see [1, 3, 4, 8, 12]) and the violation of expectations. More specifically, @*MetaphorMagnet* views the schematic structures of Lakoff & Johnson's Conceptual Metaphor Theory (or *CMT*; see [2]) as "*scripts*" in the vein of the *SSTH* (the *Semantic Script Theory of Humor*; see [1]) and the *GTVH* (the *General Theory of Verbal Humor*; see [3, 4]). In this paper we show how @*MetaphorMagnet* makes use of Twitter norms to turn metaphors into scripts, and to elevate a simple semantic opposition between scripts into a humorous social conflict.

2   Modular Concerns in Metaphor and Jokes

Metaphors and jokes share many interesting characteristics. At their best, each allows us to see a familiar situation or idea in a new and perhaps surprising light. Each involves a delicate balance of information, of what is explicitly said by the speaker and of what must be inferred by the listener. Each requires knowledge of words and of the world, and the careful packaging of ideas in a concise linguistic form. In the most thought-provoking instances, each sets out to surprise us by telling us what we already know, by spurring us to see the non-obvious ramifications of our knowledge of the familiar. And each derives a large measure of its success from its ability to evoke a palpable but ultimately resolvable semantic tension: jokes often peak with a closing incongruity that can only by resolved by an act of radical re-categorization, while metaphors present us with a demand for this re-categorization up front, by asking us to see deep similarities between ideas that are superficially very different.

Created to be a generator of novel and occasionally witty linguistic metaphors that are rich in semantic and pragmatic tension, @*MetaphorMagnet* relies on many of the same resources and processes that have been identified for joke generation. Applying the *GTVH* of Attardo and Raskin [3, 4], as a spirit guide if not a detailed blueprint, it makes good engineering sense to use a similarly modular approach to the generation of metaphors. The GTVH identifies a variety of knowledge-based modular concerns in joke-generation, called *knowledge resources* (or KRs). The six KRs posited by the GTVH are: *Target* (TA), *Language* (LA), *Narrative Strategy* (NS), *Script Opposition* (SO), *Logical Mechanism* (LM) and *Situation* (SI). Each KR has its own significant role to play in packaging a novel metaphor as an eye-catching, retweet-worthy tweet. Since a metaphor will only strike us as apt if it tells us something of its target that we already feel to be true, the *Target* (TA) resource must ground a figurative comparison in facts or beliefs that most speakers will hold to be true of both the target and the source ideas of the metaphor. *Language* (LA) searches for the most judicious wording for this comparison, to express what explicitly needs to be said and to suggestively evoke the rest, all while staying within the limits of a 140-character tweet. *Narrative Strategy* (NS) gives a logical shape to the tweet, by deciding e.g. whether a figurative conceit should be expressed as a *"what if"* counterfactual, an alternate dictionary definition (in the style of Ambrose Bierce's *The Devil's Dictionary*), a *"would you rather"* analogy, an ironic observation, a rueful reflection on a changing world, a work of flash fiction, a sophistic argument, a clash of world views, and so on. In @*MetaphorMagnet*, the LA and NS resources are tightly coupled, to ensure that the chosen narrative form can naturally be expressed in 140 characters. LA thus exploits Twitter norms such as hashtagging to squeeze maximum value from the medium, and will thus e.g. append the tag #*irony* rather than use the phrasing *"Isn't it ironic."*

@*MetaphorMagnet* employs a range of logical mechanisms (LMs) to juxtapose its knowledge so as to give rise to meaningful semantic oppositions. Consider this tweet:

#Irony: *When the scientists that construct defined models propose the vaguest abstractions.* #Defined=#Vague

The pivotal opposition here is a semantic one, pitting the property *defined* of *model* against the property *vague* of *abstraction*. This kind of stereotypical association can be harvested automatically from similes such as *"as vague as an abstraction."* Indeed, Web similes are shown in [5] to be an especially rich source of TA knowledge that can be reliably extracted in bulk from online texts. The relational statements *scientists construct models* and *models propose abstractions*, which comprise an important part of @*MetaphorMagnet*'s TA knowledge of *science*, are also extracted in bulk from the Web, specifically from the *"why do"* questions that naïve Web users frequently pose to search engines like Google; for example, *"why do scientists construct models?"* is a completion offered by Google for the partial query *"why do scientists."* In the above observational tweet, an irony-seeking LM notes a potential opposition between the ideas *model* and *abstraction* as connected by the intermediary idea *scientist*. This leads the NS module to frame the opposition as a sardonic observation about *scientists* that the LA module then suggestively labels with an additional hashtag, #Irony. Since @*MetaphorMagnet* assumes that connected facts typically belong to the same domain and to the same script (e.g. the domain *science*, or the script *scientist doing science*), the opposition above does not rise to the level of a true Script Opposition. A practical realization of SO that views scripts not as sequences of actions but as figurative world views, and which is thus more appropriate to metaphor generation, is presented in Sect. 4. This SO will be further elaborated to bring in the additional participants and props of a narrative setting that will serve to anchor a tweet in its own Situation (SI).

3 Logical Mechanisms for Metaphorical Conceits

Big-budget movies hire specialized individuals to oversee every facet of a production, whereas those on a tight budget force a small number of people to wear multiple hats. So if it seems arbitrary to define a medium like Twitter by something so superficial as its constrictive 140-character limit on texts, this constraint truly does force modular concerns such as LA, NS, SI and LM to work so tightly together than they hardly deserve the label "*modular*". Not only must NS work hand-in-hand with LA to squeeze its mini-narratives into the cramped confines of a tweet, or perhaps a pair of tweets linked by a shared hashtag that are issued in quick succession, but LM and NS must also be implemented as two sides of a very slim coin. It is not the case that any of @*MetaphorMagnet*'s LMs – each of which is designed to seek out a different kind of meaningful opposition in the system's knowledge of familiar topics (its TA) – can work with any of its NS forms. Rather, different LMs are designed to provide material for specific NS strategies that in turn employ specific LA rendering methods.

Consider the interaction of LM, NS and LA that produced the following tweet:

#Irony: *When some high priests manage "welcoming" churches the way jailers manage stifling prisons.* #High_priest=#Jailer #Church=#Prison

The tweet is built upon an analogical chassis by a figurative LM that best corresponds to the GTVH's LM of *False Analogy* (see [4]). TA knowledge of *priests* and *jailers* indicates that each *manages* a very different kind of building, that each carries very different affect (*priests* are respected and carry positive affect, *jailers* are feared and carry negative affect), and that an interesting opposition exists between the property *welcoming* of churches and the property *stifling* of prisons. This opposition would undermine a conventional analogy, but here it offers a sound basis for the logic of false analogy, which in turn offers a sound basis for a narrative strategy that uses the opposition to rail against modern hypocrisy. NS is abetted in this gambit by LA, which affixes an #*Irony* tag to the tweet and puts the word *welcoming* in scare quotes. The combination suggests a failure of expectations, an indictment of those priests who should be welcoming congregants as guests but instead oppress them as sinners. That *welcoming* is the mutable property here, rather than *stifling*, is signaled by the use of scare quotes, a decision of the LA that is tightly managed by both the NS and the LM.

Consider the following @*MetaphorMagnet* tweet, the fruit of a very different LM:

Love causes the arguments that create conflicts. Discord causes the confrontations that cause conflicts. Take your pick. #Love=#Discord?

This LM might be called *causal and moral equivalence*: if TA knowledge of a target idea leads a system to conclude that this target is causally similar in some respect to a very different idea – such as one with a very different affective profile – this system might conclude (with a touch of sophistry) that the two ideas are morally equivalent. Thus, because *Love* (a typically positive idea) and *Discord* (a typically negative idea) each cause their own share of conflicts, they might well be considered the same thing. *@MetaphorMagnet* employs a simple logical calculus to reason about logical ends (see [6, 12]) in which semantic triples (such as *love causes arguments*) can be chained together to reveal the unexpected distal effects of a familiar idea. More generally, the triples $A \rightarrow r1 \rightarrow B$, $B \rightarrow r2 \rightarrow C$ and $C \rightarrow r3 \rightarrow D$ can be chained to yield the chain $A \rightarrow r1 \rightarrow B \rightarrow r2 \rightarrow C \rightarrow r3 \rightarrow D$. Causal propagation rules are used to reason about the effect of the head of a causal chain (e.g. A) on the end of a chain (e.g. D). For instance, if $r1$ and $r2$ have positive causality and $r3$ has negative causality, a system can reason that more A causes more B with causes more C which causes less D, so more A ultimately causes less D. Though a TA's representation of an idea A may not directly link A to D, *@MetaphorMagnet* can infer the causal consequences of A on D.

What makes a chain humorous and/or thought-provoking? *@MetaphorMagnet* employs a simple but effective criterion: a provocative inference chain is one that links an idea A to another idea D by coherently chaining multiple triples together, where there is a bisociative tension between worlds with more A and worlds with more D. We expect a positive idea (such as *Love, Beauty, Romance, Art*, etc.) to have positive consequences on the world, by which we mean the proliferation of other positive ideas and the diminution of negative ideas. Likewise, we expect negative ideas (like *War, Hate, Jealousy, Pain*) to have negative consequences on the world, and to diminish the effect of positive ideas. So a chain $A \rightarrow \ldots \rightarrow D$ that shows how a positive idea A can have a positive causal effect on a negative idea D (so more A means more D), or shows how a negative idea A can have a positive causal effect on a positive idea D (so less A means less D), is considered interesting. A provocative chain will thus show how a target idea can reside in two mutually incongruous frames of reference – one that is desirable and one that is undesirable – thereby conforming to Arthur Koestler's definition of bisociation: *"the perceiving of a situation or idea in two self-consistent but habitually incompatible frames of reference"*[8]. The following tweet from *@MetaphorMagnet* illustrates just such a bisociation of views:

Spouses embrace marriage. Prostitutes profit from the sex that nurtures marriages.
Who is better? #Prostitute=#Spouse

To support this degree of reasoning by LMs, *@MetaphorMagnet*'s TAs assign coarse ± sentiment classes to individual ideas, and coarse ± causal classes to individual relations, so that an LM can infer the broad causal effects of the idea at the head of a chain on the idea at its end. Moreover, we have empirically verified our hypothesis (in [6, 12]) that an inferential chain is more likely to be seen as surprising if there is a clear affective incongruity between the head and the tail of a causal chain.

4   Script Opposition as a Clash of World Views

The *script* is a necessarily elastic notion in humour research, one that stretches from the frame-like organization of case-roles and fillers in Raskin's SSTH [1] to the altogether more pliant graph-theoretic structures of the GTVH as re-imagined by Attardo, Hempelmann and Di Maio [4]. There are few conventions in language or thought that cannot be subverted for humorous effect, and the notion of *script* in a theory of humour must accommodate them all. The central schematic structure in metaphor theory is the conceptual metaphor [2, 7], making this – the conceptual metaphor schema – the figurative equivalent of the *script*. These schemas, such as *Life Is A Journey* or *Politics is a Game*, serve not only as productive deep-structures for the generation of whole families of linguistic metaphors, but also provide the conceptual mappings that shape our habitual thinking about such familiar concepts as *Life, Love, Emotion* and *Politics*. The SSTH and GTVH view jokes as carefully-crafted texts that set out to trick their audiences into applying a script that is only superficially appropriate, one that ultimately lacks enough explanatory power for subsequent developments in the joke. Politicians and philosophers employ conceptual metaphor schemas to frame an issue and shape our expectations; when a schema fails to match our own experience, we likewise reject it and switch to a more apt schema. So a metaphor-generating bot can seek out thought-provoking incongruity by pitting a metaphor schema against another that advocates a conflicting view of the world. The following tweet from @*MetaphorMagnet* contrasts two views on *#Democracy*:

To some voters, democracy is an important cornerstone. To others, it is a worthless failure. #Democracy=#Cornerstone #Democracy=#Failure

The schema *Democracy is a Cornerstone* (of civilization) is frequently used to frame political discussions, and can be seen as an elaboration of the schema *Society is a Building*, which in turn elaborates the more primary schema *Organization is Physical Structure* [7]. Yet the importance of cornerstones to the buildings they anchor finds a sharp contrast in the assertion that *Democracy is a Failure*. Each of these affective claims is so commonly asserted that it can be found in the Google n-grams [9], a large database of short fragments of frequent Web texts. Thus the 4-gram "*democracy is a cornerstone*" has a frequency of 91 in the Google n-grams while the 4-gram "*democracy is a failure*" has a frequency of 165. Once again, the stereotypical view of *cornerstones* as *important* and *failures* are *worthless* are themselves derived from Web similes (as in [5]). The following tweet employs a similar metaphorical LM, but renders the conflict of metaphor schemas using a different NS:

Remember when tolerance was promoted by crusading liberals? Now, tolerance is violence that only fearful appeasers can avoid.

The LM here – which is guided by the suggestive Google 3-gram "*Tolerance for Violence*" (freq = 1353) does not directly contrast the ideas #Tolerance and #Violence, but examines the juxtaposition at an analogical remove, to find an interesting double conflict, between advocates and opponents and between the advocates of #Tolerance (*crusading* liberals) and the opponents of #Violence (*fearful* appeasers). The LA module omits the hashtags #Tolerance = #Violence from this tweet as it lacks sufficient space to include them within Twitter's 140-character limit. But LA chooses to split the following conceit across two successive tweets to create space for extra hashtags:

> *Remember when research was conducted by prestigious philosophers?*
> #Research=#Fruit #Philosopher=#Insect

> *Now, research is a fruit eaten only by lowly insects.* #Research=#Fruit
> #Philosopher=#Insect

Twitter offers other affordances that allow us to heighten the contrast in metaphorical tweets and to elevate this contrast into a dramatic social situation. So rather than talk of nameless voters or liberals or appeasers, we can give these straw men real names, or at least invent names that look like the real thing and which, in their choice of Twitter handles, appear wittily apt. The reification of conceptual types into imaginary individuals turns an abstract metaphor into a concrete situation, with its own colorful participants. This is the role of the SI (Situation) KR in @*MetaphorMagnet*: to bring a metaphor to life by imagining its central conceit as the subject of a vigorous debate by real people. Consider the imaginary debate in this tweet from @*MetaphorMagnet*:

> .@war_poet *says history is a straight line*
> .@war_prisoner *says it is a coiled chain*   #History=#Line #History=#Chain

The handles @war_poet and @war_prisoner are invented by @*MetaphorMagnet*'s SI to suit, and thereby amplify, the metaphorical views that they are fictively advanced in the tweet, again by using a mix of TA knowledge and LA data (Web n-grams). Since poets write poems about the wars that punctuate history, and these poems contain lines, the 2-gram "*war poet*" is recognized as an apt handle for an imaginary Twitter user who would advance the view of *history as a line*. In this case the handle @war_poet actually denotes a real Twitter user, but this only adds to the sense that Twitterbot confections are a new kind of interactive theatre and performance art [10]. Note that the more profound aspects of this metaphorical contrast are not appreciated by @*MetaphorMagnet* itself, or at least not yet. For example, the system does not yet appreciate what it means for history to be a straight line, and while it knows enough to invent the intriguing handle @war_prisoner, neither does it appreciate what it might mean to be a prisoner of history, enslaved in a repeating cycle of war. Our bots will always evoke in a human follower much more than they themselves can understand, but this, in the end, is a key ingredient of the allure of Twitterbots, smart or otherwise.

5   Evaluation

We argue that @*MetaphorMagnet* is a "*next-generation*" Twitterbot for a number of important reasons. Its actions are informed by, and grounded in, some well-developed theories, from Lakoff & Johnson's *Conceptual Metaphor Theory* (CMT, [2] to the *Semantic Script Theory of Humour* (SSTH) of Raskin [1] and the *General Theory of Verbal Humour* (GTVH) of Attardo and Raskin [1, 3, 4]. Since the bot aims to craft original tweets that are both metaphorically apt and humorously provocative, it represents a practical marriage of CMT and the SSTH/GTVH. Indeed, the bot draws on considerable semantic and linguistic resources to make this marriage work, from a large knowledge-base of conceptual relationships and stereotypical beliefs – which inform its TA (Target) KR – to the rich diversity of the Google n-grams which inform its LA (Language) KR. All of @*MetaphorMagnet*'s tweets – all its hits and its misses – are open to public scrutiny on Twitter. But to empirically evaluate the success of the bot as a generator of novel, meaningful and retweet-worthy metaphors, we turn to the crowdsourcing platform *CrowdFlower*. To determine just how much of its success can be attributed to its use of CMT/GTVH mechanisms and knowledge resources, we perform a comparative analysis between this knowledge-based bot and a knowledge-*free* bot called @*MetaphorMinute* (designed by noted bot-maker Darius Kazemi) that uses a wholly aleatoric approach to metaphor generation. @*MetaphorMinute* crafts its metaphors by filling a template with nouns and adjectives that are chosen more-or-less at random, to produce tweets such as "*a doorbell is a sportsman: fleetwide and infraclavicular.*" Though it generates inscrutable outputs such as these *every two minutes*, @*MetaphorMinute* is a popular bot that currently has over 500 followers.

We chose 60 tweets at random from the outputs of each Twitterbot. CrowdFlower annotators were not informed of the origin of any tweet, but simply told that each was collected from Twitter because of its metaphorical content. For each tweet, annotators were asked to rate its metaphor along three dimensions, *Comprehensibility*, *Novelty* and likely *Retweetability*, and to rate all three dimensions on the same scale, ranging from *Very Low* to *Medium Low* to *Medium High* to *Very High*. CrowdFlower was used to solicit ten annotations per tweet (and thus, per dimension), though scammers (non-engaged annotators) were later removed from this pool. Table 1 presents the distributions of mean ratings per tweet, along each dimension and for each Twitterbot.

Table 1. Comparative Evaluation of the @*MetaphorMagnet* and @*MetaphorMinute* bots

Rating	*Comprehensibility*		*Novelty*		*Retweetability*	
Metaphor System	*Metaphor Magnet*	*Metaphor Minute*	*Metaphor Magnet*	*Metaphor Minute*	*Metaphor Magnet*	*Metaphor Minute*
Very Low	11.6%	**23.9%**	**11.9%**	9.5%	15.5%	**41%**
Med. Low	13.2%	**22.2%**	**17.3%**	12.4%	**41.9%**	34.1%
Med High	**23.7%**	22.4%	**21%**	14.9%	**27.4%**	15%
Very High	**51.5%**	31.6%	49.8%	**63.2%**	15.3%	9.9%

Note how more than half of @*MetaphorMagnet*'s tweets are ranked as very highly comprehensible, while less than a third of @*MetaphorMinute*'s tweets are so ranked.

Even though only 1 in 4 of @*MetaphorMagnet*'s metaphors is rated as being hard or somewhat hard to comprehend, this is an area of performance that can be improved.

More surprising is the result that raters found more than half of @*MetaphorMinute*'s wholly random metaphors to be of medium-high to very-high comprehensibility. The bot's use of abstruse terminology, like *fleetwide* and *infraclavicular*, may be a factor here, as might the bot's use of the familiar copula template for metaphors, which may well seduce raters into believing that an apparent metaphor really does have a comprehensible meaning, if only one were to expend enough effort to discern it.

The dimension *Novelty* yields results that are equally thought-provoking, for while one half of @*MetaphorMagnet*'s metaphors are ranked as very-highly novel, almost two-thirds of @*MetaphorMinute*'s metaphors are so ranked. Nonetheless, we should not be overly surprised that @*MetaphorMinute*'s bizarre combinations of rare words, as yielded by its unconstrained use of aleatoric techniques, are seen as more unusual than those word combinations arising from @*MetaphorMagnet*'s controlled use of Web n-grams and stereotypical knowledge. As demonstrated in [11], novelty is not in itself a source of pleasure or a reliable benchmark of creativity. Pleasurability derives from *useful* novelty, that is, novelty that can be understood and usefully exploited.

In this case of Twitter, useful exploitation is frequently a matter of social reach. A tweet is novel and useful to the extent that it attracts the attention of Twitter users and is deemed worthy of re-tweeting to others in their social circles. Our third dimension, *Re-Tweetability*, reflects the likelihood that an annotator would consider re-tweeting a given metaphor to others. Though we ask annotators to speculate here – neither bot has enough followers to perform a robust statistical analysis of actual retweet rates – the results largely conform to our expectations. Retweetability, it seems, is a matter of novelty *and* comprehensibility, and not novelty alone. Though raters are not generous with their *Very-High* ratings for either bot, @*MetaphorMagnet*'s tweets are deemed to be significantly more re-tweetable than the random offerings of @*MetaphorMinute*.

This is just as well, given the considerable gap in complexity and sophistication that exists between the two bots. But this is an encouraging result not just for theory-informed Twitterbots like @*MetaphorMagnet* and their creators, but for Twitter itself. Twitter offers a compelling platform for research in interactive humour and metaphor, not least because its human users appreciate these phenomena when they see them.

References

1. Raskin, V.: Semantic Mechanisms of Humor. Reidel, Dordrecht (1985)
2. Lakoff, G., Johnson, J.: Metaphors We Live By. University of Chicago Press, Chicago (1980)
3. Attardo, S., Raskin, V.: Script theory revis(it)ed: joke similarity and joke representational model. Humor Int. J. Humor Res. **4**(3), 293–347 (1991)
4. Attardo, S., Hempelmann, C.F., Di Maio, S.: Script oppositions and logical mechanisms modeling incongruities and their resolutions. Humor Int. J. Humor Res. **15**(1), 3–46 (2002)
5. Veale, T., Hao, Y.: Comprehending and generating apt metaphors: a web-driven, case-based approach to figurative language. In: Proceedings of AAAI-2007, the 22nd AAAI Conference of the Association for the Advancement of Artificial Intelligence (2007)

6. Veale, T., Valitutti, A.: A world with or without you* (*terms and conditions may apply). In: Proceedings of AAAI-2014 Fall Symposium Series on Modeling Changing Perspectives: Re-conceptualizing Sensorimotor Experiences, Arlington, VA (2014)
7. Grady, J.: Foundations of Meaning: Primary Metaphors and Primary Scenes. University of California, Berkeley (1997)
8. Koestler, A.: The Act of Creation. Penguin Books, London (1964)
9. Brants, T., Franz, A.: Web 1T 5-gram Version 1. Linguistic Data Consortium, Philadelphia (2006)
10. Dewey, D.: What happens when @everyword ends? Washington Post, Intersect column, May 23rd edition (2014)
11. Giora, R., Fein, O., Kronrod, A., Elnatan, I., Shuval, N., Zur, A.: Weapons of mass distraction: optimal innovation and pleasure ratings. Metaphor Symbol **19**(2), 115–141 (2004)
12. Veale, T.: Running with scissors: cut-ups, boundary friction and creative reuse. In: Proceedings of ICCBR-2014, the 22nd International Conference on Case-Based Reasoning, Cork, Ireland, September 2014
13. Burroughs, W.S.: The cut-up method. In: LeRoi Jones, (ed.) The Moderns: An Anthology of New Writing in America. Corinth Books, New York (1963)

Author Index

Printed in the United States
By Bookmasters